Novels
for Students

Novels for Students

Presenting Analysis, Context and Criticism on
Commonly Studied Novels

Volume 1

Diane Telgen, Editor

Carol Jago, Santa Monica High School, Advisor
Kathleen Pasquantonio, Novi High School, Advisor

Foreword by Anne Devereaux Jordan, Teaching and Learning Literature

GALE

DETROIT · NEW YORK · TORONTO · LONDON

STAFF

Diane Telgen, *Editor*

Anne Boyd, Stacy Bushey, Jane Elizabeth Dougherty, Stephen Germic, Jeremy W. Hubbell, David Levine, Lauren Long, Nancy C. McClure, Barbara J. Parker, Jordan P. Richman, Kenneth R. Shepherd, Melissa Simpson, Genevieve Slomski, Beverly West, *Sketchwriters*

Marilyn Allen, Linda R. Andres, Shelly Andrews, Joanna Brod, Sheryl Ciccarelli, Amy K. Crook, Alan Hedblad, Kevin S. Hile, Melissa Hill, Motoko Fujishiro Huthwaite, Arlene M. Johnson, Paul Loeber, Thomas F. McMahon, Andrew Seagram, Gerard J. Senick, Crystal A. Towns, Kathleen L. Witman, *Contributing Editors*

Joyce Nakamura, *Managing Editor*

Victoria B. Cariappa, *Research Team Manager*
Michele P. LaMeau, *Research Specialist*
Laura C. Bissey, Julia C. Daniel, Tamara C. Nott, Tracie A. Richardson, Cheryl L. Warnock, *Research Associates*
Alfred A. Gardner III, *Research Assistant*

Susan M. Trosky, *Permissions Manager*
Maria L. Franklin, *Permissions Specialist*
Michele M. Lonoconus, *Permissions Associate*
Mary K. Grimes, *Image Cataloger*

Mary Beth Trimper, *Production Director*
Evi Seoud, *Assistant Production Manager*
Shanna Heilveil, *Production Assistant*

Randy Bassett, *Image Database Supervisor*
Mikal Ansari, Robert Duncan, *Imaging Specialists*
Pamela A. Reed, *Photography Coordinator*

Cover design: Michelle DiMercurio, *Art Director*
Page design: Pamela A. E. Galbreath, *Senior Art Director*

⊗™ This book is printed on acid-free paper that meets the minimum requirements of American National Standard for Information Sciences—Permanence Paper for Printed Library Materials, ANSI Z39.48-1984.

ISBN 0-7876-1686-9
ISSN 1094-3552
Printed in the United States of America

10 9 8 7 6 5 4 3 2 1

Table of Contents

The Informed Dialogue:
Interacting with Literature

When we pick up a book, we usually do so with the anticipation of pleasure. We hope that by entering the time and place of the novel and sharing the thoughts and actions of the characters, we will find enjoyment. Unfortunately, this is often not the case; we are disappointed. But we should ask, has the author failed us, or have we failed the author?

We establish a dialogue with the author, the book, and with ourselves when we read. Consciously and unconsciously, we ask questions: "Why did the author write this book?" "Why did the author choose that time, place, or character?" "How did the author achieve that effect?" "Why did the character act that way?" "Would I act in the same way?" The answers we receive depend upon how much information about literature in general and about that book specifically we ourselves bring to our reading.

Young children have limited life and literary experiences. Being young, children frequently do not know how to go about exploring a book, nor sometimes, even know the questions to ask of a book. The books they read help them answer questions, the author often coming right out and *telling* young readers the things they are learning or are expected to learn. The perennial classic, *The Little Engine That Could, tells* its readers that, among other things, it is good to help others and brings happiness:

> "Hurray, hurray," cried the funny little clown and all the dolls and toys. "The good little boys and girls in the city will be happy because you helped us, kind, Little Blue Engine."

In picture books, messages are often blatant and simple, the dialogue between the author and reader one-sided. Young children are concerned with the end result of a book—the enjoyment gained, the lesson learned—rather than with how that result was obtained. As we grow older and read further, however, we question more. We come to expect that the world within the book will closely mirror the concerns of our world, and that the author will *show* these through the events, descriptions, and conversations within the story, rather than *telling* of them. We are now expected to do the interpreting, carry on our share of the dialogue with the book and author, and glean not only the author's message, but comprehend how that message and the overall affect of the book were achieved. Sometimes, however, we need help to do these things. *Novels for Students* provides that help.

A novel is made up of many parts interacting to create a coherent whole. In reading a novel, the more obvious features can be easily spotted—theme, characters, plot—but we may overlook the more subtle elements that greatly influence how the novel is perceived by the reader: viewpoint, mood and tone, symbolism, or the use of humor. By focusing on both the obvious and more subtle literary elements within a novel, *Novels for Students* aids readers in both analyzing for message and in determining how and why that message is communicated. In the discussion on Harper Lee's *To*

Kill a Mockingbird (Vol. 2), for example, the mockingbird as a symbol of innocence is dealt with, among other things, as is the importance of Lee's use of humor which "enlivens a serious plot, adds depth to the characterization, and creates a sense of familiarity and universality." The reader comes to understand the internal elements of each novel discussed—as well as the external influences that help shape it.

"The desire to write greatly," Harold Bloom of Yale University says, "is the desire to be elsewhere, in a time and place of one's own, in an originality that must compound with inheritance, with an anxiety of influence." A writer seeks to create a unique world within a story, but although it is unique, it is not disconnected from our own world. It speaks to us *because* of what the writer brings to the writing from our world: how he or she was raised and educated; his or her likes and dislikes; the events occurring in the real world at the time of the writing, and while the author was growing up. When we know what an author has brought to his or her work, we gain a greater insight into both the "originality" (the world of the book), and the things that "compound" it. This insight enables us to question that created world and find answers more readily. By informing ourselves, we are able to establish a more effective dialogue with both book and author.

Novels for Students, in addition to providing a plot summary and descriptive list of characters—to remind readers of what they have read—also explores the external influences that shaped each book. Each entry includes a discussion of the author's background, and the historical context in which the novel was written. It is vital to know, for instance, that when Ray Bradbury was writing *Fahrenheit 451* (Vol. 1), the threat of Nazi domination had recently ended in Europe, and the McCarthy hearings were taking place in Washington, D.C. This information goes far in answering the question, "Why did he write a story of oppressive government control and book burning?" Similarly, it is important to know that Harper Lee, author of *To Kill a Mockingbird,* was born and raised in Mon-

roeville, Alabama, and that her father was a lawyer. Readers can now see why she chose the south as a setting for her novel—it is the place with which she was most familiar—and start to comprehend her characters and their actions.

Novels for Students helps readers find the answers they seek when they establish a dialogue with a particular novel. It also aids in the posing of questions by providing the opinions and interpretations of various critics and reviewers, broadening that dialogue. Some reviewers of *To Kill A Mockingbird,* for example, "faulted the novel's climax as melodramatic." This statement leads readers to ask, "Is it, indeed, melodramatic?" "If not, why did some reviewers see it as such?" "If it is, why did Lee choose to make it melodramatic?" "Is melodrama ever justified?" By being spurred to ask these questions, readers not only learn more about the book and its writer, but about the nature of writing itself.

The literature included for discussion in *Novels for Students* has been chosen because it has something vital to say to us. *Of Mice and Men, Catch-22, The Joy Luck Club, My Antonia, A Separate Peace* and the other novels here speak of life and modern sensibility. In addition to their individual, specific messages of prejudice, power, love or hate, living and dying, however, they and all great literature also share a common intent. They force us to *think*—about life, literature, and about others, not just about ourselves. They pry us from the narrow confines of our minds and thrust us outward to confront the world of books and the larger, real world we all share. *Novels for Students* helps us in this confrontation by providing the means of enriching our conversation with literature and the world, by creating an *informed* dialogue, one that brings true pleasure to the personal act of reading.

Sources

Harold Bloom, *The Western Canon, The Books and School of the Ages,* Riverhead Books, 1994.

Watty Piper, *The Little Engine That Could,* Platt & Munk, 1930.

Anne Devereaux Jordan
Senior Editor, *TALL*
(*Teaching and Learning Literature*)

Introduction

Purpose of the Book

The purpose of *Novels for Students* (*NfS*) is to provide readers with a guide to understanding, enjoying, and studying novels by giving them easy access to information about the work. Part of Gale's "For Students" Literature line, *NfS* is specifically designed to meet the curricular needs of high school and undergraduate college students and their teachers, as well as the interests of general readers and researchers considering specific novels. While each volume contains entries on "classic" novels frequently studied in classrooms, there are also entries containing hard-to-find information on contemporary novels, including works by multicultural, international, and women novelists.

The information covered in each entry includes an introduction to the novel and the novel's author; a plot summary, to help readers unravel and understand the events in a novel; descriptions of important characters, including explanation of a given character's role in the novel as well as discussion about that character's relationship to other characters in the novel; analysis of important themes in the novel; and an explanation of important literary techniques and movements as they are demonstrated in the novel.

In addition to this material, which helps the readers analyze the novel itself, students are also provided with important information on the literary and historical background informing each work. This includes a historical context essay, a box comparing the time or place the novel was writ-

ten to modern Western culture, a critical overview essay, and excerpts from critical essays on the novel. A unique feature of *NfS* is a specially commissioned overview essay on each novel by an academic expert, targeted toward the student reader.

To further aid the student in studying and enjoying each novel, information on media adaptations is provided, as well as reading suggestions for works of fiction and nonfiction on similar themes and topics. Classroom aids include ideas for research papers and lists of critical sources that provide additional material on the novel.

Selection Criteria

The titles for each volume of *NfS* were selected by surveying numerous sources on teaching literature and analyzing course curricula for various school districts. Some of the sources surveyed included: literature anthologies; *Reading Lists for College-Bound Students: The Books Most Recommended by America's Top Colleges;* textbooks on teaching the novel; a College Board survey of novels commonly studied in high schools; a National Council of Teachers of English (NCTE) survey of novels commonly studied in high schools; the NCTE's *Teaching Literature in High School: The Novel;* and the Young Adult Library Services Association (YALSA) list of best books for young adults of the past twenty-five years.

Input was also solicited from our expert advisory board, as well as educators from various areas. From these discussions, it was determined that each volume should have a mix of "classic" novels (those works commonly taught in literature classes) and contemporary novels for which information is often hard to find. Because of the interest in expanding the canon of literature, an emphasis was also placed on including works by international, multicultural, and women authors. Our advisory board members—current high school teachers—helped pare down the list for each volume. If a work was not selected for the present volume, it was often noted as a possibility for a future volume. As always, the editor welcomes suggestions for titles to be included in future volumes.

How Each Entry Is Organized

Each entry, or chapter, in *NfS* focuses on one novel. Each entry heading lists the full name of the novel, the author's name, and the date of the novel's publication. The following elements are contained in each entry:

- **Introduction:** a brief overview of the novel which provides information about its first appearance, its literary standing, any controversies surrounding the work, and major conflicts or themes within the work.

- **Author Biography:** this section includes basic facts about the author's life, and focuses on events and times in the author's life that inspired the novel in question.

- **Plot Summary:** a description of the major events in the novel, with interpretation of how these events help articulate the novel's themes. Lengthy summaries are broken down with subheads.

- **Characters:** an alphabetical listing of major characters in the novel. Each character name is followed by a brief to an extensive description of the character's role in the novel, as well as discussion of the character's actions, relationships, and possible motivation.

  Characters are listed alphabetically by last name. If a character is unnamed—for instance, the narrator in *Invisible Man*—the character is listed as "The Narrator" and alphabetized as "Narrator." If a character's first name is the only one given, the name will appear alphabetically by the name.

  Variant names are also included for each character. Thus, the full name "Jean Louise Finch" would head the listing for the narrator of *To Kill a Mockingbird,* but listed in a separate cross-reference would be the nickname "Scout Finch."

- **Themes:** a thorough overview of how the major topics, themes, and issues are addressed within the novel. Each theme discussed appears in a separate subhead, and is easily accessed through the boldface entries in the Subject/Theme Index.

- **Style:** this section addresses important style elements of the novel, such as setting, point of view, and narration; important literary devices used, such as imagery, foreshadowing, symbolism; and, if applicable, genres to which the work might have belonged, such as Gothicism or Romanticism. Literary terms are explained within the entry, but can also be found in the Glossary.

- **Historical and Cultural Context:** This section outlines the social, political, and cultural climate *in which the author lived and the novel was created.* This section may include descriptions of related historical events, pertinent aspects of daily life in the culture, and the artistic and literary sensibilities of the time in which the work was written. If the novel is a historical work, information regarding the time in which the novel is set is also included. Each section is broken down with helpful subheads.

- **Critical Overview:** this section provides background on the critical reputation of the novel, including bannings or any other public controversies surrounding the work. For older works, this section includes a history of how novel was first received and how perceptions of it may have changed over the years; for more recent novels, direct quotes from early reviews may also be included.

- **Sources:** an alphabetical list of critical material quoted in the entry, with full bibliographical information.

- **For Further Study:** an alphabetical list of other critical sources which may prove useful for the student. Includes full bibliographical information and a brief annotation.

- **Criticism:** an essay commissioned by *NfS* which specifically deals with the novel and is written specifically for the student audience, as well as excerpts from previously published criticism on the work.

In addition, each entry contains the following highlighted sections, set apart from the main text as sidebars:

- **Media Adaptations:** a list of important film and television adaptations of the novel, including source information. The list also includes stage adaptations, audio recordings, musical adaptations, etc.

- **Compare and Contrast Box:** an "at-a-glance" comparison of the cultural and historical differences between the author's time and culture and late twentieth-century Western culture. This box includes pertinent parallels between the major scientific, political, and cultural movements of the time or place the novel was written, the time or place the novel was set (if a historical work), and modern Western culture. Works written after the mid-1970s may not have this box.

- **What Do I Read Next?:** a list of works that might complement the featured novel or serve as a contrast to it. This includes works by the same author and others, works of fiction and nonfiction, and works from various genres, cultures, and eras.

- **Study Questions:** a list of potential study questions or research topics dealing with the novel. This section includes questions related to other disciplines the student may be studying, such as American history, world history, science, math, government, business, geography, economics, psychology, etc.

Other Features

NfS includes "The Informed Dialogue: Interacting with Literature," a foreword by Anne Devereaux Jordan, Senior Editor for *Teaching and Learning Literature (TALL)*, and a founder of the Children's Literature Association. This essay provides an enlightening look at how readers interact with literature and how *Novels for Students* can help teachers show students how to enrich their own reading experiences.

A Cumulative Author/Title Index lists the authors and titles covered in each volume of the *NfS* series.

A Cumulative Nationality/Ethnicity Index breaks down the authors and titles covered in each volume of the *NfS* series by nationality and ethnicity.

A Subject/Theme Index, specific to each volume, provides easy reference for users who may be studying a particular subject or theme rather than a single work. Significant subjects from events to broad themes are included, and the entries pointing to the specific theme discussions in each entry are indicated in **boldface.**

Each entry has several illustrations, including photos of the author, stills from film adaptations (when available), maps, and/or photos of key historical events.

Citing Novels for Students

When writing papers, students who quote directly from any volume of *Novels for Students* may use the following general forms. These examples are based on MLA style; teachers may request that students adhere to a different style, so the following examples may be adapted as needed.

When citing text from *NfS* that is not attributed to a particular author (i.e., the Themes, Style, Historical Context sections, etc.), the following format should be used in the bibliography section:

"The Adventures of Huckleberry Finn." *Novels for Students.* Ed. Diane Telgen. Vol. 1. Detroit: Gale, 1997. 8–9.

When quoting the specially commissioned essay from *NfS* (usually the first piece under the "Criticism" subhead), the following format should be used:

James, Pearl. Essay on "The Adventures of Huckleberry Finn." *Novels for Students.* Ed. Diane Telgen. Vol. 1. Detroit: Gale, 1997. 8–9.

When quoting a journal or newspaper essay that is reprinted in a volume of *NfS,* the following form may be used:

Butler, Robert J. "The Quest for Pure Motion in Richard Wright's *Black Boy.*" *MELUS* 10, No. 3 (Fall, 1983), 5–17; excerpted and reprinted in *Novels for Students,* Vol. 1, ed. Diane Telgen (Detroit: Gale, 1997), pp. 61–64.

When quoting material reprinted from a book that appears in a volume of *NfS,* the following form may be used:

Adams, Timothy Dow. "Richard Wright: 'Wearing the Mask,'" in *Telling Lies in Modern American Autobiography* (University of North Carolina Press, 1990), 69–83; excerpted and reprinted in *Novels for Students,* Vol. 1, ed. Diane Telgen (Detroit: Gale, 1997), pp. 59–61.

We Welcome Your Suggestions

The editor of *Novels for Students* welcomes your comments and ideas. Readers who wish to suggest novels to appear in future volumes, or who have other suggestions, are cordially invited to contact the editor. You may contact the editor via e-mail at: **CYA@gale.com.** Or write to the editor at:

Editor, *Novels for Students*
Gale Research
835 Penobscot Bldg.
645 Griswold St.
Detroit, MI 48226-4094

Literary Chronology

1775: Jane Austen is born December 16, 1774, to George and Cassandra Austen, in Steventon, Hampshire, England.

1797: Mary Shelley is born Mary Wollstonecraft Godwin on August 30, 1797, to William and Mary Wollstonecraft Godwin, in London, England.

1804: Nathaniel Hawthorne is born on July 4, 1804, in Salem, Massachusetts.

1813: "First Impressions" is the original version of Jane Austen's *Pride and Prejudice* and is rejected by a London publisher in 1797. Austen revised the story, and it is published as *Pride and Prejudice* in 1813.

1814: After Percy Shelley threatens to commit suicide, Mary Godwin elopes with him to France, even though he is already married. They eventually marry and have four children, three of whom die in infancy. Percy Shelley drowns in 1822.

1817: Jane Austen dies (probably of Addison's disease) on July 18, 1817, in Winchester, Hampshire, England.

1818: Mary Shelley begins *Frankenstein; or, The Modern Prometheus* in July, 1816, while visiting Lord Byron at Lake Geneva in Switzerland with her husband, poet Percy Bysshe Shelley; Byron challenges each of his guests to write a ghost story. The novel is published in March, 1818.

1835: Mark Twain is born Samuel Langhorne Clemens on November 30, 1835, to John Marshall and Jane Lampton Clemens, in Florida, Missouri. He first uses the name "Mark Twain" on February 2, 1863.

1850: Nathaniel Hawthorne's *The Scarlet Letter,* the story of a woman who must wear a scarlet "A" because she committed adultery, is published in 1850.

1851: Mary Shelley dies of meningioma on February 1, 1851, in London, England.

1864: Nathaniel Hawthorne dies on May 19, 1864, at Plymouth, New Hampshire, and is buried on May 23, 1864, at Sleepy Hollow Cemetery, in Concord, Massachusetts.

1884: Mark Twain establishes the Charles L. Webster Publishing Co. in order to secure greater control over his books.

1884: Mark Twain begins *The Adventures of Huckleberry Finn, Tom Sawyer's Comrade* in the summer of 1876 while he is at Quarry Farm, near Elmira, New York, and finishes it in the summer of 1883. The novel is published February 18, 1884.

1899: Ernest Hemingway is born on July 21, 1899, in Oak Park, Illinois.

1902: John Steinbeck is born on February 27, 1902, in Salinas, California. His father, John Ernst, Sr., is a miller and treasurer and his mother is a former school teacher.

1908: Richard Wright is born to Nathan and Ella Wright on September 4, 1908, on a farm near Natchez, Mississippi.

1910: Mark Twain dies of angina pectoris on April 21, 1910, in Redding, Connecticut.

1914–1918: World War I. Ernest Hemingway volunteers to be an ambulance driver for the Red Cross in 1918. He is assigned to an Italian war theater, and he receives serious wounds at Fossalta, Italy. He returns from the war in 1919. Hemingway's main character in *A Farewell to Arms* is also an ambulance driver during the war.

1919: Jerome David Salinger is born January 1, 1919, to Sol and Miriam Jillich Salinger, in New York City.

1920: Ray Bradbury is born on August 22, 1920, in Waukegan, Illinois.

1923: Joseph Heller is born May 1, 1923, to Isaac and Lena Heller in the Coney Island section of Brooklyn, New York.

1928: Gabriel García Márquez is born on March 6, 1928, in Aracataca, Colombia.

1929: Ernest Hemingway's *A Farewell to Arms,* the story of an American ambulance driver and his desire for an English nurse during World War I, is published.

1931: Toni Morrison is born Chloe Anthony Wofford on February 18, 1931, to George and Ramah Willis Wofford, in Lorain, Ohio.

1932: Sylvia Plath is born October 27, 1932, to Otto Emil and Aurelia Schober Plath, in Boston, Massachusetts.

1936: Judith Guest is born March 29, 1936, to Harry Reginald and Marion Aline Guest, in Detroit, Michigan.

1937: John Steinbeck writes of the white male migrant workers who were becoming extinct from American culture in *Of Mice and Men.*

1939: World War II begins when Nazi Germany, led by Adolf Hitler, invades Poland and England and France declare war in response. The repressive Nazi regime, with its thought control and book burnings, helps inspire the society in Ray Bradbury's novel *Fahrenheit 451.*

1944: During World War II, Joseph Heller is stationed on the island of Corsica (located in the Mediterranean Sea, off the coasts of France and Italy), where he serves as a bombardier who flew sixty combat missions. His novel *Catch-22* will use a similar wartime setting.

1945: Richard Wright publishes his autobiography, *Black Boy,* in 1945. The unused portions of his original manuscript are published in 1977 as *American Hunger.*

1950: Sen. Joseph McCarthy of Wisconsin first makes the claim that there are over 200 known Communists working in the federal government, setting off the "Red Scare" that leads to government hearings and blacklisting of suspected Communists. This emphasis on conformity influences several novels of the era, including Ray Bradbury's *Fahrenheit 451* and J. D. Salinger's *The Catcher in the Rye.*

1951: J. D. Salinger's *The Catcher in the Rye* is published July 16, 1951, and Salinger avoids the publicity by traveling to Europe.

1952: Amy Tan is born on February 19, 1952, to John and Daisy Tu Ching Tan, in Oakland, California.

1953: Ray Bradbury wrote the 25,000–word novella, "The Fireman," which appeared in *Galaxy* in 1952. *Fahrenheit 451,* his first novel, is the expanded version of that novella and is published in October, 1953.

1954: Ernest Hemingway receives the Nobel Prize in Literature.

1960: Richard Wright dies of a heart attack on November 28, 1960, in Paris, France.

1961: Joseph Heller began writing *Catch-22* while working in the New York advertising business. The book is published in 1961.

1961: Ernest Hemingway commits suicide on July 2, 1961, in Ketchum, Idaho.

1962: John Steinbeck receives the Nobel Prize for Literature.

1963: Sylvia Plath publishes *The Bell Jar* in January, 1963, under the pseudonym Victoria Lucas.

1963: Sylvia Plath commits suicide on February 11, 1963, in London, England.

1968: John Steinbeck dies of a severe heart attack in New York City on December 20, 1968.

1970: Toni Morrison's *The Bluest Eye,* published in 1970, is her first novel.

1976: Judith Guest's first novel, *Ordinary People,* is published. It is the first unsolicited manuscript accepted by its publisher in twenty years.

1982: Gabriel García Márquez receives the Nobel Prize in Literature.

1985: Gabriel García Márquez's *Love in the Time of Cholera,* published in 1985, is based in part on his parents' marriage.

1989: Amy Tan's *The Joy Luck Club* is published.

1993: Toni Morrison receives the Nobel Prize for Literature.

Acknowledgments

The editors wish to thank the copyright holders of the excerpted criticism included in this volume and the permissions managers of many book and magazine publishing companies for assisting us in securing reproduction rights. We are also grateful to the staffs of the Detroit Public Library, the Library of Congress, the University of Detroit Mercy Library, Wayne State University Purdy/Kresge Library Complex, and the University of Michigan Libraries for making their resources available to us. Following is a list of the copyright holders who have granted us permission to reproduce material in this volume of *NfS*. Every effort has been made to trace copyright, but if omissions have been made, please let us know.

COPYRIGHTED EXCERPTS IN *NFS*, VOLUME 1, WERE REPRODUCED FROM THE FOLLOWING PERIODICALS:

Ball State Teachers College Forum, v. VI, Winter, 1965. © 1965, renewed 1993 Ball State University. Reprinted by permission of the publisher.

The CEA Critic, v. 36, November, 1973. Copyright © 1973 by the College English Association, Inc. Reproduced by permission.

CLA Journal, v. XXII, June, 1979. Copyright, 1979 by The College Language Association. Reproduced by permission of The College Language Association. *CLA Journal,* v. XXXVI, December, 1992. Copyright, 1992 by The College Language Association. Reproduced by permission of The College Language Association.

Critical Inquiry, v. 10, March, 1984. Copyright © 1984 by The University of Chicago. Reproduced by permission.

Los Angeles Times Book Review, April 17, 1988. Copyright, 1988, Los Angeles Times. Reproduced by permission. *Los Angeles Times Book Review,* March 12, 1989. Copyright, 1989, Los Angeles Times. Reproduced by permission.

MELUS, v. 10, Fall, 1983. Copyright, *MELUS,* The Society for the Study of Multi-Ethnic Literature of the United States, 1983. Reproduced by permission.

The Midwest Quarterly, v. XV, January, 1974. Copyright, 1974, by The Midwest Quarterly, Pittsburg State University. Reproduced by permission.

Modern Fiction Studies, v. XIV, Autumn, 1968. Copyright © 1968 by Purdue Research Foundation, West Lafayette, IN 47907. All rights reserved. Reproduced by permission of The Johns Hopkins University Press.

Modern Language Quarterly, v. XXV, December, 1964. © 1966, renewed 1994 University of Washington. Reproduced by permission of Duke University Press.

The Nation, New York, v. 246, April 23, 1988. Copyright 1988 The Nation magazine/The Nation Company, Inc. Reproduced by permission.

The New Republic, v. 164, May 8, 1971. © 1971 The New Republic, Inc. Reproduced by permission of The New Republic.

The New York Review of Books, June 10, 1976. Copyright © 1976 Nyrev Inc. Reproduced with permission from *The New York Review of Books.*

The New York Times Book Review, March 19, 1989. Copyright © 1989 by The New York Times Company. Reproduced by permission.

Nineteenth-Century Fiction, v. 19, September, 1964 for "Arthur Dimmesdale as Tragic Hero" by Bruce Ingham Granger. © 1964, renewed 1992 by The Regents of the University of California. Reprinted by permission of the publisher and the author.

Notes and Queries, v. 190, June 15, 1946 for "The Noble Savage in Mary Shelley's Frankenstein" by Milton Millhauser. © Oxford University Press. Reproduced by permission of the publisher and the Literary Estate of Milton Millhauser.

Women's Studies: An Interdisciplinary Journal, v. 12, February, 1986. © Gordon and Breach Science Publishers. Reproduced by permission.

COPYRIGHTED EXCERPTS IN *NFS*, VOLUME 1, WERE REPRODUCED FROM THE FOLLOWING BOOKS:

Adams, Timothy Dow. From *Telling Lies in Modern American Autobiography.* The University of North Carolina Press, 1990. © 1990 The University of North Carolina Press. All rights reserved. Reproduced by permission of the publisher and the author.

Baker, Carlos. From "Chapter 17," in *The American Novel from Cooper to Faulkner.* Edited by Wallace Stegner. Basic Books, 1965. © 1965 by Basic Books, Inc., Publishers. Reproduced by permission of Basic Books, a division of HarperCollins Publishers, Inc.

Brown, Julia Prewitt. From "The 'Social History' of 'Pride and Prejudice'," in *Approaches to Teaching Austen's Pride and Prejudice.* Edited by Marcia McClintock Folsom. Modern Language Association of America, 1993. Reproduced by permission of the Modern Language Association of America.

Johnson, Wayne L. From *Ray Bradbury.* Frederick Ungar Publishing Company, 1980. Copyright © 1980 by Frederick Ungar Publishing Co., Inc. Reproduced by permission.

Kneedler, Susan. From "The New Romance in 'Pride and Prejudice,'" in *Approaches to Teaching Austen's Pride and Prejudice.* Edited by Marcia McClintock Folsom. Modern Language Association of America, 1993. Reproduced by permission of the Modern Language Association of America.

Lee, Dorothy H. From "The Quest for Self: Triumph and Failure in the World of Toni Morrison," in *Black Women Writers (1950-1980): A Critical Evaluation.* Edited by Mari Evans. Anchor Press/Doubleday, 1984. Copyright © 1983 by Mari Evans. All rights reserved. Used by permission of Doubleday, a division of Bantam Doubleday Dell Publishing Group, Inc.

Neuhaus, Ron. From "Threshold Literature: A Discussion of 'Ordinary People,'" in *Censored Books: Critical Viewpoints.* Nicholas J. Karolides, Lee Burress, John M. Kean, eds. The Scarecrow Press, Inc., 1993. Copyright © 1993 by Nicholas J. Karolides, Lee Burress, John M. Kean. Reproduced by permission.

Scarseth, Thomas. From "A Teachable Good Book: 'Of Mice and Men,'" in *Censored Books: Critical Viewpoints.* Nicholas J. Karolides, Lee Burress, John M. Kean, eds. The Scarecrow Press, Inc., 1993. Copyright © 1993 by Nicholas J. Karolides, Lee Burress, John M. Kean. Reproduced by permission.

Sewall, Richard B. From *The Vision of Tragedy.* Yale University Press, 1959. Copyright © 1959 by Yale University Press, Inc. Renewed 1987 by Richard B. Sewall. All rights reserved. Reproduced by permission of the author.

Wood, Diane S. From "Bradbury and Atwood: Exile as Rational Decision," in *The Literature of Emigration and Exile.* Edited by James Whitlark and Wendall Aycock. Texas Tech University Press, 1992. Copyright 1992 Texas Tech University Press. All rights reserved. Reproduced by permission of the publisher.

PHOTOGRAPHS AND ILLUSTRATIONS APPEARING IN *NFS*, VOLUME 1, WERE RECEIVED FROM THE FOLLOWING SOURCES:

AP/WIDE WORLD PHOTOS: Clemens, Samuel (seated in a rocking chair), photograph. AP/Wide World Photos. Reproduced by permission. Guest, Judith (in striped sweater), 1976, photograph. AP/Wide World Photos. Reproduced by permission. Heller, Joseph, photograph. AP/Wide World Photos. Reproduced by permission. García Márquez, Gabriel, photograph. AP/Wide World Photos. Reproduced by permission. Morrison, Toni (bandanna on head), photograph. AP/Wide World Photos. Reproduced by permission. Morrison, Toni (accepting Nobel Prize), 1993, photograph.

AP/Wide World Photos, Inc. Reproduced by permission. Plath, Sylvia, photograph. AP/Wide World Photos. Reproduced by permission. Salinger, J. D., photograph. AP/Wide World Photos. Reproduced by permission. Tan, Amy, photograph. AP/Wide World Photos. Reproduced by permission.

ARCHIVE PHOTOS, INC.: Arkin, Alan, in the film "Catch 22," photograph. Archive Photos. Reproduced by permission. Bradbury, Ray, photograph. Archive Photos, Inc. Reproduced by permission. Hirsch, Judd, and Timothy Hutton in the movie "Ordinary People," photograph. Archive/ Paramount. Reproduced by permission. Steinbeck, John, photograph. Archive Photos, Inc. Reproduced by permission. Wright, Richard, photograph. Archive Photos. Reproduced by permission.

THE BETTMANN ARCHIVE/NEWSPHOTOS, INC.: Cooper, Gary, and Helen Hayes, in film "A Farewell to Arms," photograph. UPI/Corbis-Bettmann. Reproduced by permission. English ambulance driver (standing next to truck), c. 1918, Italy, photograph. UPI/Corbis-Bettmann. Reproduced by permission. Field hands sitting on bagged wheat, c. 1880, Moro, Oregon, photograph by W. A. Raymond. Corbis-Bettmann. Reproduced by permission. García Márquez, Gabriel (being interviewed, on couch), photograph. UPI/Corbis-Bettmann. Reproduced by permission. Gish, Lillian, and Lars Hanson in the film "The Scarlet Letter," 1926, photograph. Springer/Corbis-Bettmann. Reproduced by permission. Laborers weighing cotton, horse and wagon, c. 1910, photograph. Corbis-Bettmann. Reproduced by permission. Mississippi riverboat loading logs, print by Currier and Ives. Corbis-Bettmann. Reproduced by permission. Nazi youths burning books, 1933, Berlin, photograph. UPI/Corbis-Bettmann. Reproduced by permission. Nurse attending patient sleeping on floor, photograph. UPI/Corbis-Bettmann. Reproduced by permission. Office workers seated at desks, large windows along side, 1952, photograph. UPI/Corbis-Bettmann. Reproduced by permission. Puritan with musket standing in doorway, 1882, woodcut. Corbis-Bettmann. Reproduced by permission. Rooney, Mickey, as Huck Finn in "The Adventures of Huckleberry Finn," photograph. Springer/Corbis-Bettmann. Reproduced by permission. Shelley, Mary Wollstonecraft (daisy trim), painting by Samuel John Stump. Corbis-Bettmann. Reproduced by permission. Street scene (buses, rickshaws, carriers in street), Chungking, China, 1944, photograph. UPI/Corbis-Bettmann. Reproduced by permission. Temple, Shirley (as a child, curtseying in accordion-pleated dress), photograph. Corbis-Bettmann. Reproduced by permission. Troops of the 85th Division march through the Porta Maggiore, 1944, Rome, photograph. Corbis-Bettmann. Reproduced by permission. Two young men standing outside Swing Rendezvous club, 1955, Greenwich Village, photograph. UPI/Corbis-Bettmann. Reproduced by permission. Wright, Richard (seated, typing next to window), photograph. Corbis-Bettmann. Reproduced by permission.

BLACK STAR: Hemingway, Ernest (fringed buckskin shirt), photograph. Hans Malmberg/Black Star. Reproduced by permission.

GALE RESEARCH INC. (Detroit): Map of Colombia, illustration. Gale Research Inc. Reproduced by permission.

THE KOBAL COLLECTION: Chin, Kieu (with other cast members) in the film "The Joy Luck Club," photograph. The Kobal Collection. Reproduced by permission. Christie, Julie, and Oskar Werner in the movie "Fahrenheit 451," photograph. The Kobal Collection. Reproduced by permission. Garson, Greer and Laurence Olivier (in a scene from the 1940 motion picture "Pride and Prejudice"), photograph. The Kobal Collection. Reproduced by permission. Hassett, Marilyn (sitting on floor), in the film "The Bell Jar" by Sylvia Plath, photograph. The Kobal Collection. Reproduced by permission. Hutton, Timothy and Dinah Manoff (in a scene from the 1980 motion picture "Ordinary People"), photograph. The Kobal Collection. Reproduced by permission. Karloff, Boris (walking in village), in movie "Frankenstein," 1935, photograph. The Kobal Collection. Reproduced by permission. Sinise, Gary, and John Malkovich, in film of "Of Mice and Men" by John Steinbeck, photograph. The Kobal Collection. Reproduced by permission.

SOURCE UNKNOWN: Austen, Jane, watercolor drawing by Cassandra Austen. First illustration of the Frankenstein Monster, by Mary Shelley. Hawthorne, Nathaniel, photograph. Jane Austen's home at Chawton, photograph.

The Adventures of Huckleberry Finn

Mark Twain

1884

Although probably no other work of American literature has been the source of so much controversy, Mark Twain's *The Adventures of Huckleberry Finn* is regarded by many as the greatest literary achievement America has yet produced. Inspired by many of the author's own experiences as a riverboat pilot, the book tells of two runaways—a white boy and a black man—and their journey down the mighty Mississippi River. When the book first appeared, it scandalized reviewers and parents who thought it would corrupt young children with its depiction of a hero who lies, steals, and uses coarse language. In the last half of the twentieth century, the condemnation of the book has continued on the grounds that its portrayal of Jim and use of the word "nigger" is racist. The novel continues to appear on lists of books banned in schools across the country.

Nevertheless, from the beginning *The Adventures of Huckleberry Finn* was also recognized as a book that would revolutionize American literature. The strong point of view, skillful depiction of dialects, and confrontation of issues of race and prejudice have inspired critics to dub it "*the* great American novel." Nobel Prize-winning author Ernest Hemingway claimed in *The Green Hills of Africa* (1935), for example, that "All modern American literature comes from one book by Mark Twain called *Huck Finn....* There was nothing before. There has been nothing as good since."

Mark Twain

Author Biography

Best known as Mark Twain, Samuel Clemens was born 30 November 1835 and raised in Hannibal, Missouri. There he absorbed many of the influences that would inform his most lasting contributions to American literature. During his youth, he delighted in the rowdy play of boys on the river and became exposed to the institution of slavery. He began to work as a typesetter for a number of Hannibal newspapers at the age of twelve. In the late 1850s, he became a steamboat pilot on the Mississippi River. This job taught him the dangers of navigating the river at night and gave him a first-hand understanding of the river's beauty and perils. These would later be depicted in the books *Life on the Mississippi* and *The Adventures of Huckleberry Finn.*

After a brief stint as a soldier in the Confederate militia, Clemens went out west, where he worked as a reporter for various newspapers. He contributed both factual reportage and outlandish, burlesque tales. This dual emphasis would characterize his entire career as a journalist. During this phase of his career, in 1863, he adopted the pseudonym Mark Twain, taken from the riverboat slang that means water is at least two fathoms (twelve feet) deep and thus easily travelled.

His second book, *The Innocents Abroad* (1869), a collection of satirical travel letters the author wrote from Europe, was an outstanding success, selling almost seventy thousand copies in its first year. On the heels of this triumph, Clemens married Olivia Langdon and moved to the East, where he lived for the rest of his life. In the East, Clemens had to confront the attitudes of the eastern upper class, a group to which he felt he never belonged. Nevertheless, he did win influential friends, most significantly William Dean Howells, editor of the *Atlantic Monthly.*

Clemens's first two novels, *The Gilded Age* (1873), written with Charles Dudley Warner, and *The Adventures of Tom Sawyer* (1876), a children's book based on his boisterous childhood in Hannibal, won Clemens widespread recognition. Shortly afterwards, he began to compose a sequel to Tom's story, an autobiography of Tom's friend, Huck Finn. He worked sporadically on the book over the next seven years, publishing more travel books and novels in the meantime. When it was finally published, *The Adventures of Huckleberry Finn* was an immediate success, although it was also condemned as inappropriate for children. The book draws on Clemens's childhood in Hannibal, including his memories of the generosity of whites who aided runaway slaves, in addition to the punishments they endured when caught. In fact, in 1841, his father had served on the jury that convicted three whites for aiding the escape of five slaves.

In the 1890s, Clemens's extensive financial speculations caught up with him, and he went bankrupt in the depression of 1893-94. With an eye to paying back his many debts, he wrote a number of works, including continuing adventures of Tom Sawyer and Huck Finn. He spent his final decade dictating his autobiography, which appeared in 1924. Clemens died on 21 April 1910.

Plot Summary

Chapters 1-7: Huck's Escape

Mark Twain begins *The Adventures of Huckleberry Finn* with a notice to the reader. He identifies Huckleberry Finn as "Tom Sawyer's Comrade," and reminds the reader that this novel resumes where *The Adventures of Tom Sawyer* left off: in St. Petersburg, Missouri, on the Mississippi River, "forty to fifty years" before the novel was written (so between 1834 and 1844, before the American Civil War). He tells the reader that several different "dialects are used," which have been written "painstakingly," based on his own "personal familiarity with these several forms of speech."

The novel's title character, Huckleberry Finn, narrates the story. He summarizes the end of *The Adventures of Tom Sawyer,* in which he and Tom discovered a large amount of stolen gold. He lives now with the Widow Douglas, who has taken him in as "her son," and her sister Miss Watson. His father, "Pap," has disappeared:

> Pap hadn't been seen for more than a year, and that was comfortable for me; I didn't want to see him no more. He used to always whale me when he was sober and could get his hands on me; though I used to take to the woods when he was around.

The widow attempts to "sivilize" Huck, and teach him religion. Huck finds her ways confining. Miss Watson nags him to learn to read, to "set up straight," and to behave. Huck remains superstitious, and he mostly resists the women's influence; after bedtime, he escapes out his window to join Tom Sawyer for new adventures. The boys meet Jim, "Miss Watson's nigger," and they play a trick on him. Jim, like Huck, is superstitious, and when he wakes up he thinks that witches played the trick.

Tom, Huck, and other boys meet in a cave down the river, and form a Gang, a "band of robbers." But Huck tires of the Gang's adventures, because they are only *imaginary.* When Pap shows up in St. Petersburg, he causes Huck some *real* problems. Pap wants Huck's reward money from the end of *The Adventures of Tom Sawyer.* Signs of his son's increased civilization irritate him: the proper clothing, and the ability to read and write. Huck secures his money by "selling" it to Judge Thatcher. Huck's father brings a lawsuit against the judge, but "law" is "a slow business." Eventually Pap kidnaps Huck, and takes him up the river to a shack on the Illinois side of the river. At first, Huck enjoys the return to freedom, but living with his father has its difficulties; "by-and-by pap [gets] too handy with his hick'ry," and he either leaves Huck locked in the cabin alone, or beats him. Huck decides to escape, and cuts a hole in the cabin. After his father lays in some supplies, Huck lays his plans. He catches a canoe as it floats down the river. Left alone, Huck stages his own murder: he kills a wild pig and leaves its blood around the shack and on his jacket, then leaves a fake trail showing a body being dragged to the river. He then loads up the supplies and takes off down river. He stops to camp on Jackson's Island, two miles below St. Petersburg.

Chapters 8-18: Down the River

On the island, Huck feels liberated. Seeing his friends search for his body troubles him only slightly. After a few days, he discovers that he is not alone on the island: Jim has run away from Miss Watson, who had threatened to sell him down the river. Jim's escape troubles Huck, but together they enjoy a good life: fishing, eating, smoking, and sleeping. They find a house floating down the river, with a dead man in it, from which they take some valuables. Huck appreciates the lore that Jim teaches him, but still likes to play tricks. He leaves a dead rattlesnake on Jim's bed, and Jim gets bitten by the snake's mate. He recovers, but interprets the bite as the result of Huck touching a snakeskin—a sure bringer of bad luck. Jim suspects that there is more to come.

One night, Huck dresses as a girl and goes across to town to "get a stirring-up." He discovers that there is a reward offered for Jim and that the island is no longer a safe hiding place. He rushes back to the island, and he and Jim float down the Mississippi, sleeping by day and drifting by night. Living this way, they get to know each other, and Jim tells Huck about his children. They also have several adventures. They board a wrecked steamboat and steal some ill-gotten goods from three thieves on board, inadvertently leaving them to drown.

Huck and Jim get separated in a fog. They call out, but for hours at a time, they seem lost to each other. Huck falls asleep, and when he awakens, he sees the raft. He sneaks aboard and convinces Jim it was all a dream. When Huck points to evidence of the night's adventure and teases him for being gullible, Jim teaches Huck a lesson:

> "When I got all wore out wid work, en wid de callin' for you, en went to sleep, my heart wuz mos' broke bekase you waz los', en I didn' k'yer no mo' what become er me en de raf'. En when I wake up en fine you back ag'in, all safe en soun', de tears come, en I could 'a' got down on my knees en kiss' yo' foot, I's so thankful. En all you wuz thinkin' 'bout wuz how you could make a fool uv ole Jim wid a lie. Dat truck dah is *trash;* en trash is what people is dat puts dirt on de head er dey fren's en makes 'em ashamed."
>
> .... It was fifteen minutes before I could work myself up to go and humble myself to a nigger; but I done it, and I warn't ever sorry for it afterwards, neither. I didn't do him no more mean tricks, and I wouldn't done that one if I'd 'a' knowed it would make him feel that way.

From the film The Adventures of Huckleberry Finn, *starring Mickey Rooney, MGM, 1939.*

Chapters 19-33: The King and Duke

Huck and Jim plan to drift down to Cairo, Illinois, and then steamboat North, but they realize that they passed Cairo in the fog. A steamboat crashes into their raft and separates them again. Huck swims ashore and is taken in by the Grangerford family, who are embroiled in a feud with another local family, the Shepherdsons. He lives with the Grangerfords, while Jim hides in a nearby swamp and repairs the raft. When the feud erupts into new violence, and Huck's new friend, Buck Grangerford, is killed, Huck and Jim set off once again down the river.

Huck and Jim rescue two "rapscallions," who identify themselves as a duke and a king. They take the prime sleeping quarters on the raft and expect Jim and Huck to wait on them. They employ different schemes to make money along the river. They attend a religious camp-meeting, and the king takes up a collection for himself. In "Arkansaw," they rent a theater and put on a Shakespearean farce called "The Royal Nonesuch." Next, a boy they meet confides that an inheritance awaits one Mr. Wilks, an English gentleman, in his town. Seeing their opportunity, the king and duke assume the identity of Mr. Wilks and his servant, and go to claim the money. Huck feels increasingly uneasy

about their unscrupulous behavior, and vows to protect their victims. He hides the cash they try to steal. When the real Mr. Wilks arrives, Huck and Jim try—but fail—to escape without the rascally "king" and "duke."

Next, the king and duke betray Jim as a runaway slave, and "sell" their "rights" to him to a farmer, Silas Phelps. Huck realizes what has happened and determines to rescue Jim. He seeks the Phelps farm. By a stroke of luck, they are relatives of Tom Sawyer's, and mistakenly identify Huck as Tom, come to pay a visit. When Tom arrives a few hours later, he falls in with Huck's deception, pretending to be his brother Sid.

Chapters 34-43: Jim's Rescue

Tom agrees to help Huck rescue Jim. He insists that the escape follow models from all of his favorite prison stories: he smuggles in items past the unwitting Phelpses. He makes Jim sleep with spiders and rats, and write a prison journal on a shirt. He also warns the Phelpses anonymously. In the escape, Tom gets shot in the leg. Jim and Huck each return and are caught in the act of seeking help for Tom.

Finally Tom reveals that Jim is in fact no longer a slave: Miss Watson died and set him free in her will. Tom's Aunt Polly arrives and clears up the case of mistaken identity. Huck, upset by the trick played on him and Jim, accepts Tom's explanation that he wanted "the *adventure*" of the escape. Tom gives Jim forty dollars for his trouble. Now that everyone knows he is still alive, Huck worries about Pap, but Jim tells him not to bother: Pap was the dead man in the house floating down the river. Huck ends the novel with a plan to "light out for the Territory ahead of the rest" before the women try again to "sivilize" him.

Characters

Aunt Polly

Tom Sawyer's guardian. She arrives at the Phelps's farm and reveals Tom and Huck's true identities.

Aunt Sally

See Mrs. Sally Phelps

Boggs

During his travels with the King and Duke in "Arkansaw," Huck meets Boggs, a drunk in

Media Adaptations

- In the 1930s, *The Adventures of Huckleberry Finn* was adapted twice as a black-and-white film under the title *Huckleberry Finn,* once in 1931 by director Norman Taurog for Paramount, and then in 1939 by MGM. The latter is the most famous of the novel's adaptations. It was directed by Richard Thorpe and starred Mickey Rooney as Huck and Rex Ingram as Jim. The 1939 film is available on video from MGM/UA Home Entertainment.

- An adaptation of the novel was produced for the "Climax" television program in 1954 by CBS. It starred Thomas Mitchell and John Carradine and is available from Nostalgia Family Video.

- Another film version of the book was released by MGM in 1960, this time in color as *The Adventures of Huckleberry Finn.* Directed by Michael Curtiz, the film starred Eddie Hodges as Huck, Archie Moore as Jim, and Tony Randall as the King. This adaptation is also available on video from MGM/UA Home Entertainment.

- PBS produced a version titled *The Adventures of Huckleberry Finn* for "American Playhouse" in 1986. The movie was directed by Peter H. Hunt and the cast included Sada Thompson, Lillian Gish, Richard Kiley, Jim Dale, and Geraldine Page. It is available from MCA/Universal Home Video.

- Walt Disney produced *The Adventures of Huck Finn* in 1993. This film, starring Elijah Wood as Huck and Courtney B. Vance as Jim, deleted racial epithets and translated the characters' dialects to suit modern tastes. It was directed by Stephen Sommers, who also wrote the screenplay. The film is available from Walt Disney Home Video.

- In 1994, the novel was updated in the film adaptation *Huck and the King of Hearts* produced by Crystal Sky Communications. In this version, Chauncey Leopardi plays Huck, who lives in a trailer park, and Graham Green plays Jim, who is a Native American con artist fleeing a hoodlum from whom he has stolen drug money. The movie was directed by Michael Keusch and written by Chris Sturgeon. It is available on home video.

- The novel has also been recorded on sound cassettes many times since 1980. Unabridged versions are available from Books, Inc. and Books in Motions. Abridged versions are available from Metacom, Listen for Pleasure Ltd., and Time Warner Audiobooks, which released a study guide along with the tape.

Bricksville. Boggs continually curses at townspeople, and despite several warnings, he provokes the wrath of Colonel Sherburn and is killed by him.

Widow Douglas

The Widow Douglas has adopted Huck and attempts to provide a stable home for him. She sends him to school and reads the Bible to him. Although at first Huck finds life with Widow Douglas restrictive, eventually he gets "sort of used to the widow's ways, too, and they warn't so raspy on me." Later, when Huck refers to her, she represents all that is good and decent to him. Nevertheless, at the close of the novel Huck decides to "light out for the Territory" instead of returning to her home.

The Duke

On their journey down the Mississippi, Huck and Jim pick up two con men who claim to be descendants of royalty. The Duke is a young, poorly dressed man of about thirty. Although they had never met before, the King and Duke soon join forces to concoct a number of scams to play on the innocent inhabitants of the various towns along the riverbanks. Even though he is aware of their true characters, Huck plays along—he has little choice, since the two men are stronger and can turn Jim in at any time. Eventually, however, Huck betrays them when they scheme to cheat the Wilks sisters out of their inheritance. The King and Duke later turn Jim in for a meager reward. The men later get their reward when they are tarred and feathered by an angry crowd. With these two characters, Twain ridicules the aristocratic pretensions of some Americans.

Huck Finn

See Huckleberry Finn

Huckleberry Finn

The narrator and hero of *The Adventures of Huckleberry Finn* is the title character, the fourteen-year-old son of the town drunk who was introduced in *The Adventures of Tom Sawyer.* At the end of that book, Huck was adopted by the Widow Douglas and her sister Miss Watson, who brought him to live in town where he could attend church and school. But at the beginning of *Adventures of Huckleberry Finn,* we learn that their attempts to "sivilize" him have been only partially successful. Huck learns to read and write, but he continues to climb out of his window at night to meet up with Tom Sawyer's gang.

Huck's life in town is abruptly ended when his father returns and kidnaps him, hoping to lay his hands on Huck's fortune. But Huck escapes by faking his own death, and he heads to Jackson's Island. There he meets up with Jim, Miss Watson's slave, who has run away because of her threat to sell him "down the river." The two of them embark on a journey down the Mississippi River and live a life of freedom on the raft, which has become their refuge from society. On their trip, Huck confronts the ethics he has learned from society that tell him Jim is only property and not a human being. By this moral code, his act of helping Jim to escape is a sin. Rather than betray Jim, though, Huck decides, "All right, then, I'll *go* to hell." Huck learns to decide for himself in various situations the right thing to do.

In the last third of the book, Huck defers to Tom Sawyer, whose outlandish schemes to free Jim direct the action. Huck is no longer in charge, and his moral quest appears to have been abandoned. But once Jim is freed, Huck decides he will "light out for the Territory" to escape the civilizing influence of another mother figure, this time Tom's Aunt Sally. For some critics, this decision redeems Huck from the charge that he has allowed Tom to distract him from discovering his inner code of ethics. To others, it means that Twain sees no hope for civilization to redeem itself: because it cannot rid itself of fundamental failures like slavery, someone like Huck must escape its influence altogether.

Pap Finn

Huck's father, Pap, is an irredeemable drunk who schemes to get Huck's fortune away from him. When he returns to find Huck living at the Widow Douglas's and going to school, he accuses Huck of trying to be better than his father. Pap kidnaps Huck and brings him to a cabin in the woods where he beats his son and confines him to their shack. Pap also submits Huck to his drunken tirades against a free black man, reflecting the attitudes poor southern whites had about blacks who had the right to vote and were highly educated. Shortly after Huck escapes, Pap is killed, although Huck does not learn this until the end of the book.

The Grangerfords

Huck is taken in by the Grangerfords after the raft is broken up by a larger boat on the river. The family is wealthy and Huck is impressed by their gaudily decorated home, although the reader is aware of their shallow faithfulness to ideals of gentility and decorum. Their feud with the Shepherdsons, based on a brutal, senseless code of honor, makes Huck "sick." He leaves after one of the Grangerfords's daughters runs off with one of the Shepherdson boys, and most of the men in the family are killed in the ensuing battle.

Buck Grangerford

The youngest son of the Grangerford family. He is Huck's age, but is killed in the feud with the Shepherdsons. Huck "haint ever heard anything" like how Buck swears after missing an opportunity to kill Harney Shepherdson. Nevertheless, he cries when he discovers Buck's body, "for he was mighty good to me."

Emmeline Grangerford

One of the Grangerfords's daughters, who died in adolescence and left behind a large number of sentimentally morbid poems and drawings that Huck admires. Her family tells Huck, "She warn't particular; she could write about anything … just so it was sadful."

Jim

Jim, a runaway slave who has escaped from his owner, Miss Watson, for fear of being sold to a plantation in New Orleans, is Huck Finn's companion as they travel on a raft down the Mississippi river. He has been recognized by critics as a complex character, at once a superstitious and ignorant minstrel-show stereotype but also an intelligent human being who conveys more depth than the narrator, Huck Finn, is aware of. As their journey progresses, however, Huck does grow to see Jim as more than a stereotype, despite comments like, "he had an uncommon level head for a nigger." Jim confronts Huck's prejudice when he scolds Huck for trying to play a trick on him without taking his feelings into consideration. Pointing to some leaves on the raft, he tells Huck, "dat truck dah is *trash;* en trash is what people is dat puts dirt on de head er dey fren's en makes 'em ashamed." On their journey, Huck becomes aware of Jim's humanity and decides he will assist Jim in his quest to become free.

In the last third of the book, Huck enlists the help of Tom Sawyer to help free Jim, only to learn at the end that Tom knew all along that Jim had been freed by Miss Watson. In this section, critics have argued, Jim is once again cast as a shallow caricature of a gullible slave, and the novel's serious theme of race relations is reduced to a farce. But other critics have seen a consistency of character in Jim throughout the book, as a slave who wears the mask of ignorance and docility as a defense against white oppression, occasionally giving Huck (and the reader) glimpses behind the mask. Forrest G. Robinson has argued that Jim learns Huck "is quite unprepared to tolerate the full unfolding of the human being emergent from behind the mask," and so the real Jim retreats in the last third of the book to ensure that Huck will continue to help him. But according to Chadwick Hansen, Jim is never a "fully-rounded character" in his own right; rather he serves the function of making Huck confront his conscience and overcome society's influence.

The King

On their journey down the Mississippi, Huck and Jim pick up two con men who claim to be descendants of royalty. The King is a bald, grey-bearded man of about seventy years. Although they had never met before, the King and Duke soon join forces to concoct a number of scams to play on the innocent inhabitants of the various towns along the riverbanks. Even though he is aware of their true characters, Huck plays along—he has little choice, since the two men are stronger and can turn Jim in at any time. Eventually, however, Huck betrays them when they scheme to cheat the Wilks sisters

out of their inheritance. The King and Duke later turn Jim in for a meager reward. The men later get their reward when they are tarred and feathered by an angry crowd. With these two characters, Twain ridicules the aristocratic pretensions of some Americans.

Mrs. Judith Loftus

A sympathetic woman whom Huck meets while he is dressed up like a girl. She sees through his costume, but inadvertently warns Huck that her husband is on his way to Jackson's Island to capture Jim.

Mrs. Sally Phelps

Tom Sawyer's aunt. When Huck arrives on the Phelps farm, they are expecting Tom, so Huck pretends to be their nephew, while Tom pretends to be his brother, Sid. She good-naturedly scolds "Sid" for pretending to be a stranger and then kissing her unasked.

Reverend Silas Phelps

Tom Sawyer's uncle. When Huck arrives on the Phelps farm, they are expecting Tom, so Huck pretends to be their nephew, while Tom pretends to be his brother, Sid. Phelps appears to be a kindly, good-natured, and trusting man, but he is holding Jim prisoner while waiting for his master to reclaim him.

Tom Sawyer

Tom Sawyer picks up where he left off in *The Adventures of Tom Sawyer* by continuing to lead the other boys in imaginative games based on his reading of romantic adventure literature. But in this novel, his antics are much less innocent and harmless. At the beginning of *Huck Finn,* he provides comic relief in Huck's otherwise straight-laced life at the Widow Douglas's. But his reappearance at the end has troubled many critics. When Tom finds out that Huck is going to free Jim, he wholeheartedly takes up the challenge, creating elaborate schemes to free the man when he could just tell the family that Jim has already been freed by Miss Watson. Neither Huck nor Jim approve of Tom's "adventures," although they feel compelled to submit to his authority in such matters. Many critics have noted the thoughtless, even cruel nature of Tom's games, as they make Jim's life miserable and terrorize Aunt Sally. But Tom is ultimately punished for his forays into fantasy; during Jim's escape he is shot and seriously wounded.

Colonel Sherburn

A Southern aristocrat who kills a drunk, Boggs, in the town of Bricksville, in "Arkansaw." He endures Boggs's taunts and gives him a warning before shooting the man in front of his own daughter. The town threatens to lynch him, but his scornful speech about the cowardice of the average American man and the mobs he participates in breaks up the crowd.

Judge Thatcher

He keeps Huck's money safely out of Pap's hands by "buying" Huck's fortune for a dollar. Later he and the Widow Douglas petition a higher court to take Huck away from his father, but the court's "new judge" says families shouldn't be separated.

Miss Watson

The Widow Douglas's sister and Jim's owner. She represents a view of Christianity that is severe and unforgiving. It is her attempts to "sivilize" Huck that he finds most annoying: "Miss Watson she kept pecking at me, and it got tiresome and lonesome." When Jim overhears her admit the temptation to sell him down South despite her promise not to do so, he runs away. Her guilt at this turn of events leads her to set Jim free in her will.

Wilks sisters

The sisters—Mary Jane, Susan, and Joanna—are orphaned when their guardian uncle, Peter, dies. The King and Duke impersonate their long-lost uncles in an attempt to gain their inheritance. Their trusting and good-hearted nature in the face of the King and Duke's fraud finally drives Huck to take a stand against the two scoundrels.

Themes

Freedom

In *The Adventures of Huckleberry Finn* both Huck and the runaway slave Jim are in flight from a society which labels them as outcasts. Although Huck has been adopted by the Widow Douglas and been accepted into the community of St. Petersburg, he feels hemmed in by the clothes he is made to wear and the models of decorum to which he must adhere. But he also does not belong to the world Pap inhabits. Although he feels more like himself in the backwoods, Pap's drunken rages and

attempts to control him force Huck to flee. At the end of the book, after Jim has been freed, Huck decides to continue his own quest for freedom. "I reckon I got to light out for the Territory ahead of the rest, because Aunt Sally she's going to adopt me and sivilize me, and I can't stand it. I been there before." Huck is clearly running from a civilization that attempts to control him, rather than running in pursuit of something tangible. He is representative of the American frontiersman who chooses the unknown over the tyranny of society.

As a slave, Jim has likewise been denied control over his own destiny, and he escapes to prevent being sold down to New Orleans, away from his wife and children. But Jim is chasing a more concrete ideal of freedom than Huck is. For Jim, freedom means not being a piece of property. Jim explicitly expresses his desire to be free as they approach Cairo and the junction with the Ohio River: "Jim said it made him all over trembly and feverish to be so close to freedom." But after they pass Cairo in the confusion of a foggy night, Jim's quest for freedom is thwarted and he must concentrate on survival. After Jim's capture, Tom and Huck attempt to free him in a farcical series of schemes that actually make escape more difficult and dangerous. Huck indicates that a simple removal of the board that covers the window would allow Jim to escape, but Tom declares that is too easy. "I should *hope* we can find a way that's a little more complicated than *that*, Huck Finn," Tom says. After Jim escapes and is recaptured, Tom reveals that he has been free all along. Miss Watson had died and left him free in her will. The irony of freeing a free man has concerned many critics, who believe Twain might have been commenting on the failure of Reconstruction after the Civil War.

Conscience

Huck's main struggle in the book is with his conscience, the set of morals with which he has been raised. As they begin to approach Cairo, and Jim looks forward to his freedom, Huck says his conscience "got to troubling me so I couldn't rest." He rationalizes that he didn't lure Jim away from his owner, but "conscience up and says every time, 'But you knowed he was running for his freedom, and you could 'a' paddled ashore and told somebody.'" During this scene he wakes up to the fact that he is helping a slave gain freedom, something he has been brought up to believe is wrong. So in an attempt to relieve his guilt, he sets off for shore, telling Jim he is going to find out if they have passed Cairo, but really intending to turn Jim in.

When he meets up with two men looking for a runaway slave, he confronts a true test of conscience, and fails, in his eyes. The two men ask him about the man on board, and Huck protects Jim by making up an elaborate tale about his father who is dying of smallpox, a highly contagious disease. When he returns to the raft, Jim rejoices in his cover-up, but Huck instead is "feeling bad and low, because I knowed very well I had done wrong." He decides that he is naturally bad, and that he only did what made him feel better. Not being able to analyze his actions, Huck fails to recognize that he has taken a stand against a morally corrupt society. Later, after Jim has been turned in by the King and Duke, Huck must again wrestle with his conscience as he decides to play an active role in freeing Jim. Up until this point he had only protected Jim from discovery; now he must help Jim escape, an even more serious crime. But rather than let his "conscience" guide him, Huck listens to his heart, which tells him that Jim is a human being, not property. He turns his back forever on society's ethics and decides he'd rather "*go to hell*" than turn his back on Jim. Through Huck, Twain attacks that part of the conscience that unquestioningly adheres to society's laws and mores, even when they are wrong.

Race and Racism

Probably the most discussed aspect of *Huck Finn* is how it addresses the issue of race. Many critics agree that the book's presentation of the issue is complex or, some say, uneven. No clear-cut stance on race and racism emerges. Despite the fact that Huck comes to respect Jim as a human being, he still reveals his prejudice towards black people. His astonishment at Jim's deep feelings for his family is accompanied by the statement, "I do believe he cared just as much for his people as white folks does for their'n. It don't seem natural, but I reckon it's so." And even after he has decided to help free Jim, Huck indicates that he still does not see black people overall as human beings. When Aunt Sally asks "Tom Sawyer" why he was so late in arriving, he tells her the ship blew a cylinder head. "Good gracious! Anybody hurt?" she asks. "No'm. Killed a nigger." "Well, it's lucky; because sometimes people do get hurt," she responds. As some critics have pointed out, Huck never condemns slavery or racial prejudice in general but seems to find an exception to the rule in Jim. Nevertheless, the fact that Huck does learn to see beyond racial stereotypes in the case of Jim is a profound development, considering his upbringing. He lived in a

Topics for Further Study

- Study the history and form of the minstrel show in the nineteenth century and find evidence in *Adventures of Huckleberry Finn* that Twain was influenced by minstrels in his creation of the novel.

- Research the history of the novel's censorship in America, and argue for or against the exclusion of *Adventures of Huckleberry Finn* from a school's curriculum.

- Using history texts and primary sources like slave narratives, research the conditions under which slaves lived in the 1840s to gain a deeper understanding of what Jim's life might have been like, and tell Jim's story from his perspective.

household with the Widow Douglas and Miss Watson where slaves were owned. And Pap's rantings over a free black man indicate his deep racial prejudice. When confronted with the fact that a free black man was highly educated and could vote, Pap decides he wants nothing to do with a government that has allowed this to happen. He wants the free man, whom he calls "a prowling, thieving, infernal, white-shirted free nigger," to be sold at auction. In other words, all black people are slaves, white man's property, in his eyes. Such are the views on race with which Huck has been raised. But there is no agreement as to what Twain's message on the subject of race is. While some critics view the novel as a satire on racism and a conscious indictment of a racist society, others stress the author's overall ambivalence about race. Critics have had a difficult time reconciling the stereotypical depictions of Jim and other slaves in the book with Huck's desire to free Jim.

Style

Narrator

The Adventures of Huckleberry Finn was a breakthrough in American literature for its presentation of Huck Finn, an adolescent boy who tells the story in his own language. The novel was one of the first in America to employ the child's perspective and employ the vernacular—a language specific to a region or group of people—throughout the book. Many critics have characterized the smoothness of Huck's language as the most unique feature of the book. Lionel Trilling sees Twain's creation of Huck's voice as a measure of his genius. He writes that Huck's language has "the immediacy of the heard voice." Shelley Fisher Fishkin has suggested that Twain created Huck's style of speech from that of a real boy, an African-American child that he met in the early 1870s, combined with dialects of white people he had heard as a child. But Huck's unique perspective is that of a lower-class, southern white child, who has been viewed as an outcast by society. From this position, Huck narrates the story of his encounters with various southern types, sometimes revealing his naivete and, at other times, his acute ability to see through the hypocrisy of his elders. Many readers have commented on Huck's unreliability as a narrator, though, especially in his admiration of the gaudy taste exhibited by the Grangerfords and his inability to see through his own prejudices when he tells Aunt Sally that no one was hurt on board the ship, although a "nigger" was killed.

Setting

Another distinctive aspect of the novel is its setting. Because it takes place when slavery was at its height in America, *The Adventures of Huckleberry Finn* addresses in a roundabout way the prejudices of southern whites that had laid the foundation for slavery and were still omnipresent in the Reconstruction South of Twain's time. The discussion of slavery in the text, then, takes on a new meaning for a post-Civil War audience. It forced them to confront the legacy of slavery in spite of their eagerness to forget its devastating impact and rid themselves of its curse. The physical setting of the novel, most specifically the river and the raft, has also drawn the attention of critics. The Mississippi River itself serves as a kind of no-man's land in the text, a place outside of society that is governed by different rules. The raft becomes a new world for Huck and Jim, where they can be themselves and make up their own rules by which to live. On either side of the river lies the shore, which represents a return to society. Significantly, it is Huck who makes excursions into towns along the

river banks for food, information, and fun. While Huck can be a kind of vagabond, travelling from one place to another without being a part of society, Jim must hide on the raft, the only place where he can be safe.

Burlesque

Burlesques, or parodies of elevated or serious forms of literature, were popular as far back as Shakespeare, but they were also the favorites of working-class theatergoers in America starting in the 1840s. In America, burlesques often poked fun at aristocratic types who were subjected to the lowly conditions of the American city or frontier, and they extolled the virtues of a democracy over the pretensions of Europe's high society. Burlesques also became associated with minstrel shows as they were incorporated into the latter in the 1850s. Mark Twain is well known for his adept adaptations of burlesques in his works. In *The Adventures of Huckleberry Finn* he used the technique to critique the aristocratic pretensions of the King and Duke, and the romantic fantasies of Tom Sawyer. In fact, the last third of the book descends into burlesque, according to the novel's critics, as Tom's outlandish schemes to free Jim take center stage. In addition, some scenes between Jim and Huck are modeled on burlesques, especially their conversation about Frenchmen, in which Jim subtly outsmarts Huck, revealing the wisdom of the supposedly ignorant.

Realism and Regionalism

Mark Twain was a major contributor to the interconnected Realist and Regionalist movements, which flourished from the 1870s to the 1920s. Realism refers to the insistence on authentic details in descriptions of setting and the demand for plausible motivations in character's behaviors. Writers of the Regionalist movement also adhered to these principles as they explored the distinct and diverse regions of post-Civil War America that they feared were being swallowed up by a national culture and economy. Realist and Regionalist techniques are exemplified in *The Adventures of Huckleberry Finn* by the specific and richly detailed setting and the novel's insistence on dialect which attempts to reproduce the natural speech of a variety of characters unique to the Mississippi Valley region. In addition, Huck's momentous decision to free Jim, even if it means going to hell, is seen as a classic episode of Realist fiction because it demonstrates

Compare & Contrast

- **1840s:** Under the Slave Codes, enacted by individual southern states, slaves could not own property, testify against whites in court, or make contracts. Slave marriages were not recognized by law.

  1884: As the result of Black Codes enacted by states during Reconstruction, African Americans could now legally marry and own property, but the codes also imposed curfews and segregation. The Fifteenth Amendment granted black men the right to vote, but individual states prohibited them from doing so.

  Today: The right to vote is universal for all citizens above the age of eighteen, and other rights are not restricted by race.

- **1840s:** The steamboat was the most popular mode of travel and the Mississippi and Ohio Rivers were the main thoroughfares in the West.

  1884: The railroad had taken over as the means of mass transportation all across America.

  Today: Most goods are transported within the U.S. by truck, and airplanes and cars allow people to travel long distances in short periods of time.

- **1840s:** Means of entertainment were beginning to flourish in America. Among the many new kinds of literature available were slave narratives and romantic adventures. The first minstrel show was staged in 1843.

  1884: The field of literature, in the form of books and periodicals, had become the province of the masses. The minstrel show continued to be popular, as did the music of ragtime which was associated with it.

  Today: Entertainment, especially film, television, and music, is a multi-billion-dollar industry.

- **1840s:** The Mississippi River ran freely, making travel dangerous, due to snags, large pieces of trees lodged in the river.

  1884: The Mississippi River Commission had been founded in 1879 to improve navigation. Over the next decades, a series of levees were built which also alleviated flooding problems.

  Today: The level of the Mississippi River and its banks are tightly controlled so that navigation is very safe and floods are less frequent.

---

the individual's struggle to make choices based on inner motivations, rather than outside forces.

Historical Context

Slavery

The issue of slavery threatened to divide the nation as early as the Constitutional Convention of 1787, and throughout the years a series of concessions were made on both sides in an effort to keep the union together. One of the most significant of these was the Missouri Compromise of 1820. The furor had begun when Missouri requested to enter the union as a slave state. In order to maintain a balance between free and slave states in the union, Missouri was admitted as a slave state while Maine entered as a free one. And although Congress would not accept Missouri's proposal to ban free blacks from the state, it did allow a provision permitting the state's slaveholders to reclaim runaway slaves from neighboring free states.

The federal government's passage of Fugitive Slave Laws was also a compromise to appease southern slaveholders. The first one, passed in 1793, required anyone helping a slave to escape to pay a fine of $500. But by 1850, when a second law was passed, slaveowners had become increasingly insecure about their ability to retain their slaves in the face of abolitionism. The 1850 Fugitive Slave Law increased the fine for abetting a run-

Currier & Ives print of a riverboat titled "Wooding up on the Mississippi."

away slave to $1000, added the penalty of up to six months in prison, and required that every U.S. citizen assist in the capture of runaways. This law allowed southern slaveowners to claim their fugitive property without requiring them to provide proof of ownership. Whites and blacks in the North were outraged by the law, which effectively implicated all American citizens in the institution of slavery. As a result, many who had previously felt unmoved by the issue became ardent supporters of the abolitionist movement.

Among those who were outraged into action by the Fugitive Slave Law was Harriet Beecher Stowe, whose novel *Uncle Tom's Cabin* (1852) galvanized the North against slavery. Dozens of slave narratives—first hand accounts of the cruelties of slavery—had shown white Northerners a side of slavery that had previously remained hidden, but the impact of Stowe's novel on white Northerners was more widespread. Abraham Lincoln is reported to have said when he met her during the Civil War, "So you're the little lady who started this big war." White southerners also recognized the powerful effect of the national debate on slavery as it was manifested in print, and many southern states, fearing the spread of such agitating ideas to their slaves, passed laws which made

it illegal to teach slaves to read. Missouri passed such a law in 1847.

Despite the efforts of southerners to keep slaves in the dark about those who were willing to help them in the North, thousands of slaves did escape to the free states. Many escape routes led to the Ohio River, which formed the southern border of the free states of Illinois and Indiana. The large number of slaves who escaped belied the myths of contented slaves that originated from the South.

Reconstruction

Although *The Adventures of Huckleberry Finn* takes place before the Civil War, it was written in the wake of Reconstruction, the period directly after the Civil War when the confederate states were brought back into the union. The years from 1865 to 1876 witnessed rapid and radical progress in the South, as many schools for blacks were opened, black men gained the right to vote with the passage of the Fifteenth Amendment in 1870, and the Civil Rights Act of 1875 desegregated public places. But these improvements were quickly undermined by new Black Codes in the South that restricted such rights. White southerners felt threatened by Republicans from the North who went south to help direct the course of Reconstruction. Most galling was the new authority of free blacks, many of whom held political office and owned businesses. While prospects did improve somewhat for African Americans during Reconstruction, their perceived authority in the new culture was exaggerated by whites holding on to the theory of white superiority that had justified slavery.

In response to the perceived threat, many terrorist groups were formed to intimidate freed blacks and white Republicans through vigilante violence. The Ku Klux Klan, the most prominent of these new groups, was formed in 1866. Efforts to disband these terrorist groups proved ineffective. By 1876, Democrats had regained control over the South and by 1877, federal troops had withdrawn. Reconstruction and the many rights blacks had gained dissipated as former abolitionists lost interest in the issue of race, and the country became consumed with financial crises and conflicts with Native Americans in the West. Throughout the 1880s and 1890s, new Jim Crow laws segregated public spaces in the South, culminating in the Supreme Court's decision in the case *Plessy v. Ferguson* in 1896, which legalized segregation.

Minstrel Shows

As the first indigenous form of entertainment in America, minstrel shows flourished from the 1830s to the first decade of the twentieth century. In the 1860s, for example, there were more than one hundred minstrel groups in the country. Samuel Clemens recalled his love of minstrel shows in his posthumously published *Autobiography,* writing, "If I could have the nigger show back again in its pristine purity and perfection I should have but little further use for opera." His attraction to blackface entertainment informed *The Adventures of Huckleberry Finn,* where, many critics believe, he used its humorous effects to challenge the racial stereotypes on which it was based.

Minstrel shows featured white men in blackface and outrageous costumes. The men played music, danced, and acted burlesque skits, but the central feature of the shows was the exaggerated imitation of black speech and mannerisms, which produced a stereotype of blacks as docile, happy, and ignorant. The shows also depicted slavery as a natural and benign institution and slaves as contented with their lot. These stereotypes of blacks helped to reinforce attitudes amongst whites that blacks were fundamentally different and inferior. The minstrel show died out as vaudeville, bur-

lesques, and radio became the most popular forms of entertainment.

Critical Overview

When it was first published, responses to *Adventures of Huckleberry Finn* were fairly nonexistent until the Concord Public Library in Massachusetts announced that it was banning the book from its shelves. This action set off a public debate over the merits of the book. The most vocal were those who deemed the book to be unsuitable for children, fearing their corruption by exposure to its lower-class hero. Howard G. Baetzhold reports that beloved children's author Louisa May Alcott said about the book, "if Mr. Clemens cannot think of something better to tell our pure-minded lads and lasses, he had best stop writing books for them." Critics who demanded that literature be uplifting cited rough language, lack of moral values, and a disrespectful stance towards authority as the book's faults. But some critics rallied behind the author and wrote reviews that praised the book as a lasting contribution to American literature.

These early reactions are a fair indication of how the book has been received ever since. On the one hand, respected scholars have claimed the book as the core text of an American literary canon, where it has enjoyed a secure position since the 1950s. As Leo Marx claims, "Everyone agrees that *Huckleberry Finn* is a masterpiece." H. L. Mencken went so far as to dub the novel "perhaps the greatest novel ever written in English." Although some have questioned the formal coherence of the novel, arguing that the ending and Tom's burlesque escapades disrupt the text's quest for freedom, the general consensus has emerged that *The Adventures of Huckleberry Finn* is one of the most important works of American fiction ever written. But despite this resounding stamp of approval from the nation's leading literary scholars, secondary schools around the country have at various times questioned its suitability for students, even going so far as to ban the book. Whereas detractors of the novel from the previous century had been primarily concerned with its lack of decency and moral values, in the wake of the Civil Rights movement, the main concern of administrators, parents, and librarians has become that it promotes racism and demeans African American children with its extensive use of the word "nigger." Ultimately, the fear is that the complexity of the racial issues in the text may be too much for schoolchildren to comprehend. As Peaches Henry explains, "Parents fear that the more obvious aspects of Jim's depiction may overshadow the more subtle uses to which they are put."

Although in the past there have been sharp contrasts between the responses of scholarly and lay readers of *The Adventures of Huckleberry Finn,* the debate over the book's racial messages has more recently become the center of debate amongst literary scholars as well. The crux of the controversy is whether or not the novel presents an indictment of racism or simply reflects the generally accepted racist attitudes of the time period in which it was written. For most critics, the issue boils down to the depiction of Jim. For some, Jim is nothing more than a minstrel show stereotype, "the archetypal 'good nigger,' who lacks self-respect, dignity, and a sense of self separate from the one whites want him to have," in the words of Julius Lester. In these critics' eyes, Twain reveals his racism when he allows Tom to derail and hence belittle Jim's serious attempts to gain freedom and Huck's efforts to overturn society's view of blacks as property. But to others, a subtle satire on slavery and racism emerges from the text and takes precedence over any stereotypical depictions of African-Americans. Eric Lott argues, for example, "Twain took up the American dilemma (of race) not by avoiding popular racial presentations but by inhabiting them so forcefully that he produced an immanent criticism of them." According to Lott, the use of minstrel show stereotypes, exaggerated and ridiculous depictions of whites's false perceptions of blacks, has the effect of "making nonsense out of America's racial structures." Many critics agree with Lott, seeing the novel itself as a critique of the racism expressed by its narrator, Huck.

For many critics, however, Twain's conscious intentions about racial messages are not the issue. They see instead a variety of perhaps unconscious effects in the novel that point to new ways to understand the text's complex evocation of America's racial predicament. For example, Forrest G. Robinson sees a depth to Jim that he thinks previous scholars have missed. Jim is both the stereotypical "darky" and the complex human being, wearing a mask of contentment and gullibility that represents the kind of prejudice whites have about him as an African American. But behind the mask, the real Jim is a shrewd agent in his own defense. In essence, Robinson argues that whether Twain was aware of it or not, Jim is a complex African American character that reflects the situation of slaves at the time as they attempted to survive in a racist so-

ciety. Such readings draw attention to the complex ways the novel addresses, in Robinson's words, "the nation's most painful and enduring dilemma." These readings accept Twain's ambivalence and contradictory responses to the issue, rather than attempting to vilify the author or insulate him from accusations of racism. In a related vein of argument, Peaches Henry declares that we may not be able to decide once and for all whether the novel is racist or subversive, but the book deserves our attention because "[t]he insolubility of the race question as regards *Huckleberry Finn* functions as a model of the fundamental racial ambiguity of the American mind-set."

Criticism

Pearl James

In the following essay, James, a doctoral candidate at Yale University, relates the history of controversy surrounding The Adventures of Huckleberry Finn *and particularly its portrayal of the slave Jim. She argues that how the reader interprets Jim's character can affect the interpretation of the novel's problematic ending.*

The Adventures of Huckleberry Finn has been a source of controversy since its publication in 1884. It was banned from many public libraries on its first appearance for being "trash." Although today it is widely regarded as a—if not *the*—classic American novel, it still poses problems for its readers. *Huckleberry Finn* has long been identified as expressing something essentially American: in the words of Bernard De Voto, "the novel derives from the folk and embodies their mode of thought more purely and more completely than any other ever written." In some ways, the debate about the Americanness of *Huckleberry Finn* reveals the larger struggle to define American identity. Those who first condemned the novel as being "trash" objected to it on grounds of both literary merit and racial, social, and economic class: they rejected its portrayal of a slave and an uneducated, poor boy as the most typical kind of American citizens. The opposite point of view, which celebrates the novel as an expression of the "folk," asserts its subject is the quintessential, or typical, American story: characters without social advantages trying to "make good."

Twain creates the impression of American folk culture through his use of dialect and phonetic spelling, which mimics speech, rather than writing.

What Do I Read Next?

- Mark Twain's *Life on the Mississippi* (revised, 1883) tells of the author's years as a steamboat pilot through a series of short articles.

- Frederick Douglass's *Narrative of the Life of Frederick Douglass* (1845) is the most prominent slave narrative written, and depicts his development from slave to free man.

- *A Short History of Reconstruction* (1990) by Eric Foner, an abridged version of his award-winning study *Reconstruction: America's Unfinished Revolution,* explains the complex reasons for the failure of Reconstruction.

- In *Slavery and Freedom: An Interpretation of the Old South* (1990), James Oakes presents a thorough history of slavery as it was practiced and preached during the period in which *Adventures of Huckleberry Finn* takes place.

- Harriet Beecher Stowe's classic *Uncle Tom's Cabin* (1852) depicts the inhumanity of an institution which separates slave families on the auction block and corrupts southern whites by giving them absolute power over their slaves.

- In his essay "On the Duty of Civil Disobedience," published in 1849, Henry David Thoreau argues that each person is responsible for acting on his own principles, no matter what the laws of the state. He applied this reasoning specifically to slavery.

As he points out in his opening notice to the reader, different characters use different dialects; in *this* world, where not everyone receives the same kind of education, people speak differently from one another. Many critics read *Huckleberry Finn* as a lesson in the way that identity is formed by social realities. They focus on the fact that Twain uses language to show that access to culture and education defines character. Depending on how you read it, the spoken language can either make characters more believable, complex, and therefore dignified, or it can make them seem merely uneducated, caricatured, and "backward."

Twain's attempt to capture the sounds of vernacular (local) speech is part of the novel's realism, part of its documentary quality. And yet, the novel also has elements of romance, which is the very opposite of realism. For instance, Twain relies on unbelievable coincidences in his plot, like the fact that the Phelpses *just happen* to be Tom Sawyer's relatives, and he *just happens* to be arriving on the same day that Huck comes to the farm. Twain manages to merge elements of these two kinds of writing by using a third literary tradition to structure his novel. This literary tradition is called the picaresque—the comedy of the road, the traveling adventure; only here, instead of on a road, the journey takes place on a river. The episodes along the river suggest that the Mississippi winds through a semi-wild frontier. Twain makes the American landscape a site of endless adventures. The river, symbolizing both the power of nature and the inevitable passing of time, is what keeps the raft, and the story, moving. This picaresque framework, although it is usually associated with romance, makes the novel's realistic, documentary moments possible. As Huck and Jim move down the Mississippi, they encounter a diverse swath of American society. Huck gives firsthand descriptions of feuding families, a camp-meeting religious revival, a lynch mob, and other complex social phenomena. Twain connects the picaresque structure, which leaves room for endless variation and adventures, with the endless variation of America's inhabitants. As in his earlier novel, *Life on the Mississippi,* Twain draws on his own childhood experience and his knowledge as a river man to give the book its convincing details. Samuel Clemens even took his pseudonym, "Mark Twain," from his life on the river.

If *Huckleberry Finn* is *the* authentically American adventure story, it also explores one of America's most lasting problems: racism. Many critics have questioned Twain's portrayal of "the nigger

Jim." Twain's consistent use of the word "nigger" is itself troubling to readers today. It is important to notice that Twain uses a great deal of irony in general, and that what Huck thinks is not the same thing that Twain thinks. There are two main questions here: does Twain simply use stereotypes? And if he does, does he do so in order to make those stereotypes seem true, or to show them as false and oversimplified? On the one hand, Jim's humanity makes him the novel's most appealing character. Jim fills a gap in Huck's life: he is the father that Pap is not; he teaches Huck about the world and how it works, and about friendship. But on the other hand, parts of Jim's character belong to a traditional stereotype of the "happy darky"—an imaginary portrayal of the slave as simple, childlike, and contented. Although Jim runs away, he does not strike the reader as overtly "rebellious" or dangerous. Jim never seems to suspect Huck's crisis of conscience about whether or not he should be helping a slave to escape. And, instead of being angry with Tom Sawyer for the trick he plays at the end of the novel, Jim is simply happy to take his forty dollars.

How we read Jim influences how we read the novel's primary structural "problem," its ending. One way of thinking about this problem is to ask whether *Huckleberry Finn* seems to go in a line, or in a circle. On the journey down the river, Huck learns that Jim has real feelings, recognizes his humanity, and vows not to play any more tricks on him. If the novel is a *bildungsroman*—a narrative about a character coming of age—this is the moment in which Huck learns his most valuable lesson. Huck seems to be traveling onward, in a line of development. But the ending chapters seem to circle us back into the childlike, irresponsible world of boyish adventure that Huck has supposedly left behind. The long and drawn out trick that Tom Sawyer plays on Jim makes the reader doubt if any real development has taken place. Which side of the joke is Huck on? Even though he does not know that Jim has been freed, he lets Tom turn the escape into a game, and seems to feel little, if any, remorse for toying with Jim's fate. He seems to have forgotten what he learned about the importance of Jim's feelings. Finally, even though Jim is technically "free," he is not recognized as a man by the other characters, or by the larger social world he inhabits. Toni Morrison argues that the novel needs Jim's enslavement to make the other characters seem free by contrast. She explains, "freedom has no meaning to Huck or to the text without the specter of enslavement, the anodyne to individualism; the yardstick of absolute power over the life of another; the signed, marked, informing, and mutating presence of a black slave." At the end of the novel, for instance, Huck plans to "light out for the Territory" in search of more adventures. But Jim's wife and children are still slaves. Because of his racial identity in a racist society, Jim always remains more confined than Huck does.

Writing *The Adventures of Huckleberry Finn* took Mark Twain several years. He began the project as a sequel to *The Adventures of Tom Sawyer,* as another children's book. But as he wrote, it became more complex; it raises questions that make it a challenging book for readers of all ages. To understand the novel's complexity, one has to take its dual historical context into account. Twain locates the action in the past, before the civil war, and before the legal abolition of slavery. But much of the novel speaks to Twain's contemporary audience, who lived during Reconstruction, a time when the South especially was trying to deal with the effects of the Civil War. The "king" and "duke" owe something of their depiction to the post-Civil War stereotype of carpetbaggers (a derogatory stereotype of Northerners come to prey on the defeated South). Jim belongs, at least partially, to a postwar Vaudeville tradition of the "happy darky," played on stage by white men in blackface, who used a parodied version of black dialect. This popular stereotype conveyed a white nostalgia, and enacted an imaginary construction of the slave before Emancipation, before the "disappointments" of Reconstruction. Twain tries to come to terms with this nostalgia, but whether he critiques it, or indulges in it, is up for debate.

During his lifetime, Twain was best known for being a humorist, a user of irony and a writer of satire. In this novel, he uses Huck as a relatively naive narrator to make ironic observations about Southern culture and human nature in general. As usual, Twain finds a likely object of satire in religious fervor, in the cases both of Miss Watson and of the visit the "king" pays to the camp-meeting. But the irony in *Huckleberry Finn* exists at several levels of narration: sometimes Twain seems to aim his irony at Huck, while other times, Huck himself is an ironic and detached observer. For instance, when the rascally "king" and "duke" come aboard the raft, Huck tells the reader:

> It didn't take me long to make up my mind that these liars warn't no kings nor dukes at all, but just low-down humbugs and frauds. But I never said nothing, never let on; kept it to myself; it's the best way; then you don't have no quarrels, and don't get into no trouble. If they wanted us to call them kings and

dukes, I hadn't no objections, 'long as it would keep peace in the family; and it warn't no use to tell Jim, so I didn't tell him. If I never learnt nothing else out of Pap, I learnt that the best way to get along with his kind of people is to let them have their own way.

This passage ironically undercuts the way we think Huck has been relating to the two frauds; he does not, in fact, "feel right and kind towards" them. In fact, the connections among the foursome on the raft are extremely tenuous. Huck's choice of metaphor compounds the irony: he compares the two men to his father, and decides to think of them as part of his "family," throwing the whole notion of "family" into an ironic light. Huck thinks he can avoid "trouble" by pretending not to know that they are frauds, but trouble is all they bring. Huck's decision to "let them have their own way" is wishful, because he really has no choice. Finally, although Huck seems to condemn them, he recognizes them as liars partially because he is one himself—he tricks people out of money on more than one occasion. This passage explicitly reminds us that Huck can dissemble and pretend, just as Twain does in his writing. As readers of *Huckleberry Finn,* we are continually challenged to locate the multiple objects of the novel's satire.

Twain's irony complicates the question of race and racism in the world of *Huckleberry Finn.* What the novel make clear, though, as their journey continually separates and reunites Huck and Jim— white and black—is that their fate is intertwined. Their destinies must be worked out in relation to each other. For Twain, *that* is the great, and greatly troubled, American adventure.

Source: Pearl James, in an essay for *Novels for Students,* Gale 1997.

Ray B. Browne

In the following excerpt, Browne discusses how Tom Sawyer, at the end of the novel, has a negative moral influence that Huck Finn must struggle to overcome.

Throughout the book Huck's attitude toward the life around him is remarkably ambivalent. Though he clearly is rebelling against respectability and civilization, he rebels because they make him uncomfortable and ill at ease. He fights them by running away. When he can no longer abide the "pecking" of the Widow and Miss Watson, and the privations they force upon him, he flees, but only to the rags and sugar-hogshead of the other side of town. He does not need to go farther. In fact, he must stay within commuting distance of respectable folk. And he quickly and easily returns when a lure

is held up to him. The agent who entices Huck back from rags to respectability is, of course, Tom Sawyer. Tom at this time clearly symbolizes Huck's ideal.

Tom seems to be a rebel. He battles the world around him. He attacks the status quo, and seemingly threatens to overturn it. Yet his battles are all shams. If he ever overthrew his paper dragons, his crusading spirit would collapse. He lives happily in his society. After the lark of playing battler, he always joyously returns to the safety and security of Aunt Polly. This clash of danger and safety appeals to Huck, and it is epitomized in the person of Tom. Huck will therefore make any sacrifice for his hero, even to giving up the comfort and freedom he so immensely enjoys. Tom has saturated and captivated Huck's consciousness. Near or far he is the older boy's evil genius.

But Huck is not satisfied or happy for long in his enslavement. Though he sees the world through Tom's rose-colored glasses, and though his spontaneous reaction to any situation is usually Tom's, Huck is restive. He is galled by his fetters and tries to break away. The fact is that he cannot live without Tom—or with him. He seeks a *modus vivendi* [a manner of living] with Tom and his world, but cannot find it. Huck's victory over this forced compromise constitutes one of the great achievements in the book.

Demonstration of Huck's ambivalence begins at the outset of the novel. Huck recounts how in *Tom Sawyer* he was adopted by Widow Douglas, could not tolerate her "sivilizing" him and therefore ran away to his rags, where he was "free and satisfied." But Tom lured him back with the promise that he could become a member of the band of robbers. "So I went back," Huck states matter-of-factly. The close bond between the two boys is further revealed when Miss Watson tries to get Huck, who is hell-bent, to reform and thus prepare for the other destination; Huck is content with hell when Miss Watson assures him that Tom will be there too: "I wanted him and me to be together."

But no sooner does Huck join the band of robbers than the two boys' incompatibility manifests itself and he begins to drag his feet. After playing robber for a month, Huck resigns. He can no longer pretend that hogs are "ingots" and turnips are "julery." He wants to see the "di'monds," A-rabs, and elephants. For his protests, Tom calls him a "numskull," and "perfect sap-head." Huck's revulsion overcomes him. "I judged that all that stuff was only one of Tom Sawyer's lies.... It had all the marks of a Sunday school." Tom the romantic dreamer, the sham adventurer, thus symbolizes everything that frightens Huck: St. Petersburg civilization, religion, romantic literature. From this monster Huck flees.

Yet fly as he will, Huck cannot shake off Tom, who is a ghost that refuses to be laid. When Huck "kills" himself to escape from Pap, he does it on Tom's terms: "I did wish Tom Sawyer was there, I knowed he would take an interest in this kind of business, and throw in the fancy touches...." Again, on the night of the storm, when Huck is trying to convince Jim to board the wrecked *Walter Scott*, the force that drives Huck aboard is not the promise of loot—of "seegars" and "solid cash"—but the irresistible urge to imitate Tom. "I can't rest, Jim, till we give her a rummaging. Do you reckon Tom Sawyer would ever go by this thing? Not for pie, he wouldn't.... I wish Tom Sawyer *was* here."

Later, in Tennessee while the King and Duke play Peter Wilks' brothers, when Huck has adroitly maneuvered Mary Jane away from the house and has satisfactorily lied to the other girls, he congratulates himself, with his inevitable comparison: "I felt very good; I judged I had done it pretty neat—I reckon Tom Sawyer couldn't a done it no neater himself." Still later, in Pikesville, when Huck discovers that the King has turned in Jim for the sum of forty dollars, he decides to write home and have Jim's owner send for him. But he automatically thinks of writing to Tom and having him tell Miss Watson where Jim is. The point is that in Huck's mind St. Petersburg—that world—and Tom are one and the same, inseparable, with Tom the symbol.

With Tom so constantly and completely—and so heavily—on his mind, Huck naturally—and not surprisingly—acquiesces in the deception when Aunt Sally mistakes him for Tom. Huck's first impulse has always been to give in to Tom. Why should he not be flattered *to be* Tom? Indeed, discovering that he was supposed to be Tom Sawyer "was like being born again," in the sense of being reborn into the world of St. Petersburg and of Tom. "Being Tom Sawyer was easy and comfortable," Huck confesses immediately. Once it is settled that Huck will be Tom and Tom will be Sid, the future looks rosy. Everything will be "easy and comfortable." Huck relaxes completely, suspending his mental processes—becoming again the blind disciple. For example, it is inconceivable that the Huck of the voyage, with his mind alerted for signs of Jim, could see a slave enter an isolated cabin with

food—part of it watermelon—and not suspect its purpose. Yet the somnolent Huck does: "Well, it does beat all, that I never thought about a dog not eating watermelon. It shows how a body can see and don't see at the same time."

But in Huck's acquiescence there immediately becomes manifest the old attraction-revulsion tug-of-war he felt in St. Petersburg. And after the initial joy of being Tom has worn off, Huck begins to protest. In the old environment, the last time the boys shared an adventure, it took Huck a month to break away. Now, however, Huck's new nature shows through quickly. When he and Tom are concocting schemes for the release of Jim, Huck gives his plan first, then sits back waiting for the "superior" one; when Tom springs his, Huck reflects ironically: "I see in a minute it was worth fifteen of mine, for style, and would make Jim just as free a man as mine would, and maybe get us all killed besides."

After this initial resistance, Huck protests each new detail of the plan, as the more mature person realizes the absurdity of Tom's childish pranks. He protests, but he gives in each time. Each protest, in fact, is weaker than its predecessor. In this increasing weakness lies Huck's downfall. His resistance—his maturity—is being abraded. He is coming more and more under the mesmeric influence of Tom. Finally he capitulates completely: "Anyway that suits you suits me," he says when Tom wants him to dress up like a servant-girl to deliver the warning of the release of Jim.

Throughout the remainder of the evasion, Huck protests not at all. During the actual escape he apparently enjoys himself. It is action, of course, instead of romantic theorizing, and therefore appeals to the pragmatic Huck. But—far more significantly—Huck's new self is being subsumed under Tom's. So fast has been the activity since Tom's arrival that Huck has not had a chance to be alone and to reflect, and it is only when he has searched his soul through active thinking that his true self emerges. Now, caught up in activity, he is becoming the old Huck again, so completely under the influence of Tom that he is ready to "slide out" with Tom and Jim and "go for howling adventures amongst the Injuns, over in the Territory, for a couple of weeks or two."

At this point Huck is faced with the greatest crisis of his life. Once before he was confronted with a mighty decision, when he had to choose between being respectable and returning Jim to Miss Watson, and being himself, listening to the voice of his heart, not returning Jim—and going to hell. He chose the latter course, but only after great soul-searching, in solitude and silence: "I ... set there thinking—thinking.... And went on thinking. And got to thinking...." In this even greater crisis if the new boy is to prevail over the old, clearly he needs time to think and think. Luckily time is provided.

Source: Ray B. Browne, "Huck's Final Triumph," in *Ball State Teacher's College Forum,* Vol. 6, No. 1, Winter, 1965, pp. 3–12.

Frances V. Brownell

In the following excerpt, Brownell explains the importance of Jim's role in the novel as not just a foil to Huck but as a "moral catalyst" who is key to Huck's moral growth.

At the beginning of the second chapter of *Huckleberry Finn,* we meet one of the most important characters in the novel: "Miss Watson's big nigger, named Jim, was setting in the kitchen door...." Jim is to play a role second only to that of Huck in this novel, but the reader is seldom conscious at any one point of the extent of Jim's importance. Even in Jim's biggest scenes, we more often than not come away thinking of Huck rather than Jim. The main point I wish to make in this paper is that Jim is not merely a noble cause or an ignoble foil, in either of which cases he would be more particularly important for the action episodes of the book than he in fact is; he is rather what one might call a moral catalyst, and thereby of central importance in the portrayal and illumination of the character of Huckleberry Finn. True, the action depends upon the presence of the runaway slave, and from this status evolves the double search for freedom which Professor [Edgar Marquess] Branch defines [in his *The Literary Apprenticeship of Mark Twain* (1950)] as the explicit theme of the book: "Huck's story of his struggle to win freedom for himself and Jim." His role as the runaway slave may certainly be argued as showing Jim's indirect importance to the varied action in the book, but it is my thesis that Jim's primary function is to further the characterization of Huckleberry Finn: by his presence, his personality, his actions, his words, to call forth from Huckleberry Finn a depth of tenderness and moral strength that could not otherwise have been fully and convincingly revealed to the reader. For Mark Twain's gift for characterization was, as Professor [Edward] Wagenknecht has observed [in his *Mark Twain: The Man and His Work*

(1935)], a very great "ability to *evoke* character, as distinct from *constructing* it." ...

It is Jim's openness, his unashamed dignity, that makes Huck's struggle with and conquest of his pride, that is, his ashamed dignity, deeply moving and fully significant. We have seen earlier in the book touches of gentleness in Huck, we have seen that he does not mean to hurt the feelings of the Widow Douglas, and later we are to see him grieving that he has deceived and brought sorrow to Aunt Sally. But it is this incident [when Huck lies to] Jim which, above all others, shows his concern about "hurting others" in its full meaning, as a deep and affectionate respect for human dignity. We have seen and are to see this concern carried far beyond respect for the visible and admirable dignity of Jim, the Widow Douglas, Mary Jane Wilks, and Aunt Sally, to include respect for the besmirched if not invisible dignity of the Duke and Dauphin as, tarred and feathered, they are ridden out of town astride a rail (Ch. XXXIII). And there is Huck's attempt to secure rescue for the stranded murderers: "I begun to think how dreadful it was, even for murderers, to be in such a fix. I says to myself, there ain't no telling but I might come to be a murderer myself yet, and then how would I like it?" Professor Wagenknecht comments: "What a triumph of Christian humility! What a triumph of understanding and imagination! It is Mark Twain's version of the generally misquoted and misattributed utterance of old John Bradford, on seeing some criminals on the way to execution: 'But for the grace of God there goes John Bradford.'"

Jim is a gentle and loyal person; he is not vengeful, he does not hate, he cannot cheat or trick another. He fears and evades violence, but he does not commit violence—as do so many of the characters in this book, whether as individuals or with the clan or mob. His most memorable speeches are characterized by an open honesty and a deep capacity for unselfish love. We recall the wounded love for Huck that brought about Jim's angry speech quoted above, and the love for his little deaf daughter in that other powerfully dramatic, though brief, narration (Ch. XXIII). In a world peopled by Pap Finn, the Duke and the Dauphin, lynchers, feuders, and murderers, Huck is almost constantly on the defensive. It is when he is alone with Jim in the secure little world of the raft drifting down the Mississippi that Huck hears a voice of love that makes sense in a world of hatred, and can reply from his own heart with his apology and with his famous moral victory: "All right, then, I'll *go* to hell." Mr. Branch has pointed out in considerable detail the significance of the Widow Douglas, but she was not a comrade to Huck. Huck was ill at ease with her, and they sometimes simply could not understand each other's thoughts and feelings. With Jim, this barrier of age, position, sex, and background does not exist. It is in response to the open tenderness in Jim that there is the opportunity and the necessity for the tender side of the "realistic" Huck Finn to be spontaneously and convincingly revealed to the reader. Mr. Branch pays tribute to the integrity that lies back of and gives strength to this tenderness in Jim: of those people in Huck's world who live consistently from the heart. "Jim, of course, is foremost in selflessness and magnanimity. Because he is incapable of deceit, his innocence, whether comic or pathetic, is haloed with grandeur. His search for freedom is carried forth in humility and sanctified by elemental justice." When Jim's dignity *is* violated without remorse, it is by the amoral Tom, not the moral Huck, and this will be discussed later in this paper.

Jim's personality is strongly influenced by his faith in superstition, especially evil omens. His first serious appearance in the novel, after his brief appearance as the butt of Tom's prank, is to cast a rather ominous prediction for Huck by means of this ox hair-ball. The reader has been prepared before this for a serious attitude on the part of the characters towards superstition, when, in the first chapter, Huck is terrified to realize that he has accidentally killed a spider. Even the simile with which he describes the atmosphere takes on the morbid touch of his fear: "I set down again, a-shaking all over, and got out my pipe for a smoke; for the house was all as still as death now, and so the widow wouldn't know." After Jim has completed his splendidly ambiguous prophecy with the disheartening sentence: "You wants to keep 'way fum de water as much as you kin, en don't run no resk, 'kase it's down in de bills dat you's gwyne to git hung," this chapter concludes with a one-line paragraph: "When I lit my candle and went up to my room that night there sat pap—his own self!" Thus enters for the first time a genuinely evil force into the novel, in the form of the malicious and dangerous town drunkard. Later, the wreck of the raft, which leads to the Grangerford feud episode, is also preceded by an evil omen: Huck carelessly handles a snake-skin. (On this is also blamed—accurately—Jim's rattlesnake bite and—inaccurately—the near disaster on the *Walter Scott*.) As a final instance of the direct role of superstition in the plot, there is the fact that the rescue episode would have been foiled at the start if the great superstitious fear

of Uncle Silas had not made communication with the prisoner Jim not only possible but relatively easy....

Jim is, as Mr. Branch observes, Huck's mentor in this dark and shifting realm. But he is more than an instructor in fear, as Mr. Branch might seem to suggest; he is here again the voice of love and conciliation in an erratically malicious and quarrelsome world, although a voice touched with fear in this realm as with grief in the human realm. Jim's only rebellion in the human realm was born of love, not hate: he planned (though futilely) to free his wife and children, to steal them away from their "rightful owners." Huck and Jim are essentially not rebels: they seek to escape, not to fight. They ask only to be left alone. This is true in the human realm, and it is true as they try to ward off "bad luck" with charms and magic formulas.

We need not smile with condescension on this superstitious response to unseen malevolence. This "mythical, fatalistic level" is merely more picturesque in Huck's world than in our present world. It would be hypocritical of us to laugh at Jim and Huck's belief in the concrete existence of evil as Evil Powers, merely because the present unwritten code observes a different form. We no longer put in our time with dead cats and salt shakers in order to save ourselves from harm. Instead, we modern realists construct fierce, nationalistic mythologies peopled with spotless heroes and mustachioed villains, the roles remaining the same, but the cast changing every twenty years. So we who have humbled ourselves before one huge fear, who accept the supremacy of Evil or Violence, and struggle to clothe ourselves most adequately in his livery, hoping that our stockpile of A-Bombs will prove the highest in the end, laugh in relieved contempt at the multitude of little fears we no longer share. Still, even this side of a graceful admission of a common weakness, the reader who reads this novel responsively is eventually saturated by the awe and humility of these people (I mean especially Huck and Jim) towards what they do not understand but feel to exist above and beyond their limited power. The reader is aware of the more-than-human struggle that tinges the novel throughout, through all the petty and tragic human struggles. And that more-than-human struggle is most often made vivid through the words and actions and personality of Jim.

Source: Frances V. Brownell, "The Role of Jim in *Huckleberry Finn,* in *Boston Studies in English,* Vol. 1, 1955, pp. 74–83.

Sources

Howard G. Baetzhold, "Samuel Longhorn Clemens," in *Concise Dictionary of American Literary Biography: Realism, Naturalism, and Local Color, 1865-1917,* Gale, 1988, pp. 68-83.

Shelly Fisher Fishkin, *Was Huck Black?: Mark Twain and African-American Voices,* Oxford University Press, 1993.

Chadwick Hansen, "The Character of Jim and the Ending of 'Huckleberry Finn'," in *The Massachusetts Review,* Vol. V, No. 1, Autumn, 1963, pp. 45-66.

Ernest Hemingway, *The Green Hills of Africa,* Scribner, 1935.

Peaches Henry, "The Struggle for Tolerance: Race and Censorship in *Huckleberry Finn,*" in *Satire or Evasion? Black Perspectives on Huckleberry Finn,* edited by James S. Leonard, Thomas A. Tenney, and Thadius Davis, Duke University Press, 1992, pp. 25-48.

Julius Lester, "Morality and *Adventures of Huckleberry Finn,*" in *Satire or Evasion? Black Perspectives on Huckleberry Finn,* edited by James S. Leonard, Thomas A. Tenney, and Thadius Davis, Duke University Press, 1992, pp. 199-207.

Eric Lott, "Mr. Clemens and Jim Crow: Twain, Race, and Blackface," in *Criticism and the Color Line: Desegregating American Literature,* edited by Henry B. Wonham, Rutgers University Press, 1996, pp. 30-42.

Leo Marx, "Mr. Eliot, Mr. Trilling, and *Huckleberry Finn,*" in *The American Scholar,* Vol. XXII, 1953, pp. 432-40.

H. L. Mencken, "Final Estimate," in his *H. L. Mencken's "Smart Set" Criticism,* edited by William H. Nolte, Cornell University Press, 1968, pp. 182-89.

Forrest G. Robinson, "The Characterization of Jim in *Huckleberry Finn,*" in *Nineteenth-Century Literature,* Vol. XLIII, No. 3, December, 1988, pp. 361-91.

Lionel Trilling, "The Greatness of *Huckleberry Finn,*" in *Huckleberry Finn Among the Critics,* edited by M. Thomas Inge, University Publications of America, 1985, pp. 81-92.

For Further Study

Anthony J. Berret, *Mark Twain and Shakespeare: a Cultural Legacy,* University Press of America, 1993.

A contextualization of Shakespeare in Twain's time: debates about authorship, Twain's identification with Shakespeare, and popular productions.

Pamela A. Boker, *The Grief Taboo in American Literature: Loss and Prolonged Adolescence in Twain, Melville, and Hemingway,* New York University Press, 1996.

In this study, Boker looks at the relationship between loss and coming-of-age issues as they are expressed in the works of several prominent American authors.

Richard Bridgman, *Traveling in Mark Twain,* University of California Press, 1987.

A study of how journeys express several themes in Twain's works.

Bernard DeVoto, *Mark Twain's America* Houghton Mifflin, 1932.

DeVoto thoroughly analyses the novel's structure and reception.

Shelley Fisher Fishkin, *Lighting Out for the Territory: Reflections on Mark Twain and American Culture,* Oxford University Press, 1997.

A new study of how Twain's focus on issues relating to the frontier reflect a uniquely American experience.

Andrew Jay Hoffman, *Twain's Heroes, Twain's Worlds: Mark Twain's Adventures of Huckleberry Finn, A Connecticut Yankee in King Arthur's Court, and Pudd'nhead Wilson,* University of Pennsylvania Press, 1988.

A study which interprets Twain's characters, including Huck Finn, according to various theories of heroism.

Randall K. Knoper, *Acting Naturally: Mark Twain in the Culture of Performance,* University of California Press, 1995.

A study which places Twain's work in the popular culture of his time, placing special emphasis on the theatrical forms of entertainment popular in Twain's day and their influence on his work.

Mark Twain: A Collection of Critical Essays, edited by Eric J. Sundquist, Prentice Hall, 1994.

A collection of scholarly essays, three of which examine *The Adventures of Huckleberry Finn* in particular. A good introduction to recent scholarly approaches to Twain's work.

Toni Morrison, *Playing in the Dark: Whiteness and the Literary Imagination,* Vintage, 1992, pp. 54-7.

Morrison interprets the importance of Jim in *The Adventures of Huckleberry Finn* and relates Twain's portrayal to other writers' fascination with and use of African-American characters in American literature.

David R. Sewell, *Mark Twain's Language: Discourse, Dialogue, and Linguistic Variety,* University of California Press, 1987.

This linguistic study uses sophisticated language theory to analyze Twain's writing. Although a scholarly study, this work is relatively free of jargon.

David Sloane and E. E. Sloane, *Adventures of Huckleberry Finn: American Comic Vision,* Twayne Publishers, 1988.

This volume in the Twayne "Masterwork Series" examines *Huck Finn* and how fits within the American tradition of comic literature.

J. D. Stahl, *Mark Twain, Culture and Gender: Envisioning America Through Europe,* University of Georgia Press, 1994.

This study looks at two trends in examining Twain's work: first, Twain's treatment of and concern with gender issues; and second, Twain's use of encounters with Europe as a mean to explore and define the American identity.

The Bell Jar

Sylvia Plath
1963

The Bell Jar was published in London, England, in January 1963, less than one month before its author, Sylvia Plath, committed suicide by asphyxiation. Published under the pseudonym of Victoria Lucas, the novel opened to some positive reviews, although Plath was distressed by its reception. In 1966, *The Bell Jar* was published in England under Plath's real name. By the early 1970s, it had been published to many favorable reviews in the United States.

The short, heavily autobiographical novel details six months in the life of its protagonist, Esther Greenwood. In the narrative's opening chapter, Esther, an overachieving college student in 1953, is spending an unhappy summer as a guest editor for a fashion magazine in New York City. After her internship ends, she returns home to live with her mother, grows increasingly depressed, suffers a mental breakdown and attempts suicide, and is institutionalized. By the book's conclusion, the hospital is about to release a somewhat improved Esther to the "real world."

The Bell Jar functions on many literary levels, but it is perhaps most obviously about the limitations imposed on young, intelligent American women in the 1950s. A brilliant woman with literary aspirations, Esther peers into the future and does not like her choices. She can learn shorthand—as her mother strongly encourages—and land some menial office job after college, or she can marry, live in suburbia, and nurture her husband. What she really wants to do—make a living

as a writer—seems unlikely, especially in a profession with so few feminine role models.

Also complicating her situation, Esther, a student on a full-time scholarship, is surrounded by people from families much wealthier than her own; not having the financial resources of her peers further limits her choices.

As we understand today, *The Bell Jar* relies heavily on Plath's own life experience. Like Esther, Plath attended Smith College on scholarship, earned top grades, published poetry at a young age, and majored in English. Like Esther, she did a summer internship in New York City, suffered a mental collapse, and was institutionalized. Both eventually recovered to the extent they were released from psychiatric units into the "real world." While Esther's future, by the novel's conclusion, remains uncertain, Sylvia Plath's recovery only lasted a decade: On February 11, 1963, she elected to end her own life.

Author Biography

Remembered today for her horrifying death as well as for her impressive body of literature, Sylvia Plath was born on 27 October 1932 in Jamaica Plain, Massachusetts, to Aurelia Schober and Otto Emil Plath. In 1940, her father, a professor of entomology, died, an event that left lasting psychological scars on Plath. References to her dead father permeate Plath's work, including *The Colossus* and *The Bell Jar*.

In 1942, Aurelia Plath found work teaching in a medical/secretarial program at Boston University. The family settled in Wellesley, Massachusetts. An excellent student, Plath showed enormous determination to get her fiction published. She submitted forty-five pieces to the magazine *Seventeen* before they published her story, "And Summer Will Not Come Again" in 1950.

At Smith College, she wrote poetry, was elected to various class offices, and received prizes for both her prose and poetry. That this gifted woman had many insecurities is obvious in one of her letters to a friend, which reveals "for the few little outward successes I may seem to have, there are acres of misgivings and self-doubts." Part of Plath's frustration lay in what she perceived as a choice between becoming a free-spirited poet or choosing the wife/mother alternative.

In the summer of 1952, she was chosen as a guest editor in *Mademoiselle*'s College Board Contest. The prize, a month of employment at the magazine in New York City, did not elevate Plath's mood. Despite the numerous frills her expense account afforded her—living at the Barbizon Hotel, expensive meals, meeting celebrities—Plath found the overall experience to be artificial. Her general disillusionment, dating experiences, and interactions with her boss and co-workers figure prominently into the first half of *The Bell Jar*.

Plath returned home after her employment ended and learned that she did not get accepted into the summer writing course that she had counted on. Her miserable subsequent months—including confused attempts to establish her career goals, a highly publicized suicide attempt, electroshock therapy, institutionalization, and recovery—are apparent in the second half of *The Bell Jar*.

Plath returned to Smith College in January 1954, graduated *summa cum laude* in June 1955, and won a Fulbright fellowship to study at Cambridge University in England. There, she met aspiring poet Ted Hughes, to whom she was immediately attracted. They married in June 1956. In 1957, the couple left England and settled in Northampton, Massachusetts, where Plath taught freshman English at Smith College. Considered an outstanding instructor, Plath also wrote poetry and worked on a preliminary draft of *The Bell Jar*.

In 1959, she and her husband returned to England; in 1960 her collection of poetry *The Colossus* was published by William Heinemann. Its initial reviews were not encouraging, although certain critics praised Plath's gifts for language. In April, 1960, she gave birth to a daughter, Frieda.

For the next year, Plath did not write much. A busy wife and mother, her health was poor, having suffered a miscarriage and an appendectomy. However, by spring 1961, she was working on *The Bell Jar*. She applied for and received a Saxon fellowship. In February, 1962, she gave birth to a son, Nicholas.

By summer 1962, her marriage to Ted Hughes was dissolving. He left Plath and their children; a devastated Plath now wrote poems at a phenomenal rate, sometimes one a day. *The Bell Jar* was published in January, 1963.

Although generally depressed in the last year of her life, Plath had one joyous experience. In December, 1962, she and her children moved into a flat in which the poet William Butler Yeats had once lived. But with her poor health, the rigors of raising two children by herself, and not having re-

Sylvia Plath

ceived the critical acclaim she desired, Plath ended her life in February, 1963.

Since her death, Plath's reputation as a writer and a cult figure has grown, and much of her work has been issued posthumously. More than thirty years after her death, Plath biographies are published with almost clock-like regularity, and critics still analyze her most famous poetry, as well as her more obscure work.

Plot Summary

New York: Chapters 1-9

Sylvia Plath's fictionalized autobiography, *The Bell Jar,* records seven months in the life of Esther Greenwood. In the summer of 1953, Esther has just finished her junior year in college. She is working in New York City as a writing intern at a fashion magazine. It is June, the same month in which Julius and Ethel Rosenberg are executed by electrocution. The Rosenbergs had been convicted of treason for allegedly selling atomic secrets to the Soviet Union (as it was then called). Esther lives at the Amazon hotel for women with other magazine interns, including Doreen. Her sarcastic remarks on the other women's primness echo Es-

ther's own feelings. Though successful and intelligent, Esther begins to doubt her own abilities to continue performing at such a high level. Her depression deepens as the summer progresses.

Esther and Doreen skip a party sponsored by the magazine, going out instead with Lenny Shepherd, a disc jockey, and his friend. Esther introduces herself as Elly Higginbottom from Chicago, in order to disassociate herself from the experience. She leaves Doreen at Lenny's apartment and returns to the Amazon. Doreen returns much later, drunk and knocking on Esther's door.

One morning, Esther muses on her depression-induced inertia: "I wondered why I couldn't go the whole way doing what I should any more. This made me sad and tired. Then I wondered why I couldn't go the whole way doing what I shouldn't, the way Doreen did, and this made me even sadder and more tired." Then her boss, Jay Cee, calls Esther into the office, concerned about her waning enthusiasm for her work. Esther tries to reassure Jay Cee, not revealing that she feels two conflicting pressures. On the one hand, she has a desire for a writing career. On the other hand, she feels that social norms are pushing her toward the more practical pursuits of shorthand and motherhood. At a luncheon sponsored by *Ladies' Day* magazine, Esther indulges in the grand spread of delicacies while she entertains memories of her own less privileged life. All the women who attend the luncheon later suffer from acute food poisoning.

Esther recalls her past relationship with Buddy Willard, a boy from her hometown who is now a medical student at Yale. Buddy visits Esther's college to go to a dance with Joan Gilling, a student there and a girl from Buddy's and Esther's town. Before the dance, however, he asks Esther for a date and later they begin regularly seeing each other. During one of the following summers, Buddy sleeps with a woman with whom he works. Esther learns of his infidelity to her just before he contracts tuberculosis and enters a sanatorium. Esther determines to avenge herself and assert her independence by sleeping with a man. When in New York, she goes on a date with a man named Constantin, but nothing happens.

As Esther waits to have her photograph taken for the magazine, she feels her sadness and uncertainty welling up. She is called to pose and she recalls:

> When they asked me what I wanted to be I said I didn't know.
>
> "Oh, sure you know," the photographer said.

"She wants," said Jay Cee wittily, "to be everything."

I said I wanted to be a poet.

Then they scouted about for something for me to hold.

Jay Cee suggested a book of poems, but the photographer said no, that was too obvious. It should be something that showed what inspired the poems. Finally Jay Cee unclipped the single, long-stemmed paper rose from her latest hat.

The photographer fiddled with his hot white lights. "Show us how happy it makes you to write a poem."

Though Esther tries obediently to smile, she bursts into tears before the photograph is taken. On her last night in New York, she accompanies Doreen to a country club dance where Esther is nearly raped by a rich man named Marco.

Suburban Boston: Chapters 10-13

In July, Esther returns to her mother's home in suburban Boston and becomes increasingly depressed. Having been denied admission to a writing course she had planned to take, she cannot decide what to do instead. For several weeks, she does not shower and is unable to read or write. She develops insomnia. On the urging of her mother, Esther sees a psychiatrist, Dr. Gordon. After one electroconvulsive therapy session, Esther becomes more and more suicidal, poring over reports of suicides in the tabloids and considering various methods of self-slaughter.

After a failed attempt to work as a hospital candystriper, Esther visits her father's grave and grieves for him for the first time in her life. Having spent the last of her savings, she determines to act on her suicidal impulses. She descends into the cellar of her mother's house, conceals herself in a remote crevice, and swallows fifty sleeping pills.

Hospitalization: Chapters 14-18

Esther, lying partially blinded in a suburban hospital, fades in and out of a coma. She is transferred to a psychiatric ward in a Boston hospital. Philomena Guinea, who had endowed the scholarship which enabled Esther to attend college, learns of Esther's situation and removes her to a private hospital in the country. Mrs. Guinea, a writer of popular novels, only intervenes because Esther's mother assures her that the root cause of Esther's suicide attempt is not emotional distress over a boy but over her writing.

At the private hospital, Esther's depression is still profound but she is intrigued by Dr. Nolan: "I didn't think they had woman psychiatrists." Though Dr. Nolan promises Esther that she will not

be subject to the kind of electroconvulsive treatment she received at Dr. Gordon's clinic, Esther is still wary.

Joan Gilling, Esther's college acquaintance who sporadically dated Buddy Willard, arrives at the hospital. She shows Esther some newspaper clippings that describe the police and her mother searching for and eventually finding the comatose Esther. The nurses give her regular insulin injections. She suffers insulin shock (which is intended to serve the same purpose as electroconvulsive therapy) and is revived with glucose treatment. Esther's mother brings her roses for her birthday, which Esther throws in the wastebasket. After that visit, Dr. Nolan informs her that she will no longer have to receive visitors, which pleases Esther.

As Esther improves, she moves to another unit in which the most stable patients live. Esther again undergoes electroconvulsive therapy, which she finds slightly less painful than her previous experience. Both Esther and Joan receive letters from Buddy Willard. Joan confesses that she has never had romantic feelings for Buddy, but that she "likes" Esther. Esther, who had accidentally discovered Joan in bed with another woman patient, rebuffs her advances.

Esther tells Dr. Nolan that she feels constrained by the thought that she will have to sacrifice her career if she were to marry and have children. The doctor arranges for Esther to be fitted with a diaphragm, which, like all birth control devices, was illegal in Massachusetts at that time. Esther feels enormously liberated.

The Bell Jar Suspended: Chapters 19-20

Esther, all but cleared to be discharged from the hospital, determines to return to college for the winter term. She lives at the hospital while she waits for the beginning of the semester, having been discouraged from living with her mother. While on a pass, she meets a young Harvard professor named Irwin. She has sex for the first time in her life with him and afterward bleeds profusely. Irwin drives Esther to the Cambridge house in which Joan has been living since her recent release from the psychiatric hospital. Joan, alarmed by Esther's hemorrhaging, takes her to the emergency room. Soon after this incident, Joan returns to the psychiatric hospital and subsequently hangs herself.

After a great snowstorm, Buddy Willard visits Esther at the hospital and she relieves him of the

From the film The Bell Jar, *starring Marilyn Hassett.*

guilt he feels over her hospitalization and Joan's suicide. She also severs her ties with Irwin and then with Joan by attending her funeral. Just as Esther is trying to devise a proper ritual "for being born twice—patched, retreaded and approved for the road," she is called into a meeting of doctors who will, she hopes, authorize her release.

Characters

Betsy

One of the guest interns at *Ladies' Day,* Betsy represents the ultimate "nice girl": an All-American girl from Kansas who will wait patiently for a husband, a big farm, and plenty of children—without losing her virginity before marriage. In *The Bell Jar,* Betsy attempts to keep Esther away from Doreen's vampish influence, and for a while Esther seems receptive. Ultimately, however, Esther cannot accept the simple naivete of Betsy, whom she comes to see as the "Pollyanna Cowgirl."

Cal

Esther's date at the beach. Like many of the men in the novel, Cal attempts to teach Esther something, in his case, the methods of suicide.

Constantin

A translator at the United Nations. Originally, Esther attempts to get him to seduce her. Unfortunately, when they actually go to bed, he simply falls asleep beside her. In the novel, he is treated as one more member of the patriarchy that ultimately disappoints Esther.

Dodo Conway

To Esther, the model of fertility: a pregnant mother who already has six children. Although it is implied that Dodo is less than an ideal mother, she is greatly admired in Esther's neighborhood simply for having so many children.

Dee Dee

A patient at the mental asylum where Esther is staying. One of the few females in the novel to demonstrate creativity, she composes a tune on the piano, about which "everybody kept saying she ought to get it published, it would be a hit."

Doreen

One of the guest editors at *Ladies' Day,* Doreen represents "the bad girl" among the group: sexy, vulgar, bored. She serves as a counterpoint to traditional "nice girl" Betsy, and Esther alternately envies both of the girls for their solid identities. Although sophisticated with Esther, Doreen dissolves into a passive sex object with the cowboy disk jockey, Lenny. After Doreen parties too much and passes out in her own vomit, Esther further distances herself from her.

Elaine

See Esther Greenwood

Eric

Esther's friend at college. Esther considers him a probable candidate for abandoning her virginity until he says she reminds him of an older sister.

Joan Gilling

A former rival for Buddy Willard's affections, Joan Gilling is eventually admitted to the same posh mental hospital where Esther is making her recovery. Although one of the novel's major characters, she materializes only toward its conclusion. Joan and Esther represent the two most complex characters in *The Bell Jar* and share many similarities. Both attend a prestigious women's college; both are intelligent, accomplished women; both come from the same hometown and went to the same church; both have suicidal tendencies. Further, both come to despise Buddy Willard for similar reasons. What distinguishes Joan and Esther most obviously is money; Joan comes from a wealthy family, whereas Esther's background is modestly middle class. Hence, Joan takes for granted many things—horseback riding, fancy clothes, private lessons—that Esther must struggle to obtain.

Although on the surface, Joan seems to represent the typical upper-class "Seven Sisters" college girl, she is really not. First, she is a physics major in college—a rather unusual choice for a woman in the 1950s. Second, she is even more nakedly ambitious than Esther and does not feign femininity in situations to please men. For example, on bike trips with Buddy Willard, she does not ask for his help ascending high hills. Third, she is not physically attractive (much to Esther's relief), and some critics have written that Joan's attraction to lesbianism can be interpreted as her realization that no man will desire her.

Like her attitude toward most of the major female characters in the novel, Esther is ambivalent toward Joan. "I looked at Joan. In spite of the creepy feeling, and in spite of the old, ingrained dislike, Joan fascinated me." Esther rebuffs Joan's sexual advances, yet turns to her for help after Esther has a terrifying bleeding experience after her first sexual experience.

After Joan commits suicide by hanging, Dr. Nolan assures Esther that it is not her fault. But some critics have linked her death with Esther's recovery and rebirth. It is also ironic that Joan, with all her social status and economic advantages, destroys herself, while struggling Esther is the survivor.

Dr. Gordon

He is the first psychiatrist to examine Esther after her breakdown. Showing little understanding or concern for her, he administers her electroconvulsive shock treatments without getting a second opinion. He then goes on vacation, referring her to a colleague. Dr. Gordon represents the respectable but artificial side of the medical profession.

Esther Greenwood

The protagonist of *The Bell Jar,* Esther Greenwood is a young, highly intelligent college student who has a breakdown. A woman from a modestly middle-class background, but surrounded by many relatively affluent people, Esther represents on the most obvious level an individual unsure of what she wants. The central conflict concerns marriage

Media Adaptations

- The movie *The Bell Jar,* based on Sylvia Plath's autobiographical novel of the same name, was directed by Larry Peerce and starred Marilyn Hassett, Julie Harris, Anne Jackson, and Barbara Barrie. Released by Avco Embassy in 1979, it was neither a critical nor commercial success, in large part because the script does not examine the reasons for Esther Greenwood's depression and mental breakdown.

and motherhood versus literary ambitions. Given her limited financial reserves, her choice is extremely important.

Her attitude toward the other major female characters in the novel is usually ambivalence. At various points in the novel, she sees Doreen, Betsy, Jay Cee, Joan Gilling, and many others as role models, but they all fail her expectations in different ways. Her feelings toward women shift quite abruptly. For example, soon after she wishes she "had a mother like Jay Cee," the ruthless editor has hurt her by criticizing her lack of ambition. Sexy, uninhibited Doreen seems like a nice contrast to the bland guest editors at *Ladies' Day,* but Esther ultimately tires of her promiscuity. Betsy's niceness and virginity strikes Esther as alternatively a blessing and a curse; Joan's lesbian advances appall Esther, but Esther turns to her in a moment of a medical emergency.

The one female character that Esther is unambivalent toward is her mother, Mrs. Greenwood. "I hate her" sums up her feelings very well. Two reasons explain Esther's loathing. First, her mother discouraged Esther from mourning over her dead father; second, Esther sees her mother as a woman who sacrificed her will for her husband's career.

Esther's attitude toward the male characters in the novel seems less confused. She sees Buddy Willard, Constantin, Cal, Irwin, Eric, Marco, and others in mostly sexual terms, candidates to lose her virginity to or potential husbands. In varying degrees, they are all unsympathetic characters, ranging from the pure misogyny of Marco to Buddy Willard's smug superiority. Soon after her date with Cal, Esther loses all interest in men as potential husbands, although she still aspires to lose her virginity.

Despite her intellect, Esther is an extremely impressionable person. That, early in the novel, she lies about her own name to a virtual stranger indicates what little identity she really has. Even her surname, Greenwood, as Linda Wagner-Martin suggests, "was satisfying for reasons both personal and symbolic, and because the novel moves toward Esther's rebirth, the image of green wood is comforting." By the conclusion of *The Bell Jar,* however, Esther represents a kind of survivor, although the extent of her mental and emotional recovery is debatable. She is more confident and able to make some of her own decisions, as evidenced by her instructing Irwin to pay her emergency room bill. Her feelings toward individuals and events are less confused, more rational: she grieves at Joan's funeral, realizes Buddy Willard is "nothing, but a great amiable boredom" to her, and is understandably apprehensive about her interview with the board of physicians. Contrast this to the earlier Esther who once threw her clothes out of a New York hotel window, ate raw meat, made an unsuccessful suicide attempt, and often stared catatonically into space.

Mrs. Greenwood

Esther Greenwood's widowed mother, Mrs. Greenwood appears periodically throughout the narrative. Although she seldom articulates it, Esther harbors great hostility toward her mother, as evidenced in the following passage: "I had always been my father's favorite, and it seemed fitting that I should take on a mourning my mother had never bothered with." A teacher of secretarial students, Mrs. Greenwood wants her daughter to learn shorthand so she will have a job after college. She does little to encourage Esther's literary aspirations. For example, after Esther returns from New York City to move back with her mother, Mrs. Greenwood unsympathetically passes on this bad news: "I think I should tell you right away, you didn't make the writing course."

Philomena Guinea

A famous and successful writer, she is also the woman who sponsors Esther's scholarship. She agrees to subsidize Esther's stay at a posh psychiatric hospital as soon as she learns Esther is not pregnant.

Elly Higginbottom

See Esther Greenwood

Hilda

Like Esther, she is a guest editor at *Ladies' Day.* A designer of hats and other accessories, she demonstrates no curiosity or any positive emotion in the brief period that Esther spends with her.

Irwin

The man to whom Esther loses her virginity. Described by Esther as "rather ugly and bespectacled," she does not have romantic feelings for him and is simply tired of being a virgin.

Jay Cee

Esther's boss at *Ladies' Day,* Jay Cee is an unglamorous, savvy editor, something of a rarity in a profession dominated by men in the 1950s. Although perceived by the summer interns as intimidating, Jay Cee does show some genuine concern for Esther by directly asking what her future plans are and by making suggestions. Esther's attitude toward her is ambivalent. While she admires Jay Cee's intelligence and claims indifference to her unattractive appearance, Esther also feels Jay Cee and some other women "wanted to teach me something … but I didn't think they had anything to teach me."

Marco

Accurately described by Esther as a "woman-hater," Marco sees women in one of two categories: Madonnas or whores. On his date with Esther, he admits to being in love with his first cousin, who intends to become a nun. Treating Esther like a whore, he gives her a diamond stickpin, throws her in a muddy ditch, and threatens to rape her.

Dr. Nolan

One of the few positive characters in the novel, Dr. Nolan is a direct yet humane psychiatrist—the opposite of Dr. Gordon—who empowers Esther after her breakdown. Through Dr. Nolan's influence, Esther comes to understand her own motivations and reconciles with her anger. Not judgmental, she empowers Esther by not criticizing or analyzing her statement toward her mother: "I hate her." When Joan Gilling commits suicide, Dr. Nolan assures Esther that it is no one's fault, certainly not Esther's. Dr. Nolan is also the first person Esther sees after her electroconvulsive shock treatments and the person who coaches her back into reality.

Mrs. Savage

One of the patients at the mental asylum where Esther is staying. She is a rich, idle woman who has apparently committed herself to shame her family.

Lenny Shepherd

An unscrupulous disk jockey who becomes sexually involved with Doreen and unconsciously intimidates Esther. In observing Doreen and Lenny, Esther becomes less impressed with Doreen as a role model.

Valerie

A lobotomized patient whom Esther meets at the mental asylum.

Mr. Willard

The father of Buddy Willard. Not as pretentious as his son, he is nonetheless in the novel to represent the patriarchy of the 1950s.

Mrs. Willard

The mother of Esther's boyfriend, Buddy Willard. A woman who has decided to live her life through her husband, she serves mostly as a negative role model for Esther.

Buddy Willard

Buddy Willard is Esther's boyfriend and a medical student. Originally, Esther enjoyed what she perceived as Buddy's lack of sexual experience ("… he made me feel I was much more sexy …"); when she learns he was having an affair with a waitress while he was seeing her, she feels disillusioned. For Esther, it is not so much the double standard (i.e, it is okay for a man to have a fling but scandalous for a woman to do so) that upsets her; she now feels inferior to Buddy because she is a virgin and he is not.

Esther is competitive with Buddy in other ways. That he, as a doctor, can give pregnant women a drug to minimize their pain during childbirth upsets Esther. To her, the doctors—all male—are depriving the expectant women of both the trauma and beauty of the birth experience simply to achieve the ends. Hence, she imagines Buddy robbing herself of all bodily forms of pleasure.

Esther's fears aside, Buddy is a rather odious character. He seems far more interested in instructing her on such matters as medicine, science, and skiing than in learning anything from her. Joan Gilling's offhand comment about Buddy ("He thought he knew everything. He thought he knew

everything about women.") captures his feelings of superiority very well. When Esther learns Buddy has contracted tuberculosis and will need to spend a year in a sanatorium, her reaction is mostly relief that he will be gone a long time. After learning that Esther has been in a mental hospital, Buddy's reaction is "I wonder who you'll marry now, Esther," implying very few men would find her desirable anymore. In light of his own long period of hospitalization for tuberculosis, the remark shows both his hypocrisy and insensitivity.

Themes

Culture Clash

Unlike most of the women who attended Smith College in 1950s, Esther Greenwood of *The Bell Jar* did not come from a wealthy family. That her family gets by on her mother's earnings as a typing teacher and on Esther's full-time scholarship explains why she does not normally have access to such luxuries as expensive clothes, travel, and summer homes. Hence, Esther is outside of the mainstream social circle at college and will never really fit in unless she marries into it. Aware of this, Esther makes many attempts to connect socially—she dates Buddy Willard mostly because he attends Yale; she baby-sits on Cape Cod to be in close proximity to wealthy people; she shops at expensive clothing stores for items on sale.

To complicate matters further, Esther comes to resent her own financial dependence on her mentor, the wealthy writer Philomena Guinea. Since Esther ultimately needs her patronage for continuing psychological care as well as for education, Esther becomes even more frustrated with her own financial dependence, although she seldom expresses this anger directly.

Yet in other ways, Esther is fairly typical of other Smith students: white, educated, attractive, and studious. That she is socially cut off from women with whom she has so much in common is one of the ironies of *The Bell Jar*.

Sex Roles

Although *The Bell Jar* is partly about the impact of economics on a brilliant student with limited financial reserves, it also concerns sex roles in the 1950s. In that decade, women, generally speaking, did not attend college to ultimately support themselves; they were expected to marry eventually. In the novel, there are three women

Topics for Further Study

- Explore some of the current career opportunities for females that did not exist in the 1950s.

- What are some of the circumstances that might lead a person to consider suicide? What are some indications that a person may be contemplating suicide? What can you do to intervene? Investigate the debate surrounding assisted suicide and argue one position.

- If a bright young person comes from a family without much money, how can that person improve his or her chances of obtaining a higher education? Is it better for that person to work full-time and put off college for a while or to work part-time and study part-time? Back up your opinion with some solid research.

who have created real identities for themselves separate from the men in their life. The unglamorous editor Jay Cee has succeeded in that, but she has also sacrificed a certain amount of femininity to get there; the writer Philomena Guinea has thrived creatively on her own terms; Esther's psychiatrist, Dr. Nolan, emerges as a caring, competent professional. However, they are exceptions in Esther's frame of reference, as well as in the male-dominated 1950s American society. More typical are wisecracking Doreen who depends on men for sex if not necessarily for marriage; traditional Betsy who patiently waits for domesticity; Dodo Conway whom Esther perceives as kind of a baby machine; and Joan Gilling whose combination of ambition and lesbianism have not made her into a happy, functional person. Even widowed Mrs. Greenwood, who earns her own money as a typing teacher, does not encourage her smart daughter to flourish: she prefers that Esther learn shorthand and eventually marry well.

Given these feminine influences, Esther channels much of her energy into men as potential husbands or as a means of losing her virginity. Nearly all of the men fall short, often because Esther resents their attempts to informally teach her something without really listening to her. Even men who are not potential lovers fancy themselves as instructors, for example, the old doctor at the sanatorium who foolishly imparts great knowledge about pilgrims. As *The Bell Jar* progresses, Esther loses most of her interest in marriage, but not in losing her virginity.

Esther also reserves much of her affection for her late father, who died when she was only nine, an event from which she has never psychologically recovered. As Lindsay Wagner-Martin wrote in *The Bell Jar: A Novel of the Fifties,* "... while it is—as she has consistently been taught—unseemly for her to be angry with her dead father, there is little stigma attached to her being angry with her living mother."

Search for Self

In *The Bell Jar,* Esther searches consistently for some kind of identity but finds her options limited as a young woman with little money of her own. After a disappointing summer as a guest editor in New York City, she fails to be accepted into a prestigious writing course and gradually loses much of her sanity and ambition. She mentally explores many wild scenarios for happiness and fulfillment (e.g., apprenticing herself to a pottery maker, finding a European lover), tries to write a novel, does such bizarre things as wearing her mother's clothes and eating raw meat, and finally attempts suicide. Obviously, she is not mentally well, but to some extent society's repressions for females and the lack of creative inspiration in her life have both contributed to her collapse.

Since society does not encourage Esther to excel—her excellent grades not withstanding—she sometimes competes in bizarre ways. For example, at a banquet for the guest interns at *Ladies' Day,* she eats ravenously as if she must consume more than any of the other interns. She also feels inferior to Buddy Willard because he lost his virginity before she did.

Esther recovers much of her mental and emotional stability by the end of the novel, but the reasons for her improvement are not entirely clear. To some extent, Dr. Nolan has empowered Esther to understand her motivations, actions, and reactions, but some would argue Esther has at least partly responded to electroconvulsive shock. At least one critic, David Holbrook in *Sylvia Plath: Poetry and Existence,* even questions to what extent Esther has recovered, when he writes, "All that her therapy achieves is symbolised by the last chapter that blankets the asylum grounds ... Sylvia Plath's insight is not deceived. 'Treatment' merely freezes her." Linda Wagner-Martin disagrees: "... Esther has indeed entered a new phase ... she enters her new birth ritual, the process of leaving the asylum for the real world, with as much confidence as an intelligent person can muster ... There is no question that Plath intended to create a thoroughly positive ending for Esther's narrative." While the extent of Esther's recovery is debatable, the search for her identity will certainly continue after she is released from the asylum.

Style

Point of View

Told in first person, Esther Greenwood narrates the entire novel *The Bell Jar*. From this perspective, the reader sees guest editor Esther in the miserable summer of 1953, her selective childhood and college memories, her romantic history, her breakdown and subsequent period of institutionalization, and her road to recovery. Despite her considerable intelligence, a careful reader will not necessarily take everything she says on faith, especially in light of her history of depression and occasionally bizarre behavior. The careful reader will also take into consideration that Esther's feelings shift quite abruptly on such subjects as role models and marriage. Though the narrative generally proceeds in a straightforward, chronological fashion, occasionally jumping back and forth in time, many questions arise. Why, for example, does Esther hate her mother so much? Why does she leave her drunken friend Doreen in the hotel hallway? Why does she reduce so many people around her to unpleasant stereotypes? Above all, why is Esther so unhappy? Part of the answer can be found in the oppressive 1950s environment, but can other factors figure into it? What factors really contributed to her recovery? After observing Esther in an assortment of situations, the reader can form his or her own impressions.

Setting

Literally, most of *The Bell Jar* takes place in either New York City or the Boston vicinity. The time is mostly the latter half of 1953, although Esther occasionally makes reference to earlier occasions in her narration. On a figurative level, much of the novel occurs in the mind of its protagonist, Esther Greenwood.

Symbolism

On the simplest level, *The Bell Jar,* Plath's only novel, refers to the social pressure for young women to marry in the 1950s. One of the causes of Esther's depression is her worry that she would not make a good wife for all of the following reasons: She cannot cook, stands too tall, and dances poorly. Unfortunately, she thinks her positive qualities—a high degree of intelligence, ambition, a literary aptitude—are actually handicaps in the marriage market. On other occasions, Esther thinks she could never be happy in any marriage, regardless of whom she finds as a husband.

The Bell Jar overflows with other symbolism; one of the most important is birth and rebirth. In one scene, Esther witnesses a birth in the teaching hospital where Buddy Willard works: "I was so struck by the sight of the table where they were lifting the woman I didn't say a word. It looked like some awful torture table, with these metal stirrups sticking up at mid-air at one end and all sorts of instruments and wires and tubes...." Her continuing description of the birthing is accurate and precise, but completely lacking in any sense of joy and wonderment. As Lynda K. Bundtzen writes in *Plath's Incarnations:* "The problem ... is that men have usurped the privilege of giving birth from women. The doctors are all male and they are entirely responsible for the emergence of a new creature into the world." So for Esther, a woman giving birth is no cause for celebration; it is symbolic of male oppression.

The subject of rebirth comes up figuratively in the conclusion of the novel. Note Esther's description of the elements: "The sun, emerged from its gray shrouds of clouds, shone with a summer brilliance on the untouched slopes ... I felt the profound thrill it gives me to see trees and grassland waist-high under flood water, as if the usual order of the world had shifted slightly, and entered a new phase."

Some critics have suggested that with the death of Joan Gilling, the character who most resembles Esther Greenwood, the latter is liberated from some of her pain. As Stan Smith notes in *Critical Quarterly,* "Esther is left wondering, at Joan's funeral, just what she thinks she is burying, the "wry black image" of her madness, or the 'beaming double of her old best self.' In a sense, the suicide of this surrogate is Esther's rebirth."

Compare & Contrast

- **1950s and 1960s:** As recently as 1950, men received approximately 76 percent of all degrees conferred in the United States. At the Master's level, men received roughly 2.5 times as many degrees as women.

  Today: In 1993, men received approximately 46 percent of all degrees conferred in the United States. Since 1986, women began receiving more Master's degrees than men, and the pattern continues.

- **1950s and 1960s:** In 1960, about 59 percent of single women were part of the American work force, about 32 percent of married women belonged to the work force, and about 42 percent of "other" (widowed, divorced, separated) women belonged to the work force.

  Today: In 1994, About 68 percent of single women were part of the American work force, about 61 percent of married women belonged to the work force, and about 48 percent of "other" (widowed, divorced, separated) women belonged to the work force.

- **1950s and 1960s:** The concept of date rape did not exist; if a woman went on a date with a man and was raped, she did not have any legal recourse.

  Today: Many more women are successfully suing men for date rape.

- **1950s and 1960s:** National Center for Health Statistics (NCHS) on suicide in America can never be entirely accurate or reliable, as many people who attempt or commit suicide often conceal their intention. Their families often conceal the suicide, too. However, NCHS statistics on suicides in 1953 reveal that men were more than three times as likely to commit suicide as women. White men in 1953 were more likely to commit suicide than any other racial/gender group; the second most likely group was nonwhite men; the third most likely group was white women; the least likely group was nonwhite women.

  Today: As of 1993, the racial/gender breakdown of 1953 had not changed; however, men are now about four times more likely to commit suicide than women.

Historical Context

Absence of Feminism in the 1940s and 1950s

It is impossible to fully understand *The Bell Jar* without a realization of the relative absence of feminism in the United States in the 1940s and 1950s. Both decades were fairly prosperous ones in American history, and women's social and financial standing usually hung on their husbands' occupation and respective income. Although more than six million women went to work when America was engaged in World War II, after the war ended, many were encouraged to leave the work force. Dr. Benjamin Spock, who published the book *Baby and Child Care,* once even proposed that the federal government subsidize housewives to discourage them from entering into the work force. In

Modern Woman: The Lost Sex (1946), authors Marynia Farnham and Ferdinand Lundberg argued that women who worked sacrificed their essential femininity. While, of course, many single women worked out of economic necessity, they were not encouraged to show naked ambition or to stay in the work force indefinitely. A married woman—with or without children—who earned as much as her husband was rare.

Of course, women who worked in menial or low-paying jobs were less of a threat to mainstream America. Hence, in *The Bell Jar,* Mrs. Greenwood encourages her daughter, Esther, to learn shorthand, because that skill will at least guarantee her some kind of job after college.

In 1963, Betty Friedan's *The Feminine Mystique* was published. At the time, as in the 1950s, there were many more men in the work force and

These patients at Rockland State Hospital have become sleepy due to drug treatments. In the 1950s, alternative therapies emerged which allowed disturbed patients to live without restraints or even outside institutions.

women earned far less money. However, this pivotal study of middle-class women's anger and some proposed solutions paved the way for a gradual redefinition of sex roles in America. In 1966, three years after Plath had taken her own life, Friedan and her colleagues established the National Organization for Women (NOW).

Mental Illness and Suicide

The Bell Jar is not simply about male oppression in the 1950s; it also tackles the topic of mental illness, although it does so in nonclinical terms. Specifically, it is about one depressed and confused woman's suicide attempt at a time when the medical profession often relied on such crude methods as electroconvulsive therapy (ECT). In ECT, a low electric charge is passed through a patient's body, to cure such illnesses as depression and schizophrenia. Like Esther in The Bell Jar, Sylvia Plath received ECT.

While many factors contribute to a person's choice in taking his or her own life, researchers have found that age, sex, and marital status are all statistically significant. For example, men are more likely to kill themselves than females today, al-

though the opposite was true at the turn of the twentieth century. By the 1960s, there was some scientific evidence that married people were less suicide-prone than single people; in turn, married people with children were not as likely to commit suicide as married or single people without children. To some extent, these statistics reflected the researcher's and society's biases. For example, Louis Dublin wrote in *Suicide: A Sociological and Statistical Study* that "the presence of children has a much greater saving effect on women than on men because the parental instinct is stronger among them." It is also important to remember that Sylvia Plath—a married (although also separated) woman with two young children—defied some of the statistical data. Finally, since there is a stigma about suicide, many families cover up the circumstances if a family member elects to take his or her own life. Hence, the official suicide statistics are not necessarily valid or reliable.

While such organizations as the National Save-a-Life League date back to 1906, the subject of suicide prevention remained shrouded in mystery for many American people for several decades. In 1958, the Suicide Prevention Center in Los Angeles began with a public grant from the U.S. Public

Health Service. It was the first agency to use only professionals for its therapy sessions.

Critical Overview

Two years before Sylvia Plath published *The Bell Jar,* her collection of poetry *The Colossus* opened to some good reviews, particularly in the United States. That Plath published *The Colossus* under her own name but published *The Bell Jar* under the pseudonym of Victoria Lucas meant the reviewers would judge the latter on its own merits. Of course, the original critics of *The Bell Jar* did not know that its author was the estranged wife of Ted Hughes, who was becoming a successful poet in his own right.

Some early reviews were encouraging. Robert Taubman, in a *New Statesman* article, called *The Bell Jar* "a clever first novel…. The first feminine novel … in the Salinger mood," referring to J.D. Salinger's famous novel *Catcher in the Rye* and some of his shorter work. Laurence Lerner in *The Listener* praised the book as "brilliant and moving," while Rupert Butler, in *Time and Tide,* found the book "terribly likeable" and "astonishingly skillful." All three critiques were published in January 1963, less than a month before Plath's suicide. By 1966, *The Bell Jar* had been published in England under Plath's real name.

Many latter reviews compared *The Bell Jar* to Plath's posthumous collection of poetry *Ariel.* C. B. Cox in a 1966 review for *Critical Quarterly* believed "the novel seems a first attempt to express mental states which eventually found a more appropriate form in poetry." However, Robert Scholes, writing for *The New York Times Book Review,* called *The Bell Jar* "a fine novel, as bitter and remorseless as her last poems." Like many other critics, he compared *The Bell Jar* to some of J. D. Salinger's work when he called the former "… the kind of book Salinger's Franny might have written about herself ten years later." (Franny is one of the fictional Glass children who appears in Salinger's *Franny and Zooey* as well as in some of his short stories.) M. L. Rosenthal wrote in the *Spectator* of the novel's "magnificent sections whose candour and revealed suffering will haunt anyone's memory."

Since its publication in 1963, *The Bell Jar* has steadily acquired a reputation as a feminist classic. In 1972, Patricia Meyer Spacks, in her *Hudson River* review, listed the ways in which the novel

concerns female sexuality, "babies in glass jars, women bleeding in childbirth, Esther herself thrown in the mud by a sadist, hemorrhaging after a single sexual experience. To be a woman is to bleed and burn…." Fourteen years later, Paula Bennett, in her book *My Life a Loaded Gun: Female Creativity and Feminist Politics,* perceived the novel as offering a brilliant evocation of "the oppressive atmosphere of the 1950s and the soul-destroying effect this atmosphere could have on ambitious, high-minded young women like Plath."

Although Sylvia Plath and her mother had feared publication of *The Bell Jar* in the United States would embarrass many of the author's friends and acquaintances, much of the American reaction was mature. Some critics, including Ronald De Feo and Ruth Bauerle, defended the book as more than thinly veiled autobiography. It eventually became a Book-of-the-Month club selection, and *Book World* considered it one of the "Fifty Notable Books" of 1971.

In light of Plath's own suicide ten years after the time *The Bell Jar* actually took place, some readers and critics have found the novel's relatively optimistic conclusion to be unconvincing. Others, disagreeing, found it to be psychologically sound. For example, Tony Tanner in *City of Words: American Fiction, 1950-1970* believed the novel was "perhaps the most compelling and controlled account of a mental breakdown to have appeared in American fiction."

In retrospect, it must be stressed that Esther's problems in *The Bell Jar* aren't entirely typical of female teenagers' troubles today. As Susan Sniader Lanser and Teresa De Lauretis have written, Plath's work is about one woman in a specific period of American history when exciting career opportunities for women were rare. Esther's dilemma—marriage and children versus successful career—cannot be so easily generalized today. Also, while many male and female teenagers today face the difficult decision of whether to lose their virginity before marriage, few obsess over it to the point that Esther does in *The Bell Jar.*

Criticism

Jeannine Johnson

In the following essay, Johnson, a doctoral candidate at Yale University, notes that while The Bell Jar *has been interpreted as representing the lack of choices facing women in the 1950s, the por-*

trayal of protagonist Esther Greenwood shows her as alienated even from other women who might be in her position. The critic also examines the possibilities created by looking at the poetic aspects of the novel.

Sylvia Plath's *The Bell Jar* (1963) was first published in England under the pseudonym Victoria Lucas, a few weeks before Plath's suicide. It was published under her own name in England in 1966, and not published in the United States until 1971. Much of the novel is based on Plath's life. Her father died when she was eight years old and at that time her family moved to Wellesley, Massachusetts, outside Boston. She attended Smith College, and during the summer of 1953 worked at *Mademoiselle* magazine in New York. Later that summer Plath suffered from depression, underwent electroconvulsive therapy, attempted suicide, and was subsequently hospitalized. However much the events of *The Bell Jar* parallel those of Plath's real life, the novel remains a fictionalized autobiography. Plath herself called it a "potboiler," acknowledging that she had employed the techniques of a fiction writer in order to achieve a certain effect and to favor particular interpretations of the events depicted. Rather than read *The Bell Jar* in terms of the author's biography, we might read it in one of two other ways: as a kind of biography of American culture in the 1950s or as a record of the uses of literature, especially poetry.

One of the most common interpretations of the novel sees Esther Greenwood's life as an example of the difficult position of educated women in America in the 1950s. In her introduction to *Sylvia Plath: The Critical Heritage,* Linda Wagner notes that *The Bell Jar* represents the "cultural alienation—and the resulting frustration—of talented women" at that time. Esther struggles with the combined rewards and stigmas of excelling in school, but she is not without humor: "I hated coming downstairs sweaty-handed and curious every Saturday night and having some senior introduce me to her aunt's best friend's son and finding some pale, mushroomy fellow with protruding ears or buck teeth or a bad leg. I didn't think I deserved it. After all, I wasn't crippled in any way, I just studied too hard, I didn't know when to stop."

Esther's intellectualism seems to be a disability to some people, perhaps including Esther herself. She benefits from the prestige associated with regularly dating Buddy Willard and she is much relieved when, just as she considers breaking up with him, he contracts tuberculosis: "I simply told every-

What Do I Read Next?

- Linda Wagner-Martin's *Sylvia Plath: A Biography,* published in 1987, provides a balanced portrait of the writer, examining both her depression and talent.

- J. D. Salinger's novel *Catcher in the Rye,* published in 1953, examines the troubled adolescence of Holden Caulfield and the phoniness he detects in most adults.

- Sylvia Plath's collection of poetry, *Ariel,* was published posthumously in 1965 and contains some of Plath's most haunting work. With the publication of these poems written toward the end of Plath's short life, the author soon acquired a cult-like reputation.

- Eileen Aird's *Sylvia Plath: Her Life and Work,* published in 1973, is a good book for students unfamiliar with Plath's poetry and reputation.

- *The Colossus* (1960), Sylvia Plath's only collection of poetry published during her lifetime, has many of her poems written in the 1950s.

- *Sylvia Plath: The Collected Poems,* published in 1981, includes all of Plath's verse, including many formerly unpublished pieces. It won the Pulitzer Prize in poetry in 1982.

one that Buddy had TB and we were practically engaged, and when I stayed in to study on Saturday nights they were extremely kind to me because they thought I was so brave, working the way I did just to hide a broken heart." Diligent study is a substitute for romance, suggesting that the two cannot exist together.

By the same token, marriage and a career appear incompatible to Esther: "I also remembered Buddy Willard saying in a sinister, knowing way that after I had children I would feel differently, I wouldn't want to write poems any more. So I began to think maybe it was true that when you were married and had children it was like being brainwashed, and afterward you went about numb as a slave in some private, totalitarian state." It is this incompatibility which she sarcastically equates with a psychological disorder: "If neurotic is wanting two mutually exclusive things at one and the same time, then I'm neurotic as hell. I'll be flying back and forth between one mutually exclusive thing and another for the rest of my days." Even though Esther insists throughout the novel that she intends never to marry, she seems unable to eliminate it altogether as a possibility. She feels hurt by the photograph on Dr. Gordon's desk, by the "hairy, ape-shaped law student from Yale" who tells her she'll be a prude at forty, and by Buddy when he visits her at the psychiatric hospital and wonders who she'll marry now. To Esther's mind, all of these men seem to mock her unmarriageability.

Esther's dissatisfactions may be typical of well-educated American women of her generation. Yet, Esther does not imagine herself as part of a community of women who suffer in the same way. Even in the psychiatric hospital, she distinguishes herself from the other women there. Esther is repulsed by Valerie, who has had part of her brain removed, and intrigued by Miss Norris, the mute, unresponsive patient. She is suspicious of the society women ten years her senior, like Dee Dee and Mrs. Savage who trade private jokes about their husbands. Joan is "the beaming double of" a person Esther used to be but from whom she is now estranged. Where Esther is uneasy, Joan "seemed perfectly at home among these women." When Joan later makes a rather tame romantic overture to her, Esther recoils and literally distances herself from Joan by walking out of the room.

Esther's tendency to identify herself in contrast to these other women indicates that this is not a "feminist manifesto," as some critics have claimed it to be. Still, she is clearly affected by a conflict between her ambitions and received roles for women. This conflict is evident in her desire for sexual experience on the one hand and, on the other, a pragmatic understanding of the advantages of chastity. When she gains access to birth control, Esther proudly reflects, "I was my own woman."

Whether or not they view *The Bell Jar* as a true personal or cultural history, many critics have demonstrated the advantages of reading Plath's poetry alongside her novel. Plath was and is known primarily as a poet, though only one of her several poetry collections was published while she was alive. (All of her poems are included in *Collected Poems* (1981), for which Plath posthumously received the Pulitzer Prize.) Reading her novel in terms of poetry shows the importance of poetry as a guiding force in the plot and in the structure of the text.

Esther Greenwood is not yet a poet, and seems to be less well-read than her creator, Sylvia Plath. When Buddy Willard mentions that he has recently discovered the work of a doctor-poet and of a "famous dead Russian short-story writer who had been a doctor too," Esther does not recognize them as William Carlos Williams and Anton Chekhov. She is hardly ignorant, even though she fears others will think her so. For instance, she compares her elite college's liberal requirements for the English major to the stricter traditional requirements of the city college where her mother teaches. Esther worries that "the stupidest person at my mother's college knew more than I did."

Nevertheless, Plath grants to Esther a strong poetic sensibility. For example, though she likes botany, she resists physics for its irreverent attitude toward language: "What I couldn't stand was this shrinking everything into letters and numbers. Instead of leaf shapes and enlarged diagrams of the holes the leaves breathe through and fascinating words like carotene and xanthophyll on the blackboard, there were these hideous, cramped, scorpion-lettered formulas in Mr. Manzi's special red chalk." These monstrous forms of words do injury to the great possibilities of language and they appear to bleed on the chalkboard. While the physics professor scratches the board with his formulas, Esther places herself at a safe distance and writes "page after page of villanelles and sonnets." It may be that Esther opposes learning shorthand not only because she sees it as a stereotypically female skill, but because its characters are, like physics formulas, shrunken parodies of poetic language.

Esther shields herself against the pressures she feels with her belief that poetry possesses a special value. One of those pressures is the supposed impracticality of a career as a poet: Buddy Willard claims that a poem is simply "a piece of dust." But Esther silently believes that "People were made of nothing so much as dust, and I couldn't see that doctoring all that dust was a bit better than writing poems people would remember and repeat to themselves when they were unhappy or sick and couldn't sleep."

She imagines that poetry can work as a kind of temporary cure for emotional distress. However, as her depression worsens, Esther has less and less access to this potential remedy. She envies the unimaginative work of a U.N. translator: "I wished with all my heart I could crawl into her and spend the rest of my life barking out one idiom after another. It mightn't make me any happier, but it would be one more little pebble of efficiency among all the other pebbles." Her mother explains to Philomena Guinea that Esther's fear of never writing again is the cause of her illness. But if her writing is the cause, it is not part of the cure. Esther makes no mention of writing or of literature during her stay in the psychiatric ward. The first person Esther encounters at the private hospital is Valerie, who is reading *Vogue.* Other than magazines, the only texts she mentions are Joan's physics books, and the nurses quickly remove them.

Though poetry disappears from the story (or the thematic level) of the text, it may remain concealed in the novel's structure. The plot organization of *The Bell Jar* has been described as episodic, that is, as consisting of associated episodes or scenes. We might also call the structure of the novel "stanzaic," or organized like the stanzas or paragraphs of a poem. The last chapter, for example, is divided into six sections depicting six different kinds of farewells. Her encounters with Dr. Nolan, Valerie, Buddy, Irwin, Joan, and the doctors' board are variations on the theme of departure. These interrelated scenes reinforce the difficulty and the importance of leave-taking for Esther. Together they compose a kind of poem, the final word on her experiences of the previous months.

The story ends suspended at this significant moment before Esther exits the hospital. In the last scene we see her enter the conference room, guided inside by the "eyes and faces" of the doctors gathered there. These points of reference may symbolize stars, which can also provide direction and guidance. Plath uses a star metaphor in the introduction she wrote as Guest Managing Editor of the August 1953 college issue of *Mademoiselle:* "We're stargazers this season.... From our favorite fields, stars of the first magnitude shed a bright influence on our plans for jobs and futures. Although horoscopes for our ultimate orbits aren't yet in, we Guest Eds. are counting on a favorable forecast with this send-off from *Mlle,* the star of the campus."

Despite Plath's rather syrupy language, her metaphor connects stars and her future literary career. In a late poem called "Words" (1963), Plath more directly compares words to stars:

Years later I
Encounter them on the road—

Words dry and riderless,
The indefatigable hoof-taps.
While
From the bottom of the pool, fixed stars
Govern a life.

Plath suggests that poetry's words can lose some of their flavor and become dry, or run wild like horses without riders. Although the poet cannot control the words as she would like, the stars reflected in a pool of water provide some order and direction for her life. But while the stars are her guide, they remain "fixed" and silent at the bottom of a pool. By contrast, words tirelessly and noisily trot over the earth. Both words and stars can direct the poet to a certain extent, but neither is entirely reliable. The poet of "Words" and Esther Greenwood are not identical people. Yet they both are drawn to the language of poetry in order to define themselves. And both discover that there are times when even poetic words fail them.

Source: Jeannine Johnson, in an essay for *Novels for Students,* Gale 1997.

Linda W. Wagner

In this excerpt, the critic discusses the protagonist, Esther Greenwood, in relation to themes in the novel, including alienation, her search for identity, and generational conflict.

One of the most misunderstood of contemporary novels, Sylvia Plath's *The Bell Jar* is in structure and intent a highly conventional *bildungsroman.* Concerned almost entirely with the education and maturation of Esther Greenwood, Plath's novel uses a chronological and necessarily episodic structure to keep Esther at the center of all action. Other characters are fragmentary, subordinate to Esther and her developing consciousness, and are shown only through their effects on her as central character. No incident is included which does not influence her maturation, and the most important formative incidents occur in the city, New York. As Jerome Buckley describes the *bildungsroman* in his 1974 *Season of Youth,* its principal elements are "a growing up and gradual self-discovery," "alienation," "provinciality, the larger society," "the conflict of generations," "ordeal by love" and "the search for a vocation and a working philosophy."

Plath signals the important change of location at the opening of *The Bell Jar.* "It was a queer, sultry summer, the summer they electrocuted the Rosenbergs, and I didn't know what I was doing in New York.... New York was bad enough. By nine in the morning the fake, country-wet freshness that somehow seeped in overnight evaporated like the tail end of a sweet dream. Mirage-gray at the bottom of their granite canyons, the hot streets wavered in the sun, the car tops sizzled and glittered, and the dry, cindery dust blew into my eyes and down my throat." Displaced, misled by the morning freshness, Greenwood describes a sterile, inimical setting for her descent into, and exploration of, a hell both personal and communal. Readers [such as Denis Donoghue in "You could say she had a calling for Death," Saul Maloff in "Waiting for the Voice to Crack," and Charles Molesworth in "Again, Sylvia Plath"] have often stressed the analogy between Greenwood and the Rosenbergs—and sometimes lamented the inappropriateness of Plath's comparing her personal *angst* with their actual execution—but in this opening description, the Rosenberg execution is just one of the threatening elements present in the New York context. It is symptomatic of the "foreign" country's hostility, shown in a myriad of ways throughout the novel.

In *The Bell Jar,* as in the traditional *bildungsroman,* the character's escape to a city images the opportunity to find self as well as truths about life. Such characters as Pip, Paul Morel, and Jude Fawley idealize the city as a center of learning and experience, and think that once they have re-located themselves, their lives will change dramatically. As Buckley points out, however, the city is often ambivalent: "the city, which seems to promise infinite variety and newness, all too often brings a disenchantment more alarming and decisive than any dissatisfaction with the narrowness of provincial life." For Esther Greenwood, quiet Smith student almost delirious with the opportunity to go to New York and work for *Mademoiselle* for a month, the disappointment of her New York experience is cataclysmic. Rather than shape her life, it nearly ends it; and Plath structures the novel to show the process of disenchantment in rapid acceleration.

The novel opens in the midst of Greenwood's month in New York, although she tells the story in flashbacks; and for the first half of the book—ten of its twenty chapters—attention remains there, or on past experiences that are germane to the New York experiences. Greenwood recounts living with the other eleven girls on the *Mademoiselle* board at the Amazon Hotel, doing assignments for the tough fiction editor Jay Cee, going to lunches and dances, buying clothes, dating men very unlike the fellows she had known at college, and sorting through lifestyles like Doreen's which shock, bewilder, and yet fascinate her. Events as predictably mundane as these are hardly the stuff of exciting fiction but Plath has given them an unexpected drama because of the order in which they appear. *The Bell Jar* is plotted to establish two primary

themes: that of Greenwood's developing identity, or lack of it; and that of her battle against submission to the authority of both older people and, more pertinently, of men. The second theme is sometimes absorbed by the first but Plath uses enough imagery of sexual conquest that it comes to have an almost equal importance. For a woman of the 1950s, finding an identity other than that of sweetheart, girlfriend, and wife and mother was a major achievement.

Greenwood's search for identity is described through a series of episodes that involve possible role models. Doreen, the Southern woman whose rebelliousness fascinates Esther, knows exactly what she will do with her time in New York. The first scene in the novel is Doreen's finding the macho Lenny Shepherd, disc jockey and playboy par excellence. Attracted by Doreen's "decadence," Esther goes along with the pair until the sexual jitterbug scene ends with Doreen's melon-like breasts flying out of her dress after she has bitten Lenny's ear lobe. Esther has called herself *Elly Higginbottom* in this scene, knowing instinctively that she wants to be protected from the kind of knowledge Doreen has. Plath describes Esther as a photo negative, a small black dot, a hole in the ground; and when she walks the 48 blocks home to the Amazon in panic, she sees no one recognizable in the mirror. Some Chinese woman, she thinks, "wrinkled and used up," and, later, "the reflection in a ball of dentist's mercury." Purging herself in a hot bath, Greenwood temporarily escapes her own consciousness: "Doreen is dissolving, Lenny Shepherd is dissolving, Frankie is dissolving, New York is dissolving, they are all dissolving away and none of them matter any more. I don't know them, I have never known them and I am very pure." Unfortunately, when Doreen pounds on her door later that night, drunk and sick, Esther has to return to the real world. Her revulsion is imaged in Doreen's uncontrollable vomit.

The second "story" of the New York experience is the ptomaine poisoning of all the girls except Doreen after the *Ladies' Day* magazine luncheon. Plath's vignette of Jay Cee is imbedded in this account; the editor's great disappointment in Greenwood (because she has no motivation, no direction) serves to make Esther more depressed. As she comes near death from the poisoning, she also assesses the female role models available to her: her own mother, who urges her to learn shorthand; the older writer Philomena Guinea, who has befriended her but prescriptively; and Jay Cee, by now an admonitory figure. Although Esther feels "purged and holy and ready for a new life" after her ordeal, she cannot rid herself of the feeling of betrayal. No sooner had she realized Jay Cee ("I wished I had a mother like Jay Cee. Then I'd know what to do") than she had disappointed her. The development of the novel itself illustrates the kind of irony Esther had employed in the preface, with the lament

> I was supposed to be having the time of my life. I was supposed to be the envy of thousands of other college girls just like me all over America....
>
> Look what can happen in this country, they'd say. A girl lives in some out-of-the-way town for nineteen years, so poor she can't afford a magazine, and then she gets a scholarship to college and wins a prize there and ends up steering New York like her own private car.
>
> Only I wasn't steering anything, not even myself.

Plath's handling of these early episodes makes clear Greenwood's very real confusion about her direction. As Buckley has pointed out, the apparent conflict with parent or location in the *bildungsroman* is secondary to the real conflict, which remains "personal in origin; the problem lies with the hero himself" (or herself).

Esther Greenwood's struggle to know herself, to be self-motivated, to become a writer as she has always dreamed is effectively presented through Plath's comparatively fragmented structure. As Patricia Meyer Spacks writes in 1981 [in *The Adolescent Idea, Myths of Youth and the Adult Imagination*] about literature of the adolescent, the adolescent character has no self to discover. The process is not one of discovering a persona already there but rather creating a persona. Unlike Esther, then, perhaps we should not be disturbed that the face in her mirror is mutable. We must recognize with sympathy, however, that she carries the weight of having to maintain a number of often conflicting identities—the obliging daughter and the ungrateful woman, the successful writer and the immature student, the virginal girlfriend and the worldly lover. In its structure, *The Bell Jar* shows how closely these strands are interwoven.

Source: Linda W. Wagner, "Plath's *The Bell Jar* as Female *Bildungsroman*," in *Women's Studies: An Interdisciplinary Journal*, Vol. 12, No. 1, February, 1986, pp. 55–68.

Saul Maloff

In the following review, Maloff traces the publishing history of The Bell Jar *and concludes that "good as it is," the novel has "an absence of weight and complexity sufficient to the subject."*

Apparent reasons for the eight-year delay in importing *The Bell Jar* from England (publication there, 1963) are not in themselves convincing. The pseudonym of Victoria Lucas was a hedge, but against what? Sylvia Plath made no secret of her authorship. Her suicide followed publication by a month, but such things have never stopped the wheels of industry from turning: she was a "property" after all, certainly following the publication of *Ariel* in 1966. Nor can we take seriously her having referred to it as a "potboiler" and therefore to be kept separate from her serious work: the oldest and most transparent of all writers' dodges. All the evidence argues against it: as early as 1957 she had written a draft of the novel; she completed the final version on a Eugene Saxton Fund fellowship and felt toward its terms an urgent sense of commitment and obligation; the painstaking quality of the writing—but above all, its subject: her own pain and sickness, treated with literal fidelity, a journal done up as a novel, manifestly re-experienced, and not from any great distance of glowing health. One of her motives was the familiar one of getting her own back, to (as her heroine says) "fix a lot of people"—among others of smaller significance, to lay the ghost of her father, and tell the world she hated her mother (the exact words of her protagonist-surrogate, spoken to her psychiatrist in a key passage).

Only the names were changed, nothing else: as much as a novel can be, it was recorded rather than imagined. Evidently she panicked as publication drew near and displayed more than the usual terror of reviewers, who were on the whole generous and patronizing in a chuckling avuncular way, though she mis-read their intention, as toward the end, one supposes, she mis-read everything. Her last awful year was marked by a miscarriage, an appendectomy, the birth of her second child, as well as a series of plaguing minor illnesses, to say nothing of separation from her husband. According to her mother, Mrs. Aurelia Plath, whose 1970 letter to her daughter's Harper & Row editor is included in a "Biographical Note" appended to the novel, Miss Plath told her brother that the book must in no circumstances be published in the U.S.

Mrs. Plath's letter is a noteworthy document, and an oddly touching one. She pleads her case by telling the editor she knows no pleas will help, though publication here will cause "suffering" in the lives of several persons whom Sylvia loved and who had "given freely of time, thought, affection, and in one case, financial help during those agonizing six months of breakdown in 1953." To them, the book as it stands in itself "represents the basest ingratitude." But, Mrs. Plath argues, her daughter didn't mean for the book to stand alone; she herself told her mother in 1962 that she'd merely "thrown together events from my own life, fictionalizing to add color," a "potboiler" to show "how isolated a person feels when he is suffering a breakdown ... to picture my world and the people in it as seen through the distorting lens of a bell jar." Her second novel, she assured her mother, "will show that same world as seen through the eyes of health." Ingratitude was "not the basis of Sylvia's personality"; the second novel, presumably, would have been one long, ingratiating, fictionalized thank-you note to the world. Of course the publisher is right to publish; but since the persons who may be slightly scorched are still alive, why eight years?

The novel itself is no firebrand. It's a slight, charming, sometimes funny and mildly witty, at moments tolerably harrowing "first" novel, just the sort of clever book a Smith summa cum laude (which she was) might have written if she weren't given to literary airs. From the beginning our expectations of scandal and startling revelation are disappointed by a modesty of scale and ambition and a jaunty temperateness of tone. The voice is straight out of the 1950's: politely disenchanted, wholesome, yes, wholesome, but never cloying, immediately attractive, nicely confused by it all, incorrigibly truth-telling; in short, the kind of kid we liked then, the best product of our best schools. The hand of Salinger lay heavy on her.

But this is 1971 and we read her analyst, too wily to be deceived by that decent, smiling, well-scrubbed coed who so wants to be liked and admired. We look for the slips and wait for the voice to crack. We want the bad, the worst news; that's what we're here for, to be made happy by horror, not to be amused by girlish chatter. Our interests are clinical and prurient. A hard case, she confounds us. She never raises her voice. To control it, she stays very close to the line of her life in her twentieth year, telling rather than evoking the memorable events; more bemused than aghast. That year she came down to New York from Smith one summer month to work as an apprentice-editor for *Mademoiselle* (here *Ladies Day*) for its college issue, a reward for being a good, straight-A girl and promising young writer; and had exactly the prescribed kind of time, meeting people and going places, eating out and dressing up, shopping and sightseeing, and thinking maybe it was about time she got laid. The closest she came to it was sleeping chastely, quite dressed and untouched, beside an inscrutable UN simultaneous translator. Throughout, the tone is prevailingly unruffled, matter-of-fact, humorously woebegone.

Prevailingly, but not quite. What should have been exciting—she was a small-town girl living in NYC for the first time on her own—was dreary, trivial, flat. She was beginning to doubt herself, her talent, her prospects. Mysteriously, as if from another work, period of life, region of the mind, images and memories startlingly appear, and just as quickly vanish; colors and events we recognize from the late poems: darkness and blackness; the world perceived as misshapen and ominous; her father (the figure of her marvelous poem "*Daddy*") remembered with love and fury, the source of her last "pure" happiness at the age of nine before he perversely left her bereft one day by cruelly dying; foetuses and blood, fever and sickness, the obsession with purity and the grotesque burden of her body of feeling itself. In the poems the pressure is terrific; she screams her pain, in a final effort to contain it; yet here it is duly noted, set down serially, linearly, as possibly interesting to those in the business of making connections, scrupulously recorded as in a printed clinical questionnaire by a straight-A girl in the habit of carefully completing forms. When she sees the dumb, staring "goggle-eyed head lines" monstrously proclaiming the execution of the Rosenbergs, she "couldn't help wondering what it would be like, being burned alive all along the nerves" and concludes flatly, "I thought it must be the worst thing in the world." A silent china-white telephone sits like a "death's head." Her hometown boy-friend, a medical student, takes her to see cadavers at the morgue and a foetus with a "little piggy smile" that reminds her of Eisenhower; and then, to round things off, they go to watch a child-birth. The woman on the "awful torture-table, with these metal stirrups sticking up in mid-air" seems to her "to have nothing but an enormous spider-fat stomach and two little ugly spindly legs propped in the high stirrups" and "all the time the baby was being born she never stopped making this unhuman wooing noise" and "all the time, in some secret part of her, that long, blind, doorless and windowless corridor of pain was waiting to open up and shut her in again." A silly simpering girl, a hat-designer idiotically pleased at the good news of The Rosenbergs' execution, reveals a "dybbuk" beneath her plump, bland exterior. But these darker notes do not accumulate to thematic denisity save in retrospect; they seem accidental dissonances, slips of the tongue.

Even the breakdown, when it comes, is generally muted, seeming from the outside as much slothfulness as madness, the obligatory junior-year interlude. The break is quantitative: tones are darker, the world somewhat more distorted and remote, the voice, almost never breezy now, is more than disaffected—it can become nasty, a trifle bitchy, even cruel, streaked with violence. She makes some gestures toward suicide—as much amusing as they are frightening; and then though she very nearly brings it off, we almost can't bring ourselves to believe it, so theatrically staged is the scene. Yet even then, after breakdown and hospitalization, electroshock and insulin, she composes the book's funniest, most charming scene—of her incidental, much-delayed defloration; and in the knowledge of its appalling consequences. The chap, accidentally encountered on the steps of the Widener (where else?) is, she carefully notes, a 26-year-old full professor of Mathematics at Harvard, name of Irwin; and ugly. Him she elects to "seduce"; and after the fastest such episode in fiction, she isn't even sure it happened at all. Wanting more direct evidence, she can only infer it from her massive hemorrhaging. Concluding now that, no longer a virgin, she has put behind her childish things, she lies down and, bleeding profusely, writes: "I smiled into the dark. I felt part of a great tradition." At the end, the tone is ambiguous but not despairing; she has been readmitted to Smith, where out of old habit she will keep getting nothing but A's; the bell jar has descended once, and may again.

She laid out the elements of her life, one after the other, and left to the late poems the necessary work of imagining and creating it: it is for this reason that we feel in the book an absence of weight and complexity sufficient to the subject.

On balance, *The Bell Jar*, good as it is, must be counted part of Sylvia Plath's juvenilia, along with most of the poems of her first volume; though in the novel as in a few of the early poems she foretells the last voice she was ever to command.

Source: Saul Maloff, "Waiting for the Voice to Crack," in *The New Republic*, Vol. 164, No. 2941, May 8, 1971, pp. 33–35.

Sources

Paula Bennett, *My Life a Loaded Gun*, Beacon, 1986.

Lynda K. Bundtzen, *"Women in The Bell Jar:* Two Allegories" from *Plath's Incarnations: Women and the Creative Process*, University of Michigan Press, 1983.

Rupert Butler, "New American Fiction: Three Disappointing Novels—But One Good Time," in *Time and Tide*, January 31, 1963, p. 34.

C. B. Cox, editorial in *Critical Quarterly*, Autumn, 1966, p. 195.

Louis Dublin, *Suicide: A Sociological and Statistical Study*, Ronald, 1963.

David Holbrook, *Sylvia Plath: Poetry and Existence*, Athlone, 1976.

Laurence Lerner, "New Novels," in *Listener*, January 31, 1963, p. 215.

M. L. Rosenthal, "Blood and Plunder," in *Spectator*, September 30, 1966, p. 418.

Robert Scholes, review in *New York Times Book Review*, April 11, 1971, p. 7.

Stan Smith, "Attitudes Counterfeiting Life: The Irony of Artifice in Sylvia Plath's *The Bell Jar*," in *Critical Quarterly*, Autumn, 1975, pp. 247-60.

Patricia Meyer Spacks, "A Chronicle of Women," in *Hudson River*, Spring, 1972, p. 164.

Tony Tanner, in his *City of Words: American Fiction, 1950–1970*, Harper & Row, 1971.

Robert Taubman, "Anti-heroes," *New Statesman*, January 25, 1963, pp. 127-28.

Linda Wagner-Martin, *The Bell Jar: A Novel of the Fifties*, Twayne, 1992.

For Further Study

Paul Alexander, editor, *Ariel Ascending: Writings about Sylvia Plath*, Harper, 1985.
    One of the first anthologies of critical essays on Plath which, overall, focus more on her literary accomplishments than on the details of her life.

Ruth Bauerle, "Plath, at Last," in *Plain Dealer*, April 25, 1971, p. H7.
    Argues that the novel is more than an autobiographical success.

Elaine Connell, *Sylvia Plath: Killing the Angel in the House*, Pennine Pens, 1993.
    A brief but competent guide to Plath's biography and her critical history, combined with some uncomplicated interpretations of Plath's works, including *The Bell Jar*.

Ronald De Feo, review in *Modern Occasions*, Fall, 1971, pp. 624-25.
    Published shortly after the novel was published in the United States, this critique perceives the novel as more than a cult classic, praising it for qualities unrelated to its autobiographical elements.

Teresa De Lauretis, "Rebirth in the Bell Jar," in *Women's Studies*, 3 (1975), pp. 173-83.
    Article suggests *The Bell Jar* must be viewed be in terms of a historical perspective.

Marynia Farnham and Ferdinand Lundberg, *Modern Woman: The Lost Sex,* Harper, 1947.
   Authors make the case for women not being in the work force.

Betty Friedan, *The Feminine Mystique,* Norton, 1963.
   Pivotal study of middle-class, American women's dissatisfaction with sex roles.

Susan Sniader Lanser, "Beyond *The Bell Jar :* Women Students of the 1970s," in *Radical Teacher,* December, 1977, pp. 41-4.
   Article stresses that Plath's novel must be viewed in the context of the 1950s.

Sheryl L. Meyering, *Sylvia Plath: A Reference Guide, 1973-1988,* G. K. Hall, 1990.
   An extensive bibliography of Plath criticism up to 1988.

Charles Newman, editor, *The Art of Sylvia Plath: A Symposium,* Indiana University Press, 1970.
   An early assortment of reviews, reminiscences, then-unpublished poems, and critical essays. Some of the essays are uniquely analytical in their approach to Plath's poetry. Includes a brief essay on *The Bell Jar* written before the novel had been published in the United States.

Sylvia Plath, *Collected Poems,* edited by Ted Hughes, Harper, 1981.
   Plath's complete poems, including juvenilia, with notes by Hughes. Winner of the 1982 Pulitzer Prize.

Sylvia Plath, *The Journals of Sylvia Plath,* edited by Ted Hughes and Frances McCullough, Dial Press, 1982.
   Selections from Plath's private journals.

Aurelia Schober Plath, editor, *Letters Home: Correspondence 1950-1963,* Harper, 1975.
   A collection of Plath's letters edited by her mother.

Ellen Rosenberg, "Sylvia Plath," in *Concise Dictionary of American Literary Biography: The New Consciousness, 1941-1968,* edited by Richard Layman and Lucia Tarbox, Gale Research Company, 1987, pp. 408-22.
   Provides biographical information on Sylvia Plath, as well as some analysis of her poetry.

Jacqueline Rose, *The Haunting of Sylvia Plath,* Virago Press, 1991.
   Focusing primarily on Plath's poetry, Rose promotes the term "fantasy" as a key term by which to understand the complexities of Plath's self-representation and her psychologized, gendered, and sexualized poetics.

Toni Salvidar, *Sylvia Plath: Confessing the Fictive Self,* Lang, 1992.
   In a study primarily of Plath's poetry, Salvidar takes issue with those who reject the "confessional" label for Plath. She argues that Plath asserts a fictive "I" by presenting selective incidents from her life in order to incarnate a real, individual self through literature.

Anne Stevenson, *Bitter Fame: A Life of Sylvia Plath,* Viking, 1989.
   Of the many Plath biographies, Stevenson's is perhaps the least speculative. It received considerable blessing from the Hughes estate, which controls Plath's writings.

Linda W. Wagner, editor, *Critical Essays on Sylvia Plath,* G. K. Hall, 1984.
   A collection of reviews and critical essays, the latter mostly written from a feminist literary perspective.

Linda W. Wagner, editor, *Sylvia Plath: The Critical Heritage,* Routledge, 1988.
   A valuable anthology of reviews and short studies of Plath's work. Includes short biographical information on the reviewers.

Black Boy

Richard Wright

1945

Richard Wright made a masterful recording of his own life in the form of the novel *Black Boy: A Record of Childhood and Youth.* The work earned him a place as "father" of the post-WWII black novel and precursor of the Black Arts movements of the 1960s. Published in 1945 as a Book-of-the-Month Club selection, *Black Boy* was received enthusiastically by the reading public and topped the best-seller lists, with 400,000 copies sold. The commercial success of this novel secured for Wright what his acclaimed novel of 1940, *Native Son,* had demanded. With these two works, Richard Wright is correctly said to be one of the most powerful forces in twentieth-century American literature. Without doubt, he is the most powerful influence on modern African American writing due to his impact on James Baldwin (*Another Country,* 1962), and Ralph Ellison (*Invisible Man,* 1953).

Black Boy is an autobiographical work in which Wright adapted formative episodes from his own life into a "coming of age" plot. In the novel, Richard is a boy in the Jim Crow American South. This was a system of racial segregation practiced in some states of the U.S., which treated blacks as second-class citizens. In his novel, Wright emphasizes two environmental forces of this system: hunger and language. He shows how hunger drives the already oppressed to even more desperate acts, and his emphasis on language explains how he managed to survive Jim Crow: by developing an attention to language as a coping mechanism for the surface world of life. Meanwhile, literature of-

Richard Wright

fered him internal release from the tensions of living without the freedom to express his dignity as a human being. Thus, Wright's novel is a powerful story of the individual struggle for the freedom of expression.

Author Biography

Richard Nathaniel Wright was born on September 4, 1908, at Rucker's Plantation in Roxie, Mississippi. His parents were Ellen Wilson, a school teacher, and Nathan Wright, a sharecropper. His brother Leon was born in 1910 and one year later they moved to Ellen's parents' house in Natchez. It is that house in which Wright's novel *Black Boy* has its opening drama.

The family moved to Memphis in 1913 and soon thereafter Richard's father deserted them. For the next few years, Ellen did her best to feed and clothe the boys, but she began a devastating cycle of illness. At one point she moved her boys to the prosperous home of her sister Maggie and brother-in-law Silas Hoskins in Elaine, Arkansas. Unfortunately, he was murdered by a white mob, and Maggie, Ellen, and the boys fled to West Helena.

Over the next few years, Ellen's illness forced the extended family to shift Richard between them while she lay abed at Grandma Wilson's. Richard

eventually went to his grandmother's house to be near his mother. In 1920, Richard attended the Seventh-Day Adventist School taught by his Aunt Aggie. He later transferred to the Jim Hill School where he made friends and skipped the fifth grade. Next, he attended Smith-Robertson Junior High and published his first short story, "The Voodoo of Hell's Half-Acre," in the *Jackson Southern Register*.

After graduating as Valedictorian in 1925, he moved to Memphis where he was joined by his mother and brother in 1927. One year later, Richard removed his family to Chicago.

Over the next decade, Richard published various stories in magazines, supervised a black youth program, and wrote for Communist newspapers. He started his first novel in 1935, but "Cesspool" (posthumously published as *Lawd Today*) was not successful. By 1938, with a $500 prize for *Fire and Cloud,* Wright had embarked on a career as an author. That year, *Uncle Tom's Children* appeared to good reviews.

Wright became established as a writer in 1940 with the publication of *Native Son.* Personally, reconciliation with his father failed and he ended his marriage with his first wife, Dhima Rose Meadman. Almost immediately, he married Ellen Poplar and had two daughters—Julia in 1942 and Rachel in 1949.

After *Native Son,* Wright published some articles and left the Communist party. In 1945, *Black Boy* was published and received excellent reviews while topping best-seller charts. After this, Richard left the United States.

Wright refused to return to racist America and the risk of subpoena by anti-Communist investigations. In 1953, he published the first American existentialist novel, *The Outsider.* In 1956 he published *The Color Curtain: A Report on the Bandung Conference.* He continued to write until a heart attack in 1960 ended his life, but he never regained the acclaim awarded him by *Black Boy.*

Plot Summary

Chapters I-IV

Richard Wright's autobiographical account in *Black Boy* opens with his earliest memory, standing before a fireplace as a four-year-old child on a rural Mississippi plantation. Warned repeatedly to "keep quiet," young Richard instead plays with fire and nearly burns his family's house down, then unsuccessfully tries to avoid being severely punished by hiding under the burning house. After the family moves to a new home in Memphis, Richard again challenges parental authority by taking literally his father's exaggerated demand that he kill a noisy kitten. Richard lynches the cat and then feels triumphant over his stern father, who can not beat Richard because he was just following orders. However, when his mother forces him to bury the animal and pray for forgiveness for his cruel act, he feels crushing guilt. These two incidents set the stage for various attempts by young Richard to express his powerful feelings and to test the limits placed on him by his family and his environment.

Richard begins to explore the world around him early on, sneaking into saloons and begging for pennies and drinks, learning to read from neighborhood school children and learning to count from the coal man, and above all, asking questions of everyone he encounters. He is witness to several disturbing scenes and events that do not make sense to his young mind. He hears that a "'black' boy had been severely beaten by a 'white' man" and he can only assume that it is because the "boy" is the white man's son, since in Richard's world fathers are allowed to beat their children and Richard does not know what "black" and "white" means. He sees a black military regiment and asks his mother to explain the meaning of "soldiers," "rifles," "Germans," "enemies," and "wars." He sees a group of "strange, striped animals" and learns that it is a chain gang of black prisoners and white guards. Finally, after learning that white men have murdered his Uncle Hoskins for his thriving business, Richard and his family flee to yet another home, trying "to avoid looking into that white-hot face of terror that we knew loomed somewhere above us."

As he grows older, Richard's life at home with his family causes him as much distress as his experience with the larger world of the South. After his mother is deserted by his father and falls ill, Richard's life becomes a continual struggle with poverty and hunger. After some time in an orphanage (from which he tries to run away), Richard and his family move from place to place, living in the cheapest lodgings they can find or with relatives. Richard begins to attend school and to develop friendships with other boys, but as his mother's health worsens, he feels more and more responsible for supporting the family by working. When his mother has a nearly-fatal stroke, Richard senses an end to his childhood. Over time, his mother's illness comes to represent all the pain and suffering of his life and shapes his outlook on the future.

My mother's suffering grew into a symbol in my mind, gathering to itself all the poverty, the ignorance, the helplessness; the painful, baffling, hunger-ridden days and hours; the restless moving, the futile seeking, the uncertainty, the fear, the dread; the meaningless pain and the endless suffering…. A somberness of spirit that I was never to lose settled over me during the slow years of my mother's unrelieved suffering, a somberness that was to make me stand apart and look upon excessive joy with suspicion, that was to make me self-conscious, that was to make me keep forever on the move, as though to escape a nameless fate seeking to overtake me.

At the age of twelve, before I had had one full year of formal schooling, I had a conception of life that no experience would ever erase, a predilection for what was real that no argument could ever gainsay, a sense of the world that was mine and mine alone, a notion as to what life meant that no education could ever alter, a conviction that the meaning of living came only when one was struggling to wring a meaning out of meaningless suffering.

After living with relatives for a short time after his mother's stroke, Richard returns to live with his mother at his grandparents' home in Jackson, Mississippi. Here the outlook on life that he has forged in response to his mother's suffering comes into conflict with his grandmother's religious belief. Although she "maintained a hard religious regime," Richard succeeds in resisting her attempts to make him "confess her God." After a more violent confrontation with his Aunt Addie, Richard finally promises his grandmother that he will try to pray to God, but try as he might, he fails: "I was convinced that if I ever succeeded in praying, my words would bound noiselessly against the ceiling and rain back down upon me like feathers." Instead, he begins to write, inventing stories full of "atmosphere and longing and death." Although he can find no one in his life who might appreciate what he has created, Richard senses that in his writing he has found a source of freedom from the pain of his life and a way of expressing himself, unhindered by the limitations of his environment or his family.

Chapters V-X

Richard's confrontations with his family over religion are reignited when his mother, recovered for a time, joins a Methodist church and pleads with him to be baptized. Forced into a position in which rejection of her Christian faith would constitute a visible and shameful rejection of his mother and the entire community, Richard relents and is baptized. Privately, however, he still finds his reading and writing of "pulp narrative" far more compelling

Richard Wright at his typewriter.

than what the church, which he rejects as a "fraud," offers.

Having once again started school and in need of money for clothes and food, Richard confronts his grandmother about her religious refusal to allow him to work on Saturdays. When he finally threatens to leave her home if not allowed to work, she yields to his demand and Richard immediately begins to seek out employment. His first job, selling newspapers to black neighbors, not only provides him with an income but also a "gateway to the world" beyond his own. However, he soon learns that the newspaper he sells endorses the doctrines of the Ku Klux Klan, and he quits the job in

shame. Various other jobs—including work at a farm, a brickyard, a sawmill, a clothing store, an optical company, and a movie theater—give Richard firsthand experience of the ways that white people live in the South and, more importantly, the ways that they expect blacks to live and behave. Finding himself unable to act out the roles expected of him, Richard fears that a wrong word or action will cost him his life, and he finally resolves to leave Mississippi for Memphis.

Chapters XI-XIV

Upon his arrival in Memphis, Richard quickly finds, to his surprise, a friendly family with whom he can lodge; but he is even more surprised when Mrs. Moss, the proprietor, pressures him to marry her daughter Bess. Richard comes to realize that the Mosses live by a "simple unaffected trust" that he knows to be "impossible" in his own life. Richard immediately begins looking for work and he finds it running errands for another optical company. While working there Richard meets several other black workers who discuss together "the ways of white folks toward Negroes," but he also recognizes that the ways of some blacks toward white folks—like Shorty, who acts like a degraded clown for money—fill him with "disgust and loathing." Against his own will, however, Richard is forced into playing a similar role when the white men he works with coerce him into fighting another black boy. The psychological tension he feels around whites makes him reject the kindness of a "Yankee" white man who wants to help him.

To feed his growing hunger for books, Richard cautiously borrows a white man's library card— something forbidden to Southern blacks—and then begins to read voraciously. Reading writers whose names he can not even pronounce, Richard finds "new ways of looking and seeing" and feels "a vast sense of distance between me and the world in which I lived." Believing that he could no longer survive in the South and inspired by his reading to seek a life of meaning and possibility in the North, Richard finally flees the South for Chicago.

Chapters XV-XX

Originally deleted by Wright's publisher and finally restored in the Library of America's 1991 edition of *Black Boy,* this section details Wright's experiences after arriving in Chicago. Continuing his quest for a meaningful way to "live a human life," Wright realizes that the lives of blacks and whites are less segregated in the North but are separated nonetheless by a great "psychological distance." For a time Wright finds meaning in the work of the Communist party, but eventually he becomes disillusioned with the party's limited role for him. He closes Part Two with the decision to write, "determined to look squarely at my life" and to "build a bridge of words between me and that world outside."

Characters

Mrs. Bibbs

Mrs. Bibbs, like most white characters in the novel, represents one facet of the oppressive soci-

Media Adaptations

- A recording of *Black Boy* was made by Brock Peters. It was made available in 1989 by Caedmon/New York.

ety that confronts Richard from birth. In this case, she articulates the white assumption that blacks are inherently suited to menial labor. Therefore, when she hires Richard to do chores around her house, she is astounded to learn that Richard cannot milk a cow.

Mr. Crane

In the novel, Mr. Crane stands for the liberal whites who are well-meaning, but ultimately too weak to stand up to the prevailing racism of their society. Mr. Crane is a Yankee business man who owns an optical company in Jackson and he wants to take on a black boy with the enlightened notion of teaching him the trade of optics. Richard shows promise because of his algebraic skill so Crane hires him as shop boy, saying that he will gradually learn the trade. Unfortunately, Crane's other workers do not want to find themselves eventually equal to a black boy. Rather than risk bodily harm, Richard leaves the job. Mr. Crane is sorry to see him go and though he promises protection in the future, Richard refuses to divulge what happened because he knows there will be repercussions outside the shop.

Ella

Not to be confused with Richard's mother Ellen, who is sometimes called Ella, this Ella is a boarder at Grandma's house. A schoolteacher with a "remote and dreamy and silent" manner, Richard is attracted to her mystery, though afraid. She is always reading and Richard desires very much to ask her about what in the books is so fascinating. After increasing antagonism from Grandma, Ella is blamed for Richard's swearing and is asked to leave the house. In this clash of characters is summed up the essence of Richard's emerging consciousness— the struggle between the conflicting power of personal expression, narrative, and storytelling versus stricter religious and cultural demands.

Ella

See Ellen Wilson Wright

Mr. Falk

Richard asks Mr. Falk if he might use his library card. This does not foster an alliance between them, only a light sympathy, but Mr. Falk does give Richard his library card without betraying him. Richard is then enabled to make regular trips to the "whites only" library.

Grandpa

See Richard Wilson

Griggs

Griggs is Richard's friend who repeatedly tries to convince Richard to take the "easier" route of conforming to white expectations of black behavior. For Richard he represents the self-enslaving nature of so many of his contemporaries, whose example he can never bring himself to follow.

Harrison

He is a shop boy who works across the street from Richard. He is beset by rumors that Richard wants to fight him while Richard is told that Harrison wants to fight him. Eventually they agree to fight, not because they have fallen for the rumors but because Harrison wants the $5. They fight once. In this episode, Wright sums up the ease with which blacks allow themselves to be pitted against other blacks for the entertainment of white society.

Mrs. Moss

Richard rents a room from Mrs. Moss and finds that she is offering more than just shelter. Mrs. Moss tries to tempt him to marry her daughter Bess. Richard doesn't want to, even if it means inheriting the house. He finds Bess too simple in her emotional outlook. Desperate to have them leave him alone, he threatens to leave. They back off and he continues to rent his room.

Mr. Olin

Mr. Olin is Richard's foreman at the Memphis Optical Company. He tries to befriend Richard by telling him that Harrison wants to fight him. He is suspicious of Mr. Olin so he talks to Harrison. Mr. Olin eventually gets his fight by paying them.

Shorty

One of the black men that Richard meets working in Memphis, Shorty operates the elevator. Shorty is an intelligent man who would flee Jim Crow for the North if he could just save enough money. Richard thinks a great deal of Shorty because he is very conscious of racism as an environmental condition. However, one day Shorty says, "Just watch me get a quarter from the first white man I see." Shorty gets his quarter by letting the white man kick him. Richard is repulsed because Shorty knows the system too well and has allowed himself to be beaten by it.

Uncle Tom

See Tom Wilson

Addie Wilson

Granny Wilson's youngest daughter Addie returns from her Seventh-Day Adventist religious school and immediately tries to rule Richard. First, she persuades Granny and Richard's mom that if Richard is to live in the house he ought to abide by religious guidance. He is enrolled in the new Seventh-Day Adventist school at which Addie is the only teacher. The showdown is quick in coming when Richard refuses to feel the pain of Addie's corporal punishment in front of the class. After school they fight again but Richard holds her off with a knife. Addie, like her mother, is in conflict with Richard because of her blinkered insistence on religious behavior.

Grandma Bolden Wilson

Richard opens his novel with Granny's white, ill, face. This face disturbs Richard as a little boy because he fails to see how such a white-skinned person could be 'black'. The most important tension Richard holds with Grandma, however, is neatly summed up at the start of the fourth chapter: "Granny was an ardent member of the Seventh-Day Adventist Church and I was compelled to make a pretense of worshipping her God, which was her exaction for my keep." Ardent is not a strong enough word. Grandma is consumed by her belief in religion and its promise to reward her in the hereafter for the suffering of the Jim Crow now. Her zealotry, Richard claims, also means ruining his life. Grandma will not let him get a job that will mean him working on Saturday (their Sabbath) and thus Richard cannot buy food, clothes, and other things necessary amongst children his age. Grandma also prevents him from reading as he would like to or even hearing stories, like *Blue-*

beard, because they are not the Bible. Indirectly, this teaches Richard all about the pretense and the hypocrisy of religion. More directly, due to a deal he makes with Grandma to pray every day, he writes his first short story when he should be quietly praying in his room and thus begins to harbor the idea of being a writer. Grandma sets the pace of the family as well as establishing its treatment of Richard. She tried to orchestrate his religious conversion but finally gives up, concluding that his inability to accept the religious view of things, the established view of things, will lead to his doom. For his questioning and intolerance of status quo, he is punished or ignored.

Clarke Wilson

Richard chooses to live with Uncle Clarke when his mother becomes too ill to care for her children. His choice is based solely on Clarke's proximity to Richard's mother. However, Aunt Jody's dislike of Richard as the product of a "broken home," plus the fright caused by the knowledge that a boy died in his bed, forces Richard back to his Grandma's house. Once more, prejudice determines his choices in life.

Richard Wilson

Grandpa was wounded while fighting for the Union Army in the Civil War. Due to his illiteracy, he asked a white officer for assistance with filling out the paperwork necessary to receiving a disability pension. The officer misspelled his name as Richard Vinson. Not knowing of the mistake, Grandpa returned home. However, as time passed and he received no pension he applied to the War Department who had no trace of him. Eventually, the above story of the "mistake" formed but the War Department demanded proof that Grandpa was in fact deserving of the pension. In consequence, Grandpa spends the rest of his life trying to convince the government he is who he said he is. Grandpa, says Richard, is just "like "K" in the Kafka novel, *The Castle.* He tries desperately to persuade the authorities of his true identity right up to the day of his death, and failed.

Grandpa is a strong male influence in Richard's life who only proves to him that "manliness" is impossible for black men in the Jim Crow South. As a warrior, Grandpa has fought and been wounded for his country, yet the army never pays him the respect—or the disability pension—he has earned. In the home, Richard is also taught that men are "impotent": despite the fact that Grandma calls Grandpa in to administer punishment, it soon be-

comes apparent that it is she, not he, who rules the house.

Tom Wilson

As his name implies, Uncle Tom is an assimilationist who only seeks to get along with racist white society. From his entrance in the novel, he views Richard as a fool by inferring that because Richard is not allowing himself to be brought up by the family in a "proper" manner he will end up at the mercy of a white mob, or a victim of the KKK. Richard refuses—with razors, no less—to learn this lesson.

Ellen Wilson Wright

Richard's mother tries her best to raise Richard after his father deserts the family. Unfortunately she falls ill and Grandma must care for her and the boys. Ella's illness forces the family to split up the boys but Richard eventually returns to Grandma's house to be near his ill mother. Her relationship with Richard is a difficult one since she is not well. At the end, she goes north because Richard sends for her.

Leon Wright

Richard's brother plays a very minor role in *Black Boy.* He is a tag-along sibling when Richard sets fire to the house in the opening scene of the book, a witness to Richard hanging the cat, and present when the rest of the family shuns Richard once he is again back at Grandma's from Maggie's. At the close of the novel, however, Leon is brought north along with mother.

Nathan Wright

Richard's father is his lawgiver and his exemplar. Nathan is the only character in the novel that Richard gives a future glimpse of. Furthermore, by granting this future view of his father, Richard also gives a view of his present, writing, self. At the end of Chapter 1 he defines his father and he defines his own conception of himself. Looking at his father twenty-five years after being deserted, Richard says:

> "I forgave him and pitied him as my eyes looked past him to the unpainted wooden shack. From far beyond the horizons that bound this bleak plantation there had come to me through my living the knowledge that my father was a black peasant who had gone to the city seeking life, but who had failed in the city; a black peasant whose life had been hopelessly snarled in the city, and who had at last fled the city— that same city which had lifted me in its burning arms and borne me toward alien and undreamed-of shores of knowing."

Richard's father left the plantation hoping for a better life for his family, but being beaten by the city, he deserted his family, left them destitute, and fled back to the plantation. Richard is ultimately able to accomplish what his father failed by leaving the plantation clay behind.

Richard Wright

Richard is the protagonist of the story—he is the "black boy." He tells his own story as if he is a victim of his surroundings, almost as if he is an existentialist given limited choice in every circumstance. There is really only one thing he is ever sure of throughout the novel and which drives him to leave the South and tell his story. That one thing is a conception of himself as a person who individually can conceive of the world. In addition to this, he knows that his awareness of having this conception of himself in the world marks him out as different. His certainty of this subjectivity is settled by the age of twelve. By then, he says at the end of Chapter 3, he had a "notion as to what life meant that no education could ever alter, a conviction that the meaning of living came only when one was struggling to wring a meaning out of meaningless suffering."

His father is a peasant who is little more than clay struggling to wrest a living out of the soil, whereas he, Richard, is aware of words, of the world, and insistent that it can be different if the difference is only that he not have to mop up after white people.

Themes

Prejudice and Tolerance
Race and Racism

Racism is not as much a theme in this novel as it is an environmental condition—an integral part of the setting. The novel tries to expose the ethical effect which the Jim Crow system had on its subjects, both black and white. *Black Boy* is a novel about individual positions within a racist mind-set. That is, the world in which Richard must live is racist, and within that world prejudice against blacks is all-pervasive. However, Richard occasionally meets with tolerant persons. Furthermore, Richard himself must be tolerant with those around him who do not have the intellect to see the world like he does. He must also endure the Jim Crow system until he has enough money to escape or else he will be killed.

Richard, having realized that his options are either to play along by being dumb or to be tolerant and escape, chooses the route of escape. However, while awaiting the chance, he spends his time trying to figure out Jim Crow in his own head at least. The novel is his retrospective exploration of the way in which he learned the values and drawbacks which constitute both prejudice and tolerance. Richard may find the coping mechanism of Shorty and Griggs repulsive but in his role as passive observer he only amounts to a chronicler of the facts of Jim Crow. To be sure, to have done more than balk at the easy manner with which a girl handles sexual harassment by a constable would have found Richard strung up like the cat or Uncle Silas. It is worth noting, therefore, that young Richard comes to understand prejudices as opinions which each of us hold no matter how incorrect they are and tolerance as that degree of openness we have to a world which does not accord with our opinions.

Richard never learns the lesson of how to be "black." Part of this is due to the confusion aroused early in Richard's consciousness by his grandmother. Her white appearance implicates that the different treatment of blacks is a treatment based on something other than color. With this hint, Richard decides that blackness is a social decision, not a real fact. For the same reason, he decides that whiteness is not a reality—just an invisible fright like a ghost or bogey. After Uncle Silas is lynched, Richard has evidence of the consequences of being seen as black, but he has not witnessed it himself. Therefore, it was not until he himself is run off a job that Richard understand that whites can be oppressors.

Even after the incident with Pease and Reynolds, Richard fails to understand racism. He doesn't begin to gain an understanding of prejudice and tolerance until he begins to play the system by borrowing Mr. Falk's library card. To use it, he writes the note in which he calls himself a nigger. The librarian questions him but he claims to be illiterate. Having fooled her, he checks out H. L. Mencken who viewed the South as "hell" on earth. The title of Mencken's work was *Prejudices* and this causes Richard to pause and wonder if he hadn't made a mistake in reading Mencken. Certainly, Richard thought to himself "a man who had prejudices must be wrong." However, he discovers that prejudice is a word for a category of thought, rather than simply another word for racism. That is, racism is but one of many prejudices.

For Richard the mind-blocks of prejudice and tolerance are also applicable to religion. This dis-

Topics For Further Study

- Read a novel by Ann Petry or any other member of the "Wright School" (Chester Himes, Willard Savoy, Philip B. Kaye etc.) and compare with *Black Boy.* In the case of Petry's *The Street,* address the difference in terms of gender and the world of the urban black in the cities of post-WWII America.

- What difference does it make whether one reads *Black Boy* or *American Hunger* to one's understanding of Wright's critical view of America? Does America "get off" easy in *Black Boy* because, after all, Wright does escape to the better life in the north?

- Research the issue of Jim Crow and then compare that environment to race relations today: do we live in a more tolerant, egalitarian, society? Discuss current issues such as: Californian challenges to Affirmative action; the declaration of English as the one and only language in some states; the unequal distribution of minorities and the effects on busing, services, insurance, health care, or any other issue.

- Think about perceptions: Wright repeatedly remarks about his refusal at first to adopt proper Jim Crow mannerisms and then the necessity of his having to do so—are there roles that we play based on gender, class, or racial perceptions and are these influenced or based upon information gathered from television sitcoms? Further, what are the perceptions taught us by media on this issue of behavior (think for example about programs like *Cops* versus a network ten o'clock news program)?

- Find some images which were around during WWII and after; get a book of posters from the library showing the overt effort to, first, get people behind the war effort and then get people in the home. After viewing these images, consider the way in which Wright presents the same era. For example, the few white women he does encounter throughout the narrative (especially in the second part of "American Hunger") do not seem to fit the images you will find in the posters. Think about the aim of "urban realism" in light of these posters; think about Wright's struggle to write for people.

---

covery brings him a great deal of grief with family members who are prejudiced towards a certain way of understanding and refuse to budge. An example comes as soon as the start of the fourth chapter where Richard listens to a fire and brimstone sermon which Granny, for one, believes. However, when Richard leaves the church and feels "the throbbing of life" then the sermon inside the church is placed in perspective—it is but one of many ways of seeing the world but a way of seeing best left inside the church. As for the Jim Crow system, Richard would like to leave it in the South.

Meaning of Life
Individualism

For Richard, a life's meaning is in the independence of the individual. That means that Richard sees life as a quest for truth. He stubbornly seeks answers where none—or no satisfactory ones—are given. Richard wants answers which will stand up to argument. Time and again, Richard finds himself at odds with the world: people beat him without justification; he has to be servile to whites; his love of words and stories, which lead him to dream of writing, brings him ridicule. Then there is religion which reveals to him how people give themselves up to groups driven by dogma—they give up, as in the case of Granny or Aunt Addie, their human rights in return for a heavenly inheritance.

Instead of certainty brought about by these beliefs, Richard finds he has something else by the end of the third chapter: "I had a conception of life that no experience would ever erase, a predilection for what was real that no argument could ever gainsay, a sense of the world that was mine and mine alone, a notion as to what life meant that no education could ever alter, a conviction that the meaning of living came only when one was struggling to wring a meaning out of meaningless suffering."

Richard goes on in the next paragraph to explain that this made him a good listener to any who would talk to him and it also made him the keen observer he needed to be in order to become the famous writer he would be. Armed with observations and experience, he relates the reality he has found in the form of words, and thus his identity is entwined with his search for the reason that people behave the way they do, especially why they behave so inhumanely. His conclusions are his novels.

Style

Narration

Taking liberty with his own life's story, Richard Wright created a masterpiece in the story of *Black Boy,* a first-person ("I") narrative portraying a boy who grows up under the oppression of Southern racism. This narration demonstrated the principles of living within the Jim Crow system which Wright had previously laid out in "The Ethics of Living Jim Crow," published in *Uncle Tom's Children.* He represented these ethics through the didactic story of *Black Boy* with the intention of altering white America's racism. Wright believed that a well-developed protagonist in a successful novel would do more for race relations than any political speech or ruling. Therefore, by the use of his own experience re-enforced by a first person persona, *Black Boy* exposes the reality of life for the black American realistically but without offering solutions.

Wright used the first-person narrative to provide an objective viewpoint that borders on the style that would come to be known as existentialism. He did this by portraying his own development in the same way that French writers like Albert Camus and Jean-Paul Sartre presented their leading protagonists. Events and characters encountered by Richard are given only what depth is required to tell Richard's story, so that, in effect, Richard is the only character. The boy in the fourth chapter who wants to save Richard's soul is only an extension of Granny's "machinery," and Granny herself is but an incarnation of the repressive system of Christianity.

An example of how Richard glosses over every character, mentioning them only when they infringe on his consciousness, is the scene where he describes a confrontation among some unnamed boys in a school yard. He terms the associations of other black boys as a fraternity; not a conscious friendship, but a spontaneous gathering. The boys find themselves easily congregated together and are just as easily called away. No emotional links are described or maintained—not even with Griggs, who behaves in such a brotherly manner to Richard. For Richard, the only important things are his own awakening consciousness, his telling of his awakening, and his escape to the North.

Structure

Black Boy is structured as a series of spliced-together episodes in the life of Richard. Thus, the novel reads much like a movie, because in a very real way, Richard makes a documentary of himself. It is as if each chapter is a scene which is cut away from and moved into the next story. The finish of each chapter is punctuated with a sense of progress but not of ending. The novel is very easily visualized by the reader, not only because it is written in a naturalistic style, but also because there are no intrusions by other voices. Key to this structuring is the awareness that Richard has a growing appreciation and use for words. The whole world is filtered through Richard's growing consciousness into an existential *Weltanschauung* (world view) understandable only through his assignation of meaning.

This can be explained by noting that Richard was not allowed free motion—running, shouting, questioning—but had to stay quiet, avoid beatings, and answer his own ceaseless quest for explanation. As a result, Richard was formed by his conscious alienation: he knew he was under restraint but had no concept of an alternative. In reaction, he is very interested in life around him for the clues it reveals about the real world. However, he maintains his interest objectively and from a distance, just like when he is hungry but pretends disinterest in food because the eating of it would remind him of his shameful hunger.

Historical Context

World War II

World War II was coming to an end when *Black Boy* was published in 1945. In fact, as the novel topped the best-seller charts, the U.S. 9th Ar-

Compare & Contrast

- **1940s:** Race relations were tense, at best, with Jim Crowism sanctioned in several states of the union as well as being practiced by the U.S. military.

  Today: Jim Crowism was killed by the Civil Rights movement. Anti-hate legislation and human rights laws are being instituted around the country and rendering the justice system intolerant of all forms of discrimination. Thus, legally things look very good but, as a recent series of black church burnings and challenges in California to affirmative action show, race relations are still imperfect.

- **1940s:** In the South, $17 of tuition was spent per black student per year and $35 per white child. Richard was not obligated nor able to go beyond the ninth grade (which, he says, was really the eighth grade).

  Today: Cuts in tuition assistance put college almost beyond the reach of the poorest students. At the grade school level, no racial distinctions are made in public schools in the matter of spending. Instead, educational spending is decreasing due to congressional cuts. Furthermore, spending is not equally distributed; wealthy districts can afford to, and do, spend a lot more on their children's educations than less wealthy ones.

- **1940s:** America attempts to keep its people working and begins to build a safety net so that no person goes hungry, without care, or is unable to retire.

  Today: From Wisconsin to California, U.S. legislators are erasing the threads which make up the American safety net.

---

mored Division and the 1st Armored Division secured Ally control on the west bank of the Rhine, and U.S. B-24 bombers were bombing Tokyo. The war in Europe ended on May 8, 1945. In the Pacific, the war dragged on until August when an atomic bomb was dropped on Hiroshima and then another was dropped on Nagasaki, Japan. World War II ended, and the loss of life was estimated at 54.8 million.

The Cold War was still a few years away, and 1945 seemed to be a year of victory for the Allies and the ideology of democratic capitalism. The United States was approaching the zenith of its industrial-economic might due to trade imbalance caused by war. Hollywood was not shy to back up the tales of U.S. Army plenty with movies showing how rich and ideal life in America was. The reality, however, was quite different. Americans were wealthy as a nation, and had shown just how wealthy they were by the immensity of the resources they had thrown behind the Allied cause, but individually things were mediocre. For the minorities in America, it was just plain bad: blacks lived under Jim Crow in the South of the United States; the Dakotan, Navajo, Apache, and other tribal groups lived in reservations little better than concentration camps; and Japanese-Americans were being released from internment camps where they had been held under suspicion while the U.S. fought Japan. For these minority groups, there was no possibility of the Hollywood image being real, and in some sense members of these minority groups who had fought in the war had it worse. Like Richard Wright's grandfather, they fought for America but had little to show for it when they came home.

In some sense these problems were only dawning in 1945, because the transition to unemployment resulting from the demobilization of the war's industrial complex into a peacetime economy had not yet arrived. During the year there were signs of the upcoming struggle. Workers in car factories went on strike and despite those strikes, the American Gross National Product approached $211 billion. New agricultural procedures increased food production both within the U.S. and around the

Weighing cotton on a plantation, c. 1910.

world, and food rationing in the U.S. ceased, although it remained a reality in Europe. It was not, and never had been, a problem of wealth in America but, as evidenced in Wright's work, a problem of distribution. America was rich in 1945 but its minorities were very poor.

A societal revolution was beginning to evolve out of this economic inequality. As troops returned home throughout the year, America began a transition back to a peace time economy, thus shifting workers away from military jobs. To succeed at this transition, images changed from encouragement of the war effort to encouragement of family and consumption. In the case of women, this meant the image not of a female in a factory, but a female at home, in a dress, with a baby. This coincided with a media revolution as America increased its private ownership of televisions from only 5,000 sets to the near-universal presence it has today. The U.S. government began its most effective and profitable investment ever—the GI Bill—which allowed the returning soldiers to go back to school or buy a home. This had two effects. First, the already painful transition to a peacetime economy in the job market was not made worse by the soldiers because they instead filled the universities. Second, after a delay there was a tremendous increase in the available numbers of college-educated workers.

The ideal of a peaceful world seemed closer than ever after World War II. Atomic power promised to deter large scale military aggression and the establishment of the United Nations in June of 1945 provided the forum for nonviolent resolutions and concerted action between the world governments. This was the hope, but the reality was being displayed in Palestine by Jewish settlers as they escalated their harassment of British forces in control of the region, and in China where the Russians and the Americans attempted to pick the right side of a battle just beginning between the revolting Communists under Mao Tse-tung and Chiang Kai-shek and his followers.

Critical Overview

When considering the critical reputation of *Black Boy* it is important to note that the novel was available only in a truncated version until 1977. In that year, the full text, *American Hunger,* was published. This work gives the reader a very different view of Richard because the hope granted by the escape to the North at the "end" of the first section is undercut by the broken American dream found in Chicago in the second part. However, *Black Boy* in its 1945 version was well received and remains a popular work to this day. Critically, the work has been viewed as Wright's masterpiece, a twentieth-century version of the slave narrative, and a work of protest against racism, censorship, and intolerance. More recently, criticism has been focused on the restored novel (the version established by the Library of America) as cultural critique and a weapon against censorship. Such recent reviews have also looked more closely at the novel as pure sociology or, as Ellison previously suggested, at the Joycean quality of Wright's writing. This latter view sees Richard as a black version of Stephen Dedalus in *Portrait of the Artist as a Young Man.*

Ralph Ellison reviewed Wright's novel for the *Antioch Review* in 1945 in an essay entitled "Richard Wright's Blues." To him the work was a "blues-tempered" lyric such as Bessie Smith might sing. Richard Wright, Ellison went on, had given himself a duplicitous role: "to discover and depict the meaning of Negro Experience; and to reveal to both Negroes and whites those problems of a psychological and emotional nature which arise between them when they strive for mutual understanding." This became the aim of the "Wright School of Urban Realism". They were a group of authors inspired by Wright to use writing, as Robert A. Bone put it in *The Negro Novel in America* (1965), as a "means of dispelling inner tensions of race … [and through a fictional protagonist] alter [white] attitude toward race."

In addition to Ellison, the novel was reviewed by Lionel Trilling for *The Nation,* on April 7, 1945. Trilling applauded Wright's effort, saying, "He has the objectivity which comes from refusing to be an object." A few months later, in an article for *Esquire* (June 23, 1945), Sinclair Lewis took a more direct approach. His review took the opportunity not to be critical of Wright but of America. Lewis defended the book against those who were made uncomfortable by it. He said there could be no reason to doubt the veracity of the book's report on living conditions for blacks given the echo found in official reports made by the NAACP, the daughter of a white Navy officer (Ruth Donenhower Wilson) in a book on Jim Crow, the U.S. government itself, and others. All told, he said, the South does in fact practice Jim Crowism and the North is not much better. Why, Lewis wonders with the NAACP, should Jim Crowism exist even within the troops and the Red Cross in the European war—within the "Army of Democracy" itself?

In the 1950s, the reputation of Wright ebbed as Ellison and Baldwin came into popularity. How-

ever, in the 1960s, black militancy preferred the forthright attitude of Wright, and his popularity rose to new heights. Ronald Sanders, in "Richard Wright and the Sixties," had nothing but praise for Wright. Saunders called *Black Boy* Wright's masterpiece but also his swan song. Critically, the novel was regarded for what it was doing as a sociological study. For example, in *The Art of Richard Wright,* Edward Margolies portrays Wright as a generalist who extrapolates a blanket statement about American minorities based on his life. Margolies goes so far as to criticize Wright for playing the innocent too much: "[Wright's] theme is freedom and he skillfully arranges and selects his scene in such a way that he is constantly made to appear the innocent victim of … tyranny." That may be, but in the 1970s, critics begin to make greater comparisons and even, as Martha Stephens does, place the pre-*Native Son* works ahead of the greater commercial successes. Stephens also returns to the questions of Ellison and Baldwin as to whether Wright has a picture of "real" negroes. The answer, she says, lies in the whole of his oeuvre.

Roger Whitlow, in his 1973 book entitled *Black American Literature,* shows Wright as a cultural mirror of blacks before the era of Civil Rights. Wright, for Whitlow, is a portrait of the blacks who made the same journey North making the same critical discoveries. *Black Boy,* according to Whitlow, echoes the theme of *Native Son:* "A man must have enough control over his environment to feel that he can mold it, if only slightly, so that it can provide him with at least a part of the realization of his dreams. When he has no such control, he ceases to be a functioning member of that environment; and he thereby divorces himself from its mores and its legal restrictions." Further, just as Richard discovered that neither the North nor South wanted the black man, he had to force his way in. Forcibly black writers, protesters, and speakers have hurled "words into darkness" though many assert that they are still waiting for the full echo of the dream of equality.

Recent views of Wright's work include an article by Maryemma Graham and Jerry W. Ward, Jr. written in 1993. There, in *"Black Boy (American Hunger):* Freedom to Remember" published in *Censored Books: Critical Viewpoints,* the authors says that *American Hunger* is a statement against censorship of all forms. The inclusiveness of Wright's stance can be seen in the novel itself where Richard reflects on how he prefers the Southerner's outright rejection of him to the Northerner's polite tolerance. This article places Wright with

Ray Bradbury, George Orwell, and other writers of anti-censorship works by saying that "these books invite us to imaginatively recreate the experience of living within closed systems. It tells us much about social breakdown and disorder in American life with a vividness sociological writing cannot provide." In other words, Graham and Ward nicely tie together the artistic place of the writer with his responsibility (that responsibility which the "Wright school" focused on) to alter the consciousness of America for the better. In Wright's specific capacity as a survivor of Jim Crow and as a black man, they say, "*Black Boy (American Hunger)* is a critique of American optimism betrayed." The novel is a display of how the American dream as product fails to live up to the claims of the advertisement. Such critique is noted but needs to be acted upon.

Criticism

Anthony Dykema-VanderArk

In the following essay, Dykema-VanderArk, a doctoral candidate at Michigan State University, examines the autobiographical nature of Wright's Black Boy *and how it shows Wright's belief in "the influence of environment on a person's actions and attitudes."*

Richard Wright's reputation as one of the most influential figures in the tradition of African-American literature rests on two works in particular, his best-selling novel, *Native Son* (1940), and his autobiography, *Black Boy* (1945). In *Native Son*, Wright depicts in graphic physical and psychological detail the realities of a young black man's life under the pressures of a racist environment. In *Black Boy*, one might say that Wright turns the novelist's gaze to his own life, providing (as his subtitle indicates) "A Record of Childhood and Youth" that is at once informative as a historical account and gripping in the same way a novel can be. Blurring the boundaries between fiction and nonfiction, Wright dramatizes various scenes from his early life, recreates dialogue that he could not possibly recall, and incorporates sections of poetic rumination that resemble haiku—but none of these inventions challenges the force and eloquence of Wright's truth-telling in *Black Boy*. Wright uses his autobiography not only to recount significant experiences in his life but also to record his emotional and psychological reactions to those experiences, his intellectual awakening, his "hunger" for a meaningful life, and his condemnation of American racism. In his attempt to capture the significance of his own life, both for himself and for the reader, Wright creates in *Black Boy* a profoundly moving "record" of his remarkable life.

Because one of Richard Wright's primary interests in all of his writing is the influence of environment on a person's actions and attitudes, it is not surprising that he begins his own story by portraying the family environment of his childhood. His mother's injunction in the opening scene that Richard "keep quiet" and his father's similar demand in a following scene suggest, in one small way, the limits that were placed on his life within the family. His response in both cases—first, "accidentally" starting the house on fire, and second, killing a noisy kitten—attest to Richard's desire, even as a young child, to express his feelings and assert his presence in his family in strong terms. Richard's responses unsettle the reader because they seem excessive, out of proportion to the situations he is in. But the scene establishes two themes that run through the whole of *Black Boy:* First, that many things in Richard's Southern environment are in fact excessive, often dangerously and violently so; and second, that Richard will go to great lengths to resist limitations placed on him and to find some means of self-expression.

These opening scenes also portray the tensions that Richard feels within his family, the psychological distance that exists between them even when living close together in cramped quarters. Richard sees his father as "the lawgiver in our family," someone whose very presence stifles his voice and laughter, and someone who remains "a stranger ... always somehow alien and remote." After his father deserts the family, Richard associates him with the "pangs of hunger" he feels, hating him with "a deep biological bitterness." Richard's distance from his mother results not from abandonment but from her illness. It is because of his mother's sickness that Richard must stay in the orphanage and later with various relatives, and after she suffers a severe stroke he feels absolutely alone in the world, unable any longer to "feel" or "react as a child." Eventually, his mother's affliction becomes a powerful symbol in Richard's mind, producing a "somberness of spirit" that sets him apart from other people and inspiring "a conviction that the meaning of living came only when one was struggling to wring a meaning out of meaningless suffering."

This outlook shapes Richard's view of his Grandmother's religious belief, which he finds a poor substitute for his own rootedness in the hard

What Do I Read Next?

- Wright's first success was *Native Son* (1940). It is the tragic tale of Bigger Thomas and explores many of the same themes as *Black Boy*.

- The 1963 novel entitled *Lawd Today* is in many ways Richard Wright's best work, although it was never as successful as *Black Boy* or *Native Son*. This story began as "Cesspool" in 1935 and tells the story of the futile life of Jake Jackson, who lives in Chicago as a postal worker.

- A member of the "Wright School," Ann Petry wrote about the trials of life on 116th Street, Harlem, in *The Street*. In that 1946 novel, Petry explores the relationship of environment and a black woman's effort to live with self-respect in the ghetto. Both written by and about a woman, it is a nice companion to Richard Wright's work.

- *Invisible Man,* the 1953 novel by Ralph Ellison, has become a classic portrayal of black experience in America.

- For a nonfictional view of what actually constituted Jim Crow, see *Jim Crow Guide: The Way It Was,* which has been recently re-published by Florida Atlantic University Press. In this work by Stetson Kennedy, the legal basis as well as the civic rules which created the system of legal discrimination are displayed. The book is highly informative and very readable.

- An account of black experience in the "democratic army" which fought in World War II has been recorded by Mary Patrick Motley in *The Invisible Soldier: The Experience of the Black Soldiers, WWII.* Motley's work is a collection of interviews with veterans of the war who told her about the fighting as well as the unfortunate existence of Jim Crow in the U.S.—a practice which other armies did not mirror.

- For further reading on race relations in the U.S. at the time of the novel, see R. Polenberg's *One Nation Divisible: Class, Race, and Ethnicity in the United States since 1938.*

---

realities of life. Although he responds to the drama and the emotion of the church service and its religious symbols, he rejects entirely its "cosmic threats" of damnation and develops "a callousness toward all metaphysical preachments." Richard rejects religion in part because it finds otherworldly causes and solutions for the real-world suffering that he cannot escape. He believes that the religion of his Aunt Addie and Granny leads people to ignore or accept passively the pain of their lives. Even the school kids he meets at his Aunt's religious school seem to live flattened-out lives, almost as if they were mentally and emotionally impaired by their religion: "These boys and girls were will-less, their speech flat, their gestures vague, their personalities devoid of anger, hope, laughter, enthusiasm, passion, or despair." Religion can also be coercive, Richard realizes, as when he is "trapped" by his mother and the entire community of her church into joining the church—or, as he puts it, into giving "the sign of allegiance" to the "tribe."

Richard understands the desire behind religious belief—as he puts it, "the hunger of the human heart for that which is not and can never be"—but his grandmother's religion offers nothing to satisfy his own "hunger," just as her sparse fare at home leaves him physically hungry to the point of sickness. What he doesn't find in religion Richard seeks elsewhere, and his "hunger" for something beyond mere food becomes a dominant motif throughout *Black Boy*. Of course, real, painful physical hunger haunts Richard at every turn, and six-year-old Richard's innocent thought—"Why could I not eat when I was hungry?"—lingers as an unanswered question throughout his narrative. Wright clearly wants the reader of *Black Boy* to *feel* Richard's "biting hunger, hunger that made my body aimlessly restless, hunger that kept me on edge," and to ask "why?" along with him. Physical hunger also causes considerable psychic suffering in Richard's life, as a sign of punishment at the orphanage, as a symbol of his father's desertion, and as a barrier between him and friends at school. But Richard also depicts ways in which deeper longings, more significant to him than physical need, define his experience of life.

At times these longings point to something healthy and positive in Richard's character, as when he senses "a new hunger" before he leaves the South for Chicago. This hunger inspires Richard's strong sense of self-reliance, his unwillingness to betray his deepest feelings, and his refusal to "surrender to what seemed wrong." But Richard also describes the longing he feels as hurtful and damaging to his personality. "Again and again," he writes, "I vowed that someday I would end this hunger of mine, this apartness, this eternal difference." Here and elsewhere Richard's hunger becomes a symbol not of his positive yearning but of his isolation and loneliness, his sense of exclusion from the world around him.

Richard doesn't always understand his sense of "eternal difference" from those around him, and clearly his temperament, his learning, and his willful separation from community institutions such as the church all play a part in his "apartness." But as he grows up, Richard increasingly sees that the racist environment of the South creates and sustains his feeling of exclusion. Richard's attitudes toward white people begin to form early on, when, for example, he watches from the kitchen as a white family eats from a "loaded table" while he and his brother wait for whatever food is leftover. Though at the time he feels only "vaguely angry" and decidedly hungry, such experiences eventually convince Richard that "white folks" are in some way responsible for his exclusion from literacy and education, from knowledge of the wider world, from justice and equality, from possibilities in life, even from meaningful relationships with other people. In his fight with Harrison, Richard realizes that the power of white people to limit his life even extends to his relationships with his black peers. He fights Harrison against his will, beating up another oppressed "black boy"—and himself—because he cannot express his shame, anger, and hatred directly to the white men responsible for his feelings.

In a racist society that wants him to be content with his spiritual as well as his physical hunger, Richard finally finds "vague glimpses of life's possibilities" only in literacy, reading, and writing. He realizes at a young age that in order to lay bare the secrets of the world around him, he must understand "the baffling black print" that he sees in the school children's books. When he does learn to read, Richard uses his ability to probe into "every happening in the neighborhood," and this includes the realities of racial prejudice and hatred. When he hears that "a 'black' boy had been severely beaten by a 'white' man," he interrogates his mother about the difference between "black" and "white," words whose full significance he cannot yet grasp. At the same time, reading stories of "outlandish exploits of outlandish men in faraway, outlandish cities" gives Richard access to an imaginary world beyond his own. When he is older, Richard's reading opens his eyes to "new ways of looking and seeing" that "made the look of the world different" and let him imagine his life under different circumstances. Richard eventually recognizes that the social system of the South strives to keep black Americans from just such ways of thinking. Thus, Richard must lie about being able to read in order to check out books with a white man's library card, and he carries his newfound knowledge with him like "a secret, criminal burden." In the end, Richard's reading and his writing do not merely open his eyes to the realities of his life in the South but also create "a vast sense of distance" between him and that world, motivating him to leave it forever.

Wright's record of his experiences after his move to the North did not appear in the initial publication of *Black Boy,* though it was part of his original manuscript. (In order to see his work published by the Book of the Month Club, Wright had to agree to print a shortened version that concludes with his flight from the South.) What Richard finds in Chicago is not, by any means, an environment free from the racism of the South but rather a more "perplexing" situation in certain ways. Wright discovers that while whites and blacks in the North may view each other as merely "part of the city landscape," this nonchalance only masks a great "psychological distance" between the races. Many of the themes he develops in the first part of his narrative reemerge in the latter part, including his feelings of emotional isolation from other people, his sense of the psychological damage caused by race—prejudice and hatred, and his hunger for knowledge and understanding of the world and of himself. But more importantly, just as reading and writing alone offer Richard both a source information about his environment and a means of escape from it, Wright seeks meaning and purpose in the North by way of books and the pen. He concludes his original version of *Black Boy,* significantly, not with the resolution of his deep hungers or the healing of his psychic wounds but with a vow to write—to "look squarely" at his life, to "build a bridge of words" between him and the world, to "hurl words into this darkness" that surrounds him. This, in a sense, is what Wright does in *Black Boy,* creating from words a "Record of Childhood and Youth" that speaks to all readers of that which is "inexpressibly human," "the hunger for life that gnaws in us all."

Source: Anthony Dykema-VanderArk, in an essay for *Novels for Students,* Gale 1997.

Timothy Dow Adams

In the following excerpt, Adams offers his interpretation of Wright's Black Boy, *arguing that its historical inaccuracies have deliberate, metaphorical purpose.*

Like the autobiographies of Gertrude Stein and Sherwood Anderson, Richard Wright's *Black Boy,* published in 1945, has confused readers because of its generic ambiguity. For many readers, the book is particularly honest, sincere, open, convincing, and accurate. But for others, *Black Boy* leaves a feeling of inauthenticity, a sense that the story or its author is not to be trusted. These conflicting reactions are best illustrated by the following representative observations by Ralph K. White and W. E. B. Du Bois. White, a psychologist, has identified [in "*Black Boy*"] "ruthless honesty" as "the outstanding quality which made the book not only moving but also intellectually satisfying." But Du Bois notes [in "Richard Wright Looks Back"] that although "nothing that Richard Wright says is in itself unbelievable or impossible; it is the total picture that is not convincing." Attempting to reconcile these opposing views, I wish to argue that both sides are correct; that the book is an especially truthful account of the black experience in America, even though the protagonist's story often does not ring true; and that this inability to tell the truth is Wright's major metaphor of self. A repeated pattern of misrepresentation becomes the author's way of making us believe that his personality, his family, his race—his whole childhood and youth—conspired to prevent him from hearing the truth, speaking the truth, or even being believed unless he lied.

For most readers, worries about *Black Boy*'s trustworthiness stem from questions of genre. Although the book was clearly not called "The Autobiography of Richard Wright," its subtitle—"A Record of Childhood and Youth"—does suggest autobiography with some claim to documentary accuracy. The following descriptions of *Black Boy* reflect the confusion of readers: biography, autobiographical story, fictionalized biography, master-

piece of romanced facts, sort of autobiography, pseudoautobiography, part-fiction/part-truth autobiography, autobiography with the quality of fiction, and case history....

Although Wright seemed unsure of his book's generic identity, he never referred to *Black Boy* as autobiography. His original title, *American Hunger,* later used for the portion of his life story that began after leaving Memphis for Chicago, came after he had rejected *The Empty Box, Days of Famine, The Empty Houses, The Assassin, Bread and Water,* and *Black Confession,* all of which sound like titles for novels. When his literary agent suggested the subtitle "The Biography of a Courageous Negro," Wright responded with "The Biography of an American Negro," then with eight other possibilities including "Coming of Age in the Black South," "A Record in Anguish," "A Study in Anguish," and "A Chronicle of Anxiety." Such titles indicate his feeling that the book he had written was less personal, more documentary—a study, a record, a chronicle, or even a biography—than autobiography. Constance Webb reports [in *Richard Wright*] that Wright was uneasy with the word autobiography, both because of "an inner distaste for revealing in first person instead of through a fictitious character the dread and fear and anguishing self-questioning of his life" and because he realized that he would write his story using "portions of his own childhood, stories told him by friends, things he had observed happening to others," and fictional techniques.

Although some readers believe Wright gave in to the "strong desire to alter facts" and "to dress up" his feelings, the book's tendency to intermix fiction and facts is clearly part of both Wright's personal literary history and the Afro-American literary tradition in which he was writing. The form of *Black Boy* in part imitates the traditional slave narrative, a literary type that allowed for a high degree of fictionality in the cause of abolition. A number of major works of literature by black Americans, such as Du Bois's *The Souls of Black Folks,* Toomer's *Cane,* and Johnson's *The Autobiography of an Ex-Coloured Man,* feature mixtures of genres; and Wright, simultaneously a poet, novelist, essayist, journalist, playwright, and actor, often used the same material in different genres. For example, *"The Ethics of Living Jim Crow"* first appeared as an essay and was later attached to the stories of *Uncle Tom's Children,* one of which, *"Bright and Morning Star,"* is retold in *Black Boy* as a tale that held the protagonist in thrall, even though he "did not know if the story was factually true or not." When "black boy" says that the story is emotionally true, he reflects exactly the kind of truth Wright wants his readers to respond to in *Black Boy*. Some of the characters in *Black Boy* have been given fictional names, whereas Bigger Thomas, the central character in the fictional *Native Son,* is the real name of one of Wright's acquaintances. That he used real names in fiction and fictional names in nonfiction is typical of Richard Wright, who further confounded the usual distinctions between author and persona by playing the role of Bigger Thomas in the first film version of *Native Son.*

Richard Wright makes clear that *Black Boy* is not meant as a traditional autobiography by presenting much of the story in the form of dialogue marked with quotation marks, a technique that suggests the unusual degree of fiction within the story. Although critics often point to Wright's first novel, *Native Son* (1940), as the other half of *Black Boy,* another model for this autobiographical work was his more recently completed *Twelve Million Black Voices: A Folk History of the American Negro in the United States* (1941). Writing *Black Boy* in the spirit of folk history seemed a reasonable thing to do, and Wright apparently saw no hypocrisy in omitting personal details that did not contribute to what he was simultaneously thinking of as his own story and the story of millions of others. Wright's claim to be composing the autobiography of a generic black child is reinforced by the narrator's particular reaction to racism: "The things that influenced my conduct as a Negro did not have to happen to me directly; I needed but to hear of them to feel their full effects in the deepest layers of my consciousness."

[Most] of the omission in *Black Boy* is designed not to make the persona appear admirable but to make Richard Wright into "black boy," to underplay his own family's middle-class ways and more positive values. Wright does not mention that his mother was a successful school teacher and that many of his friends were children of college faculty members; he omits most of his father's family background and his own sexual experiences. Also mainly left out are reactions from sensitive southern whites, including those of the Wall family to whom, we learn from Michel Fabre's biography [*The Unfinished Quest of Richard Wright*], "he sometimes submitted his problems and plans … and soon considered their house a second home where he met with more understanding than from his own family."

In addition to omissions, name changes, poetic interludes, and extensive dialogue, *Black Boy* is replete with questionable events that biographical research has revealed to be exaggerated, inaccurate, mistaken, or invented. The section of Fabre's biography dealing with the *Black Boy* years is characterized by constant disclaimers about the factuality of the story. Some omissions can be explained because the urbane ex-Communist who began *Black Boy* "wanted to see himself as a child of the proletariat," though "in reality he attached greater importance to the honorable position of his grandparents in their town than he did to his peasant background." Although these distortions are acceptable to many, especially in light of Wright's intention of using his life to show the effects of racism, numerous other manipulations are less acceptable because they are more self-serving.

Most of these incidents are relatively minor and might be judged unimportant; however, the misrepresentations in two of the book's most important episodes—the high school graduation speech and the story of Uncle Hoskins and the Mississippi River—might be less acceptable. "Black boy's" refusal to deliver the principal's graduation speech rather than his own is apparently based on truth, but the version in *Black Boy* leaves out the important fact that Wright rewrote his speech, cutting out more volatile passages, as a compromise. The story of Uncle Hoskins does not ring true, for how could a boy whose life had been so violent to that point be scared of his uncle's relatively harmless trick? He says of his Uncle Hoskins, "I never trusted him after that. Whenever I saw his face the memory of my terror upon the river would come back, vivid and strong, and it stood as a barrier between us." One reason the tale feels false is that the whole story—complete with the above revelations about Uncle Hoskins—actually happened to Ralph Ellison, who told it to Richard Wright [see Webb, p. 419].

For many critics, including Edward Margolies, these deliberate manipulations reduce *Black Boy*'s authenticity as autobiography because they set up doubts about everything, the same doubts that resonate through the remarks of black writers from Du Bois to Baldwin to David Bradley, all of whom have persisted in taking *Black Boy*'s protagonist to be Richard Wright. But, "Richard Wright is not the same person as the hero of that book, not the same as 'I' or 'Richard' or the 'Black boy,' not by several light years," argues James Olney, [in "Some Versions of Memory/Some Versions of Bios"], who refers to the book's chief character as "black boy," explaining that "by means of an encompassing and creative memory, Richard Wright imagines it all, and he is as much the creator of the figure that he calls 'Richard' as he is of the figure that, in *Native Son,* he calls 'Bigger.'" Olney's idea that the central figure be treated as a single person referred to as "black boy," a literary character representing the actual author both as a child and as an adult—the famous writer imagining himself as representative of inarticulate black children—is finally convincing. That seems to be what Richard Wright meant to do, what he said he had done, and what he did....

The opening scene suggests the whole atmosphere of the book—a desperate fear of meaningless visitations of violence without context, a life of deliberate misrepresentations of the truth and complete distrust of all people, a world in which "each event spoke with a cryptic tongue." Throughout *Black Boy,* Wright presents a lonely figure whose life does not ring true because "that's the way things were between whites and blacks in the South; many of the most important things were never openly said; they were understated and left to seep through to one." Thus all actions are tempered by a subtext, which is obvious to everyone, a strategy that the author claimed to have discovered when he delivered his Fisk University oration.

Whenever the narrator questions his mother about racial relationships, she is defensive and evasive. "I knew that there was something my mother was holding back," he notes. "She was not concealing facts, but feelings, attitudes, convictions which she did not want me to know," a misrepresentation that disturbs "black boy" who later says, "My personality was lopsided; my knowledge of feeling was far greater than my knowledge of fact." Although the narrator holds back or conceals facts, he is usually straightforward about emotional feelings, even though he can say, "The safety of my life in the South depended upon how well I concealed from all whites what I felt." Worrying less about factual truth, Wright was determined to stress the emotional truth of southern life to counteract the stereotypical myths shown in the song that prefaced *Uncle Tom's Children :* "Is it true what they say about Dixie? Does the sun really shine all the time?" ...

The actual audience must narrow the gap between the narrative and authorial audiences; the reader of *Black Boy* must strive to be like the narrator of *Black Boy,* must keep what is happening at a particular moment and the entire history of black-white relations—the content and the context—together in his or her mind. Wright's context includes the need to speak simultaneously as an adult and as a child and to remove everything from his story that, even if it happened to be true, would allow white readers to maintain their distorted stereotype of southern blacks. He was searching for a way to confess his personal history of lying, forced on him by his childhood, while still demonstrating that he could be trusted by both black and white....

Wright's words are not self-pitying; instead, he is presenting a naive youth who was never good at lying or exaggerating. The misrepresentation is so obvious that only a particularly inept liar would attempt it, a child who did not want to be good at lying. Only an outsider, such as "black boy," to the established systems of lying by both races, a representative of the many black adolescents then coming of age—what Wright hoped would be a new generation of the children of Uncle Tom, no longer willing to accept the old lie that the best way to fight racism was to lie through both omission and commission—could fail to distinguish between melodrama and genuine oppression and could be so surprised at the power of his words.

Black Boy should not be read as historical truth, which strives to report those incontrovertible facts that can be somehow corroborated, but as narrative truth. The story that Richard Wright creates in *Black Boy,* whatever its value as an exact historical record, is important both in telling us how the author remembers life in the pre-Depression South and in showing us what kind of person the author was in order to have written his story as he did. Although he is often deliberately false to historical truth, he seldom deviates from narrative truth. In *Black Boy,* Wright has made both the horrifyingly dramatic and the ordinary events of his life fit into a pattern, shaped by a consistent, metaphoric use of lying.

Source: Timothy Dow Adams, "Richard Wright: 'Wearing the Mask,'" in his *Telling Lies in Modern American Autobiography,* The University of North Carolina Press, 1990, pp. 69–83.

Robert J. Butler

In the following excerpt, Butler analyzes how the conflicting images of motion and stagnation presented in Wright's Black Boy *further the themes of human opportunity and human suffocation.*

Richard Wright is noted for his trapped heroes, especially figures such as Bigger Thomas, Fred Daniels, and Cross Damon, but he has also written powerfully of the quest for open motion. Both "*The*

Man Who Was Almos' a Man" and *"Big Boy Leaves Home "* end with bittersweet images of the heroes moving vaguely North in search of new lives which may or may not be available to them. *The Long Journey* concludes with its central character on "a journey that would take him far, far away" from a restrictive past toward new possibilities. These narratives evoke simultaneously allusions to the journey across the River Jordan celebrated by the spirituals, the odyssey down the road extolled by the blues, and the search for open space which resonates through our classic literature. All of these works, to use Whitman's phrase [from *Leaves of Grass*], "tramp a perpetual journey" toward varying degrees of freedom and independence.

Although Wright is often described as a natural genius who wrote about raw experiences unfiltered through any literary traditions, he was, as Michel Fabre has cogently argued [in *CLA Journal,* June 1973], a very well-read man who was acutely aware of the "dual heritage of the Black writer in America." *Black Boy,* which is essentially structured as a search for an open journey, drinks thirstily from the deep streams of Black folk literature and American picaresque literature. As a result, it portrays Wright's own life as very different from Bigger Thomas' trapped existence. Although he had to struggle hard against the racist environment which paralyzed many of his characters, Wright was able to liberate himself and thus give free play to what Ellison has called [in *Shadow and Act*] his "almost manic restlessness." Far from being a sign of purposelessness and incoherence, Wright's pursuit of open motion endowed his life with real energy and purpose. Indeed, it helps to account for his triumph as a man and an artist.

In its most basic terms, *Black Boy* presents a world with two basic options: 1) human suffocation which is dramatized with images of stasis, and 2) human possibility which is rendered by images of constant movement. To emphasize this polarity, Wright repeatedly contrasts scenes of motion and stasis throughout the book. For example, the terrifying opening scene of entrapment is artfully counterpointed with the Whitmanesque prose poem which immediately follows it. Unlike *Native Son,* which is telescoped by the opening scene of paralysis, *Black Boy* begins with two scenes which define the book's central drives.

Confined in a house with a bed-ridden grandmother, Wright as a four-year-old boy looks "yearningly" out into the empty street, all the while "dreaming of running and playing and shouting."

From the beginning, his protean imagination is set in opposition to a flat, enervated environment which denies his impulses any creative outlet. Wandering "listlessly" about the room, he can find nothing interesting except the "shimmering embers" and "quivering coals" of the fire. Even after he has been cautioned by his mother not to play with the fire, he feels irresistibly drawn to this fluid medium and soon sets the curtains ablaze. Although his immediate reaction is "to run away and never come back," he merely hides under the house which he falsely regards as "a place of safety." He breaks into "a wild run" when his father pulls him out of the crawl space but is easily caught and then severely beaten by his mother, to the extent that he is bed-ridden for five days. This scene ends on a note of painful ambivalence with Wright "determined to run away" but "lost in a fog of fear." As Fabre has observed [in *The Unfinished Quest of Richard Wright*], this episode left lasting scars on Wright, shattering his emotional security and initiating an "estrangement" which deepened as Wright grew older. Indeed, the "red circles" of flame which consume the curtains can be seen as a revealing symbol of Wright's early life—a trap of spreading violence which can easily destroy him if he fails to understand and find alternatives to it.

In addition, the prose poem which immediately follows this scene, gives some clues about what these alternatives might be. Here Wright is outdoors, moving in a world of imaginative, physical, and emotional freedom. Whereas in the previous scene his consciousness was blocked by fear, he now relaxes and expands his sensibilities, as experience reveals its "coded meanings" to him. Significantly, the poem is suffused with lyrical images of indefinite motion: horses clopping down a dusty road; Wright himself running through wet garden paths in the early morning; the Mississippi River winding past the bluffs of Natchez; wild geese flying South for the winter; a solitary ant moving on "a mysterious journey"; and "vast hazes of gold" which "washed earthward from star-heavy skies on silent nights." The implications of this startling juxtaposition of scenes are clear. Even in the harshly restrictive world of segregated Mississippi there are avenues of escape and development. Once liberated from society, which in *Black Boy* is always a trap, Wright can discover a protean world offering human possibilities.

As is the case in much American writing, the physical liberation literally described by the poem almost always generates emotional and spiritual freedom. Although the net effect of the opening scene is to bottle up Wright's feelings, here he feels wonder at the horses, nostalgia for the geese, and languor from the rustling leaves. These images also spring meanings which have significant spiritual overtones. The waters of the Mississippi evoke "a sense of the infinite," the movements of the lone ant are described as "mysterious," and the motion of the stars instills in him a deep religious awe. In short, motion endows life with vitality and meaning, transforming a dead world of routine into a dynamic realm of beauty where the self can be transformed.

Wright carefully develops this contrast between motion and stasis throughout *Black Boy.* The Memphis tenement in which he lives as a young man is set in opposition to the steamboat ride on the Mississippi which fires his imagination. The terror he initially feels at being locked out of his house is dissolved into fascination by his "irresistible" impulse to roam the streets of the city. The scene where he again hides under his bed to avoid a beating from his grandmother is likewise contrasted with a second prose poem filled with images of movement—chasing butterflies, observing the "rolling sweep of tall green grass," and enjoying "nights of drizzling rain." The closed world of Mississippi is always sharply differentiated from the open world of his developing spirit.

Black Boy, therefore, has a narrative structure which is complexly double, giving us two opposite but thematically related plot patterns. Wright's outer journey takes the form of a series of apparently random moves which end in paralysis. In contrast to this naturalistic fable, strongly resembling the plots of works such as *Maggie: A Girl of the Streets* and *McTeague,* is an inward narrative which is centered around the development of the hero's consciousness which will enable him eventually to move in freer, more productive ways. As such, it is a story of awakening and is closely related to Dreiser's *Dawn* and Farrell's autobiographical novels about Danny O'Neill.

An even cursory examination of the outer narrative of *Black Boy* vividly demonstrates that Wright's physical movements during his early life were a bewildering road leading nowhere. As Keneth Kinnamon has revealed [in *The Emergence of Richard Wright*], Wright lived in no less than nineteen residences in his first nineteen years. The result of this incoherent movement from one racist place to another was to strip Wright of both familial bonds and a meaningful self image, thus depriving him of any emotional center to his life. The results of such a life of perpetual drifting are clear

to Wright as he observes the people around him. His father's life is an especially painful object lesson, for he sees it as environmentally-controlled movement leading to eventual depletion:

I stood before him, poised, my mind aching as it embraced the simple nakedness of his life, feeling how completely his soul was *imprisoned* by the slow flow of the seasons, by wind and rain and sun, how *fastened* were his memories to a crude and raw past, how *chained* were his actions and emotions to the direct, animalistic impulses of his withering body. (italics added)

Since nothing directs the father's life but the restrictive motions of nature, his movements eventually wind down to a terrifying stasis. After deserting the family and wandering restlessly around the North where he becomes "hopelessly snarled" in the city, he returns to the South to live out his days in a form of slavery, sharecropping. His life then is very much like the flame described in Chapter One, a circle of necessity which consumes him.

Wright's view of his grandmother and mother are also portrayed with images of futility. Unlike his father who was associated with blind movement, the grandmother is always described in terms of an equally disastrous inertia. Initially presented as immobilized in a sick bed, she is throughout the novel mentally and spiritually imprisoned by an absolute commitment to a fundamentalist religion which separates her from anything vital in life. Her house in Jackson provides a kind of locus for Wright since it is the place to which he keeps returning after his various moves, but it is always a dead center of repression and he usually feels a sense of claustrophobia there. His deepest wish is simply to run away from such a "home" as soon as he grows old enough to do so.

An even more important image of futility is provided by his mother, whose suffering becomes a tragic epiphany of the wasted life. After a stroke leaves her partially paralyzed, she is often seen in bed or, like Dreiser's Hurstwood, rocking in a chair while gazing blankly into oblivion. Indeed, one of the central passages in *Black Boy* is Wright's agonized meditation on his mother's condition:

That night I ceased to react to my mother; my feelings were frozen.... Her illness gradually became an accepted thing in the house, something that could not be stopped or helped.

My mother's suffering grew into a symbol in my mind, gathering to itself all the poverty, the ignorance, the helplessness, the painful, baffling, hunger-ridden hours, the restless moving, the futile seeking, the uncertainty, the fear, the dread, the meaningless pain and endless suffering. Her life set an emotional tone for my life.

The forms of moral and physical paralysis characterizing the lives of his parents and grandmother become for Wright an index of the roles assigned to Blacks in Southern society, all of which result in "meaningless suffering."

It is his task to "wring a meaning" out of such suffering. Although he eventually comes to see the South as a Dantean hell where he is "forever condemned, ringed by walls," he nevertheless is able to achieve salvation of sorts by moving along his "own strange and separate road." Caught in a society which is intent on reducing his life to random drifting, disintegration, and paralysis, he is able to find a meaningful alternative in his own inwardness: "Because I had no power to make things happen outside me, I made things happen within me." Crucial to this purposeful inward narrative is Wright's gradual mastery of language through reading and writing, a process which is always associated with images of motion and release. Even the cheap pulp thrillers he reads as a boy become "a gateway to the world" because they transport him from the locked room in which he reads to "outlandish men in faraway, outlandish cities." Energizing his imagination, they provide Wright access to an open world. Ella, the boarder at his grandmother's house, can feed his starved imagination on the literature which serves as an alternative to his grandmother's mind-numbing religiosity:

> As her words fell upon my ears I endowed them with a reality that *welled up* somewhere within me.... The tale made the world around me be, *throb, live*. As she spoke, *reality changed*, the look of things altered, and the world became peopled with magical presences. My sense of life deepened.... My imagination *blazed*. (italics added)

This rich proliferation of motion images, which portrays his mind bubbling, the world throbbing and his imagination blazing, suggests that his active use of language has dissolved the harshly fixed limits of Southern life. Restrictive place has been turned into open space—a universe of growth.

Source: Robert J. Butler, "The Quest for Pure Motion in Richard Wright's *Black Boy*," in *MELUS*, Vol. 10, No. 3, Fall, 1983, pp. 5–17.

Sources

Robert A. Bone, *The Negro Novel in America*, revised edition, Yale University Press, 1965, pp. 141-52.

Ralph Ellison, "Richard Wright's Blues," in *The Collected Essays of Ralph Ellison*, ed. John F. Callahan, Modern Library, 1995, pp. 128-44.

Maryemma Graham and Jerry W. Ward, Jr., "*Black Boy (American Hunger): Freedom to Remember*," in *Censored Books: Critical Viewpoints*, edited by Nicholas J. Karolides, Less Burress, and John M. Kean, Scarecrow Press, 1993, pp. 109-16.

Sinclair Lewis, review in *Esquire*, June 23, 1945.

Edward Margolies, *The Art of Richard Wright*, Southern Illinois University Press, 1969.

Ronald Sanders, "Richard Wright and the Sixties," in *Midstream*, Vol. XIV, No. 7, August/September, 1968, pp. 28-40.

Lionel Trilling, review in *The Nation*, April 7, 1945.

Roger Whitlow, "Chapter 4: 1940-1960: Urban Realism and Beyond" in *Black American Literature: A Critical History*. Nelson Hall, 1973, pp. 107-46.

For Further Study

Harold Bloom, editor, *Richard Wright (Modern Critical Views)*, Chelsea, 1987.
    A collection of essays on all of Wright's work, including an analysis of *Black Boy*'s place in the black literary tradition.

Edward D. Clark, "Richard Wright," in *Dictionary of Literary Biography*, Volume 76: *Afro-American Writers, 1940-1955*, Gale Research, 1988, pp. 199-221.
    Clark describes Wright's position in the history of American literature as that of a father to the post-World War II black novel.

Ralph Ellison, "The World and the Jug," in *The Collected Essays of Ralph Ellison*, edited by John F. Callahan, Modern Library, 1995, pp. 155-88.
    Ellison's powerful rejoinder to Irving Howe's commentary in "Black Boys and Native Sons."

Michel Fabre, *The Unfinished Quest of Richard Wright*, William Morrow, 1973.
    A lengthy biography, translated from French, that evaluates Wright as a "representative man" and an important spokesperson of his age.

Henry Louis Gates, Jr., and K. A. Appiah, editors, *Richard Wright: Critical Perspectives Past and Present*, Amistad, 1993.
    A collection of critical essays on Wright's work written with knowledge of the untruncated version. In this collection is an essay by Horace A. Porter exploring in greater depth the similarity of Richard and Stephen Dedalus.

Donald B. Gibson, "Richard Wright: Aspects of His Afro-American Literary Relations," in *Critical Essays on Richard Wright*, ed. Yoshinobu Hakutani, G. K. Hall, 1982.
    Gibson examines why Wright's work is "so clearly distinguished" from other literature by black authors, comparing Wright in particular to Charles Chesnutt and Paul Laurence Dunbar.

Irving Howe, "Black Boys and Native Sons," in *A World More Attractive*, Horizon, 1963.

Howe's well-known essay in which he examines and compares the element of "protest" in the works of Wright, James Baldwin, and Ralph Ellison.

David Ray and Robert M. Farnsworth, *Richard Wright: Impressions and Perspectives,* University of Michigan Press, 1971.

A unique collection of writings by and about Wright, including personal impressions, reminiscences, and correspondence.

John M. Reilly, editor, *Richard Wright: The Critical Reception,* Burt Franklin, 1978.

An overview of original critical responses to Wright's work, including excerpts of more than sixty early reviews of *Black Boy.*

Sidonie Ann Smith, "Richard Wright's *Black Boy:* The Creative Impulse as Rebellion," in *The Southern Literary Journal,* Vol. V, No. 1, Fall, 1972, pp. 123-36.

In this essay, Smith presents Wright's autobiography as a slave narrative because of the commonalities of themes which the novel has with such pre-Civil War accounts.

Martha Stephens, "Richard Wright's Fiction: A Reassessment," *Georgia Review,* 1971, pp. 450-70.

Looking at all of Wright's works, Stephens ranks the works written before *Native Son* as a better display of Wright's mastery than his more profitable or later works.

Ellen Wright, and Michel Fabre, editors, *Richard Wright Reader,* Harper and Row, 1978.

A collection of some of Wright's best writings, including excerpts from his fiction, poetry, essays, and criticism.

The Bluest Eye

Toni Morrison
1970

As Toni Morrison has become one of America's most celebrated contemporary authors, her first novel *The Bluest Eye,* published in 1970, has gained increasing attention from literary critics. Most of the novel is narrated by a young black girl, Claudia MacTeer, who is part of a poor but loving black family in Lorain, Ohio, in the 1940s. However, the primary focus of the novel is on Pecola Breedlove, another young black girl who lives in very different circumstances from Claudia and her sister Frieda. Pecola's mother, Pauline, is cruel to her family because they are a constant reminder that her life can never measure up to the ideal world of the white family for which she works as a maid. Not only is her mother distant and aloof, but Pecola's father is also unreliable for any comfort or support. Cholly Breedlove drinks excessively and later rapes Pecola. She bears his child, who dies shortly after birth. Because Pecola, like Pauline, yearns to be seen as beautiful, she longs for the blue eyes of the most admired child in the 1940s: Shirley Temple. After visiting Soaphead Church, a "spiritualist" who claims he can make Pecola's eyes blue, Pecola believes that she has the bluest eyes in the world and now everyone will love her. Clearly, Pecola is the truest kind of victim. Unlike Claudia, who possesses the love of her family, Pecola is powerless to reject the unachieveable values esteemed by those around her and finally descends into insanity. *The Bluest Eye* portrays the tragedy which results when African Americans have no resources with which to fight the standards

presented to them by the white culture that scorns them.

Author Biography

From her childhood days in Lorain, Ohio, Toni Morrison learned from her parents, Ramah Willis Wofford and George Wofford, the importance of racial pride but also the tragedy that can result when a black person internalizes alien, often white, values. These lessons surface repeatedly in Morrison's first novel *The Bluest Eye* and in many of her other works.

Morrison was born Chloe Anthony Wofford on February 18, 1931, to parents who were very confident in themselves and their race. They stressed the importance of an education, which is reflected in the fact that Morrison was the only child entering her first grade class who could read. Her love of books continued as she devoured the works of European writers, including Jane Austen, Gustav Flaubert, and Leo Tolstoy, as an adolescent.

After graduating from high school in Lorain with honors, Morrison earned a B.A. in English from Howard University. Two pivotal events for Morrison occurred at Howard: she changed her name to Toni because many people could not pronounce Chloe, and she became acquainted with black life in the South while touring with the Howard University Players. In 1955, Morrison earned an M.A. in English from Cornell and taught English at Texas Southern University for two years before returning to Howard in 1957 to teach English. Again, events at Howard were pivotal as she met her husband, Howard Morrison, a Jamaican architect, there. Morrison rarely discusses her marriage, which ended in divorce after the births of two sons, Harold Ford and Slade Kevin.

Raising two sons alone, Morrison moved to Syracuse to take an editing job with a textbook subsidiary of Random House, and to combat isolation, she wrote. She first worked on a story she had begun in her writers group at Howard. This story about a little black girl who longs for blue eyes was the genesis of her first novel, *The Bluest Eye,* published in 1970.

Since the appearance of *The Bluest Eye,* Morrison's successes have multiplied. In 1970, she took an editorial position with Random House in New York and began writing regularly for the *New York Times* about black life. Her second novel, *Sula,* was published in 1973 and brought Morrison national

Toni Morrison

acclaim. In 1977, her third novel, *Song of Solomon,* was chosen as a Book-of-the-Month Club main selection, the first book by a black writer to be chosen since Richard Wright's *Native Son* in 1940. The novel also won the National Book Critics' Circle Award, and Morrison was awarded an American Academy and Institute of Arts and Letters Award, as well as an appointment by President Carter to the National Council on the Arts. Morrison appeared on the cover of *Newsweek* at the publication of her fourth novel, *Tar Baby,* in 1981. She has received the most praise for her fifth novel, *Beloved,* which earned her a Pulitzer Prize for fiction in 1988. Morrison's next novel, *Jazz,* was published in 1992. She has also written one play entitled *Dreaming Emmett,* which was performed in 1986; edited two books, *The Black Book* in 1974 and *Race-ing Justice, En-Gendering Power: Essays on Anita Hill, Clarence Thomas, and the Construction of Social Reality* in 1992; published a book of literary criticism entitled *Playing in the Dark: Whiteness and the Literary Imagination* in 1992; and published one short story, "Recitatif," in *Confirmation: An Anthology of African American Women.*

While continuing to write, Morrison has taught at such universities as State University of New York at Albany, Princeton, and Yale. Most notable of the awards she continues to garner is the Nobel Prize for Literature, which she won in 1993, making her the first African American to receive this honor.

Plot Summary

Part I

The Bluest Eye opens with a short Dick and Jane primary reader story that is repeated three times. The first time the story is written clearly. In the second telling, however, the text loses its capitalization and punctuation. By the third time through, the story has also lost its spacing. The novel then shifts to a short, italicized preface in the voice of Claudia MacTeer as an adult. She looks back on the fall of 1941. We find that this book will be the story of Claudia, her sister Frieda, and their involvement with a young black girl named Pecola, pregnant with her father's child.

Part II: Autumn

In this section, the tense shifts from present to past, indicating shifts between the nine-year-old Claudia and the adult Claudia acting as narrators. The story begins with the arrival of Mr. Henry Washington, a boarder who will live with the MacTeers. At the same time, Pecola Breedlove comes to live with the MacTeers. She has been "put outdoors" by her father, who has gone to jail and not paid the rent on their apartment. Frieda and Pecola talk about how much they each love Shirley Temple. Claudia rebels. She does not like Shirley Temple nor the white dolls she receives each Christmas with the big blue eyes. To the dismay of the adults, she dismembers these dolls, trying "to see what it was that all the world said was lovable."

The text shifts to the third person ("he"/"she") omniscient point of view and gives the reader a brief of the inside of the Breedloves' two room apartment. The whole family shares one bedroom and there is no bath, only a toilet. At the same time, the Breedlove family is introduced. The family is described as ugly: "No one could have convinced them that they were not relentlessly and aggressively ugly. Except for the father, Cholly, whose ugliness (the result of despair dissipation, and violence directed toward petty things and weak people) was behavior, the rest of the family ... wore their ugliness, put it on, so to speak although it did not belong to them."

Pecola's parents both fight and make love in front of their two children. In the midst of the turmoil, Pecola comes to believe that if she had blue eyes, she would only see the things she wanted to see. Pecola's only refuge from her life is with the three prostitutes who live upstairs and who treat her with affection, the only people who do so.

Part III: Winter

Claudia and Frieda endure the gray Ohio winter until a "disrupter of seasons," a new girl named Maureen Peale, comes to school. She is lighter skinned than either Claudia, Frieda, or Pecola, and her family is wealthy. Claudia and Frieda both hate her and love her. One day on the way home from school, the three girls encounter Pecola, who is being teased by a group of boys. Frieda rescues her, and Maureen appears to befriend her. However, Maureen soon turns on Pecola, taunting her with her blackness and her ugliness.

The focus of the book shifts to a description of the "Mobile girls," women who attempt to control and modify their blackness. In imitation of the dominant culture, they straighten their hair, control their body odors, and learn to behave in order to "do the white man's work with refinement...." Geraldine is one such woman who has moved to Lorain with her husband and son, for whom she cares, but never nurtures. Her love is spent on a cat. One day, her son Junior lures Pecola into the house and then throws the cat at her. He finally kills the cat and blames Pecola as Geraldine walks into the house. Geraldine berates Pecola: "'Get out,' she said, her voice quiet. 'You nasty little black bitch.'"

Part III: Spring

In the spring, Mr. Washington, the boarder, fondles Frieda's breasts, and Mr. MacTeer beats him up and throws him out of the house. Later, Frieda and Claudia go to visit Pecola who is at the Fishers', where Mrs. Breedlove works as a housekeeper. While the children are there, Pecola spills a pan of hot blueberry cobbler all over herself, the dress of the little Fisher girl, and the clean white floor. Mrs. Breedlove viciously abuses Pecola for the mess and comforts the little white girl.

In the next section, a third person omniscient narrator flashes back to Pauline's young adulthood and subsequent marriage. This narration also details how Pauline came to work as a servant for a white, rich family. Pauline loves the order, the plenty, and the cleanliness of the house. Interspersed in the third person narration are sections of Pauline's voice in first person. She talks of her life with Cholly and why she stays with him in spite of his drunkenness and abuse.

The narration shifts again, this time to Cholly's story. We read how he was abandoned by his mentally ill mother when he was four days old. His Aunt Jimmy raised him until she died when Cholly was a young teen. After the funeral, he took a young girl into the woods and had his first sexual experience. He and the girl are discovered by a group of white men who force him to repeat the act for their entertainment. Cholly never forgets nor forgives this humiliation. At the end of this chapter, Cholly returns to his home in Lorain, drunk, and finds Pecola washing dishes. He is overcome with both love and hatred for her; his response is to rape her. He leaves her passed out on the floor, under a quilt. Pecola awakens to her mother's angry eyes.

Again, the scene shifts, this time to the room of Soaphead Church, an educated West Indian man living in Lorain. Pecola, now pregnant with her father's child, visits Church, a "reader, advisor, and interpreter of dreams" in order to request blue eyes. He tricks her into feeding poisoned meat to his landlady's dog; Pecola reads the dog's death throes as a sign from God that her wish has been granted.

Part IV: Summer

It is summer when Claudia and Frieda hear that Pecola is pregnant with her father's child. They overhear adults talking about the child and how it will probably not survive. Claudia and Frieda seem to be the only ones who want the baby to live. They make a promise to God to be good for a whole month and plant marigold seeds that will serve as a sign for them: when the seeds sprout, they will know that everything will be all right. However, as readers we already know that "there were no marigolds in the fall of 1941" and nothing turns out right for Pecola. The next chapter is a deranged dialogue carried out between Pecola and herself in which she discusses her new blue eyes, questioning if they are the "bluest eyes" in the world. We also discover that Cholly has raped his daughter more than once. Her madness, then, appears to be a defense against the pain of living her life.

The last voice in the novel is Claudia's, now an adult looking back, trying to assign blame for the tragedy of Pecola. She tells us that Pecola's baby died soon after birth; Cholly is dead as well; that Mrs. Breedlove still works for white folks; and that Pecola spends her days talking to herself and picking at the garbage in a dump. The novel closes with an indictment of the community and the culture:

> And now when I see her searching the garbage—for what? The thing we assassinated? I talk about how I did *not* plant the seeds too deeply, how it was the fault of the earth, the land, of our town. I even think now that the land of the entire country was hostile to marigolds that year. This soil is bad for certain kinds of flowers. Certain seeds it will not nurture, certain fruits it will not bear, and when the land kills of its own volition, we acquiesce and say the victim had no right to live. We are wrong, of course, but it doesn't matter. It's too late. At least on the edge of my town, among the garbage and the sunflowers of my town, it's much, much, much too late.

Characters

Aunt Jimmy

Aunt Jimmy becomes Cholly Breedlove's guardian after rescuing the four-day-old child from the trash heap where his mother, her niece, had abandoned him. When she is ill, Aunt Jimmy is instructed to drink only "pot liquor"; however, she "[dies] of peach cobbler" after eating a piece of pie.

Cholly Breedlove

Cholly Breedlove begins his life abandoned by his mother when he is only four days old. He spends most of his life in a state of abandonment, disconnected from those around him and, as the novel describes him, "dangerously free" because of his isolation. When his guardian, Aunt Jimmy, dies, he is initiated into the world of racism as two hunters interrupt him having sex with a young black girl named Darlene and refuse to let the couple stop. He is unable to continue having sex and directs his hatred toward Darlene instead of toward the white men because, as the novel states, hatred for whites who are in a position of power would have consumed him totally and immediately. However, the hatred he directs toward Darlene gnaws at him his entire life. The day before he is to leave with the uncle appointed to be his guardian, Cholly leaves for Macon in search of his father who, when Cholly finds him, spurns him in favor of a game of craps. Cholly turns to alcohol, and although his early married life with Pauline contains some hopeful moments, for the most part, his existence is dismal. In a scene portraying a drunken Cholly's ultimate frustration at being unable to offer his children a better life than his, he rapes Pecola while visualizing her as the young Pauline. In the novel's last pages, the narrator reveals that Cholly finally dies in the workhouse.

Pauline Breedlove

Pauline Breedlove, mother of Pecola, is trapped by the same destructive force as her daugh-

Media Adaptations

- An abridged version of *The Bluest Eye* was recorded on two audio cassettes in 1994 by Morrison and actress Ruby Dee. Available from Random House Audiobooks, the cassette is three hours long.

- The unabridged text of *The Bluest Eye* was recorded in 1981 by Michelle Shay. Available from Holt, Rinehart, and Winston, the recording is distributed by National Library Service and lasts 704 minutes.

ter: the unachievable desire for beauty. After stepping on a nail as an infant, Pauline is left with a deformed foot, an event that causes her to see her entire self as deformed in some way. As an adolescent, she buys into the myth of a "prince charming" who will sweep her off her feet, and she seems to find such a man in Cholly. Although their life together begins well, it quickly declines. Pauline struggles with loneliness and a loss of self-esteem after she loses a front tooth. She turns to Cholly for consolation, but he turns to alcohol instead of to her. She begins to take solace in going to movies and imagining herself as beautiful film star Jean Harlow. After Pauline loses another tooth while eating candy at a movie, she no longer cares about her physical appearance, and her relationship with Cholly, Pecola, and Sammy becomes the way we find it at the book's beginning: abusive and full of hatred. Pauline only finds satisfaction in working for the Fishers, a white family that lives in a clean, affluent world, a world in total contrast to the one in which Pauline exists.

Pecola Breedlove

Pecola Breedlove, the protagonist of Morrison's novel, is the truest of all victims, for she is an innocent little girl born into a family that does not provide her with any support to endure society's racial prejudices. When Pecola lives temporarily with the MacTeers after her family is evicted from their apartment, we learn of her ob-

session with white female beauty when she sits at the table with Claudia and Frieda to snack on milk and graham crackers. She continues to drink quart after quart of milk just to be able to use the cup with Shirley Temple's picture on it, almost as if she was trying to drink Shirley Temple's beauty. Much like her mother, Pecola longs to be beautiful, to have blue eyes specifically, because she thinks that fulfilling white society's idea of beauty will bring her the love she has never received. Pecola's life is consumed by this desire, and after she is raped by her father, she is so desperate that she goes to the town's pedophilic fortune teller, Soaphead Church, for help in obtaining blue eyes. Even the fraudulent Soaphead pities her and writes in a letter to God that he may not have been able to give Pecola blue eyes, but she thinks she has them and will, therefore, live "happily ever after." Soaphead is, of course, horribly mistaken, and Pecola descends into madness. She continues believing that her eyes are bluer than any others, illustrating the danger for an unloved black girl who accepts white society's definition of beauty.

Sammy Breedlove

Brother of Pecola, Sammy Breedlove is a victim of his parents failed marriage and deals with their arguments by running away from home. The novel reveals that at fourteen Sammy has run away from home at least twenty-seven times, and the last mention of him in the novel states that he runs away for good some time before Pecola's descent into madness.

China

China is one of three prostitutes who lives in an apartment above the storefront where the Breedloves also live. The only trait that distinguishes China from the other two prostitutes is that she is constantly curling her hair. All three are characterized as cruel haters of men and disrespectful of women, yet these three prostitutes are among the very few characters in *The Bluest Eye* who are kind to Pecola.

Darlene

The young women with whom Cholly Breedlove has his first sexual experience on the day of his Aunt Jimmy's funeral.

Samson Fuller

Samson Fuller is Cholly Breedlove's father, who left town for Macon before Cholly was born.

When Cholly locates his father after Aunt Jimmy's death, his father rejects him, his attention totally focused on a game of craps, leaving Cholly emotionally scarred.

Geraldine

Geraldine fits the type of middle-class black woman that Morrison describes in detail just before Geraldine appears in *The Bluest Eye*. This kind of woman rejects what she views is "black" by distancing herself from the "funkiness" of life, the dirt of poverty, and ignorance. Geraldine has only a perfunctory relationship with her family and is closest to her cat, whom her son Junior throws against a wall after Pecola shows it affection. In Geraldine's eyes, Pecola represents the black lifestyle she rejects; therefore, when Geraldine discovers Pecola in her house, she throws Pecola out with the words, "You nasty little black bitch. Get out of my house."

Mr. Henry

Mr. Henry boards with the MacTeer family and endears himself to Frieda and Claudia by calling them Greta Garbo and Ginger Rogers, popular film stars of the 1940s. Mr. Henry is involved in two important scenes in the book. The first occurs when Claudia and Frieda return home from school and he gives them money for ice cream. They return before he expects them to, and they find him with China and Maginot Line, two of the town's prostitutes. When the women leave, Mr. Henry explains to the girls that these women were part of his Bible study group but that the girls should not tell their mother that the women were there. After this episode opens Mr. Henry's morality up to question, his depravity is confirmed when he is thrown out of the house for molesting Frieda.

Junior

Junior is the only son of Geraldine, an arrogant black woman who despises most other black families and, as a result, prevents Junior from playing with other black boys. Because he lives near the school, Junior claims the playground as his turf, and when he sees Pecola walking there, he invites her into his house and terrorizes her with his mother's cat.

Maginot Line

See Miss Marie

Claudia MacTeer

A nine-year-old black girl, Claudia narrates the majority of the novel. Because she and Pecola share many of the same experiences, Claudia also acts as a foil, or contrast, to Pecola. For example, Claudia hates Shirley Temple, unlike Pecola who idolizes her, and does not understand the fascination black adults have with little white girls. Claudia is also a representative of society as a whole in her attitude toward Pecola. Although she and Frieda befriend Pecola after she lives with them temporarily, they have no contact with her after her father rapes and impregnates her. Claudia hopes that her baby will live simply to "counteract the universal love of white baby dolls"; however, the baby dies, and Claudia and Frieda avoid Pecola from then on. As an adult, Claudia realizes that she, like those around her, made Pecola into a scapegoat, hating Pecola in order to make her life appear much better in comparison.

Frieda MacTeer

Frieda is the sister of Claudia, the narrator of the novel. She is a minor character, largely in the shadow of Claudia, but shares in most of her experiences and is, therefore, also part of the coming of age motif in the novel. However, she is distinguished from Claudia a few places in the novel, such as when she knows that Pecola has begun menstruating when Pecola and Claudia have no idea why Pecola is bleeding, and also she appears apart from Claudia when she is molested by the MacTeer's boarder, Mr. Henry.

Miss Marie

The prostitute called Miss Marie by Pecola and Maginot Line by Claudia and Frieda is overweight and obsessed with food, a quality revealed in her passion at describing a meal eaten in the distant past and her habit of using food related nicknames for Pecola. She also has a knack for storytelling and amuses Pecola with stories of her former "boyfriends."

M'Dear

M'Dear, a midwife and practitioner of folk medicine, instructs Cholly's Aunt Jimmy to drink only "pot liquor" during an illness. People in the community believe M'Dear possesses supernatural abilities and summon her when all other remedies are ineffective.

Maureen Peal

Maureen is a light-skinned, wealthy, African American girl who attends the same school as

Pecola, Claudia, and Frieda. The girls resent her because she is adored by teachers and students, both black and white alike. Claudia and Frieda make up names for her, such as "Six-finger-dog-tooth-meringue-pie," to express their resentment, but they are alone in their ridicule. Maureen does try to befriend Pecola, but she later turns against Pecola, calling her ugly and taunting her with accusations that she has seen her father naked.

Poland

Another of the prostitutes living above the Breedloves, Poland is characterized by her singing and her soundless laugh.

Polly

See Pauline Breedlove

Soaphead Church

A pedophile and misanthrope, Soaphead Church bills himself as a spiritualist, an interpreter of dreams, and a miracle worker, while in reality he is a fraud. The book details his sexual preferences for young girls as well as his family background, former professions, and failed marriage. He despises his landlady's mangy dog Bob, and when Pecola comes to him asking for blue eyes, he sees the perfect opportunity to rid himself of Bob. He gives Pecola poisoned meat to give to Bob, telling her that if the dog reacts to the meat, her eyes have become blue. Of course, the dog dies, leaving Pecola to believe that she truly does have blue eyes. In a letter to God, Soaphead admits that he did not attempt to molest Pecola because he truly pities her and actually wishes he could perform miracles.

Rosemary Villanucci

Rosemary Villanucci is a young white girl who lives next door to the MacTeers and always tattles on Claudia and Frieda.

Elihue Micah Whitcomb

See Soaphead Church

Pauline Williams

See Pauline Breedlove

Themes

Beauty

Morrison has been an open critic of several aspects of the Civil Rights Movement of the 1960s,

and she has stated in numerous interviews that a primary impetus for *The Bluest Eye* was the "Black is Beautiful" slogan of the movement, which was at its peak while Morrison wrote her first novel. Even though *The Bluest Eye* is set in the 1940s, Morrison integrates this pressure that blacks feel to live up to white society's standards of beauty with racism in general, and the reader sees quickly that several characters are indeed "in trouble" as a result of their obsession with beauty, especially Pecola and Pauline.

Of course, as the title indicates, Pecola's one desire is to have blue eyes, which to her are central to being beautiful and would enable her to transcend the ugliness of her life and perhaps change the behavior of her parents. Pecola worships the beautiful, white icons of the 1940s: she drinks three quarts of milk at the MacTeer's house so that she can use the cup with Shirley Temple's picture on it, buys Mary Janes at the candy store so that she can admire the picture of the blond haired, blue eyed girl on the wrapper, and even resorts to contacting Soaphead Church, thinking that perhaps he can make her eyes blue. By the novel's end, Pecola truly believes she has blue eyes, and her delusion is a tragic picture of the damage the ideals of white society can have on a young black girl who, seeing no other options, embraces them.

The situation of Pecola's mother is little better. Pauline's life is already marred in her eyes when as a child she steps on a nail and her foot is left deformed. After she marries Cholly, their life in Lorain, Ohio, does not turn out to be the fairy tale she expected, so she alleviates her loneliness by going to the movies. There, she is introduced, as the novel states, to the ideas of physical beauty and romantic love, "probably the most destructive ideas in the history of human thought. Both originated in envy, thrived in insecurity, and ended in disillusion." Pauline buys into the fantasy world she views in the theaters, even going so far as to wear her hair like the popular white actress Jean Harlow. Pauline's illusion is broken when she loses a tooth while eating candy at a movie. From then on, she "settled down to just being ugly" but finally finds a job working for a white family so that she can have the "beauty, order, cleanliness, and praise" absent from her own family. For example, when Pecola knocks a hot pie off the counter at the Fisher home, Pauline slaps and verbally abuses her because she disrupts her clean, white world; on the other hand, she comforts the weeping Fisher girl who is startled by the incident. Although Pauline does not become insane like Pecola does, her decline is still obvious, for she is unable to see beauty in herself or her family but only in the surrogate family which makes her feel "white."

Unlike Pecola and Pauline, Claudia MacTeer, the novel's main narrator, is able to overcome the standards for beauty society pushes upon her. Claudia hates Shirley Temple and cannot understand the fascination blacks have for little white girls. Much to the dismay of her family members who see her actions as ungrateful, Claudia dismembers a white doll she receives for Christmas "to see of what it was made, to discover the dearness, to find the beauty, the desirability that had escaped me, but apparently only me." Claudia does struggle with self-image, as all in her community do, and she comments that they all made Pecola into a scapegoat because "we were so beautiful when we stood astride her ugliness." However, as she relates Pecola's story to the reader, she regrets their treatment of Pecola and realizes that even though she herself later learned to "worship" Shirley Temple, the change was "adjustment without improvement."

Coming of Age

The Bluest Eye has often been labeled by critics as a *bildungsroman,* or a novel that chronicles the process by which characters enter the adult world. As critic Susan Blake has stated, the novel is "a microscopic examination of that point where sexual experience, racial experience, and self-image intersect." For Pecola, this experience is not a pleasant one. Physically, when she begins to menstruate in the novel, Morrison uses this pivotal event in the life of any young girl to reveal the absence of love in Pecola's life. When Frieda confirms Pecola's suspicion that she can now conceive, Frieda tells her that someone has to love her for that event to occur. In one of the most poignant scenes of the novel, she asks Frieda, "How do you do that? I mean, how do you get somebody to love you?" Foreshadowing Pecola's future, Frieda falls asleep without answering Pecola's question, leaving the reader to conclude that Pecola will never find love. Indeed, her mother rejects her and her father rapes her, leaving her to conceive a child who dies at birth. Of course, Pecola's realization that society defines ideal beauty in a figure completely opposite from the one she sees in the mirror every day also contributes to her initiation into adulthood. Again, she meets only destruction as she descends into insanity after the death of her child, finding emotional nourishment in her belief that she not only has blue eyes but has the bluest of them all.

Topics for Further Study

- Research the life and career of Shirley Temple, the child star whom Pecola sees as the epitome of female beauty. What about Shirley Temple made her idolized by white society? Then, examine Pecola's admiration of Shirley Temple. How does Pecola's admiration of Shirley Temple affect her throughout the novel?

- Many critics consider *The Bluest Eye* to be a *bildungsroman,* a story outlining the maturing process of a character. Analyze the ways in which Claudia and Pecola both mature. Why do they mature into very different people even though they share many of the same experiences?

- Although *The Bluest Eye* does not take place in the South, many characters in the novel are victims of racism. Investigate life for African Americans, in both the North and South, during the 1940s, and compare your findings to the treatment of characters in the book.

Fortunately, the process of growing up is much more productive for Claudia and Frieda MacTeer. They share numerous experiences with Pecola, but the way in which their family copes with certain situations reveals that they will not be eternally traumatized by the hardships of growing up but will become solid adults because of the love and stability of their family. For example, when Mr. Henry, the family's boarder, fondles Frieda, Mr. MacTeer kicks him out of the house, throwing a tricycle at him, and even shoots at him. On the other hand, not only does Cholly Breedlove not protect Pecola, but he is the very one who violates her, seeing in her the Pauline he once loved and transferring his self-hatred and lack of ability to provide a better life for his children into sexual aggression. Fortunately for Frieda and Claudia, their family is not crippled by negative emotions but able to cope with love.

Toni Morrison accepting the Nobel Prize, 1993.

Race and Racism

The fact that Pecola, Pauline, and Claudia must struggle with the fact that they do not fit white society's idea of beauty is part of the racism toward blacks that has existed ever since they were brought to the United States as slaves. As much as Morrison concentrates on this aspect of white racism, she includes other aspects of racism that involve black attitudes toward each other as well as white attitudes toward blacks.

First, Morrison presents white characters who treat black characters in a racist fashion. For example, when Pecola goes to the candy to store to buy Mary Janes, Mr. Yacobowski immediately expresses disgust at her presence. The narrator makes some allowances for his actions by emphasizing that he is simply different than Pecola, "a fifty-two-year-old white immigrant storekeeper with the taste of potatoes and beer in his mouth." However, he is also presented as a representative of all whites, as Pecola thinks to herself that she has seen this same disgust and "glazed separateness ... lurking in the eyes of all white people."

Another example of racism by whites against blacks is a pivotal moment in the coming of age process for Cholly Breedlove. On the day of his Aunt Jimmy's funeral, Cholly goes with a neighborhood girl, Darlene, into the woods, and they

have sex. This is Cholly's first sexual experience, and it becomes a defining moment in his life when two white hunters find him and Darlene together. The hunters force Cholly to continue having sex with Darlene as they observe and laugh. Cholly's humiliation makes him impotent, but he does not turn his hatred toward the white men because he knows that "hating them would have consumed him, burned him up like a piece of soft coal, leaving only flakes of ash and a question mark of smoke." Instead, he turns his hatred toward Darlene, one of his own kind, over whom he can feel power. This experience leads Cholly to search for his father, and when his father rejects him, he becomes "dangerously free" because he has nothing more to lose since he has lost his family and his dignity. This "freedom" Cholly finds is important later in the book, for while she reflects on Cholly's "love" for Pecola, Claudia states that "Love is never any better than the lover. Wicked people love wickedly, violent people love violently, weak people love weakly, stupid people love stupidly, but the love of a free man [Cholly] is never safe."

Not all of the racist acts and attitudes in the novel are between whites and blacks, however. Several important instances involve racism among black characters. First, Morrison presents the character Maureen Peal, a "high-yellow dream child with long brown hair braided into two lynch ropes that hung down her back." Maureen has everything that Pecola, Claudia, and Frieda lack: wealth, nice clothes, and beauty which brings her the admiration of whites and blacks alike. Claudia remarks that she and Frieda were fascinated but irritated by Maureen, and they do anything they can to make her ugly in their minds—call her names and make fun of her few physical flaws. At one point, Maureen comes to the defense of Pecola, who is being harassed by a group of black boys because of her own blackness and the rumor that her father sleeps naked. Maureen seems genuine in her attempts to befriend Pecola, but when the paranoid Pecola mentions her father when Maureen asks her if she has ever seen a naked man, Maureen begins to make fun of Pecola as well. Claudia tries to beat up Maureen, mistakenly hitting Pecola instead, and leaving Maureen to shout at them, "I *am* cute! And you ugly! Black and ugly e mos. I *am* cute." Not only are Claudia, Frieda, and Pecola victimized by their peers who degrade them in favor of Maureen, but even Maureen uses her beauty against them because they refuse to bow to her. However, in an interview with author Gloria Naylor entitled, "A Conversation: Gloria Naylor and Toni Morrison," Morrison states that Maureen suffers as much as Pecola does because she receives her self-esteem from society's approval of her beauty, not because she is confident and secure in who she is.

Finally, Morrison presents the character Geraldine, a representative of blacks who wish to "move up" in the world and assimilate into white culture and scorn anything or anyone that reminds them they are black, an issue she also addresses in her novels *Song of Solomon* and *Tar Baby*. Morrison saw this kind of person as a problem in the wake of the Civil Rights Movement, the time during which she wrote *The Bluest Eye,* as she explains in her essay "Rediscovering Black History": "In the push toward middle-class respectability, we wanted tongue depressors sticking from every black man's coat pocket and briefcases swinging from every black hand. In the legitimate and necessary drive for better jobs and housing, we abandoned the past and a lot of the truth and sustenance that went with it." Geraldine is exactly this kind of woman, which Morrison describes in *The Bluest Eye* as "brown girls" who go to any length to eliminate the "funkiness" in their lives, anything that reminds them of the dirt, poverty, and ignorance that they associate with being black. Specifically, Geraldine keeps her son Junior from playing with "niggers" and even makes a distinction between "niggers" and "colored people": "They were easily identifiable. Colored people were neat and quiet; niggers were dirty and loud." When Junior invites Pecola into his house and torments her with his mother's cat, Geraldine immediately hates her, seeing her as one of the little black girls she had seen "all her life. Hanging out of windows over saloons in Mobile, crawling over the porches of shotgun houses on the edge of town.... Hair uncombed, dresses falling apart, shoes untied and caked with dirt." In her mind, Pecola is like a fly who has settled in her house and expels her with the words, "Get out.... You nasty little black bitch. Get out of my house," leaving Pecola rejected again because of what others perceive as ugliness.

Style

Point of View and Structure

The point of view in *The Bluest Eye* is dominated by first person ("I") through the mind of Claudia MacTeer, sometimes narrating as a nine-year-old child and sometimes as an adult. The instances in which Morrison uses the adult Claudia as narrator serve as points of reflection for Claudia. For example, because Claudia is the same age as Pecola, she should be able to empathize with her; however, as an adult, she looks back at the manner in which she and her community cast Pecola as a scapegoat and is able to see that they did not love her as they should have. A third person, omniscient, anonymous narrator also exists in the novel. For example, this narrator presents to us the childhoods and early adulthoods of Cholly and Pauline, providing a means for the reader to understand the path which has taken Cholly and Pauline to such depths of self-loathing. The narrative as a whole is the adult Claudia's flashback, framed by her adult musings and interspersed with scenes presented by the third person narrator. The novel is divided into four parts to correspond with the four seasons, an appropriate structure since the main characters, nine-year-old girls, would measure time by passage of the seasons.

Setting

The setting of *The Bluest Eye* is a fictionalized Lorain, Ohio, in the 1940s. Morrison grew up in Lorain, the daughter of Southerners who had moved North to find employment, much as the Breedloves and MacTeers have done in the novel. Of course, schools are still segregated, and everyone is trying to recover from the Depression. Little is mentioned of the white neighborhoods in Lorain, although the book is scattered with white characters like Rosemary Villanucci and Mr. Yacobowski, who appear as reminders that this world does exist. Instead, Morrison focuses on the world in which the MacTeers and Breedloves live. Although both families are poor, the MacTeers are much better off, for the family is loving and stable. For example, early in the book, Claudia describes their home as "old, cold, and green … peopled by roaches and mice." However, whatever the home might lack materially is made up for by the love that exists in the family. For example, although Mrs. MacTeer complains when an ill Claudia vomits on her bed, her love for her daughter is clear as during the night, "feet padded into the room, hands repinned the flannel, readjusted the quilt, and rested a moment on [Claudia's] forehead." The Breedloves are equally as poor, but their family is characterized by violent physical battles between an angry Pauline and a drunken Cholly, not a love for their children and or one another.

Symbolism

The most obvious symbols found in *The Bluest Eye* are the popular female film stars of the 1940s who are mentioned throughout the novel: Jean Harlow, Greta Garbo, Ginger Rogers, and especially Shirley Temple. These women, of course, represent the standard of ideal beauty held up by white society, a standard that ultimately destroys Pecola.

Aside from these, three other important symbols operate in the novel: marigolds, the seasons, and the "Dick and Jane" reader. Marigolds are mentioned twice in the novel, at its beginning and at its end. In Frieda and Claudia's minds, the fact that the marigolds they plant do not grow results from the fact that Pecola is pregnant with Cholly's child. Although this take on the failure of the marigolds is an insightful one, Claudia herself makes a statement that leads the reader to a wider perception of the marigolds. After blaming herself and Frieda for the marigolds' failure, Claudia says, "It never occurred to either of us that the earth itself might have been unyielding." The unyielding earth is an appropriate parallel for the world in which Pecola, Claudia, and Frieda live, a world that scorns blackness and worships white beauty. Claudia and Frieda manage, through the love of their family, to survive, but Pecola is devastated and cannot thrive in such a world, just as the marigold seeds cannot survive in this particular soil. In the last paragraph of

the novel, Claudia says of the earth, "Certain seeds it will not nurture, certain fruit it will not bear, and when the land kills of its own volition, we acquiesce and say the victim had no right to live." Although she is describing the earth, her words are an apt description of Pecola's situation. She is killed emotionally and mentally by her own father, by a white world, and in the end, the members of the community do not turn their scorn toward Cholly or toward white standards but toward Pecola, the ultimate victim.

Another aspect of nature, the seasons of the year, also operate symbolically in the novel. Morrison divides the novel into four sections, each corresponding to a season of the year. Appropriately, the novel begins with autumn: for children like Claudia, Pecola, and Frieda, autumn is a time of "beginnings," especially marked by the beginning of the school year. Indeed, this section does contain many "beginnings," for in this section, Claudia and Frieda first meet Pecola. Winter, of course, is traditionally a time of barrenness, and it is in winter that the girls become acquainted with Maureen Peal, a reminder to them that life is barren without beauty that brings admiration. This is also the section in the book in which Pecola is terrorized by Geraldine and her son Junior. One would hope for rebirth in the section entitled Spring. However, this title works ironically, for here, degradation occurs as Frieda is fondled by Mr. Henry and Pecola is abused by her mother for spilling the cobbler at the Fisher home and raped by her father. This is also the section in which the reader learns of the steady decline that has occurred in the lives of Pauline and Cholly Breedlove since their childhoods. The section entitled Summer is the shortest section of the book and does not present gleeful children reveling in the pleasures of summer but an isolated, insane Pecola.

Finally, Morrison uses clips from the Dick and Jane reader symbolically. The book opens with three excerpts from the Dick and Jane reader, which was the textbook used to teach every child to read from the 1940s through the 1960s. According to critic Phyllis R. Klotman, the three versions of the reader presented on the first page of *The Bluest Eye* represent the three lifestyles presented in the novel. The text of the first version is the standard text, with correct capitalization and punctuation, and represents the ideal white family represented in the novel by the Fishers. The second version contains the same words as the first but contains no punctuation or capitalization; this version symbolizes the MacTeer family, which is stable and loving but economically below a family like the Fishers. The final version, however, is completely disjointed, containing no punctuation or capitalization, not even spaces between words. This version, of course, represents the dysfunctional Breedlove family. A newspaper article commemorating the seventieth birthday of the "Dick and Jane" series says that the authors realize that the life presented in the series was very different from the life many children lived in the 1940. However, they believe, "When such deprived children lose themselves in stories about Dick, Jane, and Sally, and live for a time with these happy storybook characters, they experience the same release from their problems that the adult does when he loses himself in a good book or movie." Morrison, on the other hand, has recognized what these authors have not: that being inundated with a fantasy world that your family can never achieve does not provide release but leads to self-hatred, misanthropy, and insanity. As critic Susan Blake has written, "Pecola's story is a parody of the general fairy tale that she and her mother believe in," a fairy tale much like the lives of Dick and Jane.

Shirley Temple, the movie icon of childhood from the 1930s and 1940s, curtseys.

Historical Context

Civil Rights and Race Relations

Although Toni Morrison set her novel *The Bluest Eye* in the 1940s in the North, the thoughts that gave rise to the novel are centered in the Civil Rights Movement, which was waning in the late 1960s when she was writing *The Bluest Eye*. Many historians mark the peak year of the Civil Rights Movement at 1963 because of the pivotal events which took place during this year: the assassination of NAACP (National Association for the Advancement of Colored People) leader Medgar Evers, mass demonstrations led by Dr. Martin Luther King, Jr., in Birmingham, Alabama, the attempt by Alabama Governor George Wallace to stop integration of Alabama's schools, and the March on Washington marked by Dr. King's "I Have a Dream" speech. When Morrison published *The Bluest Eye* in 1970, the Civil Rights Movement was far from over; however, following its peak in 1963, white backlash increased. In addition, national attention turned to other events, such as the continuing Paris peace talks to end the Vietnam War, war protests by college students at Kent State University and other colleges, and the exposure of the massacre of unarmed civilians in My Lai, South Vietnam, by American troops. With such events

taking place, the March on Washington must have seemed like decades ago to black activists who found it increasingly difficult for their voices to be heard. Progress seemed to halt as Congress approved bills designed to stop bussing of students to create racial balance in integrated schools and Governor Wallace encouraged governors across the South to ignore integration orders from Washington. As historian Harvard Sitkoff explains in his book *The Struggle for Black Equality: 1954-1992,* "The movement had secured basic civil rights for African-Americans, yet much remained to be done."

One of the most important slogans of the Civil Rights Movement was "Black is Beautiful," an attempt to raise the self-esteem of blacks who felt inferior to white standards of beauty. Morrison, however, found fault with this slogan, as she explains in her 1974 essay, "Rediscovering Black History": "The slogan provided a psychic crutch for the needy and a second (or first) glance from whites. Regardless of those questionable comforts, the phrase was nevertheless a full confession that white definitions were important to us (having to counteract them meant they were significant) and that the quest for physical beauty was both a good and worthwhile pursuit. When the strength of a people

Compare
&
Contrast

- **1940s:** The United States became involved in World War II in 1941 after the bombing of Pearl Harbor. The war ended the Great Depression as well as American isolationism. The United States government's fear of the Soviet Union as a major communist force marked the beginning of the Cold War.

   1960s: The United States became involved in several international conflicts, including the 1961 Bay of Pigs invasion in Cuba, the Cuban Missile Crisis in 1962, and the Vietnam War beginning in 1965. Low public opinion of American involvement in Vietnam was marked by protests across the country, especially on college campuses. In 1968, United States involvement hit its peak with approximately 500,000 troops in Vietnam. Approximately 58,000 United States troops were killed in the war.

   Today: Foreign relations in the 1990s have been marked by the fall of communism in Russia and eastern Europe, heralding the end of the Cold War. The only major military conflict in which the United States had been involved extensively was the Persian Gulf War in 1991.

- **1940s:** Most households listened to the radio an average of 4.5 hours per day during World War II, with 30 percent of air time devoted to war coverage. However, serials starring heroes like Dick Tracy and Superman also aired. Movies also continued to be popular, with around 100 million people attending each week.

   1960s: Television took the place of radio and provided footage of the Vietnam War, the Civil Rights Movement, and American politics. By 1970, 95 percent of American homes owned a television, a higher percentage than owned a refrigerator or an indoor toilet. Popular television shows were family-oriented sitcoms like "Leave It to Beaver" and police dramas such as "The Untouchables."

   Today: Televisions continues to be an integral part of life, bringing news events into our homes as they happen. According to Nielsen Media Re-

search, Americans in 1995 watched over eighteen hours of television per week. Also, the advent of video cassette recorders has made taping television programs or watching movies in one's own home popular. Computers have provided another form of entertainment, as Americans spend hundreds of hours playing computer games, sending or receiving electronic mail, or "surfing" the Internet.

- **1940s:** Unemployment plummeted from a high of 14.6 percent in 1940 to 1.9 percent in 1945 as the need for supplies and the absence of soldiers at war created jobs, especially for women and minorities.

   1960s: Unemployment held steady at around 5 percent, taking a slight drop in the late 1960s as a result of the Vietnam War.

   Today: Throughout the 1990s, the unemployment rate has remained steady at 5 percent to 7 percent, as American is centered in an economy reliant on global commerce.

- **1940s:** Public schools remained segregated. Segregation in the armed forces officially ended in 1948, and new laws aimed at stopping discrimination in hiring practices were put into place. In practice, however, segregation and discrimination continued.

   1960s: The 1960s were marked by the Civil Rights Movement, which included activities such as lunch counter sit-ins, integration of schools and colleges, and nonviolent protests led by Dr. Martin Luther King, Jr., all aimed at procuring equal rights for black Americans. The Civil Rights Act of 1964 officially outlawed discrimination in all public accommodations and in hiring practices.

   Today: Race relations remain tense. Public schools are integrated, but issues of achieving racial balance still plague school districts. Tensions often erupt into civil unrest, such as the riots in Los Angeles after an all white jury acquitted four police officers of all but one charge in the beating of black motorist Rodney King.

rests on its beauty, when the focus is on how one looks rather than what one is, we are in trouble." Morrison's hope at the time was that blacks would instead rely on the strength of their communities, instead of power, wealth, or beauty, an issue she explores further in her novel *Song of Solomon.* While the creators of the "Black is Beautiful" slogan were most assuredly well-intentioned, Morrison's point of view shows that the emphasis on physical beauty can be deadly for black children like Pecola Breedlove, whether in the 1970s or the 1940s or even the 1990s, who see all those around them bow to the Shirley Temples of the world and aspire to possess that kind of beauty in order to solve life's problems.

Critical Overview

The Bluest Eye received an appreciative nod from critics at its appearance in 1970. Although Morrison was virtually unknown at the time, she seems to have taken offense at what she perceived as neglect of the book, for she wrote in the afterword to a 1993 edition of the novel, "With very few exceptions, the initial publication of *The Bluest Eye* was like Pecola's life: dismissed, trivialized, misread." Clearly, however, as Morrison's reputation as an author has grown, *The Bluest Eye* has received increased recognition and respect as a poignant portrayal of a black girl trapped by white society's ideals.

One aspect of the book that caught critical attention at the book's publication and continues to be a focal point for critics of Morrison's work is her use of language, which is often referred to as "poetic prose." John Leonard of the *New York Times* described the novel as containing "a prose so precise, so faithful to speech and so charged with pain and wonder that the novel becomes poetry." However, others, such as *New York Times Book Review* contributor Haskel Frankel, described Morrison's prose not as poetic but as inexact, marred by "fuzziness born of flights of poetic imagery."

Like many readers, critics seemed disturbed by the book's content, not because it was irrelevant or trivial but because, as Liz Gant wrote in *Black World,* it is about "an aspect of the Black experience that many of us would rather forget, our hatred of ourselves." In *Freedomways,* African American actress Ruby Dee described the novel's events as "painfully accurate impressions" which cause the reader to "ache for remedy."

Morrison's reputation has grown as she has garnered numerous honors and awards, including the Pulitzer Prize in 1988 for her novel *Beloved* and the Nobel Prize for Literature in 1993; however, critics have not neglected *The Bluest Eye.* Contemporary assessments of the book tend to focus on the same matters of the early reviews: Morrison's writing style and the novel's portrayal of black victimization in America. For example, in her 1988 article in *The New Criterion,* Martha Bayles contends that "the book has flaws, but at its best it is an extraordinary fusion of poetic language and moral clarity" that is "even timelier today than it was eighteen years ago." Not all assessments are as favorable as Bayles', however. For example, in a 1987 article, Carol Iannone states that Morrison "crudely manipulates the assignment of judgment and blame in this book, refusing to transcend black and white as categories of good and evil.... Instead of exploring the universal theme which she herself has set into play—the fatal and terrifying lapses of love in the human heart—Miss Morrison sticks doggedly to her shallow dichotomies."

Not only has *The Bluest Eye* become a standard text in many colleges and universities in America, but it is often taught to high school students. As Ken Donelson reports in his article "'Filth' and 'Pure Filth' in Our Schools—Censorship of Classroom Books in the Last Ten Years," *The Bluest Eye* came under attack at least four times between 1986 and 1995, according to the American Library Association's *Newsletter on Intellectual Freedom.* Those who wish to ban the book from the classroom tend to focus on its explicit language and sexual content. One principal involved in a 1995 incident said, "It was a very controversial book, it contains lots of very graphic descriptions and lots of disturbing language." Despite such responses, the book continues to flourish and was reissued in 1994 with a new afterword by Morrison.

Criticism

Diane Henningfeld

Henningfeld is a professor of English at Adrian College. In the following essay, she examines the critical history of The Bluest Eye *and how various aspects such as characterization, plot, and structure contribute to its portrayal of racism and the search for identity.*

Toni Morrison's first novel, *The Bluest Eye* was published in 1970. Set in Morrison's home-

What Do I Read Next?

- Alice Walker's Pulitzer Prize-winning novel *The Color Purple,* printed in 1982, uses Celie's letters to God to chronicle her rise from a browbeaten woman, who is forced by her abusive father to marry an abusive husband and is separated from her sister and only friend, Nettie, to a self-confident business woman who learns to love others and herself, largely through her friendship with her husband's lover, Shug Avery.

- Maxine Hong Kingston's 1976 novel, *The Woman Warrior,* records the struggles of the narrator who must reconcile the values of her Chinese immigrant parents, especially her mother, and her own adopted American values.

- Published in 1977, Toni Morrison's novel *Song of Solomon* presents the geographical and psychological journey of Milkman Dead from a life of empty affluence to self-knowledge and reunion with community as he rediscovers his family's past.

- Leslie Marmon Silko's novel *Ceremony,* printed in 1977, illustrates cultural conflict faced by Tayo, a young man of Native American and white parentage. As a result, Tayo must become reconnected with his Native American roots. After returning from World War II, Tayo finds that he is no longer respected by whites as a soldier and former POW but is imprisoned by prejudice of the white community.

- Ralph Ellison's 1952 novel *Invisible Man* presents the struggle of a nameless narrator who, after experiencing various traumas because of his race, comes to the awareness that being black in a white society makes one invisible, or a nonentity.

- Published in 1969, *I Know Why the Caged Bird Sings* is the first of Maya Angelou's many autobiographies and chronicles her experiences living with her grandmother in rural Stamps, Arkansas, being shuffled between her parents, being raped by her mother's boyfriend, and eventually giving birth as a teenager to her own son.

town of Lorain, Ohio, the novel tells the story of Pecola Breedlove, a young black girl convinced of her own ugliness who desires nothing more than to have blue eyes. On the first page of the novel, Morrison tells the reader in advance everything that will happen in the pages to follow. Indeed, Morrison alludes to the central event of the book in the first two sentences: "Quiet as it's kept, there were no marigolds in the fall of 1941. We thought, at the time, that it was because Pecola was having her father's baby that the marigolds did not grow." Morrison places importance not so much on *what* happens as on *how* and *why* Pecola Breedlove descends into inevitable madness.

Early reviews of *The Bluest Eye* were favorable, if subdued. Morrison, in an afterword to the 1994 edition of the novel, expresses her dissatisfaction with the reception the novel initially received: "With very few exceptions, the initial publication of *The Bluest Eye* was like Pecola's life: dismissed, trivialized, misread." And it has taken twenty-five years for her to gain respect for this publication.

Critical attention to *The Bluest Eye* was also slow in coming. The subsequent publication of her novels *Sula* in 1973, *Song of Solomon* in 1977, and *Tar Baby* in 1981 increased dramatically the volume of studies on Morrison's work. Certainly, after Morrison's selection as a Pulitzer Prize winner following the publication of *Beloved* in 1987, critics turned their gazes back to her earlier novels, looking for the origin of themes and controlling images that found expression in Morrison's later work.

In an early critique of *The Bluest Eye,* Chikwenye Okonjo Ogunyemi concentrates on the structure of the novel, noting the "triadic patterns,"

patterns that appear in threes, present in the work. Further, this writer examines the scapegoating in the novel, ranging from Geraldine's cat, to Bob the dog, and finally to Pecola herself. More recently, Terry Otten, in his book *The Crime of Innocence in the Fiction of Tony Morrison,* published in 1989, argues that the theme of *The Bluest Eye* is "failed innocence." Further, he believes that Morrison "depicts how American Society has substituted beauty for virtue." Likewise, Denise Heinze in her 1993 *The Dilemma of "Double-Consciousness": Toni Morrison's Novels* examines the ideas of beauty and ugliness in *The Bluest Eye.* She argues that the African-American community in the novel has internalized "the insidious and lethal standard of westernized beauty" symbolized by blue eyes. Finally, in a long article appearing in the winter 1994 issue of *MELUS,* Patrice Cormier-Hamilton takes as her subject self-realization. She writes, "A universal characteristic of Morrison's published novels has been her depiction of male and female protagonists failing or succeeding on the difficult journey to freedom through self-awareness."

Toni Morrison herself offers readers insight to her book in the afterword included in the 1994 edition of *The Bluest Eye.* She recalls how at the time she started elementary school, a young friend told her that she wanted to have blue eyes. Morrison writes, "*The Bluest Eye* was my effort to say something about that; to say something about why she had not, or possibly ever would have, the experience of what she possessed and also why she prayed for so radical an alteration. Implicit in her desire was racial self-loathing. And twenty years later I was still wondering about how one learns that. Who told her? Who made her feel that it was better to be a freak than what she was? Who had looked at her and found her so wanting, so small a weight on the beauty scale? The novel pecks away at the gaze that condemned her."

Morrison also discusses the problems she had with writing the novel as well as describing places she feels the novel does not succeed. She expresses dissatisfaction with her solution to the problem of placing so much of "the weight of the novel's inquiry on so delicate and vulnerable a character...." In addition, although Morrison writes that she was "pressing for a female expressiveness" in the novel, she believes that she was unable to achieve this expressiveness, except, ironically, in the section describing Cholly's abuse by the white men who forced him to have sex with his young girlfriend.

Obviously, there are any number of possible starting places for a reading of *The Bluest Eye.* At the heart of the novel are the themes of racism, within and outside of the African-American community; the loss of innocence and its consequences; and the implications of the way a culture defines beauty and ugliness. Morrison explores these themes through her characters, her plot, her dialogue, and through the framing devices she chooses the structure the novel.

The first framing device strikes the reader immediately upon opening the book. In a sort of preface to the book, Morrison has written a parody of the Dick and Jane primary reader story. In this preface, Morrison first writes the story of Dick and Jane in perfect, primer prose. The images are of a happy, "normal," family. Without a pause, Morrison launches into the second telling of the story, identical to the first, but absent punctuation and capital letters. In the third telling, the prose is rendered nearly unintelligible because of the absence of not only punctuation and capital letters, but also of spaces between the words. Thus, in just three paragraphs, Morrison demonstrates the destruction of the "normative" model of American life into a mad jumble of letters on a page.

Morrison returns to the Dick and Jane story several times through the text to head a chapter. These headings provide a foreshadowing of what the chapter will bring. For example, the first heading is "HEREISTHEFAMILYMOTHERFATHERANDWHITWHITEHOUSETHEYAREVERYH." The chapter that follows is a description of life inside the two room apartment where the four Breedloves lives in abject and violent poverty. We see immediately that the headings of the chapters are used ironically, to contrast the "ideal" world of the primary school picture book family with that of the Breedloves of Lorain, Ohio. It is the disparity between the way the picture book family lives and the way the Breedloves live that propels the novel.

The second appearance of the Dick and Jane heading begins "SEETHECATITGOESMEOW MEOW." In this chapter, Morrison describes a particular type of African-American woman who comes from the South to the North, determined to wipe all traces of blackness from her life. These women work their whole lives trying "to get rid of the funkiness. The dreadful funkiness of passion, the funkiness of nature, the funkiness of the wide range of human emotions." Morrison creates Geraldine in this mold in order to represent the ways in which "Mobile women" have internalized the ideals and values of the majority culture. Geraldine's violent rejection of Pecola in the belief that the child has killed her cat demonstrates the way that she wants to reject everything associated with her own cultural heritage. Further, her rejection of Pecola and blackness illustrates again to Pecola her own lack of worth.

Morrison chooses carefully the subsequent chapters she heads with fragments of the Dick and Jane story. In two of these chapters she gives biographical information about Pauline and Cholly to illustrate how far their lives are from the "ideal" world of Dick and Jane. Significantly, the chapter headed with "SEEFATHERHEISBIGANSTRONG FATHERWILLYOUPLAYWITHJANE …" includes Cholly's rape of Pecola. In each instance, the chapter heading signals the reader that an illustration of the disintegration of the Breedlove family is to follow. Further, in each instance, Morrison is providing both the "how" and the "why" of Pecola's ultimate madness.

Morrison writes, "LOOKLOOKHERECOMES AFRIENDTHEFRIENDWILLPLAYWITHJANE …." as the heading for last chapter. This chapter opens with what appears to be a dialogue between Pecola and someone else. However, it becomes clear that this is not a dialogue between two people, but rather a dialogue between Pecola and herself. Now insane, she contemplates her new blue eyes with her "friend." We find through this "dialogue" that Cholly has continued to abuse his daughter and that Pauline no longer even speaks to her daughter. We also find that the disintegration of Pecola and her family is complete.

In addition to the Dick and Jane story, Morrison frames her story by using Claudia as an adult narrator at the beginning and the end of the story. Through Claudia's adult voice, we come to understand that the events of the novel have happened in the past. Like all stories, this one has achieved significance with time. We can see that Claudia's childhood understanding of the events in Pecola's life are different with the truths she now reads in the story: "For years I though my sister was right: it was my fault. I had planted them too far down in the earth. It never occurred to either of us that the earth itself might have been unyielding…. What is clear now is that of all of that hope, fear, lust, love, and grief, nothing remains but Pecola and the unyielding earth." The adult Claudia seems to be able to absolve herself of her childhood guilt over the death of Pecola's baby and over Pecola's fate.

Nevertheless, in the epilogue, when the adult Claudia's voice returns to close the story, it is as if she reassumes the guilt, making it universal, mak-ing the entire community complicit in the disintegration of one small black child. "All of our waste which we dumped on her and which she absorbed. And all of our beauty, which was hers first and which she gave to us. All of us—who knew her—felt so wholesome after we cleaned ourselves on her. We were so beautiful when we stood astride her ugliness." In the final paragraphs, Claudia indicts all of us for our easy acceptance of outward appearance as measure of worth, for our blind willingness to define beauty as white, blonde, and blue-eyed, and for our inability to love and nurture a child.

Source: Diane Henningfeld, in an essay for *Novels for Students,* Gale 1997.

Dorothy H. Lee

In the following excerpt, Lee interprets Morrison's The Bluest Eye *as a failed quest for self.*

One of the more interesting characteristics of Toni Morrison's four novels—*The Bluest Eye* (1970), *Sula* (1974), *Song of Solomon* (1977), and *Tar Baby* (1981)—is that each is a part of a whole. They reveal a consistency in Morrison's vision of the human condition, particularly in her preoccupation with the effect of the community on the individual's achievement and retention of an integrated, acceptable self. In treating this subject, she draws recurrently on myth and legend for story pattern and characters, returning repeatedly to the theory of *quest* as a motivating and organizing device. The goals her characters seek to achieve are similar in their deepest implications, and yet the degree to which they attain them varies radically because each novel is cast in unique human terms. Moreover, the theme of quest is always underscored by ironic insights and intensely evocative imagery. An exploration of these distinguishing qualities, technical and thematic, enhances one's appreciation of her achievement.

The Bluest Eye, Morrison's first novel, presents a failed quest culminating in madness. The young Pecola Breedlove searches painfully for self-esteem as a means of imposing order on the chaos of her world. Because a sense of self-worth and the correlative stability that would accompany it are unavailable to her in the familial or wider environment, she retreats to a subjective world of fantasy.

The novel is framed in several ways, first by the young narrator Claudia, then by chronological time. The story spans a year, moving through "Autumn," "Winter," "Spring," and "Summer." By means of the seasonal cycle and the fact that the girls are entering puberty, Morrison suggests a tale of growth and the eventual fruition of "Summer." The imagery of the prologue, however, immediately undercuts this promise:

> Quiet as it's kept, there were no marigolds in the fall of 1941. We thought, at the time, that it was because Pecola was having her father's baby that the marigolds did not grow. A little examination and much less melancholy would have proved to us that our seeds were not the only ones that did not sprout; nobody's did.... It never occurred to either of us that the earth may have been unyielding.

The newly matured Claudia realizes in retrospect that the environment was "unyielding" to both marigold seeds and Pecola Breedlove.

The familiar elementary school story of Dick and Jane provides another ironic frame for Pecola's circumstances:

> Here is the house. It is green and white. It has a red door. It is very pretty. Here is the family. Mother, Father, Dick, and Jane live in the ... house. They are very happy.... Who will play with Jane? See the cat.... See Mother. Mother is very nice ... Mother laughs ... See Father. He is big and strong.... Father is smiling.... See the dog.... Here comes a friend. The friend will play with Jane....

For each segment of this idealized picture of secure family life, Morrison offers in counterpoint the bleak specifics of Pecola's existence: shabby home, bitter and hostile parents, and two encounters with animals that are death-giving to her spirit and sanity.

Her parents' problems forecast defeat for Pecola's quest before her birth, and the coming of children only gives them a target for their frustrations. The father's life is a study in rejection and humiliation caused and intensified by poverty and Blackness. He learns early to deal with his hatred against those who cause his impotence by turning it against those who witness it. The mother's love for him decays as insistently as specks appear in her untreated teeth and in proportion to his inability to fill the spaces of loneliness within her. She avenges herself on Cholly by forcing him to indulge in the weaknesses she despises and seeks redemptive suffering through enduring him. Neglecting her own house, children, and husband, she derives satisfaction only from the house in which she is a maid for it offers her a pathetically illusory sense of "power, praise and luxury." After all, she is conceived to be the "ideal servant" there. Gentle with her employers' children, into her own daughter she beats "a fear of life." Neither parent

possesses a sense of self-esteem which might be communicated to the child. Their name—Breedlove—is almost too obviously ironic.

The abandoned store in which this family "festers together in the debris of a realtor's whim" can offer no gratification. The furniture, like the store, has the advantage of being affordable. The fabric of the sofa, like that of their lives, "had split straight across the back by the time it was delivered".

Morrison speaks often of the ugliness of the Breedloves, of their "wearing" this ugliness, out of "conviction," a belief confirmed for them by the responses of their world to them. Pecola's search for an acceptable face, that is to say self, as she shrinks beneath this "mantle," "shroud," "mask," of ugliness is the center of this novel. Her failure to find it other than in fantasy is Morrison's indictment of the society which deprives her of any sense of self-worth. The ugliness leads us to the image in her title. In order for Pecola to feel acceptable, she must ensure her self by possessing not only blue eyes but the bluest eyes created. Anything less is to live precariously, on the edge of an abyss.

The bluest eyes which represent the epitome of desirability to Pecola are possessed by the doll Claudia receives one Christmas. Claudia resents the doll and destroys it but comes to feel shame for her violence and hatred of both it and her similarly favored Shirley Temple cup. She sublimates her dislike in "fraudulent love." Pecola worships more truly, taking every opportunity to drink out of it "just to handle and see sweet Shirley's face." In these autumn days she also spends her pennies for Mary Janes, which bear a smiling white face, "Blond hair in gentle disarray, blue eyes looking at her out of a world of clean comfort.... To eat the candy is somehow to eat the eyes, eat Mary Jane, Love Mary Jane, Be Mary Jane."

Winter brings intensified chill outside and within Pecola as she increasingly rejects herself. It seems briefly that she will find acceptance with her peers minimally compensatory for the other voids in her life. She is attached to Maureen Peal, the "high yellow dream child with long brown hair braided into two lynch ropes that hung down her back." This relationship fulfills the metaphor's violent promise when Maureen, herself threatened, takes refuge in her beauty and attacks Pecola's ugliness. Responding, Pecola "seemed to fold into herself, like a pleated wing." Folding inward is the direction her quest takes. When her parents fight, "Please God [she whispers], please make me disappear. She squeezed her eyes shut. Little parts of her body faded away." One by one they all go un- til only her eyes remain. "Only her tight, tight eyes were left. They were always left." If she could make those eyes beautiful, "she herself would be differ- ent." When she had bought the Mary Janes, she had sensed she was invisible to the storekeeper, sensed "his total lack of human recognition." She is in- visible as an individual, of course, but the metaphor is reified in Pecola's consciousness. Her sense of being is literally in danger.

Through a chance encounter, she enters the house of a lighter-skinned middle-class boy whose caste-conscious mother ejects her with soul-killing words. To this woman, a type of character recur- rent in Morrison's work, Pecola represents all the dirt and disorder which she has managed to shut out of her artificial but neat environment, and she is therefore vicious.

In "Spring," ironically, Pecola's growth is in- creasingly stunted as she draws nearer her personal abyss. Her mother confirms the child's sense of re- jection as she throws her out of the spotless kitchen in which she is employed. She threatens the peace in this one ordered space of Mrs. Breedlove's life. Finally her father violates her body as the others have violated her spirit. Guilt, impotence, and— strangely—tenderness motivate his drunken rape of Pecola. His body is, after all, all he has to offer his daughter and with it he tries to penetrate to her soul. Instead, he pushes her into final withdrawal. The waning days of the season detail Pecola's encounter with Soaphead Church, who is a study of alien- ation, loss of identity and self-respect, and, once more, the futile search for order. He, like other characters in this and the other novels, compensates for a lack of self-worth with a pathological hatred of disorder and decay. Because he is a neighbor- hood seer, Pecola comes to him petitioning for blue eyes. Because she so "lowers herself" to come to him, he "gives" them to her by means of a con- trived "miracle." Thus is Pecola re-created: per- manently blue-eyed—and mad.

What could be left for "Summer"? The quest surely has ended. Yet Morrison gives us a closer look at the child and in so doing intensifies the pain with which this novel leaves us. We see Pecola, fragmented, engaged in a dialogue with self, i.e., the imaginary friend she has created. We hear her plea for reassurance that her eyes are the blu*est* and that her "friend" will not abandon her. "The dam- age done was total," Claudia says. "A little black girl yearns for the blue eyes of a little white girl, and the horror at the heart of her yearning is ex- ceeded only by the evil of fulfillment."

She spent her days, her tendril, sapgreen days, walk- ing up and down, her head yielding to the beat of a drummer so distant only she could hear. Elbows bent, hands on shoulders, she flailed her arms like a bird in an eternal, grotesquely futile effort to fly. Beating the air, a winged but grounded bird, intent on the blue void it could not reach—could not even see—but which filled the valleys of the mind.

There is a resonance to "blue" and to "void" and to the images of flight that we will encounter again in *Sula* and *Song of Solomon* as they point us toward the quest for selfhood.

Morrison concludes *The Bluest Eye* with Clau- dia's indictment of the society which "cleaned it- self" on Pecola. As the girl searches the garbage for "the thing we assassinated" (her self?), Claudia reflects that "this soil is bad for certain kinds of flowers. Certain seeds it will not nurture, certain fruit it will not bear, and when the land kills of its own volition, we acquiesce and say the victim had no right to live." The novel thus comes full circle to the images of infertility with which it began, and this search for a whole self is finished. We also un- derstand that Pecola's doomed quest is but a height- ened version of that of her parents, of Church, and of countless others in her world....

That Toni Morrison's novels constitute a con- tinuum seems evident. She has, beginning with *The Bluest Eye,* been interested in the effect of com- munity acceptance or rejection on the individual. She has consistently focused on the quest for self- acceptance and wholeness as seen again in *Sula.* In *Song of Solomon,* she asks that we come to terms with origins and acquire an awareness of false stan- dards of evaluation. In *Tar Baby,* all of these themes reappear. Yet, though there are unifying as- pects in her novels, there is not a dully repetitive sameness. Each casts the problems in specific, imaginative terms, and the exquisite, poetic lan- guage awakens our senses as she communicates an often ironic vision with moving imagery. Each novel reveals the acuity of her perception of psy- chological motivation—of the female especially, of the Black particularly, and of the human generally.

Source: Dorothy H. Lee, "The Quest for Self: Triumph and Failure in the Works of Toni Morrison," in *Black Women Writers (1959–1980): A Critical Evaluation,* edited by Mari Evans, Anchor Press/Doubleday, 1984, pp. 346–60.

Jacqueline de Weever

In the following excerpt, de Weever explores the crisis of black identity when cultural values are defined by a white society in Morrison's novel The Bluest Eye.

It used to be that black magazines like *Ebony* and *Jet,* barometers of the levels of black consciousness, carried advertisements for bleaching creams and hair-straighteners. Since the growth of black appreciation of natural color and texture and the advent of the slogan "Black is Beautiful," formed in protest to white standards of beauty, notices for bleaching creams no longer appear, although those for hair-straighteners still do. These illustrate the black woman's dilemma in a world where her white sisters are admonished: "Be a blond." "If you have one life to live, live it as a blond." Occasionally, one sees a black "blond" in the street or in the subway, vividly proclaiming the contradictions of her identity and of her society.

Bombarded on all sides to conform to an impossible standard of beauty, some women become confused and succumb to a psychological crisis. Black male writers have dealt with the crisis in different ways, [Richard] Wright in *Native Son* and [Ralph] Ellison in *Invisible Man,* presenting it in terms of the hero's conception of himself and of his place in society, while the identity crisis in women's lives appears only briefly. The narrator in *Invisible Man* notices a sign in a shop-window in Harlem:

> You too can be truly beautiful. Win greater happiness with whiter complexion. Be outstanding in your social set.

The narrator feels a savage urge to push his fist through the pane, but does not apply the admonition to himself. Ellison does not examine the ramifications of the sign, keeping his focus on the male hero, whose identity problems take a different form.

The apparent "throw-away" lines in Ellison's novel become the main theme of Morrison's first novel, *The Bluest Eye.* A woman may whiten her skin, straighten her hair and change its color, but she cannot change the color of her eyes. The desire to transform one's identity, itself an inverted desire, becomes the desire for blue eyes and is a symptom of Pecola's instability. She goes mad at the end of the novel. In Morrison's second novel, *Sula,* the identity crisis becomes the attempt to create a self where there is none. The heroine fails, and dies although not as a direct result of her failure. Morrison presents an inverted world in both novels; her two heroines find no help as they grope towards possession of an identity. Neither the inner nor outer world provides any support because both appear to have turned upside down.

The Bluest Eye introduces the reader to this topsy-turvy world at the very beginning with a paragraph from the First Grade Reader. Printed at first with the structure of simple sentences, it is repeated without punctuation, then without spaces between the words:

> Here is the house. It is green and white. It has a red door. It is very pretty. Here is the family, Mother, Father, Dick, and Jane live in the green-and-white house. They are very happy. See Jane. She has a red dress. She wants to play. Who will play with Jane? See the cat. It goes meow-meow....

The sentences lay out the clear, simple, synthetic world of the storybook. Repeated, without punctuation, this world is still recognizable:

> Here is the house it is green and white it has a red door it is very pretty here is the family mother father dick and jane live in the green-and-white house they are very happy....

The third time the paragraph appears, there are no boundaries of spacing or punctuation; the sentences approach the psychic confusion of the novel:

> Hereisthehouseitisgreenandwhiteithasareddooritisvery prettyhereisthefamilymotherfatherdickandjanelive inthegreenandwhitehousetheyareveryhappyseejaneshe hasareddressshewants toplaywhowillplaywithjane ...

Individual space has disappeared as it does in the novel; the father intrudes on and violates the child's space. The clear structure of the storybook world is wrecked as Pecola's life is wrecked. All the elements of the novel are here. The cat and the dog of the Reader appear in sinister form in the novel: the black cat has blue eyes, the blue eyes which haunt Pecola, and the dog writhes as it dies of poison, the sign Pecola must look for that her eyes have become blue. Then Pecola, who is Jane of the First Grade Reader, invents the friend who comes to play with her as she enters the world of insanity.

The Bluest Eye is divided broadly into two parts. Claudia, the narrator of one part, appears with her sister Frieda in the sections marked *Autumn, Winter, Spring, Summer;* the time of the novel spans one year. Claudia tells the story from her point of view, presenting the world of three little black girls who are given presents of white, blue-eyed, yellow-haired dolls, and whose cups are adorned with Shirley Temple's dimpled face. Claudia thinks that Shirley Temple is squint-eyed, and that the dolls have moronic eyes, pancake faces, and orangeworms hair. Her revulsion protects her from the deadly seduction which claims Pecola at the end of the novel. Claudia destroys the dolls, taking them apart to discover their secret as she would like to take apart little white girls to discover *their* secret. What did they possess to make even black women consider them cute, sweet, beautiful? Why were not Claudia and Frieda beautiful? Claudia thus articulates the theme of the novel. She and Frieda confront the same world which destroys Pecola, but a stable family life supports them. Pecola has no support.

The Breedloves, Pecola's family, are the people of the Reader. Mother, Father, Dick, and Jane are Mrs. Breedlove, Cholly, Sammy, and Pecola, and their story forms Part Two of the novel. Sentences from the Reader introduce this story, indicating their inner confusion and general desolation. Just as the lines from the Reader run together, without boundaries or punctuation, so the family lives together without the structure of a strong relationship or the punctuation of loving gestures or deeds.

HEREISTHEHOUSEITISGREENANDWHITEITHAS
AREDDOORITISVERYPRETTYITISVERYPRETTY
PRETTYPRETTYP

This heading introduces the description of the Breedloves's apartment. It is not a pretty house, but a storefront apartment. Each section on the Breedloves appears under the appropriate sentences from the Reader printed the same way. The fight between Mrs. Breedlove and Cholly is introduced by:

HEREISTHEFAMILYMOTHERFATHERDICKAND
JANETHEYLIVEINTHEGREENANDWHITE
HOUSETHEYAREVERYH

The Breedloves breed not love but disgust in each other. Pauline Breedlove, lame in one foot, believes she is ugly, and bears children she thinks are ugly.

> ... Although their poverty was traditional and stultifying, it was not unique. But their ugliness was unique. No one could have convinced them that they were not relentlessly and aggressively ugly.... You looked at them and wondered why they were so ugly; you looked closely, and could not find the source. Then you realized that it came from conviction, their conviction.

Mrs. Breedlove, Mother of the Reader, does not play with Pecola; she knocks her down in the kitchen of her white employers when she spills the blueberry cobbler, but turns, immediately, to soothe the little white girl who calls her Polly. No tenderness for her own black child, but tenderness for the white one. This is Pecola's inverted world. Pecola and Mrs. Breedlove are not very happy in their storefront apartment or in their relationship to each other.

Mrs. Breedlove is an artist at heart, fascinated with colors. Lacking paints and crayons, she cannot express her rainbow. She retreats into the fantasy world of movies, combs her hair like Jean Harlow's, pretends she is Jean Harlow, and thinks:

> "The onliest time I be happy seem like was when I was in the picture show."

Sex with Cholly causes the colors to rise, to float up, within her, but she does not know how to express them. In her frustration and belief in her own ugliness, she fights Cholly and beats her daughter.

When her parents fight, Pecola thinks that if she had blue eyes her parents would do lovely things for her eyes to see. Her consolation is buying and eating her favorite candy, the Mary Jane with Mary Jane's picture on the wrapper: white face, blond hair, blue eyes, the same combination that Claudia so ardently destroys.

> To eat the candy is somehow to eat the eyes, eat Mary Jane, Love Mary Jane, be Mary Jane.

This symbolic cannibalism is a sign of Pecola's latent instability. The desire for blue eyes is evidence of Pecola's dissatisfaction with her identity, with her world, and of her longing for something better, which, at twelve years old, she has no way of providing for herself. The desire for blue eyes is part of the inverted quality of her world; in wanting blue eyes, Pecola wants, in fact, to be white.

Reinforcing Pecola's sense that she is ugly are the episodes of Maureen Peal and Geraldine. Maureen Peal is "a high-yellow dream child with long brown hair braided into two lynch ropes that hung down her back." Maureen, a different shade of black, is everything Claudia and Frieda are not. She knows it, and screams at them:

> "You are ugly. Black and ugly black e mos. I *am* cute."

She forces Claudia to ask: "What was the secret? What did we lack?" In asking the question, Claudia admits her acceptance of Maureen's standard of beauty; yet by describing Maureen's braids as "lynch ropes" the author indicates a sinister quality of such beauty, at the same time acknowledging the white ancestor responsible for those ropes. The episode leads into the section on plain, brown Geraldine, who represents still another shade of black. She belongs to the "colored people," different from niggers. "Colored people are neat and quiet; niggers are dirty and loud." In Geraldine's beautiful gold and green house, Pecola meets the black cat with blue eyes, and the blue eyes in the black face hold her. Geraldine, however, tells her to get out of her house: "Get out," she tells her in a quiet voice, "You nasty little black bitch."

The men in the novel form part of the inverted world. Cholly is big and strong, like Father, but he does not smile, and he rapes his daughter. Mr. Henry, the roomer who gives the impression that he is "picky" with women, entertains the town whores in Mrs. McTeer's living room, and snatches at Frieda's budding breasts. Soaphead Church, of decayed West Indian aristocratic family, lives behind the candy store and gives readings. But he also entertains little girls, to whom he gives mints and money, and who eat ice cream while he plays with them. The sweat, the smells, the groans of adult women disgust him; there is none of that with little girls. Pecola's rape is set in this context of varying degrees of child molestation, and thus seems almost inevitable.

Everyone wants Pecola's baby dead before it is born in a world of universal love of white baby dolls, Shirley Temple cups, and Maureen Peals. Pecola, left alone, invents the friend who comes to play with her:

LOOKLOOKHERECOMESAFRIENDTHEFRIEND
WILLPLAYWITHJANETHEYWILLPLAYAGOOD
GAMEPLAYJANEPLAY

Pecola retreats into her mad world to enjoy her blue eyes, bluer than any other, and Claudia voices the psychic contradictions of the sane:

We were so beautiful when we stood astride her ugliness. Her simplicity decorated us, her guilt sanctified us, her pain made us glow with health, her awkwardness made us think we had a sense of humor. Her inarticulateness made us believe we were eloquent. Her poverty kept us generous. Even her waking dreams we used—to silence our own nightmares. And she let us, and thereby deserved our contempt.

... Morrison's novels depict the helplessness of Pecola and Sula before the ambiguities and paradoxes of their lives. Both suggest that the struggle to establish identity in a world which does not acknowledge one's existence is sometimes lost. The inverted world in which Pecola finds herself gives no support or guidance to a twelve-year-old struggling to find a self; the inverted quality of Sula's life leads to the great negation, death. It is a bleak vision that Morrison presents.

Source: Jacqueline de Weever, "The Inverted World of Toni Morrison's *The Bluest Eye* and *Sula*," in *CLA Journal,* Vol. XXII, No. 4, June, 1979, pp. 402–14.

Sources

Martha Bayles, "Special Effects, Special Pleading," in *The New Criterion,* Vol. 6, No. 2, January, 1988, pp. 34-40.

Susan L. Blake, "Toni Morrison," in *Dictionary of Literary Biography: Afro-American Fiction Writers After 1955,* edited by Thadious M. David and Trudier Harris, Vol. 33, Gale, 1984, pp. 187-99.

Patrice Cormier-Hamilton, "Black Naturalism and Toni Morrison: The Journey Away from Self-Love in *The Bluest Eye*," *MELUS,* Vol. 19, winter, 1994, pp. 109-28.

Ruby Dee, "Black Family Search for Identity," in *Freedomways,* Vol. XI, 1971, pp. 319-20.

Ken Donelson, "'Filth' and 'Pure Filth' in Our Schools—Censorship of Classroom Books in the Last Ten Years," in *English Journal,* Vol. 6, No. 2, February, 1997, pp. 21-25.

Haskel Frankel, "Toni Morrison's *The Bluest Eye*," in *New York Times Book Review,* November 1, 1970, p.46.

Liz Gant, "*The Bluest Eye*," in *Black World,* Vol. 20, May, 1971, pp. 51-2.

Denise Heinze, *The Dilemma of "Double-Consciousness": Toni Morrison's Novels,* University of Georgia Press, 1993.

Carol Iannone, "Toni Morrison's Career," in *Commentary,* Vol. 84, No. 6, December, 1987, pp. 59-63.

Phyllis R. Klotman, "Dick-and-Jane and the Shirley Temple Sensibility in *The Bluest Eye*," in *Black American Literature Forum,* Vol. 13, No. 4, winter, 1979, pp. 123-25.

John Leonard, "First Three Novels on Race," in *New York Times,* November 13, 1970, p. 35.

Karen MacPherson, "It's Time for Cat, Moon, Dick, and Jane to celebrate," in *Arkansas Democrat Gazette,* March 2, 1997, J1,8.

Toni Morrison, "Rediscovering Black History," in *New York Times Magazine,* August 11, 1974, pp. 14-24.

Toni Morrison, "Afterword," in *The Bluest Eye,* Plume, 1994, pp. 209-216.

Gloria Naylor, "A Conversation: Gloria Naylor and Toni Morrison," in *Conversations with Toni Morrison,* edited by Danille Taylor-Guthrie, University Press of Mississippi, 1994, pp. 188-217.

Chiwenye Okonjo Ogunyemi, "Order and Disorder in Toni Morrison's *The Bluest Eye, Critique, Studies in Modern Fiction,* Vol. 19, no. 1, 1977, pp. 112-120.

Terry Otten, *The Crime of Innocence in the Fiction of Toni Morrison,*University of Missouri Press, 1989.

For Further Study

Carolyn C. Denard, "Toni Morrison," in *Modern American Women Writers,* edited by Elaine Showalter, Lea Baechler, and A. Walton Litz, Macmillan, 1993, pp. 209-27.
    Denard's essay contains thorough treatment of each of Morrison's novels as well as biographical information.

Anne Koenen, "The One Out of Sequence," in *History and Tradition in Afro-American Culture,* edited by Gunter H. Lenz, Campus Verlag, 1984, pp. 207-21.

In her interview with Koenen, Morrison comments on motherhood, romantic love, her frustration at having to explain the black life she writes about for the benefit of whites, and the Black liberation movement of the 60s.

Jane Kuenz, "*The Bluest Eye:* Notes on History, Community, and Black Female Subjectivity," *African American Review,* Vol. 27, no. 3, fall, 1993, pp. 421-32.

Study of the ways in which participation in mainstream culture can cause "an abdication of self" by members of minorities.

Wilfred D. Samuels and Clenora Hudson Weems, *Toni Morrison,* Twayne, 1990.

An excellent introduction for student to the work of Morrison; includes an extensive bibliography.

Harvard Sitkoff, *The Struggle for Black Equality: 1954-1992,* Noonday, 1993.

Sitkoff's book chronicles important events and examines the lives of important figures in the Civil Rights Movement.

Amanda Smith, "Toni Morrison," in *Publishers Weekly* August 21, 1987, pp. 50-51.

In Smith's interview, Morrison discusses strength of family and community in her childhood and how she made the change from editing to writing.

Catch-22

Joseph Heller
1961

Set toward the end of World War II in 1944, on an island off the coast of Italy, Joseph Heller's *Catch-22* is a satirical antiwar novel. It features black humor, an unusual narrative structure, surrealism (a genre which features strange imagery and events), and a not-so-heroic protagonist who struggles to deal with the insanity of war and concludes that the only sane response to it is not to participate in it. Heller began writing *Catch-22* in 1953, and a chapter from the still-in-progress novel was published in an anthology in 1955. The completed novel was published in 1961.

American army pilot John Yossarian is an antihero, that is, a protagonist lacking some traditionally heroic qualities. He is obsessed with being rotated out of active flight duty. His commander, Colonel Cathcart, keeps raising the number of missions the men in the squadron must fly before they can be rotated out. Consequently, Yossarian is desperate to find another way out of his dilemma. He asks the squadron's doctor, Doc Daneeka, to declare him unfit for duty by reason of insanity. Doc refuses, citing the mysterious Catch-22: if Yossarian asks to be let out of his duties, he must be sane. Only a crazy man would want to continue to fly missions, but the only way Daneeka can ground him, according to Catch-22, is if he asks to be grounded—which would indicate his sanity. The circular reasoning of this "catch" is the central metaphor for the absurdity of war and the military bureaucracy.

Joseph Heller

Yossarian's questions and responses to his situation show that he is indeed a sane man in an insane situation. Heller uses black humor, absurd and even surreal events, and a nonlinear narrative structure in which events are arranged by theme rather than by chronology, to drive home his point that institutions such as the military, big business, government, and religion are corrupt and individuals must find their own responses to this corruption. Heller's questioning of these respected institutions, and of war in general, foreshadowed the social protests and antiwar movements of the late 1960s, and made it one of the most popular and enduring novels of its time.

Author Biography

Joseph Heller was born in Brooklyn, New York, in 1923 and grew up in Coney Island. This oceanside town had a large population of Russian Jewish immigrants, including Heller's parents, and was known for its amusement park. Heller's biting sense of humor may have been influenced by growing up in this somewhat surrealistic, carnival-like neighborhood.

After his 1941 high school graduation, Heller worked in an insurance office for a short time. The next year, 1942, he enlisted in the Army Air Corps, and in 1944, the year in which *Catch-22* is set, Heller was stationed on the island of Corsica (located in the Mediterranean Sea, off the coasts of France and Italy). There he was a bombardier who flew sixty combat missions, earning an Air Medal and a Presidential Unit citation. After the war ended in 1945, Heller married Shirley Held and went to college, eventually earning a B.A. in English from New York University and an M.A. from Columbia University. He then attended Oxford University in England as a Fulbright Scholar for a year, then moved to Pennsylvania, where he taught English at Pennsylvania State University for two years. Heller then changed careers, working as an advertising copywriter from 1952 to 1961 at such popular magazines as *Time, Look,* and *McCall's.* These jobs influenced his 1974 novel *Something Happened.* While working as a copywriter, Heller wrote short stories and television and film screenplays, and began writing *Catch-22.*

The first chapter of *Catch-22* was originally published in an anthology in 1955, and the entire work was published in 1961. After the novel's great success, Heller quit his copywriting job and concentrated on writing. In December 1981, he contracted a rare disease of the nervous system, which he wrote about in his book *No Laughing Matter* (1986) with his friend Speed Vogel. Heller has written other novels, many of which employ the plot of an individual battling against a powerful institution such as the military, government, or a corporation. These works capture Heller's basic pessimism about the power of the individual to fight society's corruption. Heller has also written a play, *We Bombed in New Haven,* about a group of actors who are supposed to play an Air Force squadron in an unnamed war, but who question their roles in the play. Heller also adapted *Catch-22* for the stage, but critics consider the book much better than the play. To date, none of the author's writings have achieved the acclaim or success of *Catch-22,* which is still considered a modern classic for its black humor and absurd portrayal of war. Heller continues to write, and lives in New York.

Plot Summary

The "Catch-22"

Joseph Heller's satirical war novel *Catch-22* depicts the absurdity and inhumanity of warfare through the experiences of Yossarian, a bombardier pilot stationed on the island of Pianosa (near Italy) in World War II. Heller does not tell Yossarian's story chronologically. Instead, the novel revolves around episodes in Yossarian's life (particularly the gruesome death of Snowden, a young airman) and employs flashbacks and digressions to jump back and forth between events.

Yossarian is terrified of flying bombing missions and attempts throughout the novel to escape this duty. He is thwarted, however, by his superiors and by "Catch-22," an ever-changing rule that keeps people subjected to authority. Early on, "Catch-22" works to keep all the men flying bombing missions, as Doc Daneeka explains to Yossarian:

"Sure, I can ground Orr [who is considered crazy]. But first he has to ask me to."

"That's all he has to do to be grounded?"

"That's all. Let him ask me."

"And then you can ground him?" Yossarian asked.

"No. Then I can't ground him."

"You mean there's a catch?"

"Sure there's a catch," Doc Daneeka replied. "Catch-22. Anyone who wants to get out of combat duty isn't really crazy."

There was only one catch and that was Catch-22, which specified that a concern for one's own safety in the face of dangers that were real and immediate was the process of a rational mind. Orr was crazy and could be grounded. All he had to do was ask; and as soon as he did, he would no longer be crazy and would have to fly more missions. Orr would be crazy to fly more missions and sane if he didn't, but if he was sane he had to fly them. If he flew them he was crazy and didn't have to; but if he didn't want to he was sane and had to. Yossarian was moved very deeply by the absolute simplicity of this clause of Catch-22 and let out a respectful whistle.

The book's final "Catch-22" is the most direct and the most sinister: "Catch-22 says they have a right to do anything we can't stop them from doing."

Life in the Squadron

The novel begins with Yossarian in a military hospital faking a liver ailment. He spends his time censoring letters until a talkative Texan drives him from the safety of the hospital. Upon Yossarian's return to active duty, we learn about the various men in his unit. We meet Orr, Yossarian's short, mechanically-gifted tentmate who keeps being shot down during bombing runs but wants to keep flying; McWatt, who likes to fly low and buzz Yossarian's tent in order to terrify him; Nately, a naive boy in love with a prostitute in Rome (who is only referred to as "Nately's whore") who barely notices

him; Doc Daneeka, a depressed doctor continuously lamenting the loss of his lucrative practice in America; Yossarian's navigator, Aarfy, who calmly smokes a pipe and talks while Yossarian yells hysterically during bombing runs; Major Major Major Major, the pitiable squadron commander who resembles Henry Fonda and who avoids contact with everyone, leaping through his office window when people try to see him; Colonel Cathcart, a man so obsessed with promotion that he keeps increasing the men's bombing missions so that he might impress his commander, General Dreedle; and Milo Minderbinder, the unit's morally blind mess officer, a financial genius who believes only in unrestricted capitalism and who forms the M & M Enterprises syndicate, which eventually controls almost all black market commerce in the hemisphere.

Yossarian has been promoted to Captain to cover up the disaster at Ferrara, where six days passed without the squadron destroying a bridge; on the seventh day, Yossarian led a mission on a dangerous second bombing run which destroyed the target but resulted in the deaths of several men. During another incident before Yossarian's stay in the hospital, the men become panicked when they learn they must bomb Bologna, Italy, which they believe is heavily fortified. When they finally fly the Bologna mission, Yossarian pretends his plane is malfunctioning and turns back to Pianosa. Yossarian finds upon the squadron's return, however, that Bologna was a "milk run," an easy mission that involved no enemy resistance. Yossarian is the lead bombardier on the next Bologna mission. To everyone's astonishment, they encounter heavy enemy fire, which Yossarian frantically tries to avoid. Many planes are shot down. After the mission, Yossarian packs and flees to Rome on leave, where he spends his time in a brothel.

On a trip with Milo Minderbinder, Yossarian and Orr fly between countries on various trading missions of Milo's devising. They discover that Milo makes enormous profits buying and selling goods, often to and from himself. Milo reasons that the more he earns, the more the syndicate earns, and every soldier owns a share of the syndicate, though they themselves never see any money from it. Soon, Milo's fleet of planes fly everywhere, including enemy territory. For Milo, no country is an enemy because they all belong to the syndicate (except communist Russia). Milo even begins contracting with both sides to simultaneously attack and defend target sites, which leads to the death of many men. Milo does not blame himself for these deaths because he is merely a middleman, some-

From the film Catch-22, *starring Alan Arkin.*

one making a fair profit off inevitable attacks. Milo's main worry is unloading stockpiles of Egyptian cotton that he bought and now cannot sell. To alleviate his financial straits, Milo contracts with the Germans to bomb his own unit, wreaking great destruction. Milo escapes punishment when he opens the books to his military superiors and reveals the tremendous profit the syndicate realized on this deal.

Casualties of War

Soon, a series of tragedies hits the unit. McWatt, while jokingly flying low over the beach, accidently kills a member of the squad, Kid Sampson, with a propeller. McWatt flies the plane into a mountain rather than land. Colonel Cathcart responds to these deaths by raising the missions to sixty-five. Yossarian returns to Rome. Also in Rome, Nately finds the prostitute with whom he is in love and, instead of sleeping with her, allows her to sleep for eighteen hours. When she awakes, she suddenly discovers she loves him. Nately volunteers to fly more missions so he can stay near Rome. On one of these, Nately dies when another plane collides with his. When Yossarian tells Nately's whore of Nately's death, she tries to kill him. Yossarian escapes, but he must keep watch because she continually attempts to ambush him.

In response to Nately's death, Yossarian vows to fly no more missions. The men in his unit secretly tell him they hope he succeeds. Then Yossarian learns that Nately's whore and her younger sister have disappeared after the police cleared out the brothel. Yossarian goes AWOL (absent without leave) and flies to Rome, feeling remorse and guilt over his lost friends, including Orr, whose plane went down after the Bologna mission.

Yossarian begins looking for Nately's whore and her kid sister. In a passage reminiscent of a descent into the Underworld, Yossarian walks the streets and witnesses scenes of horrific brutality. He returns to his room, only to find that Aarfy has raped a woman and then thrown her out the window, killing her. Aarfy's indifference appalls Yossarian. Yet when the police arrive, they arrest Yossarian for being AWOL and apologize to Aarfy for the intrusion.

The Final Catch

On Pianosa, Colonel Korn, Cathcart's assistant, informs Yossarian that they are sending him home. Yossarian is a danger to his superiors because he has given the men hope that they, too, can stop flying missions. Yossarian's release comes with one condition: he must become his superiors' "pal" and never criticize them. Yossarian agrees to this "odious" deal. On his way out, Nately's whore attacks him, stabbing him in the side.

While sitting in the hospital, Yossarian recalls in full Snowden's death. During a mission, Snowden is wounded and Yossarian tries to treat him, discovering a large wound in Snowden's upper leg. Snowden keeps complaining that he is cold, even after Yossarian bandages the wound. Yossarian cautiously looks for another wound and removes Snowden's flak suit. Snowden's insides pour out. This moment traumatizes Yossarian, causing him to watch Snowden's funeral from a distance while sitting nude in a tree. Snowden's death has taught Yossarian a secret: "Man was matter.... The spirit gone, man is garbage.... Ripeness was all."

Major Danby from Yossarian's unit comes to see him. Yossarian tells him that he is refusing the "odious" deal, but Danby informs him that if he refuses to cooperate, Korn and Cathcart will court-martial him on a variety of charges, some real, most invented. Still, if he takes the deal, Yossarian would violate the memory of his friends and would hate himself. The squad's Chaplain Tappman rushes in and informs them that Orr was not killed when his plane crashed, but rowed to Sweden in a life boat. Yossarian realizes that all of Orr's crash landings were practice runs for this escape. Yossarian decides to escape as well, first to Rome to save Nately's whore's kid sister, then to Sweden. He is afraid but feels very good. As he leaves the hospital, Nately's whore jumps out, misses him with a knife, and he runs.

Characters

Captain Aarfy Aardvaark

Yossarian's navigator, Aardvaark pretends he can't hear Yossarian's commands and laughs when Yossarian or anyone else is in trouble, because deep down he's a sadist. Captain Aardvaark is well-mannered and respectful of the ladies on the surface, but he turns out to have a sinister side, coldly pushing a young girl out the window after raping her. What's one Italian girl's life worth, he asks Yossarian calmly. Against the horror of war, his question is a disturbing one, because we know that the answer is: not much.

The Chaplain

See Captain Albert Taylor Tappman

Appleby

He is as all-American as apple pie, and "everything Appleby did, he did well." Although "everyone who knew him liked him," the men tease him with the absurd charge that he has flies in his eyes, and Yossarian despises him.

Captain Black

The squadron intelligence officer, Captain Black aspires to be squadron commander, even though he is not on combat duty. Outraged by Major Major's naming as commander, he starts the Glorious Loyalty Oath Crusade and refuses to allow Major Major to sign the voluntary oath. His power trip is ended by Major —— de Coverley, who demands to be fed after he is asked to sign an oath.

Colonel Cargill

General Peckem's forceful yet inept troubleshooter. It's Cargill's job to get the troops excited about the lame U.S.O. shows that Peckem organizes, for example. Ruddy-complexioned, he is an aggressive man who made quite a good living in civilian life as a marketing executive, hired by firms that needed to lose money for tax purposes. He is a "self-made man who owed his lack of success to nobody."

Colonel Chuck Cathcart

Cathcart is the squadron's colonel. In order to increase his chances of promotion, Cathcart keeps raising the number of missions the men must fly before getting rotated. Because he is obsessed with being promoted to general, his priorities are absurd. For example, he asks the chaplain to lead the men in prayer before missions because it might attract the attention of the *Saturday Evening Post,* and a nice article on Cathcart and his squadron might boost his promotion chances. He is less concerned with his pilots' safety than that they create tight bombing patterns that will make "nice photographs" to impress his superiors. Also, he promotes Yossarian to cover for Yossarian's insubordination, lest anyone blame Cathcart for Yossarian's bombing run gone awry. He is a symbol of military corruption and blind ambition.

Cathcart's self-absorption also causes him to go into business with Milo Minderbinder, who will trade the men's valuable supplies just to make a quick buck. Cathcart also builds a skeet-shooting range for the officers—not because it will help them be better soldiers, but just because he loves shooting skeet. Thus, he represents not just mili-

Media Adaptations

- A film of *Catch-22* was released in 1970 in the U.S., directed by Mike Nichols, screenplay by Buck Henry, starring Alan Arkin (as Yossarian), Martin Balsam, Richard Benjamin, and Art Garfunkel. Available on videotape from Paramount Pictures.

- *Catch-22: A Dramatization* was a one-act play based on the novel, produced in East Hampton, New York, at the John Drew Theater, July 23, 1971. Script published by Samuel French, New York, 1971.

- *Catch-22,* a sound recording on two cassettes (approx. 120 minutes); abridged by Sue Dawson from the novel by Joseph Heller, read by Alan Arkin. Published by Listen for Pleasure, 1985.

- *Catch-22,* an unsold pilot for a television comedy series, was created in 1973. Written by Hal Dresner, directed by Richard Quine, it starred Richard Dreyfuss as Yossarian.

---

tary corruption, but the self-absorbed American businessman. Down deep, he is insecure, and relies on Colonel Korn to help him succeed. He hates Yossarian for standing up to him.

Clevinger

One of the members of the squadron, he is not "clever" as "Clevinger" suggests, but rather slow-witted. He argues with Yossarian about Yossarian's paranoid and dark attitude and calls him crazy, which carries no weight with Doc Daneeka when Yossarian wants to be released from duty. The war is a black-and-white issue for Clevinger, who conducts educational sessions for the men and disappears on the Parma mission.

The Controller

See Doc Daneeka

Major Danby

The group operations officer whose name suggests that he is namby-pamby, meaning he's weak-willed and unable to make decisions. He's sort of like a babbling university professor, concerned with ideas and unable to act. Danby argues with Yossarian about idealism and the ethics of deserting, and then helps Yossarian to go AWOL once and for all. General Dreedle threatens to shoot him.

Doc Daneeka

Doc Daneeka, the squadron doctor, looks out for himself first and foremost. He tells Yossarian he will scratch Yossarian's back if Yossarian will scratch his, but Doc's self-interest prevents him from doing what Yossarian really wants, which is to sign papers saying Yossarian is too crazy to fly (in contrast to Doctor Stubbs, who does this for some pilots). Doc delegates many of his duties to two men named Gus and Wes. This leaves Doc free to fret over his life. He is a hypochondriac, constantly having his assistants take his temperature. He is also worried about being transferred to the Pacific, with its unusual diseases. Back home, Doc's private practice had been struggling until the war came along and all his competitors were drafted. He thrived until he was drafted himself, and he complains about having lost the business he built up. Doc earns extra money, or flight pay, by having the pilots sign documents saying that he is on flights that he isn't on. This leads the Army to assume he is dead when one of his "flights" crashes, despite his obvious living presence on base. Heller ironically describes Doc as a warm and compassionate man who is fearful and never stops feeling sorry for himself.

Major —— de Coverley

The mysterious de Coverley's first name is never given, and no one seems to know exactly what his job or rank is. An inspiring figure, he has some sort of godlike power; for instance, he is able to march into the mess hall and end Captain Black's Great Loyalty Oath Crusade with a simple command: "Gimme eat!" An older man, de Coverley has one eye, loves to play horseshoes, and has a skill for obtaining luxury apartments in recently re-captured cities. About halfway through the novel, he mysteriously goes off to Florence and is not heard from again.

Dobbs

A pilot. He flies with Huple on the Avignon mission in the number two seat and grabs the controls midair. When Colonel Cathcart raises the number of missions, Dobbs tries to assassinate him but is stopped by Yossarian.

General Dreedle

The wing commander, General Dreedle, is a solid military man who is moody but only requires that the men "do their work; beyond that, they were free to do whatever they pleased." He employs his annoying son-in-law, Colonel Moodus, to assist him. His nurse-mistress accompanies him everywhere, and he demands that people show her respect. He is constantly up against General Peckem, who is vying for Dreedle's job, but ex-P.F.C. Wintergreen helps Dreedle as much as he can until Peckem finally wins and replaces Dreedle. He is not upset when Yossarian goes naked, and he dislikes Colonels Korn and Cathcart. He seems more benevolent than the other authority figures in the novel, but his hands-off attitude allows Cathcart to keep increasing the number of missions the men must fly.

Nurse Sue Ann Duckett

A nurse in the Pianosa hospital who takes care of Yossarian and later has an affair with him. Her name suggests that she ducks out of his embraces when she's not in the mood. A serious and practical young woman who also enjoys sensual pleasures, she ends up marrying a doctor who will make a lot of money.

Lieutenant Dunbar

A fighter-pilot captain, Dunbar is Yossarian's companion in the hospital more than once, and even trades beds with the soldier named A. Fortiori to be near his pal Yossarian. He tries to make time "go more slowly," a twist on the idea that people want time to fly, so that he doesn't have to return to combat. He is a man of ethics, so he and McWatt get upset when they're instructed to bomb a defenseless village just to block a road. After this protest, Dunbar disappears. Yossarian wonders if it has something to do with the mysterious soldier in white who appears in a hospital bed. Is there a conspiracy to shut up Dunbar? he asks himself.

Captain Flume

Flume is a public relations officer who is terrorized by his roommate Chief Halfoat's threats to slit his throat. At one point, he is so traumatized that he moves to the woods, where he lives alone, eating strawberries.

A. Fortiori

A mysterious soldier who is involved in several mix-ups over identity. A. Fortiori's name is a Latin term used in logic for a conclusion that is more reliable than the previous conclusion or reasoning it is based on.

Chief White Halfoat

Halfoat is a semi-illiterate assistant intelligence officer who drinks a lot, beats up Colonel Moodus (which is just fine with Moodus's father-in-law, General Dreedle), and makes his roommate Flume crazy. Halfoat, whose Indian-sounding name is reminiscent of "half-crocked" or "half-nuts," is indeed a little wacky, with reason. He is a half-blooded Creek Indian. Halfoat says that the government used to chase his family around Oklahoma. Inevitably, wherever they settled, oil was found, so they kept moving on, to the point where the government wouldn't even let them settle in before they started digging. He resents having had his family exploited in this way. He is set in his ways, from hating foreigners to insisting that he will die of pneumonia, which he does.

Captain Havermeyer

Havermeyer is the best bombardier in the squadron, according to Colonel Cathcart, who defends Havermeyer's upsetting habit of shooting field mice at night with a gun stolen from the dead man in Yossarian's tent. Cathcart likes Havermeyer because he flies straight toward a target, taking no evasive actions that might make his bombing less accurate and his men more safe. As a result, the men can't stand flying with him.

Hungry Joe

Another member of the squadron, Hungry Joe is a woman chaser, pretending he is a photographer (which he really was in civilian life) as a come-on. He has nightmares on nights when he doesn't have a bombing run scheduled the next day, suggesting that while bombing runs are terrifying for the men, there is some perverse comfort in the ritual of bombing. In fact, his nightmares disappear when Cathcart increases the number of missions he must fly. Despite his anxieties over the war, Hungry Joe ends up being killed by his roommate Huple's cat, which smothers him.

Huple

Huple is the underage roommate of Hungry Joe who only fifteen years old; his cat kills Hungry Joe. Huple, a pilot, flies the Avignon mission on which Snowden is killed.

The Kid Sister

She is the twelve-year-old sister of Nately's whore. She tries to be seductive, like her big sister, but Yossarian and Nately look out for her because they see her as a child growing up too quickly.

Lieutenant Colonel Blackie Korn

Lt. Colonel Korn is Colonel Cathcart's assistant. He runs the farm he and Cathcart co-own, which Milo provided to them. His name is reminiscent both of corn, the crop, and "corny," meaning overly sentimental and cloying. Colonel Cathcart is annoyed by Blackie Korn, but he relies on him for help, since Korn is smarter and more devious. For example, Korn is the one who suggests that they give Yossarian a medal for his ill-fated bombing run over Ferrara in order to spare the military any embarrassment.

Kraft

Kraft is a young pilot who is killed on the Ferrara mission, which makes Yossarian feel terribly guilty, for he was the one who ordered a second pass on the target. Kraft only wanted to be liked. His name suggests craft, or skill, which is a joke because he is too inexperienced to have gained any skill as a pilot before he dies.

Luciana

Yossarian's Italian girlfriend whom he sees at the officers' club. Her name is derived from the Italian word for "light." She seems, at times, to know Yossarian better than he knows himself and what he will do. She laughs off his proposal of marriage.

Major Major Major Major

Major Major Major Major is the long and bony squadron commander who resembles actor Henry Fonda and is deliberately never in his office. The military insists on making him a major because they can't keep straight that Major Major Major is the man's given name, not his rank (it was a joke on his father's part). Major Major is not much of a leader, and now that he's an officer he misses being just one of the men. A timid man, he's afraid to ask Major — — de Coverley which of the two outranks the other. To relieve his boredom, he begins his own secret rebellion, signing orders as "Washington Irving" (the American novelist) and later as "John Milton" (the British author of "Paradise Lost").

McWatt

A crazy pilot who shares a tent with Clevinger and then Nately, McWatt relieves his stress by buzzing people—flying as low as possible over them—just for fun. His stunts end in his accidentally killing Kid Sampson, who is on the raft; after this McWatt intentionally crashes his plane, killing himself. While he's crazy—"the craziest combat man of them all probably, because he was perfectly sane and still did not mind the war"—he isn't a bad person. After all, he, along with Dunbar, protests when ordered to bomb a defenseless village just to block a road.

Lieutenant Milo Minderbinder

The ultimate capitalist, he is a mess officer turned businessman, trading all sorts of supplies on the black market and assuring everyone not to worry, they'll all be rich by the end of the war. He takes essential supplies from the planes but says that because everyone has a "share" in his business, it's for their own good. At one point, he makes a deal with the Germans in which he will have the Americans bomb their own base. He is Heller's symbol of capitalism at its most corrupt as well as its most powerful. As Milo's German bombing affair shows, wars come and go, but business goes on as usual.

Colonel Moodus

Moodus is General Dreedle's son-in-law and assistant. He is so annoying that Dreedle actually hires Chief Halfoat to punch him.

Mudd

Mudd is the dead man in Yossarian's tent. Actually, he's not really there. He's a pilot who died on a mission before he even checked in at Pianosa. Mudd's name is forever linked with the clutter that Yossarian's roommates find and throw out. The military insists Mudd is still alive because of their bureaucratic ineptness.

Lieutenant Nately

A squadron member, Nately is a gentle, sheltered nineteen-year-old kid from a wealthy family. He romanticizes his relationship with a whore he wants to save from prostitution and argues about the purpose of war and life with the old man in the whorehouse. He is killed, along with Dobbs, on the La Spezia run.

Nately's whore

An Italian prostitute, Nately's whore is too exhausted from her hard life to care about Nately, even though he's completely infatuated with her. She just uses him for his money, which supports her and her kid sister. However, one night after a good eighteen hours' sleep she wakes up and realizes she does love him after all. When Nately is killed, she blames Yossarian, who had broken

Nately's nose but isn't really responsible for his death. Yossarian is, to her, a symbol of the war and all the pain it has caused her, so she tries to stab him to death. Her surrealistic pursuit of Yossarian, and the fact that she stabs him just when he makes his deal with Cathcart and Korn, suggest that she is a symbol for Yossarian's conscience.

The Old Man in Rome

The old man runs the whore house and lectures Nately on the meaning of war and life. His philosophy is the opposite of the young pilot's: he believes it is better to live on your knees than die on your feet. He also attacks and blinds Major —— de Coverley, to everyone's astonishment.

Orr

Yossarian's roommate, Orr is a handyman who builds many projects with Yossarian. His tinkering with mechanical objects sometimes irritates Yossarian. Orr is a skilled pilot as well, but he keeps getting shot down in his plane and ending up in the ocean. He is nonchalant about this, even though no one wants to ride in his plane because they feel he has tremendously bad luck. Orr eventually crashes near Italy and while his crew rows toward shore, he rows his own raft to Sweden, where he sits out the war. Yossarian realizes this was Orr's plan all along, because Orr had made mysterious comments about his crashes being "good practice." Orr's name is reminiscent of "oar," a tool he uses to row to freedom, and the word "or," which reminds the reader of options and choices.

General P. P. Peckem

In charge of Special Operations/Services, General Peckem is an ambitious military man given to issuing silly orders, such as insisting that the men in Italy pitch their tents with their openings facing the Washington Monument in the United States. His assistant, Colonel Cargill, helps him in his effort to take over command from General Dreedle. His name suggests "pecking order," or hierarchy, as well as a certain part of the male anatomy.

Captain Piltchard

See Captain Wren

Kid Sampson

A pilot who is killed by McWatt in a violent accident while he is standing on the raft in the ocean.

Lieutenant Scheisskopf

A pompous but ambitious officer who is promoted to general when General Peckem takes over command from General Dreedle and who eventually becomes Peckem's superior. Scheisskopf, whose name is German for "shithead," loves parades and organizes one to honor Yossarian. He also has a very sexy, promiscuous wife that the men drool over.

Snowden

The young gunner on Yossarian's B-52 who dies a gruesome death as Yossarian tries in vain to save his life. His horrible death haunts Yossarian throughout the book. A sad symbol of the sheer waste of war, Snowden is so anonymous that at his funeral no one can give a eulogy because none of the commanding officers remember much about him.

The Soldier in White

Covered from head to toe in bandages, he is supposedly Lieutenant Schmulker, but no one can tell for sure. His appearance in the hospital coincides with the disappearance of Dunbar, which makes Yossarian suspicious that he's really some sort of spy, especially since his body seems to be a slightly different size the second time he shows up.

Doctor Stubbs

Doctor Stubbs is a flight surgeon who resents having to treat wounded men only to have them fly again and expose themselves to danger. Unlike Doc Daneeka, Stubbs will help pilots get excused from duty, and he is punished by being sent to the Pacific.

Captain Albert Taylor Tappman

Everyone calls Captain Tappman "Father," but as he tells them, he's not Catholic but an Anabaptist. He's not the sort to push the point, however, being very sweet-natured and shy. He's uncomfortable around officers and hates to have to eat in the officers' mess tents, especially since he has a hard time keeping track of which tent he's supposed to eat in each day. He lives alone in his own tent, and misses his wife and child back home. He often wonders about philosophical questions, "yet they never seemed nearly as crucial to him as the question of kindness and good manners."

Because he is quiet and unassuming, sometimes people take advantage of him, but he stands up for things that are important. He asks Colonel Cathcart to stop sending the men on so many missions, and he insists that Corporal Whitcomb not send form condolence letters to the families of men killed in combat. He puts himself on the line for others, as when he claims to be the forger instead of pointing his finger at the real culprit—Yossarian.

Corporal Whitcomb

The assistant to Chaplain Tappman, he's an opportunist, looking to advance his career, and an atheist. He doesn't get along well with his boss. For example, he wants to send form letters to the families of dead soldiers, which horrifies the sensitive Chaplain. He initiates the C.I.D. investigation of the Chaplain, fingering his boss as the forger.

Ex-P.F.C. Wintergreen

A former private first class (P.F.C.), he is the mail clerk at the 27th Air Force Headquarters who tosses Peckem's silly orders into the waste basket and processes Dreedle's orders, which he thinks are written in better prose. He's constantly being promoted and then demoted, and goes AWOL (absent without leave) regularly. By taking it upon himself to forge and discard documents, he gains a lot of power over the squadron. His name suggests that he never goes away, like an evergreen that stays green in winter.

Captain Wren

Along with Captain Piltchard, one of the squadron's operations officers whose job it is to organize combat missions. Piltchard and Wren have petty ambitions, as their names suggest ("pilchard" means sardine, and a wren is a small bird).

Yo Yo Yossarian

See Captain John Yossarian

Captain John Yossarian

The central character of *Catch-22* is Yossarian, a bombardier who is a captain with the 256th squadron. He is well-liked by his fellow bombardiers, and the Chaplain admires him, and even covers for him when he forges a document. Yossarian has friendships and people value his opinion (Dobbs and Milo ask him for advice, for example), but he considers himself a loner. Physically, he is big and strong and twenty-eight years old, but we learn no more than that. Yossarian also has an off-beat sense of humor, which he uses to cope with his frustration over being unable to get out of flying any more missions. He's an intelligent, complex character, honest and not given to deluding

himself. He is familiar with world literature and identifies with the loners in great works of the past. Yossarian is the kind of man who is uncomfortable interacting with a woman sexually unless he is in love with her, and he cares about kids, as we can see by how he treats the kid sister of Nately's whore. He even goes AWOL (absent without leave) to find her when she's missing.

Despite his intelligence and influence, Yossarian feels powerless because his superiors keep increasing the number of missions he needs to fly before he can go home. Though he feels helpless and angry about the situation, he asks very pointed questions of the people in charge about why things are the way they are. Yossarian's questions are Heller's; they show the illogic and futility of war. His attitude toward the war and the military angers Colonel Cathcart, who resents that Yossarian, for all his powerlessness, does not cave in to the values the military promotes, such as blind obedience and unquestioning patriotism. Yossarian has a moral center that he cannot put aside for the convenience of the military, which is why he makes the squadron bomb the ocean instead of an Italian town that has no military or strategic value. He hates war and cannot ignore its horrors, and he cannot stop reliving the horror of Snowden's death. When given a final "Catch-22"—either accept a honorable discharge by lying about his refusal to fly or face a court martial—Yossarian finally discovers a way out. By following Orr to Sweden, Yossarian can finally live with his conscience. As he tells Major Danby, "I'm not running *away* from my responsibilities, I'm running *to* them."

Themes

Individual vs. Society

Joseph Heller's *Catch-22* traces the efforts of Yossarian, an American bombardier in World War II, to escape participation in a war that seems meaningless. Yossarian represents the individual against a huge, corrupt institution of any sort, whether it is the army or a large corporation. The bureaucracy and rules of such large institutions, Heller suggests, often exist for their own sake, not for a good reason. Milo Minderbinder's M & M enterprises represents the corrupt corporation. In the pursuit of profits and wealth, he will trade anything, even life rafts or morphine that is needed to save the lives of the pilots, with anyone, including the enemy. The obvious question is, if we can communicate enough with the enemy to make business deals, why can't we settle our differences instead of killing each other? Negotiating peace is not the concern of Milo or his customers, however. Thus, Heller suggests that some businesspeople value money even more than human life. When Milo actually has the American pilots bomb their own base as part of a business deal with the Germans, it is perfectly logical and at the same time completely unethical. Yossarian, the sane individual, recognizes that this act is insane and evil.

The other corrupt institution in *Catch-22* is, of course, the military. Yossarian is the voice of reason. He is stunned by the priorities of the army, which at best are absurd and at worst evil, such as when the military police care about his going AWOL more than Captain Aardvaark's rape and murder of the Italian girl. Many of the orders issued by the men in power serve only to secure their own positions. Yossarian is constantly questioning the foolish arbitrary military rules and decisions and even sabotages his plane's communications systems in order to abort a mission that he feels is wrong. Individual men such as Yossarian are powerless to fight the army's corruption, which is why Yossarian decides he must leave rather than be a part of it.

Sanity and Insanity

The outrageous military regulation called Catch-22 captures Heller's attitude toward sanity and insanity. It is, he suggests, impossible to exist as a sane person in an insane environment. Heller portrays life for the men in the squadron as completely crazy. They are at the mercy of ambitious commanders who care more about their own careers than the men's lives. Their sanity is challenged by military rules that make no sense but which they must blindly obey. They see ethics thrown out the window, by Milo in pursuit of profit, for example, or by the old man in Rome, who lives only for pleasure. They are asked to endanger their lives, and begin to question why this is necessary, especially when they are asked to bomb an innocent village just to block a road.

The men deal with this insanity in different ways. Yossarian fakes illness to hide out in the hospital. McWatt buzzes people with his plane. Most of the men visit the whorehouse and have meaningless sex–"banging" women, as Yossarian calls it—to distract themselves from their fears and their deep-rooted feeling that they are risking their lives for foolish reasons.

Only Orr seems to cope well, to stay sane amid the madness, and the reader later learns it is be-

Topics for Further Study

- Research the antiwar movements of the 1950s and 1960s. Compare the reasoning antiwar activists presented for their opposition to war with the ideas presented in *Catch-22*.

- Discuss the themes of greed and corruption in the business world in *Catch-22*. Find a real-life case of a disaster caused by corporate greed and compare it to Milo Minderbinder's actions.

- Research the military justice system. Investigate under what circumstances a soldier may be charged with disobeying orders or desertion and what the penalties are. Then analyze how Yossarian's actions in *Catch-22* would have been charged and penalized.

- Discuss how Heller uses language itself to show that war is absurd. Use examples from several characters and be sure to take quotes from the text to support your analysis.

cause he has been focused on a plan to escape, and has even been practicing that escape. When Yossarian realizes what Orr has been doing, he makes the choice to escape as well. Despite the tremendous odds against the success of Yossarian's plan, Heller suggests it is not a crazy but a sane response to an insane situation over which Yossarian has no control.

Heroes and Heroism

The protagonist of a novel is generally called the hero because he or she usually has heroic, admirable qualities. An antihero, however, is someone who does not have heroic qualities such as courage and selflessness, but is still admirable because he has qualities that may mean just as much to the reader. Yossarian is certainly not courageous: he will do anything to get out of combat, even fake illness. He's not selfless; in fact, he's obsessed with saving himself from danger. Note that Heller chose as his setting World War II, an unambiguously "good" war to most Americans. Yossarian is rebelling against fighting a just war against a very evil empire, Nazi Germany. In theory, the reader should not like or identify with such a protagonist.

However, the war that we see in the book is not the Allies versus the Axis powers but the individual against the bureaucracy. Again and again, the military and business bureaucracies steal the dignity and hope of the men in Yossarian's squadron. The reader can understand Yossarian's point of view and empathize with him because he can never reach the number of missions he must fly before he goes home; the number will constantly be bumped up—not because that is what is necessary to stop the enemy, but because more missions will help the individual ambitions of one man gunning for a promotion. The reader sees Yossarian helpless against an absurd militaristic bureaucracy, held hostage and even physically endangered by the mercenary, money-grubbing business dealings of M & M Enterprises. The reader comes to like and respect Yossarian for standing up to the absurdity, refusing the dishonesty of betraying his fellow men by taking Cathcart and Korn up on their offer (he'll be discharged if he lies and tells people he never refused to fly or challenged his superiors). Under the circumstances, Yossarian's character flaws are no match for his decency and honesty, traits which seem utterly absent in the military.

Absurdity
Language and Meaning

While the purpose of language is to communicate, Heller shows that corrupt people and institutions misuse language in order to confuse and manipulate others and avoid responsibility. The characters' bizarre and illogical uses of language help create an atmosphere of absurdity—a state in which unreal, irrational things happen every day. In the beginning of the book, readers may be confused by the seemingly illogical discussions of flies in Appleby's eyes or Orr's story of stuffing crab apples or horse chestnuts in his cheeks to make them rosy, but soon it's clear that the men's unorthodox use of language mirrors that of their commanding officers'. Colonel Cargill tries to instill pride in the men, saying, "You're American officers. The officers of no other army in the world can make that statement." This self-evident statement has no real meaning. Captain Black says signing his loyalty oath is voluntary, but anyone who does not sign will be starved to death. And Major Major tells his assistant "I don't want anyone to come

in to see me while I'm here." While the sentence is grammatical, it makes no sense. It is just a roundabout way of saying he doesn't want to see anyone, ever, which of course is absurd. He has to talk to people to do his job. Circular logic and redefining words, Heller shows, allows people to avoid the reality of situations, or to twist reality to suit their purposes. No wonder that when asked if Appleby has flies in his eyes, Yossarian thinks this impossibility might be true because "it made as much sense as anything else."

Style

Setting

Catch-22 is set on an army air force base on the island of Pianosa off the coast of Italy in 1944, toward the end of World War II. The majority of the action takes place on the base itself, in the B-52 bomber planes as they go on raids, and in the local whorehouse, where the men relax; there are also flashbacks to training camps in America and some scenes in Italy. The island is real, but there was not a base on it in WWII. Note that the 256th is an army squadron of pilots; the army and navy both had air forces during the war but a separate U.S. Air Force was not created until 1947.

Point of View

The story is told in third person. Sometimes the narrative is omniscient ("all-knowing"), meaning that readers can see the large picture and everything that goes on. Sometimes, however, the narrator's vision is somewhat limited: we see things as if through a particular character's eyes. For example, the first several chapters are really from the point of view of Yossarian, but then in chapter nine we pull back and see the larger picture. This switching from limited to omniscient narration allows Heller to focus on the big picture or just one character.

Structure

Catch-22 is not a linear novel in which events follow each other chronologically. Instead, to underscore his points, Heller has the narrative jump around in time, using flashbacks and *déjà vu*—a French term for repetition meaning "already seen." This allows the author to juxtapose scenes that have a strong connection to each other thematically. The reader can follow the chronological chain of events by noting the references to Cathcart's continual raising of the number of missions the men must fly; the growth of M & M enterprises, which becomes increasingly powerful over time; and the revelations about the gruesome death of the young pilot named Snowden, a singular event that serves as an epiphany for Yossarian, that is, a moment that makes him "see the light." After he finally relives the event in full, he is determined to escape the insanity of war rather than try to find a way to cope with it.

The scrambling of scenes serves a second purpose as well: to reflect the state of mind of a combat pilot. Life in the military is in certain ways controlled and orderly, even dull, but it is intermingled with the sheer terror of death, which is completely unpredictable. Heller wants the reader to understand that time itself has a different meaning for someone in this situation, that what is important is not each day's separate events but the themes that are apparent in so many different situations at different times: the absurdity of bureaucracy, the callousness of ambitious men, the difference between reality and appearance.

Irony, Satire, and Black Humor

Writers often combine irony, satire, and black humor to express their themes and ideas, because the three techniques work together well. Heller uses all of these techniques liberally in *Catch-22*. One definition of irony is the use of words to express something other than their literal meaning—or even the opposite of their meaning. Thus, naming a pilot who is inexperienced at his craft "Kraft" is an ironic choice. Satire is the holding up of human vices and follies to ridicule or scorn through wit and sarcasm. *Catch-22* is a social satire, ridiculing targets such as the military (an example would be Scheisskopf's absurd obsession with military parades) and big business (witness the success of Milo's M & M Enterprises: countries that are actually at war with each other hypocritically do business with each other as well). Satire usually involves extremes, and certainly much of the absurdity in *Catch-22* is due to extreme examples of bureaucracy run amok, or capitalism at its most corrupt. The absurdity Heller creates is also funny, although not in a lighthearted way. Heller uses black humor, that is, humor with a dark tone to it, or an edge. Joking about death, for example, is a form of black humor. Thus, when Heller makes the army unable to recognize that Mudd is dead and Doc is alive (because they have more faith in the military's records than in the reality of one dead and one live body), it is black humor.

Allusion

Allusions are subtle references authors make to other books or events that are relevant to the point at hand, or to other events within the book itself. Throughout *Catch-22*, Joseph Heller makes references to literature, the Bible, and other writings and historical events. So, for example, when Yossarian censors letters in an absurdly nonsensical way, he signs off on them as "Washington Irving" or "Irving Washington." Washington Irving, a nineteenth-century novelist and essayist, often used black humor, and created the famous character Rip Van Winkle, who was, like Yossarian, an antihero (a protagonist whose admirable qualities are not the usual ones). This allusion points out to the reader that Yossarian identifies with the antihero Van Winkle and with Irving's black humor.

Allusion can also achieve a comic effect. At one point, Heller turns around Shakespeare's classic proclamation that "some men are born to greatness" and "some men have greatness thrust upon them" by writing that Major Major Major was "born to mediocrity" and had "mediocrity thrust upon him." The reader, remembering the loftiness of the original quote and its source, is meant to see the humor in changing "greatness" to "mediocrity," as if mediocrity, like greatness, could be stunningly admirable and spoken of with the utmost respect.

Finally, allusions to events within the novel itself remind readers of thematic connections between the events. Heller makes many such allusions to drive home his themes.

Historical Context

Italy in World War II

Catch-22 takes place on an American Army Air Force base on an island off the coast of Italy. Italy had been drawn into World War II by Benito Mussolini, a former Socialist who had come to power in 1925. His fascist government, marked by strict government control of labor and industry, ended civil unrest in the country but limited the rights of its citizens. Mussolini was constantly engaged in military campaigns, conquering Ethiopia in 1936, for example, and that same year he signed an agreement with Nazi Germany's Adolf Hitler to cooperate on a mutually beneficial foreign policy. When Germany invaded Poland in 1939, Great Britain and France declared war, and Italy officially joined Germany in the alliance of Axis Powers in 1940.

Compare & Contrast

- **1940s:** The U.S. invades Normandy, France, in June, 1944, while massively bombing Japan. Two atom bombs dropped on Japan in August will lead to Japan's surrender. The war ends in 1945.

  1960s: In November 1961, President Kennedy begins increasing the number of American advisers in Vietnam, which will grow from 1,000 to 16,000 over the next two years. Two U.S. Army helicopter companies, the first direct American military support of South Vietnam, arrive in Saigon. In 1965, President Johnson will begin sending combat troops, without getting the approval of Congress.

  Today: Recent police actions, such as Operation Desert Storm in 1991 and the 1983 invasion of Grenada (an island in the Caribbean), have been publicly questioned by Americans even as these actions were taking place. Congress must now vote on such actions.

- **1940s:** Jim Crow laws in the South are the most obvious evidence that blacks are expected to keep their distance from whites. Throughout the country, African Americans have fewer educational and economic opportunities.

  1960s: The Civil Rights movement is in full swing, as African Americans forced the federal government to pass the Civil Rights Act in 1957. Movement leaders like Martin Luther King, Jr.,

  advocate peaceful civil disobedience, but others, such as Malcolm X and the Black Panthers, suggest that armed resistance against white oppression should not be ruled out.

  Today: Racism continues to afflict America, as the different responses between African Americans and whites to the O. J. Simpson trial pointed out. African Americans still have higher rates of infant mortality, joblessness, and poverty than whites do.

- **1940s:** While many men are off at war, women work as "Rosie the Riveters," taking jobs in the war industry. For many women, this is the first time they have entered the work force and earned their own money.

  1960s: Betty Friedan publishes *The Feminine Mystique* in 1963, launching the modern-day feminist movement. The movement focuses on individual women at first, and only begins to be a major political force toward the end of the Vietnam War in the early 1970s.

  Today: The term "feminism" has become so loaded with contradictory meanings that many women who are technically feminists (anyone who believes in political, social, and economic equality of the sexes) avoid it. Women make up 46% of the work force but still only make 75 cents for every dollar men earn.

Italy had neither the economic or strategic resources to succeed for long, and by mid-1943 the Allied Forces of the United States and Great Britain had begun occupying Italian territory. By this time, Mussolini was in political trouble, and he was exiled and eventually executed in 1945. A new government of Italian businessmen and workers signed an armistice with the Allies, and in October 1943 declared war on Germany. The Germans, however, still controlled the northern part of the country and Italy now found itself divided. By the time that

Yossarian and his combat crew entered the war, Italy had largely withdrawn from the war and Germany still occupied portions of the country. Although the war with Germany ended on May 7, 1945, the Allies would continue to occupy Italy until a peace treaty with the country was finally signed in 1947.

U.S. War Involvement

Italian territory occupied by Allied forces provided good locations for air force divisions, which

U.S. troops from the 85th Division marching through the Porta Maggiore in Rome, 1944.

played a key strategic role during World War II. The United States Army Air Force employed two types of military bombers: the smaller fighter bombers, and the strategic bombers, which were large, long-range planes that could attack targets deep in enemy territory. They generally held between two and eight people. In the novel, Yossarian flies aboard a B-25, one model of this type of strategic bomber. The men on board these planes had distinct duties. Seated in the nose of the plane were the bombardier and the navigator. While the navigator directed the plane toward its destined target, the bombardier timed the release of the plane's bombs to most effectively destroy that target. These two men had to work closely with each other to facilitate the exchange of in-flight information. Above and behind the nose was the pilot's compartment. Here the pilot and copilot steered the plane toward its destination and through any enemy fire, or "flak." The body of the plane held the bomb bay and the radio compartment. Radio operators generally worked as communication men as well as gunners. Also on the planes were men who worked as aerial engineer gunners and armorer gunners, whose mechanical backgrounds would come into play when planes suffered damage. Altogether, though each of them held a different post

and their ranks varied, the crew worked as a unit each time its members entered the sky.

Catch-22 is set at the end of World War II, the so-called "good war" because almost all Americans supported it. Any reluctance to join the Allies in their battle against Germany's Adolf Hitler and the Axis powers was erased in 1941 when the Japanese bombed Pearl Harbor in Hawaii. Having already been through a world war, however, Americans realized that wars rarely settled political grievances; they were becoming more cynical about war in general. The Korean War (technically only a "police action" that lasted from 1950 to 1953) left Americans wary about the futility of entering "limited" wars in other countries. The Vietnam War, which America began to enter in the late 1950s, was not yet unpopular in 1961, but Americans after the Korean War would soon embrace Heller's absurdist, antiwar message as strongly as they did his satire of Cold War America.

The Cold War

While *Catch-22* takes place in 1944, in it Heller makes frequent allusions to events in America in the 1950s, even using anachronisms (things out of time) such as computers and helicopters so that people would think of the Korean War as well as WWII. Heller felt that the Cold War era, far from being an ideal, peaceful time, was filled with tension and paranoia. Allusions to the 1950s abound: the C.I.D. (a representative of the CIA or FBI) accuses the Chaplain of hiding documents in a plum tomato stolen from Cathcart's office. Absurd though it sounds, Heller was drawing upon the story of real-life state department official Alger Hiss, who was accused of being a communist and of hiding documents in a hollowed-out pumpkin. Captain Black starts a loyalty oath "crusade," and Chief Halfoat makes references to being "red"— talking about communism, not skin color. When Milo claims "what's good for the syndicate is good for the country," he is echoing a member of President Eisenhower's cabinet, who said, "what's good for General Motors is good for the country." These are ideas that Americans would come to question in the 1960s.

The Zeitgeist *of the 1960s*

Readers of *Catch-22* responded to the novel's celebration of the individual and its satire of institutions such as the government, the military, and business corporations. Yossarian stands up against absurd and corrupt authority, dismisses the shallow values of ambition and materialism, recognizes the hypocrisy of the army, and bravely makes up his own mind about how to respond to a demoralizing situation. He wrests control of it, and overcomes his powerlessness.

These themes would become a crucial part of the *zeitgeist,* or spirit of the age, in the 1960s. American youth were questioning the idea that American institutions and politicians were completely trustworthy and free from corruption. The communist witch-hunts of the 1950s led by Senator Eugene McCarthy, in which people were hounded and blacklisted from their professions because they were suspected communists, had made many Americans rethink their blind trust in politicians and the government. This distrust would build to a peak in the early 1970s, when the Watergate scandal of the Nixon administration eroded the public's faith in the presidency. Meanwhile, in the 1960s, the Vietnam War took increasingly more American lives and became even more violent and bloody. People started to question why politicians had led the country into it initially, and why they were still there, especially since there was no end in sight. Had the U.S. become involved for idealistic reasons, or because of business deals between the country and Vietnam? Why was there still fighting if there did not seem to be any progress? Could

it be that politicians just didn't want to admit they had been wrong, and were letting young men die in Vietnam rather than being honest about the situation? As more Americans asked these difficult and important questions, they began to rethink other issues as well. They stopped taking for granted that the status quo (the way things are) was the best that it could be.

Racism and Sexism

Until the late 1950s and early 1960s, few white Americans gave any thought to the plight of black Americans. "Negroes" were, after all, a minority, and segregation kept them in different neighborhoods, different schools, and in the South, even in different restaurants, bus seats, and bathrooms. However, black Americans were beginning to take action against the treatment they received. Their "separate but equal" schools were inferior to white students' schools. A 1954 Supreme Court ruling, *Brown vs. the Board of Education,* forced school integration, and helped launch the Civil Rights movement. The movement, which would be led by Dr. Martin Luther King, Jr., began to gather power, inspiring the Civil Rights Act of 1957, which created the Civil Rights Commission and spelled out penalties for voting rights violations, and the Voter's Rights Act of 1965, which guaranteed black Americans access to the voting booths. Other black leaders and organizations, from Malcolm X to the Black Panthers, demanded respect and power for their people. Heller alludes to the growing civil rights movement when he has Colonel Cathcart claim that he would never let his sister marry an enlisted man—in other words, an inferior. This summed up many white American's attitude towards blacks: they would claim to have many Negro friends, but in the end, they wouldn't want a relative to actually marry a black person.

As the Civil Rights movement gained momentum, the feminist movement was just beginning. In 1963 journalist Betty Friedan published a best-selling book called *The Feminine Mystique,* which pointed out that housewives were on the whole an unhappy lot, unfulfilled because their lives were built around men's. The book launched an entire movement, as women began questioning what they needed and wanted for themselves as individuals outside of their relationships to others. In 1961, Heller's portrayal of military women, prostitutes, and nurses seemed funny, honest, and dead-on. It would be several years before most people would notice that the female characters in *Catch-*

22 are mostly shallow, portrayed as sex-starved and preoccupied with men.

Critical Overview

When a chapter of *Catch-22* was first published as a novel-in-progress in 1955, Joseph Heller got several letters of encouragement from editors. Then, when the finished book was published in 1961, Orville Prescott of the *New York Times* described it as "a dazzling performance that will outrage nearly as many readers as it delights." Half the reviews were positive, but the other half were negative, and some were downright scathing. *New York Times Book Review* contributor Richard G. Stern said the novel "gasps for want of craft and sensibility," "is repetitious and monotonous," "is an emotional hodgepodge" and certainly no novel, and, finally, that it "fails." The structure was problematic for some: acclaimed author Norman Mailer said in *Esquire:* "One could take out a hundred pages anywhere from middle ... and not even the author could be certain they were gone." *New Yorker* critic Whitney Balliett said it "doesn't even seem to have been written; instead, it gives the impression of having been shouted onto paper," and that "what remains is a debris of sour jokes." Further, the critic said Heller "wallows in his own laughter and finally drowns in it."

The last laugh was on these reviewers, however, because although the book did not win any prizes or appear on any best-seller lists, it soon became an underground hit and sold extremely well in paperback. More and more critics began to see in it what readers saw. The book had quickly become a favorite of the counterculture because of its antiauthoritarian and antiwar attitude. As Eliot Fremont-Smith said in the *Village Voice* (New York City's progressive counterculture newspaper), "[*Catch-22*] came when we still cherished nice notions about WWII. Demolishing these, it released an irreverence that had, until then, dared not speak its name." While *Catch-22* was set in World War II, its message was very contemporary. As some critics pointed out, in *Catch-22* the real enemy is bureaucracy, and Vietnam was a war in which the real enemy seemed to be not the Viet Cong but the U.S. military and big business, which dehumanize people. Carol Pearson wrote in the *CEA Critic* that the book captures how people "react to meaninglessness by renouncing their humanity, becoming cogs in the machine. With no logical explanation

to make suffering and death meaningful and acceptable, people renounce their power to think and retreat to a simpleminded respect for law and accepted 'truth.'" Jean E. Kennard wrote in *Mosaic,* "Heller's horrifying vision of service life in World War II is merely an illustration of the human condition itself."

Raymond M. Olderman wrote in *Beyond the Waste Land* that the key scene of the novel is when the M.P.s arrest Yossarian for being AWOL while they overlook the murdered young Italian girl lying in the street. This incident, Olderman said, symbolizes "much of the entire novel's warning—that in place of the humane ... we find the thunder of the marching boot, the destruction of the human, arrested by the growth of the military-economic institution." This institution is personified by Milo Minderbinder, the wheeling and dealing businessman who values money and business deals above all else. In the *Canadian Review of American Studies,* reviewer Mike Frank said that "for Milo, contract, and the entire economic structure and ethical system it embodies and represents, is more sacred than human life." After all, Milo even trades away the men's life rafts and makes a deal with the Germans to bomb the Americans' own base.

Critics pointed out that Yossarian's sense of powerlessness in the face of large institutions such as the military, the government, and big business are experienced by people everywhere. Yossarian became a timeless symbol of rebellion and reason, and his decision to take the moral high ground and defect despite the odds against him was embraced by many. Olderman noted that Yossarian's choice in the end was more admirable than it appears on the surface. As he points out, Yossarian's choices are that "He can be food for the cannon; he can make a deal with the system; or he can depart, deserting not the war with its implications of preserving political freedom, but abandoning a waste land, a dehumanized, inverted, military-economic machine."

Critics also noticed Heller's distinctive use of language. Kennard of *Mosaic* wrote that in the novel, "Reason and language, man's tools for discovering the meaning of his existence and describing his world, are useless." Language, Heller reveals, can be easily manipulated to the point where it doesn't reflect reality but instead has the power to "divest itself from any necessity of reference, to function as a totally autonomous medium with its own perfect system and logic," as Marcus K. Billson II pointed out in the *Arizona Quarterly.* Of course, the most memorable misuse of language is in the circular logic of the fictional military rule called "catch-22."

While Heller's novel is humorous, he said he wanted the reader to be ashamed that he was amused and to see the tragedy. Morris Dickstein in the *Partisan Review* pointed out that Milo's antics, which are funny at first, "become increasingly somber, ugly and deadly—like so much else in the book—that we readers become implicated in our own earlier laughter." Nelson Algren in the *Nation* also saw the more serious side of the novel: "Below its hilarity, so wild that it hurts, *Catch-22* is the strongest repudiation of our civilization, in fiction, to come out of World War II."

Today, more than ten million copies of the book have been sold, and *Catch-22* is considered a classic novel. As Richard Locke said in the *New York Times Book Review*, "It is probably the finest novel published since World War II ... the great representative document of our era, linking high and low culture." Indeed, the term "catch-22" has entered the language itself and can be found in many dictionaries.

Criticism

Darren Felty

Felty is a visiting instructor at the College of Charleston. In the following essay, he discusses how Catch-22 *explores larger issues of social order and individual responsibility within the context of a war novel.*

As most critics recognize, *Catch-22* offers more than a critique of World War II, despite its focus on the destructiveness of warfare. Instead, Joseph Heller employs this setting to comment upon the condition of mid-century American life. His satire targets not just the military but all regimental institutions that treat individuals as cogs in a machine. His central character, Yossarian, recognizes the insanity of social institutions that devalue human life and tries to rebel against them, first in minor ways and finally through outright rejection of them. Yet Yossarian is not, as some have contended, an immoral or non-idealistic man. He is a man who responds to human suffering, unlike characters such as Colonel Cathcart and Milo Minderbinder, who ignore the human consequences of their actions. Yossarian's perceptions conflict with most everyone else's in the book. Thus, his encounters with people inevitably lead to mutual misunderstandings, to Yossarian labelling everyone else crazy, and to a sense of pervasive lunacy. This lack of rationality creates wild comedy in the novel, but, ultimately, it drives the book toward tragedy.

Yossarian sees the conflicts of the war in purely personal terms. To him, his enemies, which include his superior officers, are trying to murder him. Those who believe in the war cannot comprehend his reduction of its conflicts to personal assaults. The young airman Clevinger, for instance, refuses to accept Yossarian's views that people are trying to kill him:

> "No one's trying to kill you," Clevinger cried.
>
> "Then why are they shooting at me?" Yossarian asked.
>
> "They're shooting at *everyone*," Clevinger answered. "They're trying to kill everyone."
>
> "And what difference does that make?"
>
> Clevinger was already on the way, half out of his chair with emotion, his eyes moist and his lips quivering and pale.... There were many principles in which Clevinger believed passionately. He was crazy.

Yossarian reduces the war to its barest elements and refuses to see himself as one component in a wider cause, which befuddles the "principled," patriotic Clevinger. Yet Yossarian does not reject the aims of the war (stopping the spread of Nazism); he reacts the way he does because he sees that the aims have been perverted. The men no longer serve a cause; they serve the insane whims of their superiors.

Men with authority in the novel do not focus on a common goal (which Clevinger believes), nor do they recognize the humanity of those they command. They value only the power they hold in the military (or the medical, religious, or commercial professions). To gain more power, these men corrupt and exploit the founding principles of the institutions they serve. For instance, instead of fighting to stop totalitarian regimes that would eliminate freedom, the military itself has imposed totalitarian rule. To maintain it, they utilize "Catch-22," a rule that they can change to fit their needs and that keeps the men trapped in their current roles. "Catch-22" grows more sinister as the novel progresses. It begins as a comic absurdity reflecting the essential powerlessness of those in the squadron since it keeps them flying the additional missions Colonel Cathcart orders:

> There was only one catch and that was Catch-22, which specified that a concern for one's own safety in the face of dangers that were real and immediate was the process of a rational mind. Orr [who wants

What Do I Read Next?

- *One Flew Over the Cuckoo's Nest* (1962) by Ken Kesey is another novel about a man caught in an insane institution, in this case literally. Randall Patrick McMurphy was sent to an insane asylum as part of a plea bargain arrangement, and must fight to retain his sanity and sense of himself when he is confronted with the brutal authoritarian figure of Big Nurse, who runs the ward.

- *Slaughterhouse-Five* (1969) by Kurt Vonnegut is another semi-autobiographical, satirical novel that uses a nonlinear structure to make its points about the horror and absurdity of war. The main action is set during the Allied bombing of Dresden, Germany, in World War II, and the main character, Billy Pilgrim, like Yossarian, is a bombardier.

- *Going after Cacciato* (1979) is an antiwar novel by Tim O'Brien, set during the Vietnam War. In it, the main character, Cacciato, like Yossarian, tries to escape the war, in this case Vietnam, and arrive in a safe place, Paris. O'Brien, like Heller, uses black humor and surrealism to bring out his themes.

- *V.* (1963) by Thomas Pynchon is a novel about a mysterious woman who shows up at key points in European history. Pynchon uses black humor to point out the flaws in American values in the 1950s. He also shows, like Heller, that language can serve to confuse people rather than clearly communicate. Also, like *Catch-22, V.* has an unusual narrative structure that jumbles chronology.

- *The Best of Abbie Hoffman: Selections from "Revolution for the Hell of It," "Woodstock Nation," "Steal This Book," and New Writings* (1990) by Abbie Hoffman, edited by Daniel Simon. Abbie Hoffman was a highly influential political activist, radical, and counterculture hero of the 1960s who, like Joseph Heller, used humor to make important points about American society and values, as well as to criticize the war and big business. He believed that "street (guerilla) theater" got people's attention in the television age, so he arranged stunts such as dropping dollar bills on the Stock Exchange and threatening to have people meditate en masse, causing the Pentagon to levitate. He explained his ideas in several nonfiction books, excerpted in this collection.

- *M*A*S*H**, like *Catch-22*, was a satirical movie about the insanity of war, released in 1970 in the U.S., directed by Robert Altman, screenplay by Ring Lardner, Jr., starring Donald Sutherland, Elliot Gould, Sally Kellerman, and Robert Duvall. Available on video from 20th Century-Fox.

---

to keep flying] was crazy and could be grounded. All he had to do was ask; and as soon as he did, he would no longer be crazy and would have to fly more missions.

When Yossarian attempts to go over Colonel Cathcart's head to division headquarters, the rule simplifies further. Despite the fact that he has flown the number of missions needed to complete his tour of duty, as specified by Cathcart's superiors, he still must obey Cathcart because "Catch-22" "says you've always got to do what your commanding officer tells you to." The soldiers, who see no alternative to these rules, accept them. Thus, everyone (except Yossarian and a scant few others) is insane because they ascribe to insane principles. They see not reality but the "reality" constructed by those who manipulate them. And they die, not to stop the Germans, but to fulfill the ambitions of their superiors and to maintain the institutions that abuse them.

Of even wider significance than military authoritarianism, however, is Milo Minderbinder's capitalistic fervor and the excesses he commits in its name. Through Milo, Heller condemns the unscrupulous expansion of commercial interests that exploit people for profit or even reduce them to the status of commodities. Milo himself acts not out maliciousness, but out of blindness. He recognizes only the right to profit, which forms his very morality. Milo embodies an American ideal. He is an individualist who believes in initiative, hard work, and opportunism, and these principles make him rich. But he is also the ultimate organization man. He forms the M & M Enterprises syndicate on the premise that every man owns a share. Thus, by supposedly incorporating everyone into his ventures, he monopolizes the black market and ensures the cooperation of those he manipulates. His vision proves destructive, however, because it excludes any notion of humanity. For instance, he contracts with the Allies and the Germans to both bomb and defend a bridge at Orvieto, and he even bombs his own squadron to make money to offset his losses in the Egyptian cotton market. When Yossarian criticizes him for his actions at Orvieto, Milo replies, "Look, I didn't start this war.... I'm just trying to put it on a businesslike basis. Is anything wrong with that? You know, a thousand dollars ain't such a bad price for a medium bomber and a crew." Here, Milo unwittingly reveals his purely economic intelligence, which equates men with machinery. His agreements also betray his notions of loyalty: neither the Allies nor the Germans are his enemies because they both belong to the syndicate. He remains loyal only to his economic empire, in which the sanctity of a contract means more than the sanctity of life.

The catastrophic results of the callous misuse of power in the novel find their most wrenching expression in "The Eternal City" chapter. This chapter loses all vestiges of comedy and becomes a nightmare vision of brutality run amuck. Yossarian wanders through Rome encountering a succession of horrors and thinks, "Mobs with clubs were in control everywhere." He also learns the essence of "Catch-22": "Catch-22 says they have a right to do anything we can't stop them from doing." Power is all. And the power to control belief is even more valuable than the power to kill, since, as Yossarian realizes, "Catch-22" works because people *believe* that it exists when it actually does not. Like Milo Minderbinder's capitalistic rationalizations, it serves to "bind" people's minds. Therefore, they accept the abuses heaped upon them and the world turns absurd.

In such a world, Colonel Cathcart can keep raising missions and Milo can brazenly bomb his own squadron. Hence, the restraints governing commerce and the military have completely collapsed. Survival becomes all that matters, and one must look to save himself because the institutions that supposedly support him actually look to cannibalize him. Yossarian learns this lesson most forcefully through the death of Snowden, an event that haunts him throughout the book but which he only fully understands at the novel's end. When Snowden's insides spill out as Yossarian is trying to save him, Yossarian discovers a secret: "Man was matter.... Bury him and he'll rot like other kinds of garbage. The spirit gone, man is garbage." He graphically encounters human vulnerability and comprehends the essential need to understand another's humanity, to see his "spirit," not to view him as only an expendable object.

Thus, the more Yossarian understands the abuses of those who wield power, and the more he sees people suffer because of these abuses, the more stubborn he becomes in his refusal to participate in the war. When he finally decides to desert from the military altogether, he does not run from the defense of principles of freedom, individuality, and justice. He, like his dead comrades, defended those ideals. His only recourses besides desertion are imprisonment or accepting Cathcart and Korn's deal to become their "pal." Both options ultimately defend Cathcart and Korn's actions and spur others to continue fighting. If imprisoned, Yossarian implicitly validates his superiors' "right" to punish him. If he accepts their deal, he would advocate murder, since men are now dying not for the cause but to help maintain their superiors' hold on authority. As Victor J. Milne contends, Yossarian's flight affirms "that an individual has no right to submit to injustice when his action will help to maintain an unjust system." Instead, Yossarian tries to flee the system itself. However futile this effort, he refuses to sanction corrupt officials and become, like them, an exploiter of others for personal gain, thereby preserving his own moral character.

Source: Darren Felty, in an essay for *Novels for Students,* Gale 1997.

Louis Hasley

In the following essay, Hasley explores how Heller uses a dramatic contrast between humorous and harrowing incidents to heighten the horror of the novel.

A book that was widely acclaimed a classic upon its appearance and that has suffered no loss of critical esteem deserves many critical examinations. Now, more than ten years after its first publication in 1961, Joseph Heller's *Catch-22* may justify another attempt to fix certain qualities in it more precisely than has yet been done. My special concern here is the pattern of dramatic tension between the preposterous events of the story and the built-in dimension of laughter. It is part of the pattern that the laughter, intermittent and trailing away just before the end, contributes to a catharsis in which the grimness of war provides the dominant memory.

It is part of the book's greatness that its hilarious force comes so near to a stand-off with the grimness. Heller has achieved his declared purpose, mentioned elsewhere, not to use humor as a goal, but as a means to an end. "The ultimate effect is not frivolity but bitter pessimism," he said (*Time,* Mar. 4, 1966). And yet the alternating play of humor and horror creates a dramatic tension throughout that allows the book to be labeled as a classic both of humor and of war. It is not "a comic war novel" despite the fact that comedy and war are held more or less in solution, for the war is *not* comic but horrible—this we are not allowed to forget. The laughter repeatedly breaks through the tight net of frustration in which the characters struggle only to sink back as the net repairs itself and holds the reader prisoned in its outrageous bonds.

Right here the unskillful reader may protest that *Catch-22 is* a comic war novel. For who could believe that war is conducted as the novel pictures it—realism blandly ignored, motivations distorted beyond recognition, plausibility constantly violated. Even conceding that war is not peace, that the conditions of any war are abnormal, could any serious work stray so far from what we know of human character?

The answer lies in an artistic strategy relating to the thesis of the novel, which, put simply, is this: War is irrational; and the representative things that happen in war are likewise irrational, including man's behavior in war. This thesis is an underlying assumption, a donnée, illustrated not documentarily but imaginatively throughout the book. It is, in terms of the book, unarguable—you take it or leave it—for the author has seen to it that all the evidence favors his thesis. What he asks, and it is everything, is that his readers accept the credibility of his characters and their actions, if not at face value, then as wild, ingratiating exaggeration that nevertheless carries the indestructible truth that war is irrational.

It would be an uncritical reader indeed who would accept at face value the greater part of what

is related in this hilarious, harrowing book. For the absurd, the ridiculous, the ludicrous, are pyramided, chapter after chapter, through the lengthy book's entire 463 pages.

Starting with the opening page in which Captain Yossarian, the book's non-hero, is goldbricking in a hospital bed and censoring letters which he as censoring officer signs "Washington Irving" and sometimes with variant whimsicality "Irving Washington," to the last page in which "Nately's whore" makes a final but unsuccessful attempt to stab Yossarian because he had told her of Nately's death—through all this the predominance of the outré in events and behavior is unchallenged. One such episode has Yossarian appearing naked in formation to be pinned with the Distinguished Flying Cross by General Dreedle. Another has Lieutenant Milo Minderbinder directing his buddies in the bombing of their own camp and leaving the runways and the mess halls intact so they could make a proper return landing and have a warm snack before retiring. But it is useless to enumerate. "So many monstrous events were occurring that he [the chaplain] was no longer positive which events *were* monstrous and which *were* really taking place." That quoted sentence can stand as characterizing the events of the entire book.

The effect of such wildly imagined actions is an artistic triumph in which the reader perceives the author's attitude as overtly playful in expression and managed event, this being the only way, or at least a meritoriously acceptable way, of facing the fundamental inhumanity and irrationality of war. The author begins with an *absurdum,* though the reader does not always recognize it as such, and makes it into a further and unmistakable *reductio ad absurdum.* It thus becomes unabashed hyperbole; its literary costume is familiar to one who has read Cervantes, or Rabelais, or Swift, or the American humorists of the Old Southwest and their principal heir, Mark Twain, who could be as darkly pessimistic as is the author of *Catch-22.*

Heller's comic genius, however, does not come to rest in the mere contrivances of exaggeration, daft though the exaggerations are. No part of the whole texture of objectively rendered dialogue, narrative, description, and introspective characterization fails to enhance the total artistry. Of random examples, let us cite first a bit of comic circularity—not hard to find—such as this one in which the staff psychiatrist, Major Sanderson, questions Yossarian:

"Hasn't it ever occurred to you that in your promiscuous pursuit of women you are merely trying to assuage your subconscious fears of sexual impotence?"

"Yes, sir, it has."

"Then why do you do it?"

"To assuage my fears of sexual impotence."

Even in a paragraph of only ten lines, Heller
can blend a telling bit of narrative with characterization and cynical reflective analysis:

> Nately was a sensitive, rich, good-looking boy with
> dark hair, trusting eyes, and a pain in his neck when
> he awoke on the sofa early the next morning and won-
> dered dully where he was. His nature was invariably
> gentle and polite. He had lived for almost twenty
> years without trauma, tension, hate, or neurosis,
> which was proof to Yossarian of just how crazy he
> really was. His childhood had been a pleasant, though
> disciplined, one. He got on well with his brothers and
> sisters, and he did not hate his mother and father,
> even though they had both been very good to him.

Verbal humor crops up with considerable fre-
quency in *Catch-22*. Yossarian, for example, said
he "would rather die than to be killed in combat."
A certain apartment maid in Rome (who wore lime-
colored panties) "was the most virtuous woman
alive: she laid for *everybody,* regardless of race,
creed, color or place of national origin...." Often
the irony is both humorous and grim, as in Corporal Whitcomb's form letter for Colonel Cathcart's
self-serving and hypocritical condolence:

> Dear Mrs., Mr., Miss, or Mr. and Mrs.: Words can-
> not express the deep personal grief I experienced
> when your husband, son, father or brother was killed,
> wounded or reported missing in action.

Much of the verbal humor still more acutely
serves Heller's almost constant preoccupation with
characterization, as when Colonel Cathcart adjures
his men to attend a U.S.O. show.

> "... Now, men, don't misunderstand me. This is all
> voluntary, of course. I'd be the last colonel in the
> world to order you to go to that U.S.O. show and
> have a good time, but I want every one of you who
> isn't sick enough to be in a hospital to go to that
> U.S.O. show right now and have a good time, and
> *that's an order!*"

Some indication of the mixture of horror and
hilarity appears in examples already cited. But not
enough to show how the cumulus of horror maintains itself against the pull of hilarity and finally
establishes its ascendancy. Reappearing periodically throughout is Yossarian's memory of the
bombing flight over Avignon when Snowden is
mortally wounded and Yossarian as bombardier
bandages a thigh wound of Snowden only to find
that "whole mottled quarts" of Snowden's guts fall

out when Yossarian rips open the injured man's
flak suit. Memory of this experience recurs to Yossarian at intervals throughout the book, but it is so
metered that it is only in the second to the last chapter that the horrible trauma experienced by Yossarian is brought home to the reader, helping to provide a clinching explanation of his refusal to obey
any further flying orders and his decision to desert.

But there are other notable horror scenes of a
different kind. In a chapter called "The Eternal
City," Yossarian wanders through the bombed ruins of Rome compassionately in search of a twelve-
year-old girl who has been made homeless. It is a
dark night of the soul, a nightmare of the bizarre
and the surrealistic typified by a blue neon sign
reading: "TONY'S RESTAURANT. FINE FOOD
AND DRINK. KEEP OUT." As Yossarian tramps
the streets in the raw, rainy night,

> A boy in a thin shirt and thin tattered trousers walked
> out of the darkness on bare feet.... His sickly face
> was pale and sad. His feet made grisly, soft, sucking
> sounds in the rain puddles on the wet pavement as
> he passed, and Yossarian was moved by such intense
> pity for his poverty that he wanted to smash his pale,
> sad, sickly face with his fist and knock him out of
> existence because he brought to mind *all* the pale,
> sad, sickly children in Italy.... He made Yossarian
> think of cripples and of cold and hungry men and
> women, and of all the dumb, passive, devout moth-
> ers with catatonic eyes nursing infants outdoors that
> same night with chilled animal udders bared insen-
> sibly to that same raw rain.

Other similarly pathetic sights whip up in Yossarian a tide of frenzied anguished questions.

> The night was filled with horrors, and he thought he
> knew how Christ must have felt as he walked through
> the world, like a psychiatrist through a ward full of
> nuts, like a victim through a prison full of thieves.

Another dramatically moving horror scene
centers on an unfortunate character whose name,
given him by a father with a bizarre sense of humor, is Major Major Major. By the whim of an
IBM machine he is vaulted from private to major
in four days; later he is arbitrarily named squadron
commander by Colonel Cathcart, whereupon Major Major Major Major is dogged by ineptitude,
loneliness, and ostracism. In a desperate attempt at
fellowship he joins in an outdoor basketball game,
first disguising himself with dark glasses and a false
moustache. The scene that follows gradually takes
on the ritual killing of a scape-goat reminiscent of
Shirley Jackson's brilliant horror story, "The Lot-
tery."

> The others pretended not to recognize him, and he
> began to have fun. Just as he finished congratulating
> himself on his innocent ruse he was bumped hard by

one of his opponents and knocked to his knees. Soon he was bumped hard again, and it dawned on him that they did recognize him and that they were using his disguise as a license to elbow, trip and maul him. They did not want him at all. And just as he did realize this, the players on his team fused instinctively with the players on the other team into a single, howling, bloodthirsty mob that descended upon him from all sides with foul curses and swinging fists. They knocked him to the ground, kicked him while he was on the ground, attacked him again after he had struggled blindly to his feet. He covered his face with his hands and could not see. They swarmed all over each other in their frenzied compulsion to bludgeon him, kick him, gouge him, trample him. He was pummeled spinning to the edge of the ditch and sent slithering down on his head and shoulders. At the bottom he found his footing, clambered up the other wall and staggered away beneath the hail of hoots and stones with which they pelted him until he lurched into shelter around a corner of the orderly room tent.

Of course, Yossarian is no King Lear whose single tragic fault causes him to fall from on high. He lies, goldbricks, fornicates, cheats at gambling, even for a time goes about naked. Yet he is more sinned against than sinning. The military organization, commanded by a vain, selfish publicity seeking, ambitious, greedy and unscrupulous authoritarian, has persecuted his squadron beyond endurance by periodically raising the number of missions required before a flier can be sent home. The number starts at twenty-five and moves by stages up to eighty. It is only after Yossarian points out that he has now flown seventy-one "goddam combat missions" that his rebellion becomes final and he refuses to fly any more missions.

The central actions of Yossarian are nevertheless not to be seen as those of a strong-minded individualist. The entire sense of the book is that war, in itself irrational, makes everyone connected with it irrational. There are no good guys in this book. Just about everyone of the approximately two score characters of some importance is called crazy at one time or another. Not only can Nature be hostile ("There was nothing funny about living like a bum in a tent in Pianosa between fat mountains behind him and a placid blue sea in front that could gulp down a person with a cramp in a twinkling of an eye"); the Deity is likewise roundly vituperated by Yossarian. In an adulterous visit to Lieutenant Scheisskopf's wife (on Thanksgiving!) he argues with her about God.

> "And don't tell me God works in mysterious ways," Yossarian continued.... "There's nothing so mysterious about it. He's not working at all. He's playing. Or else he's forgotten all about us. That's the kind of God you people talk about—a country bumpkin, a clumsy, bungling, brainless, conceited, uncouth hayseed.... What in the world was running through that warped, evil, scatalogical mind of His when He robbed old people of power to control their bowel movements? Why in the world did he ever create pain?"

Even the chaplain is not immune from what seems the universal corruption of war. He

> had mastered, in a moment of divine intuition, the handy technique of protective rationalization, and he was exhilarated at his discovery. It was miraculous. It was almost no trick at all, he saw, to turn vice into virtue and slander into truth, impotence into abstinence, arrogance into humility, plunder into philanthropy, thievery into honor, blasphemy into wisdom, brutality into patriotism, and sadism into justice. Anybody could do it; it required no brains at all. It merely required no character. With effervescent agility the chaplain ran through the whole gamut of orthodox immoralities....

The responsive reader of *Catch-22* is thus made to walk a tight-rope as he leans first to riotous humor and then tips to the side of black tragedy. There is much in the book that illustrates Charlie Chaplin's dictum that humor is "playful pain." "The minute a thing is overtragic," says Chaplin, "it is funny." And he is supported emotionally, if not logically, by W. C. Fields, who said: "I never saw anything funny that wasn't terrible. If it causes pain, it's funny; if it doesn't it isn't." The humor in *Catch-22*, we are forced to conclude, is only secondary. Where Heller comes through in unalleviated horror is where the message lies. The book's humor does not alleviate the horror; it heightens it by contrast.

It is not therefore the disinterestedness of pure humor that we find in *Catch-22*. It does not accept the pain of life with wry resignation. Instead it flaunts in bitterness the desperate flag of resistance to the wrongs of this life—wrongs suffered, not by the wholly innocent, but by the insufficiently guilty. And the wrongs are perpetrated not only by unscrupulous, ignorant, and power-hungry men, but also by the inscrutable Deity.

Source: Louis Hasley, "Dramatic Tension in *Catch-22*," in *The Midwest Quarterly*, Vol. 15, No. 2, January, 1974, pp. 190–197.

Walter R. McDonald

In the following excerpt, McDonald places Yossarian's character within the tradition of "American rebels" such as Huck Finn, Hester Prynne, and Ike McCaslin.

Yossarian of Joseph Heller's *Catch-22* has been called a coward, an amoralist, a cop-out, a traitor. Others see him as a casualty, an individualist, a prophet of love, the last soul true to himself. The first readers object primarily because he "takes off," claiming this is artistically, patriotically, or morally no way to end the book.

Yet Yossarian gives up safety, rewards, and a hero's homecoming when he flees. He is in fact following an American tradition—escaping, or trying to escape, in order to save himself from absurdity, compromise, or despair. In what Hemingway called the source of modern American literature, *Huckleberry Finn,* Twain's puckish hero (after surviving a river's length of encounters with man's hideous inhumanity to man) also "lights out" for the Indian Territory. The similarity is striking when we realize that Yossarian leaves rather than be comfortably tamed and returned as a hero to the civilized States (for the glory of Colonels Cathcart and Korn) and that Huck leaves to avoid the comfortable (but to him confining and compromising) civilized family life.

There is in American fiction a tradition of heroes who "take off," or who renounce ease, or who deny themselves pleasure in quest of individual rather than conventional fulfillment. This radical individualism—absurd, perhaps, or ascetic--shows Yossarian at the end of the story to be not a cop-out, but one of many rebels in a tradition of rebels.

Thoreau set the tradition's example and gave it voice in the concluding chapter of *Walden:* "If a man does not keep pace with his companions, perhaps it is because he hears a different drummer. Let him step to the music which he hears, however measured or far away." Such a code romanticizes Natty Bumppo, for example, who refuses the comfort of the Effinghams' cabin in *The Pioneers,* preferring the free wilderness (and see his Lone Ranger solitude in the other Leatherstocking tales, as well).

In a spirit of free renunciation and penitence, Hester Prynne resumes her symbol in *The Scarlet Letter,* long after anyone requires it. Hawthorne speculates that Pearl would "most joyfully" have entertained her mother in England in regal comfort. But Hester hears a drum no others hear.

However much we may think Lambert Strether's ethics are precious and overstrained at the end of *The Ambassadors,* we recognize in him another American individualist denying himself pleasure (marriage to Miss Gostrey) in order to save his concept of honor.

As if reading Thoreau's urging as a command ("Enjoy the land, but own it not," from "Baker Farm" in *Walden*), Faulkner's Ike McCaslin re-

nounces his birthright to save himself and, he hopes, the land, which has been cursed by slavery. Repeatedly, his cousin McCaslin Edmonds urges him to inherit the land and demands a reason for his refusal. The involuted Part IV of "The Bear" is Ike's attempt to explain the call of the different drummer he hears. Finally, even the temptation of his bride's sweet body is not enough to break his resolve, and Ike becomes uncle to half a county and father to none.

With Frederick Henry the tradition begins to involve patriotism rather than mere personal gain. But since it is the Italian Army, most readers easily allow him to take his farewell to Italian arms without rebuke. His desertion seems hardly that, justified as it is by the absurd circumstances. Justified also by this American code of individualism, he deserves to escape, deserves better surely than the tragic end, his farewell to Catherine Barkley's English arms.

Because life in those times played such dirty tricks on individuals, we even allow an American like Jake Barnes to exile himself in Europe after the war (*The Sun Also Rises*). Life in exile may not have been as simple as a hero's return; it may, in fact, have required a certain asceticism for Jake Barnes to endure the sad desperate crowd of his lost generation. But it is his solitary choice, preferring his troubled priestly life among the lost to the sterile homecoming of young Krebs in "Soldier's Home."

But it is Yossarian himself, literally marching backwards with his gun on his hip, who is the fullest example of Thoreau's man marching to a different drummer. At this same time of rebellion, he refuses to fly any more missions because, as the final blow, Nately has been killed. It is this point, it would seem, which critics would object to, rather than his actual desertion. For it is at this time, not when he runs away, that Yossarian quits the fight.

When he refuses to fly, his superiors have two choices: to court-martial him or to let it pass. Seeing a chance for profit to themselves, Colonels Cathcart and Korn offer him a deal: as Yossarian summarizes for the chaplain, "They'll let me go home a big hero if I say nice things about them to everybody and never criticize them to anyone for making the rest of the men fly more missions." It is such a "good deal" that Colonel Korn says, "'You'd have to be a fool to throw it all away just for a moral principle.'"

But that is exactly what Yossarian does. The passage is Heller's *donnée,* the stipulation of the rules the rest of his fiction is to be played by. The "deal" is what takes Yossarian out of the war. He does not desert from combat; he takes off from a "luxurious, privileged existence" that he would "have to be a fool" to turn down.

At first, even though he knows it would be "a pretty scummy trick" he would be playing on the men in his squadron who would have to remain, Yossarian leaves his new "pals" the colonels exhilarated. "He was home free: he had pulled it off; his act of rebellion had succeeded; he was safe, and he had nothing to be ashamed of to anyone."

But after Nately's whore stabs him and as he is recovering in the hospital, Yossarian cannot go through with "the odious deal." The colonels have even compounded the lie by writing in the official report that Yossarian has been stabbed while heroically saving his colonels from a Nazi spy. Yossarian's "moral principle" which Colonel Korn has scorned interferes: "'Let them send me home because I flew more than fifty missions,' Yossarian said, 'and not because I was stabbed by that girl, or because I've turned into such a stubborn son of a bitch.'"

But by now he is trapped: as Major Danby explains, "'If you don't go through with the deal, they're going to institute court-martial proceedings as soon as you sign out of the hospital.'" If he goes through with the deal, he violates his moral principle, dupes his country, and betrays his fellows. If he refuses and is court-martialed, he risks becoming another Billy Budd, whom Captain Vere martyred to preserve discipline. For if Yossarian is found innocent, "'Other men would probably refuse to fly missions, too … and the military efficiency of the unit might be destroyed. So in that way,'" Major Danby concludes, "'it *would* be for the good of the country to have you found guilty and put in prison, even though you *are* innocent.'"

Here, Heller is carefully plotting, ethically walking the thin line between anarchy and individualism, and even doing so conservatively. Yossarian is in an absurd dilemma; he is faced with preposterous alternatives. Given such a situation, he invents a compromise: he does not want "to destroy the military efficiency of the unit"; neither does he want to be the pampered bellwether of the colonels' flock. So he says, "'I can run away…. Desert. Take off. I can turn my back on the whole damned mess and start running.'" Even before he hears that Orr has arrived in Sweden, Yossarian has decided to light out for the Territory. Orr's escape merely injects more hope into him.

Yet it is no life of ease Yossarian seeks in Sweden now, as he once has yearned for. Before things come to a crisis, Sweden has represented Elysium to him: Yossarian "would certainly have preferred Sweden, where the level of intelligence was high and where he could swim nude with beautiful girls with low demurring voices." But Sweden then "was out of reach," and at the story's close it may still be. Though the movie makes Yossarian ridiculous, rowing hopelessly away in his tiny raft for Sweden, the novel's Yossarian is more realistic:

"'You'll never get there,'" Major Danby warns. "'You can't run away to Sweden. You can't even row.'"

"'But I can get to Rome,'" Yossarian says, "'if you'll keep your mouth shut when you leave here and give me a chance to catch a ride.'"

Rather than swimming nude with beautiful girls, Yossarian's goal is more spartan now, to live accordingly to his "moral principle" or "responsibilities"—to march not in Scheisskopf's parade nor in Cathcart's and Korn's, but to the beat of his own drummer—specifically, at first, to rescue Nately's whore's kid sister from the hell of "The Eternal City" and save her life by taking her with him to Sweden.

He has chosen the harder way. Although he refuses the martyrdom of a court-martial, he has also renounced the free trip home to a hero's welcome. "'Your conscience will never let you rest,'" Danby warns, but Yossarian laughs: "'God bless it…. I wouldn't want to live without strong misgivings.'" Yossarian has not bought a ticket to safety, either. The last time we see him, that latter-day fury Nately's whore slashes out at him. "The knife came down, missing him by inches."

"He took off," therefore, running not away from but toward his own honor. Like many in American fiction before him, by rebelling, he denies himself the easy, comfortable way. When I asked Heller if he was conscious of this radical tradition of renunciation, he replied in a letter dated February 8, 1971:

> I conceived the ending to my book first and wrote the book; and it was only in the years since that I dwelled upon it as being in an old tradition of alienation and renunciation. To the protagonists you mention [see above, Huck, Hester, Ike, etc.] can be added Ahab, Bartleby, Hightower (again Faulkner), to name a few.
>
> The difference, though, is that Yossarian does not make good his escape, but only tries, and that this attempt is illegal and turns him into a fugitive, thereby instituting a struggle between him and the authorities

in the environment he repudiates. It may have been an easy way out for me, but definitely not for him, who could have more safely and comfortably accepted the offer of the Colonels to turn him into a hero and send him home. My purpose was to raise a question rather than answer one; his action institutes a conflict rather than evades one. And if his mood is one of elation at the end, it is mainly because he has moved off dead center finally and begun to act for himself.

Yossarian, marching backwards by himself and then renouncing a hero's comfortable role, is our clearest dramatization of Thoreau's man who steps to the beat of a different drummer. In Heller's intention, Yossarian is not copping out, is not taking the easy way, but rather "moved off dead center finally." And in his peculiar world of horror and absurdity, he is ironically a "traditional" American rebel, like so many other cultural mavericks who have made their separate, principled peace.

Source: Walter R. McDonald, "He Took Off: Yossarian and the Different Drummer," in *The CEA Critic,* Vol. 36, No. 1, November, 1973, pp. 14–16.

Sources

Nelson Algren, "The Catch," in *Nation,* Vol. 193, November 4, 1961, pp. 357–58.

Whitney Balliett, in a review of *Catch-22,* in *The New Yorker,* December 9, 1961, p. 247.

Marcus K. Billson II, "The Un-Minderbinding of Yossarian: Genesis Inverted in *Catch-22,*" in *Arizona Quarterly,* Vol. 36, No. 4, Winter, 1980, pp. 315–29.

Morris Dickstein, "Black Humor and History: The Early Sixties," in *Partisan Review,* Vol. 43, No. 2, 1976, pp. 185–211, reprinted in his *Gates of Eden: American Culture in the Sixties,* Penguin, 1977, 1989, pp. 91-127.

Mike Frank, "Eros and Thanatos in *Catch-22,*" in *Canadian Review of American Studies,* Spring, 1976, pp. 77-87.

Eliot Fremont-Smith, "Kvetch-22," in *Village Voice,* March 5, 1979, pp. 74–75.

Jean E. Kennard, "Joseph Heller: At War with Absurdity," in *Mosaic,* Vol. IV, No. 3, Spring, 1971, pp. 75–87.

Richard Locke, "What I Like," in *New York Times Book Review,* May 15, 1997, pp. 3, 36–37.

Norman Mailer, "Some Children of the Goddess," in *Esquire,* July, 1963, reprinted in *Contemporary American Novelists,* edited by Harry T. Moore, Southern Illinois University Press, 1964, pp. 3–31.

Raymond M. Olderman, "The Grail Knight Departs," in *Beyond the Waste Land: A Study of the American Novel in the Nineteen-Sixties,* Yale University Press, 1972, pp. 94-116.

Carol Pearson, "*Catch-22* and the Debasement of Language," in *The CEA Critic,* November, 1974, pp. 30-5.

Orville Prescott, review of *Catch-22,* in *New York Times,* October 23, 1961, p. 27.

Richard G. Stern, "Bombers Away," in *New York Times Book Review,* October 22, 1961, p. 50.

For Further Study

Alex Cockburn, review in *New Left Review,* Vol. 18, January-February, 1963, pp. 87-92.
    Cockburn praises Heller's humor but criticizes him for never moving beyond parody into satire.

Review in *Daedalus: Journal of the American Academy of Arts and Sciences,* Vol. 92, No. 1, Winter, 1963, pp. 155-65.
    A scathing review of the novel, focusing on its immoral underpinnings and Heller's faults as a writer.

Gary Lindberg, "Playing for Real," in *The Confidence Man in American Literature,* Oxford University Press, 1982. 231-58.
    Lindberg contrasts Yossarian and Milo as confidence-men figures, and favorably compares Yossarian to Huckleberry Finn.

Robert Merrill, "The Structure and Meaning of *Catch-22,*" in *Studies in American Fiction,* Vol. 14, No. 2, Autumn, 1986, pp. 139-52.
    Merrill focuses on Heller's use of cyclical repetition of episodes that "move from the comic to the terrible" in the novel, causing the reader to reevaluate his own reactions to these episodes.

Robert Merrill, *Joseph Heller,* Twayne, 1987.
    Merrill examines Heller's thematic and technical concerns in his work.

Victor J. Milne, "Heller's 'Bologniad': A Theological Perspective on *Catch-22,*" in *Critique: Studies in Modern Fiction,* Vol 12, No. 2, 1970, pp. 50-69.
    This critical article examines Heller's use of the mock-epic form, as well as Heller's asserting a humanistic Christian ethic over a destructive competitive ethic.

James Nagel, editor, *Critical Essays on Joseph Heller,* G. K. Hall, 1984.
    A collection of critical essays on Heller's work.

George J. Searles, "Joseph Heller," in *Dictionary of Literary Biography, Volume 28: Twentieth Century American-Jewish Fiction Writers,* edited by Daniel Walden, Gale, 1984, pp. 101-107.
    An overview of the author's works and career.

David Seed, *The Fiction of Joseph Heller: Against the Grain,* Macmillan, 1989.
    A full-length study of Heller's body of work.

Leon F. Seltzer, "Milo's 'Culpable Innocence': Absurdity as Moral Insanity in *Catch-22,*" in *Papers on Language and Literature,* Vol 15, No. 3, Summer, 1979, pp. 290-310.
    Seltzer provides an in-depth study of Milo, focusing on his extreme commitment to capitalistic ideals and

the moral blindness that results from this commitment.

Jan Solomon, "The Structure of Joseph Heller's *Catch-22*," in *Critique,* Vol. 9, No. 2, 1967, pp. 46-57.

Solomon asserts that the differing time sequences of Yossarian's and Milo's stories reinforce the absurdity of the novel.

Jeffrey Walsh, "Towards Vietnam: Portraying Modern War," in *American War Literature 1914 to Vietnam,* Macmillan, 1982, pp. 185-207.

Walsh contends that the novel's satire, themes, and form distinguish it from the traditional war novel.

The Catcher in the Rye

J. D. Salinger

1951

Although *The Catcher in the Rye* caused considerable controversy when it was first published in 1951, the book—the account of three disoriented days in the life of a troubled sixteen-year-old boy—was an instant hit. Within two weeks after its release, it was listed number one on *The New York Times* best-seller list, and it stayed there for thirty weeks. It remained immensely popular for many years, especially among teenagers and young adults, largely because of its fresh, brash style and anti-establishment attitudes—typical attributes of many people emerging from the physical and psychological turmoil of adolescence.

It also was the bane of many parents, who objected to the main character's obscene language, erratic behavior, and antisocial attitudes. Responding to the irate protests, numerous school and public libraries and bookstores removed the book from their shelves. Holden simply was not a good role model for the youth of the 1950s, in the view of many conservative adults. Said J. D. Salinger himself, in a rare published comment, "I'm aware that many of my friends will be saddened and shocked, or shock-saddened, over some of the chapters in *The Catcher in the Rye*. Some of my best friends are children. In fact, all my best friends are children. It's almost unbearable for me to realize that my book will be kept on a shelf out of their reach." The clamor over the book undoubtedly contributed to its popularity among the young: It became the forbidden fruit in the garden of literature.

For some reason—perhaps because of the swirling controversies over his written works—Salinger retreated from the New York literary scene in the 1960s to a bucolic New Hampshire community called Cornish, where he has lived a very private life and avidly avoided the press. Despite the fact that he has granted few interviews, there is a substantial body of critical and biographical works about Salinger and his all-too-brief list of literary creations.

Author Biography

Born in 1919 to a prosperous Manhattan family, Jerome David Salinger grew up in a New York City milieu not unlike that of young Holden Caulfield. Being a diligent student was never his first priority: After he flunked out of several prep schools, including the prestigious McBurney School, his parents sent him to Valley Forge Military Academy in Pennsylvania, from which he graduated in 1936. (Many people believe he modeled Pencey Prep, the fictional school attended by Caulfield, after Valley Forge.) He briefly attended Ursinus College, also in Pennsylvania, and New York University, where he stayed one month.

It was not until he took a short story course at Columbia University that Salinger officially launched his literary career. His teacher, Whit Burnett, was the founder and editor of *Story* magazine, which gave a headstart to a number of mid-century fiction writers. Salinger's first published piece appeared in *Story*. Then he moved rapidly into the big time of slick commercial magazines, writing short pieces for *Collier's, Saturday Evening Post, Esquire, Good Housekeeping, Cosmopolitan* and the upscale *New Yorker.*

Salinger has consistently refused to allow anyone to republish his early stories—those written between 1941 and 1948. (However, they may still lurk among the microfilm or microfiche copies of old magazines in local libraries.) Several are about draftees in World War II and may mirror Salinger's own military experiences in that war. He served in the Army Signal Corps and the Counter-Intelligence Corps from 1942 to 1945, participating in the Normandy campaign and the liberation of France. Winner of five battle stars, he still found a way to keep writing during this period, toting a portable typewriter around in the back of his Jeep (as did Holden's brother, D. B., in the novel).

J. D. Salinger

The extant body of Salinger's work therefore consists (in addition to *The Catcher in the Rye*) of three collections of short stories: *Nine Stories* (1953), *Franny and Zooey* (1955) and *Raise High the Roof Beams* (1963)— plus, of course, his more recent book, *Hapworth 16, 1924* (1997), which is a republication of a former *New Yorker* novella.

Since the early 1960s, Salinger has lived in seclusion in rural New Hampshire, his privacy fiercely protected by loyal friends and neighbors. Married twice, he has two children, Margaret Ann and Matthew, from his second marriage. Both marriages ended in divorce.

Plot Summary

Part I—Holden Flunks out of Pencey Prep School

The Catcher in the Rye tells the story of Holden Caulfield, a teenage slacker who has perfected the art of underachievement. The novel begins with Holden flunking out of school for the fourth time. During the last days before his expulsion, he searches for an appropriate way to conclude his school experience, but he ends up getting so annoyed with his school and schoolmates that he leaves in the middle of the night on the next train home to New York City. Arriving home a few days earlier than his parents expect him, he hangs out in the city to delay the inevitable confrontation with his parents. When his money runs out, he considers hitchhiking out west, but he ultimately returns home, mainly to be with his younger sister Phoebe.

The first few chapters describe Holden's last days at Pencey Prep School in Agerstown, Pennsylvania. Advertisements portray Pencey as an elite school that grooms boys into sophisticated men, but Holden sees it as a nightmare of adolescence run amok. Fed up with everything about Pencey, Holden skips the football game against Pencey's rival to say good-bye to his history teacher, Mr. Spencer. He vaguely hopes that Spencer might give him some comfort and useful advice, but Spencer is a sick old man who simply lectures him with a thousand platitudes about not applying himself. Like Spencer, the other teachers and administrators rarely spend any time mentoring boys because they are too busy spouting off platitudes or kissing up to the wealthy parents visiting the school.

Moreover, Pencey's students do not fit the prep school ideal any more than its teachers do. Holden's classmate Robert Ackley, for example, is the quintessential adolescent nerd. His acne and unbrushed teeth make him physically repulsive, while his annoying social habits—such as barging into the room uninvited, asking annoying questions, and refusing to leave when asked—make him a general nuisance. Other students, like Holden's roommate Ward Stradlater, initially appear sophisticated, but even they are really phonies. Stradlater seems good-looking, but he is secretly a slob who never cleans his rusty old razor. He also appears to be a successful student, but he is really an ungrateful egotist who gets other people to do his assignments. Nevertheless, Holden still feels a certain affection even for these annoying phonies. He is annoyed by Ackley but still invites him to the movies, and he sees through Stradlater's phoniness but also notices his occasional generosity.

The tension between Holden and his classmates eventually climaxes in a fight between Holden and Stradlater. Stradlater annoys Holden by asking him to write his English paper, so he can go on a date with Jane Gallagher, an old friend of Holden's. Stradlater really angers Holden, however, when he returns from the date and begins insinuating that he did all kinds of stuff with Jane in the back seat of a car. Fed up with Stradlater's phony nice-guy image, Holden picks a fight. Strad-

later easily defeats the weaker Holden and gives him a bloody nose. After the fight, Holden retreats into Ackley's room to forget about Stradlater, but Ackley only makes Holden more lonely. Then Holden goes into the hall to escape Ackley, but the hall is just as lonely. Surrounded by Pencey's all-pervasive loneliness, Holden decides to return home immediately instead of waiting for school to finish. He quickly packs and heads for the train station late at night, but before departing he vents his frustration with his schoolmates one last time. Yelling loud enough to wake everyone, he screams his final farewell to his moronic classmates.

Part II—Holden's Adventures in New York City

The middle section of the novel describes Holden's adventures in New York City. As soon as he arrives in New York, he looks for something to do, since it is too late to call his friends. He calls Faith Cavendish, a stripper recommended by a friend, but she does not want to meet a stranger so late. After a failed attempt to get a date with some girls in the hotel bar, he takes a cab to another bar in Greenwich Village. When he returns to his hotel, a pimp named Maurice sets him up with a prostitute named Sunny, but Holden is too nervous to do anything with her. The next day Holden asks his old girlfriend, Sally Hayes, to a show. While waiting to meet her, he has breakfast with two nuns and buys a blues record for his sister. When he finally meets Sally, they go to a concert and go skating, but they eventually get into a fight and split up. After their fight, Holden meets an old classmate, Carl Luce, at the Wicker Bar, where they have a brief discussion until Holden gets drunk and starts asking inappropriately personal questions. After Carl leaves, the still-drunk Holden calls up Sally and makes a fool of himself.

Part III—Holden Returns Home

The last section of the novel describes Holden's return home. At first, Holden only wants to briefly say good-bye to his sister, Phoebe, so he sneaks into his house late at night in hopes of avoiding his parents. He successfully sneaks into the room where his sister sleeps, aided by the lucky coincidence that his parents are not home. At first, Phoebe is delighted to see Holden, but she gets upset when she realizes that he has flunked out again. She asks him why he flunked out, and he blames it on his terrible school. After listening to Holden's excuses, Phoebe criticizes him for being too pessimistic. Holden tries to deny this by explaining

Men at the Swing Rendezvous club in Greenwich Village, 1955.

how he likes lots of things, but he can only think of a few: his dead brother Allie, a kid named James Castle who died at one of his schools, and Phoebe. In the end, Phoebe forces Holden to admit that he is a rather pessimistic failure. In the passage that gives the book its title, Holden explains that he cannot imagine himself fitting into any of the roles that society expects him to perform, like growing up to be a lawyer or scientist. Instead, he can only imagine being a catcher in the rye who stands at the edge of a large rye field watching over and protecting little kids from danger.

> "You know that song, 'If a body catch a body comin' through the rye'? I'd like—"
>
> "It's 'If a body *meet* a body coming through the rye'!" old Phoebe said. "It's a poem. By Robert *Burns*."
>
> "I *know* it's a poem by Robert Burns."
>
> She was right, though. It *is* "If a body meet a body coming through the rye." I didn't know it then, though.
>
> "I thought it was 'If a body catch a body,'" I said. "Anyway, I keep picturing all these little kids playing some game in this big field of rye and all. Thousands of little kids, and nobody's around—nobody big, I mean—except me. And I'm standing on the edge of some crazy cliff. What I have to do, I have to catch everybody if they start to go over the cliff— I mean if they're running and they don't look where

they're going I have to come out from somewhere and *catch* them. That's all I'd do all day. I'd be the catcher in the rye and all. I know it's crazy, but that's the only thing I'd really like to be. I know it's crazy."

In this passage, Salinger brilliantly blends the two sides of Holden's character. On the one hand, Holden admits that he *is* a failure: he is incapable of even imagining himself functioning in the adult world. On the other hand, however, Holden is not *only* a failure: he is also a deeply sensitive and compassionate person, albeit in an unorthodox way. In particular, he understands and cares about people who are outcasts or powerless. Phoebe seems to understand and accept this unorthodox sensitivity because she eventually reconciles herself to him, and they celebrate their reconciliation by dancing until their parents return and Holden has to sneak back out of the house.

After sneaking out of the house, Holden spends the night with his favorite teacher, Mr. Antolini, but he leaves early in the morning when he wakes up to find Mr. Antolini stroking his hair. Confused by such unusual behavior, Holden spends the morning wandering the streets until he eventually decides to hitchhike out west. He leaves a note at Phoebe's school telling her to meet him at the museum so they can say good-bye, but Phoebe shows up carrying her own belongings in a suitcase because she wants to go with Holden. At this point, Holden realizes how important they are to each other, and he finally decides to return home and face his parents. The novel never actually describes what happens next, but it suggests that Holden faces the dreadful confrontation with his parents and then later experiences some sort of nervous breakdown. The novel concludes with Holden looking back at all the people he has described and fondly remembering how he likes them despite their annoying and phony qualities.

Characters

Robert Ackley

Holden's unpleasant dormmate, whose personal habits are dirty and whose room stinks. Holden suspects that Ackley does not brush his teeth and describes them as mossy. Cursed with acne, Ackley constantly picks at the sores. Ackley dislikes Stadlater, calling him a "son of a bitch." Holden finds Ackley disgusting but appears to feel sorry for him at the same time.

Mr. Antolini

Holden's former English teacher, Mr. Antolini, "the best teacher I ever had," invited Holden to come right over, even though Holden probably woke him and his wife up in the middle of the night. Mr. Antolini asked why Holden was no longer at Pencey, warned him about heading for a fall, and wrote down a quote on paper for him: "The mark of the immature man is that he wants to die nobly for a cause, while the mark of the mature man is that he wants to live humbly for one." Later that night, after falling asleep on the couch, Holden wakes up to find Mr. Antolini patting his head in the dark. Holden leaps up, convinced Mr. Antolini is a pervert, and rushes out of the apartment. Later Holden is unsure whether his reaction was mistaken.

Allie Caulfield

Allie Caulfield is Holden's younger brother. While he has died of leukemia, he is very much alive throughout the book. Holden refers to him as still living and even talks to him. Bright and charming, Allie is/was Holden's best friend other than Phoebe.

D. B. Caulfield

D.B. Caulfield is Holden's and Phoebe's older brother. He is a successful and financially secure screenwriter in Hollywood. But Holden feels that D.B. has prostituted his art for money and should instead be writing serious works. While D.B. shows great solicitude for Holden, the relationship between the brothers is distant.

Holden Caulfield

Holden Caulfield is a deeply troubled sixteen-year-old boy who is totally alienated from his environment and from society as a whole. He looks on people and events with a distaste bordering on disgust. The reader can view him either as an adolescent struggling with the angst of growing up (the Peter Pan syndrome) or as a rebel against what he perceives as hypocrisy (phoniness) in the world of adults (i.e., society).

The novel is the recollection of three depressing days in Holden's life when his accumulated anger and frustration converge to create a life crisis. The events of this long weekend eventually propel him to a hospital where he is treated for both physical and mental disorders. Since the book is written in the first person, we see all people and events through Holden's eyes. He tells his story from the vantage point of the 17-year-old Caulfield, who is still in a California hospital at the outset of the book.

He begins with a statement of anger that includes the reader in its sarcasm:

> "If you really want to hear about it, the first thing you'll probably want to know is where I was born, and what my lousy childhood was like, and how my parents were occupied and all before they had me and all that David Copperfield kind of crap, but I don't feel like going into it, if you want to know the truth.... I'm not going to tell you my whole goddam autobiography or anything. I'll just tell you about this madman stuff that happened to me around last Christmas just before I got pretty run-down and had to come out here and take it easy.... Where I want to start telling about is the day I left Pencey Prep."

Holden has once again flunked out of prep school, where he failed every subject but English. On this day, he says goodbye to his history teacher, Mr. Spencer, who is home with the grippe. He views the sick man with both sympathy and disgust and escapes hastily after the teacher begins to lecture him about flunking out of three prep schools.

The novel continues with equally flawed encounters with two fellow students, Bob Ackley and his playboy roommate, Ward Stradlater. Holden decides to leave Pencey that very night.

He packs his belongings, heads to the railroad station and grabs a train to New York City. There he embarks on a harrowing weekend staying at hotels, frequenting bars, and trying desperately to communicate with everyone he meets—the mother of a classmate (to whom he lies about his identity), hangers-out in bars, taxi drivers, a prostitute and her pimp, and two nuns in a restaurant. His two most memorable encounters are with his old friend, the pseudo-sophisticated Sally Hayes, and a former schoolmate, Carl Luce. Both take place on Sunday.

Late Sunday night—thoroughly chilled from sitting in Central Park and having used up most of his money and everyone else's patience—Holden sneaks into his family's apartment. He wakes up his engaging ten-year-old sister, Phoebe. Phoebe is the only human being with whom Holden can communicate except for the memory of Allie, for whom he continually grieves. Phoebe represents the innocence and honesty of childhood, which is all Holden truly respects—a viewpoint shared in part by Salinger himself. (In contrast, Holden sees his older brother, D.B., as a "prostitute" because he has sold out his art, becoming a Hollywood scriptwriter instead of what Holden views as a serious writer.)

Phoebe is direct and blunt. When she learns that Holden has been expelled from yet another private school, her instant comment is, "Daddy'll *kill* you." And of course that's what Holden has been running away from all weekend—confronting his parents about his expulsion. Later, Phoebe tells him: "You don't like anything that's happening … You don't like any schools. You don't like a million things. You *don't.*" Holden is stunned and defensive. When he tries to think of something he likes, he finally comes down to nothing but Allie and Phoebe. He tells Phoebe that he's going to hitchhike to Colorado and start a new life there.

Still avoiding his parents, he arranges to spend the rest of Sunday night with a former favorite English teacher, Mr. Antolini, and his somewhat frowsy wife. During the night, he awakes to find Antolini stroking his hair. He immediately panics, deciding that Antolini is just another pervert in a world full of twisted people, and flees the Antolini apartment.

On Monday, he goes to Phoebe's school to leave a message for her to meet him at the Museum of Natural History. He wants to say goodbye. When Phoebe shows up, she is dragging a huge suitcase along the sidewalk. She intends to go with him. This is not in his plan at all. Instead, he takes her to the Central Park Zoo. While watching her ride on the merry-go-round, he worries that she'll fall off while trying to catch the gold ring. "The thing with kids is, if they want to grab for the gold ring, you have to let them do it, and not say anything. If they fall off, they fall off, but it's bad if you say anything to them," muses Caulfield. This, in a way, is the end of a dream he has told Phoebe:

> " … I keep picturing all these little kids playing some game in this big field of rye and all. Thousands of little kids, and nobody's around—nobody big, I mean—except me. And I'm standing on the edge of some crazy cliff. What I have to do, I have to catch everybody if they start to go over the cliff—I mean if they're running and they don't look where they're going. I have to come out from somewhere and *catch* them. That's all I'd do all day. I'd just be the catcher in the rye and all. I know it's crazy, but that's the only thing I'd really like to be. I know it's crazy."

Is this a turning point in Holden's withdrawal from the world—a point at which he know he has to accept the inevitable realities of life and people? Or will he continue to run away toward his dream of saving the world?

We leave Holden where we found him—or he found us—in the California hospital. When he is well, his brother D.B. will drive him back East, where he will attend yet another school.

Holden Caulfield is both tragic and funny, innocent and obscene, loving and cruel, clear-sighted yet viewing the world from a warped perspective, an expert in identifying phonies and the greatest phony himself. Of course, how you see Holden depends upon your own point of view. For many young readers of the book, especially in the 1950s and '60s, Holden still represented the true reality—the innocent abroad in a corrupt world. For older readers, he represents the angst of adolescence in its nightmarish extreme. For the ultraconservative, he still remains a threat to the status quo.

Phoebe Caulfield

Phoebe Caulfield, Holden Caulfield's pretty, redheaded ten-year-old sister, is straightforward and independent. She says exactly what she means. She does not share Holden's disenchanted view of the world. Quite the opposite, she scolds Holden for not liking anything at all. This hurts him very much because Phoebe is his favorite person—the only one with whom he can truly communicate. Phoebe is bright, well-organized, and creative. She keeps all her school work neatly in notebooks, each labeled with a different subject. She also loves to write books about a fictional girl detective named Hazle [sic] Weatherfield, but according to Holden, she never finishes them. Holden delights in taking her to the zoo and the movies and other places, as did their dead brother, Allie. Her directness and honesty are both refreshing and amusing.

Faith Cavendish

Faith Cavendish is the first person Holden calls when he gets to New York City. He met her previously at a party, where she was the date of a Princeton student. A burlesque stripper, she is supposed to be an "easy" conquest. She turns down Holden's invitation to get together and wishes him a nice weekend in New York.

Jane Gallagher

While she does not appear in the book, Jane Gallagher is very much present. Holden has a crush on this attractive and interesting young woman, who dances well and plays golf abominably. He resents the fact that his roommate, Stadlater, takes her out on a date and suspects that Stadlater, who likes to brag about his alleged sexual conquests, has forced her to have sex with him. When he first arrives in New York, Holden wants to call her up, but he never actually does so.

Sally Hayes

Sally Hayes is Holden's very attractive ex-girl-friend. He considers her stupid, possibly because she has an affected, pseudo-sophisticated manner. But he makes a date with her anyway. They go ice skating in Rockefeller Center, then go to a bar. Holden asks her to go away with him to Massachusetts or Vermont. She refuses, pointing out that they are much too young to set up housekeeping together and that college and Holden's career come first.

Holden doesn't want to hear about a traditional career. He becomes angry and tells Sally she's a "royal pain in the ass." She "hit the ceiling" and left. Later, drunk, he calls her late at night to tell her that, yes, he will come to help trim her family's Christmas tree.

Horwitz

Horwitz is the second taxi driver Holden encounters in New York City. Holden tries to strike up a conversation with him about where the ducks in Central Park go when the water in the lake freezes over. But Horwitz obviously considers Holden somewhat of a loony and is abrupt with him.

Carl Luce

Carl Luce, Holden's former schoolmate, ostensibly his Student Adviser, was about three years older and "one of these very intellectual guys—he had the highest I.Q. of any boy at Whooton."

Holden called him, hoping to have dinner and "a slightly intellectual conversation," but Luce could only meet him for a drink at the Wicker Bar at ten that evening.

He arrived saying he could only stay a few minutes, ordered a martini, kept trying to get Holden to lower his voice and change the subject. Before leaving, he suggested that Holden call his father, a psychoanalyst, for an appointment.

Mrs. Morrow

Mrs. Morrow is the mother of Holden's classmate, Ernest. Holden runs into her on the train to New York. They have a superficial conversation in which Mrs. Morrow is very friendly. So is Holden— but he lies about his identity because he doesn't want Mrs. Morrow to know he has been kicked out of school.

Piano Player in the Wicker Bar

Holden encounters the Wicker Bar's "flitty" piano player in the men's room. He asks him to find out whether the waiter delivered his message to the singer, Valencia, whom Holden wanted to invite to his table. The piano man, seeing how drunk Holden is, tells him to go home.

Lillian Simmons

Lillian Simmons is D.B.'s ex-girlfriend. Holden's main observation about her: "She has big knockers." Holden encounters her in Ernie's, a Greenwich Village hangout, where she introduces Holden to her companion, Navy Commander "Blop."

Mr. Spencer

Mr. Spencer is Holden Caulfield's history teacher at Pencey. Before leaving on Saturday of his long weekend, Holden goes to Spencer's house to say goodbye. Spencer, ill with the grippe, is wearing pajamas and a bathrobe. Holden finds old men dressed this way to be pathetic, with their pale, skinny legs sticking out under their bathrobes and their pajama tops askew, revealing their pale, wispy chests. Spencer obviously likes Caulfield, but he cannot resist giving him a lecture on his poor performance in history. Holden listens, agrees, and leaves as soon as he can.

Ward Stradlater

Ward Stradlater is Holden's obnoxious roommate at Pencey Prep. A playboy, he asks Holden to write an essay on a room or a house for him while he goes out on a date with Jane Gallagher, the girl Holden really cares about. A resentful Holden writes an essay about his brother Allie's baseball glove, on which Allie scribbled Emily Dickinson poems. A secret slob (he shaves with a dirty, rusty razor), Stradlater makes a good appearance. Smooth and slick, he likes to boast about his alleged sexual prowess. When he returns from his date, he is irate because Holden has written an essay about a baseball glove instead of a house. Holden tears it up, has an argument with Stradlater, and ends up in a fistfight with him.

Sunny

Sunny is the prostitute Holden requests. When she comes to his room in the Edmont Hotel, she discovers that Holden just wants someone to talk with. She leaves in disgust. Later, she returns with her pimp, Maurice, the hotel's elevator operator. They demand another five dollars for her time. Holden protests, and after she takes the money from his wallet.

Three girls from Seattle

After checking in and calling Faith Cavendish, Holden goes to the bar of the Edmont Hotel—"a goddam hotel" that was "full of perverts and morons," comments Holden. In the bar, he strikes up a conversation with three thirty-ish girls from Seattle who are spending their vacation touring New York City. He dances with them all, one by one, but the whole experience fizzles and he leaves the bar, calls a cab, and goes to Ernie's, a night club in Greenwich Village.

Two Nuns

Two nuns with whom Holden strikes up a conversation in a restaurant. They are both school teachers, and Holden charms them with his expressions of enthusiasm about English literature. Since they have a wicker collection basket with them, Holden gives them $10 as a contribution to their charity.

Themes

Alienation and Loneliness

The main theme that runs through this book is alienation, whether the book is read as the funny/tragic account of a deeply troubled, rebellious, and defensive teenager or as a commentary on a smug and meaningless social milieu. Phoebe sums up Holden's sense of separateness from and anger at other people when she tells him he doesn't like anything. Holden's red hunting cap, which he dons when he is most insecure, is a continuing symbol throughout the book of his feeling that he is different, doesn't fit into his environment, and, what's more, doesn't want to fit in.

Failure

A second theme is that of failure. Holden continually sets himself up for failure, then wears it like a badge of courage. Thus he fails in every encounter with other people in the book with the exception of Phoebe. Why would a sixteen-year-old want to fail? Failure serves as a great attention-getting device. And perhaps, more than anything, Holden wants attention from his parents, the absent characters in the book. What Holden really longs for, most likely, is acceptance and love.

Guilt and Innocence

Holden is deceitful and manipulative in most of his dealings with others. And he knows this all too well and even boasts of his prowess as a liar. But throughout the book we glimpse another Holden, the one who feels sorry for the people he cons. His basic kindness comes through in glimpses, particularly in the passage where he reveals that the only thing he would like to be is a "catcher in the rye" protecting innocent children from falling into the abyss of adulthood.

Anger

Holden is angry at everyone except Allie and Phoebe and perhaps the ducks in the pond in Central Park. Anger, of course, is the flip side of hurt. Holden is wounded by his disappointment in the faults of the world and frustrated because he finally realizes that he can't fix them. His failures may also be a way of acting out his anger at his parents and society at large.

Sexuality

Holden struggles with his emerging sexuality. He is unable to relate in any meaningful way to the girls he encounters along the way, writing them off as sex objects. He writes off other males as perverts or morons and views their sexuality with disgust. Confusion about sexual identity is common in adolescents. For Holden, it is terrifying.

Topics for Further Study

- Investigate current research on adolescent psychology. According to current theory, argue whether Holden Caulfield is a typical troubled adolescent or a seriously mentally ill young man.

- Is Holden Caulfield a reliable narrator? Why or why not?

- Compare Holden's generation of the 1940s to today's generation. How are the two cultures similar and different?

Courage

Courage is one of the subtle themes running throughout the novel. Holden, in his own twisted way, confronts the demons in his life and, therefore, stands a chance of wrestling them to the floor.

Style

Narrator

In essence, we have three narrators of the events that take place in this book. The first is the author, J. D. Salinger, who was looking back in anger (or in creativity) from his thirty-two-year-old vantage point. The second is the seventeen-year-old Holden, still institutionalized, who tells the story as a recollection. And the third, and most immediate, is the sixteen-year-old Holden who does all the talking. The form of the narration is first person, in which a character uses "I" to relate events from his or her perspective.

Stream of Consciousness

The technique of the narration is a form known as "stream of consciousness." While the book proceeds in a rough chronological order, the events are related to the reader as Holden thinks of them. Wherever his mind wanders, the reader follows. Notice how his language often appears to be more like that of a ten-year-old than that of a smart six-

teen-year-old. This is a continuing demonstration of Holden's unwillingness to grow up and join the hypocritical adult world that he despises. Holden's conversation in the Wicker Bar with Luce demonstrates this reluctance aptly, when Luce expresses annoyance at Holden's immaturity.

Setting

The settings for *The Catcher in the Rye*—Pencey Prep and New York City—were the settings for J. D. Salinger's early life as well, although the novel is not strictly autobiographical. Through his description of Holden's history teacher, Mr. Spencer, and his portrayals of Holden's fellow students, Salinger recreates the stifling atmosphere of a 1940s prep school, where a sense of alienation often resulted from not conforming to narrow social standards. The New York City where Holden spent his nightmare weekend is the same Manhattan where Salinger grew up—smaller, a little homier, and a lot less glitzy than the New York City of today. And Holden's home and family are similar to those of Salinger. However, Salinger had only one sibling, a brother. From the taxi ride, to the seedy hotel where Holden stayed, to Rockefeller Center to Central Park, Holden's New York is tangible, real, and plays an active role like any other character in the book. The descriptions of places and events are colorful and immediate. Salinger entices us into Holden's world whole and without resistance. He is a master of vivid story telling.

Symbolism

The book is rich in symbolism. The author drops hints of the meaning of its title twice before we find out what it is. The first time, Holden hears a little boy in New York sing-songing "If a body meet a body comin' through the rye," an Americanization of Robert Burns's poem and the song it inspired. The second time, Holden is with Phoebe and brings up the topic, referring to the song as "If a body *catch* a body comin' through the rye." Phoebe corrects him. But Holden's dream of being a catcher in the rye (derived from the second line of the poem) persists. He will save the children from adulthood and disillusionment.

Holden's red hat is an abiding symbol throughout the book of his self-conscious isolation from other people. He dons it whenever he is insecure. It almost becomes his alter ego. After he gives it to Phoebe, she gives it back to him. We do not know at the end of the book whether he still needs this equivalent of a security blanket.

Historical Context

Postwar Prosperity

The events in *The Catcher in the Rye* take place in 1946, only a year after the end of World War II. Adults at this time had survived the Great Depression and the multiple horrors of the war. Paradoxically, the war that wounded and killed so many people was the same instrument that launched the nation into an era of seemingly unbounded prosperity. During the postwar years, the gross national product rose to $500 billion, compared with $200 billion in prewar 1940. In unprecedented numbers, people bought houses, television sets, second cars, washing machines, and other consumer goods. No wonder the nation wanted to forget the past and to celebrate its new beginnings. The celebration took the form of a new materialism and extreme conservatism. Traditional values were the norm. People did not want to hear from the Holden Caulfields and J. D. Salingers of the era. They were in a state of blissful denial.

Holden has withdrawn from this society enough to see it from a different perspective. He abhors the banality and hypocrisy he sees in the adult world and is therefore reluctant to participate in it, so his behavior, while that of an adolescent trying to affirm his own identity, also symbolizes the perceived shallowness of people and society. Most of the things Holden fears peak in the 1950s, when conservatism, rigid morality, and paranoid self-righteousness held the nation in a tight grip. Small wonder that 1950s parents assailed Salinger's novel when it hit book stores and libraries in 1951. It undermined the foundations of their beliefs and threatened to unsettle their placid but pleasant existence, which was sustained by their hatred of an outside enemy—communism.

Cold War Concern

Despite the materialistic prosperity of the 1950s, many people were concerned about what appeared to be a troubling future. The Soviet Union acquired nuclear technology soon after the war, and the successful launch of the first artificial satellite, Sputnik, in 1957 appeared to give the Russians a threatening advantage over the United States. Americans also questioned the success of their educational system, which had failed them in the space race. The fear of nuclear war became so pervasive that students were regularly drilled on how to "duck and cover" in the case of an attack, and many families built bomb shelters in their back-

yards and stocked them with food and other supplies to survive a possible holocaust.

Education

In 1950 about ten percent of all children were educated in Catholic schools, which at the time received federal funding. This became a topic for debate as people disputed whether or not private institutions should receive taxpayer money. Public schools that employed Roman Catholic nuns as teachers also became a target of debate, as some states, such as Wisconsin, denied these schools public support. Such actions were supported by the National Education Association, which took a strong antireligious stance. On the other hand, the National Catholic Educational Association argued that Catholic citizens supported public schools, and so it was unfair to deny parochial schools funding when they were meeting the same educational goals. Religion was more prevalent in public schools during the 1950s; religious topics were routinely taught in public schools: students listened to Bible readings (which were required in twelve states and the District of Columbia), and many students were given "released-time" breaks, during which they were allowed to leave school for one hour a week to attend religious classes.

Pressure to Conform

Social pressures to conform were intense in the 1950s, not only in politics but also within the nation's educational system, which enjoyed multiple infusions of government funds. A college education became the passport to prosperity, especially after the G.I. bill of 1944 helped pay for war veterans' higher education. Corporations grew rapidly to meet the increasing demands of consumers and sopped up the growing number of skilled employees. Dress codes and embedded company cultures muted individualism. Jobs for white males were secure, while women stayed home and raised the many children ushered in by the postwar "Baby Boom."

The Growing Generation Gap

The "Baby Boom" caused Americans to pay more attention to the younger generation. While *Catcher in the Rye* was somewhat before its time in this regard, the subject had particular relevance in the years after its publication. Lifestyles began to change dramatically as teenagers began to date and become sexually active at a younger age. Teenagers became more rebellious, a trend that their parents viewed to be strongly influenced by a

Compare & Contrast

- **1950s:** Religion is an integral part of many classrooms. Bible readings and regular lessons about religious topics are included in course plans.

  Today: The separation of Church and State is rigorously upheld and children do not study religious texts; prayer in schools becomes a burning issue, and there is growing pressure from religious factions to have educators teach creationism to counterbalance lessons in Charles Darwin's theory of evolution.

- **1950s:** Only about 58% of students finish high school, but jobs are so plentiful that employment rates remain high. Employer loyalty is the norm, and employees often remain with one company until they retire.

  Today: Most employers that offer jobs with living-wage incomes require employees to have college degrees, even for low-level positions. Routine layoffs and downsizing largely eliminate company loyalty, and it becomes common for workers to switch jobs and even careers.

- **1950s:** Classroom curricula focus on basic skills, including reading, writing, and arith-

metic, but the inclusion of science in classes becomes a growing priority as the educational system tries to prepare students for the needs of a more technology-oriented world.

  Today: Educators aim to give students well-rounded educations that include sex education and an emphasis on multicultural studies; parents become concerned that children are not being taught the basics and that high school students are graduating without knowing how to read. Educators recognize the need to train students in the use of computers, which become common equipment in classrooms and libraries.

- **1950s:** Postwar prosperity brings with it a preoccupation with material goods as the middle-classes enjoy unprecedented buying power; children begin to rebel against this crass materialism and conservatism, and nonconformist icons like actor James Dean become popular.

  Today: Adults who were the rebellious children of the 1950s and 1960s long for a return of the "family values" of the 1950s; "family values" becomes a campaign buzz phrase for politicians as the American people return to conservative beliefs.

---

new, decadent form of music called rock 'n' roll. This new attitude of rebelliousness was typified by Hollywood actors such as James Dean and Marlon Brando, the bohemian lifestyle of the beatniks, and later in the literature of Jack Kerouac and Alan Ginsberg. Juvenile delinquency became an alarming problem and was considered a major social issue. Teens were skipping classes and committing crimes, and parents were alarmed by their children's lack of respect for authority.

Critical Overview

Mixed reviews greeted J. D. Salinger's first novel, *The Catcher in the Rye,* published on July

16, 1951. *New York Times* critic Nash K. Burger, for example, lauded the book as "an unusually brilliant first novel," and *Chicago Tribune* reviewer Paul Engle called the novel "engaging and believable." In contrast, T. Morris Longstreth stated in the *Christian Science Monitor* that "the book was not fit for children to read." Regarding Holden Caulfield, the book's teenage narrator and protagonist, Longstreth wrote: "Fortunately there cannot be many of him yet. But one fears that a book like this given wide circulation may multiply his kind—as too easily happens when immorality and perversion are recounted by writers of talent whose work is countenanced in the name of art of good intention." In the novel's defense, critic James Bryan wrote in *PMLA:* "The richness of spirit in

Lever House on Park Avenue, a typical 1950s office in New York City.

this novel, especially of the vision, the compassion and the humor of the narrator, reveal a psyche far healthier than that of the boy who endured the events of this narrative. Through the telling of his story, Holden has given shape to, and thus achieved control of, his troubled past."

It can be argued that *The Catcher in the Rye* is as much a critique of society as a revelation of the rebellion and angst of a teenage boy. The book takes potshots at a post-World War II society full of self-righteousness and preoccupied by the pursuit of the "American Dream" of everlasting prosperity. Salinger depicts this goal as being empty and meaningless. Commented the great American novelist William Faulkner, who praised Salinger's novel, "When Holden attempted to enter the human race, there was no human race there."

The reader never finds out how Holden turns out. Will he compromise with the realities of people and society, becoming like the people he despised? Will the banality of everyday events engulf his reluctant coming of age, leaving him a tormented misfit for the rest of his life? Or will he become a superhero, leading others out of the slough of the ordinary and into a more enlightened view of life? The reader will never know unless Salinger writes a sequel. His most recent novel, *Hapworth 16, 1924,* released in the spring of 1997, is a re-

publication of a long short story that appeared in the *New Yorker* in the 1960s. The featured character in the new book is Seymour Glass, member of another well-to-do fictional New York family depicted in a number of Salinger short stories. For some readers and critics, however, the endless saga of the eccentric Glass family eventually wore out its welcome. *The Catcher in the Rye* and *Hapworth 16, 1924* are the only two novels Salinger has thus far written. But he did write a wealth of short stories for such magazines as the *New Yorker, Saturday Evening Post,* and *Collier's.*

If *The Catcher in the Rye* were introduced as a new book today, it would certainly not be considered as shocking now as it was in the 1950s. But it would still be viewed as a true and vivid portrait of adolescent angst. It can therefore rightly take its place among the literary classics of the twentieth century.

Criticism

Robert Bennett

In the following essay, Bennett, a doctoral candidate at the University of California—Berkeley, argues that despite its status as a "minor" classic, The Catcher in the Rye *is a work with literary sig-*

What Do I Read Next?

- *The Member of the Wedding* (1946) by Carson McCullers tells of an awkward young girl living in a southern town as she suffers the pangs of growing up and feelings of isolation.

- In her influential first novel, *The Outsiders* (1967), S. E. Hinton writes of how two gangs—the Socs, who are teens from well-off families, and the Greasers, who come from lower-income homes—come to blows that lead to murder. Hinton, who was a teenager when she wrote the novel, creates remarkable, sympathetic portraits of the troubled teens in the Greasers gang.

- In Judith Guest's *Ordinary People* (1976), a disturbed teenager comes to grips with the events underlying his attempted suicide with the help of his psychotherapist.

- *Three Friends* (1984), by Myron Levoy, in which an intelligent fourteen-year-old boy who enjoys chess and psychology becomes involved with Karen, a feminist activist, and her artistic friend, Lori; all three consider themselves outsiders and develop complex and troubled relationships with each other.

---

nificance that rewards the reader with several types of interpretations.

Even though *The Catcher in the Rye* is usually considered only a "minor" classic of American fiction, it is a very popular novel that frequently provokes strong reactions—both positive and negative—from its readers. In fact, *The Catcher in the Rye* is one of the most widely read and discussed works in the American literary canon. Despite its widespread popularity and significant reputation, however, some critics argue that it is too vulgar, immoral, and immature to be considered serious literature. Moreover, a few teachers and parents have censored the novel because they feel that it will corrupt children who read it. While there are undoubtedly subversive, or corrupt elements in the

novel, arguments for censoring it generally misrepresent its more nobler intentions and greatly exaggerate its subversive designs. Putting aside the overinflated claims of the novel's most extreme critics and supporters, the diversity and intensity of readers' reactions to *The Catcher in the Rye* suggest that the issues it raises are significant ones. Consequently, it seems likely that readers will continue to have heated discussions about this "minor" classic for a long time to come.

One of the issues that has been debated ever since the novel's initial publication is whether or not it qualifies as a significant work of literature. Does it offer significant insights into the complexities of human existence and the development of American culture, or does it simply appeal to vulgar adolescent minds with its obscene language, complaining about everything without developing any positive insights of its own? While some of the initial reviews of *The Catcher in the Rye* were negative, critics later acknowledged it as a significant literary work and demonstrated how the novel's narrative structure, themes, and character development resemble other great works of literature. For example, Arthur Heiserman and James E. Miller's essay, "J. D. Salinger: Some Crazy Cliff," helped establish the literary significance of *The Catcher in the Rye* by showing how it belonged to the long tradition of epic quest narratives in western literature. Similarly, Charles Kaplan's essay, "Holden and Huck: The Odysseys of Youth," points out similarities between *The Catcher in the Rye* and Mark Twain's *Huckleberry Finn.* Both novels are about a young man who tells the story of his own personal odyssey using his own comical wisdom and colloquial everyday language. Critic Lilian Furst compares *The Catcher in the Rye* to Russian novelist Fyodor Dostoyevsky's novels in the *Canadian Review of Comparative Literature.* Helen Weinberg compares it to Franz Kafka's novels in *The New Novel in America* while John M. Howell in his essay "Salinger in the Waste Land," compares it to T. S. Eliot's poetry.

Perhaps the most interesting aspect about *The Catcher in the Rye,* however, is that it redefines the focus of the literary text. Instead of focusing primarily on plot development like most traditional novels, *The Catcher in the Rye* focuses more on character development. In fact, most of the plot is mundane and uneventful; it only becomes interesting because Salinger makes the character of Holden and the perspective through which Holden narrates the story interesting. Consequently, when reading *The Catcher in the Rye* it is important to pay attention to how Salinger represents Holden's character, language, and world view. While some critics simply dismiss Holden's character as purely negative, vulgar, whining, and cynical, a more balanced reading of the novel could indicate that there is something more to Holden than his academic failures and adolescent cynicism: He is perceptive, sensitive, creative, and even intelligent in his own way.

There are several ways that critics have attempted to describe Holden's positive characteristics, including rather obvious childlike innocence. This quality is evident in a number of passages, including when Holden expresses his desire to be a catcher in the rye who protects little children from falling over the edge of a cliff, his fight with Stradlater for making sexual advances to Jane Gallagher, his inability to have sex with a prostitute, and his tender dance with his sister. In his essay "The Saint as a Young Man," Jonathan Baumbach, as other critics have, notes that Holden acts like a saint or savior of the innocent. It is this sensitive, innocent, and childlike side of Holden that makes him a complex and endearing character in spite of his vulgarity and immaturity.

Another way that critics have tried to show the positive side of Holden is by focusing on his demonstrated ability to use language creatively. After all, the one course that Holden passes is English. Not only does Holden write a good essay for himself but he also writes a good one for his roommate Stradlater. In addition to writing, Holden is a natural actor and storyteller. He is often seen imitating his classmates or mimicking roles from the movies. In fact, A. Robert Lee goes so far as to argue in his essay "Flunking Everything Else Except English Anyway" that Holden continually performs himself by endlessly putting on a new mask and new identity for each new situation. In the train scene for example, Holden makes up stories about one of his classmates in order to please his classmate's mother; he not only adopts a new identity for himself, but he also fabricates a whole new fictional history of life at Pencey. Speaking is another area of importance. Even if Holden may not amount to much else, he is always a smooth talker who can keep the reader interested simply by the way in which he creatively tells his story using the vernacular slang that American teenagers used in the early 1950s.

While such positive interpretations of Holden correct reductive interpretations that simply dismiss Holden as an immature cynic, Duane Edwards's essay, "Holden Caulfield: Don't Ever Tell Anybody Anything," advances an even more complex interpretation of Holden. Instead of trying either to redeem Holden as a saint or to condemn him as a pessimist, Edwards argues that Holden is an ironic character who critiques his phony culture but ends up participating in the same phony culture that he condemns. His argument becomes even more interesting when readers remember that Holden is the novel's narrator. By making such an unorthodox and unreliable character as Holden the narrator, Salinger subtly suggests that maybe readers cannot completely trust everything Holden tells them about himself and the world in which he lives. Obviously, the perspective of a cynical failure like Holden cannot be trusted completely as an accurate description of the way things really are, but neither can his compassionate wit be dismissed entirely. Consequently, the reader must always read between the lines like a detective looking for hints and clues that might help explain which of Holden's insights are valid and which are as phony as the phoniness he condemns.

Moving beyond purely literary interpretations, *The Catcher in the Rye* can also be interpreted from the perspective of the social sciences. In particular, many critics have advanced psychoanalytic interpretations of the novel because it repeatedly explores questions relating to death, sexuality, and processes of both psychological development and psychological breakdown. In general, these psychoanalytic interpretations usually try to get beneath the surface of Holden's psyche to discover some hidden force that explains why Holden thinks and acts the way that he does. One way to uncover the hidden layers of Holden's mind is to look back on his childhood in order to find some significant or traumatic event that might explain his current state of being. Clearly, one of the most traumatic, formative moments in Holden's childhood was the death of his brother Allie. Throughout the novel, Holden repeatedly thinks about his dead brother. For example, when Holden agrees to write a paper for his roommate Stradlater, he writes about Allie's baseball mitt. Or when Holden starts to have a breakdown while walking around New York City, he pleads in his mind with Allie to protect him. Perhaps as a result of this traumatic childhood experience involving death, Holden seems to be somewhat obsessed with it. For example, when Phoebe asks Holden to name people that he enjoys, the only people other than Phoebe that he can think of are all dead: Allie and James Castle, a boy who died at Holden's school. This obsession with death, therefore, might be one clue that can offer insight into the inner workings of Holden's mind.

Another place where one might find clues about Holden's psychological make-up is in his relationships with other people and especially in his sexual or almost sexual relationships with women. Throughout the novel, Holden is continually obsessed with women, but he rarely does anything about it. He likes Jane Gallagher, but they never get beyond holding hands. He even orders a hooker to his hotel room, but he decides that he only wants to talk. Instead of developing sexual or even intimate relationships with women, Holden seems to focus most of his emotional energy on his younger sister, Phoebe. While some critics have interpreted this as evidence of Holden's repressed incestual desires and psychological immaturity, others have interpreted it as simply an affectionate bond between siblings that demonstrates Holden's innocence. While the novel may not provide any definitive explanation of Holden's sexuality, sexuality is clearly an important and interesting aspect of his character.

A final way to interpret *The Catcher in the Rye* is to read it from a sociological perspective. Instead of simply analyzing Holden's individual psychological make-up, a sociological analysis probes deeper into the social and economic contexts that shape Holden's personality. Carol and Richard Ohmann's essay, "Reviewers, Critics, and *The Catcher in the Rye*," offers an excellent example of such an interpretation. In their Marxist analysis, the Ohmanns argue that critics' narrow focus on moral issues causes them to overlook how these moral issues are related to broader social and economic contexts. By situating the novel in its broader historical context at the beginning of the cold war, the Ohmanns argue that the novel is less about the morality of Holden's internal psychological character than it is about the capitalist economic system that produces Holden's character. As the Ohmanns point out, the people who Holden criticize are virtually all representatives of a corrupt capitalist society: Mr. Haas is the phony headmaster who gets money for the school by kissing up to wealthy parents while ignoring poorer parents; Mr. Ossenburger is the phony funeral parlor owner who makes money off of personal tragedies; and the majority of Holden's classmates are simply the spoiled children of similar bourgeois money-grabbers. As the Ohmanns demonstrate, Holden consistently directs his strongest criticisms against the evils of capitalism: the commercialization of culture, class-based social hierarchies, exploitative sexuality, phony image-minded people, etc. From a socioeconomic perspective, therefore, *The Catcher in the Rye* portrays the manners and follies of the rising

American bourgeois class during the post-World War II era of rapid capitalist expansion, and Holden represents a sensitive social critic who reveals the evils of this phony bourgeois society.

Source: Robert Bennett, in an essay for *Novels for Students*, Gale, 1997.

Susan K. Mitchell

In the following excerpt, Mitchell considers the significance of Holden Caufield being an unreliable narrator.

In the work, Holden has analyzed his family as a representative slice of society and has concluded that adult society is phony and corrupt. But can we really trust his observations of his family after he has told us that he lies? Is he not, like the Cretan who declared that all Cretans were liars, a person declaring that all people are phony? If everyone is phony, then he is phony, too! Although Holden has claimed that he is a liar, he does not always realize whether he is lying or telling the truth. The distinctions between truth and falsehood become blurred as he often adds the phrase "to tell you the truth" onto whatever he is saying. But does this catch phrase ensure that his words are any more truthful? This unambiguous rhetorical statement is restated in an even more paradoxical way when Holden tells Sally that he loves her and then comments to the reader, "It was a lie, of course, but the thing is, I *meant* it when I said it." Again we are forced to read the work, as de Man suggests [in his essay "Semiology and Rhetoric," appearing in *Contemporary Literary Criticism,* edited by Robert C. Davis, 1986], in "two entirely coherent but entirely incompatible" ways. Is he lying, or does he "mean" it? First we may claim that Holden is telling the truth: he is a liar, people are phony, society is corrupt. Or we may claim that Holden is lying: he is truthful, people are genuine, and society is untainted.

There are obvious problems with both sides of this paradox. Can Holden, people, and society be entirely unchanging—always lying, always corrupt, always phony? Or are there internal forces within each that cause them to change (un)willingly? Holden would argue that each is unchanging, labeled forever. In fact, this is how he presents his information to us. He may go out with Sally, but he does not harbor any hope that she will cast off her phoniness. He may loan Stradlater his coat, but he still believes Stradlater is a phony.

Because we view all of the events in the book through the eyes of one narrator, our observations are necessarily biased. Holden is an unreliable narrator not only because he is a self-proclaimed liar but also because he perceives reality in a simplistic way. In his work *S/Z* [1974], Roland Barthes outlines two ways of perceiving reality: *readerly* and *writerly.* Barthes explains these ideas in terms of reading books. He claims that the only way to read a different story is to reread the same book. By rereading, a person can learn how this book differs from itself rather than how it differs from other books. When a reader rereads a work, he is perceiving writerly. When a reader refuses to reread, Barthes maintains that he is condemned to "read the same story everywhere." Holden refuses to reread as he perceives reality readerly, seeing only the surface differences between people, not the underlying differences within each person. To perceive a person readerly would be to perceive in terms of overt, easily distinguishable differences.

Because Holden avoids investigating deeply, he sees the same story everywhere. Everyone is phony, he insists. But can we honestly believe him? Is he telling the truth? Even so, he is not passing on false or limited information since he has not gone to the trouble to read one story well. To approach accuracy, Holden would have to perceive a person writerly, to judge the fragmentation, the differences within the person, the covert, often contradictory intentions that war within and cause overt actions. We can draw conclusions only from the data which Holden perceives and selects to reveal to us (and he does select carefully as when he refuses to discuss his childhood or his parents); hence, we must be astute readers indeed lest we miss the multidimensionality of the characters that he develops. His readerly perception creates blinkers for the reader.

Throughout the novel, Holden tries to lull us into accepting his view of surrounding life as he makes statements that seem to make sense, but which, upon closer inspection, do not bear up to a writerly view. This simplistic mode of perception is revealed particularly through his description of his family. First of all, the Caulfield parents are described in such a way as to cause the blinkered reader to view them uncompromisingly as irresponsible, alienated, skittish parents. For example, the parents are off at work away from their children, who are scattered throughout the country: D. B. in Hollywood, Allie dead, Phoebe at home, and Holden at Pencey Prep. Mr. and Mrs. Caulfield seem to be isolated characters. The reader never meets Mr. Caulfield and only hears Mrs. Caulfield when Holden is hiding in Phoebe's room. Holden

will not tell much about his parents beyond his veiled opinion that they both are phony hypocrites. The reader is not even told their first names. From the beginning we are led to believe that they are hypersensitive about Holden's revealing their personal life because they want to protect their created image of conformed perfection. Because Mrs. Caulfield is a nervous woman who has smoked compulsively ever since Allie's death, Holden avoids confrontation about his being kicked out of Pencey Prep. He therefore hides from her as he stays in a hotel or in Mr. Antolini's apartment. Each of these examples appears to show that Mrs. Caulfield does not really communicate with her children. On the other hand, Mr. Caulfield is a lawyer. Holden makes no bones about his opinion of lawyers: they "make a lot of dough and play golf and play bridge and buy cars and drink Martinis and look like a hot-shot" and are phony but can't know it.

Holden's warped view of his parents denigrates them without even considering that the Caulfields may be blameless. Can we really trust Holden's view of his parents? Isn't he unethically stacking the deck so that we are prohibited from obtaining an objective view of them? We are given so few facts and scenes to describe them that we have trouble refuting Holden, except that we know he is holding something back from us. No couple could merit such a denunciation from a son. If what he has revealed about the Caulfields is true, carefully selected though the information may be, can we blame them for their anger, hysteria, and desire for privacy? These would be logical reactions if an offspring were so apathetic as to be kicked out of several reputable schools and then became anxious to write a book about his family while recovering from insanity. And what is wrong about working hard to support children, to enable them to have the best education possible? What exactly is phony about being a lawyer? Even though Holden's vagueness works well for him, making his parents appear base, mercenary, isolated, distant, and careless, it denies any redeeming qualities that would upset Holden's persuasive thesis that adult society is corrupt.

According to Holden, D. B. represents wholehearted acceptance of society's norms. In Holden's caustic terms, D. B. is a "prostitute" who lives in Hollywood, where he makes buckets of money producing popular movies, such as the Annapolis love story, which might prevent him from joining the family at Christmas. D. B. appears to symbolize the successful all-American man since he lives in Hollywood, one of the most prestigious areas of the country, displays a noticeable sign of wealth by owning a Jaguar, and has a "good-looking" albeit affected English girlfriend. However, D. B.'s own name is revealing of both society's worst qualities and his embracing of its values. Like many of the movies that he is writing, D. B.'s name is abbreviated, easy to remember, and void of significant meaning. The very fact that D. B.'s name is compressed into two initials makes one wonder what lies behind them. Just as his name used to mean something, he used to have something to say. But now as D. B. apparently bows to society's pressure and to his desire to pursue the American Dream, he loses the meaning in his life and therefore cannot communicate the message he once had, the message he once published in his short story, "The Secret Goldfish," one of Holden's favorites.

After being bombarded with these loaded examples of D. B.'s phoniness, we must ask certain questions to reveal whether Holden is right to condemn his brother. For instance, we should ask why it is wrong to display signs of wealth. Don't the signs reveal a truth about D. B.—that he is indeed wealthy? Also, does his meaningless name necessarily mean that he has no message of truth and beauty? D. B. is actually an unselfish, caring brother, as demonstrated by his numerous visits ("practically every week") with a recovering Holden. He does have other commitments, a girlfriend and work, that do keep him from devoting himself wholeheartedly to his immediate family; it is to his credit that he finds as much time as he does to visit his family. However, to prove his thesis, Holden holds fast, emphasizing that because D. B. has rejected an accepted art form and taken up the mass media that a technological society promotes, he has become visibly corrupt. But what is so corrupt about writing movies? Is it the medium that makes the difference? Can paper itself be any more artistic than celluloid? And is Holden really as against movies as he claims to be? If so, why does he volunteer to see so many? By seeing movies, Holden embraces that which he says he rejects. Although he distinguishes between "good" movies and "lousy" movies, he still claims that they are all phony. But what is the difference between a good movie and a good book? Holden does not answer our question. He doesn't follow his proclaimed norms; he is phony.

In Holden's readerly view, Allie represents immunity from the dangers of society. Allie is dead, escaped from the clutches of a culture that ultimately requires that children give up their inno-

cence and individuality. Fascinated with Allie's solution to the problem, Holden defies him, preserving him in his memory by carrying Allie's uniquely poem-laden baseball mitt, praying aloud to him, and remembering his good-natured innocence. At the beginning of the novel, Allie is Holden's ally, his closest friend and kin. Holden *wants* to ally himself with Allie, to lie down, subside, become extinct, to simply leave this corrupted Eden. Throughout the novel, Holden contemplates physical death in innumerable scenes, such as when he writes about Egyptian mummies in his history class, when he asks what the ducks do during winter, and when he remembers the suicide of James Castle.

However, does he want to unite himself with Allie because Allie truly is perfectly pure, or simply to assuage free-floating feelings of guilt associated with Allie's death? His guilt seems to arise primarily from an incident that occurred when Allie was alive. Holden and a friend decided to have a picnic and shoot their BB guns, and Allie wanted to go with them. However, Holden called him a child and would not let him come along. Now that Allie is dead, whenever Holden gets depressed, he does penance, telling Allie out loud, "Okay. Go home and get your bike and meet me in front of Bobby's house. Hurry up." Holden's recurring feelings of guilt distort his (and our) image of Allie. Did Holden refuse to allow Allie to join him on the expedition because Allie was not perfect? Looking back on the incident, Holden states, "[Allie] didn't get sore about it—he never got sore about anything—but I keep thinking about it anyway, when I get very depressed." Or was Holden the guilty party by refusing without a good reason to allow Allie to come along? In his guilt, Holden paints Allie larger than life.

Phoebus, the name of Apollo, means the genius of poetry. This association is not lost on Phoebe as she writes a synthesized gothic-detective thriller in which her protagonist, Hazle Weatherfield, is an orphan detective who has a father. Holden believes that Phoebe is also an orphan who has parents, but because they are alienated, they do not offer the example, guidance, and support that true parents should. Of course Holden proves this neglect as he chooses to tell us that although Phoebe is to play Benedict Arnold in "A Christmas Pageant for Americans," her father plans to fly to California on that day anyway. Also, her mother, instead of lecturing Phoebe when she admits to smoking, simply closes the subject with the irrelevant question "Do you want another blanket?" Because Phoebe is still young and alive, Holden transfers many of his guilt feelings about Allie to her, causing her to grow, in Holden's perception, more and more innocent and uncorrupted. She trusts Holden wholly as she gives him her Christmas money and packs a suitcase to run away with him. In spite of his guilt over Allie, he commits the same guilt-inducing act with Phoebe as he refuses to allow her to accompany him on the new expedition.

As pure as Holden makes Phoebe appear, she has a wisdom that belies her years. She shrewdly sees through Holden's facade of well-being, realizing that he doesn't like anything. When she tests him to prove her theory, he cannot name anything "really" that he likes. She is also a very literate young lady. She is able to identify Holden's song as belonging to Robert Burn's poem and to correct the miswording in it. She perceives reality writerly, as shown when she writes the same story over and over again. When her mother smells smoke and assumes that Phoebe has been smoking cigarettes, Phoebe is too quick—she, like Holden, lies about the truth, saying that she only took one puff of the cigarette when it was actually Holden who had been smoking. Again, when Mrs. Caulfield complains of a headache, Phoebe promptly supplies the remedy: "Take a few aspirins." Does Phoebe's covert wisdom support Holden's premise that society is corrupt? Does the thesis prove truer than he wants it to be? Holden wants to hold out for children, to proclaim their Edenic innocence. However, his flawed readerly perception blinds him to the writerly truth: not all is as easily categorizable as it appears.

Naturally, Holden is the only character shown to be heroically struggling with exactly how to relate to society. He is locked into a self that desires to be genuine but finds no way to return to the pastoral ideal. He believes that he is holed in, trapped by the games of phoniness that society requires its citizens to play. He tries to escape this trap by flunking out of school and by searching for a quiet retreat, only to discover that there is no pure retreat on earth—log cabins are distant and lonely, deserted museum rooms are corrupted with permanent obscenities, private hotel rooms lure prostitutes and pimps. Frustrated by the readerly evidence which he has gathered to support his thesis, Holden is himself fragmented and ravaged by the warring forces within him. For instance, within Holden, the desire to reject others conflicts with the desire to be accepted by others; he doesn't want to lend Stradlater his coat, but his overt actions belie this covert, warring want; he despises Ackely, but he invites him to see a movie; he hates movies, be-

lieving them to foster phoniness in society, but during the three days of the book he sees or talks about several; he craves truth, but he tells blatant lies. Despite his own inherent writerliness or differences within, Holden still perceives only readerly. He views himself as a liar, but he refuses to acknowledge that this means that he is phony, too....

What does this mean for us? What is Salinger trying to prove? Perhaps by making Holden unreliably readerly, he is saying that society is both phony and necessary. Holden's unreliability forces us to question everything about the subject: Holden's view, society's view, our own view as readers. The apparently stable themes are radically unstable; Holden does change, and society can, too, for society is neither entirely phony nor wholly pastoral. Instead, it is both one and the other. It cannot be placed in a fixed category since it is writerly.

[Although some critics believe] that there is a coherent, knowable meaning of a work, they refuse to analyze why the meaning varies so radically from one critic to the next. Of course, some of them would rationalize that one critic may not be as intelligent or educated as another. This is possible but does not really answer the fundamental question satisfactorily. Therefore the meaning is ultimately undecidable. Since this is a writerly text, a text that splits down the middle into positive and negative factions, the ultimate meaning of it is undecidable. The reader's expectations of having an orderly, coherent world of meaning are unraveled by the thread that holds the work together. Salinger places his story *en abyme,* to use [J. Hillis] Miller's term [as quoted from "Stevens' Rock and Criticism as Cure, II," in *Georgia Review,* 1976], so that it becomes undecidable. Society now appears genuine, now phony, now genuine again, and so on endlessly. There is an endless freeplay of meaning because the book lacks a genuine center—the apparent center of the book is actually phony. Therefore, the meaning of *The Catcher in the Rye* can never be totalized.

Source: Susan K. Mitchell, "To Tell You the Truth…" in *CLA Journal,* Vol. 36, No. 2, December, 1992, pp. 145–56.

Jonathan Baumbach

In the following excerpt, Baumbach explores the meaning of "innocence" in The Catcher in the Rye.

J. D. Salinger's first and only novel, *The Catcher in the Rye* (1951), has undergone in recent years a steady if overinsistent devaluation. The more it becomes academically respectable, the more it becomes fair game for those critics who are self-sworn to expose every manifestation of what seems to them a chronic disparity between appearance and reality. It is critical child's play to find fault with Salinger's novel. Anyone can see that the prose is mannered (the pejorative word for stylized); no one actually talks like its first-person hero Holden Caulfield. Moreover, we are told that Holden, as poor little rich boy, is too precocious and specialized an adolescent for his plight to have larger-than-prepschool significance. The novel is sentimental; it loads the deck for Holden and against the adult world; the small but corrupt group that Holden encounters is not representative enough to permit Salinger his inclusive judgments about the species. Holden's relationship to his family is not explored: we meet his sister Phoebe, who is a younger version of himself, but his father never appears, and his mother exists in the novel only as another voice from a dark room. Finally, what is Holden (or Salinger) protesting against but the ineluctability of growing up, of having to assume the prerogatives and responsibilities of manhood? Despite these objections to the novel, *Catcher in the Rye* will endure both because it has life and because it is a significantly original work, full of insights into at least the particular truth of Holden's existence. Within the limited terms of its vision, Salinger's small book is an extraordinary achievement; it is, if such a distinction is meaningful, an important minor novel.

Like all of Salinger's fiction, *Catcher in the Rye* is not only about innocence, it is actively for innocence—as if retaining one's childness were an existential possibility. The metaphor of the title—Holden's fantasy-vision of standing in front of a cliff and protecting playing children from falling (Falling)—is, despite the impossibility of its realization, the only positive action affirmed in the novel. It is, in Salinger's Manichean universe of child angels and adult "phonies," the only moral alternative—otherwise all is corruption. Since it is spiritually as well as physically impossible to prevent the Fall, Salinger's idealistic heroes are doomed either to suicide (Seymour) or insanity (Holden, Sergeant X) or mysticism (Franny), the ways of sainthood, or to moral dissolution (Eloise, D. B., Mr. Antolini), the way of the world. In Salinger's finely honed prose, at once idiomatically real and poetically stylized, we get the terms of Holden's ideal adult occupation:

> Anyway, I keep picturing all these little kids playing some game in this big field of rye and all. Thousands of little kids, and nobody's around—nobody big, I mean—except me. And I'm standing on the edge of some crazy cliff. What I have to do, I have to catch everybody if they start to go over the cliff—I mean if they're running and they don't look where they're going I have to come out from somewhere and *catch* them. That's all I'd do all day. I'd just be the catcher in the rye and all. I know it's crazy, but that's the only thing I'd really like to be. I know it's crazy.

Apparently Holden's wish is purely selfless. What he wants, in effect, is to be a saint—the protector and savior of innocence. But what he also wants, for he is still one of the running children himself, is that someone prevent *his* fall. This is his paradox: he must leave innocence to protect innocence. At sixteen, he is ready to shed his innocence and move like Adam into the fallen adult world, but he resists because those no longer innocent seem to him foolish as well as corrupt. In a sense, then, he is looking for an exemplar, a wise-good father whose example will justify his own initiation into manhood. Before Holden can become a catcher in the rye, he must find another catcher in the rye to show him how it is done.

Immediately after Holden announces his "crazy" ambition to Phoebe, he calls up one of his former teachers, Mr. Antolini, who is both intelligent and kind—a potential catcher in the rye.

> He was the one that finally picked up that boy that jumped out of the window I told you about, James Castle. Old Mr. Antolini felt his pulse and all, and then he took off his coat and put it over James Castle and carried him all the way over to the infirmary.

Though Mr. Antolini is sympathetic because "he didn't even give a damn if his coat got all bloody," the incident is symbolic of the teacher's failure as a catcher in the rye. For all his good intentions, he was unable to catch James Castle or prevent his fall; he could only pick him up after he had died. The episode of the suicide is one of the looming shadows darkening Holden's world; Holden seeks out Antolini because he hopes that the gentle teacher—the substitute father—will "pick him up" before he is irrevocably fallen. Holden's real quest throughout the novel is for a spiritual father (an innocent adult). He calls Antolini after all the other fathers of his world have failed him, including his real father, whose existence in the novel is represented solely by Phoebe's childish reiteration of "Daddy's going to kill you." The fathers in Salinger's child's-eye world do not catch falling boys—who have been thrown out of prep school—but "kill" them. Antolini represents Holden's last chance to find a catcher-father. But his inability to save Holden has been prophesied in his failure to save James Castle; the episode of Castle's death provides an anticipatory parallel to Antolini's unwitting destruction of Holden.

That Antolini's kindness to Holden is motivated in part by a homosexual interest, though it comes as a shock to Holden, does not wholly surprise the reader. Many of the biographical details that Salinger has revealed about him through Holden imply this possibility. For example, that he has an older and unattractive wife whom he makes a great show of kissing in public is highly suggestive; yet the discovery itself—Holden wakes to find Antolini sitting beside him and caressing his head—has considerable impact. We experience a kind of shock of recognition, the more intense for its having been anticipated. The scene has added power because Antolini is, for the most part, a good man, whose interest in Holden is genuine as well as perverted. His advice to Holden is apparently well-intentioned. Though many of his recommendations are cleverly articulated platitudes, Antolini evinces a prophetic insight when he tells Holden, "I have a feeling that you're riding for some kind of a terrible, terrible fall"; one suspects, however, that to some extent he is talking about himself. Ironically, Antolini becomes the agent of his "terrible, terrible fall" by violating Holden's image of him, by becoming a false father. Having lost his respect for Antolini as a man, Holden rejects him as an authority; as far as Holden is concerned, Antolini's example denies the import of his words. His disillusionment with Antolini, who had seemed to be the sought-for, wise-good father, comes as the most intense of a long line of disenchantments; it is the final straw that breaks Holden. It is the equivalent of the loss of God. The world, devoid of good fathers (authorities), becomes a soul-destroying chaos in which his survival is possible only through withdrawal into childhood, into fantasy, into psychosis....

Obliquely searching for good in the adult world, or at least something to mitigate his despair, Holden is continually confronted with the absence of good. On his arrival in the city, he is disturbed because his cabdriver is corrupt and unsociable and, worst of all, unable to answer Holden's obsessional question: where do the Central Park ducks go when the lake freezes over? What Holden really wants to know is whether there is a benevolent authority that takes care of ducks. If there is one for ducks, it follows that there may be one for people as well. Holden's quest for a wise and benevolent authority, then, is essentially a search for a God-principle. However, none of the adults in Holden's world has any true answers for him. When he checks into

a hotel room, he is depressed by the fact that the bellboy is an old man ("What a gorgeous job for a guy around sixty-five years old"). As sensitized recorder of the moral vibrations of his world, Holden suffers the indignity of the aged bellhop's situation for him, as he had suffered for Spencer's guilt and Ackley's self-loathing. Yet, and this is part of his tragedy, he is an impotent saint, unable either to redeem the fallen or to prevent their fall....

After his disillusionment with Antolini, who is the most destructive of Holden's fathers because he is seemingly the most benevolent, Holden suffers an emotional breakdown. His flight from Antolini's house, like his previous flights from school and from the hotel, is an attempt to escape evil. The three are parallel experiences, except that Holden is less sure of the justness of his third flight and wonders if he has not misjudged his otherwise sympathetic teacher.

> And the more I thought about it, the more depressed I got. I mean I started thinking maybe I *should've* gone back to his house. Maybe he *was* only patting my head just for the hell of it. The more I thought about it, though, the more depressed and screwed up about it I got.

The ambivalence of his response racks him. If he has misjudged Antolini, he has wronged not only his teacher, but he has wronged himself as well; he, not Antolini, has been guilty of corruption. Consequently, he suffers both for Antolini and for himself. Holden's guilt-ridden despair manifests itself in nausea and in an intense sense of physical ill-being, as if he carries the whole awful corruption of the city inside him. Walking aimlessly through the Christmas-decorated city, Holden experiences "the terrible, terrible fall" that Antolini had prophesied for him.

> Every time I came to the end of a block and stepped off the goddam curb, I had this feeling that I'd never get to the other side of the street. I thought I'd go down, down, down, and nobody'd ever see me again. Boy, did it scare me. You can't imagine. I started sweating like a bastard—my whole shirt and underwear and everything.... Every time I'd get to the end of a block I'd make believe I was talking to my brother Allie. I'd say to him, "Allie, don't let me disappear. Allie, don't let me disappear. Allie, don't let me disappear. Please, Allie." And then when I'd reach the other side of the street without disappearing, I'd *thank* him.

Like Franny's prayer to Jesus in one of Salinger's later stories, Holden's prayer to Allie is not so much an act of anguish as an act of love, though it is in part both. Trapped in an interior hell, Holden seeks redemption, not by formal appeal to God or Jesus, who have in the Christmas season been falsified and commercialized, but by praying to his saint-brother who in his goodness had God in him.

Like so many heroes of contemporary fiction—Morris' Boyd, Ellison's Invisible Man, Malamud's Frank, Salinger's Seymour—Holden is an impotent savior. Because he can neither save his evil world nor live in it as it is, he retreats into fantasy—into childhood. He decides to become a deaf-mute, to live alone in an isolated cabin, to commit a kind of symbolic suicide. It is an unrealizable fantasy, but a death wish nevertheless. However, Holden's social conscience forces him out of spiritual retirement. When he discovers an obscenity scrawled on one of the walls of Phoebe's school, he rubs it out with his hand to protect the innocence of the children. For the moment he is a successful catcher in the rye. But then he discovers another such notice, "*scratched* on, with a knife or something," and then another. He realizes that he cannot possibly erase all the scribbled obscenities in the world, that he cannot catch all the children, that evil is ineradicable.

This is the final disillusionment. Dizzy with his terrible awareness, Holden insults Phoebe when she insists on running away with him. In his vision of despair, he sees Phoebe's irrevocable doom as well as his own, and for a moment he hates her as he hates himself—as he hates the world. Once he has hurt her, however, he realizes the commitment that his love for her imposes on him; if he is to assuage her pain, he must continue to live in the world. When she kisses him as a token of forgiveness and love and, as if in consequence, it begins to rain, Holden, bathed by the rain, is purified—in a sense, redeemed.

A too literal reading of Holden's divulgence that he is telling the story from some kind of rest home has led to a misinterpretation of the end of the novel. Holden is always less insane than his world. The last scene, in which Holden, suffused with happiness, sits in the rain and watches Phoebe ride on the merry-go-round, is indicative not of his crack-up, as has been assumed, but of his redemption. Whereas all the adults in his world have failed him (and he, a butter-fingered catcher in the rye, has failed them), a ten-year-old girl saves him—becomes his catcher. Love is the redemptive grace. Phoebe replaces Jane, the loss of whom had initiated Holden's despair, flight, and quest for experience as salvation. Holden's pure communion with Phoebe may be construed as a reversion to child-like innocence, but this is the only way to re-

demption in Salinger's world—there is no other good. Innocence is all. Love is innocence.

The last scene, with Holden drenched in Scott Fitzgerald's all-absolving rain, seems unashamedly sentimental. Certainly Salinger overstates the spiritually curative powers of children; innocence can be destructive as well as redemptive. Yet Salinger's view of the universe, in which all adults (even the most apparently decent) are corrupt and consequently destructive, is bleak and somewhat terrifying. Since growing up in the real world is tragic, in Salinger's ideal world time must be stopped to prevent the loss of childhood, to salvage the remnants of innocence. At one point in the novel, Holden wishes that life were as changeless and pure as the exhibitions under glass cases in the Museum of Natural History. This explains, in part, Holden's ecstasy in the rain at the close of the novel. In watching Phoebe go round and round on the carrousel, in effect going nowhere, he sees her in the timeless continuum of art on the verge of changing, yet unchanging, forever safe, forever loving, forever innocent.

Source: Jonathan Baumbach, "The Saint as a Young Man: A Reappraisal of *The Catcher in the Rye*," in *Modern Language Quarterly,* Vol. 25, No. 4, December, 1964, pp. 461—72.

Sources

James Bryan, "The Psychological Structure of *The Catcher in the Rye*," *PMLA: Publications of the Modern Language Association,* Vol. 89, no. 5, 1974, pp. 1065-74.

Nash K. Burger, "Books of *The Times*," in *New York Times,* July 16, 1951, p. 19.

Paul Engle, "Honest Tale of Distraught Adolescent," in *Chicago Sunday Tribune Magazine of Books,* July 15, 1951, p. 3.

William Faulkner, "A Word to Young Writers," in *Faulkner in the University: Class Conferences at the University of Virginia 1957–1958,* edited by Frederick L. Gwynn and Joseph L. Blotner, University of Virginia Press, 1959, pp. 244–45.

T. Morris Longstreth, "New Novels in the News," in *Christian Science Monitor,* July 19, 1951, p. 11.

For Further Study

Jonathan Baumbach, "The Saint as a Young Man: A Reappraisal of *The Catcher in the Rye*," in *Modern Language Quarterly,* Vol. 25, no. 4, December, 1964, pp. 461-72.

This defense of *The Catcher in the Rye* valorizes Holden's childlike innocence as a form of saintly idealism.

Harold Bloom, "Introduction," in *Major Literary Characters,* edited by Harold Bloom, Chelsea House, 1996, pp. 1-4.

A general analysis of the character Holden Caulfield which situates him relative to other literary figures.

Donald P. Costello, "The Language of *The Catcher in the Rye,*" in *American Speech,* Vol. 34, no. 3, October, 1959, pp. 172-81.

An analysis of how Salinger's use of language realistically portrays American teenage slang during the 1950s.

Duane Edwards, "Holden Caulfield: Don't Ever Tell Anybody Anything," in *English Literary History,* Vol. 44, no. 3, Fall, 1977, pp. 556-67.

This analysis of the character of Holden Caulfield emphasizes how Holden is an ironic character who exemplifies the same kind of phoniness that he criticizes in others.

Warren French, *J. D. Salinger, Revisited,* Twayne Publishers, 1988.

This book provides an overview of Salinger's life and fiction, and one of its chapters also contains an excellent introduction to the themes and issues raised in *The Catcher in the Rye.*

Lilian Furst, "Dostoyevsky's *Notes from Underground* and Salinger's *The Catcher in the Rye,*" in *Canadian Review of Comparative Literature,* Vol. 5, no. 1, Winter, 1978, pp. 72-85.

An analysis of parallels between *The Catcher in the Rye* and Dostoyevsky's *Notes from Underground.*

Arthur Heiserman and James E. Miller, Jr., "J. D. Salinger: Some Crazy Cliff," in *Western Humanities Review,* Vol. 10, no. 2, Spring, 1956, pp. 129-37.

An analysis of *The Catcher in the Rye* which shows how it belongs to the western literary tradition of epic quest narratives.

John M. Howell, "Salinger in the Waste Land," in *Critical Essays on J. D. Salinger's* The Catcher in the Rye, edited by Joel Salzberg, G. K. Hall & Co., 1990, pp. 85-91.

An analysis of parallels between *The Catcher in the Rye* and T. S. Eliot's poetry.

Charles Kaplan, "Holden and Huck: The Odysseys of Youth," in *College English,* Vol. 18, no. 2, November, 1956, pp. 76-80.

A comparison of *The Catcher in the Rye* to Mark Twain's *Huckleberry Finn.*

Robert A. Lee, " 'Flunking Everything Else Except English Anyway': Holden Caulfield, Author," in *Critical Essays on J. D. Salinger's* The Catcher in the Rye, edited by Joel Salzberg, G. K. Hall, 1990, pp. 185-97.

An analysis of Holden's character which focuses on his artistic creativity.

Carol and Richard Ohmann, "Reviewers, Critics, and *The Catcher in the Rye,*" in *Critical Inquiry,* Vol. 3, no. 1, Autumn, 1976, pp. 15-37.

A Marxist analysis of how capitalist social and economic strategies influence the development of Holden's character.

Jack Salzman, "Introduction," in *New Essays on* The Catcher in the Rye, edited by Jack Salzman, Cambridge University Press, 1991, pp. 1-22.

An overview of critical interpretations of *The Catcher in the Rye.*

Mary Suzanne Schriber, "Holden Caulfield, C'est Moi," in *Critical Essays on J. D. Salinger's* The Catcher in the Rye, edited by Joel Salzberg, G. K. Hall, 1990, pp. 226-38.

A feminist analysis of the critical reception of *The Catcher in the Rye* which argues that male critics inflate the significance of the novel because they identify with Holden as a representation of their own male adolescence and because they ignore female perspectives.

Helen Weinberg, *The New Novel in America: The Kafkan Mode in Contemporary Fiction,* Cornell University Press, 1970.

An analysis of parallels between *The Catcher in the Rye* and Franz Kafka's fiction.

Fahrenheit 451

Ray Bradbury
1953

Of the hundreds of stories Ray Bradbury has written, none are better known than *Fahrenheit 451*. Published in 1953 during the Cold War and McCarthy Eras, the novel reflects Bradbury's concerns about censorship and conformity during a period when free expression of ideas could lead to social and economic ostracization. The book expands the concept of a short story that Bradbury wrote in 1947 under the title "Bright Phoenix," which was published in a revised form in the *Magazine of Fantasy and Science Fiction* in 1963. *Galaxy* published an expanded version of the premise under the title of "The Fireman" in 1951. *Fahrenheit 451* is twice as long as "The Fireman." Book burning and the memorization of texts for preservation are the central actions of all three versions of the story.

While viewed as a science fiction work, *Fahrenheit 451* has led to mainstream critical acclaim for Bradbury's ability as a prose stylist and as a writer of ideas. The novel is often compared to other dystopias—works which create societies where people lead dehumanized and often dangerous lives—such as Aldous Huxley's *Brave New World* and George Orwell's *1984*. Bradbury has been praised for the richness of his imagery in *Fahrenheit 451*. The thematic elements of the novel have gained it the reputation as a book of social criticism which focuses particularly on American consumerism and cultural decline.

Author Biography

Born on the 22nd of August, 1920, in Waukegan, Illinois, Raymond Douglas Bradbury spent his childhood in this small town located north of Chicago. Many of his stories are set in towns similar to Waukegan. As a young child he was exposed to the horror movies of the period, such as *The Phantom of the Opera* and *The Hunchback of Notre Dame*. Like Montag in *Fahrenheit 451,* the heroes of these stories are social outcasts. Many of the themes found in *Fahrenheit 451* are related to Bradbury's early exposure to books by an aunt and his regular trips to the Waukegan Public Library with his brother. His family moved to Los Angeles in 1934 and Bradbury completed his education at Los Angeles High School, graduating in 1938. He began writing stories at the age of fifteen and in 1937 he joined the Los Angeles Science Fiction League. In 1938 he published his first short story, "Hollerbochen's Dilemma." During the 1940s, Bradbury wrote for pulp magazines such as *Weird Tales* and *Amazing Stories*. His first collection of short stories, *Dark Carnival,* was published in 1947. Even these early fantasy stories reveal elements of Bradbury's concern for the value of human imagination.

When *The Martian Chronicles* was published in 1950, Bradbury was hailed as a sophisticated science fiction writer. While it is a collection of related stories set on Mars, critics often discuss the book as a novel. Bradbury uses the framework of the settling of Mars to present issues like censorship, technology, racism, and nuclear war. The book has been praised for its allegorical treatment of important social issues. Other collections of stories by Bradbury that have received critical attention are *The Illustrated Man,* published in 1951, and *I Sing the Body Electric!,* published in 1969. His other novels include *Something Wicked This Way Comes* (1962) and *Dandelion Wine* (1957). Many of his stories have been televised on shows like *The Twilight Zone, Alfred Hitchcock Presents,* and the *Ray Bradbury Theater*. The sheer volume of Bradbury's science fiction writing guarantees his importance in that genre. *Fahrenheit 451* remains one of his best known works. The human values he explores in that work and his many other writings also assures his place among the other noted writers of dystopias, or works that suggest negative futures where humanity is oppressed.

Bradbury married Marguerite Susan McClure in 1947 and they had four daughters. Among his numerous literary awards are the O. Henry Prize in

Ray Bradbury

1947 and 1948 and a PEN Body of Work Award in 1985. Many of his stories have also been adapted to the theater and received drama awards. Besides short stories and novels, Bradbury has written for the theater, television, and film—including a noted adaptation of Herman Melville's *Moby Dick* for director John Huston—and has written more than a dozen volumes of poetry and many nonfiction essays, and has edited several collected stories by other writers.

Plot Summary

Part I: The Hearth and the Salamander

Guy Montag is a thirty-year-old fireman experiencing an intellectual awakening. For ten years now he has protected the sanity and comfort of the community by setting fire to books. He and his wife Mildred live comfortably in the suburbs of a large city. All Mildred needs to make her life complete is a fourth TV wall, so she can be surrounded by the characters she watches and interacts with everyday in her living room. True, an international war has been brewing, but nobody much cares as long as they're comfortable.

One evening, after having taken great pleasure in burning a house full of dangerous books, Montag meets Clarisse McClellan. Clarisse, a seventeen-year-old "oddball" neighbor, likes to talk about the world around her. She challenges Montag's authority as a guardian of their way of life. She questions his purpose, practically tells him that he cannot think, and asks him, "Are you happy?" These questions bring to his mind the dissatisfactions which up to now he has only vaguely felt. Going into the house, he finds Mildred lying in bed, practically dead from an overdose of sleeping pills, and he realizes that Mildred's happiness is only a mask, too. The "technicians" who come to fix her up are so casual about it that Montag realizes that something has happened to everybody, that under the "mask of happiness" lies a great emptiness.

Montag's doubt about his way of life begins to show at work. At the fire station they have a Mechanical Hound, which is usually employed to track people with illegal book collections. Now, however, the Hound seems to get suspicious and begins striking at Montag when he comes to work. Captain Beatty promises to fix the Hound, but it continues to sniff around Montag and strike its needle-nose full of poison at him.

One night the station's fire alarm sounds, and the firemen are called out to burn an attic full of books. The firemen chop down the unlocked doors, slap the helpless old woman down, and douse the piled-up books with kerosene. Before they can set the blaze, however, the woman kneels in her piled books, strikes the match, and burns herself with her books. The scene strikes Montag numb—so numb, in fact, that his hands, as if with a mind of their own, steal and hide a book under his arm, which he carries home.

The incident with the unnamed woman only aggravates Montag's doubt and alienation. He is so upset that he lays awake all night, so upset that by morning he feels too sick to go to work. Alerted by Montag's absence, Captain Beatty comes to call on him. Beatty understands his curiosity about the fireman's job and tells him the history of firemen. He tells him that the masses of people wanted the books burned because the differing ideas and information in books confused them and caused conflict. Anytime there was conflict, there was discomfort. All the people wanted was pleasure, so they made the firemen the guardians of their comfort.

"Yes, but what about the firemen, then?" asked Montag.

"Ah." Beatty leaned forward in the faint mist of smoke from his pipe. "What more easily explained and natural? With school turning out more runners, jumpers, racers, tinkerers, grabbers, snatchers, fliers, and swimmers instead of examiners, critics, knowers, and imaginative creators, the word 'intellectual,' of course, became the swear word it deserved to be. You always dread the unfamiliar. Surely you remember the boy in your own school class who was exceptionally 'bright,' did most of the reciting and answering while the others sat like so many leaden idols, hating him. And wasn't it this bright boy you selected for beatings, and tortures after hours? Of course it was. We must all be alike. Not everyone born free and equal, as the Constitution says, but everyone *made equal.* Each man the image of every other; then all are happy, for there are no mountains to make them cower, to judge themselves against. So! A book is a loaded gun in the house next door. Burn it."

After Beatty leaves, Montag reveals to Millie that he has secretly been hoarding books taken from his fires. He begins reading to her to see what might be in them that would cause such love and fear, but she can find no meaning in them.

2. The Sieve and the Sand

Montag continues to read from the books all during the afternoon while something, maybe the Mechanical Hound, scratches at the door, and war jets scream across the sky. Millie argues that the books have no meaning—they aren't "people," as the characters in her television programs are.

Having such a late start in his life, Montag cannot understand much of what he reads, so he decides that he needs a teacher. He remembers an old man, Faber, whom he had met months ago in the city park, a man who had suspiciously hidden something from him as he approached and seemed to be able to quote poetry. On his way to see Faber, he tries to memorize the *Book of Ecclesiastes* from the Bible, but the constant blaring of a Denham's Dentifrice commercial on the train's sound system interferes.

At first suspicious, Faber listens to Montag sympathetically and helps Montag to understand what books can and cannot do for humans. Faber tells Montag he is wasting his time, he can only "nibble the edges," for the coming war will destroy society and people will rebuild as they always do, but books cannot prevent the cycle from repeating. Montag suggests sabotaging firemen by planting copies of books in their houses and turning them in as traitors, and finally shames Faber into helping him. They make a plan in an effort to save Montag and save the books. First, they will try to make copies of the

Bible which Montag had stolen from the fire the previous night. Second, Montag will return to the fire station as a spy with Faber monitoring and analyzing the situation through the use of a two-way listening device placed in both their ears.

Under threatening sounds of jets in the skies overhead, Montag returns home and is impatient with Millie's bland, soulless friends, Mrs. Bowles and Mrs. Phelps. He forces them to listen to a reading of Matthew Arnold's poem "Dover Beach," against Faber's advice. He throws them out of the house and returns to the fire station and a knowing Captain Beatty. When Montag gets back to the fire station, there is an alarm, but this time they go to Montag's house.

3. Burning Bright

They arrive just as Mildred is leaving home for good. Captain Beatty baits and teases Montag until Montag burns his own house down. All this time, Faber has been trying to help Montag by whispering in his ear, but now Beatty discovers the ear-radio and takes it away. In his confusion, Montag's hands again move on their own and turn the flamethrower on Beatty, killing him. Suddenly, the Mechanical Hound appears, and Montag turns the flame onto it even though the Hound manages to get a partial injection of anesthetic into Montag before its circuitry is burned.

Now, Montag limps through the back alleys, stopping only to rescue a few unburned books. Despite the manhunt, he stops to plant some of them in the house of Black, a fellow fireman, in order to cast suspicion on firemen in general. He then moves on to Faber's house, where from Faber's tiny TV they learn that Montag has become the subject of a massive manhunt and a media event using helicopters and a sophisticated new Mechanical Hound. They also learn that war has been declared.

They decide on a new course of action. Faber will go to St. Louis to visit a printer he knows, and Montag will head for the countryside. In a desperate attempt to prevent the Hound from following his scent into Faber's house, they take measures to try to confuse the Hound's sense of smell. Montag manages to stay ahead of the manhunt and makes it to the river. He plunges into the river, listening to the confusion of the hunt approach the bank and watching the helicopter sweep the river. His tactics for throwing the Hound off the scent have worked, and the hunt turns back into the city while Montag floats on downstream.

Still from the film Fahrenheit 451, *starring Oskar Werner and Julie Christie, 1966.*

He drifts until nearly dawn. When he climbs out onto the bank, he stumbles up to the old railroad tracks and begins to follow them away from the city. Montag doesn't go very far before he hears voices, and he sneaks up to listen to a conversation. They know he is there, however, and they know who he is, having watched the chase on a small portable TV. One of them, the leader Granger, calls him out and offers him coffee and a bottle of chemical which will change his body's chemical signature so the Hound won't be able to find him. They all sit and watch the end of the manhunt, which is now focused on an innocent scapegoat. The authorities can't disappoint the viewing public.

It turns out that these wanderers are "book covers," each having a book memorized and ready for recitation. They plan to pass this knowledge onto their children and wait until society needs that knowledge again. They don't have long to wait, because several bombs hit the city while they are hiking that day. After weathering the shock waves from the blast, they turn back; civilization needs them. On the way, Montag begins to remember *Ecclesiastes*.

Characters

Captain Beatty

The captain of the firefighters and Montag's superior. Beatty's character, who represents those who rationalize the bookburnings of the firemen, contrasts with Montag's. It is Beatty who explains the history of firefighting in the story and who fully embraces its justification, ironically quoting from literature to support his arguments. Beatty leads Montag and other firefighters to bookburnings. When Montag fails to show up for work, Beatty visits him in his home and tries to talk him back to "health." When Beatty leads Montag to his own house for a book burning, he goads Montag into doing the job; Montag then kills Beatty.

Black

A fellow fireman who works with Montag. When Montag asks about the time when firemen put out fires instead of starting them, Black and Stoneman pull out their rule books and read to Montag from a section on the history of firemen in America. They show Montag the section where Benjamin Franklin had burned English-influenced books in 1790, making Franklin the first American fireman. (Franklin actually founded the first volunteer fire-fighting company in the United States in 1736.) After killing Captain Beatty, Montag plants several books in Black's house and then reports him to the firemen.

Mrs. Bowles

One of Mildred Montag's friends who talks about her Caesarian births during her social visits at the Montag home. She denounces Montag when he makes a scene in her presence by reading a poem, Matthew Arnold's "Dover Beach," after he begins to doubt his role as a fireman.

Fred Clement

One of the book people that Montag meets after his escape from the city. Clement was a former English professor at Cambridge University. He was a specialist in the works of English poet and novelist Thomas Hardy.

Professor Faber

Montag met Faber, who is a retired English professor, in the park a few months prior to the events in the novel. After Montag begins doubting his role as a fireman, he turns to Faber for guidance. Although Faber tells Montag that he will not find the answers he needs in books, he agrees to help the fireman. Faber places an electronic transmitter into Montag's ear so that they can have continuous communication. Montag begins behaving recklessly, reading poetry to his wife and her friends, despite Faber's warnings. After Montag snaps at his house, he burns the transmitter along with Captain Beatty. It is Faber Montag turns to when he must flee; "he just wanted to know that there was a man like Faber in the world," he rationalizes. However, it is Montag who ends up inspiring Faber to fight back against the firemen—to "do the right thing at last."

Granger

Granger is the man Montag meets after his escape from the city. Granger offers him a drink to change the chemistry of his perspiration so that the Mechanical Hound will not be able to find him. Granger is able to show Montag on a portable viewer how the chase for him is progressing, but assures him they will not find him. They witness his supposed capture on the viewer. Granger then introduces Montag to a number of the book people and explains to him how they keep the books alive by memorizing books or parts of them in order to preserve and hand them on to others. By using this oral tradition, the book people feel the content will not be lost, even if all the books are burned. While Montag is in the wilderness with Granger and the book people, war breaks out and the city is annihilated. Granger meditates at the end of the novel about the mythical creature known as the Phoenix that rises from its own funeral ashes to be reborn.

Clarisse McClellan

A teenage girl who is a neighbor of Montag's. Clarisse represents innocence. She questions the rationale of the ideas that govern Montag's life and is the stimulus that makes Montag begin to doubt what he is doing. Clarisse is shown in contrast to Montag's wife, who totally accepts the values of the society, even when it is harmful to her health. Clarisse does not like the social activities that most people in the society like. She describes her family to Montag as liking to sit around and talk. Clarisse's family disappears later in the novel, and she is said to have been killed by a car.

Mechanical Hound

A robotic dog that can detect the location of illegal books and is also able to destroy people. With the representation of the Mechanical Hound,

Bradbury is able to convey how technological advances can be used for destructive purposes. The Hound is central to several scenes involving the locating and burning of books. It also plays a role in the search for Montag after he kills Beatty and escapes the city. When Montag is rescued in the forest, he is given a drink that will confuse the Hound and make the former fireman safe from capture. The Mechanical Hound is described in almost life-like terms when it is first introduced in the book. Early in the novel, for instance, Montag passes the Hound and it snarls at him. It is a creature Montag comes to fear even more when he begins breaking away from his society.

Guy Montag

The central character of the novel and its hero. *Fahrenheit 451* is about the transformation of Montag from an obedient servant of the state to a questioning human being. As a fireman, Montag's job is not to put out fires but to start them, in order to burn books that are illegally harbored by wayward citizens. Montag is at first unquestioning. He takes pride in his work, which is carefully described in the opening scenes of the novel. He becomes curious, however, after meeting and talking to his young neighbor, Clarisse McClellan. Montag begins to question the values of his society, particularly in relation to his wife, who spends most of her time watching the large screen television in their living room and gossiping with her friends. After his meeting with Clarisse McClellan and after his wife takes an overdose of pills, Montag begins to question his role as a book burner. He has already taken a few books illegally from the fires he has started and he begins to read them. Montag's fire chief, Captain Beatty, becomes suspicious of Montag. Beatty defends book burning to Montag, but Montag is determined to read the books he has hidden in his home. Through his contact with a former English professor, Faber, whom he met earlier in the park, Montag is further exposed to the content of books. Faber equips him with a monitoring device in his ear that enables the two to remain in constant contact. When Montag is on a call to start a fire that leads to his own house, he finally makes his break. He burns his own house and then turns his flamethrower on Captain Beatty, killing him. Montag then makes his escape from the city and finds the book people, who give him refuge from the firemen and Mechanical Hound that is searching for him. He is then invited to join their society, where he may become the *Book of Ecclesiastes*, which resides in his memory.

Media Adaptations

- *Fahrenheit 451* was adapted as a film by the French director Francois Truffaut in 1966. It starred Oskar Werner as Montag, Cyril Cusak as Captain Beatty, and Julie Christie played the dual roles of Clarisse McClellan and Mildred Montag. It is available as a video through MCA/Universal Home Video.

- A musical production of *Fahrenheit 451* opened at the Colony Theater in Los Angeles in 1979.

- *Fahrenheit 451* has also been produced as a sound recording by Books On Tape in 1988 and by Recorded Books in 1982. Michael Prichard reads the 1988 version and Alexander Spencer the 1982 version.

- Georgia Holof and David Mettere adapted the book as an opera. It was produced at the Indiana Civic Theater in Fort Wayne in November of 1988.

Millie Montag
See Mildred Montag

Mildred Montag

Montag's wife, Mildred, represents those who completely accept the basic beliefs of the society. She is presumably content with her life, a good bit of it spent watching inane programs on the big screen television in her home. She considers the characters of her various programs that absorb her as her "family." She feels threatened by her husband's growing interest in illegal books, or any idea that suggests going beyond the narrow restrictions of society. After Mildred takes an overdose of sleeping pills and her life is threatened, Montag becomes aware that she may not be as happy with her life as he had assumed. Mildred's relationship with Montag is only viable as long as he is content with his job of fireman. When he begins to question what he is doing, Mildred becomes upset, particularly when he argues and recites poetry openly in front of her friends. His relationship with Millie in the novel is a contentious one. It is apparent that it is not safe to express his ideas even in his own home to his wife. To do so shakes the foundation of the beliefs they have been compelled to embrace.

Reverend Padover

One of the book people that Montag meets after his escape from the city. Padover was a practicing minister until he lost his congregation because of his views.

Mrs. Clara Phelps

A friend of Mildred's. She keeps Mildred company along with Mrs. Bowles as they watch the programs in the television room of Montag's house. As Montag's views are transformed, he becomes increasingly impatient with the attitudes of his wife and her friends. When Montag insists on reading from Matthew Arnold's poem "Dover Beach" to Mildred and her friends, Mrs. Phelps breaks into tears and a scene follows where Montag practically kicks the women out of the house.

Dr. Simmons

One of the book people that Montag meets after his escape from the city. Simmons is introduced as a former specialist in the works of Ortega y Gasset, a Spanish philosopher, writer, and statesman. The professor taught at UCLA. He has committed to memory the works of Marcus Aurelius, the stoic philosopher who was also a Roman emperor.

Stoneman

A fellow fireman who works with Montag. When Montag asks about the time when firemen put out fires instead of starting them, Stoneman and Black pull out the rule book and read to Montag from a section on the history of firemen in America. They show Montag the section where Benjamin Franklin had burned English-influenced books in 1790, making Franklin the first American fireman. (In reality, Franklin founded America's first volunteer fire-fighting force.)

Unnamed woman

Although she is never named, this woman holds great significance for Montag. A bookburning takes place at her house. After the firemen pour kerosene over her books, the woman ignores Montag's pleas to come away, and ignites the fire herself. She dies with her books. This event helps raise Montag's consciousness about his work.

Professor West

Montag meets the professor after he kills Beatty and escapes to the hideout of the book people. Professor West was teaching ethics at Columbia University before becoming one of the book people.

Themes

Alienation and Loneliness

An atmosphere of alienation is established by Bradbury in the opening scenes of *Fahrenheit 451,* which details a "fireman's" growing dissatisfaction with his conformist society. Montag's pleasure in his work of burning books is quickly challenged in his conversation with his neighbor, Clarisse McClellan. As they walk home together, she asks Montag if he is happy. His first reaction is to tell himself that, of course, he is happy. After leaving her and wandering around inside his house looking for his wife, Montag answers Clarisse's question in the negative. When he discovers that his wife Mildred has taken an overdose of sleeping pills, his alienation is intensified. Bradbury uses the roar of jets overhead as a counterpoint to Montag's scream, thus pitting his character's human sounds and feelings against the roaring sounds of technology. With the introduction of other mechanical devices, such as the equipment used on Mildred by the medics, the television parlors, and the Mechanical Hound, Montag's alienation from a society that has embraced mass culture and thoroughly discouraged individual thinking intensifies. In scene after scene, Montag becomes emotionally alienated from his work, his wife, and the people he works with. As this alienation increases, he reaches out to books and to the people who value them. His escape from the city to the refuge of the book people offers hope. He has escaped the alienation of the mechanical society he left behind. Perhaps he will help establish a better one by remembering the words in the book he will commit to memory. The suggestion Bradbury makes is that by staying connected to books, which are a reflection of other people's thinking, we stay connected as human beings one to the other. Books, then, are an antidote to alienation.

Apathy and Passivity

By portraying many characters as passive figures who never even wonder about their lot in life, *Fahrenheit 451* seems to imply that apathy is a very important element in the decline of Montag's society. Millie is content to receive whatever "entertainment" that comes from her television, unable to distinguish between programs that are numbing in their sameness. She has no real concept of what the coming war might mean to her—she only worries it might interrupt her precious television programs—and her friends are similarly unconcerned. Montag's colleagues laugh at him when he wonders aloud about the history of the firemen, and are satisfied with the reasons provided in their handbooks. The only action these characters take is to maintain the *status quo*—the way things are. In contrast, Clarisse, Montag, and Faber are individuals who wonder about their world and, in the case of Montag and Faber, are able to make attempts to change things. Even the book people who live outside of society are eventually able to take action, for after the destruction of the city it is implied they are the ones who will help rebuild the world.

Change and Transformation

The transformation of Montag's character from obedient fireman to outcast creates the central tension of the novel. Since the smallest act of deviation is the same as an act of civil disobedience, the reader worries from the beginning of the novel to its final pages about Montag's safety and survival. In the beginning of the story, the only action Montag can take is in his work as fireman. He follows the rules of the fireman's code until he begins to doubt his work. Throughout the story there is little will to action taken by the characters. It is as if they have all become paralyzed from conformity. Mildred and her friends are mesmerized by the programs they watch in the television parlor. The relationship between Montag and Beatty is a passive one. Beatty talks to Montag to rationalize the work of the firemen when he begins to suspect Montag's discontent with his work. The main scenes of action involve the book burnings and Montag's pursuit by the Mechanical Hound. Other than these action scenes, Montag's transformation is one of thought. In one sense he is thinking mechanically in the beginning of the story. In the end, he has opened his mind to the ideas he finds in books. It is the beginning of his transformation. The reader cannot help wondering what action his new thinking might lead to. Bradbury leaves us with the hope that through these books, society will bury some of its destructive force. By ending the book in a fire storm of bombs, there is the sense that this old society of conformity will die and a new one will be born out of the ashes, like the mythical phoenix to which Granger refers. "A time to break

Topics for Further Study

- Research the history of book burning in Nazi Germany, the censorship of books in the Soviet Union, the banned book index of the Catholic Church, and other historical instances of banned books or book burnings. Compare and contrast the reasons these institutions have given for censorship.

- Find instances of book censorship in schools and libraries that is going on today in the United States. What groups want to restrict the books held in school and public libraries and student access to them? Which books have been listed for censorship and what reasons are given?

- Research counter cultures like the "flower children" of the 1960s and modern militia groups of the 1990s. Describe what they object to in society and the role society plays in their lives.

- Research the developments in atomic weapons since World War II. Argue whether people today should feel more or less safe today than they did during the Cold War of the 1950s and 1960s.

down, and a time to build up. Yes. A time to keep silence, and a time to speak," Montag thinks as the book people move up the river at the end of the story.

Style

Structure

Bradbury has structured *Fahrenheit 451* into three parts which parallel the stages of Montag's transformation. Part One is called "The Hearth and the Salamander." Montag enjoys his work as a fireman in this section, but he also begins to find his inner voice as doubts set in. While Clarisse and Mildred are introduced in this section, the other main character is Captain Beatty. Montag's conflict with the captain begins in Part One. Part Two is called "The Sieve and the Sand." In this section Montag has taken steps away from social conformity. He is reading books. He has established an alliance with Faber, who has equipped him with a two-way communication device. Montag's dialogues become angry and incoherent as he is torn between listening to people around him and to the voice of Faber in his ear. This section of the book ends with Montag in front of his own house, where he has come to burn books. His illegal activities have been exposed. In Part Three, "Burning Bright," Montag commits his final acts of transformation. He kills Beatty after burning down his own house and is chased by the Mechanical Hound as he makes his escape down the river. The other important character in Part Three is Granger, who introduces the work of the book people. The book ends with his meeting the book people, the bombing of the city, and a note of hope for the future.

Point of View

The book is written in the third person ("he") with its central focus on the thoughts and actions of Montag. Much of the excitement in the story, though, comes from the descriptive passages of the setting, action, and characters. Through his poetic descriptions, Bradbury makes the unreal world he describes seem real. He is able to make the fantastic seem real and reality seem fantastic, which establishes a tension that moves the story along. The narrative is interspersed with dialogue between characters. Some of the dialogue is didactic—that is, somewhat preachy—and tends to delay the action. These instructive passages, however, do reveal Bradbury's basic point of view, which passionately embraces the importance of books for human beings. Clearly, he has written *Fahrenheit 451* in order to express this opinion. His purpose is not merely entertainment, although readers do find the novel an enjoyable work of fiction.

Symbolism

Fire, the salamander, the Mechanical Hound, and the number of the title are important symbols that Bradbury exploits in the novel. At 451 degrees Fahrenheit, paper will burn. Fire is a primary image in the book. In the work of the fireman it is seen as a destructive force. It stamps out books and the freedom of thought that books represent. In the beginning, Montag enjoys its qualities. He even likes the soot that it leaves behind. Later, when he is with the book people, fire is used constructively to warm people. When the Phoenix myth is used

in the book, fire becomes a symbol of renewal. Out of the ashes, the mythical bird will be renewed. The suggestion is that a new society will be born from the ashes of the old one. The symbol of the Phoenix is used in contrast to the earlier use of the salamander. The dangerous fire lizard of myth, a symbol of the firemen's society from which Montag escapes, the salamander represents the destructive uses of fire. The most frightening symbol Bradbury uses is that of the Mechanical Hound, which represents the dehumanizing side of technology. This fierce creature seems to have powers greater than human ones; it has inescapable tracking capabilities, and can capture its victims with just one sting of anesthetic. Bradbury has made the creature seem so real that it exists in the novel as an important character. When the Mechanical Hound pursuing Montag is destroyed, another one is sent in its place, suggesting that technology used destructively cannot be easily demolished.

Historical Context

Book Burnings

Bradbury had a number of recent historical events on which to base *Fahrenheit 451* when he wrote the book in the early 1950s. The book burnings of the Nazi regime in Germany during the 1930s had been widely shown after World War II. These book burnings became a major symbol of the repression that followed in Nazi Germany. The importance of books and the freedom to read them was a central concern of liberal-minded people during the 1950s. As the Senate hearings of Joseph McCarthy began to focus on writers and film makers, the question of artistic freedom troubled many people and became the subject of debate. It was within this context of artistic repression that Bradbury expanded his story "The Fireman" into a full length novel. The fact that the book was reprinted forty-eight times over a twenty-five year period after its publication is indicative of the fact that Bradbury hit a vital nerve center of public consciousness. Unlike many of the characters in *Fahrenheit 451,* the American reading public ultimately rejected the idea of thought control that was present during the McCarthy hearings.

Censorship

While Americans are guaranteed free speech and a free press in the Bill of Rights to the Con-

A Nazi book-burning during the 1930s.

stitution, a history of censorship has nevertheless existed in this country. Censorship was at times allowed and even enforced by the United States government. In the early years of film making, censorship was allowed on the grounds that movies were entertainment and not an expression of free speech. Senator Joseph McCarthy's hearings into the political background of artists led to the "blackballing" of several prominent Hollywood writers during the 1950s. While the Supreme Court decision allowing censorship of films was overturned in 1952, strict regulation of film content persisted into the 1960s. Today, the attempt to censor artistic products comes mainly from organized pressure groups. Ironically, Bradbury's publishers, unknown to him, bowdlerized *Fahrenheit 451*—that is, "cleaned up" or deleted some of the language that Bradbury used—in order to make the book saleable to the high school market. Since the advent of films, television, and the internet, efforts to limit access by children to certain types of material in these media has persisted to this day. The general method has been to have producers of these media rate the programs and place the burden of responsibility on parents to censor what children see in the movies, watch on television, or have access to on computers.

Political Repression and Conformity

Besides the repression that took place during the Nazi regime in Germany during the 1930s and 1940s, similar political repression and dictatorship had been taking place in the Soviet Union. After World War II, Western Europe and the United States entered into what has been called the Cold War—a struggle pitting the ideals of democracy and communism against each other—with the Soviet Union. Frequent reports of Soviet repression of writers and censorship of books were in the news. In his dystopian novel *1984,* George Orwell had satirized what he called "big brother," a government figure who was always watching the public. Orwell also used two-way television to illustrate how the new technology could be used against the public. Bradbury presents television in *Fahrenheit 451* as a drug that stupefies its viewers. Much of the pressure to conform in the United States during the Cold War was derived from the holdover of a wartime psychology that was strong during World War II. The mobilization during the war spilled over into the postwar era. As the United States and Europe went through a period of rebuilding domestic markets, the Cold War also stimulated a military economy. Opportunities for advancement abounded. Jobs were plentiful and

Compare & Contrast

- **1950s:** During the McCarthy hearings, artists and writers lost their jobs for their politically liberal and left-wing leanings.

  Today: More outlets exist for artists with out-of-the-mainstream views, both liberal and conservative, but when most media companies are owned by giant business corporations, these individuals are less likely to be heard by many people.

- **1950s:** The fear of nuclear conflict with the Communist Soviet Union was at its height.

  Today: Fear that atomic bomb capability will fall into the hands of terrorists prevails.

- **1950s:** Censorship was accepted by many as an unofficial good and is allowed by the federal government in cases like motion picture content.

  Today: While government-sponsored censorship is considered a threat to personal freedom, more people are inclined to support the restriction of exposure of pornographic and violent media material to children. These forms of expression, it is believed, corrupt the values of society.

- **1950s:** Most people conform to the social norms of the day. Social outcasts like the "beats" are small in number.

  Today: Multiculturalism flourishes as various ethnic and cultural groups celebrate their differences from "mainstream" society while at the same time a backlash can be seen in groups like the "English [Language] First" movement.

- **1950s:** Television made a technological impact on how people entertained themselves.

  Today: Computers compete vigorously with television as an entertainment source. The film industry has been reinvigorated both at the movie theater and as producers of videos for home entertainment.

---

people were encouraged to "work hard and get ahead." The image of the "organization man" was prevalent. If you "followed orders, you would succeed" was the conventional wisdom of the day. This attitude is reflected in Bradbury's portrayal of Montag in the opening scenes of *Fahrenheit 451.*

Technology

From the early days of television in the 1950s, when every American scrambled to have one in the home, to this day, watching television has competed with reading books. In the 1950s, schools began to use television in the classroom, because it was becoming apparent that children's reading levels were dropping. Bradbury, who had been nurtured as a child on books, used this in his novel to show how literature was begin reduced to the simplest, most general terms. "Out of the nursery into the college and back to the nursery; there's your intellectual pattern for the past five centuries or more," Captain

Beatty tells Montag and his wife when he tries to rationalize the work of the firemen.

More than any other aspect of the technological revolution that has taken place since World War II, none has had a greater impact than the development of the atomic bomb and atomic energy. During the 1950s and up until the fall of the Soviet Union, the fear of nuclear war was a real threat in the minds of people. The fear of damage from nuclear waste remains an environmental threat. The fear that destructive atomic power might fall into the hands of terrorists is also an issue that compels political discourse and action. It is within an atmosphere of fear that repression can flourish. In *Fahrenheit 451,* Bradbury re-creates the atmosphere of fear and repression that prevailed when he was writing the book.

Another technological advance that Bradbury deals with in his book is the development of robots. In the Mechanical Hound he presents a robot that is more powerful than a human being in its ability to "sniff out" its prey. This representation reflects a commonly held view that the nature of robots is to be feared because they do not possess human qualities and might even be able to take control over human beings. Many science-fiction "mad scientist" movies of the 1950s capitalized on this fear by portraying monstrous creatures created by misused technology as well as technology itself revolting against its creators. This fear of technology was pervasive during the 1950s.

Critical Overview

Reception to *Fahrenheit 451* has been mixed. While praising the book for its effective prose style and handling of important social issues, several aspects of the work have been criticized. Obscure references, such as those to the Phoenix myth and the sixteenth-century martyr Master Ridley, have been faulted for being inappropriate for general readers. References such as these and the novel's emphasis on the value of literature over that of mass culture have also led to attacks on Bradbury for being an elitist. Another area of criticism is that the author pits intellectuals against ordinary people. The book people, represented mostly by scholars, will save humanity, while ordinary people like Mildred contribute to the degradation of society by falling victim to social conformity.

In spite of these criticisms, many analysts find a great deal to praise in the book. John Colmer, in an essay in *Coleridge to Catch-22,* is struck by Bradbury's ability to convey horror. Bradbury is successful "in creating the horror of mechanized anti-culture," Colmer believes. "The burning scenes have intense power and the pursuit of Montag by the Mechanical Hound ... is in the best tradition of Gothic pursuit; mysterious, but relentless," the critic adds. Colmer, though, is one of the critics who finds Bradbury's allusions to culture forced and sentimental. "Bradbury cannot rely on his readers picking up his allusions. He ... explain[s] laboriously." He continues: "A writer who has to explain all his allusions and symbols for the benefit of lowbrow readers is at a considerable disadvantage." Colmer does find the message of *Fahrenheit 451* important, that "books create diversity and harmony," he explains. As a result the novel "is an intensely serious work of popular Science Fiction."

A major area of praise for Bradbury's work is his style. In his essay in *Ray Bradbury,* David Mo-

gen claims that *Fahrenheit 451* and the collection *The Martian Chronicles* are "destined to survive as Bradbury's best-known and most influential creations, the most sustained expressions of his essentially lyrical treatment of science-fiction conventions." While Mogen acknowledges the criticism of sentimentality and vagueness in *Fahrenheit 451,* he maintains that the work "remains one of the most eloquent science-fiction satires, a vivid warning about mistaking" mindless happiness for progress. Mogen also praises Bradbury for his ability to use the fireman as a central metaphor in the story.

In discussing the development of Montag in his essay *Ray Bradbury,* Wayne Johnson finds that the premise of a fireman starting rather than putting out fires is "farfetched." Johnson adds, however, that Bradbury "keeps such a tight focus on the developing awareness of fireman Guy Montag that we can successfully overlook the improbability of his occupation." Johnson praises Bradbury for maintaining "a certain detachment in the book, so that basic themes ... can be developed and explored without becoming either too realistic or too allegorical."

The thematic elements in *Fahrenheit 451* have received much praise. "Bradbury's rage against censorship and book burning reached its fullest and most eloquent expression ... when he expanded 'The Fireman' to novel length," says George Guffey in an essay in *Coordinates: Placing Science Fiction and Fantasy.* Gary K. Wolfe, in his essay on Bradbury in the *Concise Dictionary of American Literary Biography,* praises *Fahrenheit 451* as a "passionate attack on censorship ... equally an attack on the growing power of mass culture, particularly television ... which consistently falls prey to the demands of special interest groups." Wolfe observes that the "new culture" of the book people "seems to care as little for the individual as the mass culture from which Montag has escaped," but "the new society allows for a multiplicity of viewpoints and hence holds out some hope for the eventual revival of the human imagination." It is the glimmer of hope that Bradbury presents which has earned him the label of optimist. "Bradbury's novel does risk lapsing at the very close into a vague optimism," writes Donald Watt in his discussion of *Fahrenheit 451* as a dystopia (a work presenting a dehumanized society) in *Ray Bradbury.*

Among the highest praise Bradbury has achieved for his work is the recognition of his stylistic excellence. "On the whole, *Fahrenheit 451* comes out as a distinctive contribution to the speculative literature of our times, because in its multiple variations ... it demonstrates that dystopian fiction need not exclude the subtlety of poetry," comments Donald Watt. "Bradbury is above all a humanist ... ," says Wolfe. "Whatever the final assessment of Bradbury's later work, his historical importance both in popularizing science fiction and making it respectable cannot be denied," Wolfe writes in *Twentieth Century Science-Fiction Writers*.

Criticism

Edward E. Eller

Eller is an assistant professor at Northeast Louisiana University. In the following essay, he explores the historical climate that helped create Fahrenheit 451 *and its protests against mindless conformity and censorship.*

Bradbury developed *Fahrenheit 451* during the late 1940s and published it in 1950 just after World War II and during America's growing fear of communism. During World War II, Hitler and the Nazis had banned and burned hundreds of thousands of books. However, the Nazis went further; using new technologies, they attempted one of the largest mind control experiments in history by setting up state controlled schools and a propaganda machine which censored all ideas and information in the public media. To make matters worse, after the war the Soviet Union developed its own propaganda machine, created an atomic bomb, and invaded Eastern Europe. All this time, new technological innovations allowed these fascist states to more effectively destroy the books they didn't find agreeable and produce new forms of communication implanted with state-sanctioned ideas.

Finally, and most significantly for Bradbury, the U.S. government responded to its fear of growing communist influence with attempts to censor the media and its productions, including literature. In other words, it responded with the same tactics of tyranny implemented by Nazi Germany and the Soviet Union. The McCarthy hearings in the early fifties attempted to rein in what it saw as communist sympathies among authors and Hollywood producers. The FBI investigated the *potential* disloyalty of U.S. citizens. The federal government began attempts to restrict the free speech of judges and university professors by requiring loyalty oaths.

Fahrenheit 451 appeared in this political climate of technologically supported suspicion and

censorship, a climate which seemed to promise the possibility of the mass conformity in our citizenry. It is no surprise, then, that these concerns are central to the book's themes.

Montag and his wife, Mildred, live in what Bradbury imagines as the culture which might be produced if such trends continued. They live in a futuristic community that uses technology to control what they think and feel by controlling what they see and hear. They are encouraged to use sedatives to keep themselves docile and their senses dull. They have all the latest entertainment technology—three walls of their "living room" display soap operas, "seashell thimble" radios pump high fidelity sound directly into their ears, and two-hundred-foot billboards line the freeway, blocking out the natural landscape and replacing it with advertisements. There is one telling scene in which Montag attempts to read and remember the *Book of Ecclesiastes* while riding on the train to see Faber, his newfound teacher. He cannot, however, manage it because the train's sound system plays an advertisement for Denham's Dentifrice over and over: "Denham's does it" with a bouncy jingle that interferes with his ability to think and remember. Everywhere he goes in these controlled spaces the system is there to limit and shape what he thinks by feeding him sights and sounds.

Mildred is the end product of this system. Mildred, as does most of the community, immerses herself in the media provided for her to consume. Whenever she is not at the TV, she plugs in her earphones, always soaking up the artificial stimulus and messages someone else feeds to her. The result is that she is literally incapable of thought and remembering. When Montag questions her about an argument that the characters are having on the wall TV, she can't remember what it was about even though it happened only one minute past. When he is sick and asks Mildred to get him some aspirin, she leaves the room and then wanders back a few minutes later, not a thought in her head.

The situation is so serious for Mildred that she might as well be an empty shell, a corpse, or a machine herself. As it turns out, Mildred is literally on the verge of being a corpse, having almost overdosed on sedatives. Montag comes home after a satisfying book-burning, only to find that his house feels like a "mausoleum" and his wife "cold" and himself "with the feeling of a man who will die in the next hour for lack of air." The oppressive atmosphere of death and emptiness is aggravated by the visit of the hospital "technicians" who come to

What Do I Read Next?

- Bradbury's 1950 collection of linked stories, *The Martian Chronicles,* uses the conventional settings of science fiction to address issues such as racism, censorship, technology, and nuclear war. The framework of the collection is the human colonization of Mars, and the individual stories look at how individuals try to build and fit into a new society. The collection is marked by Bradbury's distinctive poetic style, and is widely considered a classic.

- Margaret Atwood's 1985 novel *The Handmaid's Tale* depicts a future American society where behavior is strictly controlled. People are given specific tasks to perform and must conform to assigned behavior. This futuristic society is one in which men dominate women, who are restricted to domestic roles. The handmaid's job is to bear children, which will be turned over to the privileged class of women who are the wives of the governing men. As in *Fahrenheit 451,* the central character is ultimately able to escape through an underground network. A manuscript is found several centuries later and is presented at a scholarly convention, which tries to identify some of the characters in the story. This final section satirizes scholarly inquiry.

- In *Looking Backward, 2000–1887,* Edward Bellamy criticizes American capitalism as he saw it in 1888. His novel depicts an American society in the year 2000 that has become a cooperative commonwealth where there is no longer any competition. Bellamy advocated the nationalization of public services in his "brave new world." Bellamy's book helped stimulate the socialist movement in America.

- *A Clockwork Orange* was written by Anthony Burgess in 1962. It is a futuristic novel that centers on thought control and the methods used by a totalitarian regime to brainwash people.

- Aldous Huxley's utopian novel, *Brave New World* was written in 1932. Huxley depicts a world in which genetically specialized test tube babies are developed to perform specific jobs. Recreation is done on a group basis only. Any form of individualism is fully discouraged. Those who do not conform or are too old are sent to live on reservations. The book is a satire of the modern world, which is depicted as an anti-feeling, anti-human, and anti-emotional place.

- *Animal Farm,* George Orwell's 1945 novel, is an allegory of the dictatorship of Josef Stalin in Russia. The characters are all farm animals, with the pigs taking power since they are the most intelligent creatures.

- Orwell's novel *1984* was published in 1949. It presents a stark picture of the world in 1984, a time when thought control fully regulates every aspect of life. The world is divided into three spheres of power that try to maintain that balance through police state methods. Two-way television enables those in control to monitor the activities of the populace. History is rewritten, computer data banks keep track of everyone, and a new language, "newspeak," reverses truth to accommodate the political structure.

- *Free Speech for Me—But Not for Thee* is noted free-speech scholar and young adult novelist Nat Hentoff's 1992 study of censorship.

---

the house to service Mildred. They treat her like an extension of the snakelike machine they use to "take out the old and put in the new." He finds out that they act as causally as "handymen" doing a fix-it-up job because they clean out nine to ten stomachs a night. In other words, people are no

more than extensions of machines; they are machines themselves. The "technicians" treat them appropriately, as either broken, like Mildred, or in good repair. Technology violates their humanity.

The most complete violation of humanity would be the replacement of the human with a machine in perfect conformity with the system which created it. This may not be possible with humans, but it makes the Mechanical Hound the perfect creature of the system. It makes the Hound a fail-safe against the possibility that a human member of the mass society will be tainted by individuality and independent thought. The Hound cannot be so tainted. It lacks the two key ingredients which might allow it individuality and independence—its own thoughts and true sensations. As Beatty says, "It doesn't think anything we don't want it to think … a fine bit of craftsmanship." Later, Montag describes it as a thing in the world which "cannot touch the world." It lacks the mind of its own and body that feels. This makes the Hound the best guardian of their way of life. As a result, when Montag grows more aware of how the system has deprived him of sensation and thought, the Hound grows more aware of Montag. The Hound may not be able to touch the world, but it recognizes the smell of thought, it recognizes that Montag does not belong to the same system it does.

All is not lost, though. Montag's teachers lead him out of this controlled and sterile world. Clarisse, the young seventeen-year-old "oddball," is his first teacher. Clarisse prods him back into experiencing the outside world's sensations, especially smells as simple as "apricots" and "strawberries," "old leaves" and "cinnamon," smells which up to now have always been dominated by the odor of kerosene. She entices him out of the insulated "walls" of their house and into the rain, away from the rule books and 3-D comics whose content is strictly controlled so as to ensure that everything is agreeable—that is, all packaged to promote conformity and consumerism. She ignores his authority by openly questioning whether he can even think and challenges his smug superiority by seeing through his "mask" of happiness and into his deeper discontent. She tells him how she eavesdrops on others and finds that young "people don't talk about anything" except to trade the brand names of clothes and cars. She points out that the two-hundred-foot billboards hide the real world. She teaches him that he and everyone else are subject to the dictates of others, that their thoughts and experiences are controlled.

When Clarisse "disappears," Captain Beatty, Montag's superior, ironically becomes his "teacher." Even though Beatty's purpose is to bring Montag back into conformity with the system, he drives Montag farther away during his "history lesson" on the origins and purpose of the firemen book-burners. Beatty tells him that the condition of the world and the rejection of "books" and their ideas was a "mass" phenomenon. Not only did the population find it easier to read condensed versions of literature and digests rather than whole works, but it was also more "agreeable." Books are notorious for their slippery and contradictory ideas. It becomes easier and safer to do away with them altogether; this is the job of the fireman. Over time, substitutions displaced books altogether: photography and film, rule books, sports, and trivial information. Fill them up with "non-combustible" stuff so they feel "absolutely brilliant" but lack any thought which may have "two sides … no philosophy or sociology," says Beatty. Then we can have a perfect tyranny of technology over the comfortable and thoughtless. The problem, however, is that if books are the way to "melancholy" and unhappiness, then why is Mildred so deeply depressed and Montag so angry?

Montag's third "teacher" explains the source of their unhappiness. Faber, the old college English teacher, argues that the "telivisor" is irresistible. Furthermore, if you "drop a seed" (take a sedative) and turn on the televisor, "[It] grows you any shape it wishes. It *becomes* and *is* the truth." It makes a people into what it wants them to be, a conforming mass all acting in unison. Perhaps the most frightening image in the book makes this idea of thoughtless masses under the direction of technology concrete for us. At the end of the chase scene when the Mechanical Hound closes in and Montag approaches the river, the broadcaster asks the whole population to rise and go to the door and everybody look out at the street at the same time. Montag has a vision of the population acting in near perfect unison under the direction of a technological device—a truly frightening vision of humans turned into conforming automatons.

Faber argues, however, that books have a "quality" or "texture of information." Books have a depth of imaginative experience and completeness of information which the media soaps lack. This "texture of information," along with the leisure time to absorb it and the freedom to act on what it allows us to discover, is what Montag needs to make him, if not happy, then at least satisfied. In a sense, Montag's awakening sensations, his growing awareness of smells other than kerosene, his new appreciation for rain and the light of the moon, symbolize the "quality" found in books. Throughout the book, we get hints about this. After his wife's mishap with the sedatives, he feels suffocated and empty, and in a fit of desire for something more, he throws the sealed windows of the bedroom to let the moon's light fill the room. When he is trying to memorize the *Book of Eccle-siastes* and the Denham's Dentifrice advertisement interferes, he has this urge to run out of the train and experience anything, any sensation, even if its the pain of a pounding heart and lungs gasping for air. When he lay in his bed the night of the old woman's burning, he feels that he "never ... quite ... touched ... anything." Parallel to his yearning for the "texture of information" in books, he has a yearning for deeper and richer bodily experiences and sensations.

All in all, the idea is that if Montag is to escape the technological cocoon which the culture has built for him, he must do it in mind and body, in books and sensations. This is no new idea, that the mind and body are one. If this is true, then it is also true that if you control the experiences of the body so, too, will the mind be controlled. And vise-versa, if you control the depth of ideas and smooth out the "texture of information" in the media, the body will lose its ability to absorb a wide range of sensation. We see this effect on Montag when he finally climbs up out of the river. Having been deprived of deep and textured sensations most of his life, he was "crushed" by the "tidal wave of smell and sound." He experiences an onslaught of odor: musk, cardamom, ragweed, moss, blood, cloves, and warm dust. The narrator tells us, "enough to feed on for a lifetime"; there are "lakes of smelling and feeling and touching."

It is both the mind and the body of the population which the prevailing union of politics and technology has repressed in Montag's culture. The book people Montag discovers at the end of the novel show that you must abandon the system and get "outside" the technological cocoon. You must internalize the conflicting, richly textured information and ideas of books before you can be an individual not subject to the repressive conformity of the masses. The book people are literally outside in nature as well as figuratively outsiders alienated from the culture. They have literally internalized books as well as figuratively become "book covers." They have brought the book and the body, thought and sensation together. Maybe this is why Bradbury was so outraged by the book burnings in Nazis Germany. Maybe this is why he says "that when Hitler burned a book I felt it as keenly, please forgive me, as his killing a human, for in the long sum of history they are one and the same flesh."

Source: Edward E. Eller, in an essay for *Novels for Students,* Gale 1997.

Diane S. Wood

In the following essay, Wood compares Fahrenheit 451 *with Margaret Atwood's* The Handmaid's Tale, *focusing on their historical context and respective treatment of conformity and institutionalized repression.*

Ray Bradbury's *Fahrenheit 451* and Margaret Atwood's *The Handmaid's Tale* depict the rational decision to go into exile, to leave one's native land, that is, the pre-exile condition. These novels present horrifying views of the near future where societal pressures enforce rigid limitations on individual freedom. Their alienated characters find their circumstances repugnant. Justice and freedom are denied them, along with the possibility for enriching their lives through intellectual pursuits. These speculative novels like Orwell's *1984* are dystopian in nature, showing how precarious are today's constitutional rights and how necessary it is to preserve these liberties for future generations. They depict ordinary people, caught in circumstances that they cannot control, people who resist oppression at the risk of their lives and who choose exile because it *has* to be better than their present, unbearable circumstances. Voluntary exile necessitates a journey into the unknown as an alternative to the certain repression of the present.

Both novels offer a bleak possible future for the United States. Bradbury, writing in the McCarthy era of the 1950s, envisions a time when people choose to sit by the hour watching television programs and where owning books is a crime. Atwood, in the 1980s, foresees a time when, in the wake of changes begun during the Reagan Administration, women are denied even the most basic rights of working and owning property. Both novels thus present "political" stances in the widest sense of the word. In her address on Amnesty International, Atwood defines the word "politics" and how it comes to be incorporated into a writer's work:

> By 'politics' I do not mean how you voted in the last election, although that is included. I mean who is entitled to do what to whom, with impunity; who profits by it; and who therefore eats what. Such material enters a writer's work not because the writer is or is not consciously political but because a writer is an observer, a witness, and such observations are the air he breathes. They are the air all of us breathe; the only difference is that the author looks, and then writes down what he sees. What he sees will depend on how closely he looks and at what, but look he must.

To Atwood being "political" is part of the moral stance of the writer as truth teller. In his 1966

Introduction to *Fahrenheit 451,* Bradbury expresses moral outrage concerning bookburning: "when Hitler burned a book I felt it as keenly, please forgive me, as his killing a human, for in the long sum of history they are one and the same flesh. Mind or body, put to the oven, is a sinful practice...." He sees the necessity to guard constantly against such practices:

> For while Senator McCarthy has long been dead, the Red Guard in China comes alive and idols are smashed, and books, all over again, are thrown into the furnace. So it will go, one generation printing, another generation burning, yet another remembering what is good to remember so as to print again.

Atwood stresses the qualities of authors which make them a danger to oppressive governments: "The writer, unless he is a mere word processor, retains three attributes that power-mad regimes cannot tolerate: a human imagination, in the many forms it may take; the power to communicate; and hope."

The novels by Bradbury and Atwood examine the personal response of an individual who is in conflict with the majority in his society and whose occupation is abhorrent to him. *Fahrenheit 451* centers upon the personal crisis of Montag, a young fireman whose job consists of burning books. He finds his life increasingly meaningless and eventually comes to reject the too-simple, cliched values of his milieu. He experiences loneliness in a society where people are constantly entertained without time given to reflexion and personal development, activities often associated with the reading process. The more complicated nuances of the world of books are available to him only when he leaves his reductionistic society....

In both novels the population is strictly regulated and the conduct of individuals is highly regimented. Indeed, in these repressive circumstances, it is not surprising that the protagonists would wish to flee, especially since, by the end of the novels, they have broken laws which would bring the death penalty if they were apprehended. "Mechanical Hounds" use scent to hunt down lawbreakers in Bradbury's fiction. The hounds tear apart their prey. Montag narrowly escapes this fate but the police do not admit being outwitted. They stage his death for the benefit of the huge television audience which follows the developing story of his evasion. The authorities murder an innocent derelict in Montag's place, so as not to disappoint the viewers and appear ineffectual. The authorities are motivated by the desire to maintain power at any cost and blatantly violate human rights....

The major task of both Bradbury and Atwood is to portray convincingly in their futuristic novels how the abridgement of freedom evolved in the United States. As such, the novels are strong political statements warning of the consequences of what seem dangerous trends to the authors. One has only to look at the statistics for television watching, witness the decline of interest in reading among our students, and read current reports about ecological damage to verify the gravity of the dangers this country faces at the present time. In the world of *Fahrenheit 451* people have given up thinking for mindless pursuits. No revolution or *coup d'etat* brings about the loss of freedom. Rather, individual laziness precipitates a gradual erosion. This evolution takes place long before the birth of Montag, who grows up in a society where books are proscribed. His superior, a fireman, explains the trend of increasing simplification as the result of the influence of the mass media: "Things began to have *mass*.... And because they had mass, they became simpler.... Once, books appealed to a few people, here, there, everywhere. They could afford to be different. The world was roomy. But then the world got full of eyes and elbows and mouths." In a vast generalization which is itself a simplification, he tells how the modern era brought a movement to speed up and condense everything:

> Then, in the twentieth, century, speed up your camera. Books cut shorter. Condensations. Digests. Tabloids. Everything boils down to the gag, the snap ending.... Classics cut to fit fifteen-minute radio shows, then cut again to fill a two-minute book column, winding up at last as a ten-or twelve-line dictionary resume.... Do you see? Out of the nursery into the college and back to the nursery; there's your intellectual pattern for the past five centuries or more.

The rich value of books is thus denied when they are reduced to brief summaries. Happiness to this fireman comes from eliminating all dissension, especially that caused by books: "'Colored people don't like Little Black Sambo. Burn it. White people don't feel good about Uncle Tom's Cabin. Burn it. Someone's written a book on tobacco and cancer of the lungs? The cigarette people are weeping? Burn the book. Serenity, Montag. Peace, Montag. Take your fight outside. Better yet, into the incinerator.'" Yet this society does not produce happiness. Montag is perpetually lonely and his wife attempts suicide.

Whereas Atwood's society ceremonializes violence, in Bradbury's book the society eliminates all cause for unhappiness and sweeps unpleasantness away, including those which are an integral part of the human condition: "'Funerals are unhappy and pagan? Eliminate them, too. Five minutes after a person is dead he's on his way to the Big Flue, the Incinerators serviced by helicopters all over the country. Ten minutes after death a man's a speck of black dust. Let's not quibble over individuals with memoriams. Forget them. Burn all, burn everything. Fire is bright and fire is clean.'" Television concerns itself with the ephemeral present and thus follows the trend toward forgetting the past. Books by their very essence preserve and memorialize those who have lived before. Bradbury would probably agree with Atwood's comments that all repressive governments eliminate authors because they are so dangerous. The fireman views fire as a means of purging and cleansing emotions in his society. Political dissension is eliminated by giving only one side of the argument. War is not even talked about. People are reduced to thinking about simple facts, meaningless data: "Cram them full of noncombustible data, chock them so full of 'facts' they feel stuffed, but absolutely 'brilliant' with information. Then they'll feel they're thinking, they'll get a *sense* of motion without moving. And they'll be happy, because facts of that sort don't change. Don't give them any slippery stuff like philosophy or sociology to tie things up with. That way lies melancholy." Through simplifying and reducing ideas, he feels that the firemen produce happiness for the society: "we're the Happiness Boys, the Dixie Duo, you and I and the others. We stand against the small tide of those who want to make everyone unhappy with conflicting theory and thought. We have our fingers in the dike. Hold steady. Don't let the torrent of melancholy and dreary philosophy drown our world."

Balancing this reductionist apology are the views of another character in the novel, a retired English professor who "had been thrown out upon the world forty years ago when the last liberal arts college shut for lack of students and patronage." He traces the lack of reading to apathy: "Remember, the firemen are rarely necessary. The public itself stopped reading of its own accord. Your firemen provide a circus now and then at which buildings are set off and crowds gather for the pretty blaze, but it's a small sideshow indeed, and hardly necessary to keep things in line. So few want to be rebels anymore. And out of those few, most, like myself, scare easily." The professor's personal experience bears witness to the gradual nature of the transition from a reading to a non-reading culture. One day, there are simply no more students:

That was a year I came to class at the start of the new semester and found only one student to sign up for Drama from Aeschylus to O'Neill. You see? How like a beautiful statue of ice it was, melting in the sun. I remember the newspapers dying like huge moths. No one *wanted* them back. No one missed them. And then the Government, seeing how advantageous it was to have people reading only about passionate lips and the fist in the stomach, circled the situation with your fire-eaters....

In both novels books represent important artifacts of the past and the act of reading becomes a heroic gesture. This is not surprising since both authors are avid readers and have described the importance of books in their lives. In fact, *Fahrenheit 451* was written in the UCLA library.

One of the most crucial passages in the novel shows a woman willing to die for her books. Montag is stunned when she sets fire to her library and immolates herself along with her precious volumes. This experience causes Montag to question what there is in books that is worth dying for and ultimately leads to his becoming a preserver of books instead of a destroyer....

Each novel ends with the protagonist's escape and the beginning of his exile from repression. There is some ambiguity, however, since the alternative order is not elaborated on. Montag watches his city being destroyed by a nuclear explosion. He joins a group of vagabonds who memorize the books with which they have escaped. No attempt is made to follow his further development in these difficult circumstances or to predict the course the future holds for society or the survivors. The implication is clear, however, that intellectual freedom is worth the inconvenience of life outside the modern city. Because he left, Montag survives the death of the mindless masses who stayed behind....

The appeal of these two highly acclaimed novels stems from the main characters' difficult situation in a repressive future United States. The plausible explanations given by both Bradbury and Atwood for the ghastly turn taken by American society in the futures they portray serves as a vivid reminder that freedom must be vigilantly guarded in order to be maintained. Apathy and fear create unlivable societies from which only a few courageous souls dare escape. "Ordinary" says one of the cruel Aunts of *The Handmaid's Tale* "is what you are used to." The main characters never are able to accept the "ordinariness" of the repression which surrounds them. They are among the few who are willing to risk the difficult path of exile.

Source: Diane S. Wood, "Bradbury and Atwood: Exile as Rational Decision," in *The Literature of Emigration and Ex-*

ile, edited by James Whitlark and Wendall Aycock, Texas Tech University Press, 1992, pp. 131-42.

Wayne L. Johnson

In the following excerpt, Johnson provides concise analysis of plot, theme and elements of fantasy and social criticism in Fahrenheit 451.

Fahrenheit 451 is one of only two novels Bradbury has written. The other is *Something Wicked This Way Comes. (Dandelion Wine* and *The Martian Chronicles* are often referred to as novels, but they are really collections of separate stories unified by theme and specially written bridge passages.) *Fahrenheit 451* is a short novel, an expansion of a story, "The Fireman," originally published in *Galaxy.* The book is about as far as Bradbury has come in the direction of using science fiction for social criticism. Actually, the premise of the book is rather farfetched—that firemen in some future state no longer fight fires but set them, having become arms of a political program aimed at stamping out all literature. This purging of the written word, particularly of the imaginative sort, is found in other stories, most strikingly in "Pillar of Fire" and "The Exiles." But in these other stories the tone is clearly that of a fantasy. *Fahrenheit 451* is realistic in tone, but keeps such a tight focus on the developing awareness of fireman Guy Montag that we can successfully overlook the improbability of his occupation. In fact, the very improbability of Montag's work allows Bradbury to maintain a certain detachment in the book, so that basic themes such as freedom of speech, the value of imagination, the authority of the state, individualism versus conformity, and so on, can be developed and explored without becoming either too realistic or too allegorical.

In the course of the book, Montag goes through what today might be called consciousness raising. He begins as a loyal fireman, burning what he is told to burn, progresses through a period of doubts and questioning, and ends up rebelling against the system and doing his part to keep man's literary heritage alive. But the bones of the plot do little to convey the feeling of the book. Bradbury's world here seems much closer to the present than the future—not so much in terms of its overall structure as in terms of its more intimate details. Some of the characterizations—Montag's wife, given over to drugs and mindless television; Clarisse, an archetypal hippie or flower child; and the old woman, who defies the firemen by pouring kerosene over her books and her own body before striking a match—might have been drawn from the turbulent

political events of the sixties. It is almost necessary to remind oneself that *Fahrenheit 451* was published in 1953.

Many of Bradbury's pet themes are to be found in the novel. Metamorphosis is a major theme of the story, for in the course of it Montag changes from book-burner to living-book. Montag the fireman is intensely aware of the power of fire: "It was a special pleasure to see things eaten, to see things blackened and *changed.*" He himself is changed every time he goes out on a job: "He knew that when he returned to the firehouse, he might wink at himself, a minstrel man, burnt-corked, in the mirror."

Machines are of crucial importance. Overall, the book traces Montag's flight from the dangerous mechanical world of the city to the traditional haven of the country. Montag at first feels comfortable with machines, especially his flame-throwing equipment. The first time Montag meets Clarisse he views the scene in mechanical terms: "The autumn leaves blew over the moonlit pavement in such a way as to make the girl who was moving there seem fixed to a gliding walk, letting the motion of the wind and leaves carry her forward." But many mechanical things are repellent to Montag, particularly the equipment the medical technicians use on his wife after she has taken an overdose of sleeping pills: "They had two machines, really. One of them slid down your stomach like a black cobra down an echoing well looking for all the old water and the old time gathered there."

Montag's particular mechanical enemy is the fire station's Mechanical Hound, more like a huge spider, actually, with its "bits of ruby glass and ... sensitive capillary hairs in the Nylon-brushed nostrils ... that quivered gently, gently, its eight legs spidered under it on rubber-padded paws." As Montag becomes more fascinated with books and nearer to betrayal of his duties as a fireman, the hound becomes more suspicious of him. The hound is then symbolic of the relentless, heartless pursuit of the State.

When Montag finally flees the city, he must first cross a mechanical moat, a highway 100 yards across on which the "beetle" cars seem to take pleasure in using pedestrians for target practice. Other machines Montag grows to hate are the radio and television that reduce their audience, Montag's wife, for one, into listless zombies.

But *Fahrenheit 451* is not primarily a work of social criticism. Its antimachine and antiwar elements are there primarily as background for Montag's spiritual development. It is interesting that this development seems to be in the direction of social outcast. Granted that Montag's society has its evils, but at the end of the book we are not so sure that Montag will be completely happy with his new-found friends, the book people. What we are sure of is that Montag has entrenched himself as nay-sayer to a society that has become hostile and destructive toward the past. Montag joins the book people whose task, as Granger puts it, is "remembering." But even as he does so, he promises himself that he will one day follow the refugees from the bombed-out city, seeking, though this is not stated, perhaps his wife, perhaps Clarisse. Most of the book people are like the old man in "To the Chicago Abyss," essentially harmless, using their talents for remembering things to aid their society in whatever way they can. But Montag may perhaps be too rigid an idealist, having rejected his former society with the same vehemence as he once embraced it. Like Spender in *The Martian Chronicles,* Montag has committed murder to maintain his freedom and the integrity of his vision. Unlike Spender, but like many of Bradbury's other outsiders and misfits, Montag has successfully achieved a truce or stalemate with a world hostile to his individuality. At the end of *Fahrenheit 451,* Montag's future can go either way; toward reintegration with a new, less hostile society, or toward a continuing, perpetual alienation.

Source: Wayne L. Johnson, "Machineries of Joy and Sorrow," in *Ray Bradbury,* Frederick Ungar Publishing Company, 1980, pp. 85-8.

Sources

John Colmer. "Science Fiction" in *Coleridge to Catch-22,* St. Martin's Press, 1978, pp. 197-209.

George R. Guffey, in *Coordinates: Placing Science Fiction and Fantasy,* edited by George E. Slusser, et al, Southern Illinois University Press, 1983, pp. 99-106.

Wayne L. Johnson, in "Machineries of Joy and Sorrow," in *Ray Bradbury,* Frederick Ungar Publishing Company, 1980, pp. 85-8.

David Mogen, *"Fahrenheit 451,"* *Ray Bradbury,* Twayne Publishers, 1986, pp. 105-112.

Donald Watt, in "Burning Bright: 'Fahrenheit 451' as Symbolic Dystopia" in *Ray Bradbury,* edited by Martin Harry Greenberg and Joseph D. Olander, Taplinger Publishing Company, 1980, pp. 195-213.

Gary K. Wolfe, "Ray Bradbury," in *Concise Dictionary of American Literary Biography,* Vol. 5, Gale Research, 1989, pp. 16-32.

Gary K. Wolfe, "Ray Bradbury," in *Twentieth Century Science-Fiction Writers,* 2nd edition, St. James Press, 1986, pp. 72-5.

For Further Study

Bradbury, Ray. "Introduction" to *Fahrenheit 451,* Simon and Schuster, 1967, pp. 9-15.
Bradbury narrates the history of his book's writing.

Hoskinson, Kevin. "*The Martian Chronicles* and *Fahrenheit 451:* Ray Bradbury's Cold War Novels," *Extrapolation,* vol. 36, No. 4, Winter 1995, pp. 345-359.
One of *Fahrenheit 451*'s preoccupations is with "majority rule" which to him is the same as censorship. This essay puts that theme from the book into the historical context of the 1950s, when it was written.

Moore, Everett T. A review in the *ALA Bulletin,* vol. 55, no. 5, May 1961, pp. 403-4.
Moore explores the themes of censorship and conformity in *Fahrenheit 451.* The article includes material from an interview with Ray Bradbury in which the author ridicules the trend of watering down the classics to make them easily accessible to everyone.

Seed, David. "The Flight from the Good Life: *Fahrenheit 451* in the contest of Postwar American Dystopias," *Journal of American Studies,* Vol. 28, No. 2, August 1994, pp. 225-240.
The characters in *Fahrenheit 451* live in a consumer culture which can only work if it keeps them in a controlled environment, inside the house, the car, and the fire station. Once outdoors and away from the media which defines their secure world, the society loses control of them.

Spencer, Susan. "The Post-Apocalyptic Library: Oral and Literate Culture in *Fahrenheit 451* and *A Canticle for Leibowitz,*" *Extrapolation,* vol. 32, No. 4, Winter 1991, pp. 331-342.
This critic explores the idea in Ray Bradbury's novel that written books replace the ability to remember. Those like Captain Beatty with access to literature, as opposed to rule books and comics, have power over the lives of others.

Zipes, Jack. "Mass Degradation of Humanity and Massive Contradictions in Bradbury's Vision of America in *Fahrenheit 451,*" in *No Place Else: Explorations in Utopian and Dystopian Fiction,* edited by Eric S. Rabkin, Martin H. Greenberg, and Joseph D. Olander, Southern Illinois University Press, 1983, pp. 182-199.
This essay attempts to justify apparent ironies and contradictions in the novel by describing how it fits into the time in which it was written.

A Farewell to Arms

Ernest Hemingway

1929

Ernest Hemingway's 1929 novel, *A Farewell to Arms,* is often regarded as his best artistic achievement. It was certainly his greatest commercial success to date with 80,000 copies sold within the first four months. The money earned for the novel, though, came too late to prevent his father from committing suicide due to financial stress and a losing struggle with diabetes. The novel established Ernest Hemingway as the literary master of a style that was characterized by brisk assertive staccato, or crisp precise prose. The novel also gave rise to the infamous myth of Hemingway as the epitome of American machismo. This owed as much to the popularity of his novel and his friendship with Gary Cooper—who played Frederic Henry in the film version of the novel—as it did to Hemingway's own heroism.

The book is the story of a young American named Frederic Henry who volunteers for service with the Italian army in World War I and falls in love with his English nurse, with whom he deserts from the retreating Italian front. Having escaped to Switzerland, they live in harmony until the tragic end of her pregnancy, during which both she and the child die. Much has been said about the prose style Hemingway used and a great debate has been waged over whether the novel is about machismo and the sex object, Catherine Barkley. However, *A Farewell to Arms* is not a novel glorifying war. Instead, it is a tragic love story whose *farewell* is from Frederic to the woman whose arms held sanity in the crazy world of the Great War.

Author Biography

Ernest Hemingway was born in 1899 to Dr. Clarence Hemingway and Grace Hall Hemingway. They lived in Oak Park, Illinois, and Ernest actively pursued sports with his father and arts with his mother, but without distinction. In 1917, after graduating from high school, he took a junior position at the *Kansas City Star*. This paper started Hemingway on a writing career and trained him in his style. The paper gave its reporters a style book which demanded brief, declarative, and direct sentences—Hemingway became the master of this style.

In May of 1918, he volunteered for war duty and served as an ambulance driver on the Italian front. This experience later served as the source material for *A Farewell to Arms*. He, like his character, was wounded in the legs. However, instead of being returned to the front he was sent home, where he was greeted as a celebrity and passed his months of convalescence at the family cabin in Michigan.

Having recovered, he took a position as companion to a lame boy in Toronto in 1920. There, he again entered the world of writing through the *Toronto Star*. After marriage to Hadley Richardson, he became a correspondent with the paper. He and his wife left for Paris where Hemingway associated with those writers known as the "Lost Generation" (James Joyce, Ezra Pound, Gertrude Stein, and Ford Madox Ford). His position with the *Toronto Star* enabled him to begin writing for himself.

His first publishing success was a short story entitled *My Old Man* in 1923. For the next few years he continued to meet literary figures (F. Scott Fitzgerald among others) and edit a journal with Ford Madox Ford. Then, in 1925, he began *The Sun Also Rises* and *The Torrents of Spring*. Both were published the following year. 1926 also saw Hemingway divorce Hadley for his second wife, Pauline Pfeiffer.

In 1927, Hemingway published the short story collection *Men without Women* and began *A Farewell to Arms* in 1928. His son, Patrick, was born by cesarean section and this event influenced the writing of Catherine Barkley's fate. With the publication of *A Farewell to Arms* in 1929, Hemingway found himself flooded with success and began a very mobile life. He frequented Cuba, Florida, and France; he went on several safaris in Africa; he contributed money for ambulance ser-

Ernest Hemingway

vice in the Spanish Civil War and also covered the war for *The North American Newspaper Alliance*. In 1940 he left Pfeiffer for Martha Gellhorn and published *For Whom the Bell Tolls*. Hemingway and Gellhorn then went to China. Next, he became a war correspondent with the U.S. Fourth Infantry Division where he met Mary Welsh. In 1945, he married Mary Welsh.

Hemingway continued to publish various works until 1952, when *Old Man and the Sea* crowned his fantastic career. This story gained him the Pulitzer Prize in 1953. He was awarded the prestigious Nobel Prize for Literature the following year. Unfortunately, by the mid-1950s his adventurous life had taken its toll. Hemingway became depressed and spent time in various hospitals. Finally, he returned from a stay in the Mayo Clinic on June 30, 1961, to his home in Ketchum, Idaho. There, he took a favorite gun and committed suicide on July 2.

Plot Summary

Book One

A Farewell to Arms opens in Italy during the First World War. The novel's main character, Frederic Henry, is a young American serving as a second lieutenant in the Italian Army. He is attached to a unit in Gorizia, in which he works as an ambulance driver. In addition to Frederic, the reader is introduced to two other characters: first a priest, who Frederic's friends enjoy baiting and teasing; and second Rinaldi, a good-looking Italian surgeon and a friend of Frederic's. He shares with Frederic the typical soldier's lifestyle of heavy drinking and frequent visits to the local brothels. When Frederic returns from a leave, Rinaldi tells him that a group of British nurses have arrived in the area to set up a hospital for the wounded. Rinaldi declares that he is in love with a nurse by the name of Catherine Barkley.

Rinaldi introduces Frederic Henry to Catherine Barkley, who is described as a tall, beautiful woman with long blonde hair. She finds it odd that Frederic is an American in the Italian Army. Frederic learns that Catherine had a fiance who was killed earlier in the war. He is very much attracted to her and would like to become romantically involved with her. Although Catherine responds to his first attempt to kiss her by slapping him, they gradually become more and more interested in each other. When Frederic has to take his ambulance back to the front, Catherine gives him her St. Anthony medal for good luck. Frederic feels indifferent about the war going on around him, feeling that it has little to do with him. One day while eating macaroni with cheese and drinking wine in a dugout, a shell wounds Frederic badly, and he is taken to a field hospital where he is visited by Rinaldi and the priest.

Book Two

Frederic Henry is transferred to an American hospital in Milan. Frederic manages to find a porter whom he pays to bring him some alcohol. Soon after, Catherine comes to the hospital to visit him and eventually manages to stay and work at the hospital. Three doctors come to examine Frederic, who needs surgery on his knee, and they tell him that he will have to wait six months before he can have the operation. Asking for a second opinion, he is visited by the Italian Dr. Valentini, who tells him he can have the operation the next day. During this period, and after his operation, Frederic and Catherine begin spending nights together while she is on night-duty in the hospital. Gradually Frederic finds himself falling more and more in love with Catherine.

Frederic and Catherine spend the summer together as he recovers in the hospital. Catherine continues to visit him at night during her work shifts.

As his leg improves, they are able to go outside of the hospital and visit Milan. Several new characters are introduced, including the American couple, the Meyerses, who are fond of betting on the horse races, and Ettore Moretti, an Italian captain from San Francisco. When Frederic comes down with jaundice, the stern head-nurse, Miss Van Campen, accuses him of having brought his illness on himself by drinking, in order to avoid being sent back to the front. Eventually he must go, however, and Frederic and Catherine spend a final night together in a hotel room before parting. Before Frederic leaves for the front, Catherine announces that she is pregnant.

Book Three

Frederic Henry returns to the front and reunites with Rinaldi, realizing quickly that the men at the front have lost their spirit and drive in the war. Hemingway describes the massive Italian retreat from the town of Caporetto when the German and Austrian forces began moving against them in October, 1917. Picking up two Italian sergeants, Frederic's ambulance faces many long delays caught up in the miles of forces and equipment retreating in the rain. Eventually he tries to make some progress by driving off of the road and across the countryside, but his ambulance gets stuck in the mud. When the two sergeants refuse to help him push it out of the mud, instead breaking into a run, Frederic shoots and injures one of them. His fellow driver Bonello finishes killing the man with a bullet to the head. Frederic strikes out on foot with his three companions, Bonello, Aymo, and Piani. Aymo does not make it very far before being shot and killed by an Italian sniper.

After hiding in a barn until they feel it is safe to continue, the three men push on. Bonello decides to turn himself in to the Germans as a prisoner of war to avoid being killed. Soon Piani and Frederic come to a long wooden bridge on the Tagliamento River, where military police, the carabinieri, are seizing their own Italian officers and executing them for calling the retreat. Frederic is detained, but he breaks free and jumps into the river to escape. Frederic floats down the river and eventually jumps a train headed for Milan and Catherine. Sick of the war and finished with fighting for a nation that is not even his own, Frederic is well content to make his "farewell to arms" and to desert his post in the Italian army:

> Anger was washed away in the river along with any obligation. Although that ceased when the carabiniere put his hands on my collar. I would like to

have had the uniform off although I did not care much about outward forms. I had taken off the stars, but that was for convenience. It was no point of honor. I was not against them. I was through. I wished them all the luck. There were the good ones, and the brave ones, and the calm ones and the sensible ones, and they deserved it. But it was not my show any more and I wished this bloody train would get to Mestre and I would eat and stop thinking. I would have to stop....

I was not made to think. I was made to eat. My God, yes. Eat and drink and sleep with Catherine. To-night maybe. No that was impossible. But to-morrow night, and a good meal and sheets and never going away again except together. Probably have to go damned quickly. She would go. I knew she would go. When would we go? That was something to think about. It was getting dark. I lay and thought where we would go. There were many places.

Book Four

Frederic Henry arrives in Milan and borrows civilian clothes from Ralph Simmons, a friend studying singing in Italy and preforming under the name Enrico DelCredo. Learning that the nurses have been sent to Stresa, he travels there and finds Catherine with her friend Helen Ferguson. Frederic and Catherine spend the night together in a hotel. Frederic plays billiards and converses with Count Greffi, a kind elderly man whom Frederic had met earlier while staying in Stresa. During a rainstorm, the bartender in the hotel warns Frederic that he is in danger of being caught as a deserter by the authorities and suggests that Frederic and Catherine borrow his boat and escape across the lake into Switzerland. Frederic rows all night until his hands are too sore to continue, and then Catherine takes over the rowing. When they arrive in Switzerland, they are arrested, but Frederic explains that they are tourists and that they have come to Switzerland for the winter sports. Because they have a good bit of money and valid passports, the authorities let them go.

Book Five

Frederic and Catherine travel to Montreux and spend a happy and romantic fall in a small chalet amidst the mountain pines. The couple have many happy days discussing their future life together. Frederic proposes marriage, but Catherine wishes to wait until after their child is born. While in Switzerland, Catherine visits the doctor and learns that she may have some problems during childbirth because her pelvis is very small.

When Catherine is ready to give birth, Frederic takes her to a hospital in Lausanne. Catherine's

From the film A Farewell to Arms, *starring Gary Cooper and Helen Hayes, 1932.*

labor is extremely difficult, and the doctor gives her laughing gas to ease the pain. When it is clear that she is not going to be able to give birth to the child naturally, the doctor tries to deliver it by cesarean section, but the baby is already dead. A nurse sends Frederic out to get something to eat. When he returns, he learns that Catherine has begun to hemorrhage. The doctor is unable to stop the bleeding, and Catherine's condition gradually worsens. Once she and Frederic say good-bye, Catherine slips into unconsciousness and soon dies. Catherine is gone. Frederic walks back to the hotel alone in the rain.

Characters

Bartolomeo Aymo

Aymo is one of Frederic Henry's ambulance drivers during the Italian army's retreat. He is also the driver Frederic is closest to. During the retreat, Aymo generously picks up two peasant woman with assurances that he will not rape them. This assurance frightens them even more—they, unfortunately, only recognize the one word of Aymo's Italian. It is also Aymo who is mistakenly shot by the Italian rear guard. It is a tragic mistake both for its

Media Adaptations

- Not long after its literary success, *A Farewell to Arms* was made into a movie by Paramount pictures in 1932. The lead role of Lt. Frederic Henry was played by Gary Cooper. The heroine of the tale, Catherine Barkley, was played by Helen Hayes. Directed by Frank Borzage, the film won several Academy Awards including Best Cinematography (Charles Bryant Lang, Jr.), Best Sound (Harold C. Lewis), and received nominations for Best Art Direction and Best Picture. To Hemingway's annoyance, the film departed widely from the book.

- A remake in 1950 of the 1932 film was not successful. This version starred William Holden and Nancy Olson. It was directed by Frank Borzage and even re-titled—*Force of Arms.*

- In 1957, Rock Hudson and Jennifer Jones starred in another remake. The producer, David O. Selznick, never ceased to interfere with the production. This interference led to John Huston's replacement as director with Charles Vidor. The resulting film butchered the original story so badly that Selznick wrote a letter of apology to Hemingway. The film was con-demned immediately upon release, losing Selznick millions of dollars that he had invested in the film. In fact, the only virtue of the film was the cinematic capture of the panoramic Italian landscape. The color photography was done by Piero Portalupi and Oscar Morris.

- In 1990, Hemingway's novel was adapted as a sound recording. Published by Books on Tape of California, the novel is read by Wolfram Kandinsky.

- The story of Hemingway's romance with his nurse Agnes von Kurowsky is retold by director Richard Attenborough in his 1997 film *In Love and War.* Starring Chris O'Donnell as the nineteen-year-old Hemingway and Sandra Bullock as his twenty-six-year-old nurse, *In Love and War* explores the relationship Hemingway had with von Kurowsky during the First World War and suggests Hemingway later used this failed romance as inspiration for *A Farewell to Arms.* Produced by New Line Cinema, the film was noted for splendid views of the Italian countryside and interesting historical details.

---

stupidity and because he was Frederic's friend. Aymo's role, then, is as a symbol of innocence killed by the stupidity of war.

Catherine Barkley

An English nurse with the Red Cross, Catherine Barkley is introduced to Henry through Rinaldi in Chapter IV. Frederic perceives "Miss Barkley [as] quite tall. She wore what seemed to be a nurse's uniform, was blonde and had tawny skin and gray eyes. I thought she was very beautiful." Rinaldi, on the other hand, calls her a "lovely cool goddess." These two examples summarize the critical views of Catherine—she is thought to be either a heroine or a sex object.

Not surprisingly, Catherine prefers Frederic to Rinaldi and begins a game of love with Frederic.

She tells the story of how her fiance had been horribly killed in the battle of the Somme but Frederic doesn't say anything. "They blew him all to bits," Catherine tells Frederic, who says nothing. She had imagined something far more picturesque like a sabre cut, which she would have joyously attended to. But this is World War I—trenches, mortars, and "bits"—and its horrors are awesome. Catherine reveals, through the tale of her childhood lover's death, how much more hardened by war she is than Frederic. Certainly, she has known the tragedy more intimately.

As a nurse, Catherine is able to transfer herself to the hospital where Frederic is recovering. Then, she flees with him to Switzerland where she dies from internal bleeding resulting from a difficult childbirth. In her death she is the picture of heroism and her statements are full of dark humor. "I'm not afraid. I just hate it," is one of the final lines which leaves Frederic quiet and solitary.

Catherine is a close examination of femininity in wartime but filtered through the subjective eyes of Frederic. This being the case, any decision about the character of Catherine is also a reflection on Frederic. Even so, Catherine is a representation of women in war, both as the ideal being defended by the army and the ideal sought by the individual soldier. In response to critics who have reacted negatively to her role, it can be suggested that while Catherine is won by Frederic, becomes pregnant, and then killed in a rather typical manner of a war novel, she also shows a certain assertiveness that is certainly lacking in Frederic Henry.

Bonello

Another of Frederic's drivers, Bonello is a lively sort who is looking forward to champagne at Udine—the end of the retreat. It is Bonello who asks to kill the sergeant that Frederic shot and wounded for not obeying orders. Later, after Aymo is shot, Bonello decides he would rather risk capture by the Germans than be killed by the Italians.

Cat

See Catherine Barkley

Enrico DelCredo

See Ralph Simmons

Helen Ferguson

Helen is a Scottish nurse with the Red Cross and a friend to Catherine Barkley. She makes it a point to tell Rinaldi that there is a difference between the Scottish and English. However, the translation is not very clear and Rinaldi understands her to mean that she dislikes Catherine. Helen is protective of Catherine in the same way that Rinaldi looks out for Frederic. Helen, like Rinaldi, represents the importance of social ties that become forged in war. The two characters regret the love of Frederic and Catherine because it disrupts the social network which was making the war bearable. Thus, when Frederic deserts the army and finds Helen and Catherine in Stresa, Helen is angry. She admonishes Frederic for being so irresponsible as to "compromise" and desert Catherine, but she eventually calms down. She eventually blesses the union if only because it is Catherine's wish. Having assented to the coupling, Helen is left alone.

Gino

He is the first of the drivers and mechanics that Frederic meets upon his return to the front. They discuss the war and war tactics generally until Gino begins to patriotically call his country sacred. It is after this that Frederic reveals how uncomfortable the words of honor and glory make him. He thus labels Gino a patriot, meaning Gino is a naive boy who will not be so quick to defend war once he is in it.

Count Greffi

The Count is staying in the same hotel where Frederic and Catherine stop while in Stresa. A very old man and formerly of great political importance, Count Greffi is the clearest representative of tradition and institution in the novel. Count Greffi, whose ideals were now being questioned and abandoned, helped make that nineteenth-century world which had been the cause of the devastating war. Frederic knew the Count from before the war and understands him to represent all those values, thus, he cannot refuse a game of pool. The Count is another of Frederic's tutors who wisely tries to impart lessons the priest has already tried to share, though not as concisely. The Count tells Frederic, while he beats him in pool, that a person ought to love one's fellow citizens, not abstract values. He says that the love of abstract values leads one to a foolish pursuit of illusions.

Frederic Henry

A Farewell to Arms is Frederic Henry's story of what happened to him during the First World War. Frederic is an American serving the Italian army as an ambulance driver. While in the service of the Italians, he falls in love with an English nurse named Catherine Barkley. He is wounded and sent to a hospital in Milan. Catherine transfers to the same hospital and they spend an idyllic time together as he recovers. Once his wounds have healed, Frederic must return to the front. Soon after he arrives, the Italian line breaks, and during the retreat from the Germans, he decides he has had enough of the war and deserts rather than be killed by battle police. After reuniting with his love, they flee to Switzerland. Once safely in the neutral nation, they pass the time playing cards until Catherine's baby is due. Both she and the baby die in childbirth and Frederic is left alone.

Frederic Henry's story reveals his education by various "tutors": the priest, Rinaldi, Catherine, the mechanics, and the war. Each try to impress upon Frederic a different lesson but he merely reacts to each. For example, the priest tries to persuade Frederic onto a moral and Christian path. In doing so, he extends an invitation to Frederic to visit his family. Frederic accepts, but instead chooses the more typical adventures of an officer on leave—he goes drinking and visits the brothels. He tries to explain his decision to the priest, saying, "we did not do the things we wanted to do; we never did such things." Ultimately, Frederic must learn from his experiences and, thus, his education is self-instructed. That is, from his beginning as a rootless boy, he gains such experience that even in his position as reactor, he must react to his own collection of experience. It is this that he must finally face in Catherine's death and which leads him to write it out, like an essay in answer to a test question. It is from this position that his retrospective narration is told.

Throughout the novel Frederic maintains his curious outsider status. He is an American who volunteered. "It did not have anything to do with me. It seemed no more dangerous to me myself than war in the movies," he says early in Chapter VII. Thus, as a foreigner, he finds it possible to observe the Italians without direct involvement, but then he is wounded. He is part of it as much as an ambulance driver is a part of any war. This position, as well as his forced reaction to his various tutors, leads Frederic into his separate relation with the world and this, in turn, affords him the ability to make a separate peace with the war and withdraw his involvement. Still, though he decides this is a possibility for him, there remains the fact that Henry is a reactor to events. That is, in the key moment that ends his belonging in the Italian army, he is merely risking his life to avoid summary execution. He decides, in his first bold move of the book, to jump into the river rather than face the stupidity of the guards.

Passini

Passini is killed in the same mortar attack which wounds Frederic. Passini talks against the war from a very socialist standpoint. He believes that the class controlling the country is stupid and that is why there is war. Frederic tolerates such troublesome talk out of good humor but also because he doesn't disbelieve him. It is after this conversation about politics that the mortar hits.

Luigi Piani

Luigi Piani is an ambulance driver under Frederic's direction when he returns to the front. While of lesser rank, Piani is Frederic's equal in every other way. Though he allows Frederic to be in charge, it is Piani who finds food, who leads Frederic the right way when they have left the ambulances, and who keeps him from being roughed up by the regular troops when they approach the battle police. Piani knows what is happening so far as the war is concerned, but he can do nothing to protect Frederic as they near the police. Piani is successful in his role as the brains of the group who feeds information to the leader, thereby insuring the group's survival. It is not his fault that Frederic is such a poor leader.

Priest

The chaplain of the Italian army stationed with the forces Frederic serves with, the priest is the subject of mess-hall jokes. He senses that Frederic is sympathetic to the Christian message, and they view each other as friends. He tries to persuade Frederic to spend leave time with his family in Abruzzi so he might have time to reflect and rest from the front. Then, when Frederic is in hospital, the priest comes to visit. This visit causes the clearest moment of insight into the human condition in war according to Frederic. The topic is invoked because the Priest attributes his fatigue to disgust of the war. Still, nothing is decided, though they both agree that war is the product of lust and not love.

Lt. Rinaldo Rinaldi

A surgeon for the Italian Army, Rinaldi is Frederic's roommate and friend. He is very protective of Frederic and calls him names full of endearment, for example, often referring to Frederic as "baby". He even comes to visit Frederic in the hospital and assists in the transfer of Catherine to Milan. He tries to be a good person and strives to be the best surgeon. However, the war is stressful, and he drinks to keep his hands steady. His visits to the brothel eventually give him gonorrhea. Stereotypically, he is the romantic Italian, and the novel loses track of him in the retreat.

Ralph Simmons

Ralph Simmons is an American friend of Frederic who is trying to earn a living as a singer under the name Enrico DelCredo. He seems to have little success. His purpose in the novel is to offer an opposite of Frederic, a kind of alternate self. Ralph truly has no involvement in the war but wants to be Italian, whereas Frederic is involved in the war as an Italian but doesn't want to be. Frederic goes to Ralph after he makes his escape from the battle police. Ralph lends him some clothes and Frederic goes on his way.

Tenente
See Mr. Frederic Henry

Themes

Identity

In *A Farewell to Arms,* one of the themes of Frederic Henry's adventure as an ambulance driver during World War I is identity. This theme compounds other themes that Hemingway is exploring through the war story. Identity is important to the story because it expresses the general question of the individual in the postwar world. The First World War raised some unsettling questions about the values the war generation had inherited. People began to question the validity of their national leaders and institutions which seemed to have led directly to such an incredible loss of life and economic devastation. Frederic represents, for Hemingway, this questioning of what is man that he can cause such awful destruction and human suffering.

Frederic's identity is displaced by the late introduction of his name to the reader, the fact of his being an American in the Italian army, and his constant play with words. He speaks Italian, but not well enough to advance in rank. He also understands French and German but remains unmistakably American. None of this is surprising but because Hemingway depends on dialogue to a great extent, the play of words between languages serves to heighten such issues as alienation and patriotism. The former is heightened because jokes do not translate and thus Frederic's efforts to lighten moods fall into silence. Beyond the curious problems of voice, Frederic always seems to be in the wrong outfit. This fact is exaggerated when he borrows clothes from Ralph Simmons to make his escape and when he says that his English gas mask works—whereas the Italian models do not. He continues to be someone else until the end. Finally, Frederic attempts to identify not as himself but as lost in Catherine—"We're the same one." He is forced to give this up when she dies.

Individualism

Hemingway's novel demonstrates the demise of loyalty to traditions and institutions that had been brought forward from the nineteenth century, a refocusing on the self often referred to as "individualism." His characters, especially Catherine Barkley (in terms of her fiance's death at the hand of sophisticated infantry), all have *war disgust.* Each of them is able to avoid becoming crazy by

Topics for Further Study

- The character of Hemingway's Catherine Barkley has undergone a great deal of scrutiny. This attention has alternated from seeing her as a strong, independent, and assertive woman to a needy, weak, and dependent person. Using the text, support both sides of the position. What do these views say about Hemingway's attitude toward gender roles?

- If Catherine's position as heroine is uncertain, what about the hero Frederic Henry's? Using the text, support or reject Henry's role as hero in *A Farewell to Arms.*

- Hemingway's style has been said to be a purely masculinist form of writing. What does it mean to say a writing style is male or female? Do you agree or disagree that his style is masculinist? Why?

- *The English Patient* by Michael Ondaatje is a story about a soldier wounded in the Italy of World War II. Compare it with Hemingway's story and discuss the genre of wounded men cared for by nurses. How do these stories compare with actual historical accounts of fighting in Italy during World War I?

falling back on the self. In doing so, each person rejects the "higher callings" of tradition, society, or institution. For example, Rinaldi has the satisfaction of having become a better surgeon through practice. He is also better with women for the same reason. When prodded by Frederic's suggestion that there may be more than these two self-centered items in life, Rinaldi responds with a very existentialist statement, "We never get anything. We are born with all we have and we never learn. We never get anything new."

It is out of this effort to come to terms with the stupidity and horror of the Great War that the school of thought known as existentialism emerges, a movement which suggested that men and women should not accept society's or someone else's values, but rather examine the truth in him or herself. Hemingway was not an existentialist, but his characters clearly exhibit a great deal of alienation from each other. They cope with their situation of doubt in society by developing an acute personal meaning. In *A Farewell to Arms* this is debated once by the priest and Frederic in the latter's hospital room. Not for the first time, the reader is forced to examine the discomforting notions of love. The priest loves God and this comforts him during the war. Frederic and Catherine, alternately, display another route to coping. This one is ironic and looms large over the novel—"I want you so much I want to be you too." This statement must be compared to their actions during the childbirth—Catherine is given hell by nature, while Frederic eats. The effort to be each other is an alienation from self and a failed method of coping. Thus, Frederic faces the tragedy of his love as well as the tragedy of himself—he did not listen to any of the tutors who warned him of this inevitability. Certainly, the inevitability is seen in hindsight since Catherine, as tradition and institution, died in the ghastly war leaving the "Everyman" tragically alone with himself.

Patriotism

The novel suggests that war has become a habit, a disgusting habit. At some point, Frederic has learned that this war is not romantic, and it most certainly does not concern him personally. He does not become a war-hardened soldier, but a disgusted ambulance driver who observes more facets of war than a soldier or politician would. Consequently, the notion of the patriot is reflected upon a few times, and the reader gains a definite sense that being a patriot is never to be equated to a love of war. However, that is not to say that Frederic ever clearly denounces or supports war because it is not in his character to be so passionate.

In the most obvious instance, Frederic returns to the front after his convalescence and chats about the war's progress with one of his drivers, Gino. This driver declares himself a patriot and says he does not like to hear so many people talk of the Italians losing. Gino then launches into an invocation of patriotic language which Frederic cannot help but see as naive. It is at this point that Frederic admits his problem with words like "glorious," "sacred," and "sacrifice." Frederic compares the notion of sacrifice to the stockyards of Chicago—one large slaughterhouse. Such a comparison, to the American reader at the time, was enough to question patriotism as a reason for war. If, Frederic asks, to love one's country is to be an animal

slaughtered in the stockyards, then is it smart to be a patriot?

Doubt about the calling of every man to be a patriot is put to rest ambiguously when Count Greffi challenges Frederic to a game of pool. The wise old man tells Frederic that the slaughter does not define patriotism. Instead, a patriot is a lover of one's countrymen. However, this is ambiguous precisely because there is little of this type of love on display during the retreat. All that Frederic saw in the retreat was the stupidity of war. The men who questioned his patriotism in retreat did not love him because he was an officer, and the battle police were present to kill him for his supposed betrayal. Unfortunately, one supposes, Count Greffi is no longer in charge and his vision of love is thus retired. The reader is left with an unanswered question: whether or not patriotism is an abstract value which is no longer possible to pursue rationally given the technical sophistication of death.

War

War is not glamorized in this novel. Instead, it is presented in a very real and horrifying fashion from the perspective of the ambulance driver. At some moments, war is derided as a game for the ruling classes in which the poor suffer. It is after this discussion, in Chapter IX, that the mortar hits. War is only rarely viewed in a patriotic light and more often seen as tiresome.

However, the negative portrayal of war in the novel may have as much to do with the almost futile effort of the Italian army. Frederic comments on this several times because he says he would be ashamed to be seen by the American, English, or French in such a "silly" army. Further ironies arise when his friends attempt to get him a medal for being wounded while eating macaroni.

Catherine tries to bolster the image of bravery at the end of Chapter XXI and even says that Frederic is brave. Frederic disagrees, saying that he is only a mediocre hitter. Thus war is a game, like baseball, and Frederic is not an outstanding player, but at best someone who can only do the most basic things.

War is also a disease. Rinaldi refers to his own condition of gonorrhea and says everyone has it. However, we know from earlier discussions that everyone too has war disgust. Therefore, Rinaldi's generalization equates war to a disease. That is, war is great, but like most things, after a time of too much indulgence, even pleasurable things become tiresome. The disease spreads and all one can do is have hope for a cure—the political end to the war. However, the cure simply allows a breathing space before the next burst of the disease.

Style

In Media Res

A Farewell to Arms opens *in media res*—literally, in the middle of the thing. For the novel, this "thing," constantly referred to as "it," is the war. Hemingway is certainly not the first to use this technique to bring the reader immediately into the story. In fact, one of the greatest Western war stories of all time—Homer's *Iliad*—opens in the middle of the Trojan war. Hemingway's use of the technique sets the tone of the novel as one of disjointure and alienation. The reader steps immediately into a world described by someone remembering. However, we are given no clues about time, place, or even the characters. In fact, it takes a good deal of reading before even the name of the narrator is learned.

Persona

Originally referring to the mask worn by stage actors in ancient Greece, the persona is the image of the character as it is expressed in reaction to its environment. Hemingway reveals the persona of his main character by the way he reacts to the statements of others. This is demonstrated early in the novel by Frederic's non-reaction to Catherine's story. She describes how her fiance was "blown to bits," and Frederic's response is to say nothing. Rinaldi, on the other hand, is full of chivalry and charm because his persona is one of Italian machismo. The story is told from Frederic's point of view and thus it has his voice. However, as a further development of his persona, his voicing of the story rarely devolves to a personal—"I did this." Instead, he speaks in terms of "we" until finally he is all alone and, by default, an "I".

Black humor

Black humor is a nervous humor which famous psychologist Sigmund Freud described as a way of repressing fear through laughter. Also known as graveyard humor, it is used throughout the novel to mask the very real fear of death. The starkest use of this type of humor is by Catherine Barkley when she is dying from internal bleeding suffered from a stillbirth. Though in great pain she manages to utter "black humor" when the doctor says she must not be silly because she is not going to die. To this she repeats a phrase she used earlier in the book when Frederic was in the hospital, "All right ... I'll come and stay with you nights...." The inevitability of death and the impossibility of the decision make the comment painfully ironic.

Dialogue

Hemingway employs dialogue at the expense of narrative whenever he can. He does this in order to avoid long passages of "unnecessary prose." Thus, he reveals information about the plot through a dialogue marked by terse, direct language which could be called common speech. This effort at realism also disables any attempt to define Hemingway's actual position on any of the themes in the novel. Since the story tells itself through the characters who are involved, the reader is left with his or her own thoughts on the subject—thoughts which are influenced by the speech of the characters, not Hemingway.

According to the critic Henry Hazlitt, dialogue is best when it is *of a narrow range*. He continues, "one may think of this either as cause or result of the narrow range of the characters." This is a good thing, he says, for Hemingway's characters "are never complicated people, either emotionally or intellectually, for if they were, the casual hard-boiled Hemingway manner would be incapable of dealing with them."

Historical Context

World War I

World War I was also known as the Great War because it was war on a scale previously unimagined in modern history. The war broke out after the assassination of the Archduke Franz Ferdinand ignited an already tense territorial feud between Austria-Hungary and Serbia. France, Great Britain, and Russia joined together as the Allied powers against the Central Power alliance of Austria-Hungary and Germany. Eventually, America joined the war on the side of the Allies after Russia had withdrawn and the *Lusitania,* a British passenger ship carrying 128 American citizens, had been sunk. The conflict lasted four years, cost $350 billion, and claimed the lives of twenty-two million. Technologically, it was the most advanced war ever seen because of the number of new inventions introduced: biological weapons, mortar, improved artillery, machine guns, and barbed wire. Not until World War II, when the airplane played such a dev-

Compare & Contrast

- **World War I:** America spent around thirty billion dollars on the war effort. At war's end, due to disagreements with the allies, the United States refused to ratify the peace treaty, join the League of Nations, or be part of the European recovery.

  1929: British interest rates rose and lured capital away from America's Wall Street. Prices on the New York Stock Exchange plummeted in late October. The Great Depression set in and the American economy did not see serious improvement until the beginning of World War II.

  Today: After a severe recession during the late 1970s and early 1980s, the stock market reaches record highs in the 1990s, and the American dollar becomes very strong in foreign markets. The United States, Mexico, and Canada begin cooperating in the North American Free Trade Agreement, while Europe works towards creating a stronger European Union, a organization among European countries promoting free trade, a common policy for defense, and a single monetary unit.

- **World War I:** In 1917 Russia sued for a separate peace with Germany when the government of the Tsar, Nicholas II, was threatened by civil war. The Duma, Russia's legislative body under the czar, asked the czar to step down in March and placed Russia under a provisional government. In the fall, under the leadership of Lenin, the communists seized power, and Russia became a Soviet Union modeled on Marxist principles.

  1929: Josef Stalin expelled Leon Trotsky from the Soviet Union and began an unchallenged dictatorship of the Soviet Union.

  Today: While the Soviet Union has collapsed, twelve of fifteen former Soviet states join to form the Commonwealth of Independent States. Some former eastern European countries under the influence of the Soviets dissolve peacefully, such as the former Czechoslovakia dividing into Slovakia and the Czech Republic. However, other countries cannot agree on the future of their new nations and serious fighting erupts, especially in the former Yugoslavia.

- **World War I:** At the end of the war, the suffragette movement gained women the right to vote in Britain in 1918, and in America with the passage of the Nineteenth Amendment in 1920. The Eighteenth Amendment began Prohibition, making the drinking and manufacturing of alcoholic beverages illegal.

  1929: Organized crime violence reached an historic high; illegal drinking establishments, known as "speakeasies," surged in popularity. Prohibition was finally repealed in 1933 with the Twenty-First Amendment.

  Today: In 1972, the United States Senate approves a proposed constitutional amendment prohibiting discriminating against women because of their gender. Never receiving enough votes by states for ratification, the Equal Rights Amendment was defeated in 1982. While the consumption of alcohol remains legal, national campaigns have focused on educating adults to drink responsibly. Public awareness about the dangers of drinking and driving have increased with many Americans joining national associations, such as Mothers Against Drunk Driving (MADD) and Students Against Drunk Driving (SADD), to help keep roads free of intoxicated drivers.

---

astating role, would the destructive power of these new weapons be surpassed.

In the novel *A Farewell to Arms,* Frederic Henry is serving in the Italian army. The role of Italy in World War I was as decoy. Traditionally, Italy was an ally of Germany and Austria. However, the allies promised Italy the land it had requested from Austria—the region of South Tyrol,

English ambulance driver in Italy, during World War I, c. 1918.

several islands in the Adriatic, and assistance with expansion of its colonies in Africa—if it would switch sides. The only role of Italy's ill-equipped army was to attempt to divert the force of the Austrians from helping the Germans in France, a role which caused the death of 500,000 Italians in 1916 alone. It is in that year that Frederic Henry is wounded. Surprisingly, Italy was able to turn back the Austrians and rightfully claim their share in the spoils of victory with the Allied cause.

The Roaring Twenties

The 1920s were marked by what Joseph Wood Krutch labeled as *The Modern Temper.* This was a "temper," or zeitgeist (spirit of the age), which viewed traditional beliefs of progress, perfectibility, and the success of democracy as dead on the battlefield. Consequently, other philosophies of life were being looked at, such as the growing popularity of Freudian psychoanalysis. This new method of treating the self reinforced a belief in individualism in the United States. For the same insistence on the self it was banned from Communist Russia. The decade of the twenties is also often seen as a wild decade of jazz, flappers, and the "speakeasy," gathering places which served banned alcohol. Jazz became popular music throughout America. Women finally gained the

vote on August 26, 1920, with the passage of the Nineteenth Amendment. Their new freedoms were epitomized by the more unconventional girls who were known as "flappers," identified by their short, bobbed hair and daringly short (for the time) dresses. Prohibition and the Eighteenth Amendment made alcohol illegal in 1920, but organized crime invented the "speakeasy" (with the many bribes it involved) to provide a place for Americans to find the outlawed drink. The economy, both legal and black-market, was stable, and unemployment low. Things were almost too good; after the Great War, Americans were ready to enjoy themselves. Few could forecast or believe what loomed ahead for the United States.

The Stock Market Crash

The year 1929 destroyed the momentum of the twenties. The roaring Jazz Age ground to a virtual halt in October when the New York Stock Exchange began to nosedive. After the First World War, America enjoyed a healthy economy in the 1920s, and many investors saw opportunities to make money on the stock exchange. Investors often purchased stock on credit, expecting to pay off any loan with the profits they reaped as stock prices climbed. However, after several days of falling stock prices in late October, panicky investors began to sell whatever stock they held at any price. As the market flooded with stock for sale, prices plummeted and many investors could not sell their stock at high enough prices to pay off their creditors. Investors went bankrupt, businesses lost capital, and banks failed. Unlike in previous years when the stock market fell but quickly recovered, the early 1930s became increasingly worse for Americans with millions of men and women out of work and struggling to survive.

Europe also suffered a severe economic downturn. Never fully recovered from World War I, European countries struggled with high rates of joblessness and inflation. In Britain unemployment rates exceeded twelve percent; in Germany over six million people were unemployed by 1932. Due to the sudden collapse of the American economy, aid to Germany was halted. Consequently, with no jobs, little food, and no money, the German people lost confidence in their postwar government, the Weimar Republic. Faced with a disintegrating economy, Germans began to take interest in the ideas of a rising young fascist, Adolph Hitler. Promising a return to prosperity, Hitler and the Nazi party were voted into power in 1933.

Critical Overview

Hemingway's second novel, *A Farewell to Arms,* is viewed as his finest artistic accomplishment because the subject matter is finely blended with his method. To the critics, by and large, Hemingway had become a master of the short, staccato style of writing by this novel. Further, this mastery made Hemingway the most celebrated American writer of the twentieth century. This celebration is both enhanced and questioned by his reputation as a bold warrior, whose depiction of women is often negative. Such an aura is no doubt partially the responsibility of the movie industry, which felt encouraging his legend and the identification with Gary Cooper would only help the marketing of army stories in general and Hemingway films specifically.

In 1929, when *A Farewell to Arms* was first released, the critics were impressed because it surpassed his first work dramatically. However, not every critic enjoyed the novel, and many were bothered by its diction. Robert Herrick of the *New York World* called the novel "dirt" on account of its vulgarity. He was not the only one upset by the then-unprintable words. This led to an edited version of

the novel, with words like *testicles* and *shit* removed from the text. Fortunately, the dialogue was sound enough without this soldier talk and the novel functioned without them. Still, other critics could not say enough in praise of the best-selling work.

Henry Hazlitt's review in the *New York Sun* got right to the point: "In the year of our Lord 1929 Ernest Hemingway is the single greatest influence on the American novel and short story." Further, Hazlitt put Hemingway ahead of other writers who also employed sparse prose, saying, "Hardboiled novels, monosyllabic novels, novels without commas … are like Hemingway." In a *Chicago Daily Tribune* article, Fanny Butcher also praised Hemingway's terse writing style. After comparing Hemingway with Gertrude Stein, she said, "*A Farewell to Arms* [uses] a technique which is purely subjective, and a style which is articulate entirely in its bones and not at all in its flesh." Thus, when compared to literature of the 1920s, Hemingway was a master in capturing the essence of the story and eliminating nonessential elements often employed by less talented writers.

The praise for Hemingway continued with few exceptions. Critics, such as Ray B. West, Jr., summed up the work as a reflection of a society disturbed by war. However, in the 1950s and 1960s, more attention was given to the individualist philosophy being expressed by the novel. Earl Rovit, in his essay "Learning to Care," said that the novel is not a tragedy in any sense, since the individual protagonist learns "who he is." Apparently, for Rovit the point of the novel, as well as of life, is that one realizes what is significant in life. By this recognition one can come to terms with what one's life is. Having followed these various lessons, one can live a fulfilled life. "The total effect of the story depends on the degree of Frederic's self-realization or acceptance of the implicit meanings in his experience … the identity of man is measured by the processive recognitions of his meaningful experience." Understandably, readings of a story which ends in the death of the heroine after giving birth to a stillborn child combined with the masculinist mythos which surrounded Hemingway caused a critical revolt. However, by the 1970s, debate had shifted, concentrating more on condemning the ideas of Rovit and critics like him rather than responding to Hemingway's story of Frederic and Catherine.

From the start, Hemingway was heralded as a genius. Such an early reception into fame also led to Hemingway being the most widely recognized and photographed writer (featured in both *Time* and *Life* magazines). This reputation stayed with his works until feminist critics took hold of Hemingway. They denounced his portrayal of women and summed up the Catherine Barkley character as a one-dimensional sex object. This was a sharp departure from the earlier view of Catherine as a brave woman. During the 1970s, Hemingway was viewed as the epitome of the chauvinist male who viewed women as secondary creatures whose proper place is in the home. Unfortunately, the application of this view of Hemingway's myth affected the reading of his novels unjustly. That is, much of the reading of, for example, Catherine Barkley as simply a pasteboard figure came from a justifiable loathing of Hemingway's misogynist cult, rather than from any textual basis.

Throughout the 1980s, there has been a gradual renewal of the possible readings of Hemingway. This has partly been the result of Judith Fetterley's 1978 work *The Resisting Reader: A Feminist Approach to American Fiction.* New directions have now been taken that no longer focus on the simple gender polarity. In fact, the posthumous publication of Hemingway's *The Garden of Eden* led to examinations of Hemingway's interest in androgyny, the state of having both male and female characterisics. Now, rather than being fought over, Catherine Barkley is widely regarded as a complex figure.

Most recent criticism on *A Farewell to Arms* has focused on some of the more curious aspects of Hemingway's work. For example, critics are interested in Hemingway's words as a mode of war or play. Recent criticism has not limited itself to an argument on Hemingway's sexist attitudes as much as it was in the 1970s. Instead that gender war has itself become the subject for critics like Sandra Whipple Spaniers in essays such as *Hemingway's Unknown Soldier: Catherine Barkley, the Critics, and the Great War.* Other approaches include examining slices of the uncontested strength in the novel such as Frederic Henry's narration. There is still much praise and admiration for Hemingway, and he is still regarded as influential many years after his first publication.

Criticism

Arnold A. Markley

Markley is an assistant professor at the Penn State University, Delaware County campus. In the following essay he examines Hemingway's distinctive writing style, use of his own war experiences, and examination of themes of identity as they appear in A Farewell to Arms.

Ernest Hemingway is known for his distinctive writing style, an unusually bare, straightforward prose in which he characteristically uses plain words, few adjectives, simple sentences, and frequent repetition. Nevertheless his powers of description are not diminished by his taking care to choose such simple language. Take a look, for example, at the opening paragraph of *A Farewell to Arms:*

> In the late summer of that year we lived in a house in a village that looked across the river and the plain to the mountains. In the bed of the river there were pebbles and boulders, dry and white in the sun, and the water was clear and swiftly moving and blue in the channels. Troops went by the house and down the road and the dust they raised powdered the leaves of the trees. The trunks of the trees too were dusty and the leaves fell early that year and we saw the troops marching along the road and the dust rising and leaves, stirred by the breeze, falling and the soldiers marching and afterward the road bare and white except for the leaves.

This beautifully written paragraph exemplifies the simplicity of Hemingway's language, and his tendency towards both vivid description and repetition. Hemingway worked hard to write in such a way as to give his readers highly descriptive passages without distracting them with "big words," and he hoped that his writing would leave his readers with distinct visual impressions, without their being able to recall anything unusual or memorable about the language itself. Despite the simplicity of the language in a paragraph such as the one above, the effect is quite complex. Not only does the author provide a vivid description of the geographical setting for the novel, but he also achieves a sense of the passing of time. The season gradually passes from summer into fall as the paragraph progresses, and likewise the sense of time passing is emphasized by the repeated detail of the soldiers marching by, signalling the reader to the fact that this novel is set in a time of war.

A Farewell to Arms was first published in 1929, and Hemingway had to be persistent in convincing his editor, Maxwell Perkins at Charles Scribner's Sons, not to censor language that the publishing house felt was "indecent." In addition, some contemporary readers found the novel's frank depiction of pre-marital sex to be distasteful, and the book was banned for a time in Boston due to a particular police chief's feeling that it was "sala-

What Do I Read Next?

- For a better sense of the "Lost Generation" as well as the general disillusionment brought about by the aftermath of World War I, see Hemingway's first novel, *The Sun Also Rises* (1926). The novel is also the first depiction of the American expatriates living in Paris.

- A view of America in World War I is given in John Steinbeck's *East of Eden.* The novel itself concerns a family saga, but the middle of the work was made into a movie starring James Dean. That 1954 film, *East of Eden,* focuses on Steinbeck's portrayal of the impact of the war on a small community—from the power of draft boards, to the morality of profiteering from war.

- Another view of World War I was also published early in 1929 from the perspective of a German soldier. Erich Maria Remarque's *All Quiet on the Western Front* was also a great success and found its way onto film. The idea that someone else had published on the same topic—the First World War—months before his book came out alarmed Hemingway but did not affect his sales.

- Indispensible to an understanding of the impact and the horror of the First World War, especially to Europeans, is a reading of the poetry written on the front lines and in a general response to the war. The horror of war was illustrated in ground breaking poetry by such authors as Wilfred Owen, Siegfried Sassoon and others. Some of their poetry and other poems on World War I can be found in recently republished collections, such as *World War One British Poets: Brooke, Owen, Sassoon, Rosenburg, and Others,* collected by Candace Ward and printed by Dover in 1997.

- If you want to read more about Ernest Hemingway, Jeffrey Meyers's *Hemingway: A Biography,* published in 1985, offers a thorough account of Hemingway's life.

- For a simple overview of World War I, see James L. Stokesbury's *A Short History of World War I,* published in 1981.

- A more technical insight into the growing sophistication of weaponry and the role of the ambulance in the war can be found in John S. Haller's *From Farcarts to Fords, A History of the Military Ambulance, 1790-1925,* published in 1992.

cious." Nevertheless, the novel was immediately popular, and it has enjoyed a warm reception from literary critics throughout the twentieth century. The novel was Hemingway's first big success, and it cemented his growing reputation as an author of great talent.

The novel is narrated by the central character, Frederic Henry, an American who is serving in an Italian ambulance unit during the First World War. Hemingway's style is very effective in his development of Frederic's character. Because the novel is written as if it were Frederic's autobiography, or memoirs, the events of the novel are filtered through Frederic's own consciousness. The simple style and plain language contribute to the realistic nature of Frederic's voice and his thoughts; at times it even seems as if the reader has been given access to the inner workings of Frederic's mind, as in the excerpt included in the plot summary. The fact that all of the events are seen through Frederic's eyes also means that the reader's impressions of the other characters in the novel must also come through Frederic's impressions. In fact, Hemingway relies heavily on his highly realistic dialogue in sketching portraits of the other characters, and in revealing how Frederic relates to them, and what each character experiences in the way of feelings, concerns, and motivations.

As a novel of war, based on Hemingway's own experiences in World War I, one of the work's major concerns lies in its critique of the concept of war. At the beginning of the novel Frederic Henry is nonchalant about the war that is going on around him. He is, after all, an American fighting in the Italian army, and he feels a sense of displacement and detachment as a result. Moreover, other characters, particularly Catherine Barkley, comment on the peculiarity of his being an American in the Italian army. Initially Frederic does not feel that he will be affected by this war—it has nothing to do with him, he says. He lives a hedonistic lifestyle, focusing on his pleasures—drinking and sex. Even after meeting Catherine and getting to know her, he does not initially feel that he will fall in love with her. He merely wishes to become involved with her as if in a game like bridge, but a game in which one makes moves by making statements rather than with cards.

Nevertheless, Frederic is changed by the war. When he is wounded and falls in love with Catherine over the long summer of his recuperation, he returns to the front to find conditions much changed. Things have not been going well for the Italians during his absence, and he notices a distinct difference in the attitudes of his peers—they are much more depressed and anxious about the war, even his usually carefree friend Rinaldi. The war has become darker and more threatening, and when Frederic is caught up in the chaotic retreat of the Italians from Caporetto, he is confronted with the grimmest realities of war for the first time; he watches as a companion is downed by a sniper, and he himself has a narrow brush with death when he approaches the carbinieri, or military police, as they are executing Italian officers at the bridge over the Tagliamento. Enough is enough. This isn't my war anyway, Frederic says to himself, and he makes his "farewell to arms" with no reservations about deserting his post in a war that has turned into a horrible nightmare.

Like many of Hemingway's main characters, Frederic Henry is a man who is in search of something to believe in. Robert Penn Warren called his search a search for truth and for ethical standards. Frederic detests words that are separated from actions—words like "glory" and "courage" were disgusting to him; for Frederic, it is only in one's actions that such concepts have any value or meaning. A religion, or any organized system of beliefs, has to be tried and tested before Frederic will be able to accept it, and as yet, he has found no system of beliefs or values to which to commit himself entirely. Early in the novel when his companions bait and tease the priest, Frederic nevertheless respects the humble man. Even though he doesn't agree with many of the priest's beliefs concerning Christian-

ity, he admires the priest for believing in his religion and for loving his country so strongly. As the war progresses, Frederic is better able to decide what he does not believe in—he cannot be involved with the horror of war any longer, and instead he devotes himself to his love for Catherine Barkley. And Catherine devotes herself to Frederic, even telling him that *he* is her religion at one point.

Frederic's search is also a search for home—a place where he can be comfortable and safe. Throughout the novel he finds it difficult to sleep at night, frightened by the sense of nothingness he feels then. With Catherine, he finally finds a kind of home, first in the hospital in Milan and later in their mountain chalet in Switzerland. Frederic seems to have found what he has been looking for in his love for Catherine, until Catherine suddenly and unexpectedly dies, just as they are beginning plans for their new life together. Some critics, such as Ray B. West, Jr. and E. M. Halliday, have chosen to read Hemingway's title as ironic, interpreting Hemingway's message that one cannot actually make a "farewell to arms." Frederic may have escaped the brutality and cruelty of war, but ultimately there is no way to escape pain, and solitude, and the difficult aspects of life. There is only entrapment, wherever one turns. Gerry Brenner has written that *A Farewell to Arms,* which involves an ambulance driver and a nurse and situates a number of its key scenes in hospitals, is less a novel about war or about love than it is a novel about *wounds.*

Hemingway makes use of some very important symbolism in this novel. Even as early as the first paragraph, he sets up two major symbols—the plains and the mountains—which will be in conflict throughout the story. Hemingway represents the plains as dangerous, miserable, dry, and barren. The mountains, on the other hand, represent safety, happiness, and good health. The military action that Frederic Henry witnesses takes place on the plains, and his escape, through the cleansing, baptismal ritual of jumping into the river, reaches its end in the secluded mountain chalet with Catherine. But when Frederic must take Catherine out of the mountains and back down to the city below to the hospital where she is to give birth, disaster strikes again. Rain is another important symbol throughout the novel. Often the rain suggests impending doom; there is a storm the night that Frederic learns he must leave Italy at once to avoid being arrested, Catherine dreams that she is dead in the rain, and indeed at the conclusion of the novel, it is raining when Frederic returns to his hotel. The critic Carlos Baker's essay, "The Mountain and the Plain," is an excellent source for studying these aspects of Hemingway's use of symbolism.

A Farewell to Arms is a very dramatic book. Many scholars, such as Ray B. West, Jr., have compared its five-book structure to that of the traditional English five-act play. There are similarities to be drawn between the structure of the novel and tragic drama: the first book, like the first act in a play, introduces the characters and the situation of the story, and in the second book the romantic plot is developed. Book III provides a climactic turning point: Frederic's desertion of his post in the army and his decision to return to Catherine. In Book IV it looks as if Frederic and Catherine have successfully escaped the threats of the past, only to meet a tragic end to their love in the final book, which brings the drama to a close like the last act of a tragedy. Moreover, Hemingway's heavy reliance on dialogue between his characters to develop both character and the story line makes the novel similar to a dramatic piece. Hemingway even called the novel his version of *Romeo and Juliet.* Like Romeo and Juliet, Frederic and Catherine are lovers who are kept from finding a permanent happiness together, but unlike the world view of William Shakespeare in which there is a foolish family feud to blame for the lovers' deaths, in Hemingway, there is no one to blame for Catherine's fate and Frederic's ultimate solitude. Frederic is left alone in a world in which nothing is permanent, all is subject to chance, and the best one can do, ultimately, is to face that world with acceptance. The story, like Hemingway's style of writing, is bare-boned and realistic, simple and stark.

Source: Arnold A. Markley, in an essay for *Novels for Students,* Gale, 1997.

Carlos Baker

In the following excerpt, Baker explores how Hemingway adds depth to his novel through the repetition of symbols.

Symbolic effects in this novel are achieved through a subtle process of reiterated suggestion. Among the many which might be mentioned, we shall be concerned with only three: the weather, the emblematic people, and the landscapes. The best known of these is the first: the almost poetic care with which Hemingway slowly builds up in his readers a mental association between rain and disaster. This was an association which came naturally enough to Hemingway himself. His letters throughout his life are full of complaints against rain and damp weather. He always took it personally, partly because he was susceptible to the common cold, partly because damp dark weather induced in his spirit a comparable gloom. Moreover, in his second experience of war and its effects, he had personally watched the pitiful stream of refugees plodding through mud and sodden with rain during the memorable evacuation of the civilian population from the city of Adrianople. Anyone who reads *A Farewell to Arms* with one eye on the weather will eventually marvel as he watches the author playing with falling rain as a symbol of imminent doom. Near the close of the book, when Catherine is approaching her time of confinement, the weather warms and the rains arrive. For a whole miraculous winter the lovers have gloried in their isolation, living happily in their high mountain fastness, surrounded by healthy cold air and clean snow, far from the mud and muck of war. Now at last the rains come, the time for the lying-in draws near, some great change lurks just beyond the lovers' limited horizon, and we begin to sense that Catherine is in mortal danger, as indeed she is.

A second aspect of the symbolism is the way in which Hemingway endows two of Lieutenant Henry's friends with special moral attributes. One is the young Italian surgeon, Rinaldi, a merry comrade and a capable doctor, enthusiastic about his work with the wounded, boasting of his attainments at the operating table, delighted to be of service to humanity. But Hemingway is at pains to present Rinaldi as the victim of his own virtues. The sadness and fatigue of war soon affect him. As we watch, he becomes the homeless man, without visible antecedents, cut off from saving domesticity, driven to desperate expedients in order to keep his sanity in the vast and gloomy theatre of the war. Trying to relax from the rigors of his duties, he contracts syphilis in an army brothel. The man of science is eventually victimized by the filth and disease which surround him.

The second close friend is a nameless Italian priest, a gentle little nut-brown man who seeks as well as he can to exemplify the Christian virtues in a situation where almost everything seems to conspire against them. It is he who tries to persuade Henry to visit the Abruzzi during one of his military leaves. The priest paints an idyllic picture of this mountainous region, with its clear cool air, its plump game birds, its vineyards and orchards, its flute music, its peasant population living simply and amicably as they have done for a thousand years. It is a region close to heaven—or at any rate closer than the Veneto would seem to be. "There," says the priest, "a man may love God without being satirized for his beliefs."

After the first half of the novel, Rinaldi and the priest disappear from the scene. But the qualities they stand for continue to affect the action of the story. When Henry and Catherine reach Switzerland and begin the only approximation of married life that they will ever know, it is the spirit of the priest which dominates their lives. When, on the other hand, they are compelled to leave their lofty station and descend to Lausanne, where Catherine will die, we are forcibly reminded of the world of Rinaldi—the world of doctors and hospitals and imminent death.

The third and last manifestation of symbolic intent in the novel is the subtle way in which the author plays off two levels of landscape against each other. Without following it slavishly, he carefully establishes a pattern in which plains or lowlands are associated in the reader's mind with war, death, pain, sadness, or gloom, while the high mountain regions, whether in the Abruzzi where the priest originated, or in Switzerland, high above Lausanne, where the lovers establish their temporary heartland, are just as carefully associated with pleasure and the good life, joy and health, or whatever stands opposed to the plains of the Veneto where the war is being fought and the great retreat has been made. This poetic association of the heights with pleasure and the depths with pain is Hemingway's version of the *paysage moralise,* the moralized landscape which he was teaching himself to use as a backdrop for his narratives of action.

In sum, we are suggesting that *A Farewell to Arms* is not at all the naturalistic report which we might at first take it for. One of the major reasons for its continuing freshness, its proven power of survival, is the care which Hemingway lavished on its structure and texture by the symbolic use of weather and character and moralized landscape.

As we approach the end of this demonstration, there is just time to consider one more point about *A Farewell to Arms.* This is the famous conclusion where Catherine dies and her lover says a silent farewell before he walks back to the hotel alone in the falling rain. For years it has been rumored that Hemingway rewrote the closing pages of the novel some thirty-seven times. The figure is very likely exaggerated. But whatever it was, there can be no doubt that Hemingway spent considerable effort on the conclusion, and that the final version, familiar to readers since 1929, is almost infinitely superior to the penultimate version, which has only recently come to light.

In the accepted and familiar version, Hemingway's hero stays with Catherine until her death. Then he goes out to speak to the surgeon: "Is there anything I can do tonight?" The doctor replies that there is nothing to be done and offers Henry a ride back to his hotel. Henry says that he will stay for a while at the hospital. "It was the only thing to do," says the surgeon, apologetically, speaking of the fatal Caesarean section. "The operation proved—"

> "I do not want to talk about it," says Henry. The doctor goes away down the corridor and Henry opens the door to the room where Catherine's body lies.
>
> "You can't come in now," says one of the nurses in charge.
>
> "Yes, I can."
>
> "You can't come in yet."
>
> "You get out," says Henry. "The other one, too."

But after he has got them out and closed the door and turned off the light, he discovers that it is no good. It is like saying good-bye to a statue. After a while he goes out and leaves the hospital, and walks back to the hotel in the rain.

This is where the novel ends. Much has been made of this justly famous and tight-lipped conclusion. To many readers it has seemed to be one of the high points of lonely bereavement in modern fiction, a peak of tragic lostness from a generation which suffered thousands of similar deprivations during and after World War I. It has also been seen as the epitome of stoic acceptance of the inevitable. There can be no doubt that this was precisely the effect Hemingway sought to achieve during all his rewritings of the conclusion.

The penultimate version is another matter entirely, and it is very revealing. In place of the laconic interchange between Henry and the attending surgeon, the visit to the room to say goodbye, and the lonely walk back to the hotel in the rain, we have three quite different paragraphs. Henry talks about the difficulty of making funeral arrangements in a foreign country, then of the postwar destinies of the priest and Rinaldi and one or two more, and finally of the return to the hotel, where he falls asleep to awake in the morning to his sense of loss. All the sharp poignancy of the final version is here blunted and destroyed. What is worse, the words themselves seem moist with self-pity.

Hemingway wrote, in the simulated character of Frederic Henry:

There are a great many more details, starting with my first meeting with an undertaker, and all the business of burial in a foreign country, and going on with the rest of my life—which has gone on and seems likely to go on for a long time.

I could tell how Rinaldi was cured of the syphilis and lived to find that the technic learned in wartime surgery is not of much practical use in peace. I could tell how the priest in our mess lived to be a priest in Italy under Fascism. I could tell how Ettore became a Fascist and the part he took in that organization. I could tell how Piani got to be a taxi-driver in New York and what sort of a singer Simmons became. Many things have happened. Everything blunts and the world keeps on. It never stops. It only stops for you. Some of it stops while you are still alive. The rest goes on and you go on with it.

I could tell you what I have done since March, 1918, when I walked that night in the rain back to the hotel where Catherine and I had lived and went upstairs to our room and undressed and slept finally, because I was so tired—to wake in the morning with the sun shining in the window; then suddenly to realize what had happened. I could tell what has happened since then, but that is the end of the story.

The difficulty with this conclusion is that it drowns us with words and moisture. The rather garrulous self-pity, so visible here, when we juxtapose it with the far more objective stoicism of the final version, offers us a hint that may be worth developing. It suggests what I believe to be true, that the stoicism of the last version was only a mask, adopted and assumed for dramatic show, while under it Hemingway's still wounded feelings were bleeding and suppurating almost as intensively as they had been doing ten years before. Within the short space of seven months, he had been badly smashed up in both war and love. Now, much later, his double wound of body and soul rose to the surface of his memory, and manifested itself in the trial conclusion which we have just examined.

There is no time to expand further upon the matters here. Yet the idea of the stoic mask, assumed as a facade to conceal the psychic warfare which is going on beneath, may help us to explain and to understand much of the braggadoccio which struck his detractors as all too apparent in Hemingway's later life. It may also explain his espousal of the stoic code as a standard of behavior —a standard to which he required all his later heroes to conform. But these are hypotheses better suited to the biographer than to the literary critic. If the next-to-last conclusion of *A Farewell to Arms* betrays a kind of psychological quicksand just below the surface, the final version does not…. Whatever Hemingway's future reputation, *A Farewell to Arms* will surely stand for at least another forty years as the best novel written by an American about the First World War.

Source: Carlos Baker, "Ernest Hemingway: *A Farewell to Arms*," in *The Merrill Studies in* A Farewell to Arms, edited by John Graham, Charles E. Merrill Publishing Company, 1971, pp. 27–38.

Daniel J. Schneider

In the following excerpt, Schneider reveals how Hemingway systematically uses images of rain, desolation, and impurity to reinforce the events in the novel.

Hemingway's *A Farewell to Arms* is I think one of the purest lyric novels ever written. But if we are fully to appreciate its power—and the power of a number of other works by Hemingway—we are driven to examine the poetics of this lyricism and to assess, if we can, the extent to which Hemingway has exploited the possibilities of the type….

In *A Farewell to Arms* the dominant state of mind—the sense of death, defeat, failure, nothingness, emptiness—is conveyed chiefly by the image of the rain (with all its tonal associates, *mist, wet, damp, river, fog*), by images and epithets of desolation (chiefly *bare, thin, small,* and *fallen leaves*), and by images and epithets of impurity and corruption (chiefly *dust, mud, dirt,* and *disease*). Hemingway's method of working with the images is surprisingly uniform….

The images are repeated so frequently that they begin to toll like bells in the mind. Virtually every sentence says, "Death, despair, failure, emptiness," because virtually every sentence contains an image or symbol associated with the dominant state of mind.

The novel begins with this state of mind, and it is established so firmly, through the repetition of the central symbols, that any emotions other than bitterness and despair may thereafter intrude only with difficulty. The typical procedure, as in lyric poetry, is to intensify the dominant emotion by means of a simple contrast of images. Thus the images of purity and vitality, introduced in the second sentence of the novel, are contrasted throughout the chapter with the images of dirt and failure:

In the late summer of that year we lived in a house in a village that looked across the river and the plain to the mountains. In the bed of the river there were pebbles and boulders, dry and white in the sun, and the water was clear and swiftly moving and blue in the channels. Troops went by the house and down the road and the dust they raised powdered the leaves of the trees. The trunks of the trees too were dusty and the leaves fell early that year and we saw the troops marching along the road and the dust rising and leaves, stirred by the breeze, falling and the soldiers marching and afterward the road bare and white except for the leaves.

Purity has been defiled, the life-force has been thwarted and defeated. The leaves are "powdered" by dust; the trunks too are "dusty"; the leaves fall "early"; and the empty road, "bare and white except for the leaves," becomes a perfect correlative of the inner desolation. The defilement and violation of life is further suggested by a reference to camouflage ("There were big guns that passed in the day drawn by tractors, the long barrels of the guns covered with green branches and green leafy branches and vines laid over the tractor") and by a reference to the cartridge-boxes bulging under the capes of the soldiers "so that the men, passing on the road, marched as though they were six months gone with child." And these bitter ironies are reinforced by the introduction of the dominant symbol of the rain: not life-giving rain causing the leaves to grow but the autumnal and winter rain causing them to fall, a rain associated with darkness, mud, and death:

> There was fighting for that mountain too, but it was not successful, and in the fall when the rains came the leaves all fell from the chestnut trees and the branches were bare and the trunks were black with rain. The vineyards were thin and bare-branched too and all the country wet and brown and dead with the autumn. There were mists over the river and clouds on the mountain and the trucks splashed mud on the road and the troops were muddy and wet in their capes; their rifles were wet....

The sense of failure and impotence is also reinforced by the studious avoidance of action-verbs. Almost invariably Hemingway employs the copulative *to be,* and the expletives *there were* and *there was* occur ten times in the twenty-one sentences of the chapter, six of the sentences being introduced by them. The repetitions give a sense of endless sameness and weariness: abandon hope, all ye who enter here.

The concluding paragraphs of the chapter reinforce what has already been established powerfully. The guns, the tractors, the motor-cars show a ruthless power, and it is as if life, in the presence of these overwhelming forces of death, had withered and shrunk. The "very small" king, sitting in the speeding motor-car "between two generals," becomes a fine correlative of the sense of impotence:

> There were small gray motor cars that passed going very fast; usually there was an officer in the seat with the driver and more officers in the back seat. They

splashed more mud than the camions even and if one of the officers in the back was very small and sitting between two generals, he himself so small that you could not see his face but only the top of his cap and his narrow back, and if the car went especially fast it was probably the king. He lived in Udine and came out in this way nearly every day to see how things were going, and things went very badly.

> At the start of the winter came the permanent rain and with the rain came the cholera. But it was checked and in the end only seven thousand died of it in the army.

With this last paragraph the sense of doom is complete. The rain is "permanent" and the apparent consolation, the fact that the cholera is checked, is viciously undercut by the irony that "*only* seven thousand died of it in the army."

The mood of the first chapter is thus established powerfully through the proliferation of associated images, images written in a single key. But to continue in this way—that is, to continue to present events and people as the objectification of feeling through the modulation of images—would of course be to drive narrative out of the novel; there would be no "story," only bitterness distilled. Hemingway's artistic problem accordingly becomes that of presenting action and conflict in such a way that the central emotion will not be shattered by the inclusion of elements hostile to it. As I have indicated, action must be converted into passion; characters must become embodiments of the central bitterness. When it becomes necessary, then, in Chapter II, to introduce characters and to develop a scene whose essential quality is potentially uncongenial to the established emotion, Hemingway must take pains to weaken or nullify the inharmonious effects and to absorb character and scene into the dominant mood. So it is that when the priest, the captain, and the other soldiers are introduced, Hemingway guards against any dilution of the central emotion by framing the scene with a description expressive, once again, of the profound regret and bitterness:

> Later, below in the town, I watched the snow falling, looking out of the window of the bawdy house, the house for officers, where I sat with a friend and two glasses drinking a bottle of Asti, and, looking out at the snow falling slowly and heavily, we knew it was all over for that year. Up the river the mountains had not been taken; none of the mountains beyond the river had been taken. That was all left for next year. My friend saw the priest from our mess going by in the street, walking carefully in the slush, and pounded on the window to attract his attention. The priest looked up. He saw us and smiled. My friend motioned for him to come in. The priest shook his head and went on. That night in the mess after the spaghetti

course ... the captain commenced picking on the priest.

In the scene that follows, the captain's baiting of the priest takes its tone from the frame and is anything but humorous. The "good fun" is swallowed up by the pervasive sadness and bitterness, and the episode acts upon the reader in much the same way as an episode in *The Waste Land* affects Eliot's readers: dialogue, narrative, description are all viewed as expressions of the central fears and desires. The characters introduced are not important in themselves; their development as characters does not interest the writer. They are aspects of the hero's state of mind, and represent, covertly, the conflicts of his soul....

The depression of Frederic Henry continues into Chapter III, but by this time the impressions of bitterness and failure have accumulated so densely that one is ready for a shift to an opposite state of mind. Returning from his leave, Frederic finds everything at the front unchanged. He has not gone to Abruzzi, as the priest urged him to, and, as the symbolism suggests delicately, he is mired in moral filth and inertia. Rinaldi, after kissing him, says: "You're dirty.... You ought to wash," and in Chapter IV Frederic observes, "I was very dusty and dirty and went up to my room to wash." In truth he needs a kind of purification. Thus when he sees Catherine Barkley for the first time in the garden of the British hospital, the imagery hints at the purity, the Edenlike peace that Frederic most deeply craves: "Miss Barkley was in the garden. Another nurse was with her. We saw their white uniforms through the trees and walked toward them." But the first conversation of the lovers, with its truncated, tight-lipped exchanges, only reiterates the desperation and despair that have already pervaded the novel. Once a key word has been sounded, Hemingway modulates it beautifully in half a dozen different shadings, until the conversation, like the descriptions already quoted, becomes a refrain on the theme of failure:

> "Yes," she said. "People can't realize what France is like. If they did, it couldn't go on. He didn't have a sabre cut. They blew him all to bits."
>
> I didn't say anything.
>
> "Do you suppose it will always go on?"
>
> "No."
>
> "What's to stop it?"
>
> "It will crack somewhere."
>
> "We'll crack. We'll crack in France. They can't go on doing things like the Somme and not crack."

> "They won't crack here," I said.
>
> "You think not?"
>
> "No. They did very well last summer."
>
> "They may crack," she said. "Anybody may crack."
>
> "The Germans too."
>
> "No," she said. "I think not."

Catherine here exists almost as the echo of Frederic's own bitterness and despair. She is Despair turning desperately to the religion of love. She has no past beyond the absolute minimum required for plausibility. Like another Catherine, [Emily] Bronte's Catherine Earnshaw, she *is* her lover: her temperamental affinity to Frederic is so marked that their right to each other is accepted almost from the first moment of meeting. Thus she is, in a sense, not a distinct character at all but Frederic's bitterness or his desire objectified. She will presently become the peace or bliss that stands at farthest remove from the war: the white snows of the mountaintops, the idyllic serenity of Switzerland, the Beatrice of the *Paradiso*. To lose her will be to lose Love. The lyric novel requires no deeper characterization.

Source: Daniel J. Schneider, "Hemingway's *A Farewell to Arms*: The Novel as Pure Poetry," in *Modern Fiction Studies,* Vol. XIV, No. 3, Autumn, 1968, pp. 283–96.

Sources

Carlos Baker, editor, *Ernest Hemingway: Critiques of Four Major Novels,* Scribners, 1962.

Harold Bloom, editor, *Modern Critical Views: Ernest Hemingway,* Chelsea, 1985.

Fanny Butcher, "Here is Genius, Critic Declares of Hemingway," in *Chicago Daily Tribune,* September 28, 1929, p. 11.

Judith Fetterley, *The Resisting Reader: A Feminist Approach to American Fiction,* Indiana University Press, 1978.

Henry Hazlitt, "Take Hemingway," in *New York Sun,* September 28, 1929, p. 38.

Robert Herrick, "What Is Dirt?", in *Bookman,* November, 1929, p. 258–62.

George Monteiro, editor, *Critical Essays on Ernest Hemingway's A Farewell to Arms,* G. K. Hall, 1994.

Earl Rovit, "Learning to Care," in *Twentieth Century Interpretations of A Farewell to Arms,* edited by Jay Gellens, Prentice-Hall, 1970, pp. 33-40.

Sandra Whipple Spanier, "Hemingway's Unknown Soldier: Catherine Barkley, the Critics, and the Great War," *New Essays on A Farewell to Arms,* Cambridge University Press, 1990, pp. 75-108.

For Further Study

Matthew J. Bruccoli, *Conversations with Ernest Hemingway,* University Press of Mississippi, 1986.

Contains interviews with Hemingway that provide the author's point of view on a variety of issues concerning his life and works.

Scott Donaldson, *The Cambridge Companion to Hemingway,* Cambridge University Press, 1996.

Contains a wealth of background information on Hemingway and his writings.

Scott Donaldson, editor, *New Essays on A Farewell to Arms,* Cambridge University Press, 1990.

A collection of four outstanding recent interpretations of the novel, as well as a useful introduction by the editor.

Jay Gellens, editor, *Twentieth Century Interpretations of A Farewell to Arms,* Prentice-Hall, 1970.

Contains seven critical interpretations of the novel, including a "symposium" bringing together four critics' views on Hemingway's use of symbolism. Also includes six shorter critical "View Points" on various aspects of the work.

Peter Hutchinson, "Love and War in the Pages of Mr. Hemingway," in *New York Times Book Review,* September 29, 1929, p. 5.

This critic reminds the audience that Hemingway did not invent the prose style he is known for. However, he continues, Hemingway has proven to be the master of the style.

Robert W. Lewis, *A Farewell to Arms: The War of Words,* Twayne, 1992.

A recent review of the themes, characters, and techniques of *A Farewell to Arms.* Lewis also reviews the critical reception of the work and provides a chronology of Hemingway's life.

Miriam B. Mandall, *Reading Hemingway: The Facts in the Fictions,* Scarecrow, 1995.

A valuable reference tool for the study of any of Hemingway's novels; contains detailed annotations and commentary for *A Farewell to Arms,* among other works.

Jeffrey Meyers, *Hemingway: A Biography,* Harper and Row, 1985.

A thorough and detailed biography of the author that provides a great deal of insight into the composition of his major works.

James Nagel, "Ernest Hemingway," in *Dictionary of Literary Biography,* edited by James J. Martine, Vol. 9, Gale, 1981, pp. 100-120.

Nagel presents an overview of Hemingway's life and his major works.

Michael S. Reynolds, *Hemingway's First War: The Making of A Farewell to Arms,* Princeton University Press, 1976.

Surveys the experiences that led to Hemingway's writing of the novel, including analyses of Hemingway's manner of composing the work, the structure of the novel, critical responses, and an essay on *A Farewell to Arms* as travel literature.

Arthur Waldhorn, *Reader's Guide to Ernest Hemingway,* Farrar, Straus and Giroux, 1972.

An excellent resource for information on Hemingway's life and his style of writing, including material on *A Farewell to Arms* and his other works.

Frankenstein

Mary Shelley

1818

Mary Shelley made an anonymous but powerful debut into the world of literature when *Frankenstein, or The Modern Prometheus* was published in March, 1818. She was only nineteen when she began writing her story. She and her husband, poet Percy Bysshe Shelley, were visiting poet Lord Byron at Lake Geneva in Switzerland when Byron challenged each of his guests to write a ghost story. Settled around Byron's fireplace in June 1816, the intimate group of intellectuals had their imaginations and the stormy weather as the stimulus and inspiration for ghoulish visions. A few nights later, Mary Shelley imagined the "hideous phantasm of man" who became the confused yet deeply sensitive creature in *Frankenstein.* She once said, "My dreams were at once more fantastic and agreeable than my writings." While many stage, television, and film adaptations of *Frankenstein* have simplified the complexity of the intellectual and emotional responses of Victor Frankenstein and his creature to their world, the novel still endures. Its lasting power can be seen in the range of reactions explored by various literary critics and over ninety dramatizations.

Although early critics greeted the novel with a combination of praise and disdain, readers were fascinated with and a bit horrified by the macabre aspects of the novel. Interestingly, the macabre has transformed into the possible as the world approaches the twenty-first century: the ethical implications of genetic engineering, and, more recently, the cloning of livestock in Scotland, find

echoes in Shelley's work. In addition to scientific interest, literary commentators have noted the influence of both Percy Shelley and William Godwin (Mary's father) in the novel. Many contemporary critics have focused their attention on the novel's biographical elements, tracing Shelley's maternal and authorial insecurities to her very unique creation myth. Ultimately, the novel resonates with philosophical and moral ramifications: themes of nurture versus nature, good versus evil, and ambition versus social responsibility dominate readers' attention and provoke thoughtful consideration of the most sensitive issues of our time.

Author Biography

Surrounded by some of the most famous authors in history, Mary Shelley struggled to find her own authorial voice in *Frankenstein.* She was born in August, 1797 to William Godwin, a revolutionary thinker who wrote *An Enquiry Concerning Political Justice,* and Mary Wollstonecraft, author of *A Vindication of the Rights of Women.* Shelley's freethinking parents married when Wollstonecraft was five months pregnant with Shelley. Even though both Godwin and Wollstonecraft philosophically opposed the institution of marriage, they wanted to give Mary social respectability. Unfortunately, Shelley would never witness her parents' marital relationship because Wollstonecraft died ten days after Mary's birth. A doctor (summoned by the midwife, who could not remove the placenta after Mary's delivery) infected Wollstonecraft's uterus with his unwashed hands.

Shelley turned to Wollstonecraft's books to learn about a mother she never knew. Self-taught, she also engaged herself with the books that graced her father's library shelves. The new Mrs. Godwin, Mary Jane Clairmont, affirmed Godwin's decision not to give Shelley any formal schooling, even though they both recognized Shelley's curious mind. Clairmont played a major role with other decisions in Mary's life, which gradually heightened Mary's unhappiness with her home life. In fact, Mary's upbringing mirrored certain elements of the childhood story *Cinderella* because Clairmont favored her own children above Godwin's. Clairmont harbored jealous feelings towards the offspring of two of the most progressive thinkers of the time. In addition, Clairmont resented Shelley's strong devotion to Godwin, so she limited Shelley's interaction with her father. Mary eventually transferred

Mary Shelley

her affections to Percy Shelley, another prominent literary figure of the day.

Percy Shelley and his wife, Harriet, dined with Mary's family after Percy wrote a letter of admiration to Godwin. Mary Shelley met Percy for a second time, two years later, and the pair began spending almost every day with each other. Percy was twenty-two and his wife was pregnant with their second child when Mary declared her love for him. Initially, Mary agreed not to see Percy when Godwin condemned their relationship. But Percy's dramatic threat to commit suicide convinced Mary to flee with him to France in July 1814.

The year 1816 revealed both tragedy and creativity for Shelley. Most of Mary Shelley's biographies trace 1816 as a happy year for the Shelley marriage; a son, William, was born, and the couple did extensive traveling. Mary and Percy met poet Lord Byron at his home in Lake Geneva, the infamous site where Mary gave birth to the *Frankenstein* myth. But this year also brought much grief to the couple's happiness, as both Fanny Imlay (Mary's older half-sister) and Harriet Shelley committed suicide only weeks apart from each other. Their deaths lead to a series of other deaths and produced the beginnings of Mary's depression. Both William and Clara Shelley, Percy and Mary's son and daughter, died a year apart from each other, and Percy drowned in a boating accident in 1822. Mary spent the remainder of her years in England with her only surviving son, Percy, writing five other novels and other critical and biographical writings. She died of complications from a brain tumor in 1851.

Plot Summary

Opening Letters

Frankenstein opens with Robert Walton's letter from St. Petersburgh, Russia, to his sister in England. He encourages her to share his enthusiasm about his journey to the North Pole to discover both the secret of magnetism and a passage through the pole. In additional letters he wavers between his solitude and alienation on the one hand, and his determined heart and resolved will on the other. His last letter tells the startling story of his having seen a being of gigantic stature shaped like a man, fleeing across the ice which is threatening to enclose the ship. The next day another sled appears, carrying the wasted and maddened Victor Frankenstein, who is pursuing the giant. Walton takes Frankenstein aboard. When he tells Frankenstein his purpose, how he hopes to make great discoveries, Frankenstein cautions him to leave off his mad pursuit. He asks him to listen to his story of how once he began in earnest to know all that could be known.

Victor's Story, Part I

Born in Naples, Italy, to a wealthy Swiss family, Victor Frankenstein is the only child of doting parents. When he is five, his mother brings home an orphaned girl named Elizabeth to be Victor's "sister." In Victor's happy childhood in Geneva, he and Elizabeth grow in their parents' love, and they are joined by more siblings. Victor develops a deep friendship with Henry Clerval, a fellow student. Where Clerval studies "the moral relations of things," Victor conceives a passion to discover the physical secrets of the world.

At seventeen, as he is to leave for the University at Ingolstadt, Elizabeth contracts scarlet fever. Nursed by Victor's mother, she recovers, but his mother dies. On her deathbed, she begs Elizabeth and Victor to wed. After some delay, Victor departs for Ingolstadt, where his chemistry professor so encourages him in the study of science that Victor determines to discover the secret of life, perhaps even how to create life itself. He pursues his

studies in the chemistry lab and in dissecting rooms and morgues, gathering the material for his experiment to make a creature from discarded corpses, perhaps one "like himself." Cut off from contact with all others, ignoring letters from friends and family, he exhausts himself. Finally, on a dreary November night, Victor succeeds in animating a creature. Drained of all strength, he falls asleep, only to awaken from a nightmare to find the creature staring at him. He flees in horror at what he has done.

The next day Clerval arrives and Victor's appearance and condition shock him. Victor can not tell Clerval what he has done. He believes he can keep his secret, for, on his return to his room, he discovers that the creature has fled. The nervous exhaustion into which Victor then falls lasts for several months, during which Clerval nurses him by taking him away from the lab and into the mountains on long walks.

Victor receives from his father a letter relating the death of Victor's younger brother William, strangled by someone while out walking. A necklace with a miniature likeness of Victor's mother was missing when the corpse was found. On his frantic return journey, in an electrical storm in the mountains near Geneva, Victor sees the monster and thinks that the monster might have killed William. At home Victor learns that everyone believes Justine, a family servant, to be guilty, for the necklace missing from the corpse was found on her. Victor exclaims that she is innocent, that he knows who the killer is, but does not speak up at her trial. Justine gives a forced confession and is convicted and hung. Overcome with remorse at the deaths of William and Justine, convinced of his own guilt, Victor seeks solitude. Elizabeth and his father attribute his behavior to his grief at his brother's death. He leaves the house to walk the Swiss Alps, journeying to the village of Chamounix. In a painful retreat amid the "solitary grandeur" of the mountains, he meets the monster crossing an ice field. To Victor's shocked expressions of outrage the monster replies calmly, asking Frankenstein to listen with compassion to his tale.

The Monster's Story

After fleeing from the laboratory on the night of his "birth," the monster discovers himself cold, unfed, and unbefriended in the mountains outside Ingolstadt, "a poor, helpless, miserable wretch." He searches for food and shelter, which he finally finds in a hovel adjoined to a cottage. He observes the cottage's inhabitants: an old man, a young man and woman. When he learns that the cottagers are not so happy as he believes they should be, he gathers firewood at night to replenish their woodpile and lessen their labors. Meanwhile, in the course of several seasons, he studies them, learns their names (Felix and Agatha and their father), and begins to study their language.

One day another woman arrives on horseback. Felix seems especially happy in her presence. The monster listens as Felix instructs her from a history book. He learns of human law and government, of rank and wealth, of human greatness and vileness. "Of what a strange nature is knowledge!" he exclaims. Above all, he learns of his own lonely deformity.

He later tells Frankenstein the story of this De Lacey family, a wealthy French family who suffered a reversal of fortunes, were imprisoned, and exiled to the poverty in which the monster finds them. From such books as John Milton's epic poem *Paradise Lost* the monster learns more of human virtues and vices and of his own misery.

> And what was I? Of my creation and creator I was absolutely ignorant, but I knew that I possessed no money, no friends, no kind of property. I was, besides, endowed with a figure hideously deformed and loathsome; I was not even of the same nature as man. I was more agile than they and could subsist on a coarser diet; I bore the extremes of heat and cold with less injury to my frame; my stature far exceeded theirs. When I looked around I saw and heard of none like me. Was I, then, a monster, a blot upon the earth, from which all men fled and whom all men disowned?

One day when only the old man is in the cottage, the monster enters, introducing himself as a weary traveler. He discovers that because the old man is blind, he is not repulsed by him. The monster then tells his tale of misery and loneliness; the old man responds sympathetically. When the others return, horrified at his monstrous appearance, they chase him. From seclusion in the forest, the next night he emerges to burn down the cottage. He then flees toward Ingolstadt, determined on vengeance. He comes upon young William Frankenstein out walking. When the boy repulses the monster's friendly overtures, the monster kills him. He takes from the boy a locket with the likeness of a woman and when he later meets another young woman asleep in a barn, he places the locket on her, certain that he can implicate her in the boy's murder. He concludes his tale by proposing to Victor that only Victor's creation of a female of similar deformity will grant him the happiness he cannot find among humans.

Victor's Story, Part II

The monster pleads with Victor to make him a mate, threatening him and his family if he does not. Frankenstein agrees, but only on condition that the creatures flee to uninhabitable parts of the earth where they will do no harm to humans. Victor returns to his family, more downhearted than ever. His father proposes that the long-hoped-for marriage of Victor and Elizabeth might restore Victor to happiness. Victor wishes instead to travel to England to discover from philosophers there something he believes might complete his work. He promises to marry Elizabeth on his return. His father arranges to have Clerval meet him along the way in Strasbourg, France. They walk in the mountains, then travel by boat down the Rhine River and to England. In Edinburgh, Scotland, Victor asks Clerval to permit him to travel on alone for a time. Frankenstein, convinced that the monster has been following him, seeks solitude for his work on a remote island in the Scottish Orkneys. On a moonlit night his fears are realized when he looks up from his work on the new creature to discover the monster peering at him through the window. Victor then vows to destroy his new, half-finished creation. The monster threatens him: "I will be with you on your wedding night."

Frankenstein takes the remains of the new creature and dumps them into the sea from a boat he takes offshore. When he awakens hours later, he has drifted to Ireland. Several people on shore take him to a magistrate to answer for the death of a man found murdered the previous evening. The man, to Victor's horror, is Clerval. Imprisoned for several months, Frankenstein is freed after the magistrate discovers Victor's innocence. The magistrate sends for Victor's father in Geneva to bring him home. On his return he marries Elizabeth, worried all the while about the monster's threat, "I shall be with you on your wedding night." He interprets this to mean that the monster will kill him. On the wedding night, however, the monster breaks into their room and kills Elizabeth. After he sees the monster staring through the window, grinning, Victor vows to seek revenge. He pursues the monster across the Alps, across Europe, into Russia and north to the pole, where he finds himself stranded on an ice flow before he is taken aboard Walton's ship.

Closing Letters

One week after his last letter to his sister, during which Frankenstein relates his story, Walton writes again to say that Frankenstein still intends

From the film Frankenstein, *starring Boris Karloff, 1935.*

to pursue the creature until he dies. Walton, too, is still determined to pursue his quest, although mountains of ice surround the ship and threaten to lock it in place. When his sailors ask to turn back, Walton consents to turn south. His final letter to his sister recounts Frankenstein's death and his dying advice to Walton to forego ambition and seek tranquility instead. Walton's grief over his new friend's death is interrupted by the appearance of the monster in Frankenstein's cabin, grieving over the death of his creator. The monster tells Walton how his vengeance had never been joyful to him, how he was unjustly treated by the humanity which had created him. Thus, though born in innocence

and goodness, he became malignant evil. He now lives in remorse, alone. After having said all this, he springs from the cabin window and disappears across the ice.

Characters

Henry Clerval

Victor's closest friend and companion, who balances his emotional and rational pursuits. He studies Oriental languages but passionately loves nature and life. Victor acknowledges that "[H]is wild and enthusiastic imagination was chastened by

Media Adaptations

There have been so many plays, movies, and recordings of Frankenstein that it would be difficult to list all of the productions. Therefore, the list below represents the most popular, most controversial, and most influential recordings and dramatizations:

- Recordings: *Frankenstein* phonodisc dramatization with sound effects and music, directed by Christopher Casson, Spoken Arts, 1970; *Frankenstein*, taken from a broadcast of the CBS program *Suspense*, starring Herbert Marshall, American Forces Radio and Television Service, 1976; *Frankenstein* read by James Mason, Caedmon Records, 1977; *Weird Circle*, containing Edgar Allan Poe's *The Tell-Tale Heart* and Shelley's *Frankenstein*, recorded from original radio broadcasts, Golden Age, 1978.

- Films: *Frankenstein* starred Colin Clive and Boris Karloff; it was released by Universal in 1931. *The Bride of Frankenstein*, the sequel to the 1931 film, starred Boris Karloff and Elsa Lanchester; it was released in 1935 by Universal. *Son of Frankenstein*, also a sequel to the above mentioned productions, starred Basil Rathbone, Karloff, and Bela Lugosi and was released in 1939 by Universal. All three are available from MCA/Universal Home Video.

- *The Curse of Frankenstein*, a 1957 horror film produced by Warner Brothers, included Peter Cushing and Christopher Lee as cast members; the first in a series of films inspired by Shelley's novel, it is available from Warner Home Video. *Frankenstein Must Be Destroyed!* was released in 1969 by Warner Brothers; Peter Cushing and Veronica Carlson star as the central characters. *Young Frankenstein* was released in 1974 by Fox; available from CBS-Fox Video, this comedy-horror film received Academy Award nominations for Best Adapted Screenplay and Best Sound; cast includes Gene Wilder, Peter Boyle, and director-star Mel Brooks.

- More recent films include 1985's *The Bride*, starring Sting and Jennifer Beals, available from CBS/Fox Video; famed horror director Roger Corman's 1990 work *Frankenstein Unbound*, which includes Mary Shelley as a character and stars John Hurt, Raul Julia, and Bridget Fonda, available from CBS/Fox Video; the 1993 cable production *Frankenstein*, starring Patrick Bergin and Randy Quaid, available from Turner Home Entertainment; and *Mary Shelley's Frankenstein*, released in 1994 by American Zoetrope and available from Columbia Tristar Home Video, featuring Robert De Niro and director-star Kenneth Branagh.

- Plays: *Frankenstein: A Gothic Thriller* by David Campton, published by Garnet Miller in 1973; *Frankenstein* by Tim Kelley, published by Samuel French in 1974.

---

the sensibility of his heart." And unlike Victor, who wishes to learn "the secrets of heaven and earth," Clerval aspires "to become one among those whose names are recorded in story as the gallant and adventurous benefactors of our species."

After Victor runs from the creature when the creature comes to life, Clerval nurses Victor back to health, playing the role of protector and comforter—a role Victor fails to assume for his own "child," the creature. The creature eventually strangles and kills Clerval because Victor destroys his half-created mate. Victor then vows revenge upon the creature.

The creature

Like a newborn baby reaching out to his mother, the creature reaches out to Victor when he is transformed from an inanimate to an animate being. Victor labored for two years in order to give the creature life, but he is so appalled by the creature's hideous appearance that he flees, leaving the creature to fend for himself. Shelley initially leaves her readers in suspense as to the creature's whereabouts. We do not hear his story until after he finds Victor and requests a mate for himself. He describes his life to Victor after he "awoke," explaining the difficulties he had learning basic survival techniques. The creature then describes his happiest moments watching the De Lacey family together. Living in a shack attached to the De Lacey cottage, the creature viewed the family without their knowledge. He discovered a family relationship rooted in mutual respect and benevolent love, he learned how to speak and to read as the result of Safie's efforts to learn English, and he "looked upon crime as a distant evil."

John Locke, a famous eighteenth-century philosopher, invented the concept of the "Tabula Rasa," the idea that the mind is a "blank slate" when we are born. Most critics agree that Locke strongly influenced Shelley's characterization of the creature. She wanted her readers to understand how important the creature's social conditioning was to his development as a conscious being. The creature's environment, therefore, plays a critical role in shaping his reaction to and interaction with Victor during their first meeting. While the creature uses both rational and emotional appeals to convince Victor that he deserves and needs another being like himself to share his life with, he tries to emphasize Victor's duties as a creator. The creature eventually realizes that not only has Victor rejected him, the entire race of humankind abhors his image—an image resembling no one else in existence.

The creature vows revenge against his creator and takes Victor's youngest brother, William, as his first victim. After this incident, he discovers Justine asleep in a barn, and purposely puts William's locket in her hand so that she will be accused of the murder. Clerval and Elizabeth's murders follow this incident after Victor goes back on his promise to create a mate for the creature. The creature finally appears at Victor's death bed and confesses his crimes to Walton. He assures Walton that he will fade from existence when a funeral pile consumes his body with flames and sweeps him into the dark sea.

Agatha De Lacey

Daughter of Mr. De Lacey, Agatha shows tenderness and kindness towards her family and Safie. She too, however, is horrified by the creature and faints upon seeing him.

Felix De Lacey

A hard-working son who cares for his family and his beloved Safie. He appears sad and unhappy until Safie, his fiancee, arrives at his home. His involvement with Safie's father gets him, his father, and his sister Agatha exiled from their homeland, France. Nevertheless, his unasked-for kindness to Safie's father, a foreign convict, stands in contrast to his cruel dismissal and beating of the creature, who is doing nothing but sitting at the feet of Felix's father.

Mr. De Lacey

As the blind father of Felix and Agatha, Mr. De Lacey serves as a surrogate father to the creature. The creature notes his benevolence towards his family, and notes that "he would talk in a cheerful accent, with an expression of goodness that bestowed pleasure even upon me." De Lacey and his children are in their current exile because of the aid they rendered, unasked, to a Turkish merchant who was wrongly sentenced to death; the merchant later betrayed them. Because Mr. De Lacey is blind, the creature approaches him to try to gain his sympathy and friendship. Even though Felix and Agatha return home and run the creature off, Mr. De Lacey is the only one in the book who does not judge or fear the creature.

Alphonse Frankenstein

Victor's father is described by his son as "respected by all who knew him for his integrity and indefatigable attention to public business." Alphonse met Victor's mother because of his persistence in pursuing a friend who had fallen on hard times in order to give him assistance. Alphonse is also a nurturing, loving parent, and tries many times to remind Victor that family and happiness are just as important as books and learning. It is his letters to Victor that serve as occasional reminders of the outside world while he is occupied with his experiments.

Caroline Frankenstein

Victor Frankenstein's mother, Caroline was the orphaned daughter of an impoverished merchant who was one of Alphonse Frankenstein's merchant friends. She married the much-older Alphonse two years after he completed his long search for the family. A devoted mother, she contracts the scarlet fever while caring for Elizabeth, Victor's adopted sister. She dies just before Victor leaves to attend the University.

Victor Frankenstein

Born to an affluent, loving family, Victor Frankenstein hopes to leave a lasting impression on his fellow humanity. He leaves home to attend the University of Ingolstadt, where he studies natural sciences. His professor M. Waldman inspires him to push his experiments beyond the realm of "acceptable" science, so he begins to determine the limits of human mortality. Collecting cadaver parts from graveyards, he slowly pieces together the form of a human being. It takes him two years to complete his experiment, but when he finally gives his creature the spark of life, Victor can only run in fear. The creature's hideous appearance appalls Victor, upsetting him so much that he becomes very ill. He knows nothing about the creature's whereabouts until the creature finally approaches him.

Although Victor listens to his creature's tale with a mixture of loathing and dread, he reluctantly acknowledges that he owes the creature "a small portion of happiness"; so he promises to create a mate for the creature. After much consideration, however, Victor fears the consequences of his decision and destroys what little of the female he had created. Although he honestly believes the creature despises humanity and would therefore inflict harm upon anyone and everyone, Victor is more concerned about the creature and his mate creating other "monsters" to wreak havoc upon society. Although he feels guilt for the monster's actions, realizing that by making the creature he is the cause of them, he never accepts responsibility for how he has driven the creature to vengeance.

Ironically, he continues to worry about the creature's treatment of others even when both of them slip deeper into the Arctic iceland, far away from any form of civilization, and even after he hears of the creature's benevolent efforts to help the De Lacey family survive. The ending of the novel only reaffirms Victor's truly selfish motivations, as he fails to consider the needs of Walton's crew by asking them to continue their journey in order to kill the creature. He even calls the crew members cowards for wanting to return home without completing their mission. What Victor does not realize is that his quest to conquer the unknown has left him without family or friends; he dies on Walton's ship as lonely and bitter as his unfortunate creature.

Throughout the novel, Victor's self-centered actions are shown in stark contrast to those of his family, friends, and even strangers. Whereas his parents have taken in two orphaned children and treated them as their own, Victor relinquishes responsibility for the only creature he has actually created. Unlike Elizabeth, who testifies on Justine's behalf despite the other townspeople's disapproval, Victor remains silent because he fears to be disbelieved or thought insane. Even the behavior of minor characters such as Mr. Kirwin, who exerts himself to nurse and defend a stranger who to all outward appearances is a murderer, serves to show how Victor is unnaturally selfish and as a result has performed an unnatural act.

William Frankenstein

Victor's youngest brother, who runs from the creature's presence in fear. The creature kills him, but Justine Moritz, a family friend, gets blamed for the death. Victor knows from the first that the creature is the murderer, but arrives home too late to prevent Justine from accepting blame for William's death.

Frankenstein's monster
See The creature

Mr. Kirwin

An Irish magistrate who believes Victor is responsible for Clerval's murder, for Victor is agitated on hearing the manner of the man's death. After Victor becomes bedridden upon viewing Clerval's corpse, Kirwin cares for Victor's needs and helps him recover his health. Kirwin is sympathetic to the suffering young man, even though his feverish ravings seem to indicate his guilt in the murder. He also arranges for the collection of evidence in Victor's behalf, sparing him a trial.

Elizabeth Lavenza

The Frankensteins adopt Elizabeth when she is only a girl. She and Victor share more than the typical sibling affections for each other; they love each other and correspond while Victor attends the University. In her letters to him, Elizabeth keeps Victor abreast of family and other social matters, such as town gossip. She also describes Justine's welfare, reminding Victor that orphans can blossom physically as well as mentally, given the proper love and attention. Her unselfish behavior serves as a contrast to Victor's: Elizabeth gives testimony on Justine's behalf during her trial while Victor remains silent even though he knows Justine did not murder William. Elizabeth and Victor are reunited and get married, despite the creature's threats to be with Victor on his wedding night. Elizabeth is kept ignorant of the creature's existence and his threats, and when Victor leaves the room on their wedding night, the creature kills Elizabeth.

Justine Moritz

The Frankenstein family adopts Justine because she had been abandoned by her mother. She is a favorite of Caroline Frankenstein, but returns for a time to her own mother after Caroline's death. Justine later returns to the Frankensteins, and continually reminds Elizabeth "of my dear aunt." She is found with young William's locket after his death and put on trial for his murder. Although Victor knows the creature is responsible for William's death, he says nothing at Justine's trial, reasoning that "I was absent when it was committed, and such a declaration would have been considered as the ravings of a madman and would not have exculpated her who suffered through me." Despite Elizabeth's testimony regarding Justine's good character, she is sentenced to death and then executed.

Safie

Safie becomes known to Felix through the letters of thanks she writes to him. Although her father is Turkish, her mother was a Christian Arab who had been enslaved by the Turks before marrying one of them. Safie cherishes the memory of her mother, who instructed her daughter in Christianity and fostered "an independence of spirit forbidden to the female followers of Muhammed." Against her father's wishes, Safie flees Turkey and joins Felix De Lacey and his family. Her broken English becomes a learning opportunity for the creature, because he receives the same language lessons as she does. Shelley's stereotypical treatment of Turkish Muslims in her portrayal of Sadie's situation was most likely a way to bring up the issues of women's rights that were articulated by her mother, writer Mary Wollstonecraft.

Margaret Saville

Robert Walton's sister, with whom Walton corresponds at the beginning and end of the novel.

M. Waldman

Victor's kind professor inspires him to "unfold to the world the deepest mysteries of creation." Victor hears M. Waldman's lecture on the progress of science and determines "more, far more, will I achieve." The behavior of this man of science stands in stark contrast to Victor's, for M. Waldman takes time away from his research to teach Victor and introduce him to the laboratory, whereas Victor pursues his experiments to the exclusion of all else.

Robert Walton

Walton's letters begin and end the novel, framing Victor's and the creature's narratives in such a way that Walton embodies the most important qualities found in both Victor and his creature. Walton, in other words, balances the inquisitive yet presumptuously arrogant nature of Victor with the sympathetic, sensitive side of the creature. As an Arctic explorer, Walton, much like Victor, wishes to conquer the unknown. Nevertheless, when he discovers Victor near death on the icy, vast expanse of water, he listens to Victor's bitter and tormented tale of the creature. This makes him reconsider continuing his own mission to the possible peril of his crew. When the creature appears at Victor's deathbed, Walton fails to fulfill Victor's dying wish to destroy the creature. Instead, he does what Victor continually failed to do throughout the novel: he listens to the creature's anguished tale with compassion and empathy.

Themes

Alienation and Loneliness

Mary Shelley's emphasis on the Faust legend, or the quest to conquer the unknown at the cost of one's humanity, forms a central theme of the novel. The reader continually sees Victor favor his ambition above his friendships and family. Created by a German writer named Johann Wolfgang von Goethe, the Faust myth suggested that the superior individual could throw off the shackles of traditional conventions and alienate himself from society. English Romantic poets, who assumed the status of poet-prophets, believed that only in solitude could they produce great poetry. In *Frankenstein,* however, isolation only leads to despair. Readers get the distinct feeling that Victor's inquisitive nature causes his emotional and physical peril because he cannot balance his intellectual and social interactions. For instance, when he leaves home to attend the University of Ingolstadt, he immerses himself in his experiment and forgets about the family who lovingly supported him throughout his childhood. Victor actually does not see his family or correspond with them for six years, even when his father and Elizabeth try to keep in touch with him by letters. Shelley's lengthy description of Victor's model parents contrasts with his obsessive drive to create the creature.

Margaret's correspondence with Walton at the beginning of the novel also compares with Shelley's description of Victor's home life; both men were surrounded by caring, nurturing individuals who considered the welfare of their loved ones at all times. Not surprisingly, Walton's ambition to conquer the unknown moves him, like it does Victor, further away from civilization and closer to feelings of isolation and depression. The creature, too, begins reading novels such as Goethe's *The Sorrows of Werter* and John Milton's *Paradise Lost,* claiming that an "increase of knowledge only [showed] what a wretched outcast I was." For the creature, an increase in knowledge only brings sorrow and discontent. Victor and Walton ultimately arrive at these two states because of their inquisitive natures.

Nature vs. Nurture

The theme of nurturing, or how environment contributes to a person's character, truly fills the novel. With every turn of the page, another nurturing example contrasts with Victor's lack of a parental role with his "child," the creature. Caroline nurtures Elizabeth back to health and loses her own life as a result. Clerval nurtures Victor through his illness when he is in desperate need of a caretaker after the creature is brought to life. The De Lacey's nurturing home becomes a model for the creature, as he begins to return their love in ways the family cannot even comprehend. For instance, the creature stopped stealing the De Lacey's food after realizing their poverty. In sympathy, he left firewood for the family to reduce Felix's chores. Each nurturing act contrasts strongly with Victor's gross neglect of the creature's needs. And by showing the affection between Caroline Frankenstein and her adopted daughters Elizabeth and Justine, Shelley suggests that a child need not have biological ties to a parent to deserve an abundance of love and attention.

Appearances and Reality

Victor's inquisitive probing causes him to delve beneath the appearances of "acceptable" science and create an animate being from inanimate materials. Nevertheless, he forgets to extend this inquiring sensibility toward his creature. The creature's physical appearance prompts Victor to flee from his creation; Victor never takes the time to search beneath the creature's ugliness to discover the very human qualities that the creature possesses. While Victor easily manipulates nature and natural laws to suit his own intellectual interests, he lacks an understanding of human nature, as proven throughout the novel.

In addition to the importance of the creature's appearance, Shelley emphasizes the magnificent

Topics for Further Study

- Compare and contrast Robert Walton's and Victor Frankenstein's personalities. You might draw parallels between their quest to conquer the unknown, their emotional ties to other individuals, or their loneliness.

- Research some of the prominent issues in your society that Shelley addresses in her novel, such as genetic engineering, or the effects of abandonment on children whose fathers have disappeared from their lives. Make a comparison between the novel and your discoveries and discuss observations about how your society is coping with or addressing these sensitive issues.

- Analyze the theme of justice in the novel. What does Justine's trial have to do with Victor's treatment of his creature or the creature's treatment of Victor's family and friends? How does the theme of revenge relate to issues of justice?

- Research some of the characteristics of the Romantic movement, such as isolation, an emphasis on nature, or the notion that humans are inherently good, and argue how and why Shelley's novel is an embodiment of the English Romantic movement. Or, argue why her novel is not an embodiment of the English Romantic movement.

landscape throughout the novel. This demonstrates her loyalty to the Romantic movement of her time, which often glorified nature. Although Victor often turns to nature to relieve his despondent thoughts, Clerval notices the intimate interaction between nature and humans in Switzerland. He says to Victor, "Look at that ... group of labourers coming from among their vines; and that village half-hid in the recess of the mountain." Clerval looks beyond nature's surface appearance, drawing Victor's attention to the harmonious interaction between nature and a productive society. Victor praises his friend as having a "wild and enthusiastic imagination [which] was chastened by the sensibility of his heart," a sensibility Victor ironically lacks. In the isolated Arctic, when Walton's ship is trapped by mountains of ice, he respects nature's resistance to his exploration and eventually leaves the untamed region. Like Clerval, Walton experiences life by interacting harmoniously with nature and people, as he proves when he honors his crew members' request to return home.

Duty and Responsibility

Victor's inability to know his creature relates directly to his lack of responsibility for the creature's welfare or the creature's actions. The role of responsibility or duty takes many shapes throughout the story, but familial obligations represent one of the novel's central themes. Whether Caroline nurses Elizabeth or Felix blames himself for his family's impoverished condition, Victor's dismissal of his parental duties makes readers empathize with the creature. Victor only feels a sense of duty after the creature says the famous line, "How dare you sport thus with life? Do your duty towards me, and I will do mine towards you and the rest of mankind." The creature compares himself to Adam—thus comparing Victor to God—and claims that Victor owes him a certain amount of happiness. Even though the creature temporarily convinces Victor to grant him his rights, Victor never really learns the virtues of parental or ethical responsibility.

Justice vs. Injustice

By showing how Victor ignores his responsibilities while those around him do not, Shelley invites the reader to judge his character. Themes of justice and injustice play a large role in the novel, as the author develops issues of fairness and blame. Usually those characters who take responsibility for others and for their own actions are considered fair and just. For example, Elizabeth pleads Justine's case in court after Justine is accused of William's murder. Victor knows the creature committed the crime, yet he does not—or cannot—reveal the creature's wrongdoing.

However, the most important aspect of the trial is Justine's confession. Elizabeth claims, "I believed you guiltless … until I heard that you had yourself declared your guilt." When Justine explains that she confessed after being found guilty because that was the only way to receive absolution from the church, Elizabeth accepts her at her word and tells her, "I will proclaim, I will prove your innocence." Making confessions, listening to others, and offering verbal promises all signal the highest truths in this novel. Elizabeth accepts Jus-

tine's guilt only if Justine says she is guilty; never mind the facts or evidence, never mind intuition—words reveal true belief. Except for Victor, every character listens to others: Mr. Kirwin listens to Victor's story, the creature listens to the De Lacey family, Felix listens to Safie's father, Margaret listens to Walton, and Walton listens to Victor and to his crew. Listening helps all of these characters distinguish fair from unfair. Victor's refusal to listen impartially to his creature says much about his character. Shelley suggests that Victor not only played God when he created the creature; he also unfairly played the role of judge and accuser.

Style

Narration

Instead of beginning with Victor's point of view, Shelley introduces us to Walton first. Using a frame device, in which the tale is told to us by someone who reads it or hears it from someone else, Shelley invites readers to believe Victor's story through an objective person. Shelley also uses an important literary device known as the epistolary form—where letters tell the story—using letters between Walton and his sister to frame both Victor's and the creature's narrative. Before the novel's first chapter, Walton writes to his sister about the "wretched man" he meets, building suspense about the "demon" Victor mentions at the beginning of his narrative. Once Victor begins telling his story, we slowly learn about his childhood and the eventful moments leading up to his studies at the University. Then, the creature interrupts Victor, and we get to hear all the significant moments leading up to his request for a partner. Since the theme of listening is so central to this novel, Shelley makes sure, by incorporating three different narratives, that readers get to hear all sides of the story. Walton's letters introduce and conclude the novel, reinforcing the theme of nurturing.

Setting

The majority of the novel takes place in the Swiss Alps and concludes in the Arctic, although Victor and Clerval travel to other places, such as London, England, the Rhine River which flows from Switzerland north to the Netherlands, and Scotland. All of these locations, except for the Arctic, were among the favorite landscapes for Romantic writers, and Shelley spends great care describing the sublime shapes of the majestic, snow-clad mountains. However, aside from the dark Arctic Ocean, Shelley's setting is unusual;

most Gothic novels produce gloomy, haggard settings adorned with decaying mansions and ghostly, supernatural spirits. It is possible the author intended the beautiful Alps to serve as a contrast to the creature's unsightly physical appearance. In addition to the atypical Gothic setting, Shelley also sets her story in contemporary times, another diversion from Gothic novels which usually venture to the Middle Ages and other far away time periods. By using the time period of her day, Shelley makes the creature and the story's events much more realistic and lifelike.

Romanticism

Spanning the years between 1785 and 1830, the Romantic period was marked by the French Revolution and the beginnings of modern industrialism. Most of the early Romantic writers favored the revolution and the changes in lifestyle and sensibility which accompanied it. After shaking off old traditions and customs, writers experienced the newfound freedom of turning inward, rather than outward to the external world, to reflect on issues of the heart and the imagination. In addition, writers like English poet William Wordsworth suddenly challenged his predecessors by writing about natural scenes and rustic, commonplace lifestyles. English poet Samuel Coleridge explored elements of the supernatural in his poetry.

Mary Shelley combined the ethical concerns of her parents with the Romantic sensibilities of Percy Shelley's poetic inclinations. Her father's concern for the underprivileged influenced her description of the poverty-stricken De Lacey family. Her appeals to the imagination, isolation, and nature represented typical scenes and themes explored in some of Percy Shelley's poetry. But Mary's choice of a Gothic novel made her unique in her family and secured her authorial place in the Romantic period.

Gothicism

Horace Walpole introduced the first Gothic novel in 1764 with *The Castle of Otranto: A Gothic Story*. Gothic novels were usually mysteries in which sinister and sometimes supernatural events occurred and were ultimately caused by some evil human action. The language was frequently overly dramatic and inflated. Following this movement was the Romantic movement's fascination with the macabre and the superstitious aspects of life, allowing them the freedom to explore the darkest depths of the human mind. Most critics agree that Mary Shelley's *Frankenstein* reflected her deepest

psychological fears and insecurities, such as her inability to prevent her children's deaths, her distressed marriage to a man who showed no remorse for his daughters' deaths, and her feelings of inadequacy as a writer. The Gothic novel usually expresses, often in subtle and indirect ways, our repressed anxieties. The settings usually take place far away from reality or realistic portrayals of everyday life. Shelley's setting, of course, is the exception to most Gothic novels. The fact that the creature wanders the breathtaking Alps instead of a dark, craggy mansion in the middle of nowhere either compounds the reader's fear or makes the creature more human.

Doppelganger

Many literary critics have noted the *Doppelganger* effect—the idea that a living person has a ghostly double haunting him—between Victor and his creature. Presenting Victor and the creature as doubles allows Shelley to dramatize two aspects of a character, usually the "good" and "bad" selves. Victor's desire to ignore his creature parallels his desire to disregard the darkest part of his self. The famous psychologist Sigmund Freud characterizes this "dark" side as the Id, while Carl Jung, another famous psychologist, refers to our "dark" side as the Jungian shadow. Jung claims that we all have characteristics we don't like about ourselves, yet these unsavory attributes stay with us like a shadow tailgating its leader. The creature represents Victor's "evil" shadow, just as Victor represents the creature's. When presented this way, it makes sense that so many readers confuse the creature and Victor by assuming that the creature is named Frankenstein. Both of these characters "alternately pursue and flee from one another ... [L]ike fragments of a mind in conflict with itself," as Eleanor Ty observes in the *Concise Dictionary of British Literary Biography*. But taken together as one person, Victor and his creature combine to represent the full spectrum of what it means to be human—to be joyful, compassionate, empathetic, and hateful, and also love humanity, desire knowledge, honor justice, fear the unknown, dread abandonment, and fear mortality. No other character in the novel assumes this range of human complexity.

Historical Context

The French Revolution and the Rise of Industrialism

Most of the early Romantic writers strongly advocated the French Revolution, which began in

Compare & Contrast

- **Early 1800s:** After the French Revolution ended, England turned its attention to domestic and economic concerns—particularly to problems resulting from a rapidly growing industrial nation.

  Today: Domestic and economic concerns about employment and education also stem from rapid change, as the business world moves from emphasizing industrial production to a service and information economy.

- **Early 1800s:** Scientific advancements, especially Erasmus Darwin's studies in biological evolution, caused individuals to question God's authority and inquire into matters regarding the generation of human life.

  Today: Animal scientists in Scotland successfully tweak the DNA from an adult sheep to clone another individual sheep. The U.S. government bans federal funding of experiments with cloning using human DNA.

- **Early 1800s:** Romantic writers experience a literary Renaissance as critical theory affirms the achievements of the great poets of the age. Writers enjoy literary freedom, experimenting with a bold new language and new genres like Gothicism.

  Today: Appreciation of the arts seems to be on the decrease, as most individuals spend their time with television rather than with various art mediums. Funding has been greatly reduced for the National Endowment of the Arts, and even high school music and art classes have had to be cut at many public schools.

- **Early 1800s:** Nautical explorations establish trading routes and open up communication to other cultures. Robert Walton's quest to find the North Pole mirrors the adventures of nineteenth-century scientists and explorers alike.

  Today: The continuing exploration of space that seemed so likely after the lunar landing in 1969 has slowed down, as governments can no longer afford to fund large space programs. Projects involving a space station around Earth and a manned mission to Mars are more likely to come from cooperative efforts involving several nations.

1789 with the storming of the Bastille, a prison where the French royalty kept political prisoners. The revolution signaled a throwing off of old traditions and customs of the wealthy classes, as the balance of economic power shifted toward the middle class with the rise of industrialism. As textile factories and iron mills increased production with advanced machinery and technology, the working classes grew restive and increasingly alarmed by jobs that seemed insecure because a worker could be replaced by machines. Most of England's literary thinkers welcomed revolution because it represented an opportunity to establish a harmonious social structure. Shelley's father William Godwin, in fact, strongly influenced Romantic writers when he wrote *Inquiry Concerning Political Justice* because he envisioned a society in which property would be equally distributed. Shelley's mother Mary Wollstonecraft, also an ardent supporter of the revolution, wrote *A Vindication of the Rights of Men* in response to Edmund Burke's attack on the revolution. She followed two years later with *A Vindication of the Rights of Women,* supporting equality between the sexes.

The bloody "September Massacres" in which French revolutionaries executed nearly 1200 priests, royalists, aristocrats, and common criminals, occurred in 1792. This event and the "Reign of Terror," during which the revolutionary government imprisoned over 300,000 "suspects," made English sympathizers lose their fervor. With the rise of Napoleon, who was crowned emperor in 1804, England itself was drawn into war against France during this time. After the war ended in

1815, the English turned their attention to economic and social problems plaguing their own country. Much of the reason why England did not regulate the economic shift from a farming-based society to an industrialized society stemmed from a hands-off philosophy of non-governmental interference with private business. This philosophy had profound effects, leading to extremely low wages and terrible working conditions for employees who were prevented by law from unionizing.

Science and Technology

Eventually, the working class protested their conditions with violent measures. Around 1811, a period of unemployment, low wages, and high prices led to the Luddite Movement. This movement encouraged people to sabotage the technology and machinery that took jobs away from workers. Because the new machines produced an unparalleled production rate, competition for jobs was fierce, and employers used the low employment rate against their workers by not providing decent wages or working conditions. In addition to technological advances and new machines such as the steam engine, scientific advancements influenced the Romantic period. The most significant scientist was Erasmus Darwin, a noted physician, poet, and scholar whose ideas concerning biological evolution prefigured those of his more famous grandson, Charles Darwin. Both Mary and Percy were very familiar with his description of biological evolution, which became one of the central topics at the poet Lord Byron's home when Shelley conceived her idea for *Frankenstein.* Percy and Mary also attended a lecture by Andrew Crosse, a British scientist whose experiments with electricity bore some resemblance to Frankenstein's fascinations. Crosse discussed galvanism, or the study of electricity and its applications. This lecture no doubt fueled Shelley's imagination enough for her to suggest Victor Frankenstein's step-by-step invention of the creature in her novel.

Arctic Exploration

The late 1700s also marked the beginnings of a new era of ocean exploration. England's Royal Academy, which promoted the first voyage to the South seas, appealed to scientists and travelers alike. Explorers eventually wanted to find a trade route through the Arctic that would connect the Atlantic and the Pacific Oceans. In 1818, the year that Shelley published *Frankenstein,* a Scottish explorer named John Ross went searching for the Northwest passage and discovered an eight mile expanse of

Mary Shelley's first drawing of Frankenstein's monster.

red-colored snow cliffs overlooking Baffin Bay, between Greenland and Canada. His journey reflected Walton's quest to the North pole and the era of discovery in which Shelley lived.

Critical Overview

When Mary finished her novel in May 1817, Percy Shelley sent her manuscript, under an anonymous name, to two different publishers, both of whom rejected it. Lakington, Allen, and Co. finally accepted it. Early reviews of the work were generally mixed. As quoted in Diane Johnson's introduction to the novel, a critic for *The Edinburgh Review* found that "taste and judgement [sic] alike revolted at this kind of writing," and "it inculcates no lesson of conduct, manner of morality; it cannot mend, and will not even amuse its readers unless their tastes have been deplorably vitiated." A writer from the *Monthly Review,* as quoted by Montague Summers in *The Gothic Quest,* claimed that the setting was so improbable—the story so unbelievable—that it was "an uncouth story ... leading to no conclusion either moral or philosophical." Even though this conclusion regarding the novel's lack of moral implications seems absurd to readers today, most of the earliest unfavorable reviews related to the story's grotesque or sensationalist elements. On the other hand, some early reviewers enjoyed the novel's uniqueness and praised the author's genius. As Johnson related, Sir Walter Scott stated in *Blackwood's Edinburgh* magazine that he was impressed with "the high idea of the author's original genius and happy power of expression." The rest of England seemed to agree with Scott's opinion, since so many readers enjoyed *Frankenstein.* The novel resembled many works of the popular gothic genre, but it also became one of the triumphs of the Romantic movement. People identified with its themes of alienation and isolation and its warning about the destructive power that can result when human creativity is unfettered by moral and social concerns. Even if readers did not identify the Romantic themes present in Shelley's novel, the sensationalist elements piqued interest in other forms of dramatization

In 1823, the English Opera House performed *Presumption; or, The Fate of Frankenstein,* and fourteen other dramatizations were staged within three years of the play's premiere. The Opera House, in fact, used the protests against this play to further its own interests. As Steven Forry notes in his book *Hideous Progenies: Dramatizations of Frankenstein from the Nineteenth Century to the Present,* public outrage regarding the "immoral tendency" heightened the appeal of both the play and the book. Eventually, the various dramatizations shaped Shelley's characters to fit whatever popular appeal would draw audiences to the playhouses. Even today, numerous film adaptations distort the novel's original story, especially concerning the creature's very complex response to his world.

Since the 1800s, *Frankenstein* has continued to appeal to a wide audience. Criticism of the novel represents a diverse range of approaches. These include feminist interpretations, which describe the novel as reflecting Shelley's deepest fears of motherhood. Marxist analyses explore the effects of the poor versus the bourgeois families (the De Lacey's versus the Frankenstein's). In addition, some critics have focused on psychoanalysis, interpreting Dr. Frankenstein and the monster as embodying Sigmund Freud's theory of id and ego. Today, much critical focus seems to rest on the autobiographical elements of *Frankenstein,* as critics wish to rightfully consider Shelley as one of the leading Romantic writers of her day.

Criticism

George V. Griffith

Griffith is a professor of English and philosophy at Chadron State College in Chadron, Nebraska. In the following essay, he considers Frankenstein *as a novel that both represents and goes beyond the ideas of the Romantic era.*

Perhaps no book is more of its age than *Frankenstein.* Written and published in 1816–1818, *Frankenstein* typifies the most important ideas of the Romantic era, among them the primacy of feelings, the dangers of intellect, dismay over the human capacity to corrupt our natural goodness, the agony of the questing, solitary hero, and the awesome power of the sublime. Its Gothic fascination with the dual nature of humans and with the figurative power of dreams anticipates the end of the nineteenth century and the discovery of the unconscious and the dream life. The story of its creation, which the author herself tells in a "Preface" to the third edition to the book (1831), is equally illuminating about its age. At nineteen, Mary Godwin was living in the summer of 1816 with the poet Percy Shelley, visiting another famous Romantic poet, Lord Byron, and his doctor at Byron's Swiss villa when cold, wet weather drove them all indoors. Byron proposed that they entertain themselves by writing, each of them, a ghost story. On an evening when Byron and Shelley had been talking about galvanism and human life, whether an electric current could be passed through tissue to animate it, Mary Shelley went to bed and in a half-dream state thought of the idea for *Frankenstein.* She awoke from the nightmarish vision of a "pale student of unhallowed arts" terrified by the "yellow, watery ... eyes" of his creation staring at him to stare herself at the moon outside rising over the Alps. The next morning she wrote the first sentence of chapter five: "It was on a dreary night of November that I beheld the accomplishment of my toils." With Percy Shelley's encouragement and in spite of a failed childbirth and the suicide of a half-sister, over the next several months she worked on the story. It was completed in 1817 and published the following year, the only successful "ghost" story of that evening, perhaps the most widely known ever written.

Shelley's was an age in which heart triumphed over head. Frankenstein's moral failure is his heedless pursuit to know all that he might about life without taking any responsibility for his acts. His "sin" is not solely in creating the monster, but in abandoning him to orphanhood at his birth. The monster's unnatural birth is the product of what the Romantic poet Wordsworth called humankind's "meddling intellect." Childlike in his innocence, the monster wants only to be loved, but he gets love from neither his "father" nor from any other in the human community.

Behind the novel's indictment of the intellect stand three important myths to which Shelley alludes. She subtitles her book "A Modern Prometheus," linking Victor Frankenstein to the heroic but ultimately tragic figure of Greek myth who contended with the gods, stole fire from them to give to humans, and was punished by Zeus by being chained on Mount Caucasus to have vultures eat his liver. Her husband Percy Shelley wrote a closet drama, *Prometheus Unbound,* and fellow Romantic poets Byron and Coleridge were also attracted to and wrote about a figure of defiant ambition. The story of Faust, like the Prometheus myth, also involves one who would trade everything to satisfy an aggressive and acquisitive intellect. Finally, Adam's fall from grace came of his eating of the fruit of the Tree of the Knowledge of Good and Evil. All are unhappy with the limits life places on them; all challenge those limits; all suffer great loss. Such is Victor Frankenstein's story, one which Walton appears about to replicate on his journey to the Pole. Walton tells Frankenstein,

> "I would sacrifice my fortune, my existence, my every hope, to the furtherance of my enterprise. One man's life or death were but a small price to pay for the acquirement of the knowledge which I sought, for the dominion I should acquire and transmit over the elemental foes of our race."

Frankenstein, to whom "life and death appeared ... ideal bounds" to be broken through, succeeds in his intellectual pursuit but at great cost. He loses friend, brother, and wife. He loses all contact and sympathy with the human community. At both the beginning and end of the novel, he is the most alienated figure, alone, in mad pursuit in a desolate spot on the earth.

The novel's structure enhances these ideas. It is a framed narrative with a story within a story within a story. At the outer layer the novel is framed by the letters which Walton writes to his sister while he is voyaging to the Pole, a Frankenstein-like figure consumed by an intellectual ambition, heedless of feeling, alienated and unbefriended. His drama is internal, his isolation all the more clear in the one-way communication the letters afford. The next layer is Frankenstein's story, told because he has the opportunity before his death to deter one

What Do I Read Next?

- *Dracula* by Bram Stoker was published in 1897 and horrified audiences with its tale of a blood-sucking vampire who appears at nightfall to pursue vulnerable women.

- Written by Mary Shelley in 1826, *The Last Man* is a work of science fiction that chronicles the extermination of the human race by plague.

- A work by Mary Shelley's father, William Godwin's *Caleb Williams* (1794) is the story of a man bound to and haunted by another man through his knowledge of a secret crime.

- *Prometheus Unbound,* by Percy Shelley, is a dramatized philosophical essay about the origin of evil and the moral responsibility of individuals to restore order in their world. It was published in 1820.

- Lois McMaster Bujold's Hugo-winning science-fiction novel *Mirror Dance* (1994) explores issues surrounding clones and an individual's responsibility to his clone.

- In *Genetic Engineering: Dreams and Nightmares* (1996), authors V. E. A. Russo, David Cove, and Enzo Russo present a discussion of the ethical issues surrounding modern scientific advances in genetics. The book is targeted toward the average lay reader.

like himself from the same tragic consequences. Finally, although the novel is titled *Frankenstein,* the monster is at its structural center, his voice the most compelling because the most felt. Perhaps not coincidentally, in the popular imagination, the word "Frankenstein" conjures in most minds not Victor but the monster, although popular treatments of the story on stage and film have half-misconstrued Shelley's purpose by focusing only on the monster as a terrible being.

That the monster begs for our pity, that he descends from his native-born goodness to become a "malignant devil," illustrates another notion familiar to Shelley generally in her age and particularly in her family. Her father, William Godwin, had written *Political Justice* (1793) and her mother, Mary Wollstonecraft, had written *A Vindication of the Rights of Woman* (1792), both works on social injustices. These leading philosophical radicals of the day believed that, as Rousseau put it, "Man is born free and is everywhere in chains," that in our civilizations we corrupt what is by nature innocent. The monster is not evil; he is transformed into evil by a human injustice, an Adam made into a Satan. "I was benevolent and good," he says; "misery made me a fiend." The DeLaceys, unjustly expelled from society, represent the possibility of our restoration to native goodness in retreat from society amid the sublime splendors of the Alps. Old Mr. DeLacey tells the Monster that "the hearts of men, when unprejudiced by any obvious self-interest, are full of brotherly love and charity." The monster sees in the DeLaceys the loving family he has never known and their simple cottage life is a model of the happily primitive which the Romantics idealized.

If *Frankenstein* is a book of its age, it also looks ahead to its century's end when interest in the human psyche uncovered the unconscious mind. The idea of the *Doppleganger,* the double who shadows us, had been around since the origins of the Gothic novel in the 1760s. By the end of the nineteenth century, works such as Stevenson's *Dr. Jekyll and Mr. Hyde* made the idea that we had more than one self common. Capable of both great good and evil, we had, it seemed, a "monster" always potentially within us and not always under our control. Freud's splitting of the psyche put the monster-like id at the core of our persons. Freudian readings of *Frankenstein* see the monster as the outward expression of Victor's id or his demoniacal passions. In other words, Victor and the monster are the same person. Hence, Victor must keep the monster secret. His hope to create a being "like myself" is fulfilled in the monster whose murders we must see as expressions of Victor's own desires. Victor calls himself "the true murderer" of Justine, who, along with his brother William, he labels "the first hapless victims to my unhallowed arts." Driven by remorse, he wanders "like an evil spirit," his own wandering a mirror image of the monster's. When we see both in the outer frame of the book, Victor pursues the monster, but it is the monster who has pursued Victor, whom he calls "my last victim." Since Victor's story is a story of creation, murder, investigation, and pursuit, *Frankenstein* is ultimately a book about our pursuit of self-discovery, about the knowledge of the monster within us.

Devices conventional in both gothic novels and novels of more modern psychological interest appear in *Frankenstein.* Victor's passions frequently induce lapses in consciousness; his nightmares beg for interpretation. The most powerful occurs at one in the morning on the evening he succeeds in animating the corpse. He dreams that he sees Elizabeth walking the streets of Ingolstadt "in the bloom of health," but when he kisses her, she appears deathlike and is transformed into the corpse of his dead mother. When he awakens from the horror of his sleep, his monstrous creation looms over him. Frankenstein flees. Victor creates a monster and the nightmare hints that the monster of his desire is to take Elizabeth's life, perhaps because, as some suggest, unconsciously he holds her responsible for his mother's death.

The implications of the perverse in the sexual relationships of the characters also seem well served by a Freudian reading. Frankenstein is the monster's "father," yet were he to agree to the monster's demand to create for him a bride, would his next offspring be a "sister"? That hint of the incestuous is echoed in Victor's marriage to Elizabeth. An orphan brought home by Mrs. Frankenstein, she seems to the young Victor his possession, and though they "called each other familiarly by the name of cousin," Victor acknowledges that the ambiguity of their relationship defied naming: "No word, no expression could body forth the kind of relation in which she stood to me—my more than sister, since till death she was to be mine only." The monster's threat—"I shall be with you on your wedding night"—puts the monster in the nuptial bed with his "father" and his father's "sister/bride." That the novel closes with the monster's killing of the "father" pleads for an Oedipal reading which Freud's arguments regarding infantile sexuality and the competition within the birth family for the love of the mother made possible.

Numerous psychological readings of the novel have focused on Mary Shelley's life. Ellen Moers proposed that in *Frankenstein* Shelley wrestled with the pain of birth. Her own mother died only days after she was born, and Mary's firstborn died the year before she began the novel. Later, she referred to the book as "my hideous progeny." More recent feminist interpretations, such as that by Gilbert and Gubar noting that the novel is about a motherless orphan, similarly point to Mary's youth and remind us that books and children and birth and death are so mixed in both Shelley's life and in the novel that one cannot be understood without the other.

Frankenstein shocked readers in 1818 for its monstrous impiety, but its fame seemed fixed at birth. Initial reviews, politically oriented, denounced the book as a bit of radical Godwinism, since the book was dedicated to William Godwin and many presumed that its anonymous author was Percy Shelley. A stage adaptation called *Presumption, or, The Fate of Frankenstein* appeared as early as 1823. Mary Shelley attended a performance. In Shelley's life two additional editions were published; numerous editions since then have appeared. Burlesques on stage began in the late 1840s and continued to the end of the century. Thomas Edison created a film version as early as 1910, followed by the most famous film version, in 1931, starring Boris Karloff. It fixed for several generations an idea of "the monster Frankenstein," which gave birth to numerous other films and parodies of the story which continue to the present. In film, in translation into many of the world's languages, in its presence in school curricula, and in an unending body of criticism, *Frankenstein* lives well beyond its young author's modest intentions to write an entertaining Gothic tale to pass some time indoors on a cold Swiss summer evening.

Source: George V. Griffith, in an essay for *Novels for Students,* Gale, 1997.

Joyce Carol Oates

In the following excerpt, noted American novelist, educator, and critic Oates explores literary influences on Shelley's Frankenstein *and comments on various stylistic and thematic aspects of the work.*

Quite apart from its enduring celebrity, and its proliferation in numberless extraliterary forms, Mary Shelley's *Frankenstein; or, The Modern Prometheus* is a remarkable work. A novel *sui generis,* if a novel at all, it is a unique blending of Gothic, fabulist, allegorical, and philosophical materials. Though certainly one of the most calculated and *willed* of fantasies, being in large part a kind of gloss upon or rejoinder to John Milton's *Paradise Lost, Frankenstein* is fueled by the kind of grotesque, faintly absurd, and wildly inventive images that spring direct from the unconscious: the eight-foot creature designed to be "beautiful," who turns out almost indescribably repulsive (yellow-skinned, shriveled of countenance, with straight black lips and near-colorless eyes); the cherished cousin-bride who *is* beautiful but, in the mind's dreaming, yields horrors ("As I imprinted the first kiss on her lips, they became livid with the hue of

death; her features appeared to change, and I thought that I held the corpse of my dead mother in my arms; a shroud enveloped her form, and I saw the grave-worms crawling in the folds"); the mad dream of the Arctic as a country of "eternal light" that will prove, of course, only a place of endless ice, the appropriate landscape for Victor Frankenstein's death and his demon's self-immolation.

Central to *Frankenstein*—as it is central to a vastly different nineteenth-century romance, *Jane Eyre*—is a stroke of lightning that appears to issue in a dazzling "stream of fire" from a beautiful old oak tree ("So soon the light vanished, the oak had disappeared, and nothing remained but a blasted stump"): the literal stimulus for Frankenstein's subsequent discovery of the cause of generation and life. And according to Mary Shelley's prefatory account of the origin of her "ghost story," the very image of Frankenstein and his demon-creature sprang from a waking dream of extraordinary vividness:

> I did not sleep, nor could I be said to think. My imagination, unbidden, possessed and guided me, gifting the successive images that arose in my mind with a vividness far beyond the usual bound of reverie. I saw—with shut eyes, but acute mental vision—I saw the pale student of unhallowed arts kneeling beside the thing he had put together. I saw the hideous phantasm of a man stretched out, and then, on the working of some powerful engine, show signs of life, and stir with an uneasy, half-vital motion.... The student sleeps: but he is awakened; he opens his eyes: behold the horrid thing stands at his bedside, opening his curtains, and looking on him with yellow, watery, but speculative eyes.

Hallucinatory and surrealist on its deepest level, *Frankenstein* is of course one of the most self-consciously literary "novels" ever written: its awkward form is the epistolary Gothic; its lyric descriptions of natural scenes (the grandiose Valley of Chamounix in particular) spring from Romantic sources; its speeches and monologues echo both Shakespeare and Milton; and, should the author's didactic intention not be clear enough, the demon-creature educates himself by studying three books of symbolic significance–Goethe's *Sorrows of Young Werther,* Plutarch's *Lives,* and Milton's *Paradise Lost.* (The last conveniently supplies him with a sense of his own predicament, as Mary Shelley hopes to dramatize it. He reads Milton's great epic as if it were a "true history" giving the picture of an omnipotent God warring with His creatures; he identifies himself with Adam, except so far as Adam had come forth from God a "perfect creature, happy and prosperous." Finally, of course, he identifies with Satan: "I am thy creature: I ought to be thy Adam; but I am rather the fallen angel, whom thou drivest from joy for no misdeed. Everywhere I see bliss, from which I alone am irrevocably excluded. I was benevolent and good; misery made me a fiend. Make me happy, and I shall again be virtuous.")

The search of medieval alchemists for the legendary philosophers' stone (the talismanic process by which base metals might be transformed into gold or, in psychological terms, the means by which the individual might realize his destiny), Faust's reckless defiance of human limitations and his willingness to barter his soul for knowledge, the fatal search of such tragic figures as Oedipus and Hamlet for answers to the mysteries of their lives—these are the archetypal dramas to which *Frankenstein* bears an obvious kinship. Yet, as one reads, as Frankenstein and his despised shadow-self engage in one after another of the novel's many dialogues, it begins to seem as if the nineteen-year-old author is discovering these archetypal elements for the first time. Frankenstein "is" a demonic parody (or extension) of Milton's God; he "is" *Prometheus plasticator,* the creator of mankind; but at the same time, by his own account, he is totally unable to control the behavior of his demon (variously called "monster," "fiend," "wretch," but necessarily lacking a name). Surprisingly, it is not by way of the priggish and "self-devoted" young scientist that Mary Shelley discovers the great power of her narrative but by way of the misshapen demon, with whom most readers identify: "My person was hideous, and my stature gigantic: What did this mean? Who was I? What was I? Whence did I come? What was my destination?" It is not simply the case that the demon—like Satan and Adam in *Paradise Lost*—has the most compelling speeches in the novel and is far wiser and magnanimous than his creator: he is also the means by which a transcendent love—a romantically *unrequited love*—is expressed. Surely one of the secrets of *Frankenstein,* which helps to account for its abiding appeal, is the demon's patient, unquestioning, utterly faithful, and utterly *human* love for his irresponsible creator.

When Frankenstein is tracking the demon into the Arctic regions, for instance, it is clearly the demon who is helping him in his search, and even leaving food for him; but Frankenstein is so blind—in fact so comically blind—he believes that "spirits" are responsible. "Yet still a spirit of good followed and directed my steps, and, when I most murmured, would suddenly extricate me from seemingly insurmountable difficulties. Sometimes, when nature, overcome by hunger, sunk under the exhaustion, a repast was prepared for me in the desert, that restored and inspirited me.... I may not doubt that it was set there by the spirits that I had invoked to aid me."

By degrees, with the progression of the fable's unlikely plot, the inhuman creation becomes increasingly human while his creator becomes increasingly inhuman, frozen in a posture of rigorous denial. (*He* is blameless of any wrongdoing in terms of the demon and even dares to tell Walton, literally with his dying breath, that another scientist might succeed where he had failed!—the lesson of the "Frankenstein monster" is revealed as totally lost on Frankenstein himself.) The demon is (sub)human consciousness-in-the-making, naturally benevolent as Milton's Satan is not, and received with horror and contempt solely because of his physical appearance. He is sired without a mother in defiance of nature, but he is in one sense an infant—a comically monstrous eight-foot baby—whose progenitor rejects him immediately after creating him, in one of the most curious (and dreamlike) scenes in the novel:

> "How can I describe my emotions at this catastrophe, or how delineate the wretch whom, with such infinite pains and care, I had endeavored to form? ... I had worked hard for nearly two years, for the sole purpose of infusing life into an inanimate body. For this I had deprived myself of rest and health. I had desired it with an ardor that far exceeded moderation; but now that I had finished, the beauty of the dream vanished, and breathless horror and disgust filled my heart. Unable to endure the aspect of the being I had created, I rushed out of the room, and continued a long time traversing my bed-chamber, unable to compose my mind to sleep."

Here follows the nightmare vision of Frankenstein's bride-to-be, Elizabeth, as a form of his dead mother, with "grave-worms crawling" in her shroud; and shortly afterward the "wretch" himself appears at Frankenstein's bed, drawing away the canopy as Mary Shelley had imagined. But Frankenstein is so cowardly he runs away again; and this time the demon is indeed abandoned, to reappear only after the first of the "murders" of Frankenstein's kin. On the surface, Frankenstein's behavior is preposterous, even idiotic, for he seems blind to the fact that is apparent to any reader—that he has loosed a fearful power into the world, whether it strikes his eye as aesthetically pleasing or not, and he *must* take responsibility for it. Except, of course, he does not. For, as he keeps telling himself, he is blameless of any wrongdoing apart from the act of creation itself.

The emotions he catalogs for us–gloom, sorrow, misery, despair–are conventionally Romantic attitudes, mere luxuries in a context that requires *action* and not simply *response.*

By contrast the demon is all activity, all yearning, all hope. His love for his maker is unrequited and seems incapable of making any impression upon Frankenstein; yet the demon never gives it up, even when he sounds most threatening: "Beware," says the demon midway in the novel, "for I am fearless, and therefore powerful. I will watch with the wiliness of a snake, that I may sting with its venom. Man, you shall repent of the injuries you inflict." His voice is very like his creator's—indeed, everyone in *Frankenstein* sounds alike—but his posture is always one of simple need: he requires love in order to become less monstrous, but, as he *is* a monster, love is denied him; and the man responsible for this comically tragic state of affairs says repeatedly that he is not to blame. Frankenstein's typical response to the situation is: "I felt as if I had committed some great crime, the consciousness of which haunted me. I was guiltless, but I had indeed drawn a horrible curse upon my head, as mortal as that of crime." But if Frankenstein is not to blame for the various deaths that occur, who is? Had he endowed his creation, as God endowed Adam in Milton's epic, with free will? Or is the demon psychologically his creature, committing the forbidden acts Frankenstein wants committed?—so long as Frankenstein himself remains "guiltless."

It is a measure of the subtlety of this moral parable that the demon strikes so many archetypal chords and suggests so many variant readings. He recapitulates in truncated form the history of consciousness of his race (learning to speak, react, write, etc., by closely watching the De Lacey family); he is an abandoned child, a parentless orphan; he takes on the voices of Adam, Satan ("Evil thenceforth became my good," he says, as Milton's fallen angel says, "Evil be thou my good"), even our "first mother," Eve. When the demon terrifies himself by seeing his reflection in a pool, and grasping at once the nature of his own deformity, he is surely not mirroring Narcissus, as some commentators have suggested, but Milton's Eve in her surprised discovery of her own beauty, in book 4 of *Paradise Lost:*

> I thither went
> With unexperienc't thought, and laid me down
> On the green bank, to look into the clear
> Smooth Lake, that to me seem'd another Sky.
> As I bent down to look, just opposite,

> A Shape within the wat'ry gleam appear'd
> Bending to look on me, I started back,
> It started back, but pleas'd I soon return'd,
> Pleas'd it return'd as soon with answering looks
> Of sympathy and love; there I had fixt
> Mine eyes till now, and pin'd with vain desire
>
> [ll. 455–66]

He is Shakespeare's Edmund, though unloved–a shadow figure more tragic, because more "conscious," than the hero he represents. Most suggestively, he has become by the novel's melodramatic conclusion a form of Christ: sinned against by all humankind, yet fundamentally blameless, and yet quite willing to die as a sacrifice. He speaks of his death as a "consummation"; he is going to burn himself on a funeral pyre somewhere in the Arctic wastes—unlikely, certainly, but a fitting end to a life conceived by way of lightning and electricity:

> "But soon," he cried with sad and solemn enthusiasm, "I shall die, and what I now feel be no longer felt. Soon these burning miseries will be extinct. I shall ascend my funeral pile triumphantly, and exult in the agony of the torturing flames. The light of that conflagration will fade away; my ashes will be swept into the sea by the winds. My spirit will sleep in peace; or, if it thinks, it will not surely think thus."

But the demon does not die within the confines of the novel, so perhaps he has not died after all. He is, in the end, a "modern" species of shadow or *Doppelgänger*—*the nightmare that is deliberately created by man's ingenuity* and not a mere supernatural being or fairy-tale remnant.

Source: Joyce Carol Oates, "Frankenstein's Fallen Angel," in *Critical Inquiry,* Vol. 10, No. 3, March, 1984, pp. 543–54.

Milton Millhauser

In the following essay, Millhauser considers Frankenstein's monster in relation to the tradition of the "noble savage" in literature.

The estimate of Mary Shelley's *Frankenstein* familiar to us from literary handbooks and popular impression emphasizes its macabre and pseudo-scientific sensationalism: properly enough, so far as either its primary conception or realized qualities are concerned. But it has the effect of obscuring from notice certain secondary aspects of the work which did, after all, figure in its history and weigh with its contemporary audience, and which must, therefore, be taken into consideration before either the book or the young mind that composed it has been properly assayed. One such minor strain, not too well recognised in criticism, is a thin vein of social speculation: a stereotyped, irrelevant, and apparently automatic repetition of the lessons of that school of liberal thought which was then termed "philosophical."

In the work of Godwin's daughter and Shelley's bride, some reflection of contemporary social radicalism—crude, second-hand, very earnest, already a little out of date—occurs almost as a matter of course; what deserves comment is just that this element entered the author's notion of her plot so late and remained so decidedly an alien in it; for it governs the story only temporarily and, so to speak, extraneously, and confuses as much as it promotes the development of the character of the central figure, the monster itself. Where one might have expected, from Mary's character, that it would prove a main *motif* of the narrative, it is actually both detrimental thereto and ill-assimilated, and must be discarded altogether before the story can advance to its principal effect.

For, throughout a considerable part of the book—roughly speaking, the first half of the middle section, beginning with chapter xi—the monster is so far from being the moral horror he presently becomes that it is hardly credible he should ever be guilty of wanton brutality at all. (The transformation, by the way, is effected most abruptly, without even the degree of psychological consistency appropriate to fantasy; two violent rebuffs and an astonishingly rigid logicality of temperament turn the monster from his lonely and contemplative benevolence to a course of harsh, melodramatic vengefulness.) Rather, in the solitary student of Volney, musing on the pageant of human history, or on the contrast between man's accomplishments and his failures—"Was man, indeed, at once so powerful, so virtuous and magnificent, yet so vicious and base?"—it is not hard to recognise that gentle lay-figure of late eighteenth century social criticism, the "natural man," bringing his innocence into forceful and oversimplified contrast with the complexities and contradictions of our civilisation. Or, more precisely, may we not see in him (because of his strange origin and untutored state) something approximating to that variation of the general "child of nature" pattern to which Professor Fairchild has attached the name of Noble Savage? Like the savage, the monster approaches our society as an outsider, tests it by natural impulse and unsophisticated reason, and responds to it with a mixture of bewilderment and dismay.

Now, this aspect of the monster's character is basically unnecessary to the horror-plot; he need not pass by this road to ferocity and misery. (There might, for instance, as easily have been an original moral flaw in his constitution, paralleling the physical one; he might, as in the vulgar imagination, have been *created* bestial.) Indeed, the more this phase of his development is dwelt upon, the less consistent with the later stages does it appear. Nor is his experience as a Noble Savage too closely integrated into the story; it is connected rather arbitrarily to his education in language, but the social reflections, as well as the narrative which is their more immediate occasion, are pure interpolation, and lead to nothing. This is a real flaw in the story, felt by the reader as expectation disappointed; the author fails to *make use* of all her speculative preparation. When, for instance, the monster is hurt—brutally attacked—by those he trusted, it is because of their human ignorance and natural terror, not society's injustice; so that his radical observations are irrelevant to his own fate. Before long, indeed, the author is able to forget that the monster was ever a "natural man" (and consequently gentle and just by inclination) at all, without apparent loss to the dramatic values of the story. Everything points to the whole idea's having been an afterthought, arising, perhaps, before the full detail of the book had been worked out, but well after the general mood and drift and structure of the plot had been decided. The chance for it was offered by the story, and Mary Shelley could not decline it, but it was not an essential part of her idea, and could only be fitted in as a disproportioned and almost pointless interpolation.

The temptation seems to have been offered by the problem of the monster's intellectual development. The effort to make her creature psychologically credible must have troubled Mrs. Shelley most in his early days. What the difficulty was appears as one writes of it; how is one to speak of the "youth," the "childhood," of a being that appeared upon the earth full-grown, and yet how else is one to speak of his period of elementary ignorance and basic learning? The author cannot allow him the normal protracted human infancy and gradual education, for the plot demands that he escape from his creator and fend for himself at once; yet both plot and probability demand that he escape unformed, that he be confused and ignorant in the world into which he has blundered. As a result, the author bestows upon him a curious apprenticeship (to call it that), an amalgam of two quite different rates of development: for he is at the same time both child and man, and learns alternately like each. Thus he can walk and clothe himself from the moment of his creation, yet, infant-like, has trouble for a long while in separating the effects of the various senses; he learns the use of fire (by strict inductive reasoning!) in a few minutes, yet it is years before he can teach himself to speak or read. For the most part, however, his story is that of an adult in the state of nature, with faculties full-grown but almost literally without experience, and therefore making the acquaintance of the most primitive social facts by toilsome and unguided individual endeavour. If one distinguishes the difficulties (possible to an adult) of ignorance from those (peculiar to a child) of incapacity, there is really only a single effort to make him behave like one new-born—the confusion of the senses; thereafter he is a full-grown and decidedly intelligent but extraordinarily inexperienced man.

Now this comes close to being a description of the Noble Savage: an adult, but an alien to our world. If at this point (that is, chapters xi through xv) he differs markedly from the average of the type, it is only in being not an average but an extreme; the actual savage has his own commendable if elementary civilisation that he can compare with ours, but Frankenstein's monster has only the impulses of his nature—which are, to start with, absolutely good. But this mixture of innocence with ignorance was the very point to be exhibited by the Noble Savage or the "natural man"—"man as he is not"—both forms familiar to tediousness in the literature upon which early nineteenth century ingenuous radicalism fed its mind. So that, having brought her monster, untutored and uncorrupted, into the wilderness, there to spy upon and so study civilised ways (all of which was demanded anyhow by the plot), Mrs. Shelley would have found it hard not to fall into what must have been a very familiar habit of thought. She must surely have recognised that she was straying from the plotted path, whether she identified the new influence or not; but she was trying to write a full-length novel on the basis of a rather slim idea, and in those days interpolation was not yet a sin. So, not deliberately and yet not unwillingly, she permitted the assimilation of her story and her creature into the well-worn patterns they had skirted; none the less gratefully, perhaps, because they gave the young rebel an opportunity to utter a little of what was seething in her environment—the Shelley atmosphere, crossed by Byron's sulphureous trail—and in her own eager mind.

But if the temptation was strong enough to attract her into a rather long and somewhat incongruous philosophical digression, it was still subsidiary to her initial impulse. If Godwin's daughter could not help philosophising, Shelley's wife knew

also the eerie charms of the morbid, the occult, the scientifically bizarre. Her first purpose, which was melodrama, stood. Therefore the alien figure appears in the novel only momentarily—so long as, with a little effort, the plot accommodates itself to him; when he really threatens to interfere with it, he is abandoned. But if he never dominates the story, he does figure in it, and should be reckoned with. However relentlessly the first lurid vision is finally pursued to its end, the familiar lineaments of the Noble Savage, the child of nature, did come for a little while to be visible in Frankenstein's impious creation; however sharply his hideous features and terrible career may have distinguished him from the brooding islander or haughty Indian sachem, the central theme, the uncongeniality of our actual world with a certain ideal and touchingly beautiful simplicity, served to associate his history, in some degree, with theirs, and so attract him temporarily into their form.

Source: Milton Millhauser, "The Noble Savage in Mary Shelley's *Frankenstein*," in *Notes and Queries,* Vol. 190, No. 12, June 15, 1946, pp. 248–50.

Sources

Steven Earl Forry, *Hideous Progenies: Dramatizations of 'Frankenstein' from the Nineteenth Century to the Present,* University of Pennsylvania Press, 1990.

Mary Shelley, *Frankenstein,* introduction by Diane Johnson, Bantam Books, 1991.

Montague Summers, *The Gothic Quest,* Russell & Russell, 1964.

Eleanor Ty, "Mary Wollstonecraft Shelley," in *Concise Dictionary of British Literary Biography,* Volume 3: *Writers of the Romantic Period, 1789-1832,* Gale, 1991, pp. 338–52.

For Further Study

Chris Baldick, *In Frankenstein's Shadow: Myth, Monstrosity, and Nineteenth-Century Writing,* Oxford University Press, 1987.
Treats *Frankenstein* as a modern myth and examines the effects of the book on later nineteenth-and twentieth-century writers.

Sandra Gilbert and Susan Gubar, *The Madwoman in the Attic: The Woman Writer and the Nineteenth-Century Literary Imagination,* Yale University Press, 1979.
A feminist and psycho-biographical reading which emphasizes the place of books in the novel.

M. A. Goldberg, "Moral and Myth in Mrs. Shelley's *Frankenstein,* in *Keats-Shelley Journal,* Vol. 8, 1959, pp. 27–38.

Provides the most conventional reading of Frankenstein's tale as a moral lesson to Walton.

George Levine, "*Frankenstein* and the Tradition of Realism," in *Novel,* Vol. 7, Fall, 1973, pp. 14-30.
Discusses the place of *Frankenstein* in the tradition of realism in the novel.

George Levine and U. C. Knoepflmacher, *The Endurance of 'Frankenstein,'* University of California Press, 1979.
A wide-ranging collection of essays about the novel.

Anne K. Mellor, *Mary Shelley: Her Life, Her Fiction, Her Monsters,* Methuen, Inc., 1988.
As one of the most well-known Shelley critics, Mellor draws from unpublished archival material, studying the relationships between Mary and the central personalities in her life. Her biography contains a powerful warning to parents who do not care for their children and to scientists who refuse to take responsibility for their discoveries.

Masao Miyoshi, *The Divided Self: A Perspective on the Literature of the Victorians,* New York University Press, 1969, pp. 79-89.
Discusses the *Doppelganger,* or double, in *Frankenstein.*

Ellen Moers, *Literary Women,* Doubleday, 1976, pp. 91-99.
Examines the pain of maternity in *Frankenstein,* relating the birth of the monster to Shelley's birth and her experiences as a mother.

Christopher Small, *Mary Shelley's 'Frankenstein,'* University of Pittsburgh Press, 1973.
A wide-ranging examination of Shelley, her father and husband, the novel, and her era.

Emily W. Sunstein, *Mary Shelley: Romance and Reality* Little, Brown, and Co., 1989.
A comprehensive biography which assigns Shelley her proper place among English Romantic writers. She dispels many of the myths and ill-founded prejudices against Shelley.

Martin Tropp, *Mary Shelley's Monster,* Houghton Mifflin, 1976.
A more popular treatment of the novel which emphasizes the "Mad Scientist" theme and treats film adaptations. Includes a filmography.

William Veeder, *Mary Shelley and Frankenstein: The Fate of Androgyny,* University of Chicago Press, 1986.
Includes in an appendix Percy Shelley's unpublished review of the novel.

The Joy Luck Club

Amy Tan
1989

The Joy Luck Club, published by G. P. Putnam's Sons in 1989, presents the stories of four Chinese-immigrant women and their American-born daughters. Each of the four Chinese women has her own view of the world based on her experiences in China and wants to share that vision with her daughter. The daughters try to understand and appreciate their mothers' pasts, adapt to the American way of life, and win their mothers' acceptance. The book's name comes from the club formed in China by one of the mothers, Suyuan Woo, in order to lift her friends' spirits and distract them from their problems during the Japanese invasion. Suyuan continued the club when she came to the United States—hoping to bring luck to her family and friends and finding joy in that hope.

Amy Tan wrote the *Joy Luck Club* to try to understand her own relationship with her mother. Tan's Chinese parents wanted Americanized children but expected them to think like Chinese. Tan found this particularly difficult as an adolescent. While the generational differences were like those experienced by other mothers and daughters, the cultural distinctions added another dimension. Thus, Tan wrote not only to sort out her cultural heritage but to learn how she and her mother could get along better.

Critics appreciate Tan's straightforward manner as well as the skill with which she talks about Chinese culture and mother/daughter relationships. Readers also love *The Joy Luck Club:* women of all ages identify with Tan's characters and their

conflicts with their families, while men have an opportunity through this novel to better understand their own behaviors towards women. Any reader can appreciate Tan's humor, fairness, and objectivity.

Author Biography

Amy Tan began writing fiction as a distraction from her work as a technical writer. A self-proclaimed workaholic, Tan wanted to find a way to relax. She soon discovered that not only did she enjoy writing fiction as a hobby, she liked that it provided a way for her to think about and understand her life.

Tan was born in Oakland, California, in 1952. Her first-generation, Chinese-American parents, John and Daisy Tan, settled in Santa Clara, California. As an adolescent, Tan had difficulty accepting her Chinese heritage. She wanted to look like an American—to be an American. At one point, she even slept with a clothespin on her nose, hoping to change its shape. She deliberately chose American over Chinese whenever she had the opportunity and asserted her independence in any way that she could. She dreamed of being a writer, while her parents saw her as a neurosurgeon and concert pianist.

The Tans lived in Santa Clara until first her father, then her brother, died of brain tumors. Mrs. Tan took Amy and her other brother to live in Switzerland. Amy became even more rebellious, dating a German who was associated with drug dealers and had serious mental problems. Her mother then took the children back to the United States, where Amy enrolled in a Baptist College in Oregon, majoring in pre-med. After just two semesters there, Amy went with her boyfriend back to California. There she attended San Jose City College as an English and linguistics major. Amy's mother did not speak to her for six months after this final act of rebellion.

The Joy Luck Club contains many autobiographical elements from Tan's life. Tan did not learn until she was fourteen that she has half-sisters from her mother's previous marriage. This sense of loss and her father's and brother's deaths are reflected in *The Joy Luck Club* in Suyuan Woo's loss of her twin daughters and her death. In addition, Tan has always felt that she disappointed her mother by not becoming a doctor. Like Tan, the novel's Jing-mei can not compare to Waverly Jong, the highly successful daughter of a friend of

Amy Tan

Jing-mei's mother. These and other examples from Tan's personal life lend a sensibility and sensitivity to her novel that allow the reader to experience vicariously death and solace, loss and reconciliation, disillusionment and hope.

Plot Summary

The Joy Luck Club consists of sixteen interlocking stories about the lives of four Chinese immigrant women and their four American-born daughters. In 1949, the four immigrants meet at the First Chinese Baptist Church in San Francisco and agree to continue to meet to play mah jong. They call their mah jong group the Joy Luck Club. The stories told in this novel revolve around the Joy Luck Club women and their daughters.

Feathers from a Thousand Li Away

In "The Joy Luck Club," Jing-Mei Woo remembers her recently deceased mother, Suyuan Woo, who founded the Joy Luck Club. During World War II, Suyuan Woo escapes from Kweilin on foot before the Japanese invade the city. The difficulty of the escape forces Suyuan to abandon her two twin baby girls. At the first mah jong meeting after Suyuan Woo's funeral, the Joy Luck Club "aunts" inform Jing-Mei that the twin girls are alive in China and suggest that she visit her half-sisters to bring them the news of the death of Suyuan.

The childhood of An-Mei Hsu, one of the older women, is related in "Scar." In the story, An-Mei Hsu's mother leaves her family to become a concubine of Wu Tsing, a rich merchant. An-Mei is brought up by her grandmother, Popo. In an attempt to heal Popo on her deathbed, An-Mei's mother returns to cut off a piece of flesh from her own arm to make soup for Popo, but Popo still dies.

Lindo Jong, another of the mothers, explains her own childhood in "The Red Candle," recounting her escape from an unfortunate marriage. Promised in marriage at two and delivered at twelve, Lindo Jong finds herself living with a husband who doesn't love her and a mother-in-law whose only interest is for Lindo to produce grandchildren. Finally, Lindo fabricates a dream vision which predicts the destruction of the family if the family does not annul her marriage. In the end, the family gives her enough money to fly to the United States.

In "The Moon Lady," Ying-Ying St. Clair, the third surviving mother, remembers falling into the Tai Lake, one of the largest lakes in China, during a Moon Festival boating event. The four-year-old Ying-Ying is rescued from the water by strangers and left on the shore. She wanders into an outdoor opera which stages the story of the wish-granting Moon Lady. After the opera, Ying-Ying approaches the Moon Lady to make a wish to be found by her family, only to discover that the Moon Lady is played by a man.

The Twenty-Six Malignant Gates

This section relates important childhood stories of the Joy Luck Club's American-born daughters. In "Rules of the Game," Waverly Jong recalls being a national chess champion. When she is nine, Waverly's relationship with her mother becomes tense after she tells her mother not to brag about her in the marketplace. Another difficult relationship is portrayed by Lena St. Clair in "The Voice from the Wall," as Lena remembers her mother's nervous breakdown and the noise of fights between a neighbor girl and her Italian family. At first Lena is full of pity for the Italian girl, thinking the girl has an unhappy life. Later, Lena learns that the neighbors' fighting and shouting are ways of expressing their love. However, in Lena's home, her mother lies quietly in bed or babbles to herself on the sofa.

In "Half and Half," Rose Hsu Jordan is about to be divorced from her American husband. She re-

counts how her mother lost faith in God after a failed attempt to revive her youngest son, who drowned during a family beach outing. Despite her loss of religious faith, Rose's mother insists that Rose try to have faith in her marriage. Finally, in "Two Kinds," Jing-Mei Woo remembers her mother's high expectations for her to become a prodigy. But the question plaguing her is what kind of prodigy? Her agonizing quest to meet her mother's expectations ends up in an embarrassing piano recital failure.

American Translation

This section follows the Joy Luck children as adult women, all facing various conflicts. In "Rice Husband," Lena St. Clair narrates her marital problems. She has often feared that she is inferior to her husband, who is also her boss at work and who makes seven times more than she does. Lena's husband takes advantage of her by making her pay half of all household expenses. Waverly Jong is concerned about her mother's opinion of her white fiance in "Four Directions." Waverly recalls quitting chess after becoming angry at her mother in the marketplace. Believing that her mother still has absolute power over her and will object to her forthcoming marriage with Rich, Waverly confronts her mother after a dinner party and realizes that her mother has known all along about her relationship with Rich and has accepted him.

In "Without Wood," Rose Hsu Jordan tries to sort out her own marital problems. After her husband reveals that he will be marrying someone else, Rose finally realizes she will have to fight for her rights. In the end, she refuses to sign the conditions set forth by her husband's divorce papers. Jing-Mei Woo's problems are still related to her mother. In "Best Quality," she remembers the Chinese New Year's dinner of the previous year. During the dinner Jing-Mei has an argument with Waverly over an advertisement Jing-Mei has written for Waverly's company. Realizing that Jing-Mei has been humiliated, Suyuan Woo, Jing-Mei's mother, gives her a necklace with a special jade pendant called "life's importance." After her mother dies, Jing-Mei wishes she had found out what "life's importance" meant.

Queen Mother of the Western Skies

This section of the novel returns to the viewpoints of the mothers as adults dealing with difficult choices. In "Magpies," An-Mei Hsu recalls moving to Tientsin with her mother, the third concubine of Wu Tsing, a rich merchant. In Wu Tsing's mansion, An-Mei witnesses her mother's

From the film The Joy Luck Club, *Buena Vista, 1994.*

awkward and lowly position. Finally, An-Mei's mother, fed up with her shameful life and abuse from the merchant's powerful second wife, poisons herself two days before Chinese New Year, so her "vengeful spirit" can return to haunt the family.

In "Waiting Between the Trees," Ying-Ying St. Clair remembers being abandoned by her first husband, who was a womanizer. Later, Ying-Ying marries an American whom she does not love. Marriage also figures in "Double Face," in which Lindo Jong recalls arriving in San Francisco and later working in a fortune cookie factory. In the factory, together with An-Mei Hsu, Lindo finds a fortune cookie slip which she uses to put the idea of marriage into her boyfriend's head.

The final story is a pivotal episode which brings together the experiences of mothers and daughters. In "A Pair of Tickets," Jing-Mei Woo flies to China with her father to visit the twin babies that her mother had been forced to abandon while fleeing the Japanese. Finally, after years of refusing to embrace her heritage, Jing-Mei accepts the Chinese blood in her when she meets her half sisters:

> I look at their faces again and I see no trace of my mother in them. Yet they still look familiar. And now I also see what part of me is Chinese. It is so obvious. It is my family. It is in our blood. After all these years, it can finally be let go.

Characters

An-Mei Hsu

An-Mei empowers her daughter, Rose, to stand up for her rights. Having grown up fearful of the people around her and being accustomed to self-denial, An-Mei refuses to see her own daughter endure the same unhappiness. She turns her back on her own pain and experiences, and vows to raise her daughter differently than she was raised.

An-Mei's grandparents cared for her after banning her mother for becoming another man's concubine following the death of her husband. The grandparents warned An-Mei never to speak of her mother. To them, An-Mei's mother was a ghost—someone to be forgotten entirely. An-Mei obeyed and never asked about her. An-Mei came to know her mother, however, when she returned to be with An-Mei's grandmother as she was dying. An-Mei learned from her that honor for one's mother goes much deeper than the flesh and that when you lose something you love, faith takes over.

An-Mei teaches her daughter the lessons she has learned from her own mother and from the loss of her son, Rose's brother. Rather than ignore loss, one must pay attention to it and undo the expectation. When Rose complains to An-Mei that her marriage is falling apart and she can't do anything about it, An-Mei reminds Rose of her upbringing and tells her to speak up for her rights. Rose passes An-Mei's test by advising her husband that she will not sign the divorce papers and that her lawyer will contact him about her keeping the house.

Lindo Jong

Lindo Jong tries to instill in her daughter, Waverly, a sense of both obedience and self-worth. She wants her daughter to have "American circumstances and Chinese character."

Lindo's parents promise her to her future husband, Tyan-Hu, when she is only two years old. While she sees him at various functions over the years, she does not actually go to live with him and his family until she is twelve. Always the obedient daughter, she does not question this arrangement. She recognizes immediately, however, the kind of husband Tyan-Hu will be and feels discouraged.

Lindo and Tyan-Hu marry when she turns sixteen. While they are unhappy with each other, they do not let his family know. In the meantime, Lindo devises a plan that will allow Tyan-Hu's family to release her without their losing face. Lindo pretends that she has a dream in which Tyan-Hu's ancestors tell her that their marriage is doomed; she uses existing facts to back up her story.

When she is free of the marriage, Lindo leaves for America, where she remarries and has three children. She decides that her children should live like Americans and should not have to keep the circumstances someone else gives them. While she believes that she has succeeded in teaching this idea to her daughter, Lindo thinks she has failed to teach her Chinese character. She is surprised and satisfied, however, when Waverly demonstrates Chinese character that Lindo did not know she possessed.

Waverly Jong

Waverly Jong is the figure to whom Jing-Mei is always compared by her mother, Suyuan Woo. Waverly's mother, Lindo, and Suyuan were best friends when the girls were growing up but also tried to outdo each other when comparing their children's accomplishments. Waverly continually gave her mother something to brag about. As a child, she was a national chess champion; as an adult, she is a successful tax attorney.

When Waverly was very young, her brother received a chess set as a Christmas gift. She quickly caught on to the game and was soon winning

Media Adaptations

- An abridged sound recording of *The Joy Luck Club* is three hours long, available on 2 cassette tapes. Published in 1989 by Dove Audio, the book is read by its author, Amy Tan.

- The movie version of *The Joy Luck Club* was released by Hollywood Pictures in 1993. While it does not include all the novel's stories, the film does a good job of presenting the most important scenes. The adaptation was written by Amy Tan and Ronald Bass and directed by Wayne Wang. Produced by noted filmmaker Oliver Stone, the film starred such actresses as Frances Nuyen, Rosalind Chao, Ming-Na Wen, and Lauren Tom. It is rated R, available from Buena Vista Home Video.

matches against everyone she played. Her mother taught her how to "bite back her tongue," a strategy for winning arguments that also helped her win chess games. By the time she was nine, Waverly was a national chess champion. Her mother was so proud of her that she constantly boasted of her daughter's abilities, wanting people to know that she was Waverly's mother. Waverly hated her mother's bragging, and it soon became a point of contention between them.

Not only did Waverly despise her mother's bragging, she also hated that her mother tried to take credit for Waverly's talent. Lindo would tell people that she advised Waverly on the moves she made and that Waverly wasn't really smart, she just knew the tricks of the game. Finally, Waverly told her off—in public—saying that she knew nothing, that she should shut up. After that, it was a long time before Lindo spoke to Waverly, and she no longer encouraged her to play chess. When she and her mother did start talking, Waverly found that she could no longer play chess.

Remembering her mother's reaction to her public embarrassment, Waverly was afraid to let her meet her Caucasian fiance, Rich. She did not want Rich to have to suffer the criticism she knew her mother was capable of giving without thought to his feelings. She knew the silent attacks her mother would make on Rich's character; she knew that her mother could put on a front while hiding her true emotions. She knew too well how her mother could hurt her by stabbing her in her weakest parts.

Waverly finally allows her mother to meet Rich and is not surprised by her reactions. What does surprise Waverly is that when she confronts her mother about the meeting, she learns something about herself. Not only has Waverly learned the art of invisible strength from her mother, but also she has inherited her "double-faced" approach to meeting new challenges, probably the secret to her success as an adult.

Rose Hsu Jordan

Rose Hsu Jordan, the daughter of An-Mei Hsu, marries Ted Jordan in defiance of their parents. Typically passive by nature, Rose takes charge by choosing to marry Ted, a non-Chinese. It is probably the most decisive action she has ever taken.

Ted balances her personality. Where she is weak, he bears the burden; where she is indecisive, he takes charge. Ted makes all the decisions in their married life until a professional mistake changes him. He then expects Rose to help him make the choices in their life together. When she can't change, he wants a divorce.

Rose begins to think about her mother's beliefs. Her mother had always had a firm belief in God until a family tragedy made her question God's wisdom. Her mother continues to believe, though, that a voice from above guides all people and that Rose needs to listen to that voice. When Rose had nightmares as a child, with an angry Mr. Chou telling her bad things, Rose's mother told her not to listen to him, to listen only to that voice above. She told Rose that listening to too many voices would cause her to bend when she should stand strong.

Rose remembers her mother's past advice and continues to listen to her now. Her mother tells her that she must speak up for her own rights when Ted asks for the divorce. Rose finally makes a decision on her own. When she does, she dreams of her mother and Mr. Chou smiling at her.

Lena St. Clair

Lena St. Clair grew up worrying about the mental health of her mother, Ying-Ying, who constantly battles paranoia and depression. While her father is English-Irish, Lena is more Chinese, having inherited many of her mother's Chinese traits—particularly her ability to see "with Chinese eyes." Lena could "see" the things her mother feared, but she kept them from her father by changing her mother's meanings in their translation to English.

Lena continually hoped that her mother would someday be well and that she and her mother could have the close relationship she saw in her dreams. Lena felt invisible and alone.

As an adult, Lena believes that her mother has always been able to see the terrible things that were going to happen to their family. Lena remembers that when she was eight, her mother had told her that she would marry a bad man. Now, she sees that her husband, Harold, might be the bad man her mother had envisioned.

While Lena and Harold had started out as equals in their relationship, Lena has discovered that their life together has become unbalanced. Harold has taken her business ideas and her money, yet has given little in return. He keeps a detailed accounting sheet and claims that they share everything equally. Lena, however, detects an unfairness. Where is Harold's love? Why must their relationship be reduced to columns on a ledger? Feeling invisible again, Lena yearns for something that she cannot put into words.

Ying-Ying St. Clair

Ying-Ying, mother of Lena, experiences periods of depression and paranoia. She considers herself "lost" and attributes the cause of her mental illness to a ceremony she remembers attending as a four-year-old.

The Moon Festival ceremony gives people the opportunity to see the Moon Lady and secretly ask for a wish to be granted. Four-year-old Ying-Ying is being allowed to attend the event for the first time. She is warned, however, to behave and not to speak of her wish or it will be considered a selfish desire and will not be granted.

In the excitement of the celebration, Ying-Ying falls off the boat unnoticed and is lost. She encounters a dramatic production of the Moon Lady's arrival and believes the Moon Lady can grant her wish. When she hears the Moon Lady's sad story, she loses hope. Her despair deepens when she asks the Moon Lady that she be found, then sees that the Moon Lady is really only a man in disguise. Ying-Ying's parents find her, but she feels such a sense of loss, she never believes that she is really their daughter. This sense of loss, loneliness, and despair stay with her for the rest of her life.

Ying-Ying marries a man whom she loves very much but who turns out to be abusive. In her pain, she aborts the son she is carrying. Ying-Ying later remarries but is never able to recover from the losses she has endured. She feels she has lost her chi, or spirit.

Only when Ying-Ying sees the pain in Lena's marriage does she decide to face her past and try to recover her chi. She symbolically breaks a table in her daughter's house to summon her spirit so that she can give it to her daughter.

Jing-Mei Woo

Jing-Mei, daughter of Suyuan Woo, takes her mother's place in the Joy Luck Club when her mother dies. Jing-Mei searches for her own identity, lacks confidence, and wonders how she will fill her mother's shoes.

From the time she was a child, Jing-Mei has always lived in someone else's shadow. Her mother continually compared her to other people's children, particularly Lindo Jong's daughter, Waverly. Suyuan felt that Jing-Mei could do anything that she wanted to. She gave Jing-Mei intelligence tests and piano lessons, but Jing-Mei never measured up to her mother's expectations. Jing-Mei always felt that she was disappointing her mother.

As she got older, Jing-Mei still failed to succeed at the things her mother wanted her to do. She was less than a straight-A student. She was accepted at only an average college, from which she dropped out. Jing-Mei eventually became a freelance writer, even though her mother wanted her to earn a doctorate. Jing-Mei suffers one final insult when Waverly informs her that the freelance work Jing-Mei submitted to Waverly's tax firm was not accepted.

Jing-Mei had always felt uncomfortable with her mother's Chinese ways. When Suyuan attended the Joy Luck Club in her Chinese dresses, Jing-Mei was embarrassed. She viewed the Joy Luck Club itself as a "shameful Chinese custom." Jing-Mei's view changes, however, when she joins the Joy Luck Club. The realization that these Chinese women are depending on their daughters to keep their customs alive motivates her to reawaken her sleeping Chinese heritage. At last she has a purpose. She finds a new self-respect, confidence, and peace when she returns to China to meet with her half-sisters.

June Woo

See Jing-Mei Woo

Suyuan Woo

Suyuan Woo does not tell her own story in *The Joy Luck Club.* Recently deceased when the story begins, Suyuan speaks through her daughter, Jing-Mei. Because Suyuan started the Joy Luck Club, her story provides the foundation for the novel.

Suyuan started the original Joy Luck Club in Kweilin, China, during the second Japanese invasion (the Second Sino-Japanese War) right before World War II. She and other refugees had come to Kweilin seeking safety from the Japanese troops. The crowding, constant bombing, and fear immobilized everyone. Suyuan needed something to help her keep her faith. She decided to invite a group of women to play mah jong. They met weekly to play, raise money, and eat special foods. While other people criticized their extravagance, the women forgot their troubles for a short time and enjoyed one another's company. They met to share their desire to be lucky in life. Their hope for luck was their joy. Thus, the weekly meetings became known as the Joy Luck Club.

Suyuan, however, experienced great tragedy when news of the approaching troops forced her to leave for Chungking. Having no other way to travel, she fled on foot, pushing a wheelbarrow and carrying her infant twin daughters in slings on her shoulders. Suyuan grew more weary the farther she traveled. She had to start leaving her possessions along the way. Finally, when she could go no further, she left the babies along the road, too, with a note telling their names and asking that they be cared for. When she arrived in Chungking, delirious with dysentery and grief, she found that her husband had died two weeks before.

The San Francisco version of the Joy Luck Club originated in 1949, when Suyuan and her second husband arrived from China. The couple met other Chinese couples at church functions they attended to help get acclimated to their new culture. Knowing the situations from which they had all come, Suyuan felt she and her recent acquaintances needed each others' understanding and companionship. She started the Joy Luck Club so that the new friends could have joy in their hope to be lucky in this unfamiliar land.

Suyuan's friends in the Joy Luck Club honor her by telling her daughter the complete story. They offer Jing-Mei money to travel to China to meet her half-sisters, who were located just after Suyuan's death. Suyuan's life, therefore, comes full circle.

Topics For Further Study

- In an interview with Elaine Woo for the *Los Angeles Times* (March 12, 1989), Amy Tan said that her parents wanted their children "to have American circumstances and Chinese character." Write an essay that explains what her parents may have meant. Give specific examples to illustrate the "circumstances" and "character."

- Trace the history of Chinese immigration into our country. When did the Chinese begin arriving in our country? For what reasons do the Chinese come here? Where do they choose to settle? Why do they settle there?

- *The Joy Luck Club* was published in 1989. That same year saw a major uprising by Chinese university students in Beijing's Tiananmen Square. Investigate these 1989 demonstrations. Why were these students demonstrating? How did

their country react? How did our country react? What were the effects on the Chinese who were studying in the United States at the time?

- What was the history of the "Joy Luck Club?" How did it get its name? What was its significance? Why did the Chinese-American women feel the need to have a Joy Luck Club in America?

- Compare and contrast pre-World War II China with China today. Discuss such aspects as living conditions, government, cultural aspects, education, etc.

- Investigate the psychological aspects of either generational conflict or mother/daughter relationships. Write an essay that describes your own experiences in relation to what you've learned from your research.

Themes

Choices and Consequences

The Joy Luck Club presents the stories of four Chinese immigrant women and their American-born daughters. All of their lives, the Chinese mothers in *The Joy Luck Club* have struggled to make their own decisions and establish their own identities in a culture where obedience and conformity are expected. For example, when Suyuan Woo is a refugee during the Japanese invasion, she decides that she will not be a passive victim and will choose her own happiness. She forms the Joy Luck Club to provide a distraction for herself and her friends. Thus, in a situation where there appears to be no room for disobedience, Suyuan creates an identity that she and her friends assume in order to survive. The continuation of the club in the United States helps Suyuan and her friends redefine themselves in a new culture.

The mothers want their daughters to take charge of their own lives, too. Yet the mothers find it difficult to voice their concerns and be open enough about their personal experiences to make

their advice valid with their daughters. Ying-Ying St. Clair, however, sees her daughter Lena's unhappiness in her marriage and courageously faces her own bad memories to help Lena make the decisions she needs to make to be free.

Identity

The American-born daughters have their own choices to make and their own identities to establish. While their mothers want Chinese obedience from their daughters, they do not want their daughters to be too passive. The Chinese mothers want their daughters to have American-like strength. The daughters work to find compromises their mothers can accept. Rose Hsu Jordan, for example, overcomes her passivity with the help of her grandmother's story and stands up to a husband who is trying to take everything from her.

Throughout the stories presented in *The Joy Luck Club* runs the common thread of mother-daughter connectedness and its influence on a daughter's identity formation. Tan's portrayal of the intense relationships between and among her characters shows the strength of the ties that bind culture and generation. These firmly undergird the choices the characters make and the identities they shape as a result of their decisions.

Culture Clash

The American-born daughters are ambivalent about their Chinese background. While they eat Chinese foods and celebrate Chinese traditions, they want their Chinese heritage to remain at home. They make American choices when they are in public and cringe in embarrassment when their mothers speak in their broken English. Worst of all, the American daughters do not see the importance of "joy luck"; to them, it is not even a word. They regard the Joy Luck Club as a "shameful Chinese custom."

The Chinese mothers fear the end of Chinese tradition in their families. Their American-born daughters hide their Chinese heritage and think like Americans. While the Chinese mothers want their daughters to enjoy the benefits of being Americans, they do not want them to forget their roots. They hope that their daughters will develop strong American characters yet keep positive Chinese beliefs alive. The mothers need the daughters to understand the significance of the Joy Luck Club and all that it represents.

The clash of adolescence with the American and Chinese cultures leaves the Chinese mothers without hope for their daughters' Chinese futures. Yet, time works its magic; the daughters grow up, and the mothers' dreams prevail. The Joy Luck Club survives with a daughter, Jing-Mei, continuing the tradition in place of her deceased mother, Suyuan Woo. Broken ties mend, and hope for happiness despite misfortune (what the Chinese call "joy luck") lives.

Style

Structure

In presenting the stories of four Chinese immigrant women and their American-born daughters in *The Joy Luck Club,* Tan uses "cradling," a formal literary device that can be thought of as telling a story within a story, or nesting. In other words, Tan embeds the daughters' stories within the mothers' narratives. *The Joy Luck Club* is divided into four main segments that contain sixteen stories. The first and last sections tell eight stories—two for each mother—while the middle two sections each tell a story for each of the four daughters. The entire novel revolves primarily around the stories of

Suyuan Woo and her daughter, Jing-Mei ("June"). Jing-Mei takes her mother's place in the Joy Luck Club, a club her mother created when she was in China and that she continued for her Chinese friends in America. Jing-Mei learns from her "aunties," the women who are members of the club, that they will fund her trip to China to meet with her "lost" sisters.

Setting

The Joy Luck Club is set in two places. The mothers' stories take place mostly in pre-World War II China, just before and during the Second Sino-Japanese War (1937-1945). The daughters' stories occur primarily in contemporary San Francisco, although June does visit contemporary China in the final section. These differing settings help emphasize the culture clash experienced by many of the novel's characters.

Point of View and Narration

Tan uses several first-person narrators in the novel, narrators who directly speak to the reader by using "I said"/"I did" to express events. Because three of the mothers and all of the daughters tell their own stories, the narrative shifts from a mother's point of view to a daughter's point of view. Except for Suyuan Woo, each mother speaks for herself in the first and final sections of the book; the daughters each speak for themselves in the second and third sections of the book. Since Suyuan has already died when the story opens, Jing-Mei speaks for her.

Conflict

Conflicts arise between each mother and her daughter as the result of generational and cultural differences. The mothers and daughters experience the typical difficulties in understanding each others' viewpoints. Daughters try to establish their personal identities by being like their mothers, yet different in response to contemporary pressures. These generational differences are compounded by the mothers' culture-driven views of tradition. The mothers want their daughters to be Americanized, yet they also want their daughters to honor the Chinese way of life. In Asian culture, women's identities are more often defined by their relationships to others than by their occupational success, as scholar Tracy Robinson has observed. For example, while Waverly Jong is different enough from her mother to have established herself as a successful tax attorney, she is enough like her mother that she worries that her mother will not accept her Caucasian fi-

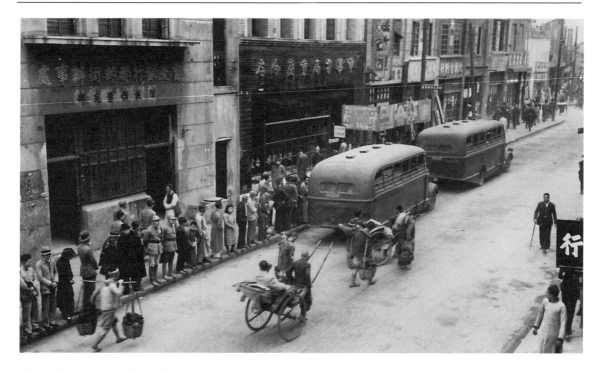

Chungking Street, China, 1944.

ance. The mothers' basic concern is that their daughters will turn their backs on their culture and their Chinese heritage will be forgotten.

Symbols

Suyuan Woo's stories tell about a woman whose allegiances were divided between her American daughter and the Chinese daughters she had lost. Suyuan's Chinese and American souls are resurrected and reunited when the daughters meet at the end of the novel. The daughters' names symbolize this rebirth and reunion. Chwun Yu (Spring Rain), Chwun Hwa (Spring Flower), and Jing-Mei (June) represent the renewing force that is connected to the seasons of spring and summer. Even Suyuan's name, meaning Long-Cherished Wish, alludes to the resolution of the conflicts she and Jing-Mei shared. Finally, the Chinese interpretation of Jing-Mei's name, "pure essence and best quality," represents Jing-Mei's learning to appreciate and coming to terms with her Chinese heritage.

Historical Context

Historical China

While *The Joy Luck Club* was published in 1989, it is set in pre-World War II China and con-

temporary San Francisco. The two settings strengthen the contrast between the cultures that Tan depicts through her characters and their relationships. Pre-World War II China was a country heavily embroiled in conflict. San Francisco, however, offered freedom and peace. In writing the novel, Tan wanted to portray not only the importance of mother/daughter relationships but also the dignity of the Chinese people.

China's history covers years of tradition, yet also decades of change. While the Chinese people consistently honor the personal qualities of dignity, respect, self-control, and obedience, they have not so continually pledged allegiance to their leaders. The first documented Chinese civilization was the Shang dynasty (c. 1523–c. 1027 BC). Various dynasties ruled over the years, ending with the Manchu dynasty in 1912. The dynasties saw peace, expansion, and technological and artistic achievement as well as warfare and chaos. Foreign intervention, particularly by Japan, created instability in the country, and internal struggles often prevented the Chinese from uniting. The area of Manchuria in northeast China, while legally belonging to China, had many Japanese investments such as railways and as such was under the control of the Japanese. This led to anti-Manchu sentiment and an eventual revolution. After civil war and addi-

Compare & Contrast

- **1930s and 1940s:** The Japanese occupied China. Full war erupted in 1945 in Beijing between the Chinese and Japanese. After the war, civil war breaks out and Communists take over the government in 1949, led by Mao Zedong.

  Today: In 1989, a pro-democracy demonstration by Chinese university students in Beijing's Tiananmen Square is put down by the Communist government. While a 1993 constitutional revision does not reform the political system, it does call for the development of a socialist market economy.

- **1930s and 1940s:** Various religions thrived in China, particularly Confucianism, Buddhism, and Taoism.

  Today: Once discouraged by Mao Zedong, religious practice has been revived to some de-

gree. In addition to the traditional religions—Confucianism, Buddhism, and Taoism—there are also smaller groups of Muslims, Catholics, and Protestants.

- **1930s and 1940s:** After a period from 1882 to 1943 that restricted Chinese immigration to the U.S., a new 1943 law extends citizenship rights and permits an annual immigration of 105 Chinese. Many refugees from the Sino-Japanese war flee to the United States.

  Today: National origin quotas were abolished in 1965, and the 1990 Immigration Act raised the immigrant quota and reorganized the preference system for entrance. Nearly 39,000 Chinese immigrants enter the U.S. in 1992, while almost 30,000 obtain visas to study at American universities.

---

tional strife, the Nationalists and Communists fought the Japanese in the second Sino-Japanese War and won when Japan was defeated by the Allies of World War II in 1945.

It is just before this victory that the mothers' stories start. Japanese aggression led to a foreign military presence on Chinese soil, and Suyuan's story in particular details the flight from the invading Japanese that was made by many Chinese. After World War II, with Japan preoccupied in recovering from their defeat, China once again became embroiled in a civil war between the Nationalists, who had been in power for several years, and the Communists, who wished to establish a new form of government. The civil war ended in 1949 with the formation of the People's Republic of China, and the Communists have held power in China since then.

Chinese Immigration to America

After the United States abolished slavery after the Civil War, freeing many of the African Americans who had worked in fields and farms, there arose a great need for manual laborers. Migrants

from China filled a large part of this need, especially in the West, where rapid expansion required people to build railroads and towns. Although greatly outnumbered by white immigrants from European nations, the number of Chinese arriving in America alarmed white settlers in the West. In 1882 Congress passed the Chinese Exclusion Act, which prohibited the immigration of Chinese laborers to the United States. Although there were less than 300,000 total Asian immigrants to the U.S. in the years between 1880 and 1909, immigration restrictions on Chinese and other Asians were tightened in 1902 and again in 1917. These laws were repealed in 1943, and in 1965 Congress passed a law which abolished immigration quotas based on national origin. In the 1980s and 1990s, China has placed in the top ten countries sending legal immigrants to the U.S. (illegal immigration is a growing problem), with almost 39,000 immigrants admitted in 1992.

Chinese immigrants often faced considerable prejudice in their new country. In the early part of the century, Chinese immigrant children attended segregated schools in the "Chinatowns" where they lived. During World War II, when Japanese Americans faced hostility and internment because of Japan's involvement in the war, Chinese Americans also encountered prejudice from people who mistook them for Japanese, although they were not deprived of property by the government. This struggle for acceptance is reflected in the novel as both mothers and daughters wish to excel in "American" society. Just as the United States has learned to value contributions of Americans of various backgrounds, the daughters in *The Joy Luck Club* learn to value their own Chinese heritage.

Critical Overview

Both critics and the reading public loved *The Joy Luck Club* from the minute it came off the press in 1989. The book successfully crosses cultures and joins separate generations. An indication of the book's appeal is its translation into seventeen languages and its place on the *New York Times* best-seller list for nine months.

Literary experts appreciate Tan's skill in storytelling. They feel that she knows what makes a good story and that she handles dialogue well. In addition, they have commented that she aptly portrays the universal life cycles of life and death, separation and reunion, uncertainty and assurance. Her ability to empathize with her characters and her subject matter, observers note, makes her stories real. Readers of all ages, genders, and cultures can appreciate her insight and honesty.

Reviewers have referred to the common sense with which Tan writes about Chinese culture. Tan explores areas of Chinese life that most other writers have not attempted. Many critics note that this novel, as well as others Tan has written, stimulates cross-culture appreciation. Readers of all cultures are able to be objective about their own predicaments while at the same time making connections between themselves and Tan's Chinese characters.

In general, Tan's treatment of the mother/daughter relationship and her understanding of her characters' ambivalence about their Chinese backgrounds provide an "intricate tapestry" that "alters the way we understand the world and ourselves, that transcends topicality," according to Michael Dorris in the *Detroit News*. Experts recognized Tan's talent, selecting her as a finalist in 1989 for the National Book Award for Fiction and nominating her for the National Book Critics Circle Award. She received not only the Bay Area Book

Reviewers Award and the Commonwealth Club Gold Award, but also $1.23 million from Vintage for paperback rights; the book was also made into a popular film in 1993.

It is no wonder that Tan has sold over three million copies of *The Joy Luck Club*. As Dorris concluded, it is "the real thing."

Criticism

Shu-Huei Henrickson

Henrickson is an instructor of English at Rock Valley College in Rockford, Illinois. In the following essay, the critic examines the popularity of The Joy Luck Club *and explores how Tan uses various narrative techniques to demonstrate the mother-daughter differences and tensions in the novel.*

Published in 1989, Amy Tan's first novel, *The Joy Luck Club*, remained nine months on the *New York Times* best-seller list. The book was considered a sensation and its success has not yet been duplicated by any other work of Asian American literature. The film adaptation of *The Joy Luck Club*, directed by Chinese American director Wayne Wang, was enthusiastically received as well. Though highly lauded, even Tan's later works *The Kitchen God's Wife* (1991), *The Moon Lady* (1992)—a children's story based on an episode from *The Joy Luck Club,* and most recently, *The Hundred Secret Senses* (1995), have not matched the legendary stature of Tan's first novel.

The success of *The Joy Luck Club*, according to Sao-Ling Cynthia Wong, is due in part to its "persistent allure of Orientalism." Other literary critics have attributed the author's achievements to Tan's excellent treatment of a prevalent theme in ethnic American literature: mother/daughter relationships. While most mother/daughter texts portray the daughter's struggles for identity, what distinguishes Tan's text from other ethnic novels, as Maria Heung points out, is the "foregrounding of the voices of mothers as well as of daughters." An analysis of Amy Tan's narrative techniques will explain how Tan brings the mothers' voices to the foreground.

The first narrative technique readers will notice is Tan's use of multiple points of view to narrate the stories, sixteen interlocking tales told from the viewpoints of four Chinese immigrant women and their four American-born daughters. (One of the mothers, Suyuan Woo, is recently deceased, so

What Do I Read Next?

• *The Kitchen God's Wife,* published in 1991 by Putnam of New York, was Tan's second novel. While many predicted that Tan would not be able to achieve the success of her first novel, this work received many accolades. It, too, deals with mother/daughter themes but also hints that male-centered social traditions hinder women's relationships with each other. Set in pre- and post-World War II China, the story portrays a woman's struggles in an abusive relationship. In writing this book, Tan tells a story that is very similar to her mother's.

• In a children's picture book entitled *The Moon Lady,* Amy Tan extends the story from the chapter of the same title in her first novel. Published in 1992 by Macmillan, *The Moon Lady* appeals to preteens as an introduction to Tan's themes and style. *The Moon Lady* is about a seven-year-old girl who attends the autumn moon festival and encounters the lady who lives on the moon and grants secret wishes.

• Published in 1995, *The Hundred Secret Senses* by Amy Tan is a story about American-born Olivia and her Chinese half-sister, Kwan. When she comes to America to live with three-year-old Olivia, Kwan is eighteen and full of stories about having "yin eyes." She convinces Olivia that she can see and communicate with the dead. The story follows the girls through adulthood and tells of the strong bond that forms between them.

• In her 1976 memoir *The Woman Warrior: Memoirs of a Girlhood among Ghosts,* Maxine Hong Kingston, an American writer born of Chinese immigrant parents, blends myth and legend with history and autobiography. Growing out of stories that Kingston's mother told her as "lessons to grow up on," the book has several parallels with Tan's most famous novel, such as profiling Kingston's mother Brave Orchid and the author's description of the difficulties she encountered as a second-generaration Chinese American.

• *The Intersections of Gender, Class, Race, and Culture: On Seeing Clients Whole* is an article that discusses identity formation in terms of race, culture, and class. The article can be found in the *Journal of Multicultural Counseling and Development,* Vol. 21, No. 1, January, 1993, pp. 50-58.

---

her story is told through her daughter, Jing-Mei (June) Woo.

Tan's technique is relatively rare in literature. What is even more unusual is the portion of stories told from the mothers' points of view. The novel is divided into four parts. The mothers' stories constitute the first and fourth parts of the novel with the second and third parts told by their daughters. In other words, the mothers tell half of the stories in the novel.

Furthermore, the mothers are all depicted as strong and determined women who play significant roles in the daughters' stories. For example, Waverly Jong's stories portray her mother's power over her, a power so great that Waverly loses her ability to win chess tournaments after she becomes angry at her mother in the marketplace. Lena St. Clair remembers her mother's "mysterious ability to see things before they happen." Rose Hsu Jordan's mother wants her to fight her divorce. And Jing-Mei Woo remembers her mother's high expectations of her becoming a child prodigy on the piano. The presence of such significant mothers is one way *The Joy Luck Club* distinguishes itself from other mother/daughter texts.

Because of their significant presences, the mothers reinforce Tan's portrayal of tension existing in the intricate relationships between mothers and daughters. Gloria Shen notes that the Joy Luck Club "mothers are possessively trying to hold onto their daughters, and the daughters are battling to get away from their mothers." Lindo Jong may be the most possessive and powerful of the mothers. In both stories narrated by her daughter, Lindo often hovers over Waverly's shoulders as she practices chess; gives Waverly instructions such as "Next time win more, lose less"; takes credit for Waverly's victories; and brags about Waverly in the marketplace. Finally, Waverly, not able to bear her mother's boasts, says, "I wish you wouldn't do that, telling everybody I'm your daughter." The tension between mother and daughter then erupts into Lindo's prophecy of Waverly's future failures at chess. Lindo's prophecy is fulfilled; Waverly eventually gives up chess at fourteen. Twenty years later, Lindo Jong's power over Waverly nearly inhibits Waverly from reporting her forthcoming second marriage for fear of Lindo's disapproval. However, the daughter's battle song about getting away from her mother has a positive finale. Waverly's narrative about the conflict between her and Lindo end with Lindo's acceptance of Waverly's fiance.

The mothers' overbearing presences in their daughters' stories are not meant to portray the mothers negatively. Almost all of the mothers' stories, in the first and fourth parts of the novel, begin with the mothers' concerns about the well-being of their daughters. In "The Red Candle," Lindo Jong addresses her story to Waverly: "It's too late to change you, but I'm telling you this because I worry about your baby." Ying-Ying St. Clair explains why she must tell her story to her daughter Lena: "All her life, I have watched her as though from another shore. And now I must tell her everything about my past. It is the only way to penetrate her skin and pull her to where she can be saved." The telling and the stories themselves demonstrate the mothers' efforts to ensure better understanding between their daughters and themselves.

Both mothers and daughters try hard to communicate with each other, but sometimes misunderstandings result from linguistic differences. As Victoria Chen points out, "The lack of shared languages and cultural logic remains a central theme throughout all the narratives in Tan's book." For example, Jing-Mei Woo laments, "My mother and I never really understood one another. We translate each other's meanings and I seemed to hear less than what she said, while my mother heard more [than what I said]."

Tan's shrewd ear for dialogue captures the linguistic differences well. The mothers' English is undoubtedly imperfect. Subjects, articles, and prepositions are often missing. Verbs often do not agree with nouns. After, for instance, Waverly be-comes angry at Lindo Jong for bragging about her at the marketplace, Lindo says, "So shame be with mother? …. Embarrass you be my daughter?" Waverly desperately tries to explain, "That's not what I meant. That's not what I say." Lindo persists, "What you say?" Further communication at this point is impossible. Mother and daughter do not talk to each other for several days after the incident. In another example, Ying-Ying St. Clair's uneasiness with the American way of life manifests itself in the way she pronounces the profession of her daughter and son-in-law: "It is an ugly word. Arty-tecky." Similarly, An-Mei Hsu cannot pronounce "psychiatrist" correctly: "Why can you talk about this with a psyche-atric and not with mother?"

As we have seen, the linguistic differences between mother and daughter are a feature of Tan's narrative technique. This language difference not only explains communication problems but also marks the cultural identity of these two generations of women. The American daughters are adapted to the customs and language of the new country; the mothers still dwell in those of China. Tan gives readers an allegory of the cultural differences between mother and daughter in the prologue to the first part of the novel, "Feather from a Thousand Li Away." The old woman in the prologue dreamt that in America she would make her daughter "speak only perfect American English." But now that the old woman's wish is fulfilled —the daughter "grew up speaking only English and swallowing more Coca-Cola than sorrow"—the old woman cannot communicate with her daughter. She waits, "year after year," for the day she can tell her daughter "in perfect American English" about a swan she brought from China with her and her good intentions. None of the Joy Luck Club mothers speaks perfect English, so they are not able to communicate their good intentions in a way that the daughters will understand.

Despite linguistic and cultural differences, the mothers are eventually able to help their daughters embrace their racial identity. Before Jing-Mei's trip to China, she denies her Chinese heritage. She remembers Suyuan Woo telling her, "Once you are born Chinese, you cannot help but feel and think Chinese." Whenever her mother says this, Jing-Mei sees herself "transforming like a werewolf." But after Suyuan's death, the rest of the Joy Luck Club mothers insist that Jing-Mei visit her half sisters in China. It is during this visit that Jing-Mei comes to terms with her true identity: "[M]y mother was right. I am becoming Chinese." Moreover, Jing-

Mei has become her mother by taking over her mother's place at the mah jong table, "on the East [side of the table], where things begin." Her trip to China culminates in her realization that both her mother and China are in her blood.

In sum, through first—person narratives and linguistic differences, Tan brings the mothers to the foreground. In other words, the heroines of *The Joy Luck Club* are the mothers. While most mothers in ethnic American literature sit silently in the background, Tan's Joy Luck Club mothers speak assertively. Disagreeing with popular assumptions that the Chinese are "discreet and modest," Amy Tan, in her article, "The Language of Discretion," urges us to reject such stereotypical views. Tan observes that "the more emphatic outbursts always spilled over into Chinese." Indeed, when asked why Chinese people commit torture, Lindo Jong, a strong, assertive Joy Luck Club mother, replies simply and emphatically, "Chinese people do many things. Chinese people do business, do medicine, do painting. Not lazy like American people. We do torture. Best torture."

Source: Shu-Huei Henrickson, in an essay for *Novels for Students,* Gale, 1997.

Carolyn See

In her assessment of The Joy Luck Club, *which she calls a "stunningly devotional tour de force," American fiction and nonfiction writer Carolyn See determines that the novel "is about the way the past distances itself away from the present." Its protagonists, See notes, are looking for their pasts— the older women for the pasts they have lost, the younger starving "for a past they can never fully understand."*

The only negative thing I could ever say about this book is that I'll never again be able to read it for the first time. *The Joy Luck Club* is so powerful, so full of magic, that by the end of the second paragraph, your heart catches; by the end of the first page, tears blur your vision, and one-third of the way down on Page 26, you know you won't be doing anything of importance until you have finished this novel.

The main narrative here is taken up by Jing-mei Woo, a first-generation American-Chinese woman whose whole tone is tuned to the fact that she is, essentially, lost. She's swimming upstream in American culture, doing the best she can, but she's gone through several jobs, she's gotten into the habit of settling for less than she should, and her own Chinese mother appears to be bitterly disappointed in her. Then, her mother dies, and Jing-mei is asked by three old family friends to take her mother's place at their mah-jongg table, at a social club they've been carrying on in San Francisco for the last 40 years.

Here is Jing-mei (who goes by the name of June, now), recording her first night as a bona-fide member: "The Joy Luck Aunties are all wearing slacks, bright print blouses, and different versions of sturdy walking shoes. We are all seated around the dining room table under a lamp that looks like a Spanish candelabra. Uncle George puts on his bifocals and starts the meeting by reading the minutes. 'Our capital account is $24,825, or about $6,206 a couple, $3,103 a person. We sold Subaru for a loss at six and three quarters. We bought a hundred shares of Smith International at seven. Our thanks to Lindo and Tinn Jong for the goodies. The red bean soup was especially delicious....'"

Not the stuff of high adventure. But the original Joy Luck Club was started in Chungking during the last of World War II by Jing-mei's mother when she was a young widow, literally setting herself and her friends the task of creating joy and luck out of unimaginable catastrophe: "What was worse, we asked among ourselves, to sit and wait for our own deaths with proper somber faces? or to choose our own happiness?... We decided to hold parties and pretend each week had become the new year. Each week we could forget past wrongs done to us. We weren't allowed to think a bad thought. We feasted, we laughed, we played games, lost and won, we told the best stories. And each week, we could hope to be lucky."

The reason that the men in the present Joy Luck Club buy stock now is so that every member can feel lucky and have some joy, because by this time it has become unacceptable to lose anything more. The four women who have consoled themselves in America for 40 years with friendship, mah-jongg and stories, have already lived lives that are, again, unimaginable. On top of all their other terrors and adversities, their pasts have been *lost* ; as if these horrors have taken place not just in another country but on another planet. Their deepest wish is to pass their knowledge, their tales, on to their children, especially to their duaghters, but those young women are undergoing a slow death of their own; drowning in American culture at the same time they starve for a past they can never fully understand.

The author leavens this *Angst* with Marx brothers humor, making you laugh, literally, even as you cry. What can you *do* with a Chinese couple who name their four boys Matthew, Mark, Luke *and* Bing? What can you tell a mother who thinks she's getting "so-so security" from the government, or (as Jing-mei remembers her own mother deep in indignation about an irate neighbor who believes that she's killed his cat) " '...That man, he raise his hand like this, show me his ugly fist and call me worst Fukien landlady. I not from Fukien. Hunh! He know nothing!' "

But the understandings don't come merely from vagaries of language. *The Joy Luck Club* is about the way the past distances itself from the present as speedily as a disappearing star on a *Star Trek* rerun. It's gone, gone, and yet the past holds the only keys to meaning in every life examined here. On her first night at the mah-jongg table, her mother's friends revealed to Jing-mei that she has two half-sisters still in China, and that the Joy Luck ladies have saved money so that she, Jing-mei, can go home to tell them about their mother. " 'What can I tell them about my mother?' " Jing-mei blurts. " 'I don't know anything....' " But the book is dedicated by the author: *To my mother and the memory of her mother. You asked me once what I would remember. This, and much more.* What results from this stunningly devotional tour de force is an entrance into eight separate lives: four women whose "real" life occurred in China, in another world in another *mind;* and four of their daughters, themselves grown women now. To say they are all products of conflicting value systems is heavy-handed inaccuracy, wimpy paraphrase.

Here, for instance, is Eurasian Lena St. Clair, Ying-ying's daughter, translating her mother's Chinese to her Caucasian father, after Ying-ying has given birth to her stillborn baby brother. Lena's mother cries out "...Then this baby, maybe he heard us, his large head seemed to fill with hot air and rise up from the table. The head turned to one side.... It looked right through me. I knew he could see everything inside me. How I had given no thought to killing my other son!" Lena translates to her sad, ignorant father: "...She thinks we must all think very hard about having another baby.... And she thinks we should leave now and go have dinner."

And, 15 or so years later, it seems inevitable that Lena should end up with a Hungarian "rice husband" (so named for all those Chinese "rice Christians" who hung around missionaries in China simply so they could get a square meal). In the name of feminism and right thinking, this husband

is taking Lena for every cent she's got, but she's so demoralized, so "out of balance" in the Chinese sense, that she can't do a thing about it.

If, so far, I haven't done justice to this book, that's because you can't turn a poem into prose, or explain magic, without destroying the magic, destroying the poem. One can only mention scraps: The four mothers come from different parts of (and times in) China, so for instance, the author allows us to see one peasant mother, Lindo Jong, who remembers she was *not* worthless: "I looked and smelled like a precious bun cake, sweet with a good clean color." Lindo, betrothed at 2, wangles her way out of a horrible marriage with courage and wit. But another mah-jongg lady, An-mei, has watched her own mother lose her honor and "face" by becoming third concubine to a hideous merchant in Tiensing. An-mei's mother times her suicide in such a way that her ghost can come back to haunt the house on New Year's Day, thus insuring a good future for her child, who, in turn, comes to America, has a daughter, Rose, who somehow rustles up the courage to defy an American husband who's trying to swindle her....

But the stories of the four mothers, the four daughters, are not really the point here. *The Joy Luck Club* is dazzling because of the *worlds* it gives us: When Lindo, old now, says, " 'Feel my bracelets. They must be 24 carats, pure inside and out,' " if you have any sense at all, you let yourself be led down a garden path into a whole other place; where a little girl in San Francisco becomes chess champion at age 6 by using her mother's "invisible strength," where a woman who comes from the richest family in Wushi (with boxes of jade in every room holding just the right amount of cigarettes) is given the name of Betty by her dopey American husband, who doesn't know she's already "dead," a "ghost...."

At the perimeters of all these stories are all the men, buying and trading in this Mountain of Gold, selling Subaru at a loss, each one of them with his own story that has yet to be told. *The Joy Luck Club* has the disconcerting effect of making you look at everyone in your own life with the—however fleeting—knowledge that they are locked in the spaceships of their own amazing stories. Only magicians of language like Amy Tan hold the imaginative keys to the isolating capsules. Which is why we have novels and novelists in the first place.

Source: Carolyn See, "Drowning in America, Starving for China," in *Los Angeles Times Book Review,* March 12, 1989, pp. 1, 11.

Orville Schell

Critic Orville Schell is recognized as an authority on China. In his review of The Joy Luck Club, *he provides some background on both the Chinese emigrants who came to America in what he calls the "great Chinese diaspora" and their children who were raised in the United States. In addition, he notes that "it is out of [the] experience of being caught between countries and cultures that writers such as ... Amy Tan have begun to create what is, in effect, a new genre of American fiction."*

In 1949, when the Red Army marched into Beijing, America's "special relationship" with China abruptly ended, and so hostile did our two countries become toward each other that people on both sides of the widening divide seemed to lose the ability even to imagine reconciliation.

Apart from the international crises, and even wars, there was another consequence, which, although more subtle, was equally tragic. Those millions of emigrants who were part of the great Chinese diaspora—beginning in the middle of the 19th century when indentured laborers went to California, and ending in the 1950's when millions of refugees fled Communism—were left almost completely cut off from their homeland. While the members of the older generation who had grown up in China before Mao Zedong were at least able to bring a sustaining fund of memory with them into exile, the younger generation was denied even this slender means of connection to the ancestral homeland. Seeing old China as hopelessly backward, and contemporary China as besmirched by Communism, many in this new generation of Chinese-Americans wanted nothing more than to distance themselves as far as possible from the *zuguo*, or motherland.

But, unlike the children of European emigrants, they had obviously Oriental features, which made it difficult for them to lose themselves in the American melting pot. Living in the confinement of Chinatowns with parents who spoke broken English ("tear and wear on car," "college drop-off") and who clung to the old Chinese way, they felt an indelible sense of otherness that weighed heavily on them as they tried to make their way into middle-class American life.

When political barriers began to fall in the 1970's, older emigrants welcomed the chance to end their long and agonizing exiles. But their sons and daughters looked with a deep ambivalence on the idea of having to awaken a dormant Chinese

side in themselves. And so, as the exterior world went about recognizing China, re-establishing diplomatic relations and initiating trade and cultural exchanges, these young Chinese-Americans found themselves wrestling with a very different and infinitely more complicated interior problem: how to recognize a country to which they were inextricably bound by heritage, but to which they had never been. It is out of this experience of being caught between countries and cultures that writers such as Maxine Hong Kingston and now Amy Tan have begun to create what is, in effect, a new genre of American fiction.

Born in Oakland, Calif., in 1952 to a father educated as an engineer in Beijing and a mother raised in a well-to-do Shanghai family, Amy Tan grew up in an American world that was utterly remote from the childhood world of her parents. In *The Joy Luck Club*, her first novel, short-story-like vignettes alternate back and forth between the lives of four Chinese women in pre-1949 China and the lives of their American-born daughters in California. The book is a meditation on the divided nature of this emigrant life.

The members of the Joy Luck Club are four aging "aunties" who gather regularly in San Francisco to play mah-jongg, eat Chinese food and gossip about their children. When one of the women dies, her daughter, Jing-mei (June) Woo, is drafted to sit in for her at the game. But she feels uncomfortably out of place in this unassimilated environment among older women who still wear "funny Chinese dresses with stiff stand-up collars and blooming branches of embroidered silk sewn over their breasts," and who meet in one another's houses, where "too many once fragrant smells" from Chinese cooking have been "compressed onto a thin layer of invisible grease." The all-too-Chinese ritual of the Joy Luck Club has always impressed her as little more than a "shameful Chinese custom, like the secret gathering of the Ku Klux Klan or the tom-tom dances of TV Indians preparing for war."

She is made uncomfortable by the older generation's insistence on maintaining old customs and parochial habits, which she views as an impediment to breaking loose from her parents' cultural gravity. What she yearns for is to lead an independent, modern and American life free of the burden of her parents' Chineseness and the overweening hopes for their children that they can't even "begin to express in their fragile English."

"At first my mother tried to cultivate some hidden genius in me," recalls June. "She did housework for an old retired piano teacher down the hall who gave me lessons and free use of a piano to practice on in exchange. When I failed to become a concert pianist, or even an accompanist for the church youth choir, she finally explained that I was late-blooming, like Einstein, who everyone thought was retarded until he discovered a bomb."

What she fears most of all is being dragged under by all that the Joy Luck Club symbolizes and transformed "like a werewolf, a mutant tag of DNA suddenly triggered, replicating itself insidiously into a *syndrome,* a cluster of telltale Chinese behaviors, all those things my mother did to embarrass me—haggling with store owners, pecking her mouth with a toothpick in public, being color-blind to the fact that lemon yellow and pale pink are not good combinations for winter clothes."

Part of June's struggle is to distance herself from the kind of helpless obedience that she recognizes in traditional Chinese women, and that she fears is manifesting itself in passivity in her own, American life. "I was raised the Chinese way: I was taught to desire nothing, to swallow other people's misery, to eat my own bitterness," says June's mother, spelling out the dangerously congenital nature of this Chinese female submissiveness. "And even though I taught my daughter the opposite, still she came out the same way! Maybe it is because she was born to me and she was born a girl. And I was born to my mother and I was born a girl. All of us are like stairs, one step after another, going up and down, but all going the same way." With a weary fatalism that speaks for June as well, her sister Lena confesses her propensity for "surrendering everything" to her American husband "without caring what I got in return."

However, after the death of June's mother a mixture of grief, guilt and curiosity, coupled with the relentless goading of the aunties of the Joy Luck Club, conspire to draw her into the very world from which she had so assiduously sought to distance herself. As the aunties talk over their mah-jongg game, even scolding June at one point for her evident lack of interest in her parents—"Not know your own mother?" asks one of them. "How can you say? Your mother is in your bones!"—June begins to see her mother's generation in a different light. Rather than viewing the aunties as expressionless aliens from an opaque and distant land who hound and embarrass their children, bit by bit she begins to understand the real dimensions of the "unspeakable tragedies they had left behind in China," and to sense how vulnerable they actually are in America. Slowly she begins to comprehend how, after all they

have endured, they might well be anxious and concerned lest all cultural continuity between their pasts and their children's futures be lost.

"Because I remained quiet for so long now my daughter does not hear me," laments one auntie. "She sits by her fancy swimming pool and hears only her Sony Walkman, her cordless phone, her big, important husband asking her why they have charcoal and no lighter fluid." It comes as a revelation to June that "they are frightened. In me, they see their own daughters, just as ignorant, just as unmindful of all the truths and hopes they have brought to America. They see daughters who grow impatient when their mothers talk in Chinese, who think they are stupid when they explain things in fractured English. They see that joy and luck do not mean the same to their daughters, that to these closed American-born minds 'joy luck' is not a word, it does not exist. They see daughters who will bear grandchildren born without any connecting hope passed from generation to generation."

When the aunties finally inform June that the two half sisters her mother had been forced to abandon during the war miraculously survived and are now living in Shanghai, she is finally jolted into feeling the ways in which her mother is, in fact, still "in her bones." But it is not until she actually leaves with her aging father for a pilgrimage to China and a rendezvous with these half sisters that the reader feels the intensity of heat building up, heat we know will finally fuse her to her hitherto elusive ancestral home. And when at last she steps off the plane to embrace these errant relatives who have grown up on the other side of the divide that once separated China from the United States so absolutely, we feel as if a deep wound in the Chinese-American experience is finally being sutured back together again:

"'Mama, Mama,' we all murmur, as if she is among us."

"My sisters look at me proudly.... And now I also see what part of me is Chinese. It is so obvious. It is my family. It is in our blood. After all these years, it can finally be let go."

As Amy Tan tells us of her own homecoming on the jacket of *The Joy Luck Club,* it was just as her mother had told her it would be. "As soon as my feet touched China, I became Chinese."

Woven into the narrative of the lives of June and her mother are the stories of the three other Joy Luck aunties and their California-born daughters. Moving back and forth across the divide between the two generations, the two continents and the two cultures, we find ourselves transported across the Pacific Ocean from the upwardly mobile, design-conscious, divorce-prone and Americanized world of the daughters in San Francisco to the World of China in the 20's and 30's, which seems more fantastic and dreamlike than real.

We come to see how the idea of China—nourished in America by nothing more than the memories of this vanished reality—has slowly metamorphosed in the minds of the aunties until their imaginations have so overtaken actual memory that revery is all that is left to keep them in contact with the past. When we are suddenly jerked by these sequences from the comforting familiarity of the United States into a scared child's memory of a dying grandmother in remote Ningbo, to remembrances of an arranged marriage with a murderous ending in Shansi or to recollections of a distraught woman abandoning her babies during wartime in Guizhou, we may readily feel bewildered and lost. Such abrupt transitions in time and space make it difficult to know who is who and what the complex web of generational Joy Luck Club relationships actually is.

But these *recherches* to old China are so beautifully written that one should just allow oneself to be borne along as if in a dream. In fact, as the story progresses, the reader begins to appreciate just how these disjunctions work for, rather than against, the novel. While we as readers grope to know whose mother or grandmother is getting married in an unfamiliar ceremony, or why a concubine is committing suicide, we are ironically being reminded not just of the nightmarishness of being a woman in traditional China, but of the enormity of the confusing mental journey Chinese emigrants had to make. And most ironic, we are also reminded by these literary disjunctions that it is precisely this mental chasm that members of the younger generation must now recross in reverse in order to resolve themselves as whole Chinese-Americans; in *The Joy Luck Club* we get a suggestion of the attendant confusion they must expect to endure in order to get to the other side.

In the hands of a less talented writer such thematic material might easily have become overly didactic, and the characters might have seemed like cutouts from a Chinese-American knockoff of *Roots.* But in the hands of Amy Tan, who has a wonderful eye for what is telling, a fine ear for dialogue, a deep empathy for her subject matter and a guilelessly straightforward way of writing, they sing with a rare fidelity and beauty. She has written a jewel of a book.

Source: Orville Schell, "'Your Mother Is in Your Bones'," in *The New York Times Book Review,* March 19, 1989, pp. 3, 28.

Sources

Michael Dorris, "'Joy Luck Club' Hits the Literary Jackpot," in the *Detroit News,* March 26, 1989, p. 2D.

Tracy Robinson, "The Intersections of Gender, Class, Race, and Culture: On Seeing Clients Whole," in *Journal of Multicultural Counseling and Development,* Vol. 21, No. 1, January, 1993, pp. 50-8.

For Further Study

Victoria Chen, "Chinese American Women, Language, and Moving Subjectivity," in *Women and Language,* Vol. 18, no. 1, 1995, pp. 3-7.

> Chen argues that Amy Tan and Maxine Hong Kingston use language differences between Chinese immigrants and their daughters to suggest "multiplicity and instability of cultural identity for Chinese American women."

Marina Heung, "Daughter-Text/Mother-Text: Matrilineage in Amy Tan's *Joy Luck Club,*" in *Feminist Studies,* Vol. 19, no. 3, 1993, pp. 597-616.

> Marina Heung argues that Tan's mother-daughter text is unique in its foregrounding of the mothers' voices.

A review of *The Hundred Secret Senses* in *Kirkus Reviews,* Volume 63, September 1, 1995, p. 1217.

> The author again relies on female relationships in this story of a Chinese-American, her Chinese half-sister, and the girls' belief in ghosts and communication with the dead. The reviewer feels that Tan spends too much time telling the story of Miss Banner but has positive words for the depiction of the Chinese sister's eccentricities and the bond between the two girls.

Gloria Shen, "Born of a Stranger: Mother-Daughter Relationships and Storytelling in Amy Tan's *The Joy Luck Club,*" in *International Women's Writing: New Landscapes of Identity,* edited by Anne E. Brown and Marjanne E. Gooze, Greenwood, 1995, pp. 233-44.

> Gloria Shen explores "the narrative strategy employed in *The Joy Luck Club* and the relationships between the Chinese mothers and their American-born daughters."

Amy Tan, "The Language of Discretion," in *The State of the Language,* edited by Christopher Ricks and Leonard Michaels, University of California Press, 1990, pp. 25-32.

> Amy Tan argues that the Chinese are not as "discreet and modest" as most people believe and that the Chinese use their language emphatically and assertively.

Sao-Ling Cynthia Wong, "'Sugar Sisterhood': Situating the Amy Tan Phenomenon," in *The Ethnic Canon: Histories, Institutions, and Interventions,* edited by David Liu Palumbo, University of Minnesota Press, 1995, pp. 174-210.

> Sao-Ling Cynthia Wong puts *The Joy Luck Club* in its "sociohistorical" context to explain the novel's success in the book market.

Love in the Time of Cholera

Gabriel García Márquez

1985

Love in the Time of Cholera (*El amor en los tiempos del cólera* in the original Spanish), published in 1985, was the first novel by Gabriel García Márquez to be published since he was awarded the Nobel Prize for Literature in 1982. As abundant publicity surrounding the book's appearance in December 1985 revealed, the author was already working on a sequel to his novel *Chronicle of a Death Foretold* when the Nobel committee's decision was announced. With the award there came numerous public commitments obliging García Márquez to interrupt the progress of his project until January 1984, when he resumed work on the existing material. *Love in the Time of Cholera* was eventually completed in August 1985 and published three months ahead of schedule.

Initial critical response took the form of summary notices and reviews, the most enthusiastic of which asserted that *Love in the Time of Cholera* was one of the great living classics of the Spanish language. It has been called a masterpiece of sensuous prose, because of its ability to summon up the textures, sensual pleasures, tastes, and smells associated with living in a particular place at a particular time. Because of this, it has been compared to other contemporary texts such as Toni Morrison's vibrant account of Harlem life *Jazz*. Overblown yet controlled, García Márquez's story of life, love, and lust in a convention-bound provincial city on the Caribbean coast of Colombia displays great imaginative and narrative freedom. In addition, it has an almost novella-like discipline in its structuring of recurrent ideas.

Author Biography

Gabriel García Márquez was born in Aracataca, Colombia, on 6 March 1928 to Gabriel Eligio García and Luisa Santiaga Márquez de Garcia. In 1940 the young García Márquez went on a scholarship to the Liceo Nacional de Zipaquira, a high school near Bogotá. Several years later he enrolled in law school at the Universidad Nacional in the capital. Political unrest closed the university in 1948, and García Márquez transferred to the Universidad de Cartagena but never graduated. Instead he became a writer for the Cartagena newspaper *Universal,* then later, from 1950 through 1952, for the *Heraldo* in Barranquilla. By 1955 he was a well-known journalist at the *Espectador* in Bogotá. From 1956 to 1958 he wrote fiction and was a freelance journalist in Paris, London, and Caracas, Venezuela. He returned to Barranquilla to marry his childhood sweetheart, Mercedes Barcha, in March 1958. They moved to Caracas, where García Márquez worked for the magazine *Momento.* In May 1959 he was instrumental in launching a branch of Prensa Latina in Bogota, where he and his wife had moved. García Márquez and his family relocated to New York City in 1961. He worked briefly at the Prensa Latina branch there but then resigned to tour the southern United States and look for filmwriting work in Mexico City. He eventually wrote for magazines there and then took an advertising job with J. Walter Thompson's Mexico City branch in 1963.

Meanwhile his fiction-writing career had begun seriously and successfully with *El coronel no tiene quien le escriba* (1961; translated as *No One Writes to the Colonel and Other Stories,* 1968). In 1967 he published what is considered his masterpiece, the novel *Cien años de soledad,* translated as *One Hundred Years of Solitude.* This work follows the strange and wonderful events surrounding six generations of the Buendía family in the imaginary Colombian town of Macondo. It was part of the "boom" of Spanish-language literature in the 1960s, when Latin American writers became increasingly known around the world. The novel, along with many of García Márquez's other works, is considered an example of "magical realism," a genre of fiction which blends mysterious, supernatural, and even surreal events with the hard political and social realities of life. When García Márquez was awarded the Nobel Prize for Literature in 1982, the Swedish Academy noted, "Each new work of his is received by critics and readers as an event of world importance, is translated into

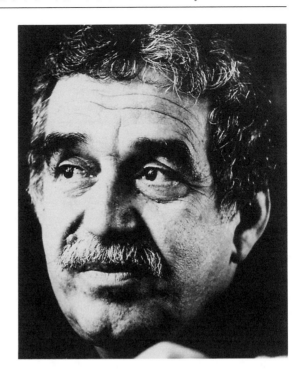

Gabriel García Márquez

many languages and published as quickly as possible in large editions." The author has published several novels since winning the Nobel, notably *Love in the Time of Cholera* in 1985, but most recently, García Márquez has pursued his interest in film. He has made a series of six films for Spanish television that have garnered both critical and popular acclaim.

Plot Summary

Part I

Love in the Time of Cholera is set between the 1870s and 1930s in an unnamed city along the Caribbean coast of Colombia. It tells the story of a man who waits fifty-one years, nine months, and four days to be with the woman he loves. The novel begins with the suicide of Jeremiah de Saint-Amour, a sixty-year-old photographer who decided long ago that he would never be old. His friend, Dr. Juvenal Urbino, 81, arrives on the scene and recognizes the lingering scent of bitter almonds left by gold cyanide—a scent that always reminds him of unrequited love. That afternoon, Dr. Urbino wakes from his siesta with the feeling that he, too, is nearing the end of his life. He dies moments later when, attempting to retrieve his parrot from a mango tree, he falls from a ladder and lands in the mud. His wife, Fermina Daza, 72, arrives just in time to hear him speak his final words. Present at both the funeral and the wake is Florentino Ariza who, at 76, is a man convinced that he has loved in silence for a much longer time than anyone else in this world ever has. After the wake, he repeats to Fermina Daza the "vow of eternal fidelity and everlasting love" he first made to her over half a century ago. Fermina Daza throws Florentino Ariza out of her house with instructions never to return. She wakes up the following morning and realizes that, while she slept, she had thought more about Florentino Ariza than about her dead husband.

Part II

Florentino Ariza first sees Fermina Daza when she is thirteen years old and begins to watch her from a hidden bench in the park she passes through every day. They see each other close up for the first time at Midnight Mass on Christmas Eve when, turning to look behind her, Fermina sees the eyes, face and lips of a boy "petrified by the terror of love." Soon afterwards, Florentino gives Fermina a letter in which he promises his perfect fidelity and everlasting love. While waiting for a response, Florentino is stricken with diarrhea and attacks of green vomit, and it is concluded that the symptoms of love are the same as those of cholera. He finally receives her answer and, after two years of continuous letter writing, Florentino makes a formal proposal of marriage. Fermina's father attempts to prevent the union by taking his daughter on an eighteen-month journey that will, he hopes, make her forget. However, Fermina and Florentino continue their correspondence and promise to marry as soon as possible. Upon her return, Fermina again comes face to face with her beloved but, instead of love, feels only the "abyss of disenchantment" and erases Florentino from her life with a wave of her hand.

Part III

Dr. Urbino first meets eighteen-year-old Fermina when it is feared she may have cholera. His physical examination reveals only an intestinal infection, but he returns to the Daza home the following week to see Fermina again. She is initially uninterested in his advances, but finally decides to respond to his letters. The news of Fermina's engagement to Dr. Urbino is crushing to Florentino, and he is quickly sent away on a curative river-journey by his mother. One night on the boat, Florentino is pulled into a dark cabin and stripped of his virginity by an unidentified woman. The expe-

rience leads to a revelation: that his illusory love for Fermina could be replaced by earthly passion. His first bedroom love is Widow Nazaret, but instead of developing into a permanent union, it becomes the first of his six hundred and twenty-two short-term liaisons. After six months with Widow Nazaret, Florentino becomes convinced that he has survived the torment of Fermina Daza—until he sees her one Sunday leaving High Mass. Fermina is now six months pregnant, and Florentino finds her more beautiful than ever, but more lost to him than she had ever been.

Part IV

On the day he sees Fermina in her sixth month of pregnancy, Florentino decides that, in order to deserve her, he will seek fame and fortune and obtains a position at the River Company of the Caribbean (R.C.C.). One day, Fermina happens to see Florentino on his bench in the park and dares to think that she might have been happier with him. Confronted with such extreme unhappiness, she talks to her husband and together they vow to look for the love they had felt during their honeymoon in Europe. Thirty years pass and, although Fermina would still think of Florentino, it is at the time when Dr. Urbino is stumbling into old age that she and her husband love each other best.

Part V

After discovering that Dr. Urbino is having an affair, Fermina leaves her husband with the determination never to return. She spends two years at her cousin's ranch before agreeing to return home. During this time, Florentino had only the rumours of an illness to explain Fermina's absence. He finally meets her and Dr. Urbino one evening at the open-air theatre and, seeing Fermina stumble, realizes that death might win an irreparable victory over love. Florentino eventually takes over complete control of the R.C.C., and, little by little, falls into a routine of visiting the same women with whom he has already established relationships. On the Pentecost Sunday when Dr. Urbino dies, he has only one lover left: fourteen-year-old América Vicuña. It is that evening that he repeats his vow of eternal fidelity and everlasting love to Fermina. Afterwards, he regrets his hasty and inappropriate act and, just when he begins to lose hope, discovers a letter from Fermina near the entrance to his house.

Part VI

Fermina's letter inspires Florentino to attempt a new method of seduction. He writes her an extensive meditation on life, love, old age and death and, two weeks after the first anniversary of Dr. Urbino's death, appears unexpectedly at Fermina's home. They continue to see each other every week until finally deciding to go on a pleasure cruise along the river. On the first night of the trip, Florentino notices that Fermina is crying and the two join hands:

> He reached out with two icy fingers in the darkness, felt for the other hand in the darkness, and found it waiting for him. Both were lucid enough to realize, at the same fleeting instant, that the hands made of old bones were not the hands they had imagined before touching. In the next moment, however, they were. She began to speak of her dead husband in the present tense, as if he were alive, and Florentino Ariza knew then that for her, too, the time had come to ask herself with dignity, with majesty, with an irrepressible desire to live, what she should do with the love that had been left behind without a master.

On the fourth day of the voyage, the boat runs out of fuel and remains stranded for over a week. The couple spend countless hours together and, after a failed first attempt, they make love. Both are left feeling disappointed. When they reach La Dorada, the last port, Florentino convinces the Captain to hoist the yellow cholera flag in order to prevent the passengers for the return trip from boarding the ship. On the final night of the return journey, Florentino and Fermina have a grand party and make "the tranquil, wholesome love of experienced grandparents." The next day, neither of them could imagine going back home and Florentino proposes that they "keep going, going, going, back to La Dorada." Asked by the Captain how long he thinks they can keep up this coming and going, Florentino's answer is simply, "forever."

Characters

Florentino Ariza

Florentino Ariza is the novel's principal romantic who lives out the very unmodern concept of a constant heart. A telegraph operator with a passion for music and books (he is a voracious reader of both classic and popular literature, especially poetry), Florentino falls in love with the teenaged Fermina, who is teaching her aunt to read. And for the next fifty-one years, nine months, and four days— for the rest of his life, in fact—he continues to love her. García Márquez based this couple on his own parents, whose courtship took a similar course. The author's father was a telegraph operator who, like Florentino, sent his sweetheart telegrams while she

Gabriel Garcia Marquez after winning the Nobel Prize in 1982.

was on a journey that was supposed to make her forget all about him. But whereas García Márquez's parents married, Florentino is spurned by his beloved, who then marries someone else. On the second of the three boat voyages that shape his life (the first is Fermina's, and the third is the final one they take together), Florentino resolves to love Fermina for the rest of his life. He then loses his virginity to another woman, which begins an erotic career that will include more than 622 liaisons. Florentino's irresistibility to women is clear. Florentino is so ruled by love that he finds himself unable to compose the simple business letters required for his job at the River Company of the Caribbean; he does, however, develop a comfortable sideline writing letters for the lovelorn. Despite his deficiency with business letters, Florentino has a highly successful career with the riverboat company, which he accomplishes in order to make himself worthy of Fermina's love. Florentino waits more than fifty years—until Urbino dies—to win Fermina back. Not deterred by Fermina's vehement rejection, he returns to his old habit of writing her long letters. While his adolescent missives were effusively ardent and handwritten, these are typewritten and reflect the contemplative wisdom of a mature man. These ruminations on life and love prove to be what Fermina needs to hear, and she finally succumbs. When they consummate their affections, Florentino tells Fermina that he has remained a "virgin" for her, and despite his voluminous sexual history he has been faithful. For her part, Fermina recognizes this fidelity even though she knows very well that Florentino is no virgin. Critics praise García Márquez enthusiastically for his compassionate portrayal of love between these two aged protagonists. The persistent Florentino attests to the existence of undying love and that love may be the most intense at the end of life, in defiance of the infirmities and indignities of old age.

Tránsito Ariza

The devotion of Tránsito Ariza, Florentino's mother, a pawnbroker who gave birth to him after an illicit affair, seems to veer into eroticism. She advises Florentino not to overwhelm young Fermina with so many ardent letters, and she later helps him recover from the cholera-like symptoms of thwarted love.

Fermina Daza

When Florentino first sees Fermina Daza, she is the beautiful, haughty young daughter of a wealthy but disreputable horse dealer. Initially dazzled by Florentino, Fermina is sent on a journey by her father in the hope that she will become disenchanted with her suitor, and indeed his behavior begins to strike her as exaggerated. Fermina's reasons for marrying Urbino, whom she does not love, are somewhat ambiguous and impress some critics as selfish or calculating. Her father has informed her that he is financially ruined, so she may be looking out for her own material protection. In addition, she has also told herself that she must be married by the age of twenty-one. In any case, her marriage begins without love but later becomes loving, and critics laud García Márquez's insightful portrayal of this ordinary yet successful union. Fermina demonstrates pride and stubbornness in the two episodes that bring about separation from her husband. The first involves her refusal to admit that she did not place soap in the bathroom. Urbino finally concedes to her. The second and longer separation occurs when her husband has an affair with another woman, but Fermina seems angriest that he took a black lover. Over the years with Urbino, Fermina admirably fulfills her role as ornament, companion, and mother of his children, even becoming something of the "great lady" her father envisioned. Yet she remains modest in her tastes and resistant to social hypocrisy, exhibiting

a trace of populism or even of rebelliousness that may derive from her own unclear origins. After Urbino's death, Fermina admits to herself that her life was borrowed from her husband, that she was essentially a highly paid servant in his house, a commentary on the options available to women of Fermina's time, place, and culture. In contrast, the elderly Fermina undertakes her relationship with Florentino in answer to her own needs and in defiance of social stereotypes.

Lorenzo Daza

The townspeople suspect Lorenzo Daza, Fermina's father, of being some kind of gangster or horse thief, but Daza turns out to be an illegal gun dealer. Lorenzo wants Fermina to become a "great lady" and sends her on a long journey so she will forget about Florentino.

Ofelia Daza

Ofelia Daza, the daughter of Fermina and Urbino, is more snobbish and morally rigid than her mother, and she banishes Fermina from her home over her mother's relationship with Florentino.

Dr. Urbino Daza

Dr. Urbino Daza, the son of Fermina and Urbino, and a physician like his father, is not as intolerant as his sister. Nevertheless, he observes that the elderly should be segregated so that they are shielded from the sadness they must feel when they are around young people.

Hildebranda

Hildebranda, Fermina's cousin, accompanies Fermina on a long journey intended to make Fermina forget about Florentino. Together they visit various telegraph offices to retrieve Florentino's messages to his sweetheart.

Leo XII Loayza

Another significant character in Florentino's life is his uncle, Leo XII Loayza, who comes from a family in which all the male children were named after popes. Leo XII owns the riverboat company for which Florentino works. When his nephew claims that he is only interested in love, Leo XII observes that "without river navigation, there is no love."

Jeremiah de Saint-Amour

The story begins with the death of Jeremiah de Saint-Amour, a photographer and chess enthusiast. The death shocks his good friend, Dr. Juvenal

Urbino. After Saint-Amour commits suicide, keeping a promise he made to himself long ago to spare himself the troubles of old age, Urbino discovers that his friend was an escaped convict who once committed a brutal crime and secretly maintained a mulatto mistress in a ghetto hovel. Several critics note that the story of Saint-Amour and his devoted lover rehearses the themes of love, devotion, and aging that are explored in the course of the novel.

Dr. Juvenal Urbino

Soon after Fermina returns from her journey and spurns Florentino, she is courted by the town's most eligible bachelor, Dr. Juvenal Urbino. He is a wealthy, refined physician who spends time overseas and prefers European ways. Well born and dapper, Urbino typifies the typical hero of a nineteenth-century romantic novel, and when Fermina does not respond, Urbino is inflamed. Just as Fermina has reasons other than love for deciding to marry him, Urbino is rational and unromantic in his desire to acquire Fermina as his wife. He knows that this lovely, charming, somewhat haughty young woman will make an appropriate mate for a prominent, upstanding citizen like himself. Although he is undoubtedly conceited, often weak, and chauvinistic in his attitude toward domestic arrangements, Urbino has significant positive qualities. His civic-mindedness and sincere desire for progress lead him to make a heroic, ultimately successful effort to combat cholera in his community. On a personal level, he treats the frightened Fermina with great tenderness during the first days of their marriage, which provides a solid foundation for love to develop. She does come to love Urbino, and on the day of his death—which occurs in a decidedly ridiculous way for such a dignified man— he manages to stay alive long enough to tell her how much he has loved her. Many critics contrast Urbino with Florentino, particularly in regard to reading. While Urbino owns a set of finely bound classics that he reads because he is supposed to read them, Florentino devours a wide variety of books with great gusto, whether they are ancient Greek poetry or the latest pulp novel.

Themes

Love

Love in the Time of Cholera tells the story of the life-long love of the illegitimate, and once poor,

Topics for Further Study

- What is the significance of the title of the novel?

- How does García Márquez debunk stereotypical notions of love in the novel?

- Discuss García Márquez's use of humor in the novel.

- Research the period of transition from colonialism to modernity in Colombian history and discuss its depiction in the novel.

Florentino Ariza for Fermina Daza. Their teenage love had been sustained largely by his letters as she was sent away by her ambitious father. But when they suddenly met after this long separation, her "illusion" of love, as she then saw it, was immediately dispelled. She rejected him to marry, although also after a period of rejection, the socially well-placed Dr. Juvenal Urbino. Much of the book is taken up with a study of this marriage and of the many affairs by which Florentino tries to fill the space left by Fermina while waiting one day to possess her. Urbino's death in his eighties allows Florentino to resume his courtship of and eventual marriage to Fermina. The novel's major themes are thus concerned with love and passion as well as aging, decay, and death.

From one point of view the marriage of Urbino and Fermina is merely a fifty-year interruption of Florentino's courtship. Yet it also proves to be the route to the final romance, since both characters develop significantly from their experiences during this period. It is the marriage that gives Fermina her realistic appreciation of romance. Marriage is not merely an obstacle. The relationship has been passionate, affectionate, boring, angry, and desperate.

The novel is thus a celebration of the many kinds of love between men and women. In part it is a brilliant account of a long marriage; elsewhere it is a tale of love finding erotic fulfillment in old age. In relating both the story of Fermina Daza's marriage and her later courtship, *Love in the Time of Cholera* is a novel about commitment and fidelity under circumstances that would seem to render such virtues absurd. It is also about a refusal to grow old gracefully and respectably.

A central idea of the novel is the primacy of passion and feeling over order, honor, duty, and authority. Love and sexual desire control, invigorate, and at times lay havoc upon lives. Sometimes the participants are burnt up as if by cholera, after which they may completely recover, may be extinguished, or, as with Florentino, may linger on in a state of perpetual convalescence. In García Márquez's work, life and love are shown as unpredictable and turbulent, forever surging and overflowing their bounds.

Aging and Decay
Death

Aside from love, the process of aging, decay, and death is *Love in the Time of Cholera*'s most important theme, and the two are linked in a defiance of society's prejudice against the sexuality of the elderly. García Márquez keenly observes the process of aging and continually brings up the details of its encroachment. At the same time he proclaims a dignified old age and the right to companionship and pleasure. Fermina Daza's two children are typical of society's cruel and thoughtless attitudes about sexuality and aging. In typical García Márquez fashion, there is a circular pattern to aging as presented in the novel, and the author observes on many occasions the return to characteristics of infancy and the reversal of the roles of parents and children.

Florentino is both intense about love and philosophical about age. Florentino sees death as a bottomless pit where memory trickles away. He is a patient man, and the delicacy with which he seduces Fermina, and the nature of their companionship during the final stage of their long lives defies shallow stereotypes. The novel is a meditation on decay, old age, and the dying process. The main characters' biographies are laid out from childhood to near death. They reveal lives actually lived, and the means by which memory can transfigure, keep alive, and obliterate both the pain and passion of the past.

Style

Narration

In *Love in the Time of Cholera*, although the narrative is in third person—the impersonal "he" or "she" performing the action—García Márquez

frequently withholds omniscient insight from his characters. In the novel the author suggests the unknowability of one's true feelings and the corresponding impossibility of summing up a relationship. Its six chapters progress smoothly along a linear path, punctuated by frequent asides and repeated flashbacks. The story is told by a single narrative voice, which recounts certain events in duplicate in order to represent the overlapping experiences of its multiple protagonists.

The letters of Florentino are a central narrative device defining the emotional ambivalence of the romantic experience. They are a way of balancing and connecting the kinds of truth and falsehood in romance. His early letters, along with Fermina's subsequent rejection of him, suggest the dangers of delusion. Yet in the long run the impulse of these letters is vindicated when he finds a newly realistic mode of expression. He has to learn that the bubble of romance bursts when its truth is too crudely counted on, or rendered literal. Fermina is so struck by the wisdom of the later letters that she decides to keep them as a series and to think of them as a book. Thus through the device of correspondence, which becomes García Márquez's book, there is a reminder of the origin of the novel in the epistolary genre—the novel of letters—from the eighteenth century.

In the eighteenth century, this device was usually a way of exploring levels of sincerity in the character's self-portrayal while retaining the illusion of reality. While Marquez does not use the letters as the narrative medium, he does firmly place them within his own third-person narrative frame. Rather than reinforcing the realistic effect of the narrative, the letters provide a brief escape from such an effect.

Using the device of the letters the narrative progresses in a series of flashbacks. From one perspective, the marriage of Urbino and Fermina is merely a fifty-year interruption of Florentino's courtship. And the flashback technique treats it as such. Yet it also proves to be the route to the final romance, since both characters develop significantly during this period. It is the marriage that gives Fermina her realistic approach to romance; thus it is not merely an obstacle. Thus the narrator is at all times humorously aware both of the fundamental struggle between romance and reality and of their inextricable connection. This is apparent in the young Florentino's business letters: "Florentino Ariza would write anything with so much passion that even official documents seemed to be about love."

Structure

Various patterns of time and structural symmetries have their indispensable role in shaping *Love in the Time of Cholera.* The narrative starts out with a death in the "present," in this case approximately 1931; a long flashback of over fifty years takes up chapters 2-4 and most of chapter 5, the concluding pages of which then pick up on the dangling thread from chapter 1; chapter 6 then proceeds with the final courtship and romance.

Many parallel threads are woven into the texture of the novel, but among the most important is the set of deflowerings of Florentino and Fermina, both in chapter 3, on his and her respective boat trips, and in each case with more experienced and aggressive sexual partners. Their own consummation of their love will likewise take place on board ship, three chapters and five decades later. The opening suicide of Jeremiah de Saint-Amour, motivated not by love but by dislike of old age, is contrasted with the suicide of rejected lover América Vicuña toward the end of the novel.

Setting

Although set ten to twenty years before the turn of the century, *Love in the Time of Cholera* shows a decidedly modern sensibility. It focuses on an urban rather than a rural society, and shows it with less mysticism and more social detail than in García Márquez's earlier works. In an unnamed Caribbean city, a "sleepy provincial capital" thought to be a composite of the actual Colombian cities of Cartagena and Baranquilla, there is a fictional leap from the imaginary village of Macondo in *One Hundred Years of Solitude* that is significant. Macondo, fully created, can stand for much larger universes, but it is mostly, fundamentally, itself. The unnamed coastal Caribbean city of the later novel can never truly remain imaginative. It seems too real. It holds the resonance and reality of many deaths before the story even begins. It is a city with a history of slavery, civil wars, and cholera epidemics for over a half century, a desolate landscape against which the destinies of the major characters are played out; and decay is part of this landscape of putrefying swamps, old slave quarters, and cadavers.

Historical Context

Colombia

Located in the northwest of South America, Colombia is a Spanish-speaking country that was part of the Spanish conquest of the sixteenth century. The landscape is dominated by the Andes Mountains in the west, the plains of the east, and the lowlands of the Caribbean coast, where most of the action of *Love in the Time of Cholera* is set. Early Spanish explorers Rodrigo de Bastidas and Francisco Pizarro first mapped the Colombian coastland, and the port city of Cartagena was founded by Pedro de Heredia in 1533. Under Spanish rule in the sixteenth, seventeenth, and eighteenth centuries, the native populations were forced into slavery or the *encomienda,* in which the taxes they paid to the Spanish government kept them in a kind of indentured servitude. Intermarriage between Spanish colonists and natives soon led to the destruction of many of the native population's special tribal characteristics, but also led to a growing class of *mestizos,* or people of mixed-race descent. Today almost 60% of Colombia's population is mestizo.

Spanish domination continued in Colombia as well as much of South America until the early 1800s. Then Colombia, as part of the viceroyalty of New Granada (which also included parts of Venezuela and Ecuador), took advantage of France's invasion of Spain to throw out their local Spanish governmental officials. A Bogotá uprising that occurred on July 20, 1810, is now celebrated as Colombia's Independence Day. Although Spain attempted to reconquer the territory in the mid-1810s, military leader Simón Bolívar led a united force of South Americans to several decisive victories over the Spanish in 1819, 1821, and 1822. The Republic of Colombia was born, and gained its present borders after the secession of Venezuela and Ecuador in 1830 and the secession of Panama in 1903.

Colombia underwent several periods of civil unrest in the 1800s, as Liberal and Conservative parties battled over the composition of the government, the role of the church, and how to share power between the two parties. The country suffered a civil war from 1840 to 1842, and again from 1899 to 1902. During this time, several constitutions were adopted, and internal political struggles often consumed the country's efforts. The most recent constitution was adopted in 1991, which provides for a system like that of the United States, with a popularly elected president, a two-body legislature, and a supreme court. Although Colombia's drug trafficking trade has received much publicity, the country currently has a diversified economy that is the most consistent on the continent, with important industries in oil, textiles, food process-

Compare & Contrast

- **Colombia:** A country of almost 37 million, Colombia has a life expectancy rate of 72.8 years, an infant mortality rate of 25.8 deaths/1,000 live births, and a literacy rate of 91.3%.

  United States: A country of over 266 million, the United States has a life expectancy rate of 75.95 years, an infant mortality rate of 6.7 deaths/1,000 live births, and a literacy rate of 97%.

- **Colombia:** With an economy based on oil and agricultural products, Colombia has a gross domestic product of $5,300 per person, one of the best in South America.

  United States: With a diverse economy involving technological, industrial, and agricul-

tural products, the United States has a gross domestic product of $27,500, the highest among major industrial nations.

- **Colombia:** After a history that includes Spanish colonial rule and several civil wars, Colombia's population is 58% mestizo (mixed white-Indian), 20% white, 14% mixed black-white, 4% black, 3% mixed black-Indian, and 1% Indian.

  United States: With a history that includes forced importation of African slaves as well as frequent immigration, recent censuses put the U.S. population at 83.4% white, 12.4% black, 3.3% Asian, and 0.8% Native American, although more and more people argue for the inclusion of "mixed-race" as a category for the next census.

---

ing, clothing, chemicals, and beverages (such as coffee).

Colonialism and Postcolonialism

Set in an unnamed town on the coast of Colombia, *Love in the Time of Cholera* spans the years from the late nineteenth century to the 1930s—the time of transition from the colonial to the modern period. On the edge of town are old slave quarters, where buzzards fight over the slaughterhouse remains. Cadavers are everywhere, some dead of cholera and others in the wars. The novel is not only about the past but also about the anachronistic lifestyle that still survives in the ruins left by nineteenth-century progress. In this respect, the novel shares the *fin de siecle,* or "end of century," mood of much contemporary Latin American writing.

The social fabric represented in the novel consists of two major groups: the Social Club (upper class) and the Commercial Club (middle class). The three main characters also embody their respective backgrounds—Dr. Urbino, with his two family names, from the old colonial elite; Fermina, the beautiful representative of the new breed of capi-

talists who seek high standing in the young republic; and Florentino, illegitimate but connected by birth to a more modern and reputable shipping enterprise that nevertheless ravages the forest environment whose populations it largely serves. In order to account for Florentino, Fermina and Juvenal's backgrounds, the novel extends some sixty years back into the past; at the same time it registers the principal social developments shaping the life of the community during the period concerned, and surveys the political history of Colombia since the country obtained independence in 1819. A still more remote perspective encompassing the period of Spanish colonial rule completes the range of temporal references in the book.

The novel thus embraces considerations of history, politics, class, race and culture, in literal as well as symbolic terms. From a detailed historical vantage point, the narrative evokes the era of Spanish colonial rule in the mid-sixteenth century as a time of prosperity for the local merchant class and, on a wider scale, as a period of slavery and abuse by the Inquisition. Hazardous open sewers inherited from the Spanish are a clear reminder of the

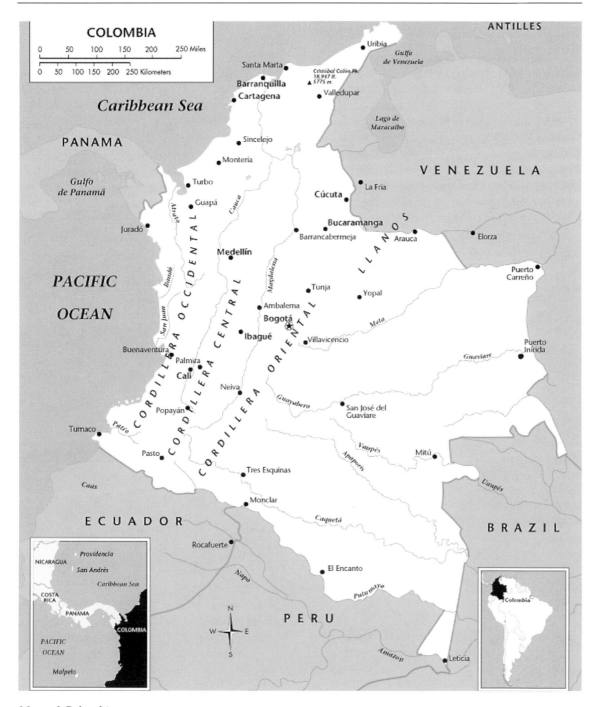

Map of Colombia.

colonial heritage of a city that "had now existed on the margins of history ... for four hundred years." The vision of inertia also holds true for the post-colonial era, as the experience of Juvenal Urbino's family illustrates: "Independence from Spanish rule, followed by the abolition of slavery, precipi-

tated the circumstances of honorable decline in which [Juvenal] was born and grew up." Marquez dramatizes the juncture in the history of families that had been influential in the past and sought refuge in the artificial order of social snobbery, racial prejudice, and political corruption.

Critical Overview

When *Love in the Time of Cholera* first appeared in 1985, it was an immediate success and won wide critical acclaim. Translated into English in 1988, it was a selection of the Book-of-the-Month Club in the United States and remained on the *New York Times* best-seller list for many weeks. García Márquez also received the *Los Angeles Times* Book Prize for fiction in 1988 for *Love in the Time of Cholera.* Critics noted the many varieties of love depicted in the novel. Jean Franco in *The Nation* stated that the novel "is not only about the past but also about the anachronistic life forms that still survive in the ruins left by nineteenth-century progress. In this respect, the novel shares in the *fin de siecle* ['end of century'] mood of much contemporary Latin American writing." In relating both the story of Fermina Daza's marriage and her later courtship, S. M. J. Minta of the *Times Literary Supplement* stated that it was a "novel about commitment and fidelity under circumstances which seem to render such virtues absurd."

Some observers claimed that García Márquez was unconvincing in his portrayal of romantic love. As Angela Carter remarked in the *Washington Post Book World,* the novel "seems to deal more with libido and self-deceit than with desire and mortality." Yet critic Michael Wood in the *New York Review of Books* wrote that "love is a disease in this book, and this is a romantic novel; but the disease is one of the self-deluding, stubborn will, a fruit of mythology and obstinacy rather than any fate beyond ourselves." He goes on to say that the novel, "like García Márquez's other novels, is an exploration of destiny but of *this* kind of destiny: the kind we invent and displace and fear and desperately live up to or die for."

Countering criticisms that the work was overemotional, S. M. J. Minta claimed that "the triumph of the novel is that it uncovers the massive, submerged strength of the popular, the cliched and the sentimental." Author Thomas Pynchon, writing in the *New York Times Book Review,* commented that "The Garcimarquesian voice we have come to recognize from the other fiction has matured, found and developed new resources." He concluded by saying, "There is nothing I have read quite like [the] astonishing final chapter," and called *Love in the Time of Cholera* a "shining and heartbreaking novel." Paul Bailey of *The Listener* said that the novel is García Márquez's most "deeply considered and satisfyingly ambitious novel—the best, in my view, that Marquez has written." According to

Mona Simpson in the *London Review of Books,* the novel "has brought a new depth to the meaning of the word 'magic.'" She continues, "This is not a story of boy meets girl, boy gets her back. García Márquez, as ever, remains stubbornly committed to the voice of the community: individual happiness is not considered an absolute good."

Later critics generally continue to extol the virtues of the work, even while pointing out some of its shortcomings. Gene H. Bell-Villada, in *García Márquez: The Man and His Work,* states that "it is perhaps no paradox that *Love* is García Márquez's most joyous book—and also his least disciplined or rigorous. Yet it is a novel that stays in the mind, producing a deep and lasting glow of satisfaction *after* being read, and the outer chapters are as beautiful and artful as anything ever fashioned by the author." Michael Bell, in *Gabriel García Márquez: Solitude and Solitary,* comments that the novel is García Márquez's "most striking attempt to square the circle; to write a genuinely popular and accessible romance while maintaining, if only to challenge, the sophistication of a high modernist consciousness."

Criticism

Jeffrey M. Lilburn

In the following essay, Lilburn, a teaching assistant at the University of Western Ontario, examines how García Márquez uses the conventions of sentimental romance stories to explore deeper themes and even satirize popular conceptions of love.

It is tempting to read Gabriel García Márquez's *Love in the Time of Cholera* as a romantic and sentimental story in which love prevails over time and death, and patience and devotion are rewarded with a happy ending. The temptation derives from García Márquez's misleading narrative that invites, or rather deceivingly manipulates readers into believing that Florentino Ariza and Fermina Daza's belated union represents a victory over individual and societal adversities, prejudices and conventions. However, disguised beneath the surface of the melodramatic plot lies a critical, sometimes satiric examination of many of the elements that appear to contribute to the novel's charm, but actually undercut much of its romanticism and sentimentality. In addition to the themes of love, aging and disease highlighted in the novel's title, the text also explores issues such as suicide, gerontophobia (the fear of ageing), dishonesty, modernization, and social and environmental responsibility. The novel does celebrate human love and sexuality—at any age—but it does so while revealing many of the repercussions that may result from false or unrealistic notions of what love is.

Critical analyses of García Márquez's novels often include a discussion of magic realism—the interweaving of realism with the fantastic and the surreal. *Love in the Time of Cholera* does contain certain elements of magic realism, but they are less prominent than in previous works. As a result, it is usually examined without an extensive discussion of magic realism. Instead, most critics tend to agree that the novel blends social realism with elements of sentimental literature. One recent discussion by Claudette Kemper Columbus, for example, has suggested that the novel, which is set in the final decades of the nineteenth century and first decades of the twentieth century, is a satire aimed at supposedly enlightened societies on the verge of entering the twenty-first century. And another critic, Robin Fiddian, has read the novel as a reflection on the moral and ideological shortsightedness that threatens the future of South America.

A need for social change is implied through the novel's opening scene. Jeremiah de Saint-Amour's suicide is motivated by the fear of growing old and alludes to a difficult and, for some, troubling question: can old age be an exciting and productive period of human life? Jeremiah de Saint-Amour obviously did not think so, and planned years ahead to end his life when he turned sixty. It becomes evident throughout the novel that Saint-Amour's fears about old age are shared by many in his society. Fermina Daza's daughter, Ofelia, becomes extremely upset when she learns that her elderly mother has a "strange friendship" with a man: "love is ridiculous at our age," she shouts to her brother and his wife, "but at theirs it is revolting." Dr. Urbino Daza, Fermina's son, initially supports the relationship because of the "good companionship" it gives his mother and begs Florentino to continue seeing her "for the good of them both and the convenience of all." However, he reveals his true feelings about the elderly when he and Florentino get together over lunch; he explains that the world would make more rapid progress without the burden of old people because "humanity, like armies in the field, advances at the speed of the slowest."

The societal attitude towards old age is perhaps best summed up by an "absent-minded voice" which is overheard making a comment about Dr.

What Do I Read Next?

- For an excellent study of old age, with considerable attention given to sexuality, see Simone de Beauvoir's *The Coming of Age* (1972).

- In *One Hundred Years of Solitude* (1970), García Márquez's best known and highly acclaimed novel, the author employs the technique of "magical realism," which blends the real with the fantastic in a comic masterpiece that chronicles six generations of a family in the town of Macondo, a microcosm of Colombia.

- *The Autumn of the Patriarch* is García Márquez's 1975 novel about the evils of despotism as embodied in a solitary dictator.

- One of his collections of short stories, *No One Writes to the Colonel and Other Stories* (1968) features García Márquez's short fiction written during the early 1960s. Critics often commend the stories in this volume.

- *Chronicle of a Death Foretold* (1982) is García Márquez's fictionalized journalistic investigation of Chile's Pinochet regime. The novella profiles a society trapped in its own myths.

- In *The Last Song of Manuel Sendero* (1987), Ariel Dorfman, a Chilean novelist and playwright, combines the real and the surreal in this novel about love, tyranny, freedom, and the anguish of exile.

- *Violence, Conflict and Politics in Colombia* (1980), by Paul H. Oquist offers some insights into the history and politics that shaped the fiction of García Márquez.

Urbino's rapidly ripening corpse: "at that age you're half decayed while you're still alive." Florentino and Fermina's union at the novel's end transcends these prejudices and unjust social conventions and suggests that one's later years can be a vital and exciting time in one's life. But transcendence does not induce change, and while Florentino and Fermina do discover that love is "always love, anytime and anyplace," their reluctance to return home at the end of their journey suggests a surrender to societal expectations.

This less than perfect ending puts into question readings of the novel that emphasize the individual happiness of Fermina and Florentino over the state of the world around them. It also forces the reader to reconsider the entire text: what may have initially appeared to be an innocent story about love, may not be. M. Keith Booker has demonstrated that the novel provides warnings against "gullibility in reading," and indeed, there are several incidents early in *Love in the Time of Cholera* that inform the reader that appearances can be deceiving. For instance, it is only after Saint-Amour's death that Dr. Urbino discovers that his friend was not the man "without a past" he thought him to be, but a fugitive from Cayenne who had eaten human flesh. The lingering aroma of gold cyanide that meets Dr. Urbino when he arrives on the scene of the suicide is also misleading. The scent of bitter almonds always reminds the doctor of unrequited love but, as the reader soon learns, Saint-Amour's suicide is not motivated by love but by submission to an all too common fear—gerontophobia. When discussing the death with his wife, Dr. Urbino reveals that it is not so much what Saint-Amour did that infuriates him, but the deception he practiced on him for so many years. Even Dr. Urbino, a man whose "narrowness of mind was out of tune with his public image," is himself an example of the ease with which appearance may be confused with reality.

Similarly, the spell Florentino Ariza falls under when he meets Fermina Daza is not what it appears to be—it is not an example of romantic love. He does not fall in love with Fermina's true virtues and sentiments, but with an image or illusion he creates by "endowing her with improbable virtues and imaginary sentiments." In other words, he idealizes her. It is this unrealistic conception of Fermina that leads to a half-century of waiting, watching and stalking. Booker has suggested that such unrealistic visions are what doom Florentino Ariza and Fermina Daza's riverboat journey at the end of the novel. Florentino Ariza had often received alarming reports about the state of the river but "never took the trouble to think about it." As a result, his plan to sail "forever" under the yellow quarantine flag is an impossibility because uncontrolled deforestation has left no trees to fuel the boat. Florentino's refusal to consider the reality of imminent environmental devastation destroys both the Magdalena River, and his own happy ending.

Critics have interpreted "the time of cholera" in the novel's title in various ways. Many equate the time of cholera with the time of romantic love and suggest that, in this text, love is a disease. The title might also be a metaphor for what Claudette Kemper Columbus describes as a "diseased society and social irresponsibility." And it is true that both Florentino Ariza and Dr. Urbino are guilty of social obliviousness and neglect. Dr. Urbino is a man of refined tastes who is up to date with all the latest European ideas and who is, as suggested by Mabel Morana, associated with modernization. But he is often blind to the realities that surround him because, for him, reality exists someplace else. Upon his return from Europe, for example, he subscribes "to Le Figaro, so he would not lose touch with reality." Florentino's social obliviousness can be explained, in part, by his susceptibility to the influence of sentimental love poetry. His letters to Fermina Daza are "inspired by the books he had learned by heart" and reveal a man who has become buried in the values of the past. But Florentino is guilty of more than simple neglect. His selfishness is often the direct cause of other people's suffering and death.

The narrator only describes a very small fraction of his six hundred and twenty-two long-term affairs, but of the ones he does relate, several offer a picture of a man less than deserving of Fermina's—or any woman's—love. It might be argued that Florentino's numerous affairs provide a positive model for free love, but he does more than fill his time with one-night-stands. One of Florentino's lovers, Olimpia Zuleta, is murdered by her husband when she inadvertently shows him the possessive inscription that Florentino painted on her belly. It is also revealed late in the novel that Florentino is a rapist who, after impregnating a maid behind his house, bribes her to put the blame on her innocent sweetheart. Perhaps most condemning is Florentino's seduction of América Vicuña, his fourteen-year-old blood relative who is entrusted to him while she attends secondary school. What is most disturbing in his relationship with this girl is the manipulation he uses to create the illusion of acquiescence. When he meets her, she is still a little girl with "the scrapes of elementary school on her knees," but Florentino spends a year cultivating her with ice cream and childish afternoons, until finally winning her confidence and affection. She commits suicide while he is on the riverboat with Fermina Daza—another of the women he manipulates.

From the time he receives Fermina's letter of insults, Florentino begins to devise a new strategy—a "new method of seduction." He plans everything "down to the last detail, as if it were the final battle." He departs from his usual imitative writing style and composes an extensive meditation on life which he disguises in the patriarchal style of an old man's memories. The letters help Fermina find new reasons to go on living, but Florentino's cunning plans complicate what she interprets as heartfelt emotions. He is also dishonest with her in person; when she asks him why he never competed in the Poetic Festivals, he "lies to her" and says that he "wrote only for her." It is true that part of his intention is to give Fermina the courage to "discard the prejudices" of society, and to "think of love as a state of grace," but his contemptible past makes it impossible to differentiate his good motives from his selfish, destructive ones.

Despite Florentino's manipulations, Fermina is the one character who recognizes that something is not quite right in her relationship with Florentino. Although she defies social conventions by entering into a romantic relationship at an age most people consider too old for such things, her repeated thoughts about another elderly couple who are murdered while vacationing on board a boat invite comparisons between the two couples. The murdered couple were clandestine lovers who maintained a relationship for forty years despite the fact that each of them was happily married to someone else. Contrasted with the love between Florentino and Fermina, a love that Fermina recognized was illusory over fifty years ago, the other couple's long-lasting relationship recalls the illicit love described by Saint-Amour's lover: hers was a life shared with a man who was never completely hers but in which she "often knew the sudden explosion of happiness." Moreover, their story shows that Florentino's plan to evade reality by refusing to ever go back home is not a viable solution. The fact that the other elderly couple are murdered on board a boat suggests that an idealistic, neverending river cruise that does nothing to break down the conventions and beliefs of the rest of society will not protect Fermina and Florentino from the prejudices that continue to exist along the shores. Eventually, those prejudices will come to them.

Source: Jeffrey M. Lilburn, in an essay for *Novels for Students*, Gale, 1997.

Jean Franco

In this review, Franco notes that in Love in the Time of Cholera *García Márquez sets his love story against a background of decay and mortality, explaining that "the humor and pathos of ag-*

ing and death are subjects that have obsessed García Márquez from his earliest writings."

In 1948, as a young journalist in Barranquilla, Gabriel García Márquez amused his readers by comparing love to a liver disease that could lead to the fatal complication of suicide. Four decades later, he recognizes that it is love that keeps readers turning the pages. That is why, despite its apocalyptic undertones, *Love in the Time of Cholera* has already sold over a million copies in Europe and Latin America.

Set in a stagnant tropical port at the turn of the century, *Love in the Time of Cholera* tells the story of Florentino Ariza's prolonged passion for Fermina Daza, a passion that is finally consummated after fifty years, nine months and four days, when they are both over 70 years old. The consummation takes place on a riverboat that flies the cholera flag in order to protect their privacy. When Fermina undresses, Florentino finds her "just as he imagined her. Her shoulders were wrinkled, her breasts sagged, her ribs were covered by a flabby skin as pale and cold as a frog's"—which does not prevent him from exploring "her withered neck with his fingertips, her bosom armored in metal stays, her hips with their decaying bones, her thighs with their aging veins." The boat cannot land because of the cholera flag, so the couple, enjoying "the tranquil, wholesome love of experienced grandparents," are destined to live out their lives perpetually journeying up and down the river through a calamitous and ruined landscape, clinging hopefully to the last vestiges of life.

The humor of this autumnal romance cannot, however, dispel the odor of mortality. On the very first page, the reader is greeted "with the aromatic fumes of gold cyanide" and the suicide of the Caribbean refugee Jeremiah de Saint-Amour. The doctor who writes the death certificate is Fermina Daza's 81-year-old husband, Juvenal Urbino, who hours later is killed falling from a ladder as he tries to coax a parrot from a tree. It is at the funeral that Florentino renews a courtship he had begun half a century earlier.

The novel retraces the story of their love and separation: Fermina's adolescence under the jealous guardianship of a father who had made his money in contraband and wanted her to be a great lady; her brief engagement to the illegitimate and lowly Florentino; her marriage to the brilliant European-educated doctor Juvenal Urbino; and her then exemplary life (marred only by a two-year separation caused by her husband's infidelity). Meanwhile, Florentino has a brilliant career with the riverboat company and becomes an impenitent and bizarre womanizer who, when he is over 60, is capable of assaulting a maid "in less time than a Philippino rooster" and leaving her in the family way. His lovers include a 50-year-old widow who receives him stark naked with an organdy bow in her hair, an escapee from the lunatic asylum and, when he is over 70, a schoolgirl "with braces on her teeth and the scrapes of elementary school on her knees."

The humor and pathos of aging and death are subjects that have obsessed García Márquez from his earliest writings. His first novel, *Leafstorm,* was about a funeral. In *One Hundred Years of Solitude,* there are dozens of tiny vignettes of death—Amaranta Úrsula preparing her own shroud, José Arcadio Buendía's dying dream of walking through room after room until he meets the man he has killed, and the matriarch, Úrsula, concealing her blindness from her children before lucidly dying. In *Love in the Time of Cholera* bodies fail long before passions are spent. Florentino goes bald when he is still young. He suffers from blennorrhea, a swollen lymph gland, four warts and six cases of impetigo in the groin. When Dr. Urbino begins to lapse into senility, Fermina "helped him to dress: she sprinkled talcum powder between his legs, she smoothed cocoa butter on his rashes, she helped him put on his undershorts with as much love as if they had been a diaper, and continued dressing him item by item, from his socks to the knot in his tie with the topaz pin." On their riverboat idyll, she helped Florentino "to take his enemas, she got up before he did to brush the false teeth he kept in a glass while he slept and she solved the problem of her misplaced spectacles, for she could use his for reading and mending." Both of them, by this time, have the "sour smell of old age."

Decay is part of the landscape. The colonial Caribbean port where Fermina and Florentino pass most of their lives is familiar García Márquez territory. It was in towns such as this that he wrote his first sketches for a novel in the late 1940s and which he chronicled as a journalist in Barranquilla and Cartagena. It was here that he collected the repertoire of legend, anecdote, small-town boredom and eccentricity that he has drawn on ever since. Not that there is any nostalgia in *Love in the Time of Cholera,* which moves from the stagnation of colonialism to the devastation of modernity in the time it takes to turn a page. Although the cobbled streets of the city recall "surprise attacks and buccaneer landings," "nothing had happened for

four centuries except a slow aging among withered laurels and putrefying swamps." On the edge of the town are the old slave quarters, where buzzards fight over the offal from the slaughterhouse. Cadavers are everywhere, some dead of cholera and others in the wars. Returning from his studies in Paris, Dr. Urbino sails into a bay "through a floating blanket of drowned animals." "The ocean looked like ashes, the old palaces of the marquises were about to succumb to a proliferation of beggars, and it was impossible to discern the ardent scent of jasmine behind the vapors of death from the open sewers." On a trip that Florentino takes upriver in an effort to forget Fermina, he sees "three bloated, green human corpses float past, with buzzards sitting on them"; when Fermina and Juvenal Urbino take a balloon ride to celebrate the year 1900, they look down on banana plantations strewn with the bodies of workers who have been summarily executed.

By the end of the novel and its "happy ending," the mood is paradoxically apocalyptic. Fermina and Florentino's love boat, which once had steamed through an idyllic landscape, now passes "calcinated flatlands stripped of entire forests." The manatees "with their great breasts that had nursed their young and wept on the banks in a forlorn woman's voice were an extinct species, annihilated by the armored bullets of hunters for sport." Natural life has almost disappeared, "the parrots, the monkeys, the villages were gone, everything was gone."

For this is the irony of García Márquez's novel—that the genial good humor disguises apocalyptic foreboding. The same civilization that idealizes lovers produces a global wasteland, and the private fantasies of romance are rafts on a sea of public devastation. Fermina and Florentino salvage their own idyll but are themselves part of the destruction, a last nineteenth-century romance that can only find a heart of darkness (not for nothing is Joseph Conrad a character in the novel; he is accused of cheating Fermina Daza's father in a shady arms deal). Fermina and Florentino's love boat, indeed, adds to the devastation, since it has polluted the river waters and consumes the last of the forests on the riverbanks. It is this ambiguous relationship of private felicity and mass destruction that provides the novel with its disturbing undertow.

In his novels, García Márquez constantly returns to one particular historical period—from independence to the first decades of the twentieth century. It is the hundred years of Macondo in *One Hundred Years of Solitude* and of the dictatorship in *The Autumn of the Patriarch.* What fascinates him, evidently, is the meeting of fierce Latin idiosyncrasy with rationalism and modernity. Yet *Love in the Time of Cholera* is not only about the past but also about the anachronistic life forms that still survive in the ruins left by nineteenth-century progress. In this respect, the novel shares the *fin de siècle* mood of much contemporary Latin American writing.

Source: Jean Franco, "Mementos Mori," in *The Nation, New York,* Vol. 246, No. 16, April 23, 1988, pp. 573–74.

Richard Eder

In the following review, Eder places Love in the Time of Cholera *in the tradition of magic realism, explaining that in the static, inert world of García Márquez's novel "the sole principle of order … consists of the extraordinary sweetness he finds in his characters."*

The city, ancient, decaying, tropical, lies at the mouth of Colombia's Magdalena River. Weeds grow in the cracks of 17th-Century palaces; the sewers are open, and the corpses of victims of endemic cholera float downstream from the hinterland. It is a city "where flowers rusted and salt corroded."

It is scene of Gabriel García Márquez's magnificent new novel, *Love in the Time of Cholera,* a book that moves a triple romance, spanning more than a half-century, through a rich, comical and totally still world that could be the dream of a prodigious sleeper lashed to the bed.

García Márquez's universe is organized around a fundamental element: stasis. It replaces oxygen, it produces a brilliant anaerobic life. It has a tacit political connotation. The evolution of liberal, capitalist, consumerist Westernism has submerged the authentic life of the Latin American Third World, while remaining alien to it. Perhaps only a revolution will deliver it. García Márquez, a leftist, doesn't say. Meanwhile, it will remain inert.

Inert in everything except the imagination. Magic realism is what moves when nothing else does. It is what a stage director looks for when he instructs a performer to keep the hands or feet still; to bind them, so that the features or shoulders can make a more expressive performance. García Márquez's art is a mighty transfiguration of these bound movements.

There is no external order. There are no proportions, limits or hierarchies of logic or feeling. Everything is tangled together, and when you fin-

ger a thread, you have no idea what it will be attached to. There are no roads in this artist's jungle because there are no destinations. There is profuse life that goes on in spite of the absurd and ramshackle forms assigned to it.

The sole principle of order belongs to García Márquez. It consists of the extraordinary sweetness he finds in his characters; a sweetness that provides energy, and does not cloy, thanks to his feverish spirit of play and his willingness to let his tall tales grow taller.

Love's 50 years center around the turn of the century. The city, loosely modeled on a mix of Cartagena and Barranquilla, is a microcosm of Colombian provincial society with its extremes of extravagantly moneyed families, abject poverty, recurring civil war between liberals and conservatives, a superficial faith in progress, and a monumental inertia.

A Spanish galleon lies, according to legend, at the bottom of the mouth of the Magdalena, with a cargo of gold and jewels valued in the billions. (As in any dream, all figures are vastly inflated; one of the three main characters numbers his love affairs at more than 600.) The image hovers throughout: a fabulous sunken treasure stuck like a plug to bottle up the energies of a people and their river.

The three sides of the love triangle are occupied by three prominent citizens. There is Juvenal Urbino, scion of a mighty family, the town's leading doctor and the herald of all kinds of progressive ideas that he has used to damp down the periodic epidemics of cholera.

Fermina Daza, his wife, is the daughter of an immigrant Spaniard, a nobody who made a fortune in various unsavory ways. Snubbed at first by local society, she has become one of its pillars and the patroness of its artistic life.

Florentino Ariza, a poet and musician by temperament, has worked his way up to wealth and power in the riverboat company founded by his uncle. He has been hopelessly in love with Fermina since they were both teen-agers, but since a man needs relief, he has prowled the city for 50 years picking up women.

So much for their public personas. But in García Márquez's country, the externals have no solidity. Juvenal, Fermina and Florentino are fey and unpredictable spirits, haunting rather than inhabiting their positions, their clothes, their habits and even their dispositions. The play of the book is the play of these free spirits in and out of their own constrained lives.

The book starts a year or two before the climax that will end it. Juvenal, in his 80s, falls off a stepladder while trying to catch his pet parrot. He dies with such an expression of terror that plans for a death mask have to be canceled. His terror is not for himself but for the thought that Fermina, after 50 years, will have to manage alone.

After the funeral, Florentino appears with his black suit, stiff collar and a strand of hair brilliantined across his bald pate. He reiterates his life-long passion to Fermina—they are both in their 70s—and in shock and outrage, she throws him out.

It is an explosive beginning, though here as always, García Márquez laces his detonations with diversions and side-trips. We then go back in time, following the trio from youth to old age. Their stories snake in and out against the tropical background.

Florentino, pale and nervous, gets a shaky start with his uncle. His business letters are poetry; he switches to telegraphy and works his way up. He is splendidly suited to business, in fact, except when it involves writing. It is the author's conceit that the poetic mind is ideal for a businessman's incursions upon reality.

Florentino spots Fermina, closely chaperoned by her aunt. He gets up the courage to write to her. They correspond passionately, even when her father finds out and sends her to stay with relatives in the backland. Florentino uses his fellow telegraphers around the country to relay messages.

The passion is total, and totally abstract. Upon her return, Fermina suddenly sees Florentino in all his awkwardness; she switches to the urbane and assured Juvenal, just back from Europe. Perhaps the finest thing in the book is García Márquez's story of a long, fractious, funny and powerful marriage. The quarrels are memorable; an argument over whether Fermina has put soap in the bathroom leads Juvenal to sleep at the hospital for several months.

All the servitude, conventionality and weight of a provincial Latin American marriage is there; yet underneath it, two free spirits flutter in utter originality. Society's two pillars are light as air, as erratic as a tropical breeze. Florentino, meanwhile, pursues his 600 affairs, many of them quite lunatic. Their chronicling eventually seems repetitious and even burdensome, despite their wit and quirkiness.

But if the richness of García Márquez's textures feels briefly excessive, the book's ending has a brilliance and audacity that more than makes up for it.

After Juvenal's death, and after Florentino's unceremonious rejection, the cycle of courtship begins all over again. He writes Fermina letter after letter. They are cool and philosophic, as befits a septuagenarian, and slowly they fill the emptiness that Juvenal's death has made in his widow's life.

Even so, it takes 140 letters—García Márquez's extravagant numbers again—before she replies. A slow courtship ensues; a seduction that is gentle, quiet and astonishingly adapted to the infirmities of two aged bodies. The author gives us geriatric sex aboard riverboat, and makes it deeply comic and deeply moving.

Finally, through a series of bizarre incidents, the ancient couple are set to cruise for the rest of their lives up and down the Magdalena. It is entirely real and entirely magical. It is not so much an ending as a triumphant departure in a balloon.

Love in the Time of Cholera, beautifully translated by Edith Grossman, may be García Márquez's best work since *One Hundred Years of Solitude.* If the tigers in his Rousseau-like moonscapes are less startling, because we are not seeing them for the first time, the moon, lighting his three lovers, is whiter, more mysterious and more transforming.

Source: Richard Eder, "The Love-Dream of a Prodigious Sleeper," in *The Los Angeles Times Book Review,* April 17, 1988, p.3.

Sources

Paul Bailey, "The Loved One," in *The Listener,* Vol. 119, No. 3069, June 30, 1988, p. 29.

Michael Bell, *Gabriel García Márquez: Solitude and Solidarity,* St. Martin's Press, 1993.

Gene H. Bell-Villada, *Gabriel García Márquez: The Man and His Work,* University of North Carolina Press, 1990.

Angela Carter, "García Márquez: Sick with Love and Longing," in *Washington Post Book World,* April 24, 1988, pp. 1, 14.

Jean Franco, "Memento Mori," in *The Nation,* New York, Vol. 246, No. 16, April 23, 1988, pp. 573-74.

S. J. A. Minta, "In Praise of the Popular," in *The Times Literary Supplement,* No. 4448, July 1-7, 1988, p. 730.

Thomas Pynchon, "The Heart's Eternal Vow," in the *New York Times Book Review,* April 10, 1988, pp. 1, 47, 49.

Mona Simpson, "Love Letters," in *London Review of Books,* Vol. 10, No. 15, September 1, 1988, pp. 22-24.

Michael Wood, "Heartsick," in *The New York Review of Books,* Vol. XXXV, No. 7, April 28, 1988, pp. 6, 8-9.

For Further Study

Isabel Alvarez Borland, "Interior Texts in 'El Amor en los Tiempos del Cólera'," in *Hispanic Review,* Vol. 59, 1991, pp. 175-86.

Alvarez Borland examines the written texts within the novel and concludes that *Love in the Time of Cholera* is a novel about writing — both in the literal sense and the figurative sense of the post-modern, self-reflexive text.

M. Keith Booker, "The Dangers of Gullible Reading: Narrative as Seduction in García Márquez' 'Love in the Time of Cholera'," in *Studies in Twentieth Century Literature,* Vol. 17, no. 2, Summer, 1993, pp. 181-95.

Booker's reading suggests that *Love in the Time of Cholera* is not a book about romance, but about politics and history and that its "saccharine surface" conceals a series of textual traps.

Claudette Kemper Columbus, "Faint Echoes and Faded Reflections: Love and Justice in the Time of Cholera," in *Twentieth Century Literature,* Vol. 38, no. 1, 1992, pp. 89-100.

This discussion of the novel invites readers to recognize that *Love in the Time of Cholera* is a satire which attacks the sentimental notions it seems to support.

Robin Fiddian, "Introduction," in *García Márquez,* edited by Robin Fiddian, Longman, 1995, pp. 1-26.

Included in Fiddian's Introduction is a discussion of the national context of Colombia, Latin American fiction and magic realism. He also provides biographical information and a brief discussion of *Love in the Time of Cholera.*

Bernard McGuirk and Richard Cardwell, editors, *Gabriel García Márquez: New Readings,* Cambridge University Press, 1987.

Editors select essays written from a variety of perspectives.

George R. McMurray, *Gabriel García Márquez,* Ungar, 1977.

The first book-length study of García Márquez in English. The author comments on all his fictional writings and provides plot summaries as well as bibliography and index.

George R. McMurray, *Critical Essays on Gabriel García Márquez,* Hall, 1987.

A collection of book reviews, essays, and articles from the 1960s to the present. There is a wide representation of critics as well as of works discussed.

Kathleen McNerney, *Understanding Gabriel García Márquez,* University of South Carolina Press, 1989.

A useful study that attempts to interpret the works of Gabriel García Márquez in light of modern and contemporary European and Latin American literature.

Stephen Minta, *Gabriel García Márquez: Writer of Colombia,* J. Cape, 1987.

Beginning with a very informative and useful chapter on Colombia, the book develops an overview of García Márquez's work within a political as well as literary context. Selected bibliography is included.

Mabel Morana, "Modernity and Marginality in 'Love in the Time of Cholera'," in *Studies in Twentieth Century Literature,* Vol. 14, No. 1, Winter, 1990, pp. 27-43.

Morana proposes that the novel juxtaposes two different social projects which are actualized in the two male characters. Urbino reflects the project of modernization, whereas Florentino incarnates the values of national culture as against European-style modernization.

K. E. A. Mose, *Defamiliarization in the Work of Gabriel García Márquez,* E. Mellen Press, 1989.

An interesting consideration of the figures of speech employed by García Márquez to "defamiliarize" his subject and present the familiar in an unfamiliar fashion.

Bradley A. Shaw and Nora Vera-Godwin, editors, *Critical Perspectives on Gabriel García Márquez,* Society of Spanish and Spanish-American Studies, 1986.

A collection of essays on various works by several scholars.

Margaret L. Snook, "The Motif of Voyage as Mythical Symbol in 'El Amor en los Tiempos del Colera' by Gabriel García Márquez," in *Hispanic Journal,* Vol. 10, No. 1, 1988, pp. 85-91.

Snook discusses the many journeys in the novel, including that of the narrative itself which reflects the movement of a journey that is interrupted and later resumed.

Raymond Williams, *Gabriel García Márquez,* Twayne, 1984.

Brief biography and description of works, including commentary on García Márquez's journalism.

Of Mice and Men

John Steinbeck
1937

Of Mice and Men is a novel set on a ranch in the Salinas Valley in California during the Great Depression of the 1930s. It was the first work to bring John Steinbeck national recognition as a writer. The title suggests that the best-laid plans of mice and men often go awry, a reference to Robert Burns's poem "To a Mouse." *Of Mice and Men* was selected for the Book of the Month Club before it was officially published, an honor that encouraged 117,000 copies of the novel to be sold before its official publication on February 25, 1937. Critical response to the novel was generally positive. There were, however, critics who were offended by the rough earthiness of the characters and their lives. By April 1937, the book was on best-seller lists across the country, and it continued to remain a top seller throughout that year. Steinbeck said that he was not expecting huge sales, and he was surprised by the substantial checks he received from his agents. In fact, Steinbeck became a celebrity with the publication of his novel, a status that he feared would negatively affect his work. Steinbeck conceived *Of Mice and Men* as a potential play. Each chapter is arranged as a scene, and each scene is confined to a single space: a secluded grove, a bunkhouse, and a barn.

With the success of the novel, Steinbeck worked on a stage version with playwright George Kaufman, who directed the play. *Of Mice and Men* opened on Broadway in New York City on November 23, 1937, with Wallace Ford as George and Broderick Crawford as Lennie. The reviews were

overwhelmingly positive, and the play ran for 207 performances, winning the prestigious New York Drama Critics' Circle Award. The action of the novel occurs over the course of three days. Steinbeck created the novel's two main characters, George Milton and Lennie Small, to portray victims of forces beyond their control. George and Lennie are two migrant agricultural workers on a California ranch who share a dream of owning their own farm someday. They take jobs at a ranch where their hopes are at first raised but then destroyed by a tragic accident. Steinbeck depicts George and Lennie as two innocents whose dream conflicts with the realities of a world dominated by materialism and greed. Their extraordinary friendship distinguishes them from other hopeless and lonely migrant farm workers. The novel portrays a class of ranch workers in California whose plight had been previously ignored in the early decades of the twentieth century. In fact, George and Lennie are like mice in the maze of modern life. The great friendship they share does not prove sufficient to allow them to realize their dream. As a young man, Steinbeck learned about migrant laborers, usually unmarried men recruited to work during harvest seasons, from his own experience as a worker on company-owned ranches. With *Of Mice and Men,* Steinbeck became a master craftsman, ready to write his masterpiece *The Grapes of Wrath* the following year.

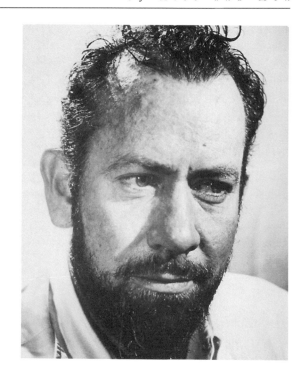

John Steinbeck

Author Biography

John Ernst Steinbeck was born on February 27, 1902, in Salinas, California. He was the third of four children—and only son—of John Ernst, Sr., and Olive Hamilton Steinbeck. Steinbeck's father managed a flour mill and later served as treasurer of Monterey County. His mother had taught in a one-room rural school. At the turn of the century, Salinas was a typical American small town. Located about one hundred miles south of San Francisco, near Monterey Bay, Salinas at the time had a population of three thousand. Steinbeck's father was a good provider, although the family was not affluent. Young John had to work to earn his own money. During high school, he worked on nearby ranches during the summer. In high school, he earned mostly B's and B-pluses and, in his senior year, he was elected president of the class. He was also an associate editor of the school newspaper, although his articles showed none of the brilliance of his later work. In 1919, Steinbeck entered Stan-

ford University in Palo Alto, about eighty miles north of Salinas. He made only average grades there, and after two years he withdrew from the university. During the following two years, he worked on a ranch south of Salinas before returning to Stanford. He attended classes off and on, sometimes suspending his studies because of illness and his indecision about what field of study to pursue. When not at school, he worked several different jobs, including one as a clerk in Oakland and as a laborer in the beet and barley fields of Salinas, an experience that he would write about fifteen years later in *Of Mice and Men.*

Steinbeck then returned to Salinas, lived at home, worked as a bench chemist at Spreckel's Sugar Company, and spent his free time writing. In January 1923, Steinbeck returned to Stanford University, where during the next three years he was a diligent student and received A's and B's. Two of his stories appeared in *The Stanford Spectator.* After five years of sporadic study, Steinbeck left Stanford in 1925 without a degree or prospects for a job. He was twenty-three. He made his first trip to New York City by freighter, hoping to establish himself as a writer. In New York he worked as a reporter for the now-defunct *New York American.* He was soon fired when his writing was judged too subjective for newspaper reporting. After his manuscript for a book of short stories was rejected, Steinbeck returned to California as a deck hand on a freighter and soon after worked as a caretaker for a lodge in the Sierras near Lake Tahoe in Nevada.

In 1930 Steinbeck married Carol Henning. She gave up a career in advertising to work as a typist, secretary, and copyreader so that her husband could write steadily. In 1931, some ten million Americans were out of work. Soup kitchen lines and closed stores were common sights across the country. The Steinbecks, however, were not desperate. Carol earned a small income, and Steinbeck's father allowed them to live in a rent-free cottage and gave his son twenty-five dollars per month. The Steinbecks and their friends discussed current events, including President Franklin Roosevelt's policies, signs of labor unrest in California, and the great number of unemployed Americans. Some of the Steinbecks' friends in the Monterey-Pacific Grove area were active in labor politics.

In 1936, Steinbeck began work on *Of Mice and Men*. Based on his ranch experiences and his firsthand knowledge of migrant workers, the novel was to be a realistic parable of farming conditions in Salinas Valley. Beginning with this novel, the works that would make him famous during the years just prior to World War II were concerned mostly with the dispossessed and farm laborers. Yet Steinbeck did not see the migrants in political terms. Although he had great concern for the plight of migrant workers, he saw himself as an artist creating works that would have universal meaning and, as art, would stand the test of time. A kind and compassionate man by nature, Steinbeck's concern for people in trouble shows clearly in his work.

Shortly after *Of Mice and Men* was published, Steinbeck worked with playwright George Kaufman on the stage version of the novel. The night the play opened on Broadway, Steinbeck was living in a migrant camp, researching and working on the early version of the novel that was to be transformed into *The Grapes of Wrath* the following year. He never saw the Broadway play of this powerful work. In 1943, Steinbeck divorced his first wife, marrying singer, writer, and composer Gwyndolyn Conger that same year. He and Gwyndolyn had two sons, Tom and John, before they divorced in 1948. Steinbeck married his third wife, Elaine Scott, in 1950.

Steinbeck's many honors during his lifetime included the U.S. Medal of Freedom and the No-

bel Prize for Literature. In 1962 Steinbeck became only the sixth American to receive the Nobel Prize. Steinbeck was elated and surprised to receive this honor, the greatest any writer can receive. His fiction of the 1930s gained national recognition, and *Of Mice and Men* and *The Grapes of Wrath* won acclaim in other countries as well. On December 20, 1968, after a series of strokes, Steinbeck died in his apartment in New York City. His ashes were buried in the family cemetery in Salinas.

Plot Summary

Of Mice and Men opens with a physical description of the topography of the Central Valley of California. "A few miles south of Soledad," the Salinas river winds through an idyllic scene of yellow sands, golden foothills, and deer that come to the shore to drink at night. It is in this setting that we first meet Steinbeck's two protagonists, George Milton and Lennie Small. George is "small and quick, dark of face, with restless eyes and sharp, strong features." Lennie is "his opposite, a huge man, shapeless of face, with large, pale eyes, with wide, sloping shoulders." They have just come from the town of Weed in Northern California where Lennie had gotten into some sort of trouble, forcing them to flee south. There they are now looking for new work on a ranch. As the two talk it becomes clear that Lennie is mentally handicapped: he cannot quite remember what had happened in Weed; he speaks with a child's vocabulary; and he bursts into tears when George makes him give up the dead mouse that he has been secretly petting in his pocket. At first George lectures Lennie on what a burden he is, with the recent events in Weed as an example:

> His voice rose nearly to a shout. "You crazy son-of-a-bitch. You keep me in hot water all of the time." He took on the elaborate manner of little girls when they are mimicking one another. "Jus' wanted to feel that girl's dress—jus' wanted to pet it like it was a mouse—Well, how the hell did she know you jus' wanted to feel her dress? She jerks back and you hold on like it was a mouse. She yells and we got to hide in an irrigation ditch all day with guys lookin' for us, and we got to sneak out in the dark and get outta the country. All the time somethin' like that—all the time. I wisht I could put you in a cage with about a million mice and let you have fun." His anger left him suddenly. He looked across the fire at Lennie's anguished face, and then he looked ashamedly at the flames.

After calming down, George repeats, at Lennie's request, the story of how they are someday going to get out of the lonely life of itinerant farm laborers and buy a piece of land where they can live by working their own small farm together.

The next day, George and Lennie arrive at the ranch and are brought by Candy the swamper (handyman) to the workers' bunk house to meet with the owner. After some discussion concerning their ability to work and Lennie's inability to speak, they are hired. A while later, the boss's son, Curley, comes into the bunk house, supposedly looking for his father. Curley is a small man and he approaches Lennie with "hands … closed into fists." "His glance [is] calculating and pugnacious," and he stands in a slight crouch. The confrontation ends with Curley leaving after telling Lennie to "answer when [he's] spoke to" in the future. As Candy explains, Curley is a good, "handy" fighter who likes to pick fights with men larger than himself; he is also very jealous of his pretty new wife who lives on the ranch and has been known to give some of the workers "the eye." Just then, Curley's wife appears momentarily at the door, pretending that she is looking for Curley. Lennie is struck by how pretty she is. Slim, the skinner (a teamster, or mule driver), also arrives and is followed by the rest of the men. The news that Slim's dog has had a litter of pups the previous night greatly interests Lennie. George promises to ask Slim if Lennie can have one.

By the next day, Slim has agreed to let Lennie have one of the pups and Lennie is out playing with them in the barn as George and Slim talk in the bunk house. Candy comes in, followed by his ancient dog and Carlson, who has just lost at horseshoes. Carlson immediately starts to complain about the smell of the feeble old dog and tells Candy that he should shoot it and take one of the new pups in its place. Candy is reluctant, but Carlson offers to shoot the dog himself and, after some deliberation, Candy agrees that it must be done. Slim leaves to fix a mule's hoof in the barn, and at the card table Whit invites George to go with the others to a brothel in town the next night. Carlson returns and begins to clean his pistol, and Lennie comes in as well. Curley then arrives, looking for his wife, and asks where Slim is. He leaves looking for them both. Slim returns shortly afterward, followed by Curley, who is apologizing for accusing him of improprieties with his wife. The men all side with Slim and tell Curley to keep her at home. Curley then attacks Lennie, who is still silently dreaming of his future ranch with George. Lennie

is surprised and terrified, but after George tells him to fight back, he grabs one of Curley's fists and crushes it.

Crooks the stableman, being black, is not allowed to live in the bunk house with the white workers; he has a bunk in the harness room of the stable. The night that the men are at the brothel Lennie wanders into Crooks' room. They talk a while: Crooks tells Lennie that he is in fact not from the South but rather a native of California. Lennie tells Crooks of his and George's plans for the future. Candy then arrives and joins the conversation. Just then, Curley's wife appears at the door asking if they have seen her husband. When she continues talking with the men despite their reluctance, Candy jumps up and shouts at her to leave. She then notices the cuts on Lennie's face and realizes that it was Lennie who broke Curley's hand. She flirts with him, and when Crooks protests she reminds him that as a black man he has no rights and that she could cause anything to happen to him that she wants. Crooks realizes that she is right and sits down. After she leaves, George arrives and Lennie and Candy leave Crooks alone in his room.

Sunday afternoon finds Lennie sitting in the barn looking at a puppy he has just accidentally killed. He is confused about how he killed the puppy and afraid of what George will do when he finds out. Curley's wife walks into the stall and kneels down in the hay beside Lennie, telling him that he gave Curley what he deserved. When Lennie is obviously reluctant to talk with her she becomes exasperated, wondering why no one will speak with her, and then she recounts the story of how she came to be Curley's wife. Lennie starts to talk about the dead puppy and how he killed it only by petting it. He says he likes to "pet nice things," and she tells him to touch her hair and feel how soft it is. When he does touch her hair he is too rough, and she tells him to stop, but he continues to clutch it. When she screams for him to let go Lennie panics and covers her mouth with his hand. As she struggles to get away Lennie tightens his grasp and breaks her neck. Slowly realizing what he has done he puts the dead pup under his shirt and creeps out of the barn. Candy then comes in, discovers Curley's dead wife, and goes to get George. George sadly decides that the only thing to do is tell everyone and to hunt down Lennie. Curley and Carlson go to get their guns, but Carlson's gun turns out to be missing, which they attribute to Lennie's having stolen it. They all go out to hunt down Lennie.

From the film Of Mice and Men, *starring Gary Sinise and John Malkovich, MGM, 1992.*

The final chapter opens with a terrified Lennie appearing from the brush in the same scene by the shore where the story opened. George then appears from the brush and tells Lennie not to worry about what has happened. He calms Lennie down with by repeating the story about their future plans and how they will always be together to care for one another. George tells Lennie to look across the river, that he can almost see their little farm. With Lennie gazing into the distance George takes out Carlson's pistol and points it at the back of Lennie's head, all the while continuing the story of their future. As the voices of the other men come within earshot, George shoots Lennie. When the men all arrive, George tells them that Lennie had the gun and that he had gotten it away from him and killed him.

Characters

Candy

Candy is the old, disabled ranch hand who is helpless to stop the shooting of his dog and who knows that he too will be banished when he is no longer useful. He is sweetly hopeful of joining Lennie and George on their dream farm, offering to contribute his savings of $350 to buy the farm.

Carlson

Carlson is a skilled worker, a mechanic at the ranch who assumes an arrogance forbidden the others. He is the one who orders Candy's dog to be put to death. Carlson has no feelings about the animal and no concept that anyone else might care about the old creature. He is insensitive, brutal, violent, and fanatical; his only contributions to the group are destructive. His callousness is especially evident at the end of the novel. Upon seeing Slim and George sadly walk off for a drink after George has shot Lennie, Carlson says, "Now what the hell ya suppose is eatin' them two guys?"

Crooks

Crooks, the despairing old Negro stable worker, lives alone in the harness room, ostracized from the ranch hands. On the one occasion when he briefly talks to Lennie and Candy, the bunkhouse worker who wants to be part of the dream farm Lennie and George are planning to buy, Crooks tells them they will never attain their dream. Crooks is excluded from the rest of the ranch hands, except at Christmas when the boss brings in a gallon of whiskey for the entire crew.

Curley

Curley, the son of the owner of the ranch where George and Lennie work, is willing to fight at the

Media Adaptations

- *Of Mice and Men* was adapted by Steinbeck as a play, which opened on Broadway on November 23, 1937, and was directed by playwright George S. Kaufman. The play won the prestigious New York Critics' Circle Award for 1937 and ran for 207 performances.

- The novel was also adapted as a film in 1939 and was nominated for three Academy Awards: Best Picture, Best Score by Aaron Copland, and Best Sound. The film starred Burgess Meredith as George and Lon Chaney Jr. as Lennie, and was released by Universal; it was directed by Lewis Mileston. As of 1997, unavailable on video.

- The novel was adapted as a film for television by ABC in 1968; it was directed by Ted Kotcheff, produced by David Susskind, and starred George Segal and Nicol Williamson.

- Another made-for-television movie version was broadcast in 1981, starring Robert Blake and Randy Quaid, and directed by Reza Badiyi. This version is available from Prism Entertainment Home Video.

- A more recent film adaptation of the novel was made in 1992. Director Gary Sinise received permission from Elaine Steinbeck, the writer's widow, to film the novel. The movie starred Gary Sinise as George and John Malkovich as Lennie; the screenplay was written by Horton Foote; it is available from MGM/UA Home Entertainment.

---

drop of a hat, yet he is really a coward. Lennie stands up to Curley and crushes his hand in his iron grip. Later, Curley organizes the posse to find Lennie after he has killed Curley's wife.

Curley's wife

Curley's wife (as the boss's son's flirtatious wife, she is not identified by any other name) wanders around the ranch searching for some human contact. She is stereotyped by the men as a "tart." Indeed, she plays the vamp, which enrages her jealous husband. George tells Lennie to avoid her, calling her "poison" and "jailbait." But she is pathetically lonely and had once had dreams of being a movie star. Both she and Crooks crave company and "someone to talk to." On Sunday afternoon, while the others are playing horseshoes, Curley's wife gets Lennie to feel her soft hair. When he begins to muss it, she panics, and he accidentally breaks her neck. When George discovers what has happened, he realizes that their dream is over.

George Milton

George Milton, a migrant laborer, is like a mouse: "small and quick, dark of face, with rest-less eyes and sharp strong features. Every part of him was defined: small, strong hands, slender arms, a thin and bony nose." George has brains and ambition. He is the most complex of the characters in *Of Mice and Men* because he has not accepted his present lot in life. He has a dream to save money, buy a small farm, and be his own boss. George is loyal in his friendship with Lennie, and he is also remarkably pure of heart. When George is driven to shoot Lennie after Lennie accidentally kills Curley's wife, he destroys his own dream, too. Its fulfillment is doomed by insensitive materialists. Along with the destruction of his dream, George loses the chance to become a better man.

Above all, George is a survivor, proving himself to be shrewdly adaptable to migratory life. Still, he has weaknesses; he yells at Lennie from time to time and needs to feel better about his own ordinariness. But George is essentially a good man. Throughout the novel, he is loyal and committed to Lennie. In fact, George takes complete responsibility for Lennie, even to the point of killing him, because he ultimately feels responsible for Lennie's actions. George had promised Lennie's aunt that he would look out for Lennie, and although George complains about having to take care of him, their friendship gives George someone with whom he can share his dream. By the end of the story, George has achieved some control over his instincts, yet, despite his obvious commitment to Lennie, the mouselike George is helpless to overcome the injustices of an imperfect world.

Slim

Slim, the mule driver, is a superior workman with "God-like eyes" who is kind and perceptive. He alone understands and tries to comfort George at the end of the novel after George has killed Lennie. Emphasis is placed on Slim's skill and craftsmanship; he does his job exceedingly well. Slim is a doer, not a dreamer. "His ear heard more than was said to him, and his slow speech had overtones not of thought, but of understanding beyond thought." Slim is the really heroic man in the novel.

Lennie Small

Lennie Small, an itinerant ranch hand like his friend, George Milton, is a tall, powerful man who is mentally handicapped. He and George share a dream of someday buying their own farm, and Lennie is excited about the prospect of taking care of the rabbits they plan to keep. For a while, it appears as if the dream might come true. Lennie is a good worker and has the strength to do much of the farm work. Yet, handicapped by his lack of adult intelligence, Lennie is doomed in the world of the migrant worker. Though an innocent and not violent by nature, he has the potential for violence; his incredible strength leads him to accidentally kill the mice and puppies whose fur he likes to stroke. Lennie is repeatedly associated with animals and described as childlike. In the opening scene, for example, he appears dragging his feet "the way a bear drags his paws," and in the book's final chapter, he enters the clearing in the brush "as silently as a creeping bear." Lennie dies because he is incapable of living within society and is in fact a menace. His contact with living creatures, from mice to puppies to Curley's wife, results in destruction. Although his weakness dooms the dream of the farm, it is his innocence that keeps it alive throughout the novel until his death. His brute strength threatens society, yet it is Lennie's extraordinary mixture of human dreams and animal passions that are important. Without Lennie, George is friendless and alone. While their partnership lasts, George and Lennie share a brotherly, mutual concern and loyal companionship. There is joy, security, and comfort in their relationship. As Steinbeck once wrote,

"Lennie was not to represent insanity at all but the inarticulate and powerful yearning of all men."

Themes

Idealism vs. Reality

Of Mice and Men tells the story of two simple men who try to escape homelessness, economic poverty, and emotional and psychological corruption. Otherwise, the fate of those who do not abandon the lives they lead as itinerant workers is bleak and dehumanizing. As George tells Slim, the mule driver: "I seen the guys that go around on the ranches alone. That ain't no good. They don't have no fun. After a long time they get mean." George and Lennie dream of owning a farm, but by the end of the novel the dream has failed. Their plan is doomed because human fellowship cannot survive in their world and also because their image of the farm is overly idealized. It is likely that even if they had obtained the farm, their lives would not have been as comfortable as they had imagined; they would not have enjoyed the fraternal harmony that is part of their dream. In fact, their dream of contentment in the modern world is impractical and does not accurately reflect the human condition. Crooks, the black stablehand, expresses his doubts about the dream. "Nobody never gets to heaven, and nobody gets no land. It's just in their head. They're all the time talkie' about it, but it's jus' in their head." Crooks is referring not only to literal ownership but to the dream of contentment about which these simple men fantasize. Implicit in the theme is the ironic idea that maturity involves the destruction of one's dreams. George "matures" by killing Lennie, thus destroying the dream that could not survive in modern civilization. George survives because he leaves behind his unrealistic dreams. Dreaming, however, is humanity's only defense against an indifferent world. The title of the novel itself implies that people are at the mercy of external forces beyond their control. Steinbeck writes with sincere compassion for the victims of these chaotic forces.

Alienation and Loneliness

Loneliness is a recurrent theme in the novel. "Guys like us," George says, "that work on the ranches, are the loneliest guys in the world. They got no family. They don't belong noplace." Lennie replies: "But not us. And why. Because ... because I got you to look after me, and you got me to look after you, and that's why." The alternative to the companionship that George and Lennie share is loneliness. George frequently affirms the fraternity between them. "He's my ... cousin," George tells the ranch boss. "I told his old lady I'd take care of him." The boss is suspicious of the bond between George and Lennie, and the other characters in turn also question this friendship: they have simply never seen anything like it. In their world, isolation is the norm. Even Slim, who is usually sympathetic and understanding, expresses surprise. "Ain't many guys travel around together. I don't know why. Maybe ever'body in the whole damned world is scared of each other." Distrust is the quality of the modern world in which people live in alienation from one another. Later, the theme of loneliness is further explored in the solitude borne by Crooks and Curley's wife, who dies as a result of seeking human companionship. Both these characters crave company and, as Curley's wife says, "someone to talk to."

Despite everyone's suspicion, the friendship between George and Lennie remains solid. In fact, Candy becomes part of their dream to buy the little farm, and later Crooks also expresses his desire to become part of the expanding fellowship. This is the high point of optimism in regard to the theme of overcoming loneliness in the modern world, when it seems most likely that alienation and loneliness will be overcome. After this point, however, the dream of fellowship on the farm begins to lose its promise, and at the moment that George and Candy discover the body of Curley's wife, they both realize that the dream is lost; their partnership dissolves. Actually, the dream was doomed from the start, because fraternal living cannot survive in a world ruled by loneliness, homelessness, and poverty.

This outcome also suggests that loneliness is an essential part of humanity's nature. This theme of loneliness has been implied from the beginning of the novel, when the author establishes the setting as "a few miles south of Soledad." Soledad is the name of a town in central California, but it is also the Spanish word for solitude. Yet Steinbeck's emphasis is on the greatness of his characters' attempt to live as brothers. Although the dream is doomed, the characters devote themselves to pursuing human fellowship.

Race and Racism

Somewhat related to the theme of loneliness is racism, which also results in personal isolation. Crooks, the old black man on the ranch, lives alone, ostracized by the ranch hands because of his race. The barrier of racial prejudice is briefly broken,

Topics for Further Study

- Research the migrant farm labor movement's attempts to organize unions in the 1930s in California and compare with the work of Cesar Chavez's United Farm Workers Union in the 1970s.

- Investigate the claims of People for the American Way that John Steinbeck's novel *Of Mice and Men* is the book most frequently challenged by school censors. Other controversial books include J. D. Salinger's *The Catcher in the Rye* and Steinbeck's *The Grapes of Wrath*.

- Research and compare how the number of farms in the United States has declined from the 1930s to the 1990s, including the average acreage of individual farms during these decades and the percentage of farms owned by corporations versus those owned by private farmers.

however, when Crooks becomes an ally in the dream to buy a farm. Crooks has a bitter dignity and honesty that illustrate Steinbeck's own criticism of American society's failures in the Depression era of the 1930s.

Class Conflict

Although George and Lennie have their dream, they are not in a position to attain it. In addition to their own personal limitations, they are also limited by their position in society. Their idealistic dream is eventually destroyed by an unfeeling, materialistic, modern society. The tensions between the characters are inherent in the nature of American capitalism and its class system. Curley, the son of the ranch owner, is arrogant and always looking for a fight. This is not merely a personality trait. His position in society has encouraged this behavior; his real strength lies not in his fighting ability but in his power to fire any worker. Similarly, Carlson, the only skilled worker among the ranch hands, is arrogant and lacks compassion. Carlson would be difficult to replace in his job as a mechanic; therefore, he feels secure enough in his status to treat the other workers sadistically. This trait is seen when he orders Candy's dog to be shot and when he picks on Lennie. The other workers go along with Carlson because they are old or afraid of losing their jobs. Lennie's mental retardation also symbolizes the helplessness of people in a capitalistic, commercial, competitive society. In this way, Steinbeck illustrates the confusion and hopelessness of the Depression era. The poor were a class of people who suddenly had captured the imagination of American writers in the 1930s. This was an example of the shift in attitudes that occurred during the Depression. Previously, American fiction had been concerned with the problems of middle-class people. Steinbeck's novel was a sympathetic portrayal of the lives of the poorest class of working people, while exposing society's injustices and economic inequalities in the hope of improving their situation.

Mental Disability

Lennie's mental limitations also serve to illustrate another way in which people separate themselves from one another. Because of his handicap, Lennie is rejected by everyone at the ranch except George. The ranch hands are suspicious of Lennie and fear him when they recognize his physical strength and his inability to control himself. For example, when Crooks maliciously teases Lennie that George might decide to abandon his friend and that Lennie would then end up in "the booby hatch," Lennie becomes enraged. Eventually, Crooks backs off in fear of what Lennie could do to hurt him. Despite Lennie's potential for hurting people, however, Steinbeck makes it clear that it is the malice, fear, and anger in other people that are to blame for Lennie's violent actions (Crooks torments Lennie out of his own frustration for being rejected because he is black). When Curly starts to hit Lennie for supposedly laughing at him, Lennie at first retreats and allows his face to become bloodied until George tells him he should fight back; and when Lennie accidentally kills Curly's wife, it is a direct result of her inappropriate advances toward him. Steinbeck's portrayal of Lennie's handicap is therefore completely sympathetic; the other characters have only themselves to blame for provoking Lennie, who is merely a child in a world of selfish adults. That Lennie has to die at the novel's conclusion is a poignant commentary on the inability of the innocent to survive in modern society.

Loyalty

George is steadfastly loyal throughout the novel, honoring his commitment to take care of the retarded Lennie. After Lennie accidentally kills Curley's wife, Curley forms a posse to lynch Lennie. George then steals a pistol and goes to the spot where he has told Lennie to hide in case there is trouble: the same spot where the novel begins. George then kills Lennie himself before the mob can find him so he can save Lennie from a lynching. Together the two men recite the dream of their farm for the last time. George mercifully kills Lennie with a shot to the head while Lennie is chanting the dream, unaware of what is about to happen to him. George, with all his personal limitations, is a man who has committed himself in a compassionate relationship. The grief he feels over the necessity of killing Lennie is also evidence of George's essential decency. Although the dream perishes, the theme of commitment achieves its strongest point in the novel's conclusion. Unlike Candy, who earlier abandoned responsibility for his old dog and allows Carlson to shoot the animal, George remains his brother's keeper. In his acceptance of complete responsibility for Lennie, George demonstrates the commitment necessary to join the ranks of Steinbeck's heroes.

Friendship

The one ingredient essential for the fulfillment of George's and Lennie's dream is friendship. And because the dream is so remarkable, that friendship must be special. There are other friendships in the novel: Slim and Carlson, Candy and Crooks, but these are ordinary friendships. The bond between George and Lennie, which goes back many years, is different. Lennie cannot survive on his own, and he needs George to guide and protect him. Without George, Lennie would live in a cave in the hills, as he sometimes threatens to do, or he would be institutionalized. George, for his part, complains regularly about having to take care of Lennie. His tolerance of Lennie also gives him a sense of superiority. At the same time, George feels a genuine affection for Lennie that he will not openly admit. Most importantly, without this friendship, neither George nor Lennie alone could sustain the dream, much less see it become a reality. The friendship lends hope to the dream, but the reality of their brutal life destroys the dream and the friendship. Although George is a survivor at the end, he is doomed to be alone.

Style

Structure

Of Mice and Men, with its highly restricted focus, is the first of Steinbeck's experiments with the novel-play form, which combines qualities of each genre. The novel thus needed few changes before appearing on Broadway. The story is essentially comprised of three acts of two chapters each. Each chapter or scene contains few descriptions of place, character, or action. Thus, the novel's strength lies in part in its limitations. Action is restricted usually to the bunkhouse. The span of time is limited to three days: sunset Thursday to sunset Sunday, which intensifies the sense of suspense and drama.

Point of View

The point of view of the novel is generally objective—not identifying with a single character—and limited to exterior descriptions. The third-person narrative point of view creates a sense of the impersonal. With few exceptions, the story focuses on what can be readily perceived by an outside observer: a river bank, a bunkhouse, a character's appearance, card players at a table. The focus on time, too, is limited to the present: there are no flashbacks to events in the past, and the reader only learns about what has happened to Lennie and George before the novel's beginning through dialogue between the characters. Thoughts, recollections, and fantasies are expressed directly by the characters, except when Lennie hallucinates in Chapter 6 about seeing a giant rabbit and Aunt Clara.

Setting

Set in California's Salinas Valley, the story takes place on a large ranch during the Great Depression. The agricultural scene in California in the 1930s, particularly in Salinas Valley, was dominated by large collective farms, or "farm factories," owned by big landowners and banks. These farm factories employed hundreds of workers, many of whom were migrants. Small farms of a few hundred acres, such as the one Lennie and George dream about, were relatively scarce. On the large farms, low wages for picking fruit and vegetables often led to economic unrest. In September 1936, thousands of lettuce workers in the Salinas Valley went on strike over low wages. The situation grew tense, and an army officer was brought in to lead vigilantes against the strikers. The strike was crushed within a month. Steinbeck covered the strike as a reporter for the *San Francisco News*.

Symbolism

The most important symbol in the novel is the bank of the Salinas River, where the novel begins and ends. In the story's opening, when George and Lennie come to the riverbank, it serves as a symbol of retreat from the world to a natural state of innocence. In this first scene, George tells Lennie that he should return to this riverbank if there is trouble at the ranch where they plan to work. The riverbank is a "safe place" for the two characters. A second symbol is the rabbits: Lennie repeatedly asks George to tell him about the rabbits, which, when they are mentioned, also come to symbolize the safe place that George and Lennie desire and dream about. The fundamental symbol is the dream itself: "a little house and a couple of acres and a cow and some pigs." This ideal place keeps the two men bonded to each other and offers hope, however briefly, to two other men whom George and Lennie will meet the next day at the ranch. When George and Lennie arrive at the ranch, the bunkhouse and farm symbolize the essential emptiness of that world, offering only minimal physical security.

Foreshadowing

Foreshadowing, where events subtly hint at things to come, serves to heighten suspense in the novel. Lennie's rough handling of the mice and the puppy, the shooting of Candy's old dog, the crushing of Curley's hand, and the frequent appearances of Curley's wife all foretell future violence. Steinbeck tells the reader about the mice and puppy, as well as the scene in which Lennie breaks the bones in Curley's hand, so that when Lennie kills Curley's wife it is completely believable and convincing—and seemingly inevitable—that this could happen. Also, at the very beginning of the book, the reader learns that George and Lennie had to leave Weed because Lennie got into trouble when he tried to touch a girl's dress. The incident in which Candy's dog is shot also foreshadows George's shooting of Lennie, an ironic comparison of the value placed on the life of a dog and a man.

Historical Context

Agriculture during the Great Depression

During the late 1930s, California was struggling not only with the economic problems of the Great Depression, but also with severe labor strife. Labor conflicts occurred on the docks and packing sheds and fields. Steinbeck wrote movingly about the struggles of migrant farm workers in three successive novels: *In Dubious Battle* (1936), *Of Mice and Men* (1937), and *The Grapes of Wrath* (1939).

Compare
&
Contrast

- **1930s:** The Great Depression and severe drought in the Midwest (leading to what became known as the Dust Bowl) forces a population shift from rural to urban areas. People leave their farms and move to the cities to find jobs. This change in demographics spurs industrialization within the cities, a trend that is accelerated in the 1940s with the beginning of World War II. Farms once owned by families begin to be bought out by corporations and consolidated into "farm factories."

  Today: Though the stock market skyrockets in the 1990s, the "Electronic Revolution" encourages more efficient business practices which, in turn, fosters corporate downsizing. Workers begin to move out of centralized urban office settings to work out of their homes in the suburbs, using computers and the Internet, while factory workers are increasingly replaced by improved automation techniques and must retrain to find jobs requiring higher skills. The number of individual farms decreases from over six million in the 1940s to two million and are largely owned by businesses.

- **1930s:** Labor unions see an incredible growth in memberships and, with the help of the federal government and dynamic union leaders like United Mine Workers president John L. Lewis, strike successfully against powerful corporations. The Roosevelt administration puts laws into effect, including the National Labor Relations Act of 1935, that facilitate unionization. Disputes among skilled versus unskilled laborers causes unskilled workers to split from the

American Federation of Labor (AFL) to found the Congress of Industrial Organizations (CIO).

  Today: The ability of large unions like the Teamsters and the United Auto Workers (UAW) to strike effectively against businesses is compromised and membership is down as federally mandated worker benefits have become widespread and public sympathy for workers diminishes. However, the practice of corporations to hire more part-time laborers in order to bypass laws that demand full-time employees receive medical and retirement benefits creates new labor problems as ordinary workers find it increasingly necessary to work two or more part-time jobs.

- **1930s:** Communism becomes a popular social movement in America and the 1930s are later dubbed the "Red Decade." Intellectuals and common workers alike support the concepts of communism, and this new social consciousness leads to support of the Social Security Act and the repeal of Prohibition. By 1936, the Communist Party favored Roosevelt's New Deal, a series of governmental programs designed to support workers with federal funds.

  Today: Communism, unpopular in America since the 1950s, collapses around the world as a political movement, especially in Europe after the breakup of the Soviet Union. However, government-funded programs have become standard in the United States, and by 1997 some 43 million Americans receive Social Security benefits and individuals become dependent on socialistic government programs.

Agriculture as a working-culture was undergoing an historic change. In 1938, about half the nation's grain was harvested by mechanical combines that enabled five men to do the work that had previously required 350. Only a short time before, thousands of itinerant single men had roamed the western states following the harvests. Their labor had been essential to the success of the large farms. By 1900, about 125,000 migrants travelled along a

route from Minnesota west to Washington state. Many traveled by rail in the empty boxcars that were later used to transport grain. At the turn of the century, the men were paid an average of $2.50 to $3 a day, plus room and board. The "room" was often a tent.

Wages had risen somewhat at the time of World War I, partly because of the Industrial Workers of the World, which established an 800-mile

Migrant field hands sitting on bags of wheat, near Moro, Oregon, c. 1880.

picket line across the Great Plains states. The "habitual" workers lived the migratory life for years until they grew too old to work. By the late 1930s there were an estimated 200,000 to 350,000 migrants: underpaid, underfed, and underemployed. The migrant worker was always partially unemployed, the nature of the occupation making his work seasonal. The maximum a worker could make was $400 a year, with the average about $300. Yet California's agricultural system could not exist without the migrant workers. It was a problem that would continue for decades. The farms in the state were more like food factories, the "farmers" were absentee owners, remaining in their city offices and hiring local managers to oversee the farming. In short, California's agriculture was not "farming" in the traditional sense. It was an industry like the lumber and oil industries. At the end of the 1930s, one-third of all large-scale farms in the United States were in California, reflecting the trend toward corporate farming. These farms had greatly fluctuating labor demands, and owners encouraged heavy immigration of low-wage foreign workers, usually Chinese, Japanese, and Filipinos. Mexicans began arriving in large numbers around 1910 and represented the largest percentage of the migrant workforce for about twenty years.

During these years, there were thousands of white Americans among the migrants, usually single men who followed the harvesting. Steinbeck writes about them in *Of Mice and Men*. These "bindle-stiffs," as they were known, had no union representation for several reasons: They had no money to pay dues, and they moved from location to location so often that it was difficult to organize them. In addition, American unionism, with its traditional craft setup, did not welcome unskilled workers like farm laborers. In 1930, the Cannery and Agricultural Workers Industrial Union, a Communist-led union, organized the first effective drive among the migrants. During 1933, the group followed the migrants and harvests, organizing a nine-county cotton pickers' strike that affected 12,000 workers. By mid-1934, the union had led about fifty strikes involving 50,000 workers. The group's leaders claimed to have a membership of 21,000 and said they had raised the basic hourly field wage from an average of 15 cents to 17.5 cents an hour in 1932 to an average of 27.5 cents in 1934.

In the summer of 1934, the union was broken up by the anti-Communist activities of employers and state authorities. Its last stand was at an apricot pickers' strike in June 1934. Deputies herded 200 strikers into a cattle pen, arrested some of the leaders, and transported the rest of the strikers out of the county. In trials, the union's president and secretary and six of their associates were convicted of treason. Five of the eight prisoners were later paroled and the other three were freed when an appellate court reversed the convictions in 1937. The existence of a strike was the greatest threat to California's growers. The harvest could wait while negotiations dragged on. Crops had to be picked within a few days of ripening or the result would be financial ruin. This situation created much social unrest. In the 1930s, vigilante activity against strikers and organizers was bloody. Many workers, as well as a number of strike breakers and townspeople, were injured. Vigilantism was not uncommon in early union activities, but in California's farming industry it was particularly vicious, which was odd because the growers could not have existed without the migrants' labor. During peak seasonal demand, growers hired as many as 175,000 workers.

Yet after the harvests most of these workers were not needed. Growers argued that they could not be responsible for paying workers year-round when they were needed only for a few weeks or months. Steady work was impossible not only because of the seasonal nature of the industry, but also because jobs were widely separated and time was lost traveling on the road. Steinbeck wrote *Of Mice and Men* at a time when he was becoming involved in California's social and economic problems. In the novel, he wrote about a group of people, the white male migrant workers, who were to shortly disappear from American culture. World War II absorbed many of the workers in the war effort in the 1940s. Although farm workers were generally exempt from the draft, the expansion of the defense industries to supply the U.S. military needs reduced the pool of surplus labor. The novel's continued popularity over the decades clearly shows that it has transcended its historical times.

Critical Overview

The critical reception of *Of Mice and Men* was the most positive that had greeted any of Steinbeck's works up to that time. The novel was chosen as a Book of the Month Club selection before it was published, and 117,000 copies were sold in advance of the official publication date of February 25, 1937. In early April, the book appeared on best-seller lists across the country and continued to be among the top ten best-sellers throughout the year. Praise for the novel came from many notable critics, including Christopher Morley, Carl Van Vechten, Lewis Gannett, Harry Hansen, Heywood Broun, and even from First Lady Eleanor Roo-

sevelt. Henry Seidel wrote in the *Saturday Review of Literature* that "there has been nothing quite so good of the kind in American writing since Sherwood Anderson's early stories." *New York Times* critic Ralph Thompson described the novel as a "grand little book, for all its ultimate melodrama."

At the time of the book's publication, critical reaction was mostly positive, although at the end of the 1930s, after Steinbeck had written *The Grapes of Wrath,* there was some reevaluation of Steinbeck's earlier work. Some critics complained that *Of Mice and Men* was marred by sentimentality. Other critics faulted Steinbeck for his portrayal of poor, earthy characters. When Steinbeck won the Pulitzer Prize for *The Grapes of Wrath,* one of his strongest critics, Arthur Mizener, condemned Steinbeck's receipt of the award, faulted the author for his love of primitive characters, and criticized his sentimentality. In 1947, an article by Donald Weeks criticized Steinbeck both for sentimentality *and* for the crude lives of his characters. Obviously, Steinbeck caused problems for many reviewers and critics, who wrote contradictory attacks on the novelist, alternately blasting him as too sentimental and too earthy and realistic for their tastes.

In addition, Steinbeck had written three novels about migrant labor in California by the end of the 1930s. Many critics at the time dismissed these novels as communist or leftist propaganda. In fact, Steinbeck's work has often been discussed in sociological, rather than literary, terms. This is unfortunate because it misses the author's intentions: whatever politics or sociology are contained in Steinbeck's works are minor elements in novels of great literary merit. After the 1930s, there were several decades of what can only be described as a critical trashing of Steinbeck's work. When the author was awarded the Nobel Prize for Literature in 1962, very few critics praised the choice. Many publications neglected to even cover the event. Writing in the *New York Times,* Arthur Mizener attacked Steinbeck in an article entitled, "Does a Moral Vision of the Thirties Deserve a Nobel Prize?" The article was published just before the Nobel Prize was presented to Steinbeck in Sweden. The article stated: "After *The Grapes of Wrath* at the end of the thirties, most serious readers seem to have ceased to read him." He went on to state that the Nobel Committee had made a mistake by bestowing the award on a writer whose "limited talent is, in his best books, watered down by tenth-rate philosophizing." Most of the critical opinion at the time was that Steinbeck's career had seriously declined since 1939. *Time* and *Newsweek* did not write favorably of the Nobel Prize to Steinbeck. An editorial in the *New York Times* went so far as to question the process of selection for the award: "The award of the Nobel Prize for Literature to John Steinbeck will focus attention once again on a writer who, though still in full career, produced his major work more than two decades ago. The award will bring back the vivid memory of the earlier books: the ... anger and compassion of *The Grapes of Wrath*, a book that occupies a secure place as a document of protest. Yet the international character of the award and the weight attached to it raise questions about the mechanics of selection and how close the Nobel committee is to the main currents of American writing. Without detracting in the least, from Mr. Steinbeck's accomplishments, we think it interesting that the laurel was not awarded to a writer—perhaps a poet or critic or historian—whose significance, influence and sheer body of work had already made a more profound impression on the literature of our age."

The irony was that Steinbeck's books were still widely read at that time, long after many of Steinbeck's contemporaries from the 1930s had been forgotten. Some critics have written that *Of Mice and Men* is one of Steinbeck's most pessimistic works. In spite of this, Steinbeck scholar Louis Owens wrote that "it is nonetheless possible to read *Of Mice and Men* in a more optimistic light than has been customary. In previous works, we have seen a pattern established in which the Steinbeck hero achieves greatness." Recent criticism, beginning in the 1980s, has acknowledged that Steinbeck's best work is timeless at its deepest level. There are questions about existence and not merely the Depression era's political agenda. Was Steinbeck a sentimentalist, or a political ideologue, or an earthy primitive? Steinbeck himself understood that the wide range of criticism of his works reflected the mindset of the individual critics. He said that many critics were "special pleaders who use my work as a distorted echo chamber for their own ideas." Jackson Benson, a Steinbeck scholar and author of *The True Adventures of John Steinbeck, Writer,* wrote that "what saved Steinbeck from constant excess was a compassion that was, in much of his writing, balanced and disciplined by a very objective view of the world and of man." Sixty years after its publication, *Of Mice and Men* is a classic of American literature read by high school and college students across the United States. It has been translated into a dozen foreign languages. Although the critics may argue for another sixty years about its merits, this "little book," as Steinbeck

called it, will continue to expand people's understanding of what the writer called "the tragic miracle of consciousness."

Criticism

Kevin Attell

In the following essay, Attell, a doctoral candidate at the University of California—Berkeley, places Steinbeck's work within the tradition of social realism and explores how the themes and concerns Steinbeck articulates in Of Mice and Men *lend themselves to this genre.*

John Steinbeck's work is most often considered in the literary tradition of Social Realism, a type of literature which concerns itself with the direct engagement with and intervention in the problematic (usually economic) social conditions in society. The height of Social Realism—and of its close relative, Naturalism, which blends social critique with a tragic narrative structure wherein a sort of natural fate irresistibly propels the characters toward their downfall—dates from the end of the nineteenth century and is represented by such authors as George Gissing, Theodore Dreiser, and Frank Norris.

By the 1930s, this literary style was already waning, having given up its position of primacy to what has come to be called Modernism, which, although not uninterested in social or political thinking, is far more experimental in the way it uses and manipulates literary and aesthetic techniques. James Joyce, Virginia Woolf, and Ezra Pound are some representative Modernist writers from Ireland, England and the United States respectively. Steinbeck's decision to forego very radical experimentation and use the more explicitly engaged realist style in his work from the 1930s may owe to the urgency of the social problems of the Great Depression and Steinbeck's desire to register an immediate and direct critical protest.

Of Mice and Men, like Steinbeck's two other major works from the 1930s, *In Dubious Battle* and *The Grapes of Wrath,* takes its subject and protagonists from the agricultural working class of California during the Great Depression. George and Lennie are itinerant laborers who roam the state looking for any sort of temporary work on large commercial ranches and farms. They work in these places as long as there is a specific task to be done—in *Of Mice and Men,* for example, George and Lennie are hired to bag the barley harvest on

What Do I Read Next?

- *The Grapes of Wrath* (1939) is Steinbeck's masterpiece about the Dust Bowl era of the 1930s which won the Pulitzer Prize. It was a timely, provocative book when published and has become a classic of American literature.

- *In Dubious Battle* (1936) is the first in Steinbeck's trilogy of books that look at the migrant labor problems in the 1930s. This is a book about labor organizers and a strike in California's apple fields. The book caused an uproar from both the political left and right. *Of Mice and Men* (1937) and *The Grapes of Wrath* (1939) followed in what has become known as Steinbeck's period of greatness.

- *A Time of Troubles* (1990), by Pieter Van Raven, is set during the Depression and tells about a boy and his father who move to California. Roy works in the orange orchards while his father tries to get a job with the growers association, and they end up on opposite sides of the labor issues there.

- *Factories in the Field* (1939), published in the same year as *The Grapes of Wrath,* is a factual account by a California state agency of the lives of migrant workers.

- *Hard Times: An Oral History of the Great Depression* (1970), by Studs Terkel, is a compilation of interviews with Americans who lived through the Depression.

- *The Unfinished Nation* (1993) is Alan Brinkley's concise history of the American people which provides a clear and readable look at the American past.

---

a farm near the city of Soledad—and when they are finished they collect their wages and move on in search of another ranch and another temporary job. In these two interrelated aspects of life in California's agricultural working class—the nomadic rootlessness of the itinerant laborer and the wage system wherein the workers are paid cash for specific tasks but are not consistently involved in the process of agricultural production from beginning to end—Steinbeck sees a problematic relation between the workers and the land that they work.

This problem provides the central thematic concern for *Of Mice and Men.* To be sure, it is a story about dreaming of the future, and this is often the thematic thread which first gets picked up in discussions of the novella. But *Of Mice and Men* is not simply about dreaming in general, for the nature of the dream at the center of this story is specifically related to Steinbeck's critical understanding of a specific aspect of society in his contemporary California. The rootlessness and alienation which Steinbeck sees in the lives of California's migrant farm laborers are the real social conditions which he chooses to structure his story, and they thus must

be considered as primary thematic concerns of the novella; that is to say, George and Lennie's dream is specifically necessitated by and responds directly to the limitations placed on their lives, and their story is meant to illuminate the social conditions which Steinbeck seeks to critique. As in all Social Realist literature, this direct engagement with the actual world in all its specificity must be rigorously considered in any thorough reading.

When the reader meets George and Lennie, their nomadic existence is one of the first things Steinbeck establishes. They have just come from the town of Weed, where they have been temporarily employed but where Lennie has gotten into trouble for scaring a young girl. They have escaped from the angry townspeople and now George is going to try to secure a new job for them on a farm near Soledad, hundreds of miles to the south. Further details here accentuate the hard travelling, the ceaseless moving that the two constantly have to undertake. For example, as they pause by the river in the opening pages George mentions that the bus they were on had left them ten miles short of their destination, forcing them to walk the rest of the way to the farm where they are not even sure they will find work. When they do arrive and are about to be taken on, George is given the bunk of a man who, as Candy indifferently says, had "just quit, the way a guy will…. Just wanted to move. Didn't give no other reason but the food. Just [said] 'gimme my time' one night, the way any guy would." Walking for miles, finding a bit of work, sleeping in a bunk house and disappearing one day, these are the exemplary images of the itinerant worker's life, the details with which Steinbeck strategically develops a precise setting and milieu for George and Lennie's story.

Against the exposition of the itinerant laborer's lonely life of moving and working, Steinbeck counterposes the dream that George and Lennie share. As mentioned above, it is not just any dream, or even simply the dream of a better life. In the opening chapter, when George repeats (as he often does) the story for Lennie he begins not by talking about their own individual plans but rather about the state of many men like them. He says: "Guys like us, that work on ranches, are the loneliest guys in the world. They got no family. They don't belong no place. They come to a ranch an' work up a stake and then they go inta town and blow their stake, and the first thing you know they're poundin' their tail on to some other ranch. They ain't got nothing to look ahead to." This is the kind of life that George and Lennie dream of leaving, and, as George suggests, the hardships of that life have primarily to do with solitude and with not having a stable place or enough money to maintain oneself. But George and Lennie have other plans for themselves. A few moments later:

> Lennie broke in. "*But not us! An' why? Because … because I got you to look after me, and you got me to look after you, and that's why.*" He laughed delightedly. "Go on now, George!" …
>
> "O.K. Someday—we're gonna get the jack together and we're gonna have a little house and a couple of acres an' a cow and some pigs and—
>
> "*An' live off the fatta the lan',*" Lennie shouted.

George then goes on to describe their modest farm, the security and freedom of having their own piece of land, and the way they will be able to work for themselves instead of for an occasional wage. A reading of these particular desires and ambitions which George and Lennie cling to, and of the particular things they want to overcome, suggests that Steinbeck rather than writing a story about "dreaming" or "hoping" in general is instead making a very precise and pointed critique of certain aspects of what it is like for many people to live in Califor-

nia, and, by extension, American society. More specifically, *Of Mice and Men* is a critique of the plight of a certain stratum of that society—the landless, poor, agricultural workers—and in the figures of George and Lennie, Steinbeck tries to dramatize on an individual level the tragic story of an entire class of people.

It is worth noting that in the story George and Lennie's dream is by no means unique to them, for it proves also to be the dream of every ranch hand to whom they tell it; Candy and Crooks, for example, each ask if they can join in on the plan. Candy, of course, is accepted, while Crooks seems to have second thoughts (Steinbeck also devotes a large part of one chapter to the figure of Crooks, and to a critical exposition of racism in rural California). The characters in *Of Mice and Men* then can be seen as archetypal insofar as their story is meant to be understood as emblematic of a larger, nonfictional story. They represent the people who work on the farms and in the factories but do not own any part of them, people who earn a wage and have little or nothing more. And in constructing the novella this way Steinbeck wants to draw the readers attention to what he sees as certain urgent and widespread social problems. This sort of direct engagement with social concerns is typical of fiction within the Social Realist tradition.

Even the dramatic climax of the story must be interpreted with an eye toward the social. Curley's wife is the catalyst for Lennie's tragic end, and through most of the story she appears as a purely menacing figure—an ominous portent, one might say. But as she recounts her personal history to Lennie the reader realizes that she, too, must be understood within the context of her surroundings. We see that insofar as she is constrained by unjust social norms, she is not unlike the figures of George and Lennie and Crooks. In her life she is trapped first by her mother's tyranny and the claustrophobia of small town Salinas (Steinbeck's own hometown), and then by her unfortunate marriage to Curley, whom, she tells Lennie, she does not even like. Her actions and her catastrophic role in the story are thus understood not simply as willful destructiveness and licentiousness, or even as the workings of an abstract "tragic fate." Her role is more concrete and complex: her actions and the events resulting from them are likewise the negative upshot of the specific norms and practices which govern society and contemporary life (in her case, the normative models of family and marriage). The novella's ending, then, further develops and indeed emphasizes Steinbeck's analysis of the ways social conventions and practices can have detrimental effects on the lives of people within that society.

Steinbeck's debt to and lineage from Social Realist and Naturalist fiction, then, is made clear through a reading of the way he constantly places his characters and narrative within the context of very specific and, more importantly, actual social situations. The narrative of *Of Mice and Men*—from George and Lennie's hopeful dreaming to the calamitous end to those dreams—is founded upon a rigorous analysis and critique of the encompassing structures of social organization and the ways they affect the people who must live within them.

Source: Kevin Attell, in an essay for *Novels for Students,* Gale, 1997.

Thomas Scarseth

In the following excerpt, Scarseth argues that despite being short and easy to read, Of Mice and Men *provides excellent examples of theme, character, and symbol.*

For *Of Mice and Men* is a Tragedy, a tragedy not in the narrow modern sense of a mere 'sad story' (though it certainly is that), but a tragedy in the classic Aristotelian/Shakespearean sense of showing humanity's achievement of greatness through and in spite of defeat.

Some people seem to believe that the function of literature is to provide vicarious "happy endings," to provide in words a sugary sweetness we would like to have but cannot always get in real life. To such people, true literary tragedy is distasteful. But the greatest writers and the best readers know that literature is not always only mere sugar candy; it can sometimes be a strong medicine: sour perhaps—at least to the untrained taste—but necessary for continued health[.]…

Some readers may object to the book's presentation of low class characters, vulgar language, scenes suggestive of improper sexual conduct, and an implied criticism of the social system. But none of this is presented indecently, or beyond the ordinary norms of contemporary literature. Compared to many modern works, (or to movies and TV) this book is tame indeed. Furthermore, these features are necessary in this book in two ways.

First, they are part of the accurate precise reporting of the reality of a particular time and place and environment. Part of Steinbeck's literary point is that this is *true to life.* As such, the dirty details are part of Steinbeck's enlargement of the realm of Tragedy, the democratization of the tragic world. Traditionally, the subjects of Tragedies have been Kings and other Great Ones: Job, Oedipus, Lear. But Steinbeck's point—a truly American point—is that all men are created equal: Tragedy exists even among the lowly of the earth; even the least of us—even a Lennie or a George—has the human potential for tragic nobility. *Of Mice and Men* is a tragedy in the modern tradition of *The Hairy Ape* and *Death of a Salesman.*

Second, the grossness is a way of presenting briefly the complex turmoil of life. This book is not stereotype melodrama. It is not a simpleminded book. There are no purely bad people in it. Conversely, there are no purely good people in it either. All the characters are complex mixtures of good and bad, or rather of bad results from good intentions. They are all—in their ability and in their outlook—limited. And they live in a gross and dirty world. Given their position in that world, they are not able to achieve much. But they are trying to do the best they can; they are trying to be good people and to have good lives. They have good intentions. They have noble aims.

The tragedy is that, limited as the characters are, the world they live in is even *more* limited; it is a world in which the simplest dream of the simplest man—poor dumb big Lennie—cannot come true. "The best laid plans of mice and men gang oft a-glae [go oft a-stray]," wrote Robert Burns in the poem which provides the book's title and its theme. And Steinbeck's story shows why: The best laid plans go oft astray because they come in conflict with one another. The simplest good intention—simply to stay alive—of a simple mouse, a simple pup, a simple young woman, is thwarted by Lennie's urge to pet something soft and beautiful. Lennie's drive to touch beauty kills the things he loves.

But his problem is the same problem that bothers Curley, the Boss's son, the closest thing to a villain in the book. Like Lennie, Curley doesn't know how to hold on to what he finds important: his young wife, his status as the Boss's son, his reputation as a man. He loses each by trying to hold on too tightly. Curley's aim to be a respected husband/boss/man is foiled by his own limited abilities.

The similar but simpler aim of Lennie and George to have a small place of their own where they can "live offa the fatta the lan'" is doomed to frustration also by their own limitations and the tragic chain of circumstance and coincidence that ends with Lennie dead by George's hand.

The point, of course, is that they all—*we* all—live in a too limited world, a world in which not all our dreams can come true, a world in which we—all of us some of the time and some of us all the time—are doomed to disappointment. The tragic dilemma is that for our basic humanity, for the goodness of our aims, we all deserve better than we get. But because of our human limitations, by our weaknesses of character, none of us is ever good enough to *earn* what we deserve. Some philosophers, seeing this dilemma, pronounce profound pessimism for humanity. Some religions promise for this world's disappointments supernatural intercession and other-worldly compensations. The tragic viewpoint (the view of Shakespeare, the Greek tragedians, the Old Testament Job, and John Steinbeck) finds in it the chance for nobility of soul: even in the blackest of disappointments, a human can achieve individual greatness. One may be defeated physically—but one need not be crushed spiritually. One can remain true to one's dream and true to one's friend. We humans may die, but we can love one another.

Friendship. Love. That too is what *Of Mice and Men* is all about. Lennie and George, disparate types, are, against all good reason, friends. They share a good dream. They love one another. They are too limited, too inarticulate, to know how to say it, but they do show it—or rather Steinbeck shows it to us readers.

So the book treats the great themes of Dreams and Death and Love with simple powerful clarity. It does so with a classically elegant structure—another reason for using the book as a teaching tool: it allows a reader—especially an untrained or beginning reader of literature—to see (or be shown) how structure supports and presents content. *Of Mice and Men* has the classic situation/complication/twist/and resolution plot structure uncluttered by diversions, distractions, or subplots. There is an inevitableness, a starkness that makes the point of the story unavoidable.

The story has the classic unities of time and place and action. It begins in a small spot of beautiful nature, a secluded camp in the woods by a stream; it moves to the buildings of a California ranch, and ends back in the woods by the stream.

The style is simple: clear, direct sentences of description and action, direct quotation of the speech of simple people. Few long words, no hard words.

The action is simple: two poor and vagrant workers, big, dumb Lennie and small, clever George, take jobs at a large ranch. Lennie has trouble with the Boss's son, Curley. Lennie accidentally—more or less—kills Curley's wife. George

kills Lennie to save him from the horrors of a lynch mob led by Curley, bent on revenge.

The settings are simple in detail, and simply powerfully symbolic. The secluded spot in the woods by the stream is the uncomplicated world of Nature; the bunkhouse is the bleak home of hired working men trying to make sense of their lives and gain comfort in a limited environment; the barn is the place of working life, of seed and harvest, birth and death; the harness room with Crook's bunk symbolizes social constraints; the "little place of our own" about which George and Lennie dream and all too vaguely plan is the Paradise on earth we all hope for.

The characters, too, are simple yet significant. "Begin with an individual, and before you know it you find you have created a type," wrote F. Scott Fitzgerald; "begin with a type, and you find that you have created—nothing." Steinbeck begins with individuals: clearly and sharply crafted characters, a whole set of individuals who are so clearly realized that *each*—without surrendering individuality—becomes a *type,* an archetype, a universal character: There is Candy, the old, one-armed worker with no place to go, as useless as his toothless dog; there is Carlson, gruffly and deliberately "unfeeling," who can coolly kill old Candy's ancient dog simply because "he stinks" and "he ain't no good to you"; and there is Crooks, the dignified "proud and aloof" but helpless and lonely victim of racial discrimination. There is Slim, calm, reasonable, compassionate, the real leader of men. And there is Curley, the arrogant but inept Boss's son. The man who could lead well does not have the position; the one who has the position and the authority is not a true leader.

Curley hides his insecurities behind a mask of macho toughness. His competitive bravado makes him push too far and Lennie, after enduring much, is given permission by George to "get him." Lennie in self-protection crushes Curley's fist in his own big hand, crippling Curley somewhat as Candy and Crooks have been crippled by the punitive harshness of life.

Curley is also the one man who has a woman. But clearly he does not—does not know how to—relate to her as a person. She is to him a thing, a possession, a sex-object and a status symbol. For the men, in braggadocio, he flaunts the sexuality of the relationship; and yet, out of his own self-doubts he is intensely jealous of the men's awareness of her.

The young woman has no name—she is merely "Curley's wife." She knows she wants—and somehow deserves—something better than this. "I don't *like* Curley," she says of her husband. She has grandiose ambitions of being a Hollywood star "in the pitchers." She is a lost little girl in a world of men whose knowledge of women is largely limited to memories of kind old ladies and rumors of casual prostitution. All these men are afraid of Curley's wife, afraid and aware that her innocent animal appeal may lead them into temptation and trouble. In self-protection they avoid her. Only Lennie, in naive goodness, actually relates to her as a person to a person. She talks to him. For a little time they share in their aesthetic sense; they both admire beauty. Unfortunately, she is too naive, and Lennie is too strong and clumsy. In trying—at her invitation—to pet her lovely hair he is panicked by her quick resistance, and ends by killing her. Just as he had earlier killed a puppy and a mouse. Curley's wife, a naive Romantic, wants love and tenderness in a harsh crude Naturalistic world; Lennie, big and ignorant, tries to give love. But he is too weak in the mind, too strong in the body. His tenderness is too powerful for weaker, unsuspecting creatures.

We readers can identify with Lennie. We sympathize; we empathize. We care. We have—most of us—been in his position; not quite able to cope with the complexities of the world around us, wanting only security, peace, comfort, and something soft and beautiful to pet and love.

Perhaps one reason that this book has evoked controversy and censorious action is that it is so simple and clear and easy to understand—and so painful! It *hurts* to read this book. And some people don't like their books to hurt them; they want soothing. But great Tragedy is *meant* to hurt. One needn't subscribe wholly to the Aristotelian doctrine of 'catharsis' by Art to see that one function of literature is to help us deal with the pain of real life by practicing with the vicarious pains of tragic art.

Of course *Of Mice and Men* contains unpleasant attitudes; there is brutality, racism, sexism, economic exploitation. But the book does not advocate them; rather it shows that these too-narrow conceptions of human life are part of the cause of human tragedy. They are forces which frustrate human aspiration.

Lennie and George have a noble dream. They are personally too limited to make it come true, but they do try. They try to help each other, and they even enlarge their dream to include old one-handed Candy and crippled black Crooks. Theirs is the American Dream: that there is somehow, somewhere, sometime, the possibility that we can make our Paradise on earth, that we can have our own self-sufficient little place where we can live off the fat of the land as peaceful friends.

What is sad, what is tragic, what is horrible, is that the Dream may not come true because we are—each and all of us—too limited, too selfish, too much in conflict with one another. "Maybe ever'body in the whole damn world is scared of each other," says Slim. And George expresses the effects of loneliness, "Guys that go around ... alone ... don't have no fun. After a long time they get mean. They get wantin' to fight all the time."

What is *ennobling* in this tragedy of mice and men is the Revelation of a way beyond that loneliness and meanness and fighting, a way to rise above our human limitations: Two men—Lennie and George—who have nothing else, do have each other. "We kinda look after each other." says George. And they do have their Dream. And the Dream is there even in the final defeat. For in the end the one thing George can do for Lennie is to make sure he's happy as he dies. He has Lennie "look acrost the river ... you can almost see [the place]." And as Lennie says, "Let's get that place now," George kills him mercifully. It's a horrible thing to do, and George knows that. And *we* know that. But in this limited world in this limited way it is all that George can do for his friend. And he does it. That is the horror and the nobility which together make up Tragedy. The Tragic pattern closes. There is a sense of completeness, of both defeat and satisfaction.

In *Of Mice and Men*, Steinbeck has shown us something about the pain of living in a complex human world and created something beautiful from it. In true great literature the pain of Life is transmuted into the beauty of Art. The book is worth reading for a glimpse of that beauty—and worth teaching as a way to show others how such beauty works.

Source: Thomas Scarseth, "A Teachable Good Book: *Of Mice and Men*," in *Censored Books: Critical Viewpoints*, edited by Nicholas J. Karolides, Lee Burress, and John M. Kean, Scarecrow Press, 1993, pp. 388–94.

Peter Lisca

In the following excerpt, Lisca details Steinbeck's use of "symbol, action, and language" in Of Mice and Men.

Shortly after sending off the manuscript for *Of Mice and Men,* Steinbeck wrote to his agents, "I'm sorry that you do not find the new book as large in subject as it should be. I probably did not make my subjects and symbols clear. The microcosm is difficult to handle and apparently I did not get it over." Despite the agents' initial disappointment, *Of Mice and Men* became a great success as novel, play, and motion picture. That Steinbeck's audience found his "subjects and symbols clear" is doubtful; that the critics did not is certain. For the most part, those critics who saw nothing beyond the obvious plot disliked the work immensely. Those who suspected more important levels of meaning were unable to offer specific and thorough explication. Today, almost twenty years later, it is generally accepted that the success of *Of Mice and Men* was an accident of history: Steinbeck merely cashed in on his audience's readiness to shed a tear, even a critical tear, over the plight of lonely migrant laborers. As one critic put it ten years later, "This is a negligible novel, seemingly written with a determined eye on the cash register" [George D. Snell, in his *The Shapers of American Fiction,* 1947].

This essay is a much belated attempt to discover just what Steinbeck's "subjects and symbols" are and how they are utilized in *Of Mice and Men,* which he once referred to as "a study of the dreams and pleasures of everyone in the world."

To present his larger subject in terms of a microcosm Steinbeck makes use of three incremental motifs: symbol, action, and language. All three of these motifs are presented in the opening scene, are contrapuntally developed through the story, and come together again at the end. The first symbol in the novel, and the primary one, is the little spot by the river where the story begins and ends. The book opens with a description of this place by the river, and we first see George and Lennie as they enter this place from the highway to an outside world. It is significant that they prefer spending the night here rather than going on to the bunkhouse at the ranch.

Steinbeck's novels and stories often contain groves, willow thickets by a river, and caves which figure prominently in the action. There are, for example, the grove in *To a God Unknown,* the place by the river in the Junius Maltby story, the two caves and a willow thicket in *The Grapes of Wrath,* the cave under the bridge in *In Dubious Battle,* the caves in *The Wayward Bus,* and the thicket and cave in *The Pearl.* For George and Lennie, as for other Steinbeck heroes, coming to a cave or thicket

by the river symbolizes a retreat from the world to a primeval innocence. Sometimes, as in *The Grapes of Wrath,* this retreat has explicit overtones of a return to the womb and rebirth. In the opening scene of *Of Mice and Men* Lennie twice mentions the possibility of hiding out in a cave, and George impresses on him that he must return to this thicket by the river when there is trouble.

While the cave or the river thicket is a "safe place," it is physically impossible to remain there, and this symbol of primeval innocence becomes translated into terms possible in the real world. For George and Lennie it becomes "a little house an' a couple of acres." Out of this translation grows a second symbol, the rabbits, and this symbol serves several purposes. By the figure of synecdoche it comes to stand for the "safe place" itself, making a much more easily manipulated symbol than the "house an' a couple of acres." Also, through Lennie's love for the rabbits Steinbeck is able not only to dramatize Lennie's desire for the "safe place," but to define the basis of that desire on a very low level of consciousness—the attraction to soft, warm fur, which is for Lennie the most important aspect of their plans.

This transference of symbolic value from the farm to the rabbits is important also because it makes possible another motif, the motif of action. This is introduced in the first scene by the dead mouse which Lennie is carrying in his pocket (much as Tom carries the turtle in *The Grapes of Wrath*). As George talks about Lennie's attraction to mice, it becomes evident that the symbolic rabbits will come to the same end—crushed by Lennie's simple blundering strength. Thus Lennie's killing of mice and later his killing of the puppy set up a motif of action, a pattern, which the reader expects to be carried out again. George's story about Lennie and the little girl with the red dress, which he tells twice, contributes to this expectancy of pattern, as does the shooting of Candy's dog, the crushing of Curley's hand, and the frequent appearances of Curley's wife. All these actions are patterns of the mice motif and predict the fate of the rabbits and thus the fate of the dream of a "safe place."

The third motif, that of language, is also present in the opening scene. Lennie asks George, "Tell me—like you done before," and George's words are obviously in the nature of a ritual. "George's voice became deeper. He repeated his words rhythmically, as though he had said them many times before." The element of ritual is stressed by the fact that even Lennie has heard it often enough to remember its precise language: "'*An' live off the fatta the lan'*'…. An' have *rabbits.* Go on George! Tell about what we're gonna have in the garden and about the rabbits in the cages and about….'" This ritual is performed often in the story, whenever Lennie feels insecure. And of course it is while Lennie is caught up in this dream vision that George shoots him, so that on one level the vision is accomplished—the dream never interrupted, the rabbits never crushed.

The highly patterned effect achieved by these incremental motifs of symbol, action, and language is the knife edge on which criticism of *Of Mice and Men* divides. Mark Van Doren, for example, sees this patterning of events as evidence of a mechanical structure: "Lennie, you see, cannot help shaking small helpless creatures until their necks are broken, just as Curley cannot help being a beast of jealousy. They are wound up to act that way, and the best they can do is to run down; which is what happens when Steinbeck comes to his last mechanical page" ["Wrong Number," *The Nation* CXLIV (6 March 1937)]. This view is shared by Joseph Wood Krutch, who insists [in his *The American Drama since 1918,* 1939] that "everything from beginning to end" is "as shamelessly cooked up as, let us say, the death of Little Nell." On the other hand, Mr. Stark Young sees this patterning as a virtue: "And instead of losing … by this evident manipulation for effect, the play gains in its total impact and imaginative compulsion. In the characters, too, we get a sense of arrangement or design, so definitely carried through that we have almost a sense of types, an almost classic designation and completeness to each" ["Drama Critics Circle Award," *The New Republic* XCIV (4 May 1938)]. Frank H. O'Hara comes to a similar conclusion [in his *Today in American Drama,* 1939], though admitting that "the constituents of melodrama are all here."

Thus while Steinbeck's success in creating a pattern has been acknowledged, criticism has been divided as to the effect of this achievement. On one side it is claimed that this strong patterning creates a sense of contrivance and mechanical action; and on the other that the patterning actually gives a meaningful design to the story, a tone of classic fate. What is obviously needed here is some objective critical tool for determining under what conditions a sense of inevitability (to use a neutral word) should be experienced as catharsis effected by a sense of fate, and when it should be experienced as mechanical contrivance. Such a tool can-

not be forged within the limits of this study; but it is possible to examine the particular circumstances of *Of Mice and Men* more closely than has been done in this connection.

Although the three motifs of symbol, action, and language build up a strong pattern of inevitability, the movement is not unbroken. About midway in the novel (chapters 3 & 4) there is set up a counter movement which seems to threaten the pattern. Up to this point the dream of "a house an' a couple of acres" has seemed impossible of realization; the motifs have been too insistent. But now it develops that George has an actual farm in mind (ten acres), knows the owners and why they want to sell it: "'The ol' people that owns it is flat bust an' the ol' lady needs an operation.'" He even knows the price—"'six hundred dollars.'" Also, the maimed workman, Candy, is willing to buy a share in the dream with the three hundred dollars he has saved. It appears that at the end of the month George and Lennie will have another hundred dollars and that quite possibly they "'could swing her for that.'" In the following chapter this dream and its possibilities are further explored through Lennie's visit with Crooks, the power of the dream manifesting itself in Crooks' conversion from cynicism to optimism. But at the very height of his conversion the mice symbol reappears in the form of Curley's wife, who threatens the dream by bringing with her the harsh realities of the outside world and by arousing Lennie's interest.

The function of Candy's and Crooks' interest and the sudden bringing of the dream within reasonable possibility is to interrupt, momentarily, the pattern of inevitability. But, and this is very important, Steinbeck handles this interruption so that it does not actually constitute a reversal of the situation. Rather, it insinuates a possibility. Thus, though working against the pattern set up by the motifs, this counter movement makes that pattern more aesthetically credible by creating the necessary ingredient of free will. The story achieves power through a delicate balance of the protagonists' free will and the force of circumstance.

In addition to imposing a sense of inevitability, this strong patterning of events performs the important function of extending the story's range of meanings. This can best be understood by reference to Hemingway's "fourth dimension," which has been defined by Joseph Warren Beach as an "aesthetic factor" achieved by the protagonists' repeated participation in some traditional "ritual or strategy," and by Malcolm Cowley as "the almost continual performance of rites and ceremonies" suggesting recurrent patterns of human experience. The incremental motifs of symbol, action, and language which inform *Of Mice and Men* have precisely these effects. The simple story of two migrant workers' dream of a safe retreat, a "clean well-lighted place," becomes itself a pattern or archetype.

Thus while John Mason Brown [in his *Two on the Aisle,* 1938] calls the play "one of the finest, most pungent, and most poignant realistic productions," Frank H. O'Hara says that "… we are likely to come away with more … feelings for the implications of the story than the story itself… sketching behind the individual characters the vast numbers of other homeless drifters who work for a toe hold in a society which really has no place for them." [In "Steinbeck of California," *Delphian Quarterly* XXIII (April 1940)] Carlos Baker sees the book as an allegory of Mind and Body. Edmund Wilson calls the book "a parable which criticizes humanity from a non-political point of view" [*The Boys in the Back Room,* 1941]. The French critic, Mme. Claude-Edmonde Magny sees George and Lennie as "l'homme et le monstre," or "la conscience et l'humanité" [*L'Age du roman américain,* 1948].

As these remarks make clear, three levels have been observed in *Of Mice and Men.* There is the obvious story level on a realistic plane, with its shocking climax. There is also the level of social protest, Steinbeck the reformer crying out against the exploitation of migrant workers. The third level is an allegorical one, its interpretation limited only by the ingenuity of the audience. It could be, as Carlos Baker suggests, an allegory of Mind and Body. Using the same kind of dichotomy, the story could also be about the dumb, clumsy, but strong mass of humanity and its shrewd manipulators. This would make the book a more abstract treatment of the two forces in *In Dubious Battle*—the mob and its leaders. The dichotomy could also be that of the unconscious and the conscious, the *id* and the *ego,* or any other forces or qualities which have the same structural relationship to each other as do Lennie and George. It is interesting in this connection that the name *Leonard* means "strong and brave as a lion," and that the name *George,* of course, means "husbandman."

The title itself, however, relates *Of Mice and Men* to still another level which is implicit in the context of [Robert] Burns' poem:

But, Mousie, thou art no thy lane,
In proving foresight may be vain:

The best laid schemes o' mice and men
Gang aft a-gley
An' leave us nought but grief an' pain
For promis'd joy.

In the poem Bums extends the mouse's experience to include mankind; in *Of Mice and Men* Steinbeck extends the experience of two migrant workers to the human condition. "This is the way things are," both writers are saying. On this level, perhaps its most important, Steinbeck is dramatizing the non-teleological philosophy which had such a great part in shaping *In Dubious Battle* and which was to be explicated in *Sea of Cortez.* This level of meaning is also indicated by the book's tentative title while it was in progress—"Something That Happened." In this light, the ending of the story is, like the ploughman's disrupting of the mouse's nest, neither tragic nor brutal but simply a part of the pattern of events. It is amusing in this regard that a Hollywood director suggested to Steinbeck that someone else kill the girl so that sympathy could be kept with Lennie.

Source: Peter Lisca, "Motif and Pattern in *Of Mice and Men,*" in *Modern Fiction Studies,* winter, 1956–57, pp. 228–34.

Sources

Jackson J. Benson, *The True Adventures of John Steinbeck, Writer,* Viking, 1984.

Arthur Mizener, article in the *New York Times Book Review,* December 9, 1962, pp. 4, 45.

Editorial in the *New York Times,* October 26, 1962, p. 30.

Louis Owens, "Of Mice and Men: The Dream of Commitment," in *Modern Critical Views: John Steinbeck,* edited by Harold Bloom, Chelsea House, 1987, p. 146

Henry Seidel, review of *Of Mice and Men,* in *Saturday Review of Literature,* February 27, 1937.

Ralph Thompson, review of *Of Mice and Men* in the *New York Times,* February 27, 1937, p. L15.

For Further Study

Jackson J. Benson, editor, *The Short Novels of John Steinbeck,* Duke University Press, 1990, pp. 39-70.
  A collection of critical essays on all of Steinbeck's work. Part 2 contains three informative essays on *Of Mice and Men.* This book also contains a very useful bibliography of Steinbeck criticism.

Paul McCarthy, *John Steinbeck,* Frederick Ungar Publishing, 1981, pp. 57-64.
  Overview of Steinbeck's life and work. Chapter 3 deals with the 1930s and pages 57-64 with *Of Mice and Men* in particular.

Joseph R. McElrath, and others, editors, *John Steinbeck: The Contemporary Reviews,* Cambridge University Press, 1996, pp. 71-94.

> An extensive collection of contemporary Reviews of all of Steinbeck's work. Pages 71-94 contain reviews of *Of Mice and Men.*

Louis Owens, *John Steinbeck's Re-Vision of America,* Georgia University Press, pp. 100-106.

> Contains a short chapter on the themes of myth and determinism in *Of Mice and Men.*

Jay Parini, *John Steinbeck: A Biography,* Henry Holt, 1995.

> A recent biography, shorter than the Benson biography.

E. W. Tedlock, and C. V. Wicker, editors, *Steinbeck and His Critics,* University of New Mexico Press, 1957.

> A large collection of critical essays dealing with many thematic and aesthetic issues in Steinbeck's fiction.

John H. Timmerman, *John Steinbeck's Fiction: The Aesthetics of the Road Taken,* Oklahoma University Press, 1986.

> Chapter 4 treats *Of Mice and Men* and *In Dubious Battle* together and discusses the thematic significance of the landscape in the two novels.

Ordinary People

Judith Guest
1976

In 1976, Judith Guest's *Ordinary People* became the first unsolicited manuscript published by Viking Press in twenty-six years. Since then the popularity of the novel has remained undiminished. It is read by adults and teenagers alike for its sensitive characterizations of the troubled teenager Conrad Jarrett and his confused father, Calvin. The story of a teenaged boy's journey back from a suicide attempt after his older brother's death in a boating accident, and the grief and guilt that tear the Jarretts apart, *Ordinary People* was an instant best-seller. It was also made into an award-winning film. Guest's themes of alienation, the search for identity, and coming of age were timely ones, as the 1970s saw a trend toward self-discovery. Thus, psychology plays a key role in the novel, as young Conrad learns to express rather than repress his emotions with the help of a psychiatrist, while his mother's inability to confront her feelings leads her to leave her husband and son. Judith Guest has been especially praised for her insight into the feelings and experiences of her adolescent male protagonist, Conrad Jarrett, as well as for her ear for dialogue. Some critics have found Guest's emphasis on surrendering control ironic, as the style of the novel is tightly controlled, though unconventional, with its shifts between the perspectives of Calvin and Conrad Jarrett. Critics have also found that Guest's ending is too contrived; the troubled relationship between Conrad and his mother is resolved through the healing power of love, even though the two are not in contact with each other. Nevertheless, *Ordi-*

nary People, with its universal insights into the grief process and the relationships between family members and its sensitive and realistic portrayals of its characters, will probably continue to be read for years to come.

Author Biography

Judith Guest does not stray too far from her own personal experiences and background in creating her fictional works. Like the characters in novels such as *Ordinary People,* she is from a white, well-to-do family and lives in the suburbs. Born March 29, 1936, in Detroit, Michigan, she is the daughter of a businessman and a housewife. Her insight into her male adolescent characters may stem from her experience raising three sons with her husband, or from her employment as a teacher in public schools.

Guest began writing at the young age of twelve, but she never showed her family her work. Later, in college, she was intimidated by the thought of taking creative writing classes at the University of Michigan. Instead, she majored in education, receiving her bachelor's degree in 1958. The summer after she graduated, she married Larry Lavercombe, a business executive. While teaching at elementary schools in Michigan, Guest began raising her children: Larry, John, and Richard. Teaching and raising her sons took up most of her time, so she did not begin writing seriously until after they had started school. When the family moved to Illinois, she tried her hand at journalism, but she did not like the constraints this kind of writing involved. She did, however, learn about meeting deadlines and editing articles to fit limited amounts of space. After taking a writing seminar, she was inspired to start writing fiction again, and she has been writing full-time since 1975.

Despite delaying a writing career while raising a family, Guest feels that this period in her life has been valuable to her fiction. While going to PTA meetings and chauffeuring her children to school and events, she was often thinking about her novels, developing plots and characters in her mind until she was ready to write them down. The content of her stories, however, was inspired by her childhood. Guest has said that her interest in cold and emotionally distant characters originates in experiences with family members. Her father did not share his feelings openly, never telling his daughter, for example, about the pain he must have felt when he was ten years old and his father died.

Judith Guest

This sort of stifled emotional anguish fills the pages of Guest's first published work. *Ordinary People* was the first unsolicited manuscript accepted by Viking Press in twenty-six years. This story of a family torn apart by the untimely death of a child was an instant success. The novel was selected by four book clubs, serialized in *Redbook,* and had paperback rights sold to Ballantine for $635,000. In 1980, Robert Redford made his directorial debut and won an Oscar when he adapted *Ordinary People* for the screen. Guest herself approved of the ending, which was more inconclusive than the ending of the book, and the acting, particularly Mary Tyler Moore's portrayal of Beth. The film adaptation created an even bigger audience for Guest's work.

Guest has written other novels, including *Second Heaven,* which appeared in 1982, *Killing Time in St. Cloud,* a 1988 work written with Rebecca Hill, and 1997's *Errands.* Like her first novel, these works present ordinary people dealing with extraordinary circumstances, struggling to maintain connections with others in the midst of loss and grief. Although Guest draws on her personal life for much of the material she puts into her novels, her characters and their experiences come from her own imagination. She has said, however, that what is most real about her characters is the feelings they experience and the emotional struggles they endure.

Plot Summary

Autumn

Ordinary People consists of two interwoven stories told from the points of view of Conrad "Con" Jarrett and his father, Calvin "Cal" Jarrett. Set in the suburbs of Chicago in the 1970s, the novel begins in the aftermath of the accidental death of Jordan "Buck" Jarrett and his brother Conrad's subsequent suicide attempt. Conrad, Calvin, and Beth Jarrett struggle throughout the novel to cope with these tragedies. The story begins with Con making an appointment with his new outpatient psychiatrist, Dr. Berger, after having been released from a mental hospital. It is evident in the first chapter that Con is still struggling with anxiety and depression.

In Chapter Two, the narrator switches to Cal's perspective. It is clear that Con and Beth's relationship is a strained one, while Cal is torn between both of them. Like Con, Cal finds Beth unknowable and distant, but he romanticizes this quality in her, even when they disagree over whether or not to go away for Christmas, as they do in Chapter Four. Cal's insistence that the family not travel during Christmas because of Con's mental and emotional state is a decision which will cause tension in the family in later chapters. Cal and Beth's mutual grief over Buck's death is not mentioned, as they both struggle to control, rather than express, their grief. This desire for control is echoed by Con in Chapter Five, when he tells Berger that he wants to feel more in control. Berger's attempts to get Con to understand that it is better to express emotions than to control them continues as a theme throughout the novel.

When Con meets a friend from the hospital, Karen, in Chapter Seven, he realizes that their relationship has changed and that he can no longer depend on his friendship with her. When he returns home from his trip to see Karen, in Chapter Eight, he is visibly tense when Cal mentions the possibility of traveling to London for Christmas. When, on the way to a party, Beth tells Cal that Con would have made the trip, Cal replies that Con did not want to go, and he feels both relief and guilt when Beth drops the subject. After the party, Beth and Cal fight over his discussion of Con's problems with friends of theirs.

In Chapter Nine, Con realizes with Berger's help that he wants to quit the swim team, and after he does so in Chapter Ten, he neglects to tell his parents because he does not want to worry them. When, in Chapter Eleven, Con brings home an "A" on a trigonometry quiz, Cal wants to believe that the work of grieving is done and that they are ordinary people again.

Winter

Chapter Twelve begins around Christmastime. With Berger's help, Con is beginning to feel better and be more at peace with himself, especially after he walks Jeannine Pratt home. But this sense of peace is short-lived as, in Chapter Thirteen, the Jarrett family explodes. Beth finds out from Carole Lazenby that Con has quit the swim team. Con becomes angry, telling her that he would have told her if he thought she cared and adding that she did not come to the hospital to visit him because she was traveling, revealing the source of his anxiety about the possible Christmas trip to London. After Con runs upstairs, Cal attempts to mediate the argument, but he gets nowhere because Con and Beth both think that he does not see their points of view. Beth and Con do not mention the fight again, but Con is able to talk about it with Berger, who tells Con to recognize Beth's limitations and to maintain a sense of perspective.

Chapter Fifteen takes place on Christmas Day. Beth and Cal fight over Con's lack of enthusiasm for his new car. When Beth tells Cal that things would have been different if they had gone away for Christmas, Cal realizes that their sense of grief underlies their argument. As Cal and Beth's relationship continues to deteriorate, Con's relationship with Berger is helping him to climb out of his depression. Cal asks Con if it's all right for him to go see Berger, and with Con's permission, he does so in Chapter Seventeen, realizing in Berger's office that he sees himself as a "fence-sitter," and that Beth and Con are possibly on opposite sides of that fence.

Chapter Eighteen takes place during Con's exam week. After one exam, he runs into Jeannine. Though he worries that she will reject him because she knows about his breakdown, he calls and asks her out on a date. Meanwhile, Cal is realizing how troubled his relationship with Beth is when his business partner tells him that the normally private Beth has told Ray's wife, Nancy, that Cal is obsessed with Con's problems.

Conrad and Jeannine's first date is the subject of Chapter Twenty. The date goes well, signaling

From the film Ordinary People, *starring Timothy Hutton and Dinah Manoff, Paramount, 1980.*

the start of their relationship. When the story switches back to Cal, he and Beth are making plans to go to a golf tournament in Dallas, but Beth is noticeably unenthusiastic, even though Cal hopes that getting away will enable them to forget their problems.

Con then attends a swim meet, where he gets into a fight with a swimmer named Kevin Stillman, who has made a crude remark about Jeannine. Con is torn by guilt over his loss of control, but he feels reassured when Cal tells him it is okay to get into an occasional fight. Cal wonders, though, why Beth did not wake Con up when she saw him sleeping on the couch.

In Chapter Twenty-four, Beth and Cal leave for Dallas. Con feels strong when he is able to comfort Jeannine, who is upset when her mother's lover unexpectedly comes to town. Con's strength is tested, however, when he finds out that Karen has committed suicide. His guilt and grief over the deaths of Karen and Buck threaten to overwhelm him. Berger gets Con to see that Buck's death is not his fault, and Con is able to finally express the pain he feels rather than trying to control it. Con feels a sense of release, just had Berger had been predicting throughout their relationship. As he tells Con, "people with stiff upper lips find it hard to smile."

As Con's story climaxes with his expression of pain and anger, Beth and Cal's story also reaches its climax, in Chapter Twenty-eight, as they fight over Con's problems. Beth says that she will never forgive Con for his suicide attempt, and admits that she can only see Con's suicide attempt in terms of how it affects her, saying that she cannot love him the way he wants her to. Cal realizes Con's breakdown has done something terrible to Beth. Though Cal knows that some action must be taken, he is afraid to face the reality of the marriage's impending breakup.

Chapter Thirty begins with Con and Jeannine making love, after which they share intimate confidences about their emotional problems. As Con achieves a new level of closeness with Jeannine, his parents' marriage is coming apart. They argue nightly, and their love is not enough to rescue the relationship. Beth leaves for a trip to Europe without saying good-bye to Conrad, and when he expresses bitterness, Cal gets angry with him, no longer metaphorically sitting on the fence. Cal realizes that Beth wants things to be like they were before Buck's death and Con's breakdown, and her inability to come to terms with these losses has destroyed the marriage. When Con tells Cal he is not at all disappointed with Cal's love for him, father and son embrace.

Summer

The epilogue begins after Con has said goodbye to Berger. He stops by his friend Lazenby's house in an attempt to repair their friendship, which has been torn apart by their mutual grief for Buck. Con remembers having found all his old school drawings when he and Cal moved, and he realizes that his mother would not have kept them so carefully if they did not mean anything to her. As Con and Lazenby go off to play golf, the novel ends on a note of optimism for Con and his relationships with others.

Characters

Karen Aldrich

Karen Aldrich is Conrad Jarrett's friend from the mental hospital. When they meet after they are released, Con feels ashamed that he's seeing a therapist while she is not. Karen tells him that she doesn't really know him, suggesting that their closeness has evaporated as Karen struggles to repress the difficulties that landed her in the hospital. Her subsequent successful suicide attempt pushes Con to the breaking point, as waves of grief and guilt wash over him. When he finally sees Dr. Berger, Con is able to use the intense grief he feels over Karen's and Buck's deaths in order to begin to heal.

Arnold Bacon

Though he does not actually appear in *Ordinary People,* Arnold Bacon is an important figure in Cal Jarrett's past. Bacon mentored Cal through college and law school, but he withdrew his support when Cal married Beth. Bacon is Cal's first true experience with loss, and Cal's inability to balance his relationships with Bacon and Beth is duplicated when he tries to mediate between Beth and Con.

Dr. Berger

Dr. Berger is the psychiatrist who is Conrad Jarrett's therapist. Gentle and eccentric, he lies on the floor with his patients during therapy sessions because he does not have a couch. His language is typically teasing and humorous, and his attitude stands in sharp contrast to the controlled and tortured Con. Berger gets Con to realize that the expression—rather than the control—of feelings is important to good mental health. Berger also helps Con to see that he is not responsible for his brother Buck's death and that he can be himself without trying to live up to Buck's legacy. Berger offers

Media Adaptations

- *Ordinary People* was adapted in 1980 as an Academy-Award winning film by Robert Redford in his directorial debut, and starred Mary Tyler Moore, Donald Sutherland, Timothy Hutton, and Judd Hirsch; the screenplay was written by Alvin Sargent, and the musical score was composed by Marvin Hamlisch. The film is available from Paramount Home Video.

Con a safe space in which to talk and to express his anger, frustration, shame, and pain. Berger is able to handle Con's emotions without being oversolicitous, unlike Con's parents, Beth and Cal. Thus, Berger helps Con retreat from the family surroundings in which he is enmeshed and gain a sense of perspective about his father, his mother, and himself.

Audrey Butler

Audrey is Ward's wife. She tries to intercede in Beth and Cal's argument and is stricken when Beth tells her that she can only talk about how to be happy if she can ensure that her kids are always going to be safe.

Ellen Butler

Ellen is Beth Jarrett's mother. Her incessant nagging causes Con and Beth to retreat emotionally and illustrates the generation gap between family members.

Howard Butler

Howard is Beth Jarrett's father. His excitement about giving Con a car for Christmas, a car that Con doesn't need or want, underscores his inability to understand Con's problems.

Ward Butler

Ward is Beth Jarrett's brother. Beth and Cal visit him in Texas in the hope of escaping their problems, but they are unable to do so and fight bitterly over Beth's inability to forgive Con. Ward and his wife, Audrey, try to mediate but are unable to help.

Marty Genthe

In *Ordinary People* Marty Genthe's questions about Con at the Murrays' party leads Beth to accuse Cal of violating the family's privacy.

Ray Hanley

Ray is Cal's law partner of many years. Ray attempts to counsel Cal after Beth tells Ray's wife that Cal is obsessed with Con's problems, just as Cal tried to mediate between Ray and his wife when Ray had an affair. Cal feels that Ray does not understand the grief he feels over his son's death and Con's hospitalization, but he feels sorry that Ray is being forced to serve as a mediator between he and Beth.

Beth Jarrett

Though one of the principal characters in *Ordinary People,* Beth remains a somewhat shadowy character throughout the novel. The reader is only given impressions of her through the perceptions of Calvin and Conrad Jarrett. Beth is described as a perfectionist, and this perfectionism does not allow for forgiveness. She sees Con's suicide attempt as a punishment directed at her, and she cannot recognize or understand Con's emotional problems. Her mysteriousness and inconsistency draw Cal to her, but it also makes it impossible for them to work out the problems in their relationship because Beth will not communicate her feelings. Cal realizes by the end of the story that she cannot accept Buck's death and wants their lives to be like they were before the accident and Con's hospitalization. Because this is impossible, she distances herself from Cal, blaming him for becoming depressed about what has happened to their family and changing into a different person. Cal sees that Beth's perfectionism and practicality function to cover up her fears about losing control. Con realizes that Beth's overbearing mother, Ellen, has probably caused her to become a private person, but Beth herself is unwilling or unable to understand herself or express her emotions. Cal and Con must therefore reconcile themselves to her loss when she leaves after Cal suggests a marriage counselor. Both Cal and Con still love Beth, but they are forced to recognize her limitations.

Buck Jarrett

See Jordan Jarrett

Cal Jarrett

See Calvin Jarrett

Calvin Jarrett

Calvin Jarrett is the father in the Jarrett family in *Ordinary People,* and like the rest of the surviving family members, he is also struggling with grief over his son Buck's death. For Cal, this struggle is particularly hard because he felt isolated during his childhood, growing up in an orphanage and only becoming a successful tax attorney through the support of his mentor, Arnold Bacon. Cal's relationship with Bacon ended after he met his wife, Beth, because he could not balance his needs between the two people he loved. Cal experiences a similar situation when he attempts to mediate between Beth and their son, Con. Cal sees himself as a "fence-sitter" and is afraid to recognize that Beth and Con are on opposite sides of the fence. Cal's concern for Con is intensified after Con tries to commit suicide, while Beth sees Con's attempt as a punishment directed at her. The difference in their approaches to Con's emotional problems ultimately leads to Cal and Beth's separation, but this is also caused by Cal's recognition of his own needs, which are not being met by his wife. Cal's desire to have a family of his own after a childhood spent in relative isolation has caused him to ignore his own needs in order to keep peace in the family. After Buck dies and Con is hospitalized, the hidden conflicts in the family become impossible to ignore, and Cal finds that he cannot turn to Beth for comfort, that the family members have become isolated in their grief. Cal's efforts to hold the family together are futile, but the novel ends on a note of reconciliation between Cal and Con. Cal finds his own voice and expresses his feelings for the first time, rather than being oversolicitous toward Con, as he has done throughout the novel.

Con Jarrett

See Conrad Jarrett

Conrad Jarrett

Conrad Jarrett is at the center of *Ordinary People,* which begins on the day he makes an appointment with his therapist. Con's suicide attempt in the wake of his brother Buck's death after a boating accident lands him in a mental hospital, where he is given electric shock treatment for severe depression. When he is finally released from the hospital, he feels alienated from family, friends, and teachers, as well as from his former self. He resents his obligations to the swim team and to his former friendships, and he feels at peace only when singing with the choir. Con's journey back to health is one of the main themes of *Ordi-*

nary People. Through his relationships with Dr. Berger and Jeannine Pratt, Conrad begins to express his repressed emotions, to find reconciliation with his parents, and to recover from the survivor's guilt he feels over his brother's death. He learns to accept his failures, his anxieties, and his fears and to act positively in spite of them. He also learns to accept others' limitations. The turning point for Con is when his friend Karen kills herself, unleashing a flood of guilt in him. In his meeting with Dr. Berger, he realizes that he is not responsible for the deaths of either Buck or Karen, and that it is okay to be himself. His relationship with his mother is less easily resolved. When his parents separate, she leaves without saying good-bye. Con feels intense anger and disappointment about this, but with Berger's help, he tries to accept that she loves him as much as she is able to. The Epilogue shows that Con's final lesson is learning that his mother does indeed love him, and that he loves her. His alienation is assuaged, and his relationships with family and friends are renewed by the end of the novel.

Jordan Jarrett

Buck Jarrett's death propels the action in *Ordinary People.* His brother, Conrad, is unable to deal with the guilt he feels at surviving the boating accident that killed Buck, while his parents' grief over losing their child haunts them throughout the novel. Buck's easygoing manner and carefree charm are contrasted with Con's guilt and feelings of responsibility, and Cal realizes that he should have worried more about Con even though he is not as apt to make trouble as Buck was. Buck's loss affects all the characters in the story and causes them to isolate themselves from each other.

Carole Lazenby

Carole Lazenby is Joe Lazenby's mother and Beth and Cal's friend. When she remarks to Beth that she didn't know Con had quit the swim team, it causes a family fight as Beth confronts Con about his dishonesty. When Cal finds out that Carole is taking a class called "Search for Identity," he realizes that even the people who seem most well-adjusted have problems.

Joe Lazenby

Joe is a friend of Conrad's from the swim team. Because of his grief over his brother's death, a grief which Lazenby shares, Con finds it painful to be around him. Con isolates himself from Lazenby un-til his friend gives up on him. It is not until the end of the novel that Con is able to renew their friendship and appreciate Lazenby's decency and good spirits.

Mrs. Pratt

Mrs. Pratt is Jeannine's mother. Her divorce from Jeannine's father and her subsequent affair with a friend of Jeannine's father propels Jeannine into depression and drug abuse.

Jeannine Pratt

Jeannine Pratt is Con's first serious girlfriend. At first, they share a relatively casual dating relationship, but they quickly become intimate friends. Jeannine and Con are drawn together by their shared struggles with depression and difficulties with family relationships. When Jeannine begins to cry over her parents' divorce, Con is there to comfort her, and he realizes that he can help others. Con and Jeannine's physical relationship brings them closer together, as Con realizes the truth of Dr. Berger's maxim that the body never lies. When Kevin Stillman makes a remark about Jeannine which cheapens Con's sense of their relationship, Con gets into a fight with him. Con feels protective of Jeannine, and his relationship with her is one of the factors which enables him to assuage his alienation from others. Jeannine is understanding and gentle with Con, as she can relate to what he has gone through.

Mike Pratt

In *Ordinary People* Mike Pratt is Jeannine's brother, whom Con and Jeannine are forced to baby-sit when Jeannine's mother's lover comes to town. Jeannine's sadness over her parents' divorce emerges as a result of encountering the man again.

Coach Salan

In *Ordinary People* Coach Salan, who coaches the swim team, causes Con to feel guilt and shame when he asks questions about Con's hospitalization, and he makes Con feel guilty about being in therapy and quitting the swim team.

Kevin Stillman

Kevin Stillman is an insensitive diver on Conrad Jarrett's swim team. His lewd remark about Con's relationship with Jeannine leads Con to get into the first fight of his life.

Topics for Further Study

- Investigate the effects of divorce on families and speculate on how life will change for the Jarrett family if Beth and Cal's separation becomes permanent.

- Investigate the lives of patients in mental hospitals today and compare with Conrad Jarrett's experiences as a psychiatric patient.

- Research the idea of "the generation gap." Discuss its historical origins and compare with the relationships among generations in *Ordinary People*.

Themes

Grief and Sorrow

One principal theme of *Ordinary People* is grief over a loved one's death. As Beth, Cal, and Con struggle to cope with Buck's fatal accident, they turn inward, causing conflicts within the family. It is only after Con comes to terms with his guilt that he is able to grieve for Buck and to realize that he is not responsible. Con's journey toward good mental health is contrasted with Beth, who never manages to deal with her sorrow. Beth is unable to accept what has happened and accuses others of changing rather than understanding that their lives have irrevocably changed. Cal's grief for Buck underlies his growing questions about his identity and his relationships with Beth and Con, as his tightly organized life has been ripped apart by the tragedy. Buck's carefree charm makes his loss that much harder for the family to accept, as his belief that he would live forever and his physical vitality convinced everyone that he would indeed live a long time. It is only when the other family members realize that there is no good explanation for Buck's loss, and no lesson to be learned from his death, that they can begin to mourn.

Atonement and Forgiveness

Closely linked to the theme of grief is the theme of atonement and forgiveness. Con is consumed by survivor's guilt over Buck's death; he feels that he should have been the one to die so that Buck could live. Though Con apologizes repeatedly for the boating accident that killed Buck, he never apologizes for his suicide attempt, and his parents must also struggle to forgive Con. Con realizes that although his mother has not forgiven him, his anger towards her indicates his lack of forgiveness for her and his refusal to accept her limitations. Cal's recognition of Beth's limitations is a milestone for him, but Beth cannot do the same. When she and Cal fight in Texas, she tells Cal that she will never forgive Con for the "bloody, vicious thing" he has done, which she feels was Con's way of punishing her. Beth does not have a capacity to forgive, and this makes a reconciliation with Con impossible. Unlike Beth, Cal only realizes the extent of his anger at Con at the end of the novel, when he remembers that Con has never apologized for his suicide attempt. Cal recognizes that Con's attempt has done something terrible to Beth, and he allows himself to get angry at Con, who reacts positively, happy that his father is no longer being oversolicitous of him. This in turn allows for a resolution of the relationship between father and son.

Alienation and Loneliness

Con's alienation and loneliness following his release from the mental hospital is obvious from the beginning of the story. He is barely able to speak with friends, teachers, or family members, and he feels depressed and anxious. Cal's alienation is less immediately apparent, but it becomes more obvious as the story progresses. Cal feels disconnected from those who share his grief and from those who do not. The person who is most likely to understand his pain, Beth, cannot listen to his feelings or express her own. Cal is struck throughout the story by the ability of language to express feelings and by the contamination that is caused by contact with others. He gets through most social encounters by drinking too much, and his attempts to connect with Beth are rebuffed. Con fares better: his relationships with Dr. Berger and Jeannine help him to open up, to trust others, and to establish communication. Through their understanding, Con becomes much more connected to others and is able to ease his feelings of isolation.

Identity

Linked to issues of alienation and loneliness is the search for identity. Buck's death has forced Cal and Con to examine their own lives. Each feels as if he has lived in the shadow of others—Con in Buck's shadow, Cal in everyone's shadow. Con looked up to Buck and tried to be like him, and he is forced to create his own identity after Buck dies. Berger identifies Con's inability to live up to Buck's legacy as the reason for his suicide attempt, and Con spends much of his time with Berger trying to figure out what kind of person he is. Berger tells Con repeatedly that he knows who he is, but he is trying so hard to hide his feelings that he represses his identity, too. It is only after Con expresses his feelings that he begins to understand who he really is. Cal is also prevented from expressing his feelings; his inability to connect with Beth forces him to discover what his needs are, and thus what his identity is. Each man is forced by circumstance to modify his identity, as the familiar roles they had played in the family vanished when Buck died. Beth's refusal to understand that life has changed for the family leads her to flee instead of transforming herself, suggesting the importance of adapting one's view of one's self in the face of difficult circumstances.

Style

Point of View

One of the concerns in *Ordinary People* is how the characters perceive their situations, and so point of view is an important part of Guest's writing technique. The point of view shifts between Conrad Jarrett and his father, Calvin, and thus the reader gets two different perspectives on the events in the story. This is most apparent with regard to their impressions of Beth. Both see her as distant, but Cal romanticizes this quality in her, while Con feels anger at her apparent lack of love for him. Con's perceptions of his mother are influenced by his sense that she loved his brother more than she loved him. This sense of being slighted as a child was caused, perhaps, by his identity as the younger, less carefree, more serious and needy child. Cal's romanticization of Beth is influenced by his isolation from his mother as a child; Beth is distant as well, but she is present in a way that Cal's mother was not. As a result, Cal feels grateful to Beth for staying with him. As each man gains perspective on the outside world, they both realize that Beth is more fragile than they had thought, but the reader's impressions of her, and of all the characters and events in the story, continues to be filtered through the points of view of Con and Cal. Their childhood

experiences affect the way that they see others and their motivations, and their subjective perceptions often prevent them from seeing events from a more objective standpoint.

Narration

The narrative technique used by Guest to present the points of view of Conrad and Calvin is that of a third-person narrator, who is omniscient only with regard to Cal and Con. Because the narrative focus shifts back and forth between Cal and Con, the narrator can only relate the thoughts of one of them at a time. Thus, during the family fight at Christmas, the reader's perceptions are filtered through Cal's subjectivity; the reader has access to Con's thoughts only through his dialogue and Cal's sense of what is going on. The narrator does not intrude or editorialize in the narrative, but rather functions as an implied narrator, presenting events as Cal and Con see them in a third-person, rather than a first-person ("I"), format.

Plot Structure

The overall structure of *Ordinary People* consists of thirty-one chapters and an epilogue. With two exceptions, the chapters alternate between the points of view of Calvin and Conrad. The story begins in the fall and extends into the spring, with an epilogue that takes place in the summer, closing the story thematically almost a year after it has begun. The story begins *in medias res* (that is, in mid-action), as Buck's death and Conrad's suicide attempt have already taken place when the story begins.

Tragic Flaw

Though the obviously tragic events of *Ordinary People*, Buck's death and Con's suicide, have already taken place when the story begins, the real tragedy of the novel lies in the inability of the characters to cope with these uncontrollable events. As Cal reflects on Beth's character, he wonders if she possesses a tragic imperfection, a personality flaw with which she was born. He speculates that she might somehow lack the capacity to forgive. Beth's congenital inability to forgive prevents her from understanding her son, thus causing problems between herself and her husband.

Conflict

Conflict is ever-present in *Ordinary People*. Because of the differing perspectives of the characters, they remain in conflict throughout the story. The conflict between Con and Beth mostly remains under the surface, only exploding at Christmas, though it has long been evident in their strained and distant relationship with each other. Cal internalizes the conflict between Con and Beth, becoming inwardly conflicted, which in turn leads to his increasing clashes with Beth. Their fights grow in intensity during the course of the novel, as Beth accuses Cal of coddling Con and becoming depressed, while Cal feels that she is cold and unforgiving towards Con. It is only in the Epilogue that Con begins to feel that love can close the rift between himself and his mother, but the different needs and viewpoints of the characters have already changed the family, perhaps forever.

Historical Context

Cultural Revolutions of the 1970s

After the political movements of the 1960s, revolutions in the 1970s took a decidedly personal turn. The concerns of *Ordinary People* reflect that shift. Decidedly apolitical and small in its scope, *Ordinary People* is not concerned with grand, sweeping political events, but rather with the shifts that accompany personal development.

The 1970s are commonly stereotyped as the "Me Decade," but this designation does reflect a shift in concerns from the political to the personal. The feminist movement, with its insistence that "the personal *is* political," influenced this trend as it gained force in the decade. Though the female characters of *Ordinary People* do not express a feminist consciousness, the influence of 1970s feminism is evident in their lives. Jeannine's mother is divorced, and Beth leaves her husband and son. These actions were just becoming acceptable in society at that time. Carole Lazenby, a housewife, is taking a college course, just as thousands of real housewives were beginning to educate themselves and go to work at that time. The efforts of women to erase the stereotypes of femininity also influenced the Sexual Revolution of the 1970s, in which traditional sexual morals were reexamined. The sexual encounter between Jeannine and Conrad is presented by Guest without any moral judgment.

If Guest is presenting any kind of moral vision, it is one that is heavily influenced by psychological principles. When the characters suffer, they do so because they are repressing their feelings and trying too hard to control themselves. This emphasis on the importance of expressing emotions represents a historical shift. Maintaining control

over oneself had been considered much more important in previous decades, especially to the generation represented by Howard and Ellen in the novel. The 1970s saw an explosion of interest in psychology and personal development, with people becoming interested in traditional psychology and in newer forms such as primal scream therapy in which people would release their pent up emotions by screaming. This widespread interest in psychology during the 1970s explains both Guest's preoccupation with it in the novel and the popularity of the novel with readers.

There are three distinct generations in *Ordinary People:* Howard and Ellen's generation, Beth and Cal's generation, and Con and Jeannine's generation. The notion of a generation gap, a term which was coined in the 1960s, becomes important in Con's relationship with his grandparents. The differences in experiences among the generations separates them from each other; when Con is having difficulties during a stay at their house, he feels that they would not understand him. The 1970s saw a widening of the generation gap, particularly between teenagers and their elders. The quality of adolescent life went down during this period, as drug use, teenage pregnancy, and juvenile delinquency increased, partly as a result of pressures on the family structure. The increased difficulty of life for adolescents is evident in the character of Jeannine, who gets involved in drugs and shoplifting after her parents' divorce.

Thus, though Guest does not deal explicitly with historical, political, or cultural events, they are evident in the choices the characters are able to make, and the experiences they have in the novel. The feminist movement, the interest in psychology, and the generation gap underlie the context of the novel, which was both written and set in the 1970s.

Critical Overview

Critical response to *Ordinary People* has been mixed. Reviewers have found much to praise and much to criticize in Guest's novel. Many have found her characterization of Conrad Jarrett, the alienated teenager just released from a mental hospital, the most impressive aspect of the novel. Lore Dickstein writes in the *New York Times Book Review* that "Guest portrays Conrad not only as if she has lived with him on a daily basis—which I sense may be true—but as if she has gotten into his head. The dialogue Conrad has with himself, his psychi-

From the film Ordinary People, *starring Timothy Hutton and Judd Hirsch, Paramount, 1980.*

atrist, his friends, his family, all rings true with adolescent anxiety. This is the small hard kernel of brilliance in the novel." Guest has acknowledged her fascination with adolescence; in an interview with former *Detroit Free Press* book editor Barbara Holliday, Guest says of adolescence, "It's a period of time ... where people are very vulnerable and often don't have the experience to draw on as far as human relationships go. At the same time they are making some pretty heavy decisions, not necessarily physical but psychological decisions about how they're going to relate to people and how they're going to shape their lives. It seems to me that if you don't have sane sensible people around you to help, there's great potential for making irrevocable mistakes."

Though Guest has been praised for her characterization of Conrad, some critics have found fault with the way Guest portrayed Beth, the distant, perfectionist mother in the story. Dorothea D. Braginsky writes in *Psychology Today* that "the mother's point of view, even though she is foremost in the men's lives, is barely articulated. We come to know her only in dialogue with her husband and her son, and through their portrayals of her. For some reason Guest has given her no voice, no platform for expression. We never discover what conflicts, fears and aspirations exist behind her

cool, controlled facade." As critics have noted, Guest's narrative style, with its shifts between the perceptions of Calvin and Conrad Jarrett, leaves the reader with an incomplete perception of Beth. A further comment about Guest's style comes from Paddy Kitchen, writing in *The Listener:* "Judith Guest takes an 'ordinary' ... family in which the son, 17-year-old Conrad Jarrett, has just returned home from a mental hospital, eight months after a suicide attempt. Her technique is to reveal information about Conrad and his parents, Calvin and Beth, in a colloquial, present-tense, piecemeal way—a method more often found in thrillers or adventure stories. She uses the technique extremely skillfully, with twist and turns that come like the proverbial unexpected cold buckets of water." Guest's "colloquial" technique has been praised by many critics for its realism. A *Kirkus Reviews* contributor writes, "where it does succeed, and succeed it does, is in communicating a sense of life both felt and experienced without ever trespassing beyond actuality. *Ordinary People* is an exceptionally real book."

Though many have praised her realism in portraying other characters, a number of critics have found Guest's portrayal of Dr. Berger, Conrad's psychologist, overly sentimental and unrealistic. They also fault her unwillingness to relinquish control over the way she tells the story, even though thematically she seems to argue against the desire to have too much control of anything. Several critics have also considered the ending to be much too neat. For example, Michael Wood writes in the *New York Review of Books* that Conrad "comes to accept his mother's apparent failure to forgive him for slashing his wrists, and his own failure to forgive her for not loving him more. It is true that she has now left his father, because he seemed to be cracking up under the strain of his concern for his son, but Conrad has learned 'that it is love, imperfect and unordered, that keeps them apart, even as it holds them somehow together.'" The critic explains: "It's an implausible conclusion, one of those secret happy ends that Hollywood weepies used to do so well: everyone dies, but they do it in the arms of the people they love, all error forgiven. Here the family is broken up, but everyone is on their way to emotional health, because they have understood their weaknesses. But then the whole novel is subtly implausible in this sense, not because one doesn't believe in the characters or in Conrad's recovery, but because problems just pop up, get neatly formulated, and vanish, as if they were performing a psychoanalytic morality play." While Melvin Maddocks praises Guest's realism, he too finds fault with the easy resolution of the novel: "the Furies in [Guest's] suburb are real, even if she seems to banish them with a spray of Airwick."

Despite the mixed critical reaction to *Ordinary People,* reviewers have found much to admire in the novel, and they have said that *Second Heaven* and *Errands,* two of Guest's succeeding books, prove that the success of *Ordinary People* was not a fluke. Moreover, *Ordinary People* was a resounding popular success, and critics have agreed that it is an excellent piece of popular fiction. It continues to be read and taught at both the high school and college level.

Criticism

Jean Dougherty

In the following essay, Dougherty, a doctoral candidate at Tufts University, explores how Guest uses perspective—both in terms of the narration and characterization—to address several themes in her novel.

In both the style and the content of *Ordinary People,* Judith Guest is concerned with issues of perspective. Perspective refers here to both point

of view and the capacity to view things as they truly are. Throughout the story, these two definitions of perspective are in conflict, and the characters are struggling to discover their own points of view as well as seeing the outside world, and their relation to it, more clearly.

The style of *Ordinary People,* appropriately enough, is one in which perspectives shift. We are given the perspectives of Conrad Jarrett, a troubled adolescent, and Calvin Jarrett, his father, in more-or-less alternating chapters. Guest uses a third-person narrator, rather than a character in the story, to relate both Con and Cal's thoughts and actions. The narrator never presents us with the thoughts of Beth Jarrett, the third major character in the story, and so the reader sees her only through the different perspectives of Cal, who doesn't know her but romanticizes her mystery and beauty, and Con, who is as private as his mother but feels both anger and longing for her. As some critics have noted, Beth's motivations remain shadowy to the reader, and so the reader is never sure what she really feels or thinks, except through the perceptions of her husband and her son, or through Beth's dialogue in the story.

Because the focus of the novel shifts back and forth between Con and Cal, it becomes clear that each man's difficulties with gaining a sense of identity are different. Con is struggling throughout to see things in their true relations rather than simply from his own point of view, and Cal is struggling to understand what his own point of view is. Though each man is trying to come to terms with the grief and guilt that he feels over Buck Jarrett's death and Con's subsequent suicide attempt, as well as trying to establish a positive identity, these private struggles are inevitably complicated by their relationships with others, particularly with Beth. Thus both Con and Cal are trying to balance their own needs with those of other people.

Con's initial perspective, then, is one of extreme isolation. He has just been released from a mental hospital, and the day on which the story opens is a "Target Day" in his recovery: he is to meet with an outpatient psychiatrist for the first time. Con's relationship with Dr. Berger is one in which he is struggles to learn how to safely express his feeling and to gain a sense of perspective by understanding the perspectives of others and their relationship to him. The following passage illustrates how Berger tries to get Con to see things from a different, or broader, perspective by getting him to see the motivations of others. The scene occurs after Con has had a fight with Beth, then realized in therapy the extent of his anger, and his lack of forgiveness for her inability to take care of him.

> Reclining on an elbow on the floor, Berger doodles on a scratch pad with his silver pen. Conrad sits beside him, his back against the wall, knees up, holding a cup of coffee in his hands. "Jesus, am I tired," he says.
>
> "Yeah, well, that's a helluva big secret you've been keeping on yourself," Berger says.
>
> "So what do I do now?"
>
> "Well, you've done it, haven't you? Revelation. She's not perfect. Recognize her limitations."
>
> "You mean, like she can't love me."
>
> "Like she can't love you enough. Like she loves you as much as she's *able*. Perspective, kiddo, remember? Maybe she's afraid, maybe it's hard for her to give love."

Here Con is beginning to be able to see other people as they really are, rather seeing them only from his point of view. A similar scene of recognition occurs when Con suddenly realizes that the reason his mother is quiet in airports and other public places is because she is afraid of strangers; he is beginning to understand that her actions originate from her emotions, that she, like him, has an internal life that drives her external behavior.

Con's difficulty with perspective is most apparent in the guilt he feels over his brother's death. He cannot see Buck's drowning from Buck's perspective, only from his own. It is only when his friend Karen kills herself that he is able to come to terms with Buck's death and the fact that Buck's inability to hold on and wait for help to arrive was not Con's fault. When, in Chapter Seven, Con met with Karen, he was unable to see things from her perspective, or understand that she, too, was suffering from depression or anxiety, which she tried to hide. Instead, he felt ashamed when she told him she had stopped seeing a counselor, because only she could help herself and solve her problems. Through his relationship with his counselor, Con is able to find a sense of perspective; Karen, on the other hand, later commits suicide. When she dies, Con is stricken with guilt and grief, which brings back his memories and feelings about his brother's death. It is only after Berger makes him see that Buck drowned because of his *own* physical or mental limitations and not because it was Con's fault, that Con can begin to heal.

If Con's quest throughout the novel is to find a clearer sense of the true relations of things, to recognize the perspectives of others, Cal's quest is the

What Do I Read Next?

- *Second Heaven,* Judith Guest's second novel, was published in 1982 and deals with some of the same themes as *Ordinary People.* At the heart of the book is a troubled teenager who is struggling to escape his abusive father with the help of his lawyer and a recently divorced woman who takes him in.

- *Errands,* Judith Guest's 1997 novel, continues her themes of suburbanites struggling to connect and heal in a story dealing with the death of a father and husband.

- *Girl, Interrupted,* Susanna Kaysen's 1993 memoir, discusses the author's hospitalization for depression at age eighteen and her transition from mental patient to productive adult.

- *A Separate Peace* (1959), by John Knowles, sensitively sketches the friendship of two adolescent boys (one of whom dies in an accident) at a prep school in New England during World War II.

- *A Map of the World* (1994), by Jane Hamilton, traces the effect of a child's death on two families and an entire community.

- *The Autobiography of My Mother* is Jamaica Kincaid's 1995 novel of an adult woman trying to understand and love her mother long after she has died, and to deal with the disappointment she felt in her relationship with her mother.

opposite: he is trying to locate his own point of view, his own perspective. When he goes to talk to Dr. Berger, he describes himself as a fence sitter, and he makes a tentative realization that Con and Beth are on opposite sides of the fence on which he sees himself sitting; after saying this, he immediately takes it back because he is afraid to acknowledge the conflict between Beth and Con. Later, after his visit with Berger stirs up old memories, Cal remembers another situation in which he felt conflicted: the time when he was forced to choose between his mentor and Beth.

Throughout the novel, Cal attempts to mediate between Con and Beth, and his own point of view is lost. When he and Beth go to Dallas, and they fight bitterly, Cal repeats to her something that Con has also said to her. When she tells him not to quote Con, he realizes that he is not quoting Con, that he is quoting himself, that he too has been angry with Beth for her inability to communicate her emotions with him. He realizes that he has needed her to get through his own grief, and she has not been there for him, because she is unwilling to come to terms with Buck's death. Her addiction to her own sense of privacy makes it impossible for them to relate as a couple; she remains a stranger to him. Beth herself recognizes that she is only able to see things from her own point of view. She finally tells Cal later how she feels about Con's suicide attempt:

> "Don't you understand what he was saying?" she asks. "He was saying 'Look! Look what you made me do!'"
>
> "Why?" he asks. "Why was he saying that?"
>
> "I don't know! I wish I knew!" She sobs, and then her voice is calm, more subdued, and she speaks slowly. "I just know how people try to manipulate other people."
>
> "Oh God, Beth, I don't believe that! I don't believe that he went all that way to try to manipulate us! What happened—what he did—he did it to him*self!* Can't you see anything except in terms of how it affects you?"
>
> "No! Neither can you! Neither does anybody else! Only, maybe I'm more honest than the rest of you, maybe I'm more willing to recognize that I do it."

Here, Beth can recognize that she is trapped in her own point of view, but she cannot recognize Con's point of view or what has motivated him other than a desire to hurt her. Con has tried to get a better sense of other perspectives through his relationships with others, but Beth cannot do this. As for Cal, he can only find his own perspective when he stops mediating between the perspectives of Con and Beth, and allows himself to speak to them from his own perspective. He is able to tell Beth that he is angry with her for not worrying enough about Conrad and to tell Con that neither he nor Con is an authority on Beth's thoughts, feelings, or actions. Because Cal is able to gain a sense of his own identity, he is able to communicate with Con in a more honest way, and Con is able to relate to Cal better because he is not so trapped in his own perspective. In the epilogue, Con even makes a gesture toward forgiving and accepting Beth's limitations, knowing that there is love between them even if it is only as much as they are both capable of expressing.

With its emphasis on relationships, personal identity, and the ways in which emotions and experience shape our perceptions, *Ordinary People* is clearly a psychological novel. Guest uses the psychological principles of emotional expression, honest communication, identity formation and professional counseling in order to drive the development of the characters, which in turn provides a framework for the plot, as the characters cope with memories and current crises. The narrator's access into the thoughts and feelings of two of the characters means that much of the plot is internal, occurring within the characters' minds. Through her use of psychological principles as the characters struggle with them, Guest provides a kind of blueprint to readers for relating, grieving, and healing. Through Guest's use of shifting perspectives, and the conflict between self and others implicit in the double meaning of "perspective," the author shows her readers how hard these processes can be, even though her conclusion is hopeful.

Source: Jean Dougherty, in an essay for *Novels for Students,* Gale, 1997.

Ron Neuhaus

In the following excerpt, Neuhaus gives an overview of the censorship challenges presented against Ordinary People, *and offers responses to the objections commonly raised.*

[When] a book like *Ordinary People* creates a fuss [because of censorship attempts], we need to make a case for it, to show that it will enrich its readers and enhance the educational environment instead of detracting from it. Can such a case be made? Of course, and a strong one. Once made, will it prevail? Well—it might or it might not. One would like to assume that the right to discretionary access carries with it the responsibility to make judgments based on a reasonably thorough consideration of a book's merits, not simply whimsy or bias. However, no one seems to relish being reminded of responsibilities, although humanists do what they can to restore that equilibrium between right and responsibility. The efforts may be fruitless, but we might remember the story of a sage who saved a scorpion from drowning in a stream. The scorpion instinctively stung the hand that had helped it and scurried back into the stream. The sage saved him again and again, and was stung each time for his efforts. A passerby, his curiosity piqued, asked the sage why he persisted in saving the scorpion. Didn't he realize the insect would keep stinging him? Replied the sage, "The scorpion stings because it is his nature." "But then why do you help him?" asked the observer. "I help him because that is *my* nature," answered the sage.

First, instead of praising this book, let's look at the worst in it. Let's lean on it hard and inventory its controversial points in a ruthless biased summary.

> *Ordinary People,* Judith Guest. The trauma as a suicidal teenager struggles for normalcy, while his parents move toward divorce. Uses obscene language, sexual scenes, nudity and violence. Includes grim representations of adolescent depression, suicide and psychosis. Contains unresolved pessimism and disillusionment.

Obviously this book would serve no purpose in the primary classrooms. But where do we go from here? What would particular groups object to? A short taxonomy of objectors may outline the problems the book presents. The five groups here identified do not encompass all objections. They represent the most salient:

Fetishists
Monkey Sees
Ostriches
Dominoes
Catchers-of-the-Raw

The first three groups tend to be the most whimsical and adamant: they need to be outvoted. The last two groups are receptive to argument and will enter into dialogue. But the substantial rationale behind their convictions makes them formidable discussants.

First of all, the Fetishists, the "booger-hunters." They will object categorically to one thing or another and let that objection harpoon the whole book. They will not compromise; all they need to know is that the word, situation, action, or relationship occurs, and the book is out—unless the objectionable parts are excised. From a censorship perspective, they're easily pleased: omit this word or that scene, bowdlerize the script, and all is well.

Ordinary People, it must be admitted, does provide grist for the fetishists. It does use a few four-letter words. Although it lacks the blase tour-de-force *a la* Henry Miller, it does not have the antiseptic diction of a Tom Swift novel. Nor would it suffer greatly if the objectionable language were removed. The question is, why do so? What harm could be done? The language would be titillating only to a grade school child delighted to see the forbidden words in print. Older readers would respond to the language in terms of its intention: to highlight the emotional state of the person using them. A similar rationale could be made for the

scenes, but fetishists don't respond to rationales, so the effort is purely for the eavesdropping allies on both sides, the principle involved, and to evoke a sense of righteousness that humanists delight in as much as Fetishists.

Next, the Monkey Sees. These assume that children will imitate selectively what they read and invariably model undesirable over virtuous behavior. There may be a germ of truth here. Huck Finn's penchant for corncob pipes inspired my own experience with smoking. But *Ordinary People* offers very little to imitate. Suicide? 24-hour-a-day depression? Guest presents these with no glamour, no allure, no factor of temptation. The harshness with which she presents her study argues for the book as a warning against the moods it explores.

The Ostriches. An endangered species who exclude certain moods and themes from any kind of consideration. These might well react to the depression and stress throughout the book by wishing their portrayal to disappear. This helps them ignore what they do not want to admit exists. They haven't experienced similar situations, nor do they see any point in contemplating them. To their extent of receptivity, this group can be answered in the same way as the next.

In these next two groups, the nature of the objections shifts. The arguments are more articulated and broader in perspective. The logic is often sound, but the assumptions create the controversy.

The Dominoes. They will admit all the merits of the book, they have no objection to it, and may even agree that it should be in the library or school. However, they fear the precedent the presence of the book will establish. They assume, and with some cause, that when a door opens for one, it's difficult to close it for others. The difficulty in responding to this is that a historical continuum exists from *Ulysses* to *Hustler,* from *Lolita* to child pornography. Here is where the negotiation and discussion play their strongest role. Apologists for a given book should make clear that acceptance of one book does not guarantee admission of another. A separate rationale must be put forward on the merits of each document; we need to be ready with an apologia when the need arises.

Last of all, the Catchers-of-the-Raw, or Holden Caulfields. These people understand and acknowledge the reality of the sensitive material portrayed in a given work but wish to guard their children from such matters as depressing experiences and sordid reality. It's a losing battle, of course, but theirs is a delaying action, not a decisive one. Yet given the inevitability of actual encounters with the sharp edges of experience, a work like *Ordinary People* can serve as a buffer that informs and actually protects—a quality of threshold literature, which prepares the sensibility through imagination for what it will soon encounter in experience.

And granted that the book does deal with depression and the more visceral moments in life, it redeems itself from being a depressing book in several ways. It makes severe depression less intimidating by examining it and revealing it as a normal reaction to abnormally stressful situations. There is even a triumph over depression, an affirmation of the reservoir of human strength. During an unexpected acceleration of his despondency, Conrad makes contact with this sense of affirmation after his analyst clarifies emotional impotence with this observation.

> Geez, if I could get through to you, kiddo, that depression is not sobbing and crying and giving vent, it is plain and simple reduction of feeling. Reduction, see? Of all feeling. People who keep stiff upper lips find that it's damn hard to smile.

Simple, straightforward advice—enough to turn the tide in Conrad's favor.

In this book people survive, endure, and mature—despite the death of the elder son, the attempted suicide of Conrad, the atrophy of Calvin and Beth's marriage. Its theme conveys the positive implication that we can survive problems, even though we may not be able to solve them. There is even a qualified "happy" ending in this endurance, an ending which ironically constitutes the major fault of the novel in that the depression gets resolved too easily. The guilt that has prompted Conrad's suicide attempt and plagued him through the novel gets neutralized in that fairly easy scene with the analyst. The answer is a bit too pat, and although the alchemical transformation of Conrad's attitude doesn't quite approach Dumbo's realization that he can fly without the feather, it's from the same school of thought—one the "catchers" always commend.

It's always gratifying to respond to objectors such as those above. There is the sense of battle for a virtuous cause against a dangerous and substantial opposition. But one cannot rely on the defensive strategy of an apologia to make the best case: better to affirm the strong points first. And *Ordinary People* has plenty, but one stands out as particularly relevant.

Some works function as thresholds. They can lead a reader into an awareness and understanding of wider dimension of the human spirit, either by expressing a situation shared by the reader or by allowing insight into the kaleidoscopic variations of the human condition. There has been little threshold literature for young adults, even though the increasing stress and diversity of living almost demands it. We can see documentaries on such problems as teenage alcoholism and pregnancy and gain only surface knowledge of the problem. Where technology provides us with a window to the externals of the world, art must keep pace by its investigation of the inner domain. Books such as the Hardy Boys and Nancy Drew novels illustrate what threshold literature is not—adventures of young adults, yet with no significant attention to how sensibilities change or mature with experience. Such stories could easily feature talking horses or bipedal Great Danes; cartoons can easily be made of them.

On the other hand, books such as those contributed by Judy Blume address the inner world, the world of emotions instead of events. Her work illustrates what threshold literature can do: create a controlled situation where the readers can encounter in fiction what they may soon experience in real situations, either as observers or participants.

Ordinary People also belongs in this category. It divides its focus between the subjective experiences of the son, Conrad, and the father, Calvin, and initiates the reader into the complementary perspectives of adolescence and maturity. Both perspectives give insight into the deserts that open up between people when they most need contact.

Teachers could well focus on Conrad as an entry-level persona. Although we would hope no reader shares his particular situation, his emotions are typical ones with which a reader could easily identify, and the motifs of his encounters are those that begin intruding into the hyperborean climate of most adolescent minds. We see the drawbacks to emotional independence—how it can lead to isolation and separation from the very forces that can heal its injuries. We also see how his awakened sense of history grows from guilt over the past to confidence in the future. The problems and tangles of evolving maturity receive insightful attention here, as do several others quite recognizable to the teenage reader: peer-pressure, school harassment, the struggle with emotions that emerge with ferocious intensity.

Although Conrad's material may be initially appealing to younger readers, Calvin's perspective may prove most enlightening. It allows them to experience the vulnerability of the adult mind, to enter a world they usually know only through a taciturn exterior. The veil of parental inaccessibility is lifted, and they can observe a correlation between the frustration and anxiety they experience and that which occurs in matured minds. While Conrad has his nest of hooks to sort out, Calvin has a similar batch. Their emotional odysseys follow roughly parallel courses. Conrad is involved with sports; Cal has his career.

Both feel the powerful influence of the past on present events.

Conrad must come to terms with the death of his brother; Calvin must deal with the breakup of his marriage. Calvin shows the adult mind charted: the relationship with a youth that Conrad has yet to encounter, the constant worry about family and career, the tragic sense of restriction in reaching out toward loved ones. The portrayal of these complementary sensibilities could well yield compassion for the younger, sympathy for the older.

The book abounds with similar entrances, and several general themes come to mind: that ordinary people often find themselves in unusually taxing situations which distort and amplify their emotions; that people in such struggles must not be seen as deviant types but representative types reacting to abnormal situations; that there is a certain haphazard nature in the universe of the human spirit, matters beyond the pat rational assumptions of post-Freudian analysis.

This all may be quite commendable stuff, but what about the questionable material exposed in the synopsis? At the risk of making an apologia for the book too simple, let me say that books of a certain style contain a built-in safety factor: they turn away any reader not mature enough to handle them. *Ordinary People* has this quality. There is nothing in it to gratify the thrill seeker. For one thing, the heavy emphasis on introspection and interior monologue generates a fairly static physical environment in order to highlight emotional dialectics. Conversation and reflection slow things down more. Most of the attention falls on the "housekeeping" aspects of life: the stress of school on Conrad, the complications of a career for Calvin.

And all of the episodes of sex and violence referred to in my synopsis are presented in a fairly discursive style, with little graphic focus. In fact, for a sexual scene between Calvin and Beth, the author ushers in language so oblique it could double as vocabulary suitable to describe a checkers match. And when Conrad and Jeannine have an intimate scene (very near the end of the book), the dialogue receives the emphasis. The entire scene serves to confirm the emerging optimism in Conrad and to strengthen him even after the news of a friend's suicide. So, if someone is looking for a book to appeal to or encourage prurient interest, *Ordinary People* holds only disappointment.

Each questionable scene has a similar explanation, and there are few such scenes, at that. In fact, if we cut out all the particular passages dealing with "sensitive" areas, they would lay out to a little over one of the book's 263 pages. So yes, the situations are there, but this book derives from a different genus than *The Valley of the Dolls*.

However, this statistical approach is not quite fair to those who would object to elements of theme and mood. The book does explore some raw wounds in the human psyche, and some people may object to such a focus in reading material even for a secondary school audience. But objections of this sort often do a great injustice to the potential literature offers. The unacknowledged premise in such a criticism is that literature functions essentially as entertainment or escapism—emotionally safe stuff that can aid reading skills. This ignores literature's potential to create a threshold by which the reader can enter a wider expanse of the human topography and develop a more mature perspective through that vision.

Threshold books reveal one of good literature's finest characteristics. Some such books even attain the status of "classic." But strangely enough, their very utility as tools of insight subjects them to attack, such as has happened with *Huckleberry Finn* and *The Scarlet Letter*. On the other hand, some books are never challenged: those that are infused with an irrelevance to a reader's personal situation and relationships. Many of the popular "classics" provide examples of this. They employ baroque, superbowl passions that engage us as awestruck observers, not emotionally involved participants. They're safe. Parents don't get into bitter debate with their children over the issues in *Crime and Punishment* or *Moby Dick*. Nor can anyone acquire credible insight into children's ingratitude from *King Lear*. We can appreciate occasional doses of inflated sentiments, however, because such experiences transport us away from the bothersome concerns of our lives. But we also need art that enters us as we are, that presents us with parameters of feeling we might actually have, with situations that we see as possible around us. As "ordinary people" we need words that can reveal insight into how we are, and where we are.

Ordinary People assays out to do that; it lacks the lofty level of intellectual melodrama possessed by the "safe" book, classic or otherwise, and that's the quality that justifies making it accessible to any heart it speaks to.

Source: Ron Neuhaus, "Threshold Literature: A Discussion of *Ordinary People*," in *Censored Books: Critical Viewpoints,* Nicholas J. Karolides, Lee Burress, John M. Kean, eds., The Scarecrow Press, Inc., 1993, pp. 414–23.

Michael Wood

In the following excerpt, Wood reviews Guest's Ordinary People.

Fiction is full of exiles from ordinary life: stranded, marginal, baffled, sulking, deluded, or violent creatures. Indeed, some sort of snag or hitch or resistance, some lapse from expectations, is probably necessary to get any story started. If Odysseus had stayed at home, there would have been no *Odyssey.* This is obvious enough, but it does mean that fiction, and perhaps even narrative, can have very little hold on ordinary life, since ordinary life, like Ithaca, is what has to be abandoned at the outset. Judith Guest's *Ordinary People,* for example, is a rather bland and far from ironic novel, yet its title hints at a complicated irony. On the one hand, the book suggests, there are no ordinary people; people are all extraordinary in their way, both finer and feebler than we think. And on the other hand, ordinary people are what we may become, if we can conquer our fear of being extraordinary. In a novel, that fear has to be acted out. In *Ordinary People,* it *is* the novel, the trace of a season of exile.

The source of the fear is an attempted suicide and an earlier accidental death. There is an actual suicide in *The 400 Eels of Sigmund Freud,* there is insanity and multiple death in *The Comatose Kids,* and there is a descent into hideous humiliation in *The Geek.* I don't take all this violence and deviation as a sign of our troubled times, or even as a sign of troubled writing minds. But I do take it as a cry for attention, a message from these writers as writers. *There is a story here,* the message says, *watch us leave ordinary life behind.* The message may reflect the youth or relative inexperience of the writers, an assumed or feared deafness in American publishers, creating the need for narrative shouts, or a more generally embattled quality in contemporary fiction, fighting off the claims of biography and transcendental meditation. Perhaps it reflects all three in different proportions in different cases. What interests me is the noise the message makes, the worry about normality that it implies.

This worry, as I have said, is the overt subject of *Ordinary People.* Conrad Jarrett, almost eighteen, has tried to kill himself, and has been in the hospital: The novel recounts his readjustment to school, friends, girls, father, mother, himself. He sheds a lot of his anxiety, weathers the suicide of a girl who was released from the hospital along with him, and comes to terms with his brother's death by drowning, which led him to the attempt on his own life. How could he, the second, less perfect brother, go on living when the paragon had given up, lost his will to live, and let go of the boat they were both hanging on to in the stormy lake? Above all, he comes to accept his mother's apparent failure to forgive him for slashing his wrists, and his own failure to forgive her for not loving him more. It is true that she has now left his father, because he seemed to be cracking up under the strain of his concern for his son, but Conrad has learned "that it is love, imperfect and unordered, that keeps them apart, even as it holds them somehow together."

It's an implausible conclusion, one of those secret happy ends that Hollywood weepies used to do so well: everyone dies, but they do it in the arms of the people they love, all error forgiven. Here the family is broken up, but everyone is on the way to emotional health, because they have understood their weaknesses. But then the whole novel is subtly implausible in this sense, not because one doesn't believe in the characters or in Conrad's recovery, but because problems just pop up, get neatly formulated, and vanish, as if they were performing a psychoanalytic morality play. "I think I just figured something out," Conrad says to his psychiatrist, and he has. It's a milestone on the road to reason.

The psychiatrist, a wisecracking cross between Groucho Marx and Philip Marlowe, is perhaps Judith Guest's major contribution to current mythology. "See, kiddo," he says, "this problem is very specific. It is not necessary to pull the whole world in on top of you, it is only necessary to finish with Tuesday night." And: "Geez, if I could get through to you, kiddo, that depression is not sobbing and crying and *giving vent,* it is plain and simple *reduction of feeling.* Reduction, see? Of all feeling." As he cuts Conrad's visits down to one a week, he murmurs, "And I just ordered a couch, how'm I gonna pay for it?" And on another occasion: "Well, okay. I'd better tell you. I'm not big on control. I prefer things fluid. In motion. But it's your money."

But I mean to suggest the limitations of the novel, not to knock it over. In spite of those quotations, which sound a good deal less bogus in context anyway, Conrad's psychiatrist, like most of the characters in the book, is very charming and very intelligent. Judith Guest has a good eye for social detail and a good ear for turns of phrase, and the breeziness of her manner ("He takes a quick look in the mirror. The news isn't good." "How about it? Illusion versus reality? All those in favor") goes with her brisk good sense. "The things which hurt don't always instruct. Sometimes they merely hurt." She measures health by a capacity for jokes, which means both a faith in shared meanings (people understand you when you say the opposite of what you think) and a sort of independence within a community (your wit pulls you out of the rut of routine).

It is a shallow notion, but not a dishonorable or an unsympathetic one, and *Ordinary People* is not a book to be condescended to. The blurb insists that it simply arrived at Viking in the mail, and that it is the first unsolicited novel to be accepted by them since 1949. But this says more about publishing practices than it does about the book, and it creates an entirely misleading picture of raw talent growing in the sticks, and then hitting the big city with its untamed narrative. *Ordinary People* is the opposite of that: a snappy, proficient novel that reads a little too smoothly for its subject; skates on thin ice without managing to give us any real sense of how very thin the ice is.

Source: Michael Wood, "Crying for Attention," in *The New York Review of Books,* June 10, 1976, p. 8.

Sources

Dorothy Braginsky, review in *Psychology Today,* August, 1976.

Lore Dickstein, review of *Ordinary People,* in *New York Times Book Review,* July 18, 1976.

Barbara Holliday, in an interview with Judith Guest, in *Detroit Free Press,* October 7, 1982.

Paddy Kitchen, "Sentimental Americans," in *Listener,* Vol. 97, No. 2494, February 3, 1977, p. 158.

Review of *Ordinary People,* in *Kirkus Reviews,* Vol. XLIV, No. 5, March 1, 1976, p. 271.

Michael Wood, "Crying for Attention, in *New York Review of Books,* June 10, 1976, p. 8.

For Further Study

Saul L. Brown, "Adolescents and Family Systems," in *Youth Suicide,* edited by Michael L. Peck, Norman L. Farberow, and Robert E. Litman, Springer Publishing Co., 1985, pp. 71-79.
> Brown discusses family systems and their relationship to the individual dynamics that may lead adolescents to commit suicide.

Fady Hajal, "Family Mythology: Ordinary People," in *Literature/Film Quarterly,* Vol. XI, No. 1, 1983, pp. 3-8.
> Hajal applies the concept of Family Mythology to Robert Redford's award-winning film adaptation of Guest's novel.

Caroline Hunt, "Dead Athletes and Other Martyrs," in *Children's Literature Association Quarterly,* Vol. 16, No. 4, Winter 1991-1992, pp. 241-45.
> An article placing *Ordinary People* in the context of adolescent literature about death and dying.

Melvin Maddocks, "Suburban Furies," in *Time,* Vol. 108, No. 3, July 19, 1976, pp. 68, 70.
> Maddox describes *Ordinary People* as a "good but thoroughly conventional novel."

Don O'Briant, "Guest Finds Noble Story in Her Family Tree," in *Atlanta Constitution,* Feb. 12, 1997, section D, p. 81.
> An article about the autobiographical origins of Guest's *Errands.*

Janet G. Stroud, "Characterization of the Emotionally Disturbed in Current Adolescent Fiction," in *Top of the News,* Vol. 37, No. 3, Spring, 1981, pp. 290-95.
> An article which favorably compares *Ordinary People* to other books containing emotionally disturbed characters.

Colleen Kelly Warren, "A Novel Worth the Long Wait," in *St. Louis Post-Dispatch,* Jan. 19, 1997, Section D, p. 52.
> A review praising *Errands* as worth the wait.

Jonathan Yardley, "Heaven & Earth: Judith Guest's Encore to 'Ordinary People,'" in *Washington Post Book World,* September 22, 1982, pp. B1, B15.
> A review of *Second Heaven* which praises it as a worthy successor to *Ordinary People.*

Pride and Prejudice

Jane Austen

1813

Jane Austen's *Pride and Prejudice* had a long and varied life before it finally saw publication on January 28, 1813. Austen began the book, originally titled *First Impressions,* in 1796. Her father submitted it to a London publisher the following year, but the manuscript was rejected. Austen continued to work on the book, and scholars report that the story remained a favorite with the close circle of friends, relations, and acquaintances she took into her confidence. She probably continued working on *First Impressions* after her family relocated to Bath in 1801 and did not stop revising and rewriting until after the deaths of both her father and a close friend in 1805. After this point Austen seems to have given up writing for almost five years. She had resumed work on the book by 1811, scholars report, and the final product appeared anonymously in London bookstalls early in 1813.

The critical history of *Pride and Prejudice* was just as varied as the evolution of the novel itself. At the time the novel was published in the early nineteenth century, most respected critical opinion was strongly biased against novels and novelists. Although only three contemporary reviews of *Pride and Prejudice* are known to exist, they are all remarkably complimentary. Anonymous articles in the *British Critic* and the *Critical Review* praised the author's characterization and her portrayal of domestic life. Additional early commentary exists in the diaries and letters of such prominent contemporary readers as Mary Russell Mitford and Henry Crabb Robinson, both of whom admired the

work's characters, realism, and freedom from the trappings of Gothic fiction. After this period, however, criticism of *Pride and Prejudice,* and of Austen's works as a whole, largely disappeared. With the exception of two posthumous appreciations of Austen's work as a whole by Sir Walter Scott and Archbishop Richard Whateley, very little Austen criticism appeared until 1870.

In 1870, James Edward Austen-Leigh, son of Jane Austen's brother James, published *A Memoir of Jane Austen, by Her Nephew.* This biography was the first major study of Austen as a person and as an artist, and it marked the beginning of a new era in Austen criticism. Although most critics no longer accept its conclusion that Austen was an "amateur genius" whose works were largely unconscious productions of her fertile imagination, it nonetheless performed a valuable service by bringing Austen and her works back into critical attention. Modern critical opinion of Austen began with the publication in 1939 of Mary Lascelles's *Jane Austen and Her Art,* which escaped from the Victorian portrait of Austen put forth by Austen-Leigh.

Jane Austen

Author Biography

Born in England on December 16, 1775, Jane Austen is widely admired for her novels about manners in eighteenth-century England. Austen's life is imbedded in the same social world as her characters—that of the "landed gentry" in England's countryside. Her father, George Austen, was a country clergyman in Steventon, Hampshire, who had advanced himself through ambition and intelligence. Her mother, Cassandra Leigh, was of much higher birth; one of her ancestors had been Lord Mayor of London under Queen Elizabeth I. "The Austen children," writes Laura Dabundo in the *Concise Dictionary of British Literary Biography,* "grew up in a close-knit family, low on financial resources but strong on education and religious principles." Two of her brothers, James and Henry, found careers in the Church of England, while two others, Francis and Charles, entered the Royal Navy and both eventually achieved the rank of admiral. Her brother Edward was adopted by a distant relative, the wealthy but childless Thomas Knight.

Because money was in such short supply, Austen and her older sister Cassandra "had little formal schooling," Dabundo continues. "The significant scholastic experiences that nurtured one of England's leading writers took place in the rectory at Steventon." Jane improved her own mind and prepared herself for a career as an author by reading widely the works of William Shakespeare, John Milton, Henry Fielding, Samuel Johnson, Samuel Richardson, and many others. By 1787, she had already begun to compose her own stories, dramas, and short novels, and in 1795 she began the first drafts of "Elinor and Marianne," which would later become *Sense and Sensibility.* However, Austen would be thirty-five years old before she ever saw her first book in print. "*Pride and Prejudice,*" writes Dabundo, "had its origins in an epistolary novel, 'First Impressions,' written between October 1796 and August 1797 and offered to a publisher by Mr. Austen in November." Eventually, *Pride and Prejudice* would be published anonymously in London on January 28, 1813.

Reverend George Austen retired from his rectory in December of 1800, and in May of 1801 he moved his family to the Regency resort town of Bath in the west of England. They remained there until Reverend Austen's sudden death in January of 1805. His death left his wife and daughters without a means of support, and they were forced to rely on the charity of the Austen sons. From 1806 to 1809 the two Cassandras and Jane lived with Frank Austen in Southampton. In the summer of 1809 they settled into Chawton, a country house in

Hampshire on the estate of Edward Austen—the brother adopted by wealthy Thomas Knight. There Jane resumed writing and began to revise her earlier manuscripts in hopes of publishing them. On January 28, 1813, *Pride and Prejudice* was published anonymously in London.

The relative success of *Sense and Sensibility* and *Pride and Prejudice* led Austen to continue to write. *Mansfield Park* and *Emma* were published during her lifetime, but *Northanger Abbey* and *Persuasion* only appeared after her death. Sometime around the end of 1815 or the beginning of 1816, she began suffering from back pain, fatigue, and nausea. "It has been speculated," declares Dabundo, "that Jane Austen had Addison's disease, destruction of the adrenal glands by tuberculosis or by tumor … but it is also possible that she had cancer or tuberculosis unrelated to Addison's disease." She had been working up to the time of her death on a final novel, *Sanditon,* but it remained unfinished on the day she died, July 18, 1817. "She was buried in Winchester Cathedral," Dabundo concludes. "Obituaries identified her for the first time as 'Authoress of Emma, Mansfield Park, Pride and Prejudice, and Sense and Sensibility.'"

Plot Summary

At Meryton

Perhaps the most famous opening lines from any nineteenth-century novel are the opening lines to Jane Austen's *Pride and Prejudice:* "It is a truth universally acknowledged, that a single man in possession of a good fortune, must be in want of a wife."

These words are spoken by Mrs. Bennet to Mr. Bennet on the news that a gentleman of fortune has just moved to Netherfield Park, a nearby estate. The Bennets begin this story with a peculiar problem: they have five unmarried daughters and no sons. Their estate is entailed, or restricted in inheritance, to Mr. Collins, a family cousin. Upon Mr. Bennet's death Mr. Collins will inherit the family lands, which will leave the Bennet daughters without a home or money. It becomes vital, therefore, that at least one of the daughters marries well in order to support and house their sisters (and mother if she is still alive) should they not be able to marry.

Shortly after arriving alone, Bingley brings to Netherfield his two sisters, Miss Bingley and Mrs. Hurst; his brother-in-law, Mr. Hurst; and his friend, Mr. Darcy, who also happens to be wealthy and unmarried. Not wanting to miss a favorable introduction to their new neighbors, Mrs. Bennet pleads with Mr. Bennet to call on Bingley so that she can begin introducing her daughters to him. Initially Mr. Bennet refuses to play any part in matching any one of his daughters with Bingley. He tells his wife that if is she is so intent on meeting the newcomers at Netherfield, she must visit Bingley herself. However, prudent manners forbade to woman call on a strange man, making Mrs. Bennet powerless to begin the process which she hopes will lead to a marriage between one of her daughters and Bingley. Following the pronouncement that Mr. Bennet refuses to call on Bingley, Mrs. Bennet despairs that her daughters will never be able to meet with the eligible bachelor. Yet Mr. Bennet does call on Bingley, beginning the family's acquaintance with him. He takes ironic pleasure in surprising Mrs. Bennet with the news after letting her believe that he would not call on him.

The Bennet girls meet the Netherfield party for the first time at a small ball. Bingley proves to be personable and polite to the local folk, making him instantly well-liked. Darcy, while handsome and noble looking, appears proud and indifferent to participating in the activities of the evening or even socializing with the other guests.

The eldest daughter, Jane, is instantly drawn to Bingley, and he seems equally attracted to her. Jane is portrayed as gentle, unselfish, and very mannerly. Elizabeth is also well mannered, but possess a very sharp wit and refuses to be intimidated by anyone. Inclined to be protective of Jane and her family, she nonetheless recognizes the faults of her parents and other sisters. At the assembly, because of a shortage of men who dance, Elizabeth is left sitting. She overhears Bingley encouraging to Darcy to dance, suggesting that he ask Elizabeth. Darcy curtly replies that "she is tolerable; but not handsome enough to tempt *me; and I am in no humour at present to give consequence to young ladies who are slighted by other men.*" Elizabeth, though insulted, refuses to give Darcy's comment any weight, instead telling the story to all her friends and ridiculing his pretentious behavior.

Jane and Bingley's relationship continues to deepen during family visits, balls, and dinners. His sisters pretend to like Jane, but are appalled by her mother's vulgarities, her younger sisters' wild, loose manners, and their lower economic position among the landed gentry. They find great amusement in making fun of the Bennets behind Jane's back. A particular point of hilarity stems from the way Kitty and Lydia chase after the young military officers stationed locally.

Jane rides on horseback through a rainstorm in acceptance of an invitation from the Bingley sisters. She consequently catches cold and must stay at Netherfield until she is well, much to Mrs. Bennet's delight. Thinking her sister might need attending, Elizabeth goes to stay with Jane until she is well. Darcy soon begins to demonstrate an interest in Elizabeth, making Miss Bingley jealous, as she has hopes of marrying him herself. In fact, Miss Bingley has a right to worry, as Darcy notes to himself that "were it not for the inferiority of [Elizabeth's] connections, he should be in some danger."

Soon Jane is well and returns home. Another visitor arrives in the person of Mr. Collins. He is a clergyman and will be the inheritor of the Bennet estate upon Mr. Bennet's death. Thinking himself generous, he decides to try to marry one of the Bennet daughters, so that any unmarried daughter will still be able to live at the family estate. His patroness, Lady Catherine de Bourgh, who is also Darcy's aunt, has urged him to marry. He obeys her, as usual, with servile haste. He becomes interested at first in Jane, but when Mrs. Bennet indicates that Jane is taken, he fastens on to Elizabeth. She refuses him, believing that a marriage without love is not a worthwhile endeavor. Mrs. Bennet breaks down in hysterics, though Elizabeth's father approves her decision. Within a day, Mr. Collins proposes to Charlotte Lucas, Elizabeth's best friend, who accepts him.

During Mr. Collins' visit, Lydia and Kitty meet an officer newly stationed in Meryton. Wickham becomes a favorite among the ladies, including Elizabeth. He claims to have grown up with Darcy, saying he is the son of the late Mr. Darcy's steward. He says that the younger Darcy has cheated him of his inheritance, forcing him into military service. Already inclined to believe the worst of Darcy, Elizabeth now believes she has proof of his poor character, never once questioning the truthfulness of Wickham's story.

The Bingleys hold a ball where all of the Bennet family's manners, with the exception of those of Jane and Elizabeth, are exposed as lacking, much to Elizabeth's mortification. Soon the Bingley party packs up and leaves Netherfield to live in London during the winter. A letter comes from Miss Bingley to Jane implying that Bingley might become engaged to Darcy's sister. Jane, while refusing to express her loss to anyone but Elizabeth, is devas-

tated. When Elizabeth learns of Bingley's near engagement, she quickly realizes that Bingley's sister does not think Jane is a good marriage partner and has persuaded her brother that Jane is not really interested in him. Unlike Jane, who faults no one but herself for Bingley's departure, Elizabeth is furious with Miss Bingley, and perhaps Darcy, for interfering with her sister's happiness.

Travelling

Thinking that a change in scenery would improve Jane's condition, Mrs. Bennet's sister-in-law, Mrs. Gardiner, suggests that she spend part of the winter in London. While there, Jane is snubbed by Bingley's sisters and never even sees Bingley. Meanwhile, Elizabeth visits Charlotte and Mr. Collins in Kent, accompanied by Charlotte's sister and father. She sees Jane on the way and is sure that Darcy is keeping Bingley from visiting Jane.

In Kent, Lady Catherine honors the visitors, as Mr. Collins repeatedly informs them, with regular invitations. Elizabeth finds the woman to be haughty and ill-mannered, constantly thrusting her opinions on the others and fully expecting that they be followed without question. Elizabeth responds coolly to the other woman's prying. Darcy soon arrives in Kent, visiting regularly at the parsonage, sparring verbally with Elizabeth. Unexpectedly, he proposes marriage to her, explaining that he loves her in spite of her low family connections. Rather than being impressed and honored that such a highborn man should be interested in her, Elizabeth is insulted and refuses. She accuses him of being ungentlemanly, of destroying her sister's happiness, and finally of treating Mr. Wickham in an miserable manner. He storms away, but the next day presents her a letter answering her charges.

In the letter he states that he did keep Bingley from Jane, referring to the improprieties of her family and his sincere belief that Jane had no feelings for Bingley. He goes on to explain how Wickham squandered all the money the late Mr. Darcy left him and how he even attempted to elope with Georgiana, Darcy's sister, for a chance at her fortune. Elizabeth acknowledges the truth of his explanation, reproaching herself for believing Wickham without once questioning the truth of his story. Slowly, her prejudice against Darcy begins to weaken. Without seeing him again, she returns home.

In spite of Elizabeth's protests, Lydia goes with one of the officer's wives to Brighton, where the regiment is now stationed. Jane returns home

Movie still from Pride and Prejudice, *starring Greer Garson and Laurence Olivier, MGM, 1940.*

from London, and Elizabeth leaves to travel with the Gardiners on a tour through the country which will take them to Derbyshire, the region where Mrs. Gardiner was born and where Darcy lives. They go to Pemberly, Darcy's home, believing that he is away and Elizabeth need not fear running into him. But he comes home earlier than expected. In spite of their mutual embarrassment, he treats Elizabeth and the Gardiners with courtesy, asking if he may introduce his sister to her. Surprised, Elizabeth agrees.

While in Derbyshire, Elizabeth enjoys her time with Darcy, Georgiana, Bingley, and Bingley's sisters. She becomes very fond of Darcy and almost

believes that he may ask for her hand once more. A letter from Jane quickly dashes Elizabeth's hopes. Lydia has eloped with Wickham. Wracked with guilt that she might have prevented this disaster if she had made known what Wickham had done to Darcy's sister, Elizabeth rushes home. It is soon discovered that the runaways are not married, but hiding in London. Wickham lets it be known that he can be bribed to marry Lydia, so Mr. Gardiner arranges a quick wedding. With no other option, Mr. Bennet must consent, though he worries how he will repay Mr. Gardiner, who is surely providing the considerable bribe to Wickham. Once they are wed, Lydia and Wickham return to the welcoming arms of Mrs. Bennet, who refuses to be embarrassed by Lydia's lack of propriety.

All Is Well

Lydia, heedlessly breaking her promise to Darcy, tells Elizabeth that Darcy attended their wedding. Elizabeth then convinces Mrs. Gardiner to give her the details. It turns out that Mr. Darcy arranged the wedding, paid off Wickham, purchased Wickham a commission in the army, and supplemented Lydia's small dowry.

Soon after, Bingley and Darcy return to Netherfield. They call on the Bennets and soon Bingley proposes to Jane, who happily accepts. Elizabeth, having developed feelings for Darcy, scrutinizes him, hoping that he still has feelings for her. But he soon leaves Netherfield.

An unexpected visit from Lady Catherine soon occurs. She has heard a wild rumor that Darcy and Elizabeth are soon to be engaged, and she wishes for Elizabeth to refute the rumor and promise never to become engaged to Darcy. It seems that she has hopes her sickly daughter will marry him. Unintimidated, Elizabeth refuses. Lady Catherine leaves in a rage, later repeating the conversation to Darcy, unwittingly giving him hope that Elizabeth is in love with him. He knows Elizabeth well enough to understand that had she "been absolutely, irrevocably decided against [him], [she] would have acknowledged it … frankly and openly." He returns to Longbourne and proposes once again. Without hesitation, she accepts.

Characters

Catherine Bennet

Catherine "Kitty" Bennet is virtually a nonentity in the Bennet family. Although she is the fourth sister, younger than Mary but older than Lydia, Austen reveals that she is "weak-spirited, irritable, and completely under Lydia's guidance … ignorant, idle, and vain." However, the end of the novel is a bit encouraging for Kitty. Jane and Elizabeth make sure that she visits both of them frequently, and they introduce her to more intelligent and entreating society. Austen notes that this change in environment has an excellent effect on Kitty.

Eliza Bennet

See Elizabeth Bennet

Elizabeth Bennet

"Elizabeth Bennet," writes Elizabeth Jenkins in her critical biography *Jane Austen: A Biogra-*

phy, "has perhaps received more admiration than any other heroine in English literature." Elizabeth is the soul of *Pride and Prejudice,* who reveals in her own person the very title qualities that she spots so easily in her sisters and their suitors. Elizabeth has her father, Mr. Bennet's, quick wit and ironic sense of humor. Unlike her older sister Jane, she resists accepting all people uncritically. She is quick to recognize most people's principal characteristics—for instance, she recognizes the stupidities of many members of her family and quickly characterizes Lady Catherine de Bourgh as a control addict and her sister's suitor Charles Bingley as a simple and good-hearted young man. But she is also, concludes Jenkins, "completely human. Glorious as she is, and beloved of her creator, she is kept thoroughly in her place. She was captivated by [George] Wickham, in which she showed herself no whit superior to the rest of female Meryton." When Elizabeth begins to accept her own impressions uncritically, she makes her worst mistakes.

Because Elizabeth is so keen an observer of other people, she recognizes her mother's silliness and vows not to be caught in the same trap as her father. This refusal, however, is itself a trap. By trusting entirely to her own observations (pride) and her own initial assessments of people (prejudice), Elizabeth threatens her future happiness with Fitzwilliam Darcy. "Above all," concludes Jenkins, "there is her prejudice against Darcy, and though their first encounter was markedly unfortunate, she built on it every dislike it could be made to bear; her eager condemnation of him and her no less eager remorse when she found that she had been mistaken, are equally lovable."

Jane Bennet

Jane Bennet is Elizabeth's older sister, the most beautiful and amiable of the Bennet sisters. Her father considers her too willing to please and believes that she lacks the character to deal with life's difficulties. He tells Jane, "You are … so complying, that nothing will ever be resolved on; so easy, that every servant will cheat you; and so generous, that you will always exceed your income." Jane eventually marries the equally amiable Charles Bingley.

Kitty Bennet

See Catherine Bennet

Lizzie Bennet

See Elizabeth Bennet

Media Adaptations

- The most famous film version of *Pride and Prejudice* is the black and white Metro-Goldwyn-Meyer production released in 1940. Directed by Robert Z. Leonard, the film featured Greer Garson as Elizabeth Bennet and Laurence Olivier as Fitzwilliam Darcy and won the Academy Award for best art direction because of its lavish sets. It is currently available as a videocassette from MGM/UA Home Entertainment.

- In 1985, the British Broadcasting Company (BBC) and director Cyril Coke adapted *Pride and Prejudice* for television as a mini-series. It starred Elizabeth Garvie and David Rintoul as Elizabeth and Darcy and was later released on video by CBS/Fox Video.

- In 1995, another BBC television adaptation of *Pride and Prejudice* was released, starring Jennifer Ehle as Elizabeth Bennet and Colin Firth as Fitzwilliam Darcy. In the United States it aired on Arts & Entertainment Television (A&E) and the Public Broadcasting Service (PBS) and is available from A & E Home Video and PBS Home Video.

- Other adaptations of *Pride and Prejudice* include the sound recordings *Pride and Prejudice*, narrated by Flo Gibson, Recorded Books, 1980 (an unabridged version of the novel); *Pride and Prejudice*, abridged by Frances Welch, read by Celia Johnson, ALS Audio Language Studies, 1981 (a "read-along" transcript); *Pride and Prejudice*, read by Jane Lapotaire, Durkin Hayes, 1992; *Pride and Prejudice: Selections*, narrated by Sheila Allen, Francia DiMase, and Roger Rees, Time Warner Audiobooks, 1994; and *Pride and Prejudice*, abridged by Elizabeth Bradbury, BDD Audio, 1994 (a BBC Radio production).

Lydia Bennet

Lydia is the youngest of the Bennet daughters and perhaps the silliest. Austen describes her as "a stout, well-grown girl of fifteen, with a fine complexion and good-humoured countenance; a favorite with her mother, whose affection had brought her into public at an early age." Rather than spend any of her day receiving any sort of education, Lydia instead devotes all of her energies to collecting gossip about their neighbors, freely spending money about the town, and flirting with young men. Although all the Bennet girls are initially attracted to George Wickham, it is the headstrong Lydia who elopes with him and who is eventually married to him. Lydia's impudent actions put her sisters' marriage prospects in jeopardy, but she shows no signs of remorse; unlike Elizabeth and Darcy, she does not learn from her mistakes.

Mary Bennet

Mary Bennet is the third Bennet daughter, younger than Elizabeth and Jane and older than Catherine and Lydia. Rather than prancing around town flirting with young men, Mary considers herself an intellectual and would rather enjoy the company of a book. But Austen reveals that she overestimates her own talents and intelligence, saying that Mary "had neither genius nor taste; and though vanity had given her application, it had given her likewise a pedantic air and conceited manner, which would have injured a higher degree of excellence than she had reached."

Mr. Bennet

Austen describes Mr. Bennet, the father of the five Bennet girls (Jane, Elizabeth, Mary, Catherine, and Lydia), as "so odd a mixture of quick parts, sarcastic, humour, reserve, and caprice, that the experience of three and twenty years had been insufficient to make his wife understand his character." He is mildly well-off. Austen reports that he has an income of two thousand pounds sterling a year, enough for his family to live comfortably—but socially he ranks toward the bottom of the scale of the landed gentry. This is one of the reasons that people like Fitzwilliam Darcy and Lady Catherine de Bourgh regard the family with some disdain.

Mr. Bennet is one of the primary means by which the author expresses her ironic wit. He shares this quality with Elizabeth, his favorite daughter. However, unlike Elizabeth's, Mr. Bennet's wit is usually expressed in sarcastic asides directed at his wife. Unlike his daughter, Mr. Bennet does not question or examine his own life, and his situation never improves. In addition, he allows his younger daughters to behave as carelessly and improperly as his wife. His inattention to his own family results in his daughter Lydia eloping with the despicable George Wickham.

Mr. and Mrs. Bennet are not well matched. Her silliness does not mix well with his sarcastic wit. Mr. Bennet recognizes this, and it is one of the reasons he instills in his daughter Elizabeth the importance of matching temperaments with her husband.

Mrs. Bennet

Mrs. Bennet, Austen reports, is "a woman of mean understanding, little information, and uncertain temper. When she was discontented, she fancied herself nervous. The business of her life was to get her daughters married; its solace was visiting and news." Mrs. Bennet is primarily concerned with the outer aspects of her society: the importance of marrying well in society without regard to the suitability of the personalities in the match. Neither does Mrs. Bennet have any regard for respecting proper manners and behavior. She is continually embarrassing Elizabeth and Jane with her inappropriate comments and schemes to marry off her daughters. Additionally, Elizabeth finds her mother's influence on the younger Bennet daughters particularly disturbing. Mrs. Bennet allows the younger girls to devote all their time searching for eligible young bachelors, neglecting any form of education. It is perhaps because of Mrs. Bennet's attitudes that her youngest daughter, Lydia, elopes with the despicable George Wickham.

Caroline Bingley

Caroline Bingley is the sister of Charles Bingley. She and her sister are very proud of her family's wealth—conveniently forgetting, Austen notes, "that their brother's fortune and their own had been acquired by trade." They are willing to go to great lengths to prevent his marriage into the poorer Bennet family. It is Caroline who reveals to Jane Bennet her plans to have Charles marry Fitzwilliam Darcy's sister Georgiana.

Charles Bingley

Charles Bingley is a friend of Fitzwilliam Darcy and the new occupant of the Netherfield estate, which neighbors the Bennet's home, Longbourn. It is through Bingley that Elizabeth first meets Darcy and is unimpressed by Darcy's manners. Bingley, whom Austen describes as "good-looking and gentlemanlike; he had a pleasant countenance and easy, unaffected manners," is very attracted to Jane Bennet. This affection distresses his sisters, including Caroline Bingley, and Darcy himself. They all believe that the Bennet family is too far down the social ladder to deserve such attention from him. Ironically, Charles himself has received his fortune by his family's interest in trade, considerably less respectable than Darcy's wealth inherited by birthright. Charles' sisters and Darcy deliberately give Elizabeth Bennet the impression that Bingley is to marry Darcy's sister, Georgiana, after he leaves for London. Eventually, however, Bingley returns to Netherfield and marries Jane.

Charlotte Collins

See Charlotte Lucas

Mr. William Collins

Mr. William Collins is Mr. Bennet's nephew and a clergyman. Because Mr. Bennet has no sons, Collins is in line to inherit Mr. Bennet's estate. Austen describes him as "not a sensible man, and the deficiency of nature had been but little assisted by education or society." Mr. Bennet enjoys Collins's visit to his home because he appreciates Collins's naive stupidity, but Elizabeth resents his attentions and rejects his marriage proposal. She is very distressed when her friend Charlotte Lucas decides to marry Mr. Collins out of interest in his estate rather than his personality.

Fitzwilliam Darcy

Fitzwilliam Darcy, like Elizabeth Bennet, combines in his character the prime characteristics of *Pride and Prejudice:* his aristocratic demeanor (pride) and his belief in the natural superiority of the wealthy landed gentry (prejudice). Darcy sometimes unconsciously assumes that a lack of money or social status are characteristics that disqualify people from marrying or loving each other. Elizabeth quickly discovers this aspect of his character, and it is her flat rejection of his first proposal of marriage that sparks his eventual change of heart. He recognizes the essential arrogance of his upbringing and repents of it; he tells Elizabeth, "By you I was properly humbled. I came to you without a doubt of my reception. You showed me how insufficient were all my pretensions to please a woman worthy of being pleased." In return for the privilege of become Elizabeth's husband, he is willing to put up with her three silly sisters, her equally silly mother, and even the scoundrel George Wickham as a brother-in-law.

Some critics maintain that this change of heart was nothing more than the uncovering of Darcy's innate characteristics. "Darcy's essential character is independent of circumstances," states Elizabeth Jenkins in her critical biography *Jane Austen: A Biography*. "He had the awkwardness and stiffness of a man who mixes little with society and only on his own terms, but it was also the awkwardness and stiffness that is found with Darcy's physical type, immediately recognizable among the reserved and inarticulate English of to-day." This analysis suggests that Darcy's character is more like that of his sister, Georgiana Darcy, a painfully shy girl. Georgiana Darcy's shyness and awkwardness and Fitzwilliam Darcy's arrogance and harshness come from the same roots. It is, however, Darcy's ability to examine his own life and recognize his flaws and his courage in approaching Elizabeth Bennet again, after she had already rejected him once, that leads to their eventual marriage and life together.

Georgiana Darcy

Georgiana Darcy is Fitzwilliam Darcy's younger sister. She is extremely shy and uncomfortable in company. Austen describes her as "tall ... and, though little more than sixteen, her figure was formed, and her appearance womanly and graceful. She was less handsome than her brother, but there was sense and good humour in her face, and her manners were perfectly unassuming and gentle." Elizabeth Bennet expects that she will dislike Georgiana just as much as she initially dislikes her brother, but she turns out to be favorably impressed. Her impressions of Georgiana are among the first intimations Elizabeth has that her conclusions about Darcy may be wrong.

Miss Anne de Bourgh

Anne de Bourgh is the only daughter of Lady Catherine de Bourgh and the late Sir Lewis de Bourgh. Her mother plans to marry the sickly Anne to her cousin, Fitzwilliam Darcy.

Lady Catherine de Bourgh

Lady Catherine de Bourgh is Fitzwilliam Darcy's aunt. A proud, unforgiving woman, she is a control addict who likes to tell everyone what to do. She is scheming to have her nephew marry her own daughter, Anne de Bourgh, whom Austen describes as "sickly and cross." Elizabeth quickly realizes that Lady Catherine is a petty tyrant, but she seizes upon this revelation as an excuse to conclude that Fitzwilliam Darcy is himself equally flawed. Lady Catherine makes a final attempt to create a breach between Darcy and Elizabeth in the final chapters of the book, but her attempt backfires and only serves to help bring them together.

Colonel Fitzwilliam

Colonel Fitzwilliam is Darcy's cousin. He is the younger son of an earl and, although "not handsome," explains Austen, "in person and address [he was] most truly the gentleman." He develops a fondness for Elizabeth Bennet, but realistically admits that as a younger son he must marry for wealth, not love.

Mr. Edward Gardiner

Mr. Gardiner is Mrs. Bennet's brother, whom Austen describes as "a sensible, gentlemanlike man, greatly superior to his sister as well by nature as education." He and his wife take Elizabeth Bennet on a tour of Derbyshire, including a side trip to Darcy's estate at Pemberley. He also tries to help Mr. Bennet locate Wickham and Lydia after they elope. Mr. Gardner and his wife are among the few relatives Elizabeth can be assured will not embarrass her.

Mrs. M. Gardiner

Mrs. Gardiner, Edward Gardiner's wife and Elizabeth Bennet's aunt, is according to Austen "an amiable, intelligent, elegant woman, and a great favourite with all her Longbourn nieces." She accompanies Elizabeth on a tour of Fitzwilliam Darcy's estate at Pemberley.

Mr. Hurst

Mr. Hurst is the husband of Mr. Charles Bingley's sister Louisa. He is lazy, says Austen, an "indolent man who lived only to eat, drink, and play at cards, who when he found [Elizabeth to] prefer a plain dish to a ragout, had nothing to say to her."

Mrs. Louisa Hurst

Louisa Hurst is the wife of Mr. Hurst and the sister of Mr. Charles Bingley and Caroline Bingley. She plots with her sister to remove their brother's affection from Jane Bennet and transfer it to someone more suitable.

Charlotte Lucas

Charlotte Lucas is Elizabeth Bennet's best friend. She distresses Elizabeth by deciding to marry William Collins, Mr. Bennet's nephew, out of interest in his estate. Up until this point Elizabeth had respected Charlotte's sensibility, but her decision to marry Mr. Collins lost her much of Elizabeth's respect.

Lady Lucas

Lady Lucas is the wife of Sir William Lucas and mother of Elizabeth Bennet's friend Charlotte Lucas. Austen describes her as "a very good kind of woman, not too clever to be a valuable neighbor to Mrs. Bennet."

Sir William Lucas

A close neighbor of the Bennets, he earned most of his income through trade. His daughter, Charlotte, marries Mr. Collins, Mr. Bennet's heir.

Mr. Philips

Mrs. Bennet's brother-in-law, Mr. Philips is an attorney. He hosts the party at which Wickham tells Elizabeth about Darcy's withholding a promised legacy. Already having a negative first impression of Darcy, Elizabeth unquestioningly accepts Wickham's story as evidence that Darcy is a miserable person. When she discovers that it is actually Wickham who wronged Darcy, Elizabeth feels terrible for allowing her pride to interfere with an objective judgement of Darcy.

Mrs. Philips

Mrs. Bennet's sister, Mrs. Philips, is described by Austen as a silly, vulgar woman.

George Wickham

Lieutenant George Wickham is an unscrupulous man who schemes to win money by marrying a wealthy heiress. He is physically quite attractive; Austen says of him that "he had all the best part of beauty, a fine countenance, a good figure, and a very pleasing address." His father was once the steward of Darcy's estates, and Wickham plays on the relationship by trying to elope with Georgiana Darcy, Fitzwilliam Darcy's sister. Darcy gave Wickham a cash payment after Wickham turned down a comfortable church position the late Mr. Darcy provided for him. After Wickham elopes with Lydia Bennet, Darcy tracks him down, bribes him into marrying Lydia, and buys him an officer's rank in the army. Wickham is presented in the novel as a man totally without principle.

Themes

Pride

The two major themes of Jane Austen's *Pride and Prejudice* are summed up in the title. The first aspect can be traced in the actions and statements of all of the work's major and many of its minor characters. Pride is the character flaw that causes Elizabeth Bennet to dislike Fitzwilliam Darcy upon their first meeting. She perceives in him a cold aloofness that she attributes to his own inflated opinion of himself. Yet Elizabeth herself also suffers from the same flaw; her pride in her own ability to analyze character is such that she refuses to reevaluate Darcy in the face of evidence in his favor.

In some characters, Austen depicts pride overtly. Lady Charlotte de Bourgh is motivated by pride in her family's status to try to break up a potential match between Elizabeth and Darcy. Mrs. Louisa Hurst and Caroline Bingley try to achieve the same effect with the relationship between their brother Charles Bingley and Jane Bennet. In each case, however, Austen depicts the pride of these minor characters as ridiculous: "Austen treats pride," writes Robert B. Heilman in "*E pluribus unum:* Parts and Whole in *Pride and Prejudice,*" "as if it were wholly unproblematic, a failing no less clear-cut than prejudice."

In the case of Elizabeth and Darcy, however, Austen treats pride less directly. On his first appearance in the novel, Darcy appears "above his company and above being pleased," reports Heilman, the "proudest, most disagreeable man in the world." The people who record these observations, the critic continues, "believe that they are seeing sense of superiority, snobbishness, excessive self-approval." However, they do not take into consideration that some of the other behavior that Darcy exhibits, such as "reserve, an apparent unresponsiveness to overtures, a holding back from conventional intercourse, pleasantries, and small talk," may actually stem from a quiet personality. So what appears to be pride may be simple shyness or awkwardness. When Elizabeth and others consider Darcy full of pride, they are also condemning him, says Heilman, for not obeying the rules of the "neighborhood social ways." For Darcy and Elizabeth, at least, pride can be more than a simple negative quality.

In fact, pride serves several different functions in the novel. In addition to the misplaced pride of the minor characters, there are characters who ne-

Topics for Further Study

- Research the changes in the English social structure during the late eighteenth and early nineteenth centuries. Show how attitudes in *Pride and Prejudice* toward the newly wealthy middle classes, who earned their money through trade and manufacturing, differed from those toward the landed gentry who inherited their generations-old wealth.

- Much of *Pride and Prejudice* centers on the question of marriage or other unions. Examine the attitudes of the different characters in the novel towards the institution of marriage and compare them to modern attitudes.

- In 1792, Mary Wollstonecraft published her book *A Vindication of the Rights of Women,* which offered the then revolutionary idea that women were the intellectual equal of men and should be educated as such. What subjects did women study during the late eighteenth and early eighteenth century? Although Austen never credited Wollstonecraft as inspiration, many of Austen's characters have qualities encouraged by Wollstonecraft. Examine Wollstonecraft's ideas and find examples of how Elizabeth fulfills many of Wollstonecraft's demands for women.

---

glect to honor their pride when they should protect it. Elizabeth's friend Charlotte Lucas decides to marry William Collins, the heir to Mr. Bennet's estate, out of a simple desire to make his estate her own. Elizabeth strongly objects to such a union; it offends her sense of pride for someone to enter into a loveless marriage for purely material purposes. The George Wickham-Lydia Bennet elopement is another example of an arrangement where pride should have been taken into consideration and was not. In this way, Heilman states, Austen defines pride as "the acceptance of responsibility. This indispensably fills out a story that has devoted a good deal of time to the view of pride as an easy and blind self-esteem." Gradually, even Darcy and Eliz-

abeth herself come to a realization of the necessity not to reject pride, but to control it.

Prejudice and Tolerance

The subject of prejudice is linked to pride in the title of *Pride and Prejudice.* It is also more directly linked to Elizabeth Bennet's character. From the beginning, states Marvin Mudrick in "Irony as Discrimination: *Pride and Prejudice,*" "Elizabeth sets herself up as an ironic spectator, able and prepared to judge and classify, already making the first large division of the world into two sorts of people: the simple ones, those who give themselves away out of shallowness (as Bingley fears) or perhaps openness (as Elizabeth implies) or an excess of affection (as Mr. Collins will demonstrate); and the intricate ones, those who cannot be judged and classified so easily, who are 'the most amusing' to the ironic spectator because they offer the most formidable challenge to his powers of detection and analysis." Elizabeth is prepared to divide the entire world into one of these two categories—an extreme example of prejudice in the "pre-judging" sense of the term. It is most evident in her judgment of Darcy; so sure is she of her powers of observation that she refuses to reevaluate Darcy even when the weight of evidence begins to turn in favor of him.

It is not until Darcy overcomes his own prejudice against those of lower social station—by treating Elizabeth and the Gardiners graciously and considerately at Netherfield—that Elizabeth's opinion of him begins to change. "Not only do Elizabeth and Darcy ... have the most serious problem of surmounting barriers of misconception and adverse feeling," Heilman declares, "but they are the most sensitive—both in susceptibility to injured feelings and in capacity for getting to the center of things—to matters of prejudice and pride." The ending "is a remarkable tracing of Elizabeth's coming around to a completely changed point of view," the critic concludes. "To Jane she acknowledges that she has cultivated her 'prejudices' and has been 'weak and vain and nonsensical.'" With this realization Elizabeth begins the process of change that will eventually bring herself and Darcy together.

Change and Transformation

The major characters of the novel suffer from a combination of the two title characteristics of *Pride and Prejudice.* What separates Elizabeth and Darcy from the silly minor characters, such as Wickham, Lydia, Mr. Collins, and Lady Catherine, and even from the good minor characters such as Mr. Bennet, Jane, and Charles Bingley, is their ability and willingness to learn and grow, to overcome their initial shortcomings. They mature and come to a better understanding of each other by the novel's end through a slow and painful growth process.

Darcy begins his process of transformation with Elizabeth's rejection of his suit. He makes his proposal to her clumsily, stressing his own wealth and position (and minimizing hers) and stating that he has tried to suppress his feelings because of the low position of her family. When Elizabeth indignantly rejects his hand, accusing him of arrogance and selfishness, Darcy begins a process of reevaluation of his behavior. When he next appears in the story—at the beginning of Volume 3—he is much friendlier and more attentive to Elizabeth. She begins to feel an attraction to him that is not fully realized until the Wickham-Lydia elopement is fully resolved. Darcy completes his transformation by swallowing his pride and proposing to Elizabeth again, in spite of the fact that her acceptance will make the silly Bennet girls his sisters-in-law and the detestable Wickham his brother-in-law.

Elizabeth's process of transformation begins later and takes longer. She realizes her own prejudices toward Darcy in Chapter 12 of Volume 2, when he gives her the letter in which he reveals the truth about Wickham and his role in the breakup of the Bingley-Jane relationship. She does not complete the change, however, until the end of Volume 3, when Lady Catherine de Bourgh demands assurances from her that she will not accept a proposal from him. Elizabeth refuses, and by doing so gives Darcy his first hint that his feelings for her are at last reciprocated. "By a slow revision of preconceptions," concludes Heilman, " … Elizabeth and Darcy 'earn' the better insight and rapport that insight makes possible."

Style

Romanticism

The novel *Pride and Prejudice* was written during the middle of the Romantic period in western literature, but it is itself rather uncharacteristic of other fictional works of the period. Unlike the great Romantic novels and poems of the period, which usually praised youthful passions, Austen's work minimizes them. Compared to Johann Wolfgang von Goethe's classic *sturm und drang* novel *The Sorrows of Young Werther* (1774), in which the young hero is unsuccessful at love and, unable to

make his inner visions conform to the reality of the outer world, finally commits suicide, Austen's works are models of restraint. Instead of the wild forces of nature, Austen concentrates on family life in small English towns. Instead of rampant emotionalism, Austen emphasizes a balance between reason and emotion. Instead of suicide and unrequited love, Austen offers elopement and marriage. Although the author does consider some of the same themes as her Romantic contemporaries—the importance of the individual, for instance—Austen's society is altogether more controlled and settled than the world presented in Romantic fiction.

Irony

Irony, or the contrast between the expected and the actual, is the chief literary device Austen uses to comment on the small, enclosed world of the English gentry in *Pride and Prejudice.* Her irony takes different forms for different characters. Perhaps the most ironic character in the entire book is Mr. Bennet, father of the five Bennet sisters. Mr. Bennet is married to a silly woman he cannot respect, who centers her life on marrying her daughters off to wealthy, well-bred men. He expresses his discontent in the marriage by criticizing his wife's stream of comments. Many of these are sarcastic and hurtful, and contribute to the misunderstandings between the couple that leave them incapable of dealing with the disastrous elopement of their youngest daughter Lydia with the detestable George Wickham. Mr. Bennet's conscious use of irony is for him a game—it serves no useful purpose.

For the author, in the persona of Mr. Bennet's daughter Elizabeth, however, irony is both a toy and a defensive weapon in the war against stupidity. The author uses Elizabeth to skewer self-important characters such as Mr. Collins and Mrs. Bennet. Yet Elizabeth is also blind to her own character faults, and her very blindness is another example of Austen's use of irony. In her misunderstandings with Darcy, she (who is blind to her own pride in her ability to read character) accuses him of excessive pride, while he (who is prejudiced against people with less money than he has) accuses her of prejudice. The on-again, off-again love between Jane Bennet and Charles Bingley is also an example of Austen's use of irony to underline messages about love and marriage. "Jane and Bingley provide us, then, with one of the book's primary ironies," writes Marvin Mudrick in "Irony as Discrimination: *Pride and Prejudice*": "that love is simple, straightforward, and immediate only for

Jane Austen's house.

very simple people." "In *Pride and Prejudice*," concludes Mudrick, "Jane Austen's irony has developed into an instrument of discrimination between the people who are simple reproductions of the social type and the people with individuality and will, between the unaware and the aware."

Other examples of Austen's use of irony abound in the novel. "Many pages of *Pride and Prejudice* can be read as sheer poetry of wit, as [Alexander] Pope without couplets," writes Reuben A. Brower in "Light and Bright and Sparkling: Irony and Fiction in *Pride and Prejudice*." "The triumph of the novel—whatever its limitations may be—lies in combining such poetry of wit," the critic concludes, "with the dramatic structure of fiction."

Historical Context

Jane Austen's England

Jane Austin's major novels, including *Pride and Prejudice,* were all composed within a short period of about twenty years. Those twenty years (1795-1815) also mark a period in history when England was at the height of its power. England stood as the bulwark against French revolutionary extremism and against Napoleonic imperialism. The

dates Austen was writing almost exactly coincide with the great English military victories over Napoleon and the French: the Battle of the Nile, in which Admiral Nelson crippled the French Mediterranean fleet, and the battle of Waterloo, in which Lord Wellington and his German allies defeated Napoleon decisively and sent him into exile. However, so secure in their righteousness were the English middle and upper classes—the "landed gentry" featured in Austen's works—that these historical events impact *Pride and Prejudice* very little.

The French Revolution and Napoleonic Wars

The period from 1789 to 1799 marks the time of the French Revolution, while the period from 1799 to 1815 marks the ascendancy of Napoleon—periods of almost constant social change and upheaval. In England, the same periods were times of conservative reaction, in which society changed very little. The British government, led by Prime Minister William Pitt, maintained a strict control over any ideas or opinions that seemed to support the revolution in France. Pitt's government suspended the right of *habeas corpus,* giving themselves the power to imprison people for an indefinite time without trial. It also passed laws against public criticism of government policies, and sup-

Compare & Contrast

- **1810s:** Europe is submerged in warfare throughout most of the decade by the struggle against the ambitions of Napoleon Bonaparte to unite the continent under French rule. Two of Austen's brothers, Frank and Charles, entered the British Navy and fought in the Napoleonic Wars.

  Today: For the first time since the Napoleonic Wars, Europe considers a single multinational government in the European Union.

- **1810s:** In the early nineteenth century, a woman's education differed greatly from that of a man. While boys attended boarding schools and studied Latin, mathematics, and science, girls were schooled at home by governesses, focusing on the fine arts, writing, reading, and sewing.

  Today: Over one hundred twenty-five million women graduated from high school in 1994 alone, while around eight hundred thousand females were enrolled in colleges and universities. Not limited to a specific gender, most American high schools and universities are open to both sexes, and course offerings are not exclusive to men or women.

- **1810s:** Because of a lack of professions for women to enter and become self-supporting, few women could afford to remain single in early 1800s. Most women elected to marry rather than depend on other family members for financial support.

  Today: Many women in America have increasingly decided to remain single. By 1994, only fifty-nine percent of women in America were married. In addition, almost sixty percent of American women over the age of sixteen were employed in the labor force, either part-time or full-time.

---

pressed working-class trade unions. At the same time, the Industrial Revolution permanently changed the British economy. It provided the money Pitt's government needed to oppose Napoleon. At the same time, it also created a large wealthy class and an even larger middle class. These are the people that Jane Austen depicts in *Pride and Prejudice,* the "landed gentry" who have earned their property, not by inheriting it from their aristocratic ancestors, but by purchasing it with their new wealth. They have few of the manners and graces of the aristocracy and, like the Collinses in *Pride and Prejudice,* are primarily concerned with their own futures in their own little worlds.

Unlike other Romantic-era writers, such as William Wordsworth and Samuel Taylor Coleridge, Austen's works are very little impacted by the French Revolution and revolutionary rhetoric. Members of Austen's own family served in the war against Bonaparte and the French; two of her brothers became admirals in the Royal Navy. The only hint of war and military behavior in *Pride and Prej-udice,* however, lies in the continued presence of the British soldiers in Meryton, near the Bennet estate at Longbourn. The soldiers include George Wickham, who later elopes with Lydia Bennet, disgracing the family. In the world of *Pride and Prejudice,* the soldiers are present only to give the younger Bennet daughters men in uniforms to chase after. Their world is limited to their own home, those of their friends and neighbors, a few major resort towns, and, far off, the city of London. There is no hint of the revolutionary affairs going on just across the English Channel in France.

English Regency Society

On the other hand, contemporary English society is a preoccupation of *Pride and Prejudice.* At the time the novel was published, King George III had been struck down by the periodic madness (now suspected to be caused by the metabolic disease porphyria) that plagued his final years. The powers he was no longer capable of using were placed in the hands of his son the Prince Regent, later George IV. The Prince Regent was widely known as a man of dissolute morals, and his example was followed by many of society's leading figures. Young men regularly went to universities not to learn, but to see and be seen, to drink, gamble, race horses, and spend money. Perhaps the greatest example of this type in *Pride and Prejudice* is the unprincipled George Wickham, who seduces sixteen-year-old Lydia Bennet. Lydia for her part also participates willingly in Regency culture; her thoughts are not for her family's disgrace, but about the handsomeness of her husband and the jealousy of her sisters.

Most "respectable" middle- and upper-class figures, such as Elizabeth Bennet and Fitzwilliam Darcy, strongly disapproved of the immorality of Regency culture. But they did participate in the fashions of the time, influenced by French styles (even though France was at war with England). During the period of the Directory and the Consulate in France (from 1794-1804), styles were influenced by the costumes of the Roman Republic. The elaborate hairstyles and dresses that had characterized the French aristocracy before the Revolution were discarded for simpler costumes. Women, including Elizabeth Bennet, would have worn a simple dress that resembled a modern nightgown. Loose and flowing, it was secured by a ribbon tied just below the breasts. Darcy for his part would have worn a civilian costume of tight breeches, a ruffled shirt with a carefully folded neckcloth, and a high-collared jacket. Even though these costumes were in part a reaction to the excesses of early eighteenth-century dress, they became themselves quite elaborate as the century progressed, sparked by the Prince Regent himself and his friend, the impeccable dresser Beau Brummel. Brummel's mystique, known as "dandyism," expressed in clothing the same idleness and effortless command of a situation that characterizes many of Austen's heroes and heroines.

Critical Overview

In the early nineteenth century, when Jane Austen published her first two novels *Sense and Sensibility* and *Pride and Prejudice,* writes B. C. Southam in his introduction to *Jane Austen: The Critical Heritage,* "fiction reviewing had no ... dignity, and in the light of prevailing standards the two novels were remarkably well-received. The reviewers were in no doubt about the superiority of these works. Although their notices are extremely limited in scope they remark on points which any modern critic would want to make." These points, in the case of *Pride and Prejudice,* include the spirited characterizations of Elizabeth Bennet and her family, Fitzwilliam Darcy, and the other major personalities of the novel. Those people that criticized the novel, however, complained that the author of the book (who was unknown at the time—Austen published her works anonymously and her authorship did not become widely known until after her death) depicted socially and morally unrefined people, that the book was simply entertaining without being uplifting, and that the realism of her book threatened their concept of literature as an idealized higher reality.

Most of the known contemporary opinions of *Pride and Prejudice* come from private journals and diaries, where important figures of the time recorded their opinions of the book as they were reading it. In January of 1813, the month of the publication of Austen's novel, however, two reviews were published anonymously in the *British Critic* and the *Critical Review.* Both reviewers praised the novel's readability, but most of the reviews are dedicated to appreciations of Austen's characterization. *Pride and Prejudice* "is very far superior to almost all the publications of the kind which have lately come before us," wrote the *British Critic* reviewer. "It has a very unexceptionable tendency, the story is well told, the characters remarkably well drawn and supported, and written with great spirit as well as vigour." "It is unnecessary to add," the reviewer concluded, "that we have perused these volumes with much satisfaction and amusement, and entertain very little doubt that their successful circulation will induce the author to similar exertions." The *Critical Review* contributor began his appreciation with the words, "Instead of the whole interest of the tale hanging upon one or two characters, as is generally the case in novels, the fair author of the present introduces us, at once, to a whole family, every individual of which excites the interest, and very agreeably divides the attention of the reader." "Nor is there one character which appears flat," the contributor concluded, "or obtrudes itself upon the notice of the reader with troublesome impertinence. There is not one person in the drama with whom we could readily dispense;— they have all their proper places; and fill their several stations, with great credit to themselves, and much satisfaction to the reader."

Those contemporaries of Austen who criticized *Pride and Prejudice* did so, says Southam, out of a feeling that the novel offended their sense of the rightness of the world. "While few readers could deny that they enjoyed reading the novels—for the vitality of the characters, the wit, the accuracy and realism of her picture of society—praise comes grudgingly, fenced round with qualifications," he states. Commentators, including Lady Darcy and Miss Mitford, complained that the characters, particularly the Bennets, are unrefined and socially mannerless. "These notions of decorum persisted throughout the nineteenth century, and created a particular unease in the reader," Southam concludes, "the sense on one hand that he was undoubtedly enjoying Jane Austen, but equally a sense that he must temper his admiration, recalling that novels so very worldly and realistic could never be great art."

Because of this common reaction to her fiction, criticism of Austen's works, including *Pride and Prejudice,* as a whole was delayed until after her death. "In 1819," writes Laura Dabundo in the *Concise Dictionary of British Literary Biography,* "Henry Crabb Robinson wrote the first of several diary entries in praise of her novels." Another contemporary reviewer, the novelist Sir Walter Scott, "recognized Austen's greatness, but his remarks also help to perpetuate the notion that her range was limited." It was the publication of James Edward Austen-Leigh's *A Memoir of Jane Austen, by Her Nephew* in 1870 that sparked a revival of Austen criticism. However, its depiction of Austen as a "spinster aunt" whose works were written primarily for her own amusement created a distorted picture of the author. "Later in the century," Dabundo explains, "George Henry Lewes argued for the unqualified excellence of her writing, comparing her accomplishment to that of Shakespeare, but nonetheless he saw her fiction as cool and unfevered." It was not until after the publication of Mary Lascelles's *Jane Austen and Her Art* in 1939 that twentieth century critics began to overturn the Victorian concept of Austen as an amateur artist uncommitted to creating great literature.

Austen criticism has exploded since 1939. Scholars turn to *Pride and Prejudice* for its portraits of late eighteenth-century society, for the technical expertise of its composition, and for its capacity to find and maintain interest in the everyday lives of small-town English society. "Increasingly, in studies like those of Dorothy Van Ghent, Reuben Brower, Marvin Mudrick, and Howard Babb," declares Donald J. Gray in his preface to *Jane Austen: Pride and Prejudice, An Authoritative Text, Backgrounds, Reviews and Essays in Criticism,* "[twentieth-century critics] study the development of characters and themes, the structure of episodes and sentences, even her very choice of words, in order to explain how novels about three or four families in a country village are also novels about the important business of making a fruitful life in a society and of a character which do not always encourage the best of even the few possibilities they permit." Austen's novels, Dabundo concludes, "deal with passionate but realistic people whose world was changing and being challenged, people who conducted their lives in the context of their immediate friends and family and a national culture that nourished and sustained them."

Criticism

Diana Francis

In the following essay, Francis, a doctoral candidate at Ball State University, relates the historical background surrounding both Jane Austen and her novel Pride and Prejudice. *She includes a critique of Austen's treatment of both male and female characters.*

Pride and Prejudice published in 1813, is Jane Austen's second, and probably best known novel, though it was originally published anonymously. Austen began *Pride and Prejudice* in 1796 under the title *First Impressions.* Her family found the novel entertaining and continued to reread it for at least two years. By 1799, she'd begun working on *Eleanor and Marianne,* which was later published as *Sense and Sensibility* in 1811. She again began revision work on *First Impressions,* though she was forced to retitle it as the name had already been used by another novelist. *Pride and Prejudice* finds its popular appeal in its control of language, wit, clever dialogue, and charming representations of human foible portrayed in characters such as Mr. Collins, Lady Catherine de Bourgh, and Mrs. Bennet. It is a far more mature and better written novel than *Sense and Sensibility.*

Known as a novel of manners, it, like *Emma* (1816), another popular Austen novel often used in the classroom, portrays the life of gentility in a small, rural society. Austen dramatizes the delicate and precarious nature of a society based on an ecology of manners. In such a society, the well-being of everyone hinges on people maintaining their proper places and behaving according to a strict code of manners. For the Bennet girls, their chances

What Do I Read Next?

- *Sense and Sensibility* (1811), Jane Austen's first published novel, looks at the contrast between reason and emotion in the persons of two of the three Dashwood sisters: Elinor and Marianne.

- Austen's *Mansfield Park* (1814), in which meek, poor Fanny Price wins through simple virtue both the love and hand of country heir Edmund Bertram.

- *Emma* (1816), in which Austen's well-to-do heroine plays matchmaker for a lower-class friend—until she realizes that she is herself in love with the man her friend has chosen.

- *Northanger Abbey* and *Persuasion* (1818), Austen's posthumously-published novels, that are respectively a sly parody of the overly-romantic Gothic novel and her examination of the transformation of the world by means of the Royal Navy.

- Sir Walter Scott's *Waverley* novels (1814). Scott was a contemporary and an admirer of Austen's work, and the *Waverley* novels—like Austen's, published anonymously—make an interesting contrast with her fiction. *Waverley* is set during the 1745 Jacobite rebellion in Scotland and is very Romantic in theme.

- *The English: A Social History, 1066-1945* (1987), by popular historian Christopher Hibbert, makes plain the evolution of the society that Austen portrays in her novels.

of marriage fall precipitously with every show of impropriety.

From the beginning, it is important to understand the very real danger that faces the Bennet girls if they do not marry. Upon Mr. Bennet's death, the girls' cousin, Mr. Collins, will inherit Longbourn. That means that the family will have no source of support and no place to live. A marriage of one of the girls to a wealthy man would provide a solution, but there is another problem, even for Jane and Elizabeth who do not suffer from ill-bred, vulgar behavior as their sisters do. Each girl possesses a negligible dowry to entice a prospective husband. Any man who chooses to marry a poor girl must do so for love or to acquire a good wife. Clearly Kitty, Mary, and Lydia will not make good wives. They have not been brought up to behave properly. Indeed, with the example of the loud, tactless Mrs. Bennet, it is a wonder that Elizabeth and Jane have managed to grow up so well.

Mrs. Bennet cannot be the only one blamed for the poor behavior of her daughters. Mr. Bennet keeps himself aloof from his wife's quirks, using them only as fodder for his dry wit. When Mrs. Bennet sends Jane on horseback to Netherfield, plotting that Jane should catch cold, Mr. Bennet, though making disparaging comments, does not attempt to stop her. He is as ineffective a parent as she is, taking no responsibility for the improprieties of the girls, until Lydia's elopement. At this point he realizes he has been derelict as a parent and attempts to change. This is part of Austen's goal: to teach the necessity of proper behavior, of taking responsibility for one's actions. Thus is it important that both Darcy and Elizabeth admit to their pride and prejudice and the mistakes that they have made. In doing so, they seek to learn from their mistakes, but also they recognize the danger of such rash opinionated behavior, such as that of Darcy's childhood friend, Wickham. Mr. Wickham was nearly the ruin of both of them and their families.

However, in spite of Wickham's and Lydia's complete break with propriety, and the danger that she places the rest of her family in, she neither learns from her mistakes, nor suffers particularly from them. In a world where so much depends on people fulfilling their positions, behaving properly, punishment is a luxury that society cannot afford. For if Lydia were punished, perhaps ostracized, the rest of the family, and through them friends and the rest of the community, would suffer. The taint of scandal and gossip serve to make women ineligible to marry. In this small community, no one could afford to associate with the Bennets. At the same time, maintaining that sort of ostracism would cause schism and the ecology of the community would be forever crippled, if not destroyed completely. Therefore, Lydia must be forgiven and her improprieties overlooked. This is only possible because she has returned to the fold, once again conforming within the bounds of acceptable behavior. Once she and Wickham have married, they have sufficiently rectified their situation and no longer pose a danger to the society.

Austen does remain cautious about marriage without some sort of attachment, or marriage between people of comparable characters. Charlotte marries Mr. Collins, suffering for the rest of her life with an obsequious fool and under the thumb of Lady de Bourgh. In exchange for security, she has given up her individuality and freedom. And while Austen does suggest that individuality must be contained within the codes and mores of society, it should not be repressed all together. Individualism has the power to add zest and charm to life, as long as it does not subvert the community. This sort of conforming individualism is best exemplified in Elizabeth. She is a unique character, abiding by the social demands of the community, yet at the same time her sharp wit and humor make her the only woman that engages Darcy's mind and heart.

Feminists have criticized Austen's portrayal of women in *Pride and Prejudice* as being too passive. None of the women ever take active control of their lives. They instead must wait until men act. Jane must wait for Bingley, and when he leaves Netherfield, she cannot contact him or ask for any explanation. Similarly, when Lydia disappears with Wickham, none of the Bennet women—who incidentally will be more fundamentally affected by the events than anyone else—are allowed to do anything to retrieve Lydia. Instead they must wait at home for news. This enforced passivity reinforces the traditional view of women as helpless and delicate. Men must take care of women since they are incapable of managing for themselves. However, it should be noted that Austen gives most of the dialogue to the women throughout the novel.

Another thing that many readers notice about Austen's novels, is that in spite of the fact that she writes during the political turmoil of the French Revolution and the Napoleonic wars, the growing Industrial Revolution, and the escalating political and social upheaval in England, except for the officers stationed in Meryton, there is no evidence of any of this strife in her novels. Austen herself notes that she knows little of the world at large and instead chooses to write about what she does know. However, it is clear that she does not know how to write male characters well. As mentioned above, much of the dialog in the novel is given to women. Some critics have suggested that Austen herself was not familiar enough with men to write believable male characters. When Elizabeth accepts Darcy's proposal, Austen only vaguely suggests his

reaction: "he expressed himself on the occasion as sensibly and as warmly as a man violently in love can be supposed to do."

Austen's writings had great influence on a number of writers throughout the century. Glimpses of Mrs. Bennet and Mr. Collins can be found in Dickens. Elizabeth's sharp wit can be found in Thackeray, Eden, and Trollope. Her exploration of manners and the constrictions of women were taken up by later women writers such as George Eliot, Sarah Grand and Elizabeth Gaskell. She helped to legitimize the novel as an art form. At the same time, she set an example for other women writers, showing them that even without the expansive education given to men, women could still make valuable contributions.

Source: Diana Francis, in an essay for *Novels for Students*, Gale, 1997.

Susan Kneedler

In the following excerpt, Kneedler explains how Pride and Prejudice *breaks conventions in its portrayals of relationships between the sexes.*

Students, like many critics, question the point of the last volume (the final 19 chapters) of *Pride and Prejudice* because they already know who will "get" whom. Many feminist scholars portray Austen's happy unions as either sexist, sellouts, or parodies. But critics' declared dissatisfaction with marriage as a narrative resolution is never reconciled with unexamined prejudices against single women.... A number of critics themselves reiterate the tired news that Austen was a "spinster," a term that Austen's books never once invoke and that hardly defends singleness as a liberating option. The twin assumptions that neither single nor married women can be powerful, useful, or happy leads to a deadlier myth: the curiously perverse axiom that suicide is woman's only "life-affirming" choice. In fact, the art—particularly Kate Chopin's *The Awakening*—and the authors—Virginia Woolf and Sylvia Plath—in vogue during the last few decades have often been seen as glorifying death as the only way out for women in an inexorably unjust culture. By implication, simply surviving, let alone coping, becomes synonymous with compromising. The last third of *Pride and Prejudice,* however, imagines an alternative: far from smothering under a shroud of "the marriage plot," Elizabeth Bennet works out a new institution of love based on a new conception of self.

After the crisis of Elizabeth's initial embarrassment at Mr. Darcy's unexpected arrival at Pemberley, including her "amaze[ment] at the alteration in his manner," Elizabeth and her aunt and uncle the Gardiners "were again surprised, and Elizabeth's astonishment was quite equal to what it had been at first, by the sight of Mr. Darcy approaching them." Elizabeth's second surprise is that "he really intended to meet them." The encounter here between Elizabeth and Mr. Darcy encapsulates the recurring action of this final volume; Elizabeth continually assumes that Mr. Darcy will "strike into some other path," but whenever the "turning" that obscures him fades away, he always turns up, "and at no great distance"—in fact, "immediately before" her. Every time that "her thoughts were all fixed on that one spot … whichever it might be, where Mr. Darcy then was," she finds that he is on an errand expressly to see or to help her.

In the woods of Pemberley, Elizabeth is far from imagining that Mr. Darcy is on such a quest. In fact, she begins an alternating pattern of distancing herself from him—fancying that her friendly praise "might be mischievously construed"—yet nevertheless bewildering herself with his mystery: "Why is he so altered? … It cannot be for *me,* it cannot be for *my* sake." Always the stunning answer is that her "reproofs at Hunsford [did] work such a change as this," because "it is [not] impossible that he should still love" her. Mr. Darcy himself later explains why he does not "avoid her as his greatest enemy," by distinguishing between hatred and anger: he could never hate her, and even his anger "soon began to take a proper direction"—at himself. Through an affecting contrast, Austen honors this man's exceptionally receptive resilience. Elizabeth's response to the events at Hunsford had been an inability to "feel the slightest inclination ever to see him again"; Mr. Darcy, however, not only wishes to continue as Elizabeth's friend but hopes that his sister, Georgiana, may come to know her as well.

The trope of Elizabeth's shock will be picked up when she is home at Longbourn, looking out the window to see Mr. Darcy riding up to the house with Mr. Bingley. The narrator explains, "Her astonishment at his coming … was almost equal to what she had known on first witnessing his altered behaviour in Derbyshire." Elizabeth's surprise is great because she has felt that the disgrace of Lydia's elopement would destroy Mr. Darcy's affection. But we also learn that although Mr. Darcy continues to astound, the shock is lessening and is now only "almost equal" to what she had felt before. The stupefaction Elizabeth experiences here, like that created by Mr. Darcy's behavior at Pem-

berley, reflects the conventional belief that men cannot be loyal and deeply attached lovers. Mr. Darcy's arrival at Longbourn enlarges Elizabeth's expectations of men's capacity to love. One measure is that when he returns yet again, after Lady Catherine de Bourgh has stormed through Longbourn vowing to separate her from Mr. Darcy, Elizabeth now only "half expect[s]" him not to come.

Back in Lambton, Elizabeth had begun to rely on Mr. Darcy's affection, or on her own "power, which her fancy told her she still possessed, of bringing on the renewal of his addresses." But that confidence is shattered by the news of Lydia Bennet's elopement. For readers swept by a growing excitement at Elizabeth's discovery of Fitzwilliam Darcy's "impossible" power "still [to] love me," the turning point at the lodgings is a careful frustration of our hopes, a transformation of exhilaration to anguish. Elizabeth mistakenly, and conventionally, reads Mr. Darcy's "earnest meditation" about how to find Mr. Wickham as a sign that "her power was sinking." The inadequacy of Elizabeth's equation of love with "power" is suggested by a sudden shift in tone. From the pathos of "she could neither wonder nor condemn," the narrator unexpectedly swells into sentimental clichés: "but the belief of his self-conquest brought nothing consolatory to her bosom, afforded no palliation of her distress." "Of course not," respond students, who readily see that women's self-sacrifice is silly. Elizabeth realizes only "now, when all love must be vain," that she "could have loved him"; yet she, at least as much as Mr. Darcy, must let go of such traditional, and false, visions of sexual relations.

At issue are assumptions about the selfishness and instability of men's love. When Elizabeth discovers that Mr. Darcy had been at Lydia's wedding, "conjectures as to the meaning of it, rapid and wild, hurried into her brain," but they "seemed most improbable." However, what she considers her most farfetched fancies will be "proved beyond their greatest extent to be true." Elizabeth's inability to conceive that Mr. Darcy could cherish a concern for her as "ardent" as hers for Jane culminates when we learn that while her new respect for Mr. Darcy is fervent, it still does not do him justice. "Elizabeth was now most heartily sorry" that she had not concealed the elopement from "all those who were not immediately on the spot." By designating Mr. Darcy as just another bystander, Elizabeth would, in her yearning for secrecy, negate her unreflecting confidence—her disclosure of how fully she has accepted his revelations about Mr. Wickham—and deprive herself of Mr. Darcy's delicately underspoken comfort. But Elizabeth's regrets are hilariously inappropriate because the joyful truth is that Lydia's problems never would have been solved had Elizabeth not confided in Mr. Darcy. Only he knew how to find Mr. Wickham.

Elizabeth's doubts about the possibility of allegiance from Fitzwilliam Darcy are hardly a private matter. Neither Austen's culture nor our own has traditionally demanded much of men as lovers. William Collins's spleen when Elizabeth refuses him reflects the customary churlishness of the disappointed suitor. Mr. Darcy's own first movement toward Elizabeth embodies the sexist view that he is a good catch who has only to choose and be accepted, that no matter how he has insulted any woman, she will be happy either to dance with or marry him whenever he can force himself to ask. The novel does not support such conventional views. Most students have been raised on the interwoven notions of women's craving for men and men's indifference to women, a trope misnamed "the battle of the sexes" and a heritage that *Pride and Prejudice* explicitly invokes in its opening torture scenes in which Mr. Bennet baits Mrs. Bennet. Readers continue to adore Mr. Bennet's bitter humor on a first reading and only later learn to reevaluate that continual breach of conjugal obligation and decorum which … was so highly reprehensible." *Pride and Prejudice* offers a vision of love in which women and men may care about each other with a passionate tenderness at least equal to that felt by strongly united sisters: the other person's well-being is simply and immediately crucial. Mr. Darcy's concern for Elizabeth is so great, so sublimely disinterested, that, whether or not she loves him, he wants to make her happy and never claim the credit.

At stake is how we recognize romance. What are the signs in others that we respond to as allure, and what are the alterations in ourselves that we identify as passion? What *Pride and Prejudice* offers to Elizabeth Bennet through Fitzwilliam Darcy is a sexuality that casts away usual power relations with their traditional alternatives of confrontation and capitulation, when men sweep women off their feet but both sides nurse an underlying narcissism as their truly dominant passion. The traditional proposal Mr. Darcy made at Hunsford betrays a masturbatory fixation with his own desires and sacrifices; however, his avowal of love in the lanes near Longbourn portrays a generous focus on Elizabeth Bennet, foretelling a relation of listening reciprocity. Mr. Darcy's reform is convincing because it is based on a goodness and generosity that Elizabeth

had never credited him with, and it is moving because it is unimaginable according to cultural ideas of men's capacity and feelings. The sexual politics of the relation between Elizabeth Bennet and Fitzwilliam Darcy locates erotic pleasure in kindnesses that any person can show another. To women Austen offers a vision in which nothing about men's honest devotion is too good to be true—a prophecy that women need not settle for less. In a final volume made up almost exclusively of characters' astonishment at how others' actions surpass or betray their expectations, the delicately crocheted chain of Elizabeth's surprises carefully builds excitement over reunions that we are asked to celebrate because they change our ideas about what love, even marriage, can mean.

Yet as Elizabeth discovers Mr. Darcy's affection, she must explore her own—in a process that protects the integrity and disinterestedness of her attachment: "She respected, she esteemed, she was grateful to him, she felt a real interest in his welfare." Her effort to "make [her feelings] out," as she "lay awake two whole hours" is a comic reversal of an earlier moment when, with "something like regret," she had toyed with envy about the position as "mistress of Pemberley," Now, as Elizabeth investigates her new tenderness for Mr. Darcy, we can delight in how she stretches out the process of committing herself. Respect, esteem, gratitude, and an interest in his welfare all add up to love. Such feelings are the origin of love based on knowledge, and, *Pride and Prejudice* shows, nothing else is love.

But Elizabeth's discerning standards for heterosexual affection display a revolution of self as well as of eros. Even at the height of her suspense about Mr. Darcy, Elizabeth asserts the worth of her own life, gloriously declaring to herself, "[I]f he is satisfied with only regretting me, when he might have obtained my affections and hand, I shall soon cease to regret him at all." Such faith that if need be she can outlive her affection for Fitzwilliam Darcy is based on the new idea that he will be unworthy if he cannot continue to love. The value for her own future, separate from her connection to a man, and her resolve to judge his rather than her own worth by his performance intensify our suspense over the test: Can Mr. Darcy justify her affection? The fulfillment of that quest comes in a love scene that readers have long depreciated as an anticlimax.…

Pride and Prejudice is a pivotal moment in our feminist heritage, an achievement whose power has in many senses been lost, as we have so often lost women's history and work. This novel offers an iconoclastic representation of women and men. Austen is a creative political thinker in her own right, but her politics must be located through attention to the relationships among her characters, between those characters and their narrator, and between narrator and reader, before we try to place her in extratextual heritages or contexts. Rather than look for politics by turning away from the text to events outside the novel, we need at last to accept that the book's explicit concerns are themselves political. *Pride and Prejudice* does more than teach us about the debates of Austen's day; it can guide us among the many urgent issues of identity and gender with which we continue to struggle. In an age when we have learned to see the battle of the sexes as one aspect of the abuse that women have been taught to label as "love," the answer is not to throw out romance altogether. *Pride and Prejudice*'s moving prophecy is that we may also make Elizabeth Bennet's demand that Fitzwilliam Darcy become worthy of her love.

Source: Susan Kneedler, "The New Romance in *Pride and Prejudice*," in *Approaches to Teaching Austen's* Pride and Prejudice, *edited by Marcia McClintock Folsom, Modern Language Association of America, 1993, pp. 152–66.*

Julia Prewitt Brown

In the following excerpt, Brown discusses how Austen offers a powerful commentary on the changes in society, gender attitudes, and class structure in early nineteenth century England.

As for the historical content of the [Austen] novels, students may not see it because they think of social history as "history with the politics left out," as G. M. Trevelyan once described it, rather than what it is: the essential foundation that gives shape to everything else. For the cultural historian Raymond Williams, for example, Austen's novels provide an accurate record of that moment in English history in which high bourgeois society most evidently interlocked with an agrarian capitalism. "An openly acquisitive society," writes Williams [in *The Country and the City,* 1975], "which is concerned also with the transmission of wealth, is trying to judge itself at once by an inherited code and by the morality of improvement." What is at stake here is not personal relations but personal *conduct:* "a testing and discovery of the standards which govern human behaviour in certain real situations." Those situations arise from the unsettled world Austen portrays, with its continual changes of fortune and social mobility that were affecting the landed families of her time. Thus, although Darcy is a landowner established for "many generations," his friend Bingley has no estate and has inherited £100,000 from his father, who made money in trade; and although Mr. Bennet has an estate, he has married the daughter of an attorney who has a brother in trade, and his estate will not pass to his own children; and so on.

Readers may glimpse the "openly acquisitive society" in the heroine's first sight of Pemberley, Darcy's beautiful estate. Deeply impressed, even awe-struck, by its elegance and grandeur, Elizabeth cannot but admit to herself that "to be mistress of Pemberley might be something!" Later Elizabeth satirizes her own response when her sister asks her to explain when she first fell in love with Darcy: "It has been coming on so gradually," Elizabeth replies, "that I hardly know when it began. But I believe I must date it from my first seeing his beautiful grounds at Pemberley." Elizabeth's wit distances her from herself, from the woman with the conventional response to Pemberley, just as the narrator's irony distances the reader from conventional responses. But before entering into a discussion of Austen's narrative irony, we may as well ask the conventional question, In what sense *would* being mistress of Pemberley "be something"?

In Austen's day England was still to a large extent an "aristocracy," or hierarchy based on property and patronage in which people took their places in a pyramidlike structure extending down from a minority of the rich and powerful at the top to ever wider and larger layers of lesser wealth to the great mass of the poor and powerless at the bottom. Together, the aristocracy and gentry owned more than two-thirds of all the land in England. In this largely agrarian society, government was conceived of as the authority of the locality, the government of parish, county, and town, whose officials were members of the gentry appointed by the Crown. In the course of the century, this system of local government was replaced by a modern bureaucracy of trained and elected administrators, but at the time Austen was writing, the gentry were the real governors of the countryside. Not until the commercial and political revolutions, accumulating full force in the eighteenth century, disrupted the solidarity of families founded on landed wealth did these ancient families, and the women who belonged to them, lose much of the power they had so long exercised. Only then did the state pass to the control of parliaments composed of men and elected by men.

Lady Catherine de Bourgh and her nephew Darcy are members of one such ancient family, and they are highly conscious of the power they possess. Both control the lives and incomes of scores of people on their estates, many of whom had no voting power until the Reform Bill of 1832. Even after that, until the secret ballot was passed in 1872, landlords could have a decisive effect on votes, since they were taken orally. Traditionally, the steward of an estate such as Darcy's would round up the tenants who could vote, take them to the polling place, and remain there while they called out their preference. A man such as Darcy, were he to run for a seat in the House of Commons, could then be sure of this built-in constituency of tenants. Wickham's chronic resentment, Austen implies, is a function of his having grown up as the son of the elder Darcy's steward, daily observing so many more advantages accrue to Darcy than to himself.

Although women in the gentry had less authority than men, a matter I take up later, some had considerable power. The tradition of primogeniture established that, under the law, property was passed to the eldest son; and English matrimonial law stipulated that, through marriage, the husband became the owner of all his wife's property. But there were ways in which the gentry could and did protect its women. Mr. Bennet cannot alter the entail requiring that his estate go to the nearest male relation, but he can settle money on his daughters that, if proper legal measures are taken, will remain their own after marriage. Because Lady Catherine's estate is not entailed from the female line, she enjoys most of the advantages of her nephew. She is patroness of the living of Mr. Collins, for example, and he is only one of many people who are dependent on her and therefore must pay court to her. Elizabeth is right when she recognizes that to join Darcy's family and become mistress of Pemberley would indeed "be something." Family and marriage occupied a far more public and central position in the social government and economic arrangements of English society than they would later. In the novels of Austen, marriage is then accurately seen as an institution that both determines and is determined by history....

[Social historian Lawrence] Stone's theory of social history suggests that only in a highly individualist society does happiness arise as an ideal: those who see themselves as living for themselves become interested in happiness. But if they view themselves as living for something beyond the self—say, the community—happiness loses its central place in human concern. That Austen re-

veals in almost every novel how difficult it is to negotiate a compromise between the drive for happiness and the necessity of a life of service all communities require of its citizens (most commonly in their role as parents) is not surprising. The question of happiness lies at the heart of the English tradition of liberal rationalism, particularly as it expressed itself in the works of Austen's contemporary Jeremy Bentham and later in the formulations of John Stuart Mill. One of Mill's major efforts was to reconcile a Benthamite faith in making happiness the supreme goal of human life with his communitarian belief in service, probably acquired through the classical education he received from his father (as Austen did from hers). In order to do so, Mill eventually insists on the existence of a private domain, set apart and separate from the demands of law and custom. This abstraction, the private domain, which we have difficulty imagining as an abstraction so much do we take Mill's ideas for granted, is the basis of the argument of *On Liberty* (1859). So little did Mill himself take it for granted, however, that a large section of *On Liberty* is devoted to establishing and defining its existence. Another example is that, until the secret ballot was passed, parliamentarians expressed their astonishment over the proposal on the grounds that no honorable person would have any reason to cast a vote in secret; the private domain was imagined only with difficulty.

These same ambiguities concerning the private self and its relation to custom and community make themselves felt in *Pride and Prejudice*. Austen tempers her affirmation of individual happiness as an ideal by means of a deep aesthetic vigilance over its possible excesses. The hero of the novel, for example, is as different in substance and temperament from the heroine as could be; he embodies the traditional self, one whose identity is based on a sense of his own position in the social hierarchy rather than on an evaluation of his inner worth. This is what Darcy means when he says to Elizabeth, after they have been united, that he was a good man in theory but not in practice. He accepted his own merit as given; until Elizabeth forces him to, he has no impulse to look critically inward. A traditional self with a strong sense of duty (as distinct from conscience), Darcy has before him a traditional— that is to say, arranged—marriage when the novel opens. Of course, contact with Elizabeth changes Darcy, but that Elizabeth ends by marrying so traditional a personality is perhaps the largest check on the modern drive for happiness (most intelligently represented by Elizabeth) in the novel.

Not all the self-seekers in the novel are as intelligent and virtuous as Elizabeth, however, which brings us to another way Austen tempers her affirmation of the pursuit of happiness. The novel continually juxtaposes to Elizabeth and Darcy's marriage the completely selfish marriage, such as the unions between Lydia and Wickham and between Charlotte and Mr. Collins, who live only for themselves and their own advancement. In contrast, Darcy and Elizabeth are envisioned at the conclusion of the novel as surrogate parents, moral guardians, and educators to Georgiana and Kitty, and as host and hostess at their ancient estate to members of the rising class of merchants, the Gardiners. The novel ends, then, on a note of affirmation of the power of marriage as an agent of constructive social change....

Feminist critics who have condemned Austen for not opening up any new vistas for the female spirit, for merely reaffirming the traditional option of marriage, may as well say to a starving person, "Man cannot live by bread alone." Like all her sisters, Elizabeth has only humiliating dependence on relations before her if she does not marry. No professions to speak of are open to her, and laws on every side are designed to restrict her independence. Within the privilege of the gentry class, wives had far less control over their lives than husbands did, and daughters had virtually none. Charlotte Lucas marries Mr. Collins because she does not wish to remain a daughter all her life; that marriage to Mr. Collins is seen as liberating by comparison with "spinsterhood" tells us all we need to know of the depth of Austen's irony on the subject of women.

What is remarkable about Austen's perspective on this subject is that she does not lapse into sentimental wish fulfillment but renders the crass, survivalist posture required of women with unfailing honesty and irony. The "honesty" and "irony" are interchangeable because of the fundamental contradiction in the gentry woman's situation: that she enjoyed tremendous privileges and relative comfort as a member of that class but that her ability to act independently within it was severely restricted. Elizabeth's refusal to marry Mr. Collins, for example, is not ponderously portrayed as an act of courage; it would take little courage to refuse so ridiculous a person as Mr. Collins. But given the situation of women and her own particular economic circumstances, to refuse him without giving way even for a moment to anxiety concerning the future shows an exceptional spirit. Elizabeth's

sangfroid is again apparent when she refuses the far more imposing Darcy; she cannot be frightened by circumstance or intimidated by power. Popular women novelists writing at the same time as Austen often show heroines engaged in far more obvious acts of heroism and have been praised over Austen by feminists for portraying more adventurous women; in one such novel the heroine travels down the Amazon River. But Austen did not have to show Elizabeth traveling down the mighty river; she walks three miles in the mud to visit an ailing sister, and the society around her (including the hero) behaves as if she had. That Elizabeth remains unfazed by their exaggerated response to this most commonplace act—Darcy's admiration no more turns her head than Miss Bingley's visible contempt ruffles her—is not the least of her virtues. It is in Austen's ironic critique of her society, with its vulgar idolatry of the "lady" combined with its brute legal and economic restriction of her independence, together with her passionate endorsement of women who live within it and still manage to retain their self-possession (*dignity* is too lofty a word) that her feminism lies....

That Elizabeth Bennet is so easy to like makes *Pride and Prejudice* the less ironic novel. But Elizabeth's marriage to Darcy, as we have seen, is not without contradiction and irony. After they are united, Elizabeth "remembered that [Darcy] had yet to learn to be laught at." Perhaps a juxtaposition of the two novels suggests more than anything else that no discussion of the social-historical context in which the heroines move can proceed without consideration of Austen's irony. The moral discrimination that forms the basis of that irony is so insistent, writes Raymond Williams, "that it can be taken as an independent value ... which is in the end separable from its social basis." After making this profound observation, Williams goes on to attach that value to the democratic social agenda: "she provided the emphasis which had only to be taken outside the park walls, into a different social experience, to become not a moral but a social criticism," such as one finds in the Victorian moralists. But we will leave it to the historical ideologists to determine the political direction Austen's emphasis would take later. Whatever one concludes, one cannot help but feel that Austen wrote more for later generations than for her own. This perception is apparent not only in her steady refusal to court the public attention she could so easily have gained but in the way the novels seem to feel themselves forward into time, articulating our own historical distance from her world by means of their irony. Historians have long been in the habit of claiming, as A. J. P. Taylor has written, that, among novelists, history began with Walter Scott, the historical novelist and contemporary of Jane Austen. But if history is a form of self-consciousness, perhaps history began with Jane Austen as well.

Source: Julia Prewitt Brown, "The 'Social History' of *Pride and Prejudice*," in *Approaches to Teaching Austen's 'Pride and Prejudice'*, edited by Marcia McClintock Folsom, Modern Language Association of America, 1993, pp. 57–66.

Sources

Reuben A. Brower, "Light and Bright and Sparkling: Irony and Fiction in *Pride and Prejudice*," in his *The Fields of Light*, Oxford University Press, 1958.

Laura Dabundo, "Jane Austen," in *Concise Dictionary of British Literary Biography*, Volume 3: *Writers of the Romantic Period, 1789-1832*, Gale, 1992.

Donald J. Gray, "Preface," in *Jane Austen: Pride and Prejudice, An Authoritative Text, Backgrounds, Reviews and Essays in Criticism*, edited by Donald J. Gray, Norton, 1966.

Robert B. Heilman, "*E pluribus unum*: Parts and Whole in *Pride and Prejudice*," in *Jane Austen: Bicentenary Essays*, edited by John Halperin, Cambridge University Press, 1975.

Elizabeth Jenkins, *Jane Austen: A Biography*, Gollancz, 1948.

Marvin Mudrick, "Irony as Discrimination: *Pride and Prejudice*," in his *Jane Austen: Irony as Defense and Discovery*, Princeton University Press, 1952.

Review of *Pride and Prejudice*, in *British Critic*, February, 1813, pp. 189-90, reprinted in *Jane Austen: The Critical Heritage*, edited and compiled by B. C. Southam, Routledge, 1968.

Review of *Pride and Prejudice*, in *Critical Review*, March, 1813, pp. 318-24, reprinted in *Jane Austen: The Critical Heritage*, edited and compiled by B. C. Southam, Routledge, 1968.

B. C. Southam, editor, *Jane Austen: The Critical Heritage*, Routledge, 1968.

For Further Study

Julia Prewitt Brown, *Jane Austen's Novels: Social Change and Literary Form*, Harvard University Press, 1979.
    Brown discusses how Austen uses contrasts between characters, themes, and narrative devices to give structure to her novel.

Marilyn Butler, *Jane Austen and the War of Ideas*, Oxford University Press, 1975, reprinted with new introduction, 1987.
    Butler argues that despite the tendency of many readers and critics, Austen's novels are not "progressive" novels, but rather novels that reinforce a conservative, orthodox thinking in tune with her era.

Sandra Gilbert and Susan Gubar, *The Madwoman in the Attic: The Woman Writer and the Nineteenth-Century Literary Imagination, Yale University Press*, 1979.
    Gilbert and Gubar explore the struggles nineteenth-century women writers endured while publishing their works and how society reacted to the ideas and perspectives of women authors.

J. David Grey, managing editor, A. Walton Litz and Brian Southam, consulting editors, *The Jane Austen Companion*, Macmillan, 1986.
    The Jane Austen Companion was published under the auspices of the Jane Austen Society and includes much scholarly information, including a chronology of Austen's life and works, her family tree, critical appraisals of her novel, and a *Dictionary of Jane Austen's Life and Works*, a concordance of important people and events in her fiction and her world.

Karl Kroeber, "*Pride and Prejudice*: Fiction's Lasting Novelty," in *Jane Austen: Bicentenary Essays*, edited by John Halperin, Cambridge University Press, 1975.
    In this essay Kroeber looks at the phenomenon of Austen's continuing popularity despite the ways in which she goes against prevailing modern literary tastes.

Robert Liddell, "Pride and Prejudice," in his *The Novels of Jane Austen*, Longmans, 1963, pp. 34–55.
    In his collection, Liddell studies various aspects of *Pride and Prejudice*, including its history, social background, and irony.

Mary Poovey, *The Proper Lady and the Woman Writer: Ideology as Style in the Works of Mary Wollstonecraft, Mary Shelley, and Jane Austen*, University of Chicago Press, 1984.
    Poovey writes about the role of women writers in society during the late eighteenth and early nineteenth centuries.

Warren Roberts, *Jane Austen and the French Revolution*, St. Martin's, 1979.
    In this study, Roberts traces the impact that the French Revolution had on Austen's own life (her brothers served in the Royal Navy in the struggle against Napoleon Bonaparte) and on the type of fiction she wrote.

LeRoy W. Smith, "*Pride and Prejudice*: No Improper Pride," in his *Jane Austen and the Drama of Woman*, Macmillan, 1983, pp. 87–110.
    This essay concentrates on the social, moral, economic, and sexual dilemmas Elizabeth must face as a middle-class woman in nineteenth-century society.

Michael Williams, *Jane Austen: Six Novels and their Methods*, St. Martin's, 1986.
    Williams discusses six Austen novels, including *Pride and Prejudice*, and concentrates on the methods Austen uses to construct her stories.

The Scarlet Letter

Nathaniel Hawthorne

1850

Nathaniel Hawthorne's *The Scarlet Letter* is famous for presenting some of the greatest interpretive difficulties in all of American literature. While not recognized by Hawthorne himself as his most important work, the novel is regarded not only as his greatest accomplishment, but frequently as the greatest novel in American literary history. After it was published in 1850, critics hailed it as initiating a distinctive American literary tradition. Ironically, it is a novel in which, in terms of action, almost nothing happens. Hawthorne's emotional, psychological drama revolves around Hester Prynne, who is convicted of adultery in colonial Boston by the civil and Puritan authorities. She is condemned to wear the scarlet letter "A" on her chest as a permanent sign of her sin. The narrative describes the effort to resolve the torment suffered by Hester and her co-adulterer, the minister Arthur Dimmesdale, in the years after their affair. In fact, the story excludes even the representation of the passionate moment which enables the entire novel. It begins at the close of Hester's imprisonment many months after her affair and proceeds through many years to her final acceptance of her place in the community as the wearer of the scarlet letter. Hawthorne was masterful in the use of symbolism, and the scarlet letter "A" stands as his most potent symbol, around which interpretations of the novel revolve. At one interpretive pole the "A" stands for adultery and sin, and the novel is the story of individual punishment and reconciliation. At another pole it stands for America and allegory, and the story

suggests national sin and its human cost. Yet possibly the most convincing reading, taking account of all others, sees the "A" as a symbol of ambiguity, the very fact of multiple interpretations and the difficulty of achieving consensus.

Author Biography

Nathaniel Hawthorne was born in the infamous village of Salem, Massachusetts, on Independence Day, July 4, 1804. His parents were Nathaniel and Elizabeth Clarke Manning Hathorne. (The surname had been written both with and without the w; Hawthorne chose to include it when he began his writing career.) Hawthorne's father, a sea captain, died far from home when Hawthorne was four years old. At the age of nine he injured his foot and could move about very little for the next two years, a time he spent reading literary "classics." In 1820, while working for his uncle as a bookkeeper, Hawthorne complained to his sister, Elizabeth, that "No man can be a Poet and a Book-keeper at the same time." This conflict between his literary interests and need to earn money would be a fact of Hawthorne's life for many years; it is made a specific subject of "The Custom House," Hawthorne's introduction to *The Scarlet Letter,* and the conflict is represented in various forms in a great deal of his works.

When he entered Bowdoin College in the fall of 1821, he wanted to be a professional author, but was well aware of the difficulties. On occasion he expressed reservedly that his forefathers, among them important Puritans, would consider such a career useless if not downright frivolous. "Why, the degenerate fellow might as well have been a fiddler": thus Hawthorne comically evokes their stern judgment in "The Custom House." But, however he joked, such forefathers were a very serious presence in Hawthorne's life and writings. One such man was John Hathorne, who was a principle prosecutor in the Salem witch trials and one of the few official judges not to acknowledge the folly of the executions after the hysteria ended.

In 1842 Hawthorne married Sophia Peabody and they resided in Concord, the geographic center of literary transcendentalism, the idealistic philosophy that opposed both Puritanical and materialistic values. They lived in a home called the Old Manse, where transcendentalist Ralph Waldo Emerson had written *Nature* in 1836. Hawthorne stayed at the Old Manse for three years, later con-

Nathaniel Hawthorne

sidering them the happiest years of his life. He wrote actively during this period, becoming hopeful that he could earn a living by his pen, but still not securing enough income from the trade. In 1845 he moved to Salem and soon took a position as surveyor of the port of Salem Custom House. When the Whigs won a national election over the Democrats (whose sponsorship secured Hawthorne's job), he was removed from office in 1849. This was a troubling moment for Hawthorne and increased his guarded stance toward potential social and political instabilities, including feminism and abolitionism. It was during this convulsive time in Salem, which included the death of his mother in July of 1849, that Hawthorne conceived and began work on *The Scarlet Letter.*

Plot Summary

Part One

The Scarlet Letter opens with an expectant crowd standing in front of a Boston prison in the early 1640s. When the prison door opens, a young woman named Hester Prynne emerges, with a baby in her arms and a scarlet letter "A" richly embroidered on her breast. For her crime of adultery, to which both the baby and the letter attest, she must proceed to the scaffold and stand for judgment by her community.

While on the scaffold, Hester remembers her past. In particular, she remembers the face of a "misshapen" man, "well stricken in years," with the face of a scholar. At this moment, the narrator introduces an aged and misshapen character, who has been living "in bonds" with "Indian" captors. He asks a bystander why Hester is on the scaffold. The brief story is told: two years earlier, Hester had preceded her husband to New England. Her husband never arrived. In the meantime, she bore a child; the father of the infant has not come forward. As this stranger stares at Hester, she stares back: a mutual recognition passes between them.

On the scaffold, Boston's highest clergyman, John Wilson, and Hester's own pastor, Rev. Dimmesdale, each ask her to reveal the name of her partner in crime. Reverend Dimmesdale makes a particularly powerful address, urging her not to tempt the man to lead a life of sinful hypocrisy by leaving his identity unnamed. Hester refuses.

After the ordeal of her public judgment, the misshapen man from the marketplace—her long lost husband—visits her, taking the name Roger Chillingworth. When she refuses to identify the father of her child, he vows to discover him and take revenge. He makes Hester swear to keep his identity a secret.

Part II

Now freed, Hester and her baby girl, Pearl, move to a secluded cabin. The narrator explains that

> There is a fatality, a feeling so irresistible and inevitable that it has the force of doom, which almost invariably compels human beings to linger around and haunt, ghost-like, the spot where some great and marked event has given the color to their lifetime.

Whether for this reason, or for others, Hester stays in the colony. She earns a living as a seamstress. Hester has "in her nature a rich, voluptuous, Oriental characteristic" that shows in her needlework. Although the Puritans' sumptuary laws (which regulate personal expenditure and displays of luxury) restrict ornament, she finds a market for her goods—the ministers and judges of the colony have occasion for pomp and circumstance, which her needlework helps supply. She uses her money to help the needy, although they scorn her in return. Hester focuses most of her love, and all of her love of finery, on her daughter, her "pearl of great price." Pearl grows up without the company of other children, a wild child in fabulous cloth-

ing. Even her mother questions her humanity and sees her as an ethereal, almost devilish, "airy sprite."

When Pearl is three, Hester discovers that certain "good people" of the town, including Governor Bellingham, seek to "deprive her of her child." She goes to the governor and pleads her case. She and Pearl find the governor in the company of Rev. Wilson, Rev. Dimmesdale, and his now close companion, Dr. Chillingworth. Pearl inexplicably runs to Rev. Dimmesdale and clasps his hand. To the men, Hester argues that God has sent Pearl both to remind her of her sin, and to compensate her for all she has lost. When they seem unswayed, Hester throws herself on Rev. Dimmesdale's mercy. He endorses her argument: Providence has bound up both sin and salvation in Pearl, whom Hester must be allowed to care for herself. The men reluctantly agree.

Since his arrival, Roger Chillingworth has assumed the identity of a physician. His scholarly background, combined with a knowledge of New World plants gained from his "Indian" captors, have prepared him well for this role. But healing masks his deeper purpose: revenge. He "devotes" himself to Rev. Dimmesdale, whose health has greatly declined. Chillingworth takes up lodging in the same house as the minister. As time passes, an "intimacy" grows up between them, and they seem to enjoy the difference in their points of view, as men of science and religion.

Unsuspected by his victim, Chillingworth digs into the "poor clergyman's heart, like a miner searching for gold." The only clue to Dimmesdale's condition lies in a characteristic gesture: he frequently presses his hand on his heart. One day, when Dimmesdale sleeps heavily (perhaps having been drugged), Chillingworth looks under his shirt. He sees something that the reader does not—something that evokes a "wild look of wonder, joy, and horror!" From that moment, their relationship changes for the worse. Having mastered Dimmesdale's secret, Chillingworth grows increasingly ugly, increasingly diabolical, and his real purpose becomes more perceptible. Many townspeople become convinced that Satan himself has sent him to torment the young minister.

Part III

Dimmesdale's secret has a paradoxical effect on his religious career. He knows himself to be the worst of sinners, and his sin makes his sermons more heartfelt, and more effective. This success intensifies his inner torment, and increases his sense

Scene from the film The Scarlet Letter, *starring Lillian Gish and Lars Hanson, 1926.*

of hypocrisy. One night he wanders out and climbs onto the scaffold. He considers waking the town and confessing his guilt. Hester and Pearl, after watching by a deathbed, find him, and join him. By this time Pearl is seven years old, and Hester's reputation has improved; now many associate the "A" with "Able," because of her good works. Pearl asks the minister if he will stand there with them the next day at noon; he promises that they will stand together—not tomorrow—but on "judgment day." A light suddenly bursts in the sky, appearing, to some, as the letter "A." Their vigil ends when Chillingworth appears and takes Dimmesdale home.

Hester, disturbed by Dimmesdale's obvious torment, confronts Chillingworth. She entreats him to stop his vengeful scheme. He refuses. Pearl guesses at the connection between the reverend and her mother, but cannot wholly understand. She fixates on her mother's scarlet "A" in an ominous way. Worried that she has corrupted her child and both men, Hester decides to intervene and to tell Dimmesdale the truth.

Hester waits for Dimmesdale with Pearl in the woods. In the forest, the sun shines on Pearl, but never on Hester, who seems always enveloped in dark and shadow. Hester tells Dimmesdale all. The

reader's suspicions about Dimmesdale are confirmed. " 'Oh Arthur,' [cries] she, 'forgive me! ... he whom they call Roger Chillingworth!—he was my husband!' " Dimmesdale realizes how full of deception his life has been. He and Hester decide to leave together and start a new life. Hester removes her scarlet letter and lets down her hair. For a moment, they are happy in their love. Seeing them, Pearl refuses to come until her mother resumes her ordinary appearance; she obstinately washes off the kiss that her father plants on her forehead. Yet the parents remain optimistic, and part with the promise to leave, secretly and by ship, in four days.

The day before their planned departure is Election Day, and Rev. Dimmesdale gives a sermon, intending it as a triumphant farewell. His spirits are strangely high. During the sermon, Hester finds their plans going awry. Chillingworth has guessed their intent and arranged to leave with them—they will never escape him. As Dimmesdale leaves the church, his strength fails him. In front of the whole community, he reaches for Hester and Pearl, and, with them, ascends the scaffold. He confesses his part in Hester's sin, and tears open his minister's collar, exposing what looks like—to some—a letter "A." He asks for the crowd's forgiveness, and in turn absolves his own tormentor, Chillingworth. Then he asks his daughter for a kiss and, when she gives it, "a spell is broken":

> The great scene of grief, in which the wild infant bore a part, had developed all her sympathies; and as her tears fell upon her father's cheek, they were the pledge that she would grow up amid human joy and sorrow, nor forever do battle with the world, but be a woman in it. Towards her mother, too, Pearl's errand as a messenger of anguish was all fulfilled.

His breast finally unburdened, Dimmesdale dies.

Chillingworth soon follows him to the grave, leaving his money to Pearl. Hester takes her daughter to Europe, but returns alone years later. Hester resumes her scarlet letter "A" and her good works. When she dies, the village buries her next to Dimmesdale.

Characters

Governor Bellingham

Governor Bellingham represents an actual person, Richard Bellingham, who came to America in 1634 and was elected as governor of the English colony in 1641, 1654, and 1655. When not acting as governor, he still held positions of power as magistrate or deputy governor. In the novel his character demonstrates that in the colony, as the narrator states in chapter two, "religion and law were almost identical." Bellingham is described as a "stern magistrate," who, in chapter eight, is convinced that Pearl should be taken from her mother in order to receive a proper moral upbringing, until Dimmesdale persuades him that the union of Pearl and Hester is a part of God's design.

Roger Chillingworth

Roger Chillingworth is the alias of Hester's husband. The two were married in England and moved together to Amsterdam before Hester preceded Chillingworth to America. Chillingworth is a man devoted to knowledge. His outward physical deformity (a hunchback) is symbolic of his devotion to deep, as opposed to superficial, knowledge. His lifelong study of apothecary and the healing arts, first in Europe and later among the Indians of America, is a sincere benevolent exercise until he discovers his wife's infidelity, whereupon he turns his skills toward the evil of revenge.

Chillingworth is introduced near the very start of the narrative, where he discovers Hester upon the scaffold with Pearl, the scarlet letter upon her chest, and displayed for public shame. After surviving a shipwreck on his voyage to America, he lived for some time among the Indians and slowly made his way to Boston and Hester. Upon discovering Hester's "ignominious" situation, Chillingworth declines to announce his identity and instead chooses to reside in Boston to find and avenge himself on Hester's lover. When Dimmesdale becomes ill with the effects of his sin, Chillingworth comes to live with him under the same roof. Reneging on an earlier promise, Hester eventually discloses Chillingworth's identity to Dimmesdale. Soon after Dimmesdale publicly confesses his sin and, as Chillingworth puts it, "Hadst thou sought the whole earth over … there was no one place so secret,—no high place nor lowly place, where thou couldst have escaped me,—save on this very scaffold!" Thus, his vengeful victory taken from him, Chillingworth soon dies, though not before leaving all of his substantial wealth to Pearl.

Arthur Dimmesdale

Arthur Dimmesdale is the young, charismatic minister with whom Hester commits adultery. Unlike Hester, who bears the child Pearl by their affair, Dimmesdale shows no outward evidence of his sin, and, as Hester does not expose him, he lives with the great anguish of his secret guilt until he confesses publicly and soon after dies near the end of the novel.

Dimmesdale is presented as a figure of frailty and weakness in contrast to Hester's strength (both moral and physical), pride, and determination. He consistently refuses to confess his sin (until the end), even though he repeatedly states that it were better, less spiritually painful, if his great failing were known. Thus Dimmesdale struggles through the years and the narrative, enduring and faltering beneath his growing pain (with both the help and harm of Roger Chillingworth), until, after his failed plan to escape to Europe with Hester and Pearl, he confesses and dies.

The Goodwives

The Goodwives are several women who discuss Hester's situation in chapter two. They generally believe the magistrates have been too easy on Hester and suggest branding or execution as appropriate punishments. One exception is a "young wife" who in this, and a later scene, feels pity for Hester.

Media Adaptations

- *The Scarlet Letter* has received several film adaptations beginning with director Victor Seastrom's 1926 silent version starring Lillian Gish as Hester Prynne. The first talkie version, directed by Robert Vignola in 1934 (produced by London Films) and starring Colleen Moore, is available from Nostalgia Family Video, though it is probably difficult to locate a rental copy.

- Recent film productions include a 1973 international version directed by Wim Wenders that received good reviews (Ingram International Films; in German with English subtitles). PBS aired a four-hour version in 1979 that stars Meg Foster as Hester and John Heard as Dimmesdale. Rick Harser's direction is faithful to the novel (PBS Home Video; four video cassettes). A similar educational version was produced in 1991 and is available from Films for the Humanities and Sciences.

- One of the great flops of recent years is the 1995 Hollywood production directed by Roland Joffe and starring Demi Moore as Hester, Gary Oldman as Dimmesdale and Robert Duvall as Chillingworth (available from Hollywood Pictures Home Video). Be careful not to embarrass yourself by relying on this film as a guide to the novel.

- There are also a number of sound recordings of the novel. Audio Partners Inc. (of Auburn, CA) published an abridged version in 1986 read by Michael Learned (the full title is *Michael Learned reads The Scarlet Letter*). The Brilliance Corporation produced an unabridged version read by Dick Hill in 1993 (8 hours). Books in Motion also published an unabridged version in 1982 read by Gene Engene (7.5 hours).

- Finally, there are two audio study guides or discussions of *The Scarlet Letter*. Lecturer Robert H. Fossum discusses the book on one 38 minute cassette in the series "19th Century American Writers," produced by Everett/Edwards (1976). Time Warner Audiobooks published a study guide narrated by Julie Amato in 1994 on one 72 minute cassette.

Mistress Hibbins

Mistress Hibbins, who makes several provoking, if short, appearances in the novel, represents the actual historical figure Ann Hibbins, who was executed for witchcraft in 1656. Mistress Hibbins tempts both Hester and Dimmesdale to enter in the league of the "Black Man," who, as a representative of the devil, haunts the wild forest. While she is very nearly a comic figure in the narrative, the fact of her historical reality and fate remind us of the grim power of Puritan regulation and paranoia.

Pearl

Pearl is the daughter of Hester Prynne and Arthur Dimmesdale. Necessarily marginal to Puritan society and scorned by other children, she grows up as an intimate of nature and the forest. Symbolically recreating the scarlet letter, Hester, in opposition to her own drab wardrobe, dresses Pearl in brilliant, decorative clothing such "that there was an absolute circle of radiance about her."

Like most characters in *The Scarlet Letter,* Pearl is complex and contradictory. On the one hand, as the narrator describes, she "could not be made amenable to rules." At one moment in the novel, her disregard of authority takes the form of a violent game where she pretends to destroy the children of the Puritan elders: "the ugliest weeds of the garden [she imagined were the elders'] children, whom Pearl smote down and uprooted, most unmercifully." On the other hand, at a climactic point in the narrative, where Hester discards the scarlet letter on the floor of the forest, it is Pearl who dramatically insists that she resume the potent symbol. The form of her insistence is particularly important, for, against her mother's request, she does not bring the letter to Hester, but obstinately has Hester fetch the letter herself. This moment demonstrates one of the central conflicted themes of the novel about the authoritarian imposition of law and the willing subjection to it, or even embodiment of it. In this scene Pearl becomes the figure of authority to whom Hester willingly, if symbolically, obeys. Pearl eventually leaves with Hester for Europe (though Hester returns), where, it is implied, Pearl stays and, with the aid of Chillingworth's inheritance, is married to nobility.

Hester Prynne

Hester Prynne is the central and most important character in *The Scarlet Letter.* Hester was married to Roger Chillingworth while living in England and, later, Amsterdam—a city to which many English Puritans moved for religious freedom. Hester preceded her husband to New England, as he had business matters to settle in Amsterdam, and after approximately two years in America she committed adultery with the Reverend Arthur Dimmesdale.

The novel begins as Hester nears the end of her prison term for adultery. While adultery was considered a grave threat to the Puritan community, such that death was considered a just punishment, the Puritan authorities weighed the long absence and possible death of her husband in their sentence. Thus, they settled on the punishment of permanent public humiliation and moral example: Hester was to forever wear the scarlet letter A on the bodice of her clothing.

While seemingly free to leave the community and even America at her will, Hester chooses to stay. As the narrator puts it, "Here, she said to herself, had been the scene of her guilt, and here should be the scene of her earthly punishment; and so, perchance, the torture of her daily shame would at length purge her soul." According to this reasoning, Hester assumes her residence in a small abandoned cottage on the outskirts of the community.

While the novel is, in large part, a record of the torment Hester suffers under the burden of her symbol of shame, eventually, after the implied marriage of her daughter Pearl and the death of Chillingworth and Dimmesdale, Hester becomes an accepted and even a highly valued member of the community. Instead of being a symbol of scorn, Hester, and the letter A, according to the narrator, "became a type of something to be sorrowed over, and looked upon with awe, yet with reverence too." The people of the community even come to Hester for comfort and counsel in times of trouble and sorrow because they trust her to offer unselfish advice toward the resolution of upsetting conflict.

Thus, in the end, Hester becomes an important figure in preserving the peace and stability of the community.

The Shipmaster

The Shipmaster is the captain of the ship on which Hester, Dimmesdale, and Pearl hope to leave America for Europe. During the Election Day sermon in chapter twelve, he is smitten by Pearl's charm. He even tries to kiss her, and, when this fails, he gives her a long gold chain.

John Wilson

Another historical figure, John Wilson was a minister who came to America in 1630. He was a strong figure of Puritan authority and intolerance. In chapter three, where Hester is on the scaffold, he prods Dimmesdale to interrogate Hester about the identity of her lover. In chapter eight he questions Pearl about her religious knowledge.

Themes

Individual vs. Society

The Scarlet Letter is a novel that describes the psychological anguish of two principle characters, Hester Prynne and Arthur Dimmesdale. They are both suffering under, while attempting to come to terms with, their mutual sin of adultery in a strict Puritan society. As critics immediately recognized upon publication of the novel in 1850, one of its principal themes involved conflict between the individual and society.

Hawthorne represents the stern and threatening force of Puritan society in the first sentence of the first chapter, where he describes a "throng of bearded men, in sad-colored garments and gray," who stand before the prison door "which was heavily timbered with oak, and studded with iron spikes," and behind which was Hester. Hawthorne symbolizes the force of the Puritan's civil and religious authority in this "prison-door," which is indeed the very name of the chapter. Yet outside the door, symbolizing Hester, the scarlet letter, and finally the individual who dissents from society, is a "wild rose-bush." This rosebush that stands just outside the prison door, Hawthorne famously suggests, "may serve ... to symbolize some sweet moral blossom, that may be found along the track, or relieve the darkening close of a tale of human frailty and sorrow."

The action of the novel (what there is of action in this notoriously unmoving narrative) maintains the conflict of the individual with society, even to the end, where Hawthorne offers a perplexing conclusion. Beginning with the above symbolic scene, Hawthorne repeatedly attaches our sympathies with the individual against social authority, setting us up for a narrative resolution where the individual breaks free from imposed constraints. Yet Hester, after she leaves America for a time, returns to the place of her punishment and willingly resumes the imposed symbol of her guilt and shame. Thus we are left with this principal thematic conflict to resolve on our own.

Change and Transformation

Closely related to the conflict of the individual and society is the theme of stability, change, and transformation. One of the important places where this theme is introduced is actually outside the proper narrative, in Hawthorne's introduction, "The Custom-House."

In "The Custom-House" Hawthorne informs us about his actual job as the commissioner of the custom house in Salem, Massachusetts. Given the job as a political appointment, Hawthorne was responsible for the inspection and regulation of merchant ships that landed in Salem. In his endless partiality to symbols, Hawthorne describes "an enormous specimen of the American eagle, with outspread wings" that "hovers" before the Custom-House entrance and appears "by the fierceness of her beak and eye and the general truculency of her attitude to … warn all citizens" of disrupting the Custom-House affairs. Here is a symbol of stable authority necessarily connected to Hawthorne himself, insofar as he is chief official of the Custom-House. Yet this firm symbol of civil authority is immediately compromised by the context of decay in which it is placed. Hawthorne notes that the wharves of Salem have been left "to crumble to ruin" and that the port "exhibits few or no symptoms of commercial life." Even the pavement around the Custom-House "has grass enough growing in its chinks to show that it has not, of late days, been worn by any multitudinous resort of business."

But these signs of creeping transformation are replaced by Hawthorne's obviously uncomfortable representation of sudden, even violent change, which in fact struck him personally. Due to the political nature of Hawthorne's appointment, when Zachary Taylor won the Presidential election of 1848, Hawthorne was promptly removed from office. Viewing himself as politically harmless, Hawthorne had felt his "prospect of retaining of-

Topics for Further Study

* Research the role of Hawthorne's relative, John Hathorne, in the Salem witch trials and discuss how this influences your interpretation of the novel.

* Read a work by one of Hawthorne's transcendentalist contemporaries (like Ralph Waldo Emerson's *Nature,* or Henry David Thoreau's *Walden*) and compare what you think to be their world view with that of Hawthorne's.

* Investigate the idea of crime and/or the role of women in colonial New England and compare your findings with Hawthorne's representation of Hester. You might want to consider what the Puritans feared that would justify their particular laws and actions.

* Look at some histories of the European revolutions of 1848 and consider why they may have caused Hawthorne some anxiety.

fice to be better than [that of his] Democratic brethren. But who can see an inch into futurity, beyond his nose? My own head was the first that fell!" With his guillotine metaphor, Hawthorne evokes the great violent revolutions then sweeping Europe. Critics now agree that he greatly feared the possibility of such dramatic change in America.

Ambiguity

Critical consensus has come to regard the issue of ambiguity and knowledge rather than ones of deception and truth, as a central, if not *the* central, theme in the novel. Truth and deception imply a firm moral order, the very possibility of which the novel repeatedly draws into question. Ambiguity, which implies the incapacity to *know* anything for certain, is much closer to what the novel describes. One of the most profound expressions of ambiguity surrounds Arthur Dimmesdale, for it is the truth of sin that he keeps hidden which makes him the very pillar of moral purity in the community. In fact, exactly because he confesses his impurity he becomes a more powerful figure of virtue: "He had told his bearers that he was altogether vile, a viler companion of the vilest, the warts of sinners, a thing of unimaginable iniquity…. They heard it all, and did but reverence him the more." The "truth" about the minister, sinner or sinless, is forever suspended. Thus, even after the narrator records Dimmesdale's public confession of his affair with Hester, the very notion that he was Hester's lover remains inconclusive. Some people maintain that they saw a stigmata of the scarlet letter on Dimmesdale's chest, others present say they saw nothing at all. Some even claim that he did not confess "the slightest connection, on his part, with the guilt for which Hester Prynne had so long worn the scarlet letter." As the narrator says, "The reader may choose among these theories."

Another moment where the lure of truth is presented yet left undisclosed occurs in chapter nineteen, where the narrator tells us that Pearl "had been offered to the world…. As the living hieroglyphic, in which was revealed the secret [Hester and Dimmesdale] so darkly sought to hide,—all written in this symbol,—all plainly manifest,—had there been a prophet or magician skilled to read the character of flame." Truth is plain, but its language is hard to interpret.

Guilt and Innocence
Sin

The Scarlet Letter is without question a novel about sin and guilt, though, as we should expect of Hawthorne, it is not a simple matter to determine who, or what, is the subject of these themes. Are Hester and Dimmesdale the principle sinners, or does their suffering, if not their love, absolve them? If we assume that the novel is an allegory, involving significant episodes and issues from American history, particularly the Salem witch trials, then is it America itself that is guilty of great sin? If this is the case (and many critics feel that it is), then we should reverse the most obvious terms of guilt and sin that the novel presents and read the representatives of authority as the principal figures of guilt. Following this line of interpretation, we can see Hawthorne attempting to individualize national sin in the actual historical characters of Governor Bellingham and John Wilson. We can even take this reading one step further and see Hawthorne attempting to absolve himself and his own family lineage when we recall that one of his own forefathers, John Hathorne, was a particularly cruel prosecutor during the witch hysteria. Whether absolution is rendered is a matter for the reader to decide.

Style

Narrator

One of the most obvious problems when discussing *The Scarlet Letter* is determining the identity of the narrator. This difficulty is clearly intentional. In the second paragraph of "The Custom-House," Hawthorne claims that he is merely "explaining how a large portion of the following pages came into [his] possession," hoping to offer "proofs of the authenticity of a narrative therein contained." Hawthorne proclaims himself only an editor, "or very little more." Yet later he states that "I have allowed myself … nearly or altogether as much license as if the facts had been entirely of my own invention," and all he is willing to verify is "the authenticity of the outline." Thus Hawthorne's characteristic use of ambiguity is both a central theme and a central technique of the novel.

Symbolism

The Scarlet Letter is rich with symbols; in fact, it is largely regarded as the first symbolic novel in America. A symbol is, like a metaphor, something that stands for, or represents, something else: an object, a person, even an idea. But the term "symbol" is used to describe a substitution with more power, or profound meaning, for which the term "metaphor" is inadequate. Of course, the scarlet letter itself is the principal symbol in the novel, but there are many others. In the first chapter the wild rosebush symbolizes dissent in its reference to the historical figure Anne Hutchinson, who led a group of religious dissenters in colonial Massachusetts. It also symbolizes Hester and even anticipates the scarlet letter that she wears. Individuals in the novel can also be understood as symbols. For instance, Arthur Dimmesdale, with all of his profound pain and suffering, is symbolic of the high value of truth and the irony of its unattainability.

Setting

Another of Hawthorne's techniques, one that so effectively immerses us in the atmosphere of his story, is his use of setting. The entire novel takes place in and around the small colonial town of Boston, Massachusetts. As Hawthorne describes it, the town is situated precariously between the sea and the great "wilderness" of unsettled America. What lies outside the town is a "black forest," strongly symbolic of moral absence and evil. Thus the narrator describes a "footpath" that straggled onward into the "mystery of the primeval forest.

This [forest] hemmed it in so narrowly, and stood so black and dense on either side ... that, to Hester's mind, it imaged not amiss the moral wilderness in which she had so long been wandering." Here we see an almost claustrophobic pressure being evoked, which alludes to not only Hester but also the community of which she is a part, always facing the possibility of moral failure.

As seen above, Hawthorne uses color adeptly in his description of settings. Besides the black wilderness there is the gray of the village and its inhabitants, who, as the narrator describes, "seemed never to have known a youthful era." Even though it was in fact a young settlement, the town jail "was already marked with weather stains and other indications of age, which gave a yet darker aspect to its ... gloomy front." In fact, it is precisely the dark and gloomy depiction of the town that helps to provide a tension with the forest, as if the town were already much like the forest and therefore more liable to be absorbed by its influence.

Ambiguity

While the importance of ambiguity as a theme has already been emphasized, it must still be described as one of Hawthorne's most important techniques. Repeatedly, where the reader expects to be given sure information, Hawthorne qualifies and withdraws assurance to the point that the reader is often left frustrated. In chapter sixteen even the small forest brook by which Hester discards the scarlet letter threatens Hawthorne's narration with the disclosure of meaning, and so, the surrounding "giant trees and boulders of granite seemed intent on making a mystery of the course of this small brook; fearing perhaps, that, with its never-ceasing loquacity, it should whisper tales out of the heart of the old forest whence it flowed, or mirror its revelations on the smooth surface of a pool." Hawthorne renders this beautiful passage to remind the reader, seemingly at every turn, that meaning, or truth, will be profoundly difficult to uncover.

Historical Context

The Transcendentalist Movement

The Scarlet Letter, which takes as its principal subject colonial seventeenth-century New England, was written and published in the middle of the nineteenth century. Hawthorne began writing the novel in 1849, after his dismissal from the Custom-House, and it was published in 1850. The discrep-

ancy between the time represented in the novel and the time of its production has often been a point of confusion to students. Because Hawthorne took an earlier time as his subject, the novel is considered a historical romance written in the midst of the American literary movement called transcendentalism (c. 1836-60).

The principle writers of transcendentalism included Ralph Waldo Emerson, Henry David Thoreau, Margaret Fuller, and W. H. Channing. Transcendentalism was, broadly speaking, a reaction against the rationalism of the previous century and the religious orthodoxy of Calvinist New England. Transcendentalism stressed the romantic tenets of mysticism, idealism, and individualism. In religious terms it saw God not as a distant and harsh authority, but as an essential aspect of the individual and the natural world, which were themselves considered inseparable. Because of this profound unity of all matter, human and natural, knowledge of the world and its laws could be obtained through a kind of mystical rapture with the world. This type of experience was perhaps most famously explained in Emerson's *Nature,* where he wrote, "I become a transparent eyeball; I am nothing; I see all; the currents of the Universal Being circulate through me; I am part and parcel of God."

Even though Hawthorne was close to many transcendentalists, including Emerson, and even though he lived for a while at the transcendentalist experimental community of Brook Farm, he was rather peripheral to the movement. Hawthorne even pokes fun at Brook Farm and his transcendentalist contemporaries in "The Custom-House," referring to them as his "dreamy brethren ... indulging in fantastic speculation." Where they saw the possibilities of achieving knowledge through mystical experience, Hawthorne was far more skeptical.

Abolitionism and Revolution

More important to Hawthorne's literary productions, and particularly *The Scarlet Letter,* was abolitionism and European revolution. These, in Hawthorne's view, were episodes of threatening instability. Abolitionism was the nineteenth-century movement to end slavery in the United States. Though it varied in intensity, abolitionism contained a very radical strain that helped to form a climate for John Brown's capture of Harpers Ferry in 1859. (John Brown intended to establish a base for armed slave insurrection.) The rising intensity and violence of abolitionism was an important cause of the Civil War. Hawthorne's conservative position in relation to abolitionism did not neces-

Compare & Contrast

- **1640s:** The Puritans believed in their mission to establish a model community for the Protestant world.

  1850s: America had developed an ideology of "manifest destiny" that held that the prosperous expansion of Americans across the continent was inevitable and ordained, and implied that the country was destined to become a great global power.

  Today: America's global power seems both assured with the splitting of the Soviet Union, and a thing of the past with the rise of countries like Japan and Germany to economic power.

- **1640s:** The colonists, though not clearly provoked, fought with the Narraganset Indians against the Pequot Indians, at one point killing seven hundred Pequot men, women, and children.

  1850s: Native land claims had all but been eliminated east of the Mississippi with President Jackson's removal of the "five civilized tribes" in the late 1830s. Their bitter march to Oklahoma is known as "The Trail of Tears."

  Today: Native peoples survive and grow in geographically dispersed areas and continue to fight legal battles over land claims.

- **1640s:** Anne Hutchinson had recently disturbed the Massachusetts Bay Colony by asserting that inward knowledge of the Holy Spirit, not outward good works, led to salvation.

  1850s: Transcendentalists disturbed orthodox religious views by claiming that God and the knowledge of his laws could be experienced by the individual open to revelation.

  Today: While religious fundamentalism is rising and many others are skeptical of religious belief, the idea that God is present in Nature, or the individual, remains popular.

- **1640s:** Women were rigidly excluded from official positions of political or religious power.

  1850s: The women's suffrage movement gained strength after the first women's rights convention took place in Seneca Falls, New York, in 1848. The two principal issues were ownership of property and voting rights.

  Today: After gaining the right to vote in 1920, women now hold political offices from mayor to senator to governor. While women have made gains in the business world, they are still underrepresented in executive positions and still encounter discrimination.

---

sarily mean that he was pro-slavery, but he did quite clearly oppose abolitionists, writing that slavery was "one of those evils which divine Providence does not leave to be remedied by human contrivances."

What Hawthorne feared were violent disruptions of the social order like those that were happening in Europe at the time he wrote *The Scarlet Letter*. The bloody social upheaval that most interested Americans began in France in 1848. This, and other revolutions of the period, pitted the lower and middle classes against established power and authority. While the revolutions eventually failed,

they were largely waged under the banner of socialism, and it was this fact that caused concern in America; as one journalist wrote, as quoted by Bercovitch, here there were "foreboding shadows" of "Communism, Socialism, Pillage, Murder, Anarchy, and the Guillotine vs. Law and Order, Family and Property." Critics have recently pointed to Hawthorne's guillotine imagery in "The Custom-House" (where he even suggests the title "The Posthumous Papers of a Decapitated Surveyor" for his tale) and metaphors of his own victimization as some evidence of his sympathies with regard to revolution and social order.

*A 1882 woodcut, "At the Church Door," showing a
Puritan Thanksgiving in the seventeenth century.*

The Puritan Colonies

The novel was written in the mid-nineteenth century, but it takes the mid-seventeenth century for the events it describes (1642-49). The Massachusetts Bay Colony was established by John Winthorp (whose death is represented near the center of the novel) and other Puritans in 1630. They sought to establish an ideal community in America that could act as a model of influence for what they saw as a corrupt civil and religious order in England. This sense of mission was the center of their religious and social identity. Directed toward the realization of such an ideal, the Puritans required a strict moral regulation; anyone in the community who sinned threatened not only their soul, but the very possibility of civil and religious perfection in America *and* in England. Not coincidentally, the years Hawthorne chose to represent in *The Scarlet Letter* were the same as those of the English Civil War fought between King Charles I and the Puritan Parliament; the latter was naturally supported by the New England colonists.

Critical Overview

Most reviewers gave Hawthorne's novel high praise at the time of its publication. Evert A. Duyckinck, one of the most influential critics of his day, called the tale a "psychological romance ..., a study of character in which the human heart is anatomized, carefully, elaborately, and with striking poetic and dramatic power." He also praised Hawthorne's departure from the overly ornate writing style popular at the time, which displayed "artifice and effort at the expense of nature and ease." Duyckinck's review was supported by that of Edwin Percy Whipple, who considered the novel "deep in thought and ... condensed in style." A striking theme common to both critics is Hawthorne's difference from French literary models. Both saw French fiction, particularly that of George Sand (a woman novelist), as far too immoral in its depiction of issues similar to those treated in *The Scarlet Letter*. Whipple wrote that the novel had "utterly undermined the whole philosophy on which the French novels rest, by seeing further and deeper into the essence both of conventional and moral laws." The terms of the anti-French attitude of those early reviewers, placing Hawthorne's positive insight into convention and morality against the French lack of such insight, is of special significance. It refers inevitably to the historical fact of the 1848 revolution in France and American anxieties about its spread overseas.

This is not to say the positive critical appraisal of Hawthorne's moral representations was unanimous. Arthur Cleveland Coxe, writing in the *Church Review,* considered Hawthorne's novel the story of "the nauseous amour of a Puritan pastor," who commits adultery with "a frail creature of his charge, whose mind is represented as far more debauched than her body." (However one interprets the moral order—or its lack—that Hawthorne describes, very few have considered Hester a "frail creature.")

Henry James's 1874 study, *Hawthorne,* stands as the first "modern" analysis of the novel, insofar as he considered it not as a work of entertainment but one of serious art. James declared that the novel was the "finest piece of imaginative writing yet put forth in the country." Yet he was put off by what he considered an almost ridiculous level of symbolic effect, writing of the scene where the scarlet letter appears in the sky above Boston as one of nearly "physical comedy" rather than high "moral tragedy." Henry James was himself a great author of literary realism, and this preference is shown in his criticism of Hawthorne's symbolism.

Most modern critics have wrangled with *The Scarlet Letter*'s unresolved tensions. One of the most insightful, F. O. Matthiessen, describes Hawthorne's method as one of "multiple choice," where different interpretive possibilities are offered by the narrator, who withholds resolution of the reader's inevitable questions. "For Hawthorne," writes Mattheissen, the value of a particular literary moment "consisted in the variety of explanation to which it gave rise." In the climactic final scene where Dimmesdale presumably confesses and exposes the stigmata on his chest, Hawthorne leaves the reader not only with a variety of options on how the letter got there, but even questions about whether there was a mark *or* confession at all.

Other critics have not been generous with Hawthorne's penchant for mystery. Frederic I. Carpenter, in an essay titled "Scarlet A Minus," calls the book a classic of a "minor order," and complains that "its logic is ambiguous." Carpenter finds the narrative generally characterized by a confusion "between romantic immorality and transcendental idealism." This unresolved tension is most obvious in the character of Hester, who is at once condemned as immoral and glorified as an ideal of courage.

Hester's courage has been the positive subject of criticism by feminist readers, including Nina Baym. Baym wrote a strong and persuasive essay against male critics, particularly of the 1950s, who read the novel as a story primarily about Arthur Dimmesdale. Baym explains the critical subordination of Hester to Dimmesdale as part a masculinist ideology which held that "it would be improper for a woman character to be the protagonist in what might well be the greatest American book." Baym shows that Hester occupies by far the greater part of the novel (including the preface) and that she clearly takes full responsibility for her actions in a way that Dimmesdale does not. In short, "Hester and her behavior are associated with the ideals of passion, self-expression, freedom, and individualism against ideals of order, authority, and restraint.... Nothing in the plot shows Hester attempting to evade responsibility for her actions."

As Baym suggests, *The Scarlet Letter* is arguably the most important work of fiction ever written in America. Naturally, it gathers enormous critical attention. Important recent works include those by Jonathon Arac, Michael Davitt Bell, and especially, Lauren Berlant and Larry J. Reynolds. These critics are highly various, but generally speaking they have examined the way the novel elaborates—that is, both represented and helped to produce—the powerful symbols and myths of dominant American structures of power. But by far the most influential of recent studies with such an emphasis is Sacvan Bercovitch's *The Office of The Scarlet Letter.*

Bercovitch maintains that the most telling point in the novel is the one sentence paragraph in chapter thirteen where the narrator tells us, "the scarlet letter had not done its office." Here, according to Bercovitch, we learn that the scarlet letter "has a purpose and a goal," thus, "Hawthorne's meanings may be endless, but they are not open-ended." So what is the "goal" of the scarlet letter? To transmute "opposition into complementarity." By this Becovitch means that the letter, in the end, defuses dissent and reestablishes unity: *The Scarlet Letter* "is a story of socialization in which the point of socialization is not to conform, but to consent. Anyone can submit; the socialized believe. It is not enough to have the letter imposed; you have to do it yourself." The scarlet letter is at first imposed on Hester by the Puritan magistrates, but this does not represent the best form of socialization because Hester does not wear it willingly but bears it as a punishment. An important turning point is the scene in the forest where she discards the letter by the brook, but then, through Pearl's imploring, takes the letter back upon her chest. Also, according to this reading, her planned escape with Pearl and Dimmesdale from Boston must fail, for leaving would represent an unwillingness to *fully* accept the letter. It is clear that the letter has finally accomplished its office when, after eventually going with Pearl to Europe, Hester willingly returns to the community of her shame. As Hawthorne writes in the Conclusion, "She had returned, therefore, and resumed,—of her own free will, for not the sternest magistrate of that iron period would have imposed it,—resumed the symbol of which we have related so dark a tale." Instead of being a figure of scorn and shame, she becomes a valued counsellor in the community, resolving conflict, as opposed to representing it. For Bercovitch this is an allegorical representation of an American method of controlling dissent: "To understand the office of the A ... is to see how culture empowers symbolic form, including forms of dissent, and how symbols participate in the dynamics of culture, including the dynamics of constraint."

Criticism

Pearl James

In the following essay, James, a doctoral candidate at Yale University, explores the historical concerns that shaped The Scarlet Letter *and how Hester Prynne's emblem serves as several types of imagery.*

Nathaniel Hawthorne envisioned *The Scarlet Letter* as a short story to be published in a collection, but it outgrew that purpose. Most critics accept Hawthorne's definition of it as a "romance," rather than as a novel. It usually appears with an introductory autobiographical essay, "The Custom House," in which Hawthorne describes working in his ancestral village, Salem, Massachusetts, as a customs officer. Hawthorne describes coming across certain documents in the customs house that provide him with the basis for *The Scarlet Letter*. But this essay fictionalizes the origins of the story in that it offers "proofs of the authenticity of a narrative therein contained." Following other literary examples in early American literature, like Washington Irving's *History of New York*, Hawthorne masks his literary invention by making it seem "historical." He calls his motivation for writing the essay "a desire to put [himself] in [his] true position as editor, or very little more." This editorial positioning indicates his interest in creating a aura of "authenticity" and historical importance for his narrative.

Not surprisingly, therefore, much criticism of *The Scarlet Letter* focuses on its relation to history. Many critics have investigated the Puritan laws governing adultery and searched for an historical Hester Prynne. Other critics have used clues within the tale to specify its context. For example, when Dimmesdale climbs on the scaffold at midnight, Hester and Pearl have been watching at the governor's deathbed. Charles Ryskamp associates this with the death of Governor Winthrop on March 26, 1649, and notices that celestial disturbances were actually recorded after his death. Similarly, Election Day, on which Dimmesdale's sermon commemorates the inauguration of a new Governor, can be located historically on May 2, 1649. To notice these dates, however, is to notice that Hawthorne takes liberties with them. ("The Minister's Vigil" chapter takes place in "early May," not March, and so on.) His role in composing *The Scarlet Letter* far exceeds that of a mere "editor." The tale is an invention, and Hawthorne's use of disparate historical details should be understood not only as significant, but also as symbolic.

Hawthorne's interest in the history of the colonies and his Puritan ancestors was deep and genuine, but complicated. He was interested in not just documenting, but *creating* an "authentic" past. In "The Custom House" and elsewhere in his writing, Hawthorne imagines an ancestral guilt that he inherits; he takes "shame upon [himself] for their sakes." (One of his ancestors, John Hathorne, ruled for executions during the Salem witch trials.) At still another level, Hawthorne invites the reader to relate *The Scarlet Letter* to contemporary politics of the 1840s. "The past is not dead"— it lives on in the custom house, and other contemporary political institutions. He writes *The Scarlet Letter* after having lost his administrative position, as a self-proclaimed "politically dead man." Hawthorne insists that the nation both enables and impedes the lives of its constituents and the telling of its histories.

In the novel's opening pages, we wait with the crowd for Hester to emerge from the prison. We overhear snatches of conversation among the women of the crowd, who express little sympathy for Hester and even wish for a harsher sentence. The narrator interrupts these bitter sentiments, which match the prison's "gloomy front," and contrasts them with a wild rosebush that blooms by the prison door. He hopes this rosebush may serve "to symbolize some sweet moral blossom, that may be found" by the reader of this "tale of human frailty and sorrow." Explicitly, then, Hawthorne identifies

What Do I Read Next?

- *The House of the Seven Gables* (1851), Hawthorne's third novel, which he personally thought was a better piece of work than *The Scarlet Letter,* about the cursed house of the Pyncheon family where the sins of fathers are passed on to their descendants.

- *The Bird Artist,* Howard Norman's recent (1994) novel about an artist in a small Newfoundland coastal village, is a story of crime and adultery in a place without the religious authority of Hawthorne's Boston.

- *The Devil in the Shape of a Woman: Witchcraft in Colonial New England* (1987) by Carol F. Karlsen shows that the violent Salem witch trials were not only directed primarily at women, but particularly women who stood to inherit property and, thus, power.

- William Cronon's *Changes in the Land: Indians, Colonists, and the Ecology of New England,* (1983) is a seminal work of environmental history that describes the impact the early settlers had on New England native peoples and the environment.

- *Life in the Iron Mills* (1861) by Rebecca Harding Davis is the powerful story of the physical and emotional oppression and struggle of a mid-nineteenth-century mill-worker. Published about a decade after Hawthorne's novel, it is even more of an anomaly in the context of literary transcendentalism.

- Henry David Thoreau's "Civil Disobedience" (1849) was originally titled "Resistance to Civil Government." He argues here for the right of the individual to refuse to pay taxes or otherwise support civil authority against his or her conscience. Thoreau spent some time in jail when he did not pay taxes in 1843 in protest of the Mexican War.

- Harriet A. Jacobs's 1861 *Incidents in the Life of a Slave Girl* is a kind of "romance" slave narrative that ties sexuality to race in pre-Civil War America.

The Scarlet Letter as a moral parable, which offers its readers a "sweet" and "moral" lesson. This lesson emerges from the faults made by the Puritans' early experiment in society, which the narrator consistently uses irony to deflate. He comments, for example, that "whatever Utopia of human virtue and happiness" the founding Pilgrims had envisioned, a cemetery and a prison both became necessary institutions. He aims his irony not at the fact that the need for a prison arose, but at the naive fantasy that it could have been otherwise. As he does in *The Blithedale Romance* (1852), Hawthorne deflates the tradition of American dreams of Utopia and new social orders. In *The Scarlet Letter,* the fault shared by the Puritan settlers, the women outside the prison, and Arthur Dimmesdale most of all, is pious hypocrisy: they naively imagine that sin, or "human frailty and sorrow," can be avoided through denial and pretense.

Chillingworth, using an assumed name and hiding his intent of revenge, becomes an increasingly diabolical villain by his own duplicity. At the other end of the spectrum, Hester Prynne, because she wears a sign of shame on the surface of her clothing, cannot feign innocence; consequently she has a greater potential for salvation and peace.

For Hawthorne, his Puritan ancestors and the society they built seemed to forget the wisdom of the great Puritan poet John Milton, author of *Paradise Lost.* Hawthorne repeatedly invokes *Paradise Lost* in order to reassert its vision of mankind as fallen, and its poetic dramatization of Adam and Eve's fall and expulsion from Eden. Fallen, with the world "all before them," they gain the potential for ultimate redemption. So Hester, let out of prison, "with the world before her," seems to have a better chance of redemption than her hypocritical neighbors.

Hawthorne's allusions to *Paradise Lost* also provide him a way of introducing the question of sexuality and woman as the site of temptation and sin. Hester Prynne repeatedly feels herself to be responsible for the sins of both Dimmesdale and Chillingworth. Dimmesdale and Chillingworth each reinforce this interpretation. The narrator dramatizes the self-serving structure of their accusations, and calls it into question. The irony of Dimmesdale's initial entreaty to Hester illustrates this:

> Be not silent from any mistaken pity and tenderness for [thy fellow-sinner]; for, believe me, Hester, though he were to step down from a high place, and stand there beside thee, on thy pedestal of shame, yet better were it so, than to hide a guilty heart through life. What can thy silence do for him, except it tempt him—yea, compel him, as it were—to add hypocrisy to sin?

Dimmesdale, as he stands at a literally high place, transfers his own responsibility to acknowledge his part in the crime to Hester. Hester serves both Dimmesdale and Chillingworth, and indeed the whole community, as a scapegoat. The "rich, voluptuous, Oriental characteristic" in her nature, which implies sexuality, is something that the community simultaneously desires and disavows. They ostracize her, but continue to consume her needlework, surreptitiously borrowing from the exotic principle she seems to symbolize.

In this way, Hawthorne directs his irony at Puritan hypocrisy. However, he softens the didacticism (intent to teach) of his tale with the other means he uses: imagery and symbolism. Again, the rosebush should "*symbolize* some sweet moral blossom"—the key word is "symbolize." The novel's most important symbol, the eponymous (name-giving) scarlet letter "A," takes on several different meanings. To the townspeople, the letter has "the effect of a spell, taking [Hester] out of the ordinary relations with humanity, and inclosing her in a sphere by herself." The spell of this scarlet letter is akin to that of *The Scarlet Letter*—the book itself. Like the community of Boston, we are invited to enter a separate sphere, where both imagination and moral growth can occur. As Hawthorne describes it in "The Custom House," modern life (of the 1840s) has a dulling effect on the mind and the spirit. In his fiction, he wants to create a richer and more challenging world. Just as the meaning of Hester's "A" gradually expands for the townspeople, meaning not just "Adultery" but also "Able," and perhaps "Angel," *The Scarlet Letter* has an ambiguity that opens possibilities of meaning for its readers. Readers continue to speculate on what the "A" additionally suggests: Arthur (Dimmesdale), Ambiguity, America, and so on.

The ambiguity of Hester's scarlet letter "A" has been used as a textbook case to illustrate the difference between two kinds of imagery in writing: allegory and symbolism. Allegory, in which the name of a character or a thing directly indicates its meaning, can be seen in Hawthorne's early story "Young Goodman Brown," about a young, good man. Symbolism, on the other hand, requires more interpretation; the "A," for instance, suggests many possibilities which are in themselves contradictory ("adultery" versus "angel"). Most critics understand symbolism as a more sophisticated technique, and see it as more rewarding for the reader, who must enter into the text in order to tease out its possible meanings. In *The Scarlet Letter,* this act of interpretation outside the text mirrors what happens in the story itself.

The narrator of *The Scarlet Letter* continually provides more than one interpretation of events. When the strange light shines in the sky during "The Minister's Vigil," it makes "all visible, but with a singularity of aspect that [seems] to give another moral interpretation to the things of this world than they had ever borne before." The narrator only reports a "light." He suggests that Dimmesdale reads it as a giant "A"—his own secret sin writ large in the heavens—because of his "highly disordered mental state." But this account is in turn undermined when the sexton and the townsfolk also read a large "A" in the sky, which they "interpret to stand for angel."

These moments suggest that part of the appeal of *The Scarlet Letter* is the act of reading itself. Hawthorne dramatizes the effect of reading most clearly through Pearl. Up until a certain point, she is more a symbol than a character. The narrator comments, as Pearl dances by, "It was the scarlet letter in another form; the scarlet letter endowed with life." But at a particular moment, Pearl ceases to be a symbol, an "it," and becomes human. That moment occurs on the scaffold, when she kisses her father; his grief transforms her, by calling upon "all her sympathies." This moment emblematizes the moral effect that aesthetic philosophers of the nineteenth century believed literature and art could have on their audiences. Hawthorne, by inscribing such a moment, puts forth high aesthetic claims for his work. The fact that Pearl—here the figure for an ideal reader—is *feminine* may suggest that Hawthorne has a feminine audience in mind. Occasionally, Hawthorne seems to voice a certain anxiety about the fact that aesthetic appreciation is "seldom seen in the masculine character after childhood or early youth," and whether or not writing might have a disturbingly feminizing effect on writers and readers. On the other hand, work as a customs officer poses a threat to "self reliance" and "manly character"—a threat Hawthorne escapes by returning to writing. In any case, the scene of Pearl's transformation, as the text's central moment of redemption and resolution, emphasizes the importance of the emotions in a richly lived *and* moral life. In this way, Hawthorne seems to bring two opposites together. Pearl, as a younger, virginal version of her mother, neutralizes the threat Hester initially posed. Hawthorne brings the possibility of sensual and feeling feminine character back into the realm of moral life.

Source: Pearl James, in an essay for *Novels for Students,* Gale 1997.

Richard B. Sewall

In the following excerpt, Sewall discusses Hawthorne's introductory essay, and the emphasis on ambiguity throughout The Scarlet Letter.

There is something reminiscent of now familiar processes in Hawthorne's account of the origin and growth of the idea of *The Scarlet Letter* in the introductory essay to the novel, "The Custom House." He tells (albeit whimsically) of finding one day the scarlet letter itself—"that certain affair of fine red cloth"—in his rummagings about the Custom House and of how it, and the old manuscript which told its story, set him to certain somber musings. The old story of a bygone, dire event and its decaying symbol rayed out meanings to his imagination as surely as the ancient myths and legends revealed new meanings to the Greek and Elizabethan dramatists. "Certainly [Hawthorne writes], there was some deep meaning in it, most worthy of interpretation, and which, as it were, streamed forth from the mystic symbol, subtly communicating it to my sensibilities, but evading the analysis of my mind." The "half a dozen sheets of foolscap" of Mr. Surveyor Pue's account of the letter, which seemed at first glance to give "a reasonably complete explanation of the whole affair," stood to the novel as (we might hazard) the ancient legend of Oedipus stood to Sophocles, or Holinshed's account of Lear's story to Shakespeare. With mock apology, Hawthorne acknowledged the liberties he took with Pue's document: "I must not be understood as affirming, that, in the dressing up of the

tale, and imagining the motives and modes of passion that influenced the characters who figure in it, I have invariably confined myself within the limits of the old Surveyor's half a dozen sheets of foolscap." Meditating upon the simple outlines of Hester's story as the old document recorded it, Hawthorne asked, as it were, the existential questions: What (to Hester) did it mean to be a woman of flesh and blood, caught in that situation of guilt but sanctioned by a kind of inner necessity, the promptings of her own high spirit, which neither she nor her pious lover could repudiate as entirely evil ("What we did had a consecration of its own.")? What did it feel like to live through a dilemma so potent with destructive possibilities? What must have been the impact on a powerful yet sensitive nature? Is there not here, too, a "boundary-situation" sufficient to call in question man's very conception of himself and what he lives by?

Hester's religious heritage and her community pronounced her utterly guilty; she had sinned "in the most sacred quality of human life." She was ostracized, imprisoned, and put on trial for her life: "This woman [said one of her persecutors] has brought shame upon us all, and ought to die. Is there not a law for it? Truly, there is, both in the Scripture and the statute-book." In her extremity, what was she to do? To accept the community's verdict of total guilt would be to renounce the element of "consecration" she knew to be true of her relationship with Dimmesdale; and yet to renounce the community in the name of her consecration was equally unthinkable. She had sinned, and she knew guilt. But hers was no passive nature and, from some mysterious promptings of her own being, she took action in the only way she knew how; in the dim light of her prison cell, she embroidered the scarlet letter—with matchless artistry and in brilliant hue.

That is, she accepted, yet defied. She wore the "A" as the sign of her sin, which she publicly acknowledged—but she wore it on her own terms. Preserving a margin of freedom, she asserted the partial justice of her cause. The letter, when she appeared in public, "had the effect of a spell, taking her out of the ordinary relations with humanity, and enclosing her in a sphere by herself." Facing the Puritan crowd, she could have cursed them—and God—and died, either spiritually, or actually by suicide (she thought of suicide in prison). She could have revealed the name of her lover and got a mitigation of sentence, or prostrated herself in guilt and got the sympathy of the community. Instead, she decided to "maintain her own ways" before the people and her judges—though it slay her. Her final answer was to live out her dilemma in full acceptance of the suffering in store.

In the penultimate chapter of the novel, as Hawthorne prepares for the climactic revelation of the scarlet letter, he himself sums up the result of his meditations on Surveyor Pue's brief summary. With Hester and Pearl headed for the scaffold to join Dimmesdale, "Old Roger Chillingworth," he writes, "followed, as one intimately connected with the drama of guilt and sorrow in which they had all been actors, and well entitled, therefore, to be present at its closing scene."

It had been the work of the Enlightenment, the Romantics, and (in America) the Transcendentalists, so to shift the perspective on man and his problems as to render needless or meaningless or irrelevant (as they thought) this "drama of guilt and sorrow" which Hawthorne saw in the old story. Emerson was aware of the contrarieties of life and of the soul's struggle, but neither he nor his fellow Transcendentalists saw in them the stuff of drama, much less tragic drama. It was for Hawthorne, who "alone in his time," writes Allen Tate [in *On the Limits of Poetry,* 1948], "kept pure, in the primitive terms, the primitive vision," to transmute "the puritan drama of the soul," which for the faithful ended in the New Jerusalem, into tragic drama. The essence of Hester's seven-year course is conflict—of Hester with her self, her society, and her God. The conflict throughout is fraught with ambiguity, with goods and bads inextricably mixed, and constantly and bitterly recognized as such by Hester. Contrarieties are never resolved, and the issues of the soul's struggles are unsettled either way. "Is not this better," murmured Dimmesdale to Hester after the confession on the scaffold, "than what we dreamed of in the forest?"—to which Hester could only reply: "I know not! I know not!"

This is the sum of Hester's seven years of penance and agonized self-questioning. The Puritan code, which tortured and yet sustained her, failed in the end to answer her question. And in the multiple ambiguities of action and character, in the prevailing "tenebrism" of the novel, in the repeated images of the maze, the labyrinth, the weary and uncertain path, Hawthorne sets (by indirection) the Emersonian promise in a harsh and tragic light. Hester and Dimmesdale had "trusted themselves"; their hearts had "vibrated to that iron string." And it was not entirely wrong, the novel says, that they should have done so. But Hawthorne, in the true vein of tragedy, dealt not with doctrinaire injunctions but with actions in their entirety, with special regard, in this instance, for their consequences—a phase to which Emerson was singularly blind. These consequences, Hawthorne saw, are never clear, they involve man not only externally as a social being but internally, to his very depths, and they can be dire....

The seven-year action which is precipitated by Hester's Antigone-like independence, or (to the Puritan judges) stubbornness, involved her and those whom it touched intimately in deep suffering and loss of irretrievable values. Hester lost her youth, her beauty, her promise of creativity, and any sure hope she might have had of social or domestic happiness. She lost Dimmesdale, whom a full confession at the outset might have brought to her side, and whose life was ultimately ruined anyway. She was the cause of Chillingworth's long, destructive, and self-destructive course of revenge. She anguished over Pearl's bleak and bitter childhood. Her own loneliness and isolation, especially for one of so warm and rich a nature, was a constant sorrow and reminder of her guilt, a kind of suffering which Antigone or Medea, who in other ways are not unlike her, never knew in similar quality or duration. And in the end, she knew not whether she had done right or wrong. She goes out of our ken, a gray figure (still wearing her scarlet letter resumed "of her own free will"), and, "wise through dusky grief," giving comfort and counsel to the perplexed or forlorn.

If a major salvage from her experience is this hard-won wisdom of Hester's, it is not the only point of light in the dark world of mysteries and riddles that the novel in general portrays. By her stand Hester asserted her own values against the inherited and inhumane dogma of her community as surely as Prometheus, in Aeschylus' play, asserted his own sense of justice against Zeus. In both instances the suffering of the hero "made a difference." Hester humanized the community that would have cast her out, even put her to death. She forced it to reassess its own severe and absolute dogmas, as Antigone forced a reassessment in Thebes, or Hamlet in Elsinore, or Prometheus on Olympus. She envisioned and in quiet corners whispered of it to those who would hear, a "brighter period ... a new truth ... to establish the whole relation between man and woman on a surer ground of mutual happiness." If Dimmesdale perished because of the ordeal her action plunged him into, it was not before he had achieved a measure of heroic strength and a new insight which in the normal course would never have been his. When he died he was "ready" as he had never been before. At his death Pearl achieved a new humanity: "The great scene of grief in which the wild infant bore a part, had developed all her sympathies; and as her tears fell upon her father's cheek, they were the pledge that she would grow up amid human joy and sorrow, nor forever do battle with the world, but be a woman in it." Hester, Dimmesdale, and now Pearl learned what it is "to be men and women in it"—what it means to be.

Dimmesdale in his faith died praising God—a religious death. Hester lived out her "tragic" existence, giving counsel but, "stained with sins, bowed down with shame," denied the prophetic voice she might have raised, still believing, yet not believing (as witness the "A" which she wore to the end) in herself. "After many, many years," she was buried with her lover, and even her burial, like everything else in her life, was ambiguous. She was buried next to Dimmesdale, "yet with a space between, as if the dust of the two sleepers had no right to mingle." No right to mingle? In the first scene of the novel, Hawthorne had said of Hester's judges: "They were, doubtless, good men, just, and sage. But, out of the whole human family, it would not have been easy to select the same number of wise and virtuous persons, who should be less capable of sitting in judgment on an erring woman's heart, and disentangling its mesh of good and evil." Had Hester's and Dimmesdale's deed a "consecration of its own," or had it not? The Puritan judges said no. Even Hawthorne, speaking through the novel as a whole, suspends judgment. "We know not. We know not." Dimmesdale, the believer, could look forward to the last day "when all hidden things shall be revealed," when "the dark problem of this life" shall be made plain. But in this life he had wandered in a maze, "quite astray and at a loss in the pathway of human existence." So, to a close and scrupulous observer like Hawthorne, it must ever be. The pathway is beset with pitfalls and dubious choices. The shrewd pick their way warily. The passionate are likely to stumble or go wrong, and "good intentions" have no bearing on the inevitable penalty, which often far exceeds the crime. This is hard, but, to the heroic in heart, no cause for despair. There is wisdom to be won from the fine hammered steel of woe; a flower to be plucked from the rosebush at the prison door "to relieve the darkening close of a tale of human frailty and sorrow." To relieve, but not to reverse or redeem.

Source: Richard B. Sewall, "The Scarlet Letter," in *The Vision of Tragedy,* new edition, Yale University Press, 1980, pp. 86–91.

Bruce Ingham Granger

Granger, a professor of English at the University of Oklahoma, maintains that The Scarlet Letter *is not Hester's story but that of Dimmesdale, whose confession bridges the gap between illusion and reality, or the ideal and actuality, thus making him a true tragic hero.*

It is my conviction that, even though Arthur Dimmesdale does not move down center until late in the action, *The Scarlet Letter* is finally his story and, what is more important, that he is a tragic hero. He alone among the major characters never functions symbolically, though he is the familiar figure of Every-Christian. Viewed thus, Hawthorne's allegorical romance centers on a good man's struggle with and eventual victory over the guilt he experiences after committing lechery. Hawthorne is saying that three courses of action are open to such a sinner: he may keep silent and suffer "eternal alienation from the Good and True," the course urged by Roger Chillingworth; or—and this implies that he will probably keep silent all the while—he may flee the scene of the crime and with it his responsibility, the course eventually urged by Hester Prynne; or he may make full and public confession, the course urged by the child Pearl. Having kept silent for more than seven years, Dimmesdale finally has his Calvinist faith put to the supreme test and, having agreed to flee Boston with Hester and their child, finds the strength to face his responsibility and confess before he dies.

Although Dimmesdale respects and, except in one instance, has never broken civil and ecclesiastical law, theocratic authority at Boston is ultimately powerless to bring him to confession. John Wilson and Governor Bellingham, the chief representatives of church and state, are ill-equipped to understand his condition and can only point to the scaffold of the pillory as the place whereon sinners must stand and reveal their sin. Is it any wonder, then, that Dimmesdale should reject their offers of assistance as he prepares to make his revelation? On the other hand, he is intimately connected with the wronged husband, the wife who was his partner in sin, and the natural child born of this sin, each of whom does in fact help him toward this revelation. And yet, were it not for his steady observance of the law, a law whose operations are symbolized by the presence of the prison, pillory, meetinghouse, and governor's hall, he could not have acted responsibly at the last. Hawthorne's Bostonians, while certainly not drawn in an altogether sympathetic light, believe that a sinner can only absolve himself of sin, God willing, by making public confession. Dimmesdale subscribes to this orthodox Calvinist belief, as he does to its corollary that good works without true faith are less than naught. Holding firmly to these beliefs, he knows from the first that nothing short of confession can bring to an end the hypocrisy he has been making of his life. He finally realizes, as Wilson and Bellingham never do, that fallen man in his search for redemption must have his faith tested by undergoing a lonely, dark, spiritual journey before he can discover the way to responsible action. No community, not even God-fearing, seventeenth-century Boston, can instruct its members what road to take. Like Job, like Bunyan's Christian, Dimmesdale feels compelled to make his way alone, realizing that the individual, seeing as the community never can how far his actual self has fallen short of his ideal, must judge himself and prescribe for his condition.

Dimmesdale began his dark journey after the moment of passion he and Hester shared in the forest. Through all the years before they meet there again, this man, a minister of God who loves the truth and loathes the lie, has known only penance—has felt from the outset the endless searing of "his inmost heart," scourges his body and fasts and keeps long vigils, feels the hypocrisy of his position mount as he stands in the pulpit on the Sabbath and utters vague confessions, and, most painful of all, makes a "mockery of penitence" by attiring himself in his vestments one obscure night in early May and standing falsely revealed in meteor light on the scaffold where Hester was once made to stand with the infant Pearl in the bright morning sun. During this long first stage of the journey Roger Chillingworth, "a chief actor, in the poor minister's interior world," is the principal motivating force in the action; indeed, he continues forceful down to the moment Dimmesdale decides to mount the scaffold in daylight and make public confession. Until Dimmesdale recognizes him as "his bitterest enemy," Chillingworth, ostensibly the friendly physician concerned for the minister's physical well-being, resembles a more familiar kind of "leech," seeking to know what guilt lies buried in his heart and, when this secret is revealed to him, corrupting "his spiritual being" and bringing him to "the verge of lunacy." In short, Chillingworth symbolizes that force within the Christian pilgrim which prompts him to conceal his sin from the world; if ever he abandons himself to this temptation, it will destroy his moral nature and he will die unrepentant.

Brought to the threshold of insanity by this never-ceasing, always secret agony, finding no spiritual relief in the acts of penance he performs, Dimmesdale enters the most critical stage of the journey. Now his faith is to be tested more severely than it has been these seven years and, as a condition of making the journey, under circumstances that are not of his own choosing. In fact, until the second forest meeting his faith has not really been tested; unlike Hester, who has long dwelt on the outskirts of the community and is critical of its institutions, he has "never gone through an experience calculated to lead him beyond the scope of generally received laws; although, in a single instance, he had so fearfully transgressed one of the most sacred of them." The great question now is whether, for all his ministerial "eloquence and religious fervor," he will prove equal to the test. Ever fearful about venturing far from the orthodox way, finding himself in the wild forest once again, he is overwhelmed by the revitalized memory of the sin of passion committed there long ago and experiences a new temptation more terrible than any he has yet known. The beautiful Hester, who has been wandering morally ever since they sinned together, is now more his enemy than the diabolical Chillingworth. Responding to the renewed strength of her love for him, he suffers temporary suspension of the will—will-lessness being a necessary state at this stage of the journey—and calls on her to be his guide: "Think for me, Hester! Thou art strong. Resolve for me!... Advise me what to do." Hester, "fixing her deep eyes on the minister's, and instinctively exercising a magnetic power over a spirit so shattered and subdued, that it could hardly hold itself erect," advises a course of action more unorthodox than that which Chillingworth long ago imposed, though not necessarily inconsistent with it: "Leave this wreck and ruin here where it hath happened!... Begin all anew!... Exchange this false life of thine for a true one.... Give up this name of Arthur Dimmesdale, and make thyself another, and a high one, such as thou canst wear without fear or shame." No Christian, certainly not if he be a Calvinist, can deny his past, indeed his very birthright, and live at peace with himself, but at this moment a will-less Dimmesdale consents to deny his.

At this point in the journey we take hope that the child Pearl, who would have the truth known to the world, will bring her orthodox father to a sense of his responsibility, as she has not been able to bring her transcendental mother. Standing at the brookside, she in effect demands as she has before that he publicly acknowledge the existence of his daughter. Realizing that he will not "go back with us, hand in hand, we three together, into the town" at this time, she runs to the brook and washes off his unwelcome kiss. Dimmesdale must journey on for a time "in a maze" before he feels ready to act in a way that will satisfy Pearl's demand. As he returns to the town he is incited at every step "to do some strange, wild, wicked thing or other...." Hawthorne offers the following explanation for his nightmarish encounters with people in the town: "Tempted by a dream of happiness, he had yielded himself with deliberate choice, as he had never done before, to what he knew was deadly sin. And the infectious poison of that sin had been thus rapidly diffused throughout his moral system." But now an epiphany is at hand. Seated before his unfinished sermon, he is ready and eager to follow the course of action Pearl has long been urging; contrite, he draws back from the state of moral anarchy into which harkening to Hester's advice had momentarily plunged him, and for the first time knows the full meaning of the verse in *Genesis,* "In the image of God made he man." "...flinging the already written pages of the Election Sermon into the fire, he forthwith began another, which he wrote with such an impulsive flow of thought and emotion, that he fancied himself inspired; and only wondered that Heaven should see fit to transmit the grand and solemn music of its oracles through so foul an organ-pipe as he." The man who had long looked down from his pulpit and seen his "flock hungry for the truth, and listening to my words as if a tongue of Pentecost were speaking" has found his tongue at last. Feeling himself that "heaven-ordained apostle" his parishioners long imagined him to be, he is enabled to pen a vision of the "high and glorious destiny for the newly gathered people of the Lord."

Hester's remark on the Election Day that follows, "a new man is beginning to rule over them," has a significance she did not intend and cannot comprehend: at this moment Dimmesdale is just such a man, even though his rule will last only for the time it takes him to deliver his sermon and make his revelation. As he proceeds to the meetinghouse, no longer will-less but surcharged with spiritual energy, she senses that she has lost the magnetic power she exercised over him in the forest. Here in the marketplace it is she who is weak and he who is strong, for in the final stage of the journey he has found his way out of the maze in which she still wanders. Pearl, who had washed off his kiss at the brook, wishes to "run to him, and bid him kiss me now, before all the people...." Knowing at last what it means to be a special instrument of God, Dimmesdale gives tongue to his prophecy; "never had man spoken in so wise, so high, and so holy a spirit, as he that spake this day...." Then, mounting the scaffold, supported by Hester and holding Pearl's hand and followed by Chillingworth, he confesses his sin and, stepping forth unassisted, reveals the stigma on his breast. Whereupon Pearl, having heard her father acknowledge her existence, kisses him willingly in his dying hour.

Arthur Dimmesdale is a tragic hero. Tragedy as I here conceive it arises from the tension between illusion and reality—illusion meaning the there and then, reality the here and now; illusion meaning the ideal and reality the actual conception one has of himself. The quality of the illusion matters greatly, the noblest being man's aspiration to free himself from his particular time and place; the aspiration, in Christian terms, to return to that state of bliss in which he existed before the Fall. But here a dilemma arises: all men require illusion to bring order out of the chaos of the present, but if a man persists in hiding behind his illusion he is incapacitated for meaningful action. Ethically meaningful, that is to say tragic, action is possible only when a man, guided by this noblest of illusions, steps out from behind it and, fronting the terrors of the here and now, acts in obedience to a secret impulse of his character. Whereas Dimmesdale's full revelation on the scaffold is tragic, Hester's dynamic but lawless behavior in the forest is at best heroically pathetic. Hester is incapable of acting in a way that is ethically meaningful. Like Dimmesdale she dreams of regaining paradise, but unlike him she finds she must forever hide behind this dream if she is to go on living. In suggesting that they three, Dimmesdale, Pearl, and she herself, exchange the New World for the Old, she seeks to fulfill a temporalized version of the Edenic illusion, Boston signifying the here and now, Europe the there and then. However noble this illusion, it provides no basis for ethically meaningful action, since she is incapable of stepping from behind it and facing the present circumstance. When Pearl demands that she fasten the letter on her bosom again and Hester, having experienced temporary freedom, does so, it is with a heavy heart. "Hopefully, but a moment ago, as Hester had spoken of drowning it in the deep sea, there was a sense of inevitable doom upon her, as she thus received back this deadly symbol from the hand of fate. She had flung it into infinite space!—she had drawn an hour's free breath!—and here again was the scarlet misery, glittering on the old spot!" Her advising them to flee Boston was irresponsible because she did not gauge the actual situation accurately and, being irresponsible, it was not ethically meaningful. Nowhere in the narrative does her transcendental morality lead to tragic action. Strong she may seem: tragic she is not.

Conversely, Dimmesdale's confession is the act of a man who is tragically great. Of course, he shares in Hester's hour of transcendental freedom. Once resolved to leave Boston with Hester and their child, he is overcome by a new sensation. "It was the exhilarating effect—upon a prisoner just escaped from the dungeon of his own heart—of breathing the wild, free atmosphere of an unredeemed, unchristianized, lawless region." What saves him in the end from the self-deception that incapacitates Hester is the fact that his version of the Edenic illusion is grounded in the infinite, not in the finite world; the fact that, except for the short time he is required to wander in a maze, he knows himself to be a sinner and never mistakes penance done on earth for penitence. Like all men tragically great he sees with unflinching honesty the distance separating his ideal from his actual self and, seeing this, tries to bridge the gap. Before his hour of freedom he tells Hester, "I have laughed, in bitterness and agony of heart, at the contrast between what I seem and what I am!" Like Young Goodman Brown, he gains insight in this critical hour. "Another man," writes Hawthorne, "had returned out of the forest; a wiser one; with a knowledge of hidden mysteries which the simplicity of the former never could have reached. A bitter kind of knowledge that!" Unlike Brown because now secure in his faith, he translates insight into meaningful action, prophesying a glorious destiny for Massachusetts and publicly repenting him of his sin. Whereas Hester believes that what they did had a consecration of its own and seeks assurance that they will be united in paradise, he must tell her in his dying breath: "The law we broke!—the sin here so awfully revealed!—let these alone be in thy thoughts! I fear! I fear! It may be, that, when we forgot our God,—when we violated our reverence each for the other's soul,—it was thenceforth vain to hope that we could meet hereafter, in an everlasting and pure reunion. God knows; and He is merciful!" Dimmesdale goes to his early grave humbled and penitent, but when Hester follows him to hers many years later she is apparently unrepentant still. Hawthorne tells us that although "one tombstone served for both," there was "a space between, as if the dust of the two sleepers had no right to mingle."

Source: Bruce Ingham Granger, "Arthur Dimmesdale as Tragic Hero," in *Nineteenth-Century Fiction,* Vol. 19, No. 2, September, 1964, pp. 197–203.

Sources

Nina Baym, "Plot in Hawthorne's Romances," *Ruined Eden of the Present,* edited by G. R. Thompson and Virgil L. Lokke, Purdue University Press, 1981, pp. 49-70.

Sacvan Bercovitch, *The Office of the Scarlet Letter,* Johns Hopkins University Press, 1991.

Frederic I. Carpenter, "Scarlet A Minus," *College English,* Vol. 5, 1944, pp. 173-80.

Arthur Cleveland Coxe, "The Writings of Hawthorne," *Church Review,* January, 1851, pp. 489-511.

Evert A. Duyckinck, Review in *Literary World,* March 30, 1850, pp. 323-25.

Henry James, *Hawthorne,* Macmillan & Co, London, 1879.

F. O. Matthiessen, *American Renaissance: Art and Expression in the Age of Emerson and Whitman,* Oxford University Press, 1941.

Edwin Percy Whipple, Review in *Graham's Magazine,* May, 1850, pp. 345-46.

For Further Study

Lauren Gail Berlant, *The Anatomy of National Fantasy: Hawthorne, Utopia, and Everyday Life,* University of Chicago Press, 1991.
    A discussion of the connections between *The Scarlet Letter* and the politics and political character of the United States in the mid-nineteenth century, including the concept of utopia as it was applied to American democracy.

Richard H. Brodhead, *The School of Hawthorne,* Oxford University Press, 1986.
    Explores the critical reputation of Hawthorne and how the prevailing literary thought of the day helped create a "school" around his work that led to his inclusion in the literary canon. A good history of Hawthorne's critical reputation.

Critical Essays on Hawthorne's 'The Scarlet Letter', edited by David B. Kesterson, G. K. Hall, 1988.
    A collection of previously published criticism on Hawthorne's novel.

Critical Response to Nathaniel Hawthorne's 'The Scarlet Letter,' edited by Gary Scharnhorst, Greenwood Press, 1992.
    Another collection of critical essays by several critics on the novel.

Louise A. DeSalvo, *Nathaniel Hawthorne,* Harvester Press, 1987.

A feminist analysis of Hawthorne's work which decries the misogyny in his texts.

Kenneth Marc Harris, *Hypocrisy and Self-deception in Hawthorne's Fiction,* University Press of Virginia, 1988.
   A study which focuses on Hawthorne's preoccupation with hypocrisy, relating it to the author's fascination with the Puritans.

Nathaniel Hawthorne's 'The Scarlet Letter' edited and with an introduction by Harold Bloom, Chelsea House Publishers, 1986.
   An edition of the novel that contains a helpful introduction by a noted literary critic.

New Essays on 'The Scarlet Letter,' edited by Michael J. Colacurcio, Cambridge University Press, 1985.
   A collection of original critical assessments of Hawthorne's novel.

Leland S. Person, *Aesthetic Headaches: Women and a Masculine Poetics in Poe, Melville, and Hawthorne,* University of Georgia Press, 1988.
   Person's analysis of these authors' difficulties in creating artistic depictions of female characters suggests the need for a "masculine poetics." Devotes a whole chapter to *The Scarlet Letter.*

Larry J. Reynolds, "The Scarlet Letter and Revolutions Abroad," *American Literature,* Vol. 77, 1985, pp 44-67.
   Reynolds shows how Hawthorne viewed and was influenced by the European revolutions that began in 1848.

Alfred F. Rosa, *Salem, Transcendentalism, and Hawthorne,* Fairleigh Dickinson University Press, 1980.
   A study of several of Hawthorne's historical influences, including the witch trials in Massachusetts and the new Transcendentalist school of religious thought.

Charles Ryskamp, "The New England Sources of *The Scarlet Letter,*" *American Literature* XXXI, November 1959, pp. 257-272.
   A look at some of the historical events that may have inspired the plot and writing of Hawthorne's novel.

Charles Swann, *Nathaniel Hawthorne, Tradition and Revolution,* Cambridge University Press, 1991.
   A literary analysis of Hawthorne's work that offers much historical background which can be applied to several readings of the author's work.

Margaret Olofson Thickstun, *Fictions of the Feminine: Puritan Doctrine and the Representation of Women* Cornell University Press, 1988.
   An excellent summary of how Puritan views of women have influenced literary works such as *The Scarlet Letter.*

Twentieth Century Interpretations of 'The Scarlet Letter': A Collection of Critical Essays, edited by John C. Gerber, Prentice-Hall, 1968.
   A collection of important and groundbreaking essays on Hawthorne's novel which discuss the novel's structure and themes and Hawthorne's technique and sources. Includes bibliography.

Glossary of Literary Terms

A

Abstract: As an adjective applied to writing or literary works, abstract refers to words or phrases that name things not knowable through the five senses.

Aestheticism: A literary and artistic movement of the nineteenth century. Followers of the movement believed that art should not be mixed with social, political, or moral teaching. The statement "art for art's sake" is a good summary of aestheticism. The movement had its roots in France, but it gained widespread importance in England in the last half of the nineteenth century, where it helped change the Victorian practice of including moral lessons in literature.

Allegory: A narrative technique in which characters representing things or abstract ideas are used to convey a message or teach a lesson. Allegory is typically used to teach moral, ethical, or religious lessons but is sometimes used for satiric or political purposes.

Allusion: A reference to a familiar literary or historical person or event, used to make an idea more easily understood.

Analogy: A comparison of two things made to explain something unfamiliar through its similarities to something familiar, or to prove one point based on the acceptedness of another. Similes and metaphors are types of analogies.

Antagonist: The major character in a narrative or drama who works against the hero or protagonist.

Anthropomorphism: The presentation of animals or objects in human shape or with human characteristics. The term is derived from the Greek word for "human form."

Antihero: A central character in a work of literature who lacks traditional heroic qualities such as courage, physical prowess, and fortitude. Antiheroes typically distrust conventional values and are unable to commit themselves to any ideals. They generally feel helpless in a world over which they have no control. Antiheroes usually accept, and often celebrate, their positions as social outcasts.

Apprenticeship Novel: See *Bildungsroman*

Archetype: The word archetype is commonly used to describe an original pattern or model from which all other things of the same kind are made. This term was introduced to literary criticism from the psychology of Carl Jung. It expresses Jung's theory that behind every person's "unconscious," or repressed memories of the past, lies the "collective unconscious" of the human race: memories of the countless typical experiences of our ancestors. These memories are said to prompt illogical associations that trigger powerful emotions in the reader. Often, the emotional process is primitive, even primordial. Archetypes are the literary images that grow out of the "collective unconscious." They appear in literature as incidents and plots that repeat basic patterns of life. They may also appear as stereotyped characters.

Avant-garde: French term meaning "vanguard." It is used in literary criticism to describe new writing that rejects traditional approaches to literature in favor of innovations in style or content.

B

Beat Movement: A period featuring a group of American poets and novelists of the 1950s and 1960s—including Jack Kerouac, Allen Ginsberg, Gregory Corso, William S. Burroughs, and Lawrence Ferlinghetti—who rejected established social and literary values. Using such techniques as stream of consciousness writing and jazz-influenced free verse and focusing on unusual or abnormal states of mind—generated by religious ecstasy or the use of drugs—the Beat writers aimed to create works that were unconventional in both form and subject matter.

Bildungsroman: A German word meaning "novel of development." The *bildungsroman* is a study of the maturation of a youthful character, typically brought about through a series of social or sexual encounters that lead to self-awareness. *Bildungsroman* is used interchangeably with *erziehungsroman*, a novel of initiation and education. When a *bildungsroman* is concerned with the development of an artist (as in James Joyce's *A Portrait of the Artist as a Young Man*), it is often termed a *kunstlerroman*. Also known as Apprenticeship Novel, Coming of Age Novel, *Erziehungsroman*, or *Kunstlerroman*.

Black Aesthetic Movement: A period of artistic and literary development among African Americans in the 1960s and early 1970s. This was the first major African-American artistic movement since the Harlem Renaissance and was closely paralleled by the civil rights and black power movements. The black aesthetic writers attempted to produce works of art that would be meaningful to the black masses. Key figures in black aesthetics included one of its founders, poet and playwright Amiri Baraka, formerly known as LeRoi Jones; poet and essayist Haki R. Madhubuti, formerly Don L. Lee; poet and playwright Sonia Sanchez; and dramatist Ed Bullins. Also known as Black Arts Movement.

Black Humor: Writing that places grotesque elements side by side with humorous ones in an attempt to shock the reader, forcing him or her to laugh at the horrifying reality of a disordered world. Also known as Black Comedy.

Burlesque: Any literary work that uses exaggeration to make its subject appear ridiculous, either by treating a trivial subject with profound seriousness or by treating a dignified subject frivolously. The word "burlesque" may also be used as an adjective, as in "burlesque show," to mean "striptease act."

C

Character: Broadly speaking, a person in a literary work. The actions of characters are what constitute the plot of a story, novel, or poem. There are numerous types of characters, ranging from simple, stereotypical figures to intricate, multifaceted ones. In the techniques of anthropomorphism and personification, animals—and even places or things—can assume aspects of character. "Characterization" is the process by which an author creates vivid, believable characters in a work of art. This may be done in a variety of ways, including (1) direct description of the character by the narrator; (2) the direct presentation of the speech, thoughts, or actions of the character; and (3) the responses of other characters to the character. The term "character" also refers to a form originated by the ancient Greek writer Theophrastus that later became popular in the seventeenth and eighteenth centuries. It is a short essay or sketch of a person who prominently displays a specific attribute or quality, such as miserliness or ambition.

Climax: The turning point in a narrative, the moment when the conflict is at its most intense. Typically, the structure of stories, novels, and plays is one of rising action, in which tension builds to the climax, followed by falling action, in which tension lessens as the story moves to its conclusion.

Colloquialism: A word, phrase, or form of pronunciation that is acceptable in casual conversation but not in formal, written communication. It is considered more acceptable than slang.

Coming of Age Novel: See *Bildungsroman*

Concrete: Concrete is the opposite of abstract, and refers to a thing that actually exists or a description that allows the reader to experience an object or concept with the senses.

Connotation: The impression that a word gives beyond its defined meaning. Connotations may be universally understood or may be significant only to a certain group.

Convention: Any widely accepted literary device, style, or form.

D

Denotation: The definition of a word, apart from the impressions or feelings it creates (connotations) in the reader.

Denouement: A French word meaning "the unknotting." In literary criticism, it denotes the resolution of conflict in fiction or drama. The *denouement* follows the climax and provides an outcome to the primary plot situation as well as an explanation of secondary plot complications. The *denouement* often involves a character's recognition of his or her state of mind or moral condition. Also known as Falling Action.

Description: Descriptive writing is intended to allow a reader to picture the scene or setting in which the action of a story takes place. The form this description takes often evokes an intended emotional response—a dark, spooky graveyard will evoke fear, and a peaceful, sunny meadow will evoke calmness.

Dialogue: In its widest sense, dialogue is simply conversation between people in a literary work; in its most restricted sense, it refers specifically to the speech of characters in a drama. As a specific literary genre, a "dialogue" is a composition in which characters debate an issue or idea.

Diction: The selection and arrangement of words in a literary work. Either or both may vary depending on the desired effect. There are four general types of diction: "formal," used in scholarly or lofty writing; "informal," used in relaxed but educated conversation; "colloquial," used in everyday speech; and "slang," containing newly coined words and other terms not accepted in formal usage.

Didactic: A term used to describe works of literature that aim to teach some moral, religious, political, or practical lesson. Although didactic elements are often found in artistically pleasing works, the term "didactic" usually refers to literature in which the message is more important than the form. The term may also be used to criticize a work that the critic finds "overly didactic," that is, heavy-handed in its delivery of a lesson.

Doppelganger: A literary technique by which a character is duplicated (usually in the form of an alter ego, though sometimes as a ghostly counterpart) or divided into two distinct, usually opposite personalities. The use of this character device is widespread in nineteenth- and twentieth-century literature, and indicates a growing awareness among authors that the "self" is really a composite of many "selves." Also known as The Double.

Double Entendre: A corruption of a French phrase meaning "double meaning." The term is used to indicate a word or phrase that is deliberately ambiguous, especially when one of the meanings is risqué or improper.

Dramatic Irony: Occurs when the audience of a play or the reader of a work of literature knows something that a character in the work itself does not know. The irony is in the contrast between the intended meaning of the statements or actions of a character and the additional information understood by the audience.

Dystopia: An imaginary place in a work of fiction where the characters lead dehumanized, fearful lives.

E

Edwardian: Describes cultural conventions identified with the period of the reign of Edward VII of England (1901-1910). Writers of the Edwardian Age typically displayed a strong reaction against the propriety and conservatism of the Victorian Age. Their work often exhibits distrust of authority in religion, politics, and art and expresses strong doubts about the soundness of conventional values.

Empathy: A sense of shared experience, including emotional and physical feelings, with someone or something other than oneself. Empathy is often used to describe the response of a reader to a literary character.

Enlightenment, The: An eighteenth-century philosophical movement. It began in France but had a wide impact throughout Europe and America. Thinkers of the Enlightenment valued reason and believed that both the individual and society could achieve a state of perfection. Corresponding to this essentially humanist vision was a resistance to religious authority.

Epigram: A saying that makes the speaker's point quickly and concisely. Often used to preface a novel.

Epilogue: A concluding statement or section of a literary work. In dramas, particularly those of the seventeenth and eighteenth centuries, the epilogue is a closing speech, often in verse, delivered by an actor at the end of a play and spoken directly to the audience.

Epiphany: A sudden revelation of truth inspired by a seemingly trivial incident.

Episode: An incident that forms part of a story and is significantly related to it. Episodes may be either self-contained narratives or events that depend on a larger context for their sense and importance.

Epistolary Novel: A novel in the form of letters. The form was particularly popular in the eighteenth century.

Epithet: A word or phrase, often disparaging or abusive, that expresses a character trait of someone or something.

Existentialism: A predominantly twentieth-century philosophy concerned with the nature and perception of human existence. There are two major strains of existentialist thought: atheistic and Christian. Followers of atheistic existentialism believe that the individual is alone in a godless universe and that the basic human condition is one of suffering and loneliness. Nevertheless, because there are no fixed values, individuals can create their own characters—indeed, they can shape themselves—through the exercise of free will. The atheistic strain culminates in and is popularly associated with the works of Jean-Paul Sartre. The Christian existentialists, on the other hand, believe that only in God may people find freedom from life's anguish. The two strains hold certain beliefs in common: that existence cannot be fully understood or described through empirical effort; that anguish is a universal element of life; that individuals must bear responsibility for their actions; and that there is no common standard of behavior or perception for religious and ethical matters.

Expatriates: See *Expatriatism*

Expatriatism: The practice of leaving one's country to live for an extended period in another country.

Exposition: Writing intended to explain the nature of an idea, thing, or theme. Expository writing is often combined with description, narration, or argument. In dramatic writing, the exposition is the introductory material which presents the characters, setting, and tone of the play.

Expressionism: An indistinct literary term, originally used to describe an early twentieth-century school of German painting. The term applies to almost any mode of unconventional, highly subjective writing that distorts reality in some way.

F

Fable: A prose or verse narrative intended to convey a moral. Animals or inanimate objects with human characteristics often serve as characters in fables.

Falling Action: See *Denouement*

Fantasy: A literary form related to mythology and folklore. Fantasy literature is typically set in non-existent realms and features supernatural beings.

Farce: A type of comedy characterized by broad humor, outlandish incidents, and often vulgar subject matter.

Femme fatale: A French phrase with the literal translation "fatal woman." A *femme fatale* is a sensuous, alluring woman who often leads men into danger or trouble.

Fiction: Any story that is the product of imagination rather than a documentation of fact. Characters and events in such narratives may be based in real life but their ultimate form and configuration is a creation of the author.

Figurative Language: A technique in writing in which the author temporarily interrupts the order, construction, or meaning of the writing for a particular effect. This interruption takes the form of one or more figures of speech such as hyperbole, irony, or simile. Figurative language is the opposite of literal language, in which every word is truthful, accurate, and free of exaggeration or embellishment.

Figures of Speech: Writing that differs from customary conventions for construction, meaning, order, or significance for the purpose of a special meaning or effect. There are two major types of figures of speech: rhetorical figures, which do not make changes in the meaning of the words, and tropes, which do.

Fin de siecle: A French term meaning "end of the century." The term is used to denote the last decade of the nineteenth century, a transition period when writers and other artists abandoned old conventions and looked for new techniques and objectives.

First Person: See *Point of View*

Flashback: A device used in literature to present action that occurred before the beginning of the story. Flashbacks are often introduced as the dreams or recollections of one or more characters.

Foil: A character in a work of literature whose physical or psychological qualities contrast strongly with, and therefore highlight, the corresponding qualities of another character.

Folklore: Traditions and myths preserved in a culture or group of people. Typically, these are passed on by word of mouth in various forms—such as legends, songs, and proverbs—or preserved in customs and ceremonies. This term was first used by W. J. Thoms in 1846.

Folktale: A story originating in oral tradition. Folktales fall into a variety of categories, including legends, ghost stories, fairy tales, fables, and anecdotes based on historical figures and events.

Foreshadowing: A device used in literature to create expectation or to set up an explanation of later developments.

Form: The pattern or construction of a work which identifies its genre and distinguishes it from other genres.

G

Genre: A category of literary work. In critical theory, genre may refer to both the content of a given work—tragedy, comedy, pastoral—and to its form, such as poetry, novel, or drama.

Gilded Age: A period in American history during the 1870s characterized by political corruption and materialism. A number of important novels of social and political criticism were written during this time.

Gothicism: In literary criticism, works characterized by a taste for the medieval or morbidly attractive. A gothic novel prominently features elements of horror, the supernatural, gloom, and violence: clanking chains, terror, charnel houses, ghosts, medieval castles, and mysteriously slamming doors. The term "gothic novel" is also applied to novels that lack elements of the traditional Gothic setting but that create a similar atmosphere of terror or dread.

Grotesque: In literary criticism, the subject matter of a work or a style of expression characterized by exaggeration, deformity, freakishness, and disorder. The grotesque often includes an element of comic absurdity.

H

Harlem Renaissance: The Harlem Renaissance of the 1920s is generally considered the first significant movement of black writers and artists in the United States. During this period, new and established black writers published more fiction and poetry than ever before, the first influential black literary journals were established, and black authors and artists received their first widespread recognition and serious critical appraisal. Among the major writers associated with this period are Claude McKay, Jean Toomer, Countee Cullen, Langston Hughes, Arna Bontemps, Nella Larsen, and Zora Neale Hurston. Also known as Negro Renaissance and New Negro Movement.

Hero/Heroine: The principal sympathetic character (male or female) in a literary work. Heroes and heroines typically exhibit admirable traits: idealism, courage, and integrity, for example.

Holocaust Literature: Literature influenced by or written about the Holocaust of World War II. Such literature includes true stories of survival in concentration camps, escape, and life after the war, as well as fictional works and poetry.

Humanism: A philosophy that places faith in the dignity of humankind and rejects the medieval perception of the individual as a weak, fallen creature. "Humanists" typically believe in the perfectibility of human nature and view reason and education as the means to that end.

Hyperbole: In literary criticism, deliberate exaggeration used to achieve an effect.

I

Idiom: A word construction or verbal expression closely associated with a given language.

Image: A concrete representation of an object or sensory experience. Typically, such a representation helps evoke the feelings associated with the object or experience itself. Images are either "literal" or "figurative." Literal images are especially concrete and involve little or no extension of the obvious meaning of the words used to express them. Figurative images do not follow the literal meaning of the words exactly. Images in literature are usually visual, but the term "image" can also refer to the representation of any sensory experience.

Imagery: The array of images in a literary work. Also, figurative language.

In medias res: A Latin term meaning "in the middle of things." It refers to the technique of beginning a story at its midpoint and then using various flashback devices to reveal previous action.

Interior Monologue: A narrative technique in which characters' thoughts are revealed in a way that appears to be uncontrolled by the author. The interior monologue typically aims to reveal the inner self of a character. It portrays emotional experiences as they occur at both a conscious and unconscious level. Images are often used to represent sensations or emotions.

Irony: In literary criticism, the effect of language in which the intended meaning is the opposite of what is stated.

J

Jargon: Language that is used or understood only by a select group of people. Jargon may refer to terminology used in a certain profession, such as computer jargon, or it may refer to any nonsensical language that is not understood by most people.

L

Leitmotiv: See *Motif*

Literal Language: An author uses literal language when he or she writes without exaggerating or embellishing the subject matter and without any tools of figurative language.

Lost Generation: A term first used by Gertrude Stein to describe the post-World War I generation of American writers: men and women haunted by a sense of betrayal and emptiness brought about by the destructiveness of the war.

M

Mannerism: Exaggerated, artificial adherence to a literary manner or style. Also, a popular style of the visual arts of late sixteenth-century Europe that was marked by elongation of the human form and by intentional spatial distortion. Literary works that are self-consciously high-toned and artistic are often said to be "mannered."

Metaphor: A figure of speech that expresses an idea through the image of another object. Metaphors suggest the essence of the first object by identifying it with certain qualities of the second object.

Modernism: Modern literary practices. Also, the principles of a literary school that lasted from roughly the beginning of the twentieth century until the end of World War II. Modernism is defined by its rejection of the literary conventions of the nineteenth century and by its opposition to conventional morality, taste, traditions, and economic values.

Mood: The prevailing emotions of a work or of the author in his or her creation of the work. The mood of a work is not always what might be expected based on its subject matter.

Motif: A theme, character type, image, metaphor, or other verbal element that recurs throughout a single work of literature or occurs in a number of different works over a period of time. Also known as *Motiv* or *Leitmotiv.*

Myth: An anonymous tale emerging from the traditional beliefs of a culture or social unit. Myths use supernatural explanations for natural phenomena. They may also explain cosmic issues like creation and death. Collections of myths, known as mythologies, are common to all cultures and nations, but the best-known myths belong to the Norse, Roman, and Greek mythologies.

N

Narration: The telling of a series of events, real or invented. A narration may be either a simple narrative, in which the events are recounted chronologically, or a narrative with a plot, in which the account is given in a style reflecting the author's artistic concept of the story. Narration is sometimes used as a synonym for "storyline."

Narrative: A verse or prose accounting of an event or sequence of events, real or invented. The term is also used as an adjective in the sense "method of narration." For example, in literary criticism, the expression "narrative technique" usually refers to the way the author structures and presents his or her story.

Narrator: The teller of a story. The narrator may be the author or a character in the story through whom the author speaks.

Naturalism: A literary movement of the late nineteenth and early twentieth centuries. The movement's major theorist, French novelist Emile Zola, envisioned a type of fiction that would examine human life with the objectivity of scientific inquiry. The Naturalists typically viewed human beings as either the products of "biological determinism," ruled by hereditary instincts and engaged in an endless struggle for survival, or as the products of "socioeconomic determinism," ruled by social and economic forces beyond their control. In their works, the Naturalists generally ignored the highest levels of society and focused on degradation: poverty, alcoholism, prostitution, insanity, and disease.

Noble Savage: The idea that primitive man is noble and good but becomes evil and corrupted as he becomes civilized. The concept of the noble savage originated in the Renaissance period but is more closely identified with such later writers as

Jean-Jacques Rousseau and Aphra Behn. See also Primitivism.

Novel of Ideas: A novel in which the examination of intellectual issues and concepts takes precedence over characterization or a traditional storyline.

Novel of Manners: A novel that examines the customs and mores of a cultural group.

Novel: A long fictional narrative written in prose, which developed from the novella and other early forms of narrative. A novel is usually organized under a plot or theme with a focus on character development and action.

Novella: An Italian term meaning "story." This term has been especially used to describe fourteenth-century Italian tales, but it also refers to modern short novels.

O

Objective Correlative: An outward set of objects, a situation, or a chain of events corresponding to an inward experience and evoking this experience in the reader. The term frequently appears in modern criticism in discussions of authors' intended effects on the emotional responses of readers.

Objectivity: A quality in writing characterized by the absence of the author's opinion or feeling about the subject matter. Objectivity is an important factor in criticism.

Oedipus Complex: A son's amorous obsession with his mother. The phrase is derived from the story of the ancient Theban hero Oedipus, who unknowingly killed his father and married his mother.

Omniscience: See *Point of View*

Onomatopoeia: The use of words whose sounds express or suggest their meaning. In its simplest sense, onomatopoeia may be represented by words that mimic the sounds they denote such as "hiss" or "meow." At a more subtle level, the pattern and rhythm of sounds and rhymes of a line or poem may be onomatopoeic.

Oxymoron: A phrase combining two contradictory terms. Oxymorons may be intentional or unintentional.

P

Parable: A story intended to teach a moral lesson or answer an ethical question.

Paradox: A statement that appears illogical or contradictory at first, but may actually point to an underlying truth.

Parallelism: A method of comparison of two ideas in which each is developed in the same grammatical structure.

Parody: In literary criticism, this term refers to an imitation of a serious literary work or the signature style of a particular author in a ridiculous manner. A typical parody adopts the style of the original and applies it to an inappropriate subject for humorous effect. Parody is a form of satire and could be considered the literary equivalent of a caricature or cartoon.

Pastoral: A term derived from the Latin word "pastor," meaning shepherd. A pastoral is a literary composition on a rural theme. The conventions of the pastoral were originated by the third-century Greek poet Theocritus, who wrote about the experiences, love affairs, and pastimes of Sicilian shepherds. In a pastoral, characters and language of a courtly nature are often placed in a simple setting. The term pastoral is also used to classify dramas, elegies, and lyrics that exhibit the use of country settings and shepherd characters.

Pen Name: See *Pseudonym*

Persona: A Latin term meaning "mask." *Personae* are the characters in a fictional work of literature. The *persona* generally functions as a mask through which the author tells a story in a voice other than his or her own. A *persona* is usually either a character in a story who acts as a narrator or an "implied author," a voice created by the author to act as the narrator for himself or herself.

Personification: A figure of speech that gives human qualities to abstract ideas, animals, and inanimate objects. Also known as *Prosopopoeia*.

Picaresque Novel: Episodic fiction depicting the adventures of a roguish central character ("picaro" is Spanish for "rogue"). The picaresque hero is commonly a low-born but clever individual who wanders into and out of various affairs of love, danger, and farcical intrigue. These involvements may take place at all social levels and typically present a humorous and wide-ranging satire of a given society.

Plagiarism: Claiming another person's written material as one's own. Plagiarism can take the form of direct, word-for-word copying or the theft of the substance or idea of the work.

Plot: In literary criticism, this term refers to the pattern of events in a narrative or drama. In its simplest sense, the plot guides the author in composing the work and helps the reader follow the work. Typically, plots exhibit causality and unity and have a beginning, a middle, and an end. Sometimes, however, a plot may consist of a series of disconnected events, in which case it is known as an "episodic plot."

Poetic Justice: An outcome in a literary work, not necessarily a poem, in which the good are rewarded and the evil are punished, especially in ways that particularly fit their virtues or crimes.

Poetic License: Distortions of fact and literary convention made by a writer—not always a poet—for the sake of the effect gained. Poetic license is closely related to the concept of "artistic freedom."

Poetics: This term has two closely related meanings. It denotes (1) an aesthetic theory in literary criticism about the essence of poetry or (2) rules prescribing the proper methods, content, style, or diction of poetry. The term poetics may also refer to theories about literature in general, not just poetry.

Point of View: The narrative perspective from which a literary work is presented to the reader. There are four traditional points of view. The "third person omniscient" gives the reader a "godlike" perspective, unrestricted by time or place, from which to see actions and look into the minds of characters. This allows the author to comment openly on characters and events in the work. The "third person" point of view presents the events of the story from outside of any single character's perception, much like the omniscient point of view, but the reader must understand the action as it takes place and without any special insight into characters' minds or motivations. The "first person" or "personal" point of view relates events as they are perceived by a single character. The main character "tells" the story and may offer opinions about the action and characters which differ from those of the author. Much less common than omniscient, third person, and first person is the "second person" point of view, wherein the author tells the story as if it is happening to the reader.

Polemic: A work in which the author takes a stand on a controversial subject, such as abortion or religion. Such works are often extremely argumentative or provocative.

Pornography: Writing intended to provoke feelings of lust in the reader. Such works are often condemned by critics and teachers, but those which can be shown to have literary value are viewed less harshly.

Post-Aesthetic Movement: An artistic response made by African Americans to the black aesthetic movement of the 1960s and early '70s. Writers since that time have adopted a somewhat different tone in their work, with less emphasis placed on the disparity between black and white in the United States. In the words of post-aesthetic authors such as Toni Morrison, John Edgar Wideman, and Kristin Hunter, African Americans are portrayed as looking inward for answers to their own questions, rather than always looking to the outside world.

Postmodernism: Writing from the 1960s forward characterized by experimentation and continuing to apply some of the fundamentals of modernism, which included existentialism and alienation. Postmodernists have gone a step further in the rejection of tradition begun with the modernists by also rejecting traditional forms, preferring the anti-novel over the novel and the antihero over the hero.

Primitivism: The belief that primitive peoples were nobler and less flawed than civilized peoples because they had not been subjected to the tainting influence of society. See also Noble Savage.

Prologue: An introductory section of a literary work. It often contains information establishing the situation of the characters or presents information about the setting, time period, or action. In drama, the prologue is spoken by a chorus or by one of the principal characters.

Prose: A literary medium that attempts to mirror the language of everyday speech. It is distinguished from poetry by its use of unmetered, unrhymed language consisting of logically related sentences. Prose is usually grouped into paragraphs that form a cohesive whole such as an essay or a novel.

Prosopopoeia: See *Personification*

Protagonist: The central character of a story who serves as a focus for its themes and incidents and as the principal rationale for its development. The protagonist is sometimes referred to in discussions of modern literature as the hero or antihero.

Protest Fiction: Protest fiction has as its primary purpose the protesting of some social injustice, such as racism or discrimination.

Proverb: A brief, sage saying that expresses a truth about life in a striking manner.

Pseudonym: A name assumed by a writer, most often intended to prevent his or her identification as the author of a work. Two or more authors may work together under one pseudonym, or an author may use a different name for each genre he or she publishes in. Some publishing companies maintain "house pseudonyms," under which any number of authors may write installations in a series. Some authors also choose a pseudonym over their real names the way an actor may use a stage name.

Pun: A play on words that have similar sounds but different meanings.

R

Realism: A nineteenth-century European literary movement that sought to portray familiar characters, situations, and settings in a realistic manner. This was done primarily by using an objective narrative point of view and through the buildup of accurate detail. The standard for success of any realistic work depends on how faithfully it transfers common experience into fictional forms. The realistic method may be altered or extended, as in stream of consciousness writing, to record highly subjective experience.

Repartee: Conversation featuring snappy retorts and witticisms.

Resolution: The portion of a story following the climax, in which the conflict is resolved. See also *Denouement*.

Rhetoric: In literary criticism, this term denotes the art of ethical persuasion. In its strictest sense, rhetoric adheres to various principles developed since classical times for arranging facts and ideas in a clear, persuasive, appealing manner. The term is also used to refer to effective prose in general and theories of or methods for composing effective prose.

Rhetorical Question: A question intended to provoke thought, but not an expressed answer, in the reader. It is most commonly used in oratory and other persuasive genres.

Rising Action: The part of a drama where the plot becomes increasingly complicated. Rising action leads up to the climax, or turning point, of a drama.

Roman a clef: A French phrase meaning "novel with a key." It refers to a narrative in which real persons are portrayed under fictitious names.

Romance: A broad term, usually denoting a narrative with exotic, exaggerated, often idealized characters, scenes, and themes.

Romanticism: This term has two widely accepted meanings. In historical criticism, it refers to a European intellectual and artistic movement of the late eighteenth and early nineteenth centuries that sought greater freedom of personal expression than that allowed by the strict rules of literary form and logic of the eighteenth-century neoclassicists. The Romantics preferred emotional and imaginative ex-

pression to rational analysis. They considered the individual to be at the center of all experience and so placed him or her at the center of their art. The Romantics believed that the creative imagination reveals nobler truths—unique feelings and attitudes—than those that could be discovered by logic or by scientific examination. Both the natural world and the state of childhood were important sources for revelations of "eternal truths." "Romanticism" is also used as a general term to refer to a type of sensibility found in all periods of literary history and usually considered to be in opposition to the principles of classicism. In this sense, Romanticism signifies any work or philosophy in which the exotic or dreamlike figure strongly, or that is devoted to individualistic expression, self-analysis, or a pursuit of a higher realm of knowledge than can be discovered by human reason.

Romantics: See *Romanticism*

S

Satire: A work that uses ridicule, humor, and wit to criticize and provoke change in human nature and institutions. There are two major types of satire: "formal" or "direct" satire speaks directly to the reader or to a character in the work; "indirect" satire relies upon the ridiculous behavior of its characters to make its point. Formal satire is further divided into two manners: the "Horatian," which ridicules gently, and the "Juvenalian," which derides its subjects harshly and bitterly.

Science Fiction: A type of narrative about or based upon real or imagined scientific theories and technology. Science fiction is often peopled with alien creatures and set on other planets or in different dimensions.

Second Person: See *Point of View*

Setting: The time, place, and culture in which the action of a narrative takes place. The elements of setting may include geographic location, characters' physical and mental environments, prevailing cultural attitudes, or the historical time in which the action takes place.

Simile: A comparison, usually using "like" or "as", of two essentially dissimilar things, as in "coffee as cold as ice" or "He sounded like a broken record."

Slang: A type of informal verbal communication that is generally unacceptable for formal writing. Slang words and phrases are often colorful exaggerations used to emphasize the speaker's point; they may also be shortened versions of an often-used word or phrase.

Slave Narrative: Autobiographical accounts of American slave life as told by escaped slaves. These works first appeared during the abolition movement of the 1830s through the 1850s.

Socialist Realism: The Socialist Realism school of literary theory was proposed by Maxim Gorky and established as a dogma by the first Soviet Congress of Writers. It demanded adherence to a communist worldview in works of literature. Its doctrines required an objective viewpoint comprehensible to the working classes and themes of social struggle featuring strong proletarian heroes. Also known as Social Realism.

Stereotype: A stereotype was originally the name for a duplication made during the printing process; this led to its modern definition as a person or thing that is (or is assumed to be) the same as all others of its type.

Stream of Consciousness: A narrative technique for rendering the inward experience of a character. This technique is designed to give the impression of an ever-changing series of thoughts, emotions, images, and memories in the spontaneous and seemingly illogical order that they occur in life.

Structure: The form taken by a piece of literature. The structure may be made obvious for ease of understanding, as in nonfiction works, or may be obscured for artistic purposes, as in some poetry or seemingly "unstructured" prose.

***Sturm und Drang*:** A German term meaning "storm and stress." It refers to a German literary movement of the 1770s and 1780s that reacted against the order and rationalism of the enlightenment, focusing instead on the intense experience of extraordinary individuals.

Style: A writer's distinctive manner of arranging words to suit his or her ideas and purpose in writing. The unique imprint of the author's personality upon his or her writing, style is the product of an author's way of arranging ideas and his or her use of diction, different sentence structures, rhythm, figures of speech, rhetorical principles, and other elements of composition.

Subjectivity: Writing that expresses the author's personal feelings about his subject, and which may or may not include factual information about the subject.

Subplot: A secondary story in a narrative. A subplot may serve as a motivating or complicating force for the main plot of the work, or it may provide emphasis for, or relief from, the main plot.

Surrealism: A term introduced to criticism by Guillaume Apollinaire and later adopted by Andre Breton. It refers to a French literary and artistic movement founded in the 1920s. The Surrealists sought to express unconscious thoughts and feelings in their works. The best-known technique used for achieving this aim was automatic writing—transcriptions of spontaneous outpourings from the unconscious. The Surrealists proposed to unify the contrary levels of conscious and unconscious, dream and reality, objectivity and subjectivity into a new level of "super-realism."

Suspense: A literary device in which the author maintains the audience's attention through the buildup of events, the outcome of which will soon be revealed.

Symbol: Something that suggests or stands for something else without losing its original identity. In literature, symbols combine their literal meaning with the suggestion of an abstract concept. Literary symbols are of two types: those that carry complex associations of meaning no matter what their contexts, and those that derive their suggestive meaning from their functions in specific literary works.

Symbolism: This term has two widely accepted meanings. In historical criticism, it denotes an early modernist literary movement initiated in France during the nineteenth century that reacted against the prevailing standards of realism. Writers in this movement aimed to evoke, indirectly and symbolically, an order of being beyond the material world of the five senses. Poetic expression of personal emotion figured strongly in the movement, typically by means of a private set of symbols uniquely identifiable with the individual poet. The principal aim of the Symbolists was to express in words the highly complex feelings that grew out of everyday contact with the world. In a broader sense, the term "symbolism" refers to the use of one object to represent another.

T

Tall Tale: A humorous tale told in a straightforward, credible tone but relating absolutely impossible events or feats of the characters. Such tales were commonly told of frontier adventures during the settlement of the west in the United States.

Theme: The main point of a work of literature. The term is used interchangeably with thesis.

Thesis: A thesis is both an essay and the point argued in the essay. Thesis novels and thesis plays share the quality of containing a thesis which is supported through the action of the story.

Third Person: See *Point of View*

Tone: The author's attitude toward his or her audience may be deduced from the tone of the work. A formal tone may create distance or convey politeness, while an informal tone may encourage a friendly, intimate, or intrusive feeling in the reader. The author's attitude toward his or her subject matter may also be deduced from the tone of the words he or she uses in discussing it.

Transcendentalism: An American philosophical and religious movement, based in New England from around 1835 until the Civil War. Transcendentalism was a form of American romanticism that had its roots abroad in the works of Thomas Carlyle, Samuel Coleridge, and Johann Wolfgang von Goethe. The Transcendentalists stressed the importance of intuition and subjective experience in communication with God. They rejected religious dogma and texts in favor of mysticism and scientific naturalism. They pursued truths that lie beyond the "colorless" realms perceived by reason and the senses and were active social reformers in public education, women's rights, and the abolition of slavery.

U

Urban Realism: A branch of realist writing that attempts to accurately reflect the often harsh facts of modern urban existence.

Utopia: A fictional perfect place, such as "paradise" or "heaven."

V

Verisimilitude: Literally, the appearance of truth. In literary criticism, the term refers to aspects of a work of literature that seem true to the reader.

Victorian: Refers broadly to the reign of Queen Victoria of England (1837-1901) and to anything with qualities typical of that era. For example, the qualities of smug narrowmindedness, bourgeois materialism, faith in social progress, and priggish morality are often considered Victorian. This stereotype is contradicted by such dramatic intellectual developments as the theories of Charles Darwin, Karl Marx, and Sigmund Freud (which stirred strong debates in England) and the critical attitudes of serious Victorian writers like Charles Dickens and George Eliot. In literature, the Victorian Period was the great age of the English novel, and the latter part of the era saw the rise of movements such as decadence and symbolism. Also known as Victorian Age and Victorian Period.

W

Weltanschauung: A German term referring to a person's worldview or philosophy.

Weltschmerz: A German term meaning "world pain." It describes a sense of anguish about the nature of existence, usually associated with a melancholy, pessimistic attitude.

Z

Zeitgeist: A German term meaning "spirit of the time." It refers to the moral and intellectual trends of a given era.

Cumulative
Author/Title Index

Cumulative Nationality/Ethnicity Index

African American

Morrison, Toni
  The Bluest Eye: V1
Wright, Richard
  Black Boy: V1

American

Bradbury, Ray
  Fahrenheit 451: V1
Clemens, Mark
  *The Adventures of Huckleberry
    Finn:* V1
Guest, Judith
  Ordinary People: V1
Hawthorne, Nathaniel
  The Scarlet Letter: V1

Heller, Joseph
  Catch-22: V1
Hemingway, Ernest
  A Farewell to Arms: V1
Morrison, Toni
  The Bluest Eye: V1
Plath, Sylvia
  The Bell Jar: V1
Salinger, J. D.
  The Catcher in the Rye: V1
Steinbeck, John
  Of Mice and Men: V1
Tan, Amy
  The Joy Luck Club: V1
Twain, Mark
  *The Adventures of Huckleberry
    Finn:* V1
Wright, Richard
  Black Boy: V1

Asian American

Tan, Amy
  The Joy Luck Club: V1

British

Austen, Jane
  Pride and Prejudice: V1
Shelley, Mary
  Frankenstein: V1

Colombian

García Márquez, Gabriel
  Love in the Time of Cholera: V1

Subject/Theme Index

Suicide
    The Bell Jar: 22–23, 25–26,
      30–34
    Love in the Time of Cholera:
      223, 229, 232–34
    Ordinary People: 263, 265–66,
      270–71, 273, 277–79
    Pride and Prejudice: 299
Supernatural
    The Scarlet Letter: 308
Switzerland
    Frankenstein: 180, 182–83, 190

T

Time and Change
    Fahrenheit 451: 138, 144–46
    Love in the Time of Cholera: 231
Tragedy
    Of Mice and Men: 256, 258
Transcendentalism
    The Scarlet Letter: 315

U

Uncertainty
    The Scarlet Letter: 307, 313–15,
      318
Understanding
    Ordinary People: 278
Upper Class
    Pride and Prejudice: 295–96
Utopianism
    The Scarlet Letter: 320

V

Vietnam War
    The Bluest Eye: 77–78
    Catch-22: 102–05

W

War
    A Farewell to Arms: 166
War, the Military, and Soldier Life
    Black Boy: 45, 53–54
    The Bluest Eye: 77–78
    Catch-22: 89–93, 98–103,
      105–07, 109–13
    The Catcher in the Rye: 125
    Fahrenheit 451: 139–41, 145–48
    A Farewell to Arms: 158–60,
      162–68, 170–77
    The Joy Luck Club: 211–13
    Pride and Prejudice: 285,
      294–96
Wealth
    The Catcher in the Rye: 118, 125,
      127
Wisdom
    Ordinary People: 276–79
    The Scarlet Letter: 323–24
World War I
    A Farewell to Arms: 158–59,
      162–63, 165, 167–70,
      172–76, 178
World War II
    Black Boy: 52–53
    The Bluest Eye: 78
    Catch-22: 89, 91, 98–103,
      105–06
    Fahrenheit 451: 146–47
    The Joy Luck Club: 204, 211,
      213–14